Fourth Edition

LEADERSHIP

Fourth Edition

LEADERSHIP

A Communication Perspective

Michael Z. Hackman
University of Colorado–Colorado Springs

Craig E. Johnson
George Fox University

WAVELAND
PRESS, INC.
Long Grove, Illinois

For information about this book, contact:
Waveland Press, Inc.
4180 IL Route 83, Suite 101
Long Grove, IL 60047-9580
(847) 634-0081
info@waveland.com
www.waveland.com

To my wife, Kim, and my children, Jane, Zachary, and Aubrey. Your love leads the way in every endeavor of my life.

—MZH

To my wife, Mary. Have I told you lately that I love you?

—CJ

About the Authors

Michael Z. Hackman is a Professor and chair of the Department of Communication at the University of Colorado-Colorado Springs. He teaches courses in communication at both the undergraduate and graduate levels, including courses supported by a grant from the U.S. Department of Education Fund for the Improvement of Post-Secondary Education (FIPSE) that allowed for the development of an online curriculum in organizational communication and leadership delivered to students and working professionals in the U.S. and Europe. In 1995, he was awarded the university-wide Outstanding Teacher Award. Dr. Hackman's research focuses on a wide range of communication issues, including: the impact of gender and culture on communication and leadership behavior, humor and communication, instructional communication in mediated contexts, and creativity. His work has appeared in such journals as *Communication Education, Communication Quarterly, Distance Education, The Journal of Leadership Studies, Perceptual and Motor Skills*, and the *Southern Speech Communication Journal*. Since 1991, Dr. Hackman has served as a Visiting Professor at the University of Waikato in Hamilton, New Zealand on four separate occasions, the most recent in 2002. He also served as an adjunct Professor at the University of Siena (Italy) and the University of Vienna (Austria). Dr. Hackman has conducted workshops on a variety of topics related to leadership and communication for numerous public and private sector organizations in Canada, the United States, Italy, the Netherlands, and New Zealand. His clients have included AARP, Agilent Technologies, Bristol-Myers Squibb, Ernst & Young, Georgia-Pacific, Harley-Davidson, Hewlett-Packard, J.D. Edwards, Telecom New Zealand, the United States Air Force, and Wells Fargo.

Craig E. Johnson is a Professor of Communication and chair of the Department of Communication Arts/World Languages/English Language Institute at George Fox University, Newberg, Oregon. He teaches a variety of communication and leadership courses, including communication theory, public relations, organizational communication, public speaking, leadership communication, interpersonal communication, and organizational communication. He also acts as faculty director of the university's interdisciplinary leadership studies minor. In 1994 Dr. Johnson received the George Fox University faculty achievement award for teaching. In 2001 he was a visiting instructor at Daystar University in Nairobi, Kenya. Dr. Johnson's research interests include leadership ethics, leadership education, cross-cultural communication, and powerful/powerless forms of speech. He is author of the book *Meeting the Ethical Challenges of Leadership: Casting Light or Shadow*. His articles have appeared in such journals as *Communication Quarterly, The Journal of Leadership Studies, Communication Education, Communication Reports*, and *The Journal of the International Listening Association*. He has served in leadership roles in several religious and nonprofit organizations.

Acknowledgements

Students and colleagues (including readers of the previous editions) provided us with many of their own leadership stories along with encouragement, advice, and support. In particular we want to recognize Alvin Goldberg, our mentor at the University of Denver, who was instrumental in igniting our interest in the topic of leadership.

Many of our associates, past and present, have also been helpful in focusing our thoughts concerning leadership. Most notably we want to thank Ted Baartmans, Jeroen Meier, and Annebeth Sieswerda of the Presentation Group in Bloemendaal, the Netherlands; Kevin Barge of the University of Georgia; Stephen Bowden, Neil Harnisch, and Ted Zorn of the University of Waikato, New Zealand; Jim Fleming, Shaun McNay, and Scott Wade of George Fox University; Nadyne Guzman and Pamela Shockley-Zalabak of the University of Colorado-Colorado Springs; and Bryan Poulin of Lakehead University, Canada. Thanks also to our editor at Waveland Press, Carol Rowe, who was a constant source of encouragement and inspiration.

The University of Colorado-Colorado Springs and George Fox University graciously granted sabbatical leave for both of us, which was instrumental in the completion of the fourth edition. Special recognition goes to the many research assistants who helped with previous editions—Almarah Belk, Marylou Berg, Carrie Brown, Joanne Desrochers, Fred Gatz, Sarah Gillespie, Gina Hallem, Peg Hutton, Misse Lampe, Ashley Lewis, Amanda Martell, Kevin O'Neill, Melissa Rowberg, Rich Seiber, Heather Smith, and Penny Whitney— and to those who helped prepare materials for this edition—Karen Bisset, Chris Cooper, Belinda Pilcher, and Hush Hancock. Our greatest appreciation, however, is reserved for our families who lovingly supported our journey to explore the latest developments in leadership.

Acknowledgements

Students and colleagues (including readers of the previous editions) provided us with many of their own leadership stories along with encouragement, advice, and support. In particular we want to recognize Alvin Goldberg, our mentor at the University of Denver, who was instrumental in igniting our interest in the topic of leadership.

Many of our associates, past and present, have also been helpful in focusing our thoughts concerning leadership. Most notably we want to thank Ted Baartmans, Jeroen Meier, and Annebeth Sieswerda of the Presentation Group in Bloemendaal, the Netherlands; Kevin Barge of the University of Georgia; Stephen Bowden, Neil Harnisch, and Ted Zorn of the University of Waikato, New Zealand; Jim Fleming, Shaun McNay, and Scott Wade of George Fox University; Nadyne Guzman and Pamela Shockley-Zalabak of the University of Colorado-Colorado Springs; and Bryan Poulin of Lakehead University, Canada. Thanks also to our editor at Waveland Press, Carol Rowe, who was a constant source of encouragement and inspiration.

The University of Colorado-Colorado Springs and George Fox University graciously granted sabbatical leave for both of us, which was instrumental in the completion of the fourth edition. Special recognition goes to the many research assistants who helped with previous editions—Almarah Belk, Marylou Berg, Carrie Brown, Joanne Desrochers, Fred Gatz, Sarah Gillespie, Gina Hallem, Peg Hutton, Misse Lampe, Ashley Lewis, Amanda Martell, Kevin O'Neill, Melissa Rowberg, Rich Seiber, Heather Smith, and Penny Whitney—and to those who helped prepare materials for this edition—Karen Bisset, Chris Cooper, Belinda Pilcher, and Hush Hancock. Our greatest appreciation, however, is reserved for our families who lovingly supported our journey to explore the latest developments in leadership.

Contents

Preface

Revising a text serves as a sobering reminder of how quickly events and organizations change. The terrorist attacks on the World Trade Center and the Pentagon and our involvement in the war in Iraq produced an almost instantaneous shift in national priorities. The Clinton scandals and the contested Bush-Gore presidential election now seem like ancient history. Of course, rapid change is not limited to the political arena. Since the third edition of this book appeared in print, a number of major corporations like Enron, K-Mart, and Global Crossing have gone bankrupt while others, like Lowe's and Apple Computer, are in better shape than they were just a few years ago.

Many of the revisions in this fourth edition of *Leadership: A Communication Perspective* address changing world conditions as well as recent developments in the fields of communication and leadership studies. We've updated examples, sources, cases and research highlights throughout. While the number of chapters remains the same, readers of the fourth edition will find additional material on such topics as emotional intelligence, transformational leadership, resisting influence, group decision making, global leadership, and ethics. There are also two new features found at the end of each chapter. The first feature—Cultural Connections—looks at the impact of global diversity on concepts covered in that chapter. Experts cited in these sections caution us against blindly transferring leadership concepts and behaviors from the United States to other cultural settings. The second feature—Leadership on the Big Screen—describes a movie or documentary that brings important chapter themes to life. You may want to review these films on your own or your instructor may ask you to analyze one of them as a class project. We highlight the chapter concepts that are illustrated in each film. However, don't limit your reflection and analysis to our lists. You'll find that every film has connections that extend beyond the chapter to material covered in the rest of the book.

Leadership: A Communication Perspective emphasizes both theory and practice because we contend that leadership is a symbolic process and that leaders are made, not born. Leadership competence is the product of communication competence. Each chapter blends discussion of research and theory with practical suggestions for improving leadership effectiveness.

The first six chapters introduce the fundamentals of leadership. Chapter 1 examines the relationship between leadership and communication with an in-depth look at the differences between leading and managing and the leader/follower relationship. Chapter 2 surveys the research on leader and follower communication styles. Chapters 3 and 4 summarize the development of leadership theory. Chapters 5 and 6 focus on two elements—power and influence—that are essential to the practice of leadership.

The next three chapters provide an overview of leadership in specific contexts. Chapter 7 introduces group leadership, contrasting groups and teams, and describing the use of self-directed work teams. Chapter 8 is a discussion of organizational leadership. Chapter 9 examines the power of public leadership.

The final three chapters look at important leadership issues. Chapter 10 describes cultural differences, how to foster diversity, and how to narrow the gender leadership gap. Chapter 11 identifies components of ethical behavior and outlines ethical perspectives that can guide both leaders and followers. Chapter 12 identifies strategies for developing effective leadership communication.

As we noted in the preface to previous editions, this text is designed as an introduction to leadership from a communication vantage point, not as the final word (as if there could be one) on the topic. Please consider *Leadership: A Communication Perspective* as our part of a continuing dialogue with you on the subjects of leading and following. Throughout the book we'll invite you to disagree with our conclusions, generate additional insights of your own, and explore topics in depth through research projects, reflection papers, and small group discussions. If we've ignored issues that you think are essential to the study and practice of leadership, let us know. Send your comments and suggestions to us via e-mail or regular mail to the addresses below or in care of Waveland Press.

Michael Z. Hackman
Department of Communication
University of Colorado-Colorado Springs
1420 Austin Bluffs Parkway
Colorado Springs, CO 80933-7150
mhackman@uccs.edu

Craig Johnson
Department of Communication
George Fox University
414 Meridian St.
Newberg, OR 97132
cjohnson@georgefox.edu

One

LEADERSHIP AND COMMUNICATION

> *Leadership is action, not position.*
> —Donald McGannon

Overview

Leadership: At the Core of Human Experience
Defining Leadership
    The Nature of Human Communication
    The Human Communication Process
    Leadership: A Special Form of Human Communication
    Leaders vs. Managers
The Leader/Follower Relationship
Willingness to Communicate/Leadership Communication Skills
    Functional Communication Skills
    Emotional Communication Competencies
Playing to a Packed House: Leaders as Impression Managers

Leadership: At the Core of Human Experience

Leadership attracts universal attention. Historians, philosophers, and social scientists have attempted to understand and to explain leadership for centuries. From Confucius to Plato to Machiavelli, many of the world's most famous thinkers have theorized about how people lead one another.[1] One reason for the fascination with this subject lies in the very nature of human experience. Leadership is all around us. We get up in the morning, open the newspaper, or turn on the radio or television and discover what actions leaders all over the world have taken. We attend classes, work, and interact in social groups—all with their own distinct patterns of leadership. Our daily experiences with leadership are not that different from the experiences of individuals in other cultures. Leadership is an integral part of human life in rural tribal cultures as well as in modern industrialized nations. Looking at your past leadership efforts can help to provide a good starting point for understanding why the success of leadership often varies so significantly. Identify your own best and worst leadership moments and what you can learn from these experiences by completing the self-assessment exercise in box 1.1.

While leadership is part of every society, there are scholars who question just how much difference one leader can make. These observers argue that a leader only accounts for a small portion of a group's success or failure and gets the credit (or blame) when other forces are really at work.[2] The fate of a business, for example, may rest more on industry trends and market conditions than on the decisions of the CEO. The best school principal can't improve the academic performance of students without committed, talented teachers.

We acknowledge that the importance of leadership can be overstated. Yet, we remain convinced that leaders do make a difference. For every study that casts doubt on the importance of leadership, several more establish that leaders have a significant impact on group outcomes.[3] Attempts to devalue leadership appear to be losing their momentum. Some skeptics who earlier doubted the significance of leaders now admit that these individuals exert strong influence on organizations and the experiences of their members.[4] Followers prosper under effective leaders and suffer under ineffective leaders whatever the context: government, corporation, church or synagogue, school, athletic team, or class project group. The effects of leadership scandals in organizations such as Rite-Aid, Tyco, and WorldCom underscore the fact that leadership does have an impact. The study of leadership, then, is more than academic. Understanding leadership has practical importance for all of us. (See the case study in box 1.2 for a dramatic example of how important leadership can be.) In this text we will examine leadership in a wide variety of situations. However, our perspective remains the same—leadership is best understood from a communication standpoint. As Gail Fairhurst and Robert Sarr explain, effective leaders use language as their most tangible tool for achieving desired outcomes.[5] Let's begin our exploration of leadership by considering the special nature of human communication and the unique qualities of leadership.

Box 1.1   Self-Assessment

Your Best and Worst Leadership Moment[6]

Everyone has enjoyed leadership success at some point. At some time—whether in high school, college, on the athletic field, in a community or religious group, or at work—we have all made things happen through other people. We have all been leaders. Looking back over your life, what is the experience that you are *most* proud of as a leader? Use the space below to capture the details of that moment.

Just as all of us have enjoyed success, we've also experienced the pain of leadership failure. Learning to be a leader requires looking back and learning from past mistakes so that you don't repeat errors. What was your most disappointing experience as a leader? Record your thoughts in the space below.

Given the best and worst leadership experiences you identified, consider the lessons you have learned about leadership in the past. In working through this assessment it can be very helpful to share your leadership stories with others so that you have a richer set of examples from which to compile a list of leadership lessons. The lessons learned from past leadership experiences might be things like: *It is difficult to succeed as a leader when followers are not motivated; leadership works best when you have a clear sense of direction;* or *a leader must be sure his or her message is understood to insure followers stay involved.* Try to identify ten leadership lessons your experiences (and, if possible, those of others) have provided.

Leadership Lessons

1.
2.
3.
4.
5.
6.
7.
8.
9.
10.

Box 1.2   Case Study

Death on Everest

Leadership in high-risk activities like whitewater rafting, rappelling, and mountain climbing can literally mean the difference between life and death. In the best selling book *Into Thin Air*, writer and alpine expert Jon Krakauer describes how poor leadership decisions contributed to disaster on Mt. Everest, the highest mountain on earth at 29,038 feet.[7]

In April 1996, Krakauer joined the Adventure Consultants expedition to write an article on the Everest climb for *Outside* magazine. Several groups were on the mountain that spring, but the Adventure Consultants team was most closely allied with an expedition organized by a company called Mountain Madness. The leaders of the two teams had very different approaches to guiding. Rob Hall, 35, the New Zealander heading Adventure Consultants, was a cautious, well-organized climber. He had a "methodical, fastidious approach" to his ascents. Because of his successful experience as an Everest guide, the leaders of other parties came to him for advice. In contrast, American Scott Fischer, head of the Mountain Madness group, took a "harrowing, damn-the-torpedoes approach." The 40-year-old Fischer refused to let injuries and sickness slow him down. He was a gregarious, energetic leader who made friends quickly. This was his organization's first guided expedition up Everest. Clients, many of them novice climbers, paid $65,000 each for the trip.

Scaling Mt. Everest is a dangerous undertaking with a fatality rate of one death for every four successful ascents. Climbers suffer from a variety of altitude-related illnesses, including frostbite, hypothermia, severe weight loss, and lung and brain damage. Many have fallen to their deaths. At the very least, the extreme altitude (the top of the mountain is at the cruising level for commercial jet aircraft) makes reasoning difficult. In more extreme cases, trekkers hallucinate and become disoriented. Ill and injured team members must be carried halfway down the mountain to where the atmosphere thickens enough to allow evacuation by helicopter.

The Hall and Fischer expeditions (twenty climbers in all) started their final ascent around midnight on Friday, May 9. Members of both parties were told to head back to camp no later than 2 P.M. even if they had not reached the summit. Staying later would exhaust the climbers' bottled oxygen supply, increasing the chances of hypothermia, frostbite, and impaired thought. Tardy clients wouldn't be able to make it back to shelter before darkness fell.

The push to the top got off to a slow start due to bottlenecks of climbers at narrow places on the trail. Krakauer made it to the summit around 1 P.M. and headed down. However, Rob Hall and Scott Fischer ignored their own deadlines, perhaps out of competitive pressure. Hall was disappointed that most of his climbers had already turned back while Fischer's party was still on the way to the top. He wanted to make sure that a client who had failed to reach the summit the year before succeeded this time. Fischer needed a successful climb to build his business. Climbers from both groups were still on the summit well after 3 P.M. Around 6 P.M. a blizzard struck with driving snow and winds of over 60 knots. Krakauer made it to safety but Hall and Fischer did not. Despite the rescue attempts of other climbing teams, the two leaders and three of their clients died. Another member of the Hall/Fischer party survived only to lose most of his fingers and his nose to frostbite.

A number of miscalculations contributed to the Everest tragedy. In addition to ignoring turn-around times, team leaders failed to anticipate and prevent delays during the climb. Hall had never faced severe weather conditions on previous expeditions. Perhaps he was overconfident. Fischer decided to press on to the top despite exhaustion and the flare-up of a chronic liver problem. His second in command, an experienced Russian guide, chose to return to the safety of camp instead of staying with his party. Clients also demonstrated poor judgment, continuing on when severe fatigue and altitude sickness should have convinced them to turn back. The harsh environment of Everest left no margin for error. Oxygen deprivation, frigid temperatures, and the sudden blizzard ("a fairly typical Everest squall") determined the fate of the combined expeditions, turning the miscues of leaders, guides, and clients into tragedy.

Discussion Questions

1. Should inexperienced climbers be allowed on Mt. Everest? Would you lead such a trip, assuming that you had the qualifications to do so?
2. What can we learn about leadership from the 1996 Everest disaster?
3. Have you ever followed a leader in a life-or-death situation? How did you determine that this person was worthy of your trust?
4. Have you ever been the leader in a high-risk activity? How did you approach this task?
5. Hall and Fischer expected clients to obey their orders. Leaders in other dangerous situations like combat and firefighting also expect obedience. Is there ever a time when followers should challenge the authority of these leaders?

Defining Leadership

As we have noted, leadership is a fundamental element of the human condition. Wherever society exists, leadership exists. Any definition of leadership must account for its universal nature. Leadership seems to be linked to what it means to be human. As communication specialists, we believe that what makes us unique as humans is our ability to create and manipulate symbols.

> *I take leadership to signify the act of making a difference.*
> —Michael Useem

The Nature of Human Communication

Communication theorist Frank Dance defines symbols as abstract, arbitrary representations of reality agreed upon by human users.[8] For example, there is nothing in the physical nature of this book that mandates labeling it a "book." We have agreed to use this label, or symbol, to represent a bound collection of pages;

this agreement is purely arbitrary. The meaning of a symbol, according to Leslie White, does not come from the intrinsic properties of the idea, concept, or object being represented. The value is "bestowed upon it by those who use it."[9] Words are not the only symbols we use; we attach arbitrary meanings to many nonverbal behaviors as well. Looking someone in the eye symbolizes honesty to many North Americans. However, making direct eye contact in some other cultures is considered an invasion of privacy. Meaning is generated through communication.

> *[Humans] differ from the apes, and indeed all other living creatures so far as we know, in that [they are] capable of symbolic behavior. With words, [humans] create a new world, a world of ideas and philosophies.*
> —Leslie White

Communication is based on the transfer of symbols, which allows individuals to create meaning. As you read this text, the words we have written are transferred to you. The meanings of these words are subject to your interpretation. It is our goal to write in a way that allows for clear understanding, but factors such as your cultural background, your previous experience, your level of interest, and our writing skills influence your perception of our message. The goal of communication is to create a shared reality between message sources and receivers.

The human ability to manipulate symbols allows for the creation of reality. Simply labeling someone as "motivated" or "lazy," for example, can lead to changes in behavior. Followers generally work hard to meet the high expectations implied in the "motivated" label; they may lower their performance to meet the low expectations of the "lazy" label. This phenomenon, discussed in detail in chapter 8, is known as the Pygmalion Effect.

Symbols not only create reality but also enable us to communicate about the past, present, and future. We can evaluate our past performances, analyze current conditions, and set agendas for the future. In addition, symbolic communication is purposive and goal driven. We consciously use words, gestures, and other symbolic behaviors in order to achieve our goals. The purposeful nature of human communication differentiates it from animal communication.[10]

The communication patterns of animals are predetermined. For example, wolves normally travel in small groups known as packs. Dominance within the pack is predetermined based on such characteristics as size, physical strength, and aggressiveness. Humans, on the other hand, consciously select from an array of possibilities for achieving their goals. Human leadership is not predetermined as in the animal world; rather, it varies from situation to situation and from individual to individual.

Leadership shares all of the features of human communication described above. First, *leaders use symbols to create reality.* Leaders use language, stories, and rituals to create distinctive group cultures. Second, *leaders communicate about the past, present, and future.* They engage in evaluation, analysis, and goal setting. Effective leaders create a desirable vision outlining what the group should be like in the future. Third, *leaders make conscious use of symbols to reach their goals.* See the case study in box 1.3 for examples of the effective and ineffective use of symbols by leaders. We will have more to say about how leaders adapt their behaviors to reach their goals later in the chapter. In the meantime, let's take a closer look at the characteristics of human communication.

> *Words can destroy. What we call each other ultimately becomes what we think of each other, and it matters.*
> —Jeane Kirkpatrick

The Human Communication Process

Noted communication scholar Dean Barnlund identified five principles that reflect the basic components of human communication.[11]

Communication is not a thing, it is a process. Communication is not constant; it is dynamic and ever changing. Unlike a biologist looking at a cell through a microscope, communication scholars focus on a continuous, ongoing process without a clearly defined beginning or end. Take a typical conversation, for example. Does a conversation begin when two people enter a room? When they first see each other? When they begin talking? Barnlund, and others, would suggest that a conversation actually "begins" with the experiences, skills, feelings, and other characteristics that individuals bring to an interaction.

Communication is not linear, it is circular. Models depicting the process of communication have evolved from a linear explanation, first developed by ancient Greek rhetoricians over two thousand years ago, to a circular explanation, offered by Barnlund. In the earliest description of the communication process, a source transmitted a message to a receiver in much the same way that an archer shoots an arrow into a target. Only the source had an active role in this model; the receiver merely accepted messages. This view, known as an action model, is diagrammed below.

An Action Model of Communication

Box 1.3   Case Study

The Importance of Symbols

Leadership is primarily a symbolic activity. The words and behaviors of leaders greatly influence the reactions of those who follow. Consider these examples:

Don Isley is the General Manager of Renco Manufacturing, a medium-sized manufacturing company producing precision components for the airline industry. The Renco plant is located in an office park near a commercial airport and parking is limited. Employee parking areas at the plant are divided into two lots. In one lot, managers and office staff park their vehicles near the main entrance to the Renco plant. On the other side of the building, those who work in the production area park near a side entrance to the plant. This parking arrangement is more informal than formal, but employees are consistent in their behavior and rarely park in the "wrong" lot. Isley parks in neither lot. He parks his vehicle, a new Corvette, directly in front of the building in a fire lane designated as a no parking area. Isley claims he needs to park in this location so that he can have easier access to his office. Some of the production workers who earn salaries just above minimum wage feel like Isley is "showing off." What do you think?

Peter Houghton is the CEO of a large privately owned utility company—Valley Electric. Houghton came to Valley Electric from a competitor where he was highly regarded for his successful management practices. Despite this reputation, employees at Valley Electric were nervous when Houghton was hired. He replaced a well-regarded CEO who had been at the helm during a period of rapid growth and profitability. Sensing this uneasiness, Houghton made the decision to spend his first month on the job meeting as many Valley Electric employees as he could. Houghton visited offices, power stations, and field sites. He introduced himself to employees, asked questions, and learned policies and procedures. At the end of his first month on the job, Houghton finally reported to his office. He felt ready to assume the challenge of leading Valley Electric. What do you think of this strategy?

Mark Ayala is the owner of a small tee-shirt printing business. His company employs about fifteen full-time staff members that are responsible for the production of a variety of custom-designed tee shirts. Most of the staff work for minimum wage, and turnover is high. The clothing produced ranges from special-order logo shirts for corporate clients to mass-produced shirts celebrating sports team championships. Ayala started the business in his garage five years ago and has built a loyal clientele by providing high-quality products that are delivered on time to his customers. Ayala and his staff must, at times, work around the clock to meet deadlines for special orders. Through his persistence and hard work, Ayala has developed a very successful business. Recently, Ayala noted that his total revenue for the year exceeded one million dollars for the first time in company history. To mark this accomplishment and to thank his employees, Ayala came in late one night and printed tee-shirts for his staff. The shirts featured a depiction of a one-million-dollar bill with Ayala's picture in the center. On the back each shirt read, "Thanks a Million." When Ayala announced the million-dollar milestone to his employees and handed out the shirts, many of his employees were appreciative. Some, however, found the tee-shirt giveaway insulting. What do you think?

Eric Littleton is the president of Bald College, a small, private, residential school in the south. Under pressure from students, Littleton recently removed the "faculty only"

designation from the parking lot next to the building that houses the offices of many professors. Soon students who live in nearby dormitories occupied most of the parking
spots, rarely moving their cars except on weekends. Faculty protested the loss of the
parking and loading spaces to the president but to no avail. Now they routinely gripe to
one another about the fact that they have to walk two or three blocks from their cars,
often carrying heavy loads of books and classroom materials. Some feel that Littleton's
refusal to reconsider his choice is a sign that he doesn't understand or appreciate his
employees. What do you think?

Margaret Gates is the superintendent of schools in the Elmwood Hills school district.
Elmwood Hills is an affluent community located in the suburbs of a large metropolitan
area. The schools in the Elmwood Hills district have an excellent reputation, and many
parents choose to live in the area so their children can attend the schools. Gates was
hired as superintendent after her predecessor (who had been in the district for thirty-
seven years as a teacher and administrator) retired. Gates was a well-regarded candidate; she had years of experience leading high-performing programs in school districts
in another state. Within two months of her arrival at Elmwood Hills, Gates assembled
all of more than 2,000 faculty and staff within the district. Although few of these teachers or staff members had met Gates yet, most were eager to hear what their new leader
had to say. In the meeting, Gates unveiled a new vision statement and a set of twelve
initiatives, including mandatory nightly homework assignments, a greater emphasis on
core academic subjects, and revamping many of the existing programs within the district. Although many of the initiatives Gates presented had merit, most of those attending the meeting left with a very negative impression of their new leader. What do you
think went wrong?

Shirley Phillips is the CEO of Hilcrest Laboratories, a multinational pharmaceutical
company. As CEO, Phillips has exhibited an antipathy toward corporate perks. Like all
other Hilcrest executives and managers, Phillips has a cubicle, not a private office.
When Phillips travels, she flies coach class and rents a subcompact car, as do all
Hilcrest executives and managers. Employees jokingly refer to the Ford Escorts they are
most often given by rental agencies as "Hilcrest limousines." Phillips's efforts are
viewed by some as merely an attempt to cut costs. Some senior managers feel they have
earned the perks of first-class travel and full-size rental cars. Others contend that
Hilcrest's profit-sharing plan is perk enough and that money shouldn't be wasted on
costly airfares and rental cars. Phillips argues her actions communicate a belief that all at
Hilcrest are equal in importance. What do you think?

After considering these five examples, think of some of the leaders with whom you
have worked in the past. Identify examples of effective or ineffective symbolic behavior
on the part of these leaders. Discuss your examples with others in class.

The action model provided an incomplete depiction of the communication
process because the response of the receiver was ignored. Reactions to messages, known as feedback, were included in the next explanation of communication—the interaction model. The interaction model described communication as a process of sending messages back and forth from sources to receivers

and receivers to sources. From this perspective, diagrammed below, communication resembles a game of tennis.

·An Interaction Model of Communication

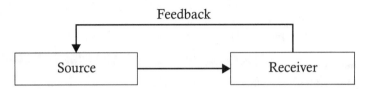

The evolution of the circular explanation of communication was completed with the development of Barnlund's transactional model. The transactional approach assumes that messages are sent and received simultaneously by source/receivers. The ongoing, continuous nature of the process of communication is implicit in this model.

A Transactional Model of Communication

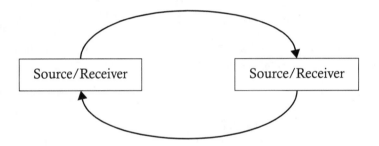

In the transactional model, communicators simultaneously transmit and receive messages. Effective communicators pay close attention to the messages being sent to them as they talk with others. The typical classroom lecture demonstrates how we act as senders and receivers at the same time. Even though only one person (the instructor) delivers the lecture, students provide important information about how the lecture is being received. If the lecture is interesting, listeners respond with smiles, head nods, and questions. If the lecture is boring, class members may fidget, fall asleep, or glance frequently at their watches. These responses are transmitted throughout the lecture. Thus, both the instructor and students simultaneously act as message source and receiver.

Communication is complex. Communication involves more than just one person sending a message to another. The process involves the negotiation of shared interpretations and understanding. Barnlund explains that when you have a conversation with another person there are, in a sense, six people involved in the conversation.

1. Who you think you are
2. Who you think the other person is
3. Who you think the other person thinks you are
4. Who the other person thinks he or she is
5. Who the other person thinks you are
6. Who the other person thinks you think he or she is

Communication is irreversible. Like a permanent ink stain, communication is indelible. If you have ever tried to "take back" something you have said to another person, you know that while you can apologize for saying something inappropriate, you cannot erase your message. Many times in the heat of an argument we say something that hurts someone. After the argument has cooled down, we generally say we are sorry for our insensitive remarks. Even though the apology is accepted and the remark is retracted, the words continue to shape the relationship. The other person may still wonder, "Did he/ she really mean it?" We can never completely un-communicate.

Communication involves the total personality. A person's communication cannot be viewed separately from the person. Communication is more than a set of behaviors; it is the primary, defining characteristic of a human being. Our view of self and others is shaped, defined, and maintained through communication.

Now that you have a better understanding of the process of human communication, we will examine the special nature of leadership communication.

Leadership: A Special Form of Human Communication

One way to isolate the unique characteristics of leadership is to look at how others have defined the term. There are three themes common to many proposed definitions of leadership. The first theme is *the exercise of influence*. To identify leaders, we need to determine who is influencing whom. For example, Paul Hersey defines leadership as "any attempt to influence the behavior of another individual or group.[12] Bernard Bass argues that "an effort to influence others is attempted leadership." When others actually change, then leadership is successful.[13] Swedish researcher Mats Alvesson focuses on the influence process from a communication perspective, arguing that leadership is a "culture-influencing activity" that involves the "management of meaning." [14]

The second definitional thread is *group context*. Leader influence attempts are neither random nor self-centered. Instead, leaders channel their influence and encourage change in order to meet the needs or to reach the goals of a group (task force, business organization, social movement, state legislature, military unit, nation). Note the group orientation in the following definitions:

- the behavior [of] an individual when he [she] is involved in directing group activities. [15]
- the process (act) of influencing the activities of an organized group toward goal setting and goal achievement.[16]

Placing leadership in the context of group achievement helps to clarify the difference between leadership and persuasion. Persuasion involves changing attitudes and behavior through rational and emotional arguments. Since persuasive tactics can be used solely for personal gain, persuasion is not always a leadership activity. Persuasion, although critical to effective leadership, is only one of many influence tools available to a leader.

> *Leadership is one of the most observed and least understood phenomena on earth.*
>
> —James MacGregor Burns

The third definitional theme emphasizes *collaboration*. Leaders and followers establish mutual purposes and work together to reach their goals. Success is the product of leaders' and followers' joint efforts. Joseph Rost highlights the interdependence of leaders/followers this way: "Leadership is an influence relationship among leaders and their collaborators [followers] who intend real changes that reflect their mutual purposes."[17]

Combining our discussion of human communication with the definitional elements above, we offer the following communication-based definition of leadership: **Leadership is human (symbolic) communication, which modifies the attitudes and behaviors of others in order to meet shared group goals and needs**. (For a sampling of how some other textbooks have defined leadership see box 1.4).

Box 1.4

Leadership Definitions: A Textbook Sampler

"Leadership is a process whereby an individual influences a group of individuals to achieve a common goal."—Peter Northouse[18]

"[Leadership is]. . . the process wherein an individual member of a group or organization influences the interpretation of events, the choice of objectives and strategies, the organization of work activities, the motivation of people to achieve the objectives, the maintenance of cooperative relationships, the development of skills and confidence by members, and the enlistment of support and cooperation from people outside the group or organization."—Gary Yukl[19]

"A leader can be defined as any person who influences individuals and groups within an organization, helps them in the establishment of goals, and guides them toward achievement of those goals, thereby allowing them to be effective."—Afsaneh Nahavandi[20]

"Leadership involves people in a relationship, influence, change, a shared purpose of achieving a desired future, and taking personal responsibility to make things happen." —Richard Daft[21]

"Organizational leadership behaviors emerge during interaction among individuals working toward a common goal or engaged in activity of mutual interest." —Patricia Witherspoon[22]

Leaders vs. Managers

Management is often equated with leadership. However, leading differs significantly from managing. Managers may act as leaders, but often they do not. Similarly, employees can take a leadership role even though they do not have a managerial position. Leadership experts James Kouzes and Barry Posner suggest the following exercise to highlight the differences between leaders and managers. Take a sheet of paper and make two columns. In the first column, identify the activities, behaviors, and actions of leaders. In the second column, list the activities, behaviors, and actions of managers. Now compare the two lists. Kouzes and Posner predict that you will associate leaders with factors such as change, crisis, and innovation and that you will associate managers with organizational stability. According to these authors, "When we think of leaders, we recall times of turbulence, conflict, innovation, and change. When we think of managers, we recall times of stability, harmony, maintenance, and constancy."[23]

Perhaps the key difference between a leader and a manager lies in the focus of each. While the manager is more absorbed in the status quo, the leader is more concerned with the ultimate direction of the group. Warren Bennis and Burt Nanus surveyed 90 successful corporate and public leaders in an attempt to better understand leadership. They found that *managers are people who do things right and leaders are people who do the right thing.*[24] As Bennis and Nanus further explain, managers are problem solvers who focus on physical resources. Leaders, on the other hand, are problem finders who focus on spiritual and emotional resources.

Efficiency versus effectiveness provides another contrast between management and leadership. Management is frequently concerned with efficiency. However, an organization can be efficiently run yet still fail if it does not respond to changing conditions or meet the needs of members. Bennis notes: "Leading does not mean managing; the difference between the two is crucial. There are many institutions that are very well managed and very poorly led. They may excel in the ability to handle all the routine inputs every day, yet they may never ask whether the routine should be preserved at all."[25]

> *You manage things; you lead people.*
> —Grace Murray Hopper

John Kotter uses three central activities to highlight the differences between management and leadership: creating an agenda, developing a human network for achieving the agenda, and executing the agenda (box 1.5).

The management process for creating an agenda involves planning and budgeting. Managers at this stage tend to focus on time frames, specific details, analysis of potential risks, and resource allocation. By contrast, leaders create an agenda by establishing direction and communicating long-range views of the big picture. This process involves developing a desirable and attainable goal for the future, oth-

---

Box 1.5   Research Highlight

Management vs. Leadership[26]

	Managers	**Leaders**
Creating an Agenda	*Planning and Budgeting*—establishing detailed steps and timetables for achieving needed results and then allocating the resources necessary to make that happen	*Establishing Direction*—developing a vision of the future, often the distant future, and strategies for producing the changes needed to achieve that vision
Developing a human network for achieving the agenda	*Organizing and Staffing*—establishing some structure for accomplishing plan requirements, staffing that structure with individuals, delegating responsibility and authority for carrying out the plan, providing policies and procedures to help guide people, and creating methods or systems to monitor implementation	*Aligning People*—communicating the direction by words and deeds to all those whose cooperation may be needed so as to influence the creation of teams and coalitions that understand the vision and strategies and accept their validity
Execution	*Controlling and Problem Solving*—monitoring results vs. plan in some detail, identifying deviations, and then planning and organizing to solve these problems	*Motivating and Inspiring*—energizing people to overcome major political, bureaucratic, and resource barriers to change by satisfying very basic, but often unfulfilled, human needs
Outcomes	Produces a degree of predictability and order, and has the potential of consistently producing key results expected by various stakeholders (e.g., for customers, always being on time; for stockholders, being on budget)	Produces change, often to a dramatic degree (e.g., new products that customers want, new approaches to labor relations that help make a firm more competitive)

---

erwise known as a vision. The actions of Herb Kelleher during his tenure as CEO of Southwest Airlines are examples of this type of leadership activity. In taking a fledgling airline to prominence in the U.S. airline industry, Kelleher had a clear vision of the strategy and leadership practices necessary to make Southwest Airlines a success (see the case study in box 1.6 for more about leadership at Southwest Airlines). The presence of a shared and meaningful vision is a central component of effective leadership. *Fortune* magazine's list of the "100 Best Companies to Work for in America" noted that two of the common features of great organizations are a visionary leader and a strong sense of common purpose.[27]

Box 1.6   Case Study

Leadership with Love at Southwest Airlines

Southwest Airlines began as a fledgling operation with four airplanes flying eighteen daily roundtrip flights among three cities in Texas. The early history of the airline led to the development of a unique leadership approach. Before Southwest ever had its first flight, a group of competitors filed a lawsuit to block the upstart airline from initiating its proposed service. The legal battle dragged on for three years before Southwest finally got off the ground in 1971. The early days were lean for the airline as flights often carried only a handful of passengers and the cost of the legal battles required to establish the company drained its resources. The CEO of Southwest Airlines from its founding until his retirement in 2001 was Herb Kelleher. An attorney by training, Kelleher turned the struggling airline into a personal crusade. To survive among its hostile and much larger competitors, Kelleher worked to develop the leadership practices that would allow Southwest to survive.

Southwest's operating strategy focuses on providing low-cost, no-frills service with frequent direct flights between cities that are an average of 400 miles, or an hour, apart. The method for achieving success in using this strategy has been to employ a revolutionary leadership approach. While many companies argue that the customer is always right, Kelleher believes employees come first. "Customers are not always right and I think that is one of the biggest betrayals of your people you can possibly commit. The customer is frequently wrong. We don't carry those sorts of customers. We write them and say, 'Fly somebody else. Don't abuse our people.'"[28]

As Southwest's corporate philosophy explains: Employees are number one. The way you treat your employees is the way they will treat your customers. The results for customers have been exceptional. Southwest has consistently been rated by the United States Department of Transportation Consumer Report as having the best on-time performance, best baggage handling, and fewest complaints of all major air carriers. In a highly competitive industry in which all carriers strive to get top ratings in any of the three reporting categories, Southwest is the only airline to ever be rated best in all three categories—a feat called the triple crown. Indeed, Southwest once held the triple crown for five consecutive years—an astonishing record considering no other airline has held the triple crown for even one month!

Other key corporate philosophies suggest that work should be fun (employees are encouraged to take their jobs and the competition seriously—but not themselves) and that employees should do whatever it takes to meet the needs of customers. As Colleen Barrett, the Executive Vice President for Customers, explains, "No employee will ever be punished for using good judgment and good old common sense when trying to accommodate a customer—no matter what our rules are."[29] Perhaps most extraordinary is Southwest's commitment to conducting its business in a loving manner. As consultants Kevin and Jackie Freiberg explain, "Southwest understands that when people feel loved they develop a greater capacity to love others. Employees bear out this belief every day in the kindness, patience, and forgiveness they extend to each other and their customers."[30] This value is so deeply ingrained in the company's culture that Southwest's stock symbol is LUV.

The results of the Southwest leadership approach have been nothing short of phenomenal. The airline has been rated as one of the nation's ten best companies to work for, and Herb Kelleher was hailed in 1994 by *Fortune* magazine as quite possibly the best CEO in the United States.[31] Each year Southwest receives over 200,000 applications for some 4,000 available jobs. The demand for employment at the airline is so great that it is easier to get accepted at Harvard than it is to become a mechanic at Southwest![32] In an industry plagued by problems associated with excessive costs, frequent labor disputes, and the often-changing whims of travelers, Southwest has been a bastion of profitability. Southwest is the only U.S. airline to have made money every year since 1973. After the September 11 terrorist attacks caused a significant downturn in the travel industry, the 2002 stock market capitalization of Southwest exceeded the *combined* value of all ten of the other major U.S. air carriers.[33] Certainly Southwest's well-defined operating strategy has contributed to its long-term success. The airline's major competitive advantage, however, appears to be its people and its leadership practices. It will be interesting to see if Kelleher's retirement has an impact on Southwest's ongoing culture. For now, the company and its leadership appear as strong as ever.

Discussion Questions

1. How do you think an organization's past history affects leadership practices?

2. Do you agree with Herb Kelleher's contention that employees should come first? Have you ever worked somewhere where you have felt that you were particularly valued as an employee? Have you had the opposite experience?

3. Do you think people are more productive and satisfied if they have fun in the workplace? Why or why not?

4. Is there a place for "love" in organizations? How can a leader build a loving environment?

5. Southwest Airlines is noted for its outstanding customer service. What are some of the organizations you have encountered that have provided the best and the worst customer service? What do you think the relation is between customer service and leadership?

Once the agenda is established, people must be mobilized to achieve the plan. Managers mobilize others through organizing and staffing. The focus of this management activity involves getting individuals with the right training in the right job and then getting those individuals to carry out the agreed-upon plan. Leaders mobilize others by aligning people. Alignment focuses on integration, teamwork, and commitment. The leadership of Apple Computer co-founder Steven Jobs exemplified this process of aligning people. During development of the Apple Macintosh computer in the early 1980s, Jobs moved his entire design team to a separate building on the Apple compound. With Jobs as project leader, and with the Jolly Roger flying over the design team's building, members of the Macintosh development team focused their attention exclusively on designing a personal computer to revolutionize the home computing industry. These "pirates" of the corporation aligned themselves to bring Jobs' compelling vision to life.[34]

The execution of the agenda from a management perspective involves controlling and problem solving. This process usually focuses on containment, control, and predictability. Leaders execute their agenda by motivating and inspiring. This process focuses on empowerment, expansion, and creativity. One organization that does an excellent job of motivating and inspiring followers is Mary Kay Cosmetics. Founded in 1963 by the late Mary Kay Ash, the company has more female employees earning over $50,000 per year than any other organization in the world. One of the most coveted awards presented to the independent agents (known as "beauty consultants") who sell Mary Kay products is a 14-carat gold brooch in the shape of a bumblebee. The bumblebee, all new recruits are reminded, has a body too big for its wings and thus should not be able to fly. But it does. Recruits are told that the ability to achieve more than seems possible is what Mary Kay Cosmetics is all about.[35]

According to Kotter, the outcomes of management and leadership differ significantly. Management produces orderly results. Leadership, on the other hand, often leads to useful change. Both these activities are important in the overall success of groups and organizations.

To be successful, organizations must consistently meet their current commitments to customers, stockholders, employees, and others, and they must also identify and adapt to the changing needs of these key constituencies over time. To do so, they must not only plan, budget, organize, staff, control, and problem solve in a competent, systematic, and rational manner, they must also establish and reestablish, when necessary, an appropriate direction for the future, align people to it, and motivate employees to create change even when painful sacrifices are required.[36]

For Kotter the key is balancing leadership and management. As he explains, not every individual is effective as both a leader and a manager. However, successful organizations nurture both. The ideal is to combine strong leadership and strong management.[37] This can be accomplished by developing both leadership and management skills within individuals or by establishing a combination of these skills among a cross-section of individuals within an organization. Despite differences in the management and leadership process, there are also some similarities. Leadership expert John Gardner observes, "Every time I encounter an utterly first-class manager he [she] turns out to have a lot of leader in him [her].[38]

Of course, an employee may assume a leadership role even though she or he is not a manager. Consider the example of a Procter and Gamble employee at a Jif peanut butter plant. While shopping at his neighborhood supermarket, the employee noticed that the labels on several jars of Jif peanut butter were crooked. He bought all of the stock with the poorly mounted labels, assuming that Procter and Gamble would not want its image tarnished by sloppy workmanship. His leadership efforts have since become part of the folklore of Procter and Gamble.[39] (For another example of a follower who took on a leadership role, see the Leadership on the Big Screen case at the end of the chapter.)

The Leader/Follower Relationship

Clarifying the relationship between leading and following is the final step in defining leadership. Earlier we noted that leaders and followers function collaboratively. Recognizing that leaders and followers work together toward shared objectives should keep us from overemphasizing the importance of leaders or ignoring the contributions of followers. Unfortunately, we generally pay a lot more attention to leaders than to followers. The revival of the Chrysler Corporation in the early 1980s is a case in point. Press accounts and business texts typically credit Lee Iacocca with saving Chrysler from bankruptcy. The company would not have returned to profitability, however, without the hard work of thousands of assembly line workers, supervisors, truck drivers, warehouse workers, secretaries, and other followers.

Shifting some of the spotlight from leadership to followership is one way to assure that followers get the credit they deserve. Yet the distinction between leading and following is not always clear. Many of the qualities of effective leaders, such as independent thought, commitment, competence, dependability, and honesty, also mark effective followers. Compounding the confusion is the fact that some scholars are reluctant to use the follower label. Joseph Rost and John Gardner argue that the term reflects a hierarchical rather than a collaborative view of leadership and relegates those who don't lead to a passive, subservient role. They recommend using such descriptors as "constituents," "stakeholders," or "collaborators" instead.[40]

> *In every moment of life, we both lead and follow.*
> —Dee Hock

Describing leaders and followers as relational partners who play complementary roles is the best way to capture what followership means.[41] Leaders exert a greater degree of influence and take more responsibility for the overall direction of the group. Followers, on the other hand, are more involved in implementing plans and carrying out the work. John Childress, CEO of the Senn-Delaney Leadership Consulting Group, calls this process of filtering leadership down to followers *distributed leadership.*[42]

Most people routinely shift between leader and follower functions during the course of the day. As a student you must follow in the classroom, but you may also lead a class project group or an intramural sports team. In recognition of this fact, we suggest that you make a mental note to think of yourself not as a leader or a follower but as a *leader-follower.* Recognize, too, that you can learn to lead by following and learn to follow by leading (see box 1.7).

Training at West Point provides one example of followership as leadership training.[43] Submission to authority is the cornerstone of leadership development at the military academy. New cadets must obey everyone else, including upperclassmen. Leadership can prepare us for followership in the same way that following prepares us for leading. By observing our followers we can gain insights into what we should (and shouldn't) do when we serve in a follower role.

Box 1.7   Research Highlight

Co-Leadership

Wise leaders create strong bonds with their key subordinates by sharing power and credit. David Heenan and Warren Bennis use the term "co-leadership" to describe these alliances. They "make the case for co-leadership" with the stories of a dozen leaders and key adjuncts from business, government, athletics, and other settings.[44] Some of these notable leader/co-leader partnerships include: Intel co-founder Andy Grove and his successor Craig Barrett; humanitarian Helen Keller and her teacher Ann Sullivan Macy; Mao Tse-Tung and his deputy Chou En-lai; and Stanford women's head basketball coach Tara VanDerveer and her assistant Amy Tucker.

The researchers' first suggestion to prospective co-leaders is: "Know thyself." Co-leaders define success in their own terms and realize that not everyone has the talent or desire to function in the top spot. Further, they recognize that being No. 2 may be tougher than being No. 1. Co-leaders may labor in obscurity, receiving little recognition when things go right but getting more than their share of the blame when things go wrong. In some cases top lieutenants are more, not less, talented than those who get more attention. General George Marshall, for example, was army chief of staff during World War II. He directed recovery efforts in Europe after the war and served as Secretary of Defense and Secretary of State under President Truman. Winston Churchill, Dwight Eisenhower, and Harry Truman are more famous than General Marshall. Yet, all three of these leaders called Marshall "the greatest man they had ever known."[45]

Other lessons for co-leaders build on the foundation of self-knowledge. According to Heenan and Bennis, prospective co-leaders should also understand their superiors and their organizations. Partnerships won't work if leaders aren't willing to share power and if co-leaders break the rules or assumptions of the organization's culture. Effective co-leaders know when to challenge their bosses, how to cope with pressures, and when to leave an organization. Finally, co-leaders recognize their dual role as leaders/followers. Top adjuncts are leaders in their own right. They are generally experts in some important organizational task and may oversee the work of thousands of followers. Craig Barrett, for instance, directed Intel's manufacturing division before replacing Andy Grove as CEO.

Heenan and Bennis believe that organizations can create cultures that foster co-leadership. Among the more important steps to a co-leadership culture: (1) celebrate the enterprise, not celebrity, by putting the emphasis on the collective work of the group rather than on one individual; (2) encourage togetherness through teamwork; (3) cultivate equalitarianism by keeping status distinctions to a minimum; (4) nurture trust and communicate hope in the future; (5) solicit dissent and put allegiance to group values above loyalty to the individual leader; and (6) share power and authority.

> *A good leader can't get too far ahead of his [her] followers.*
> —Franklin D. Roosevelt

Throughout this text we will use alternative terms like "constituents," "stakeholders" or "collaborators" to describe those responsible for carrying out the work. Yet we are not ready to completely abandon the follower label. The word is widely used, and followers are neither passive nor subservient. As you will see in chapter 2, followers play an active, vital role in the success of any group, organization, or society. We also believe that effective leadership is based on service, not hierarchy. In our discussions of transformational leadership in chapter 4 and servant leadership in chapter 11, we suggest that truly great leaders serve rather than rule because they recognize that those whom they lead entrust them with leadership responsibilities.

Outstanding leaders enable followers to become leaders themselves. Followership expert Robert Kelley sums up the work of followers and leaders this way:

> . . . in reality followership and leadership are two separate concepts, two separate roles. . . . Neither role corners the market on brains, motivation, talent, or action. Either role can result in an award-winning performance or a flop. The greatest successes require that the people in both roles turn in top-rate performances. We must have great leaders and great followers.[46]

Willingness to Communicate/Leadership Communication Skills

Viewing leadership from a communication perspective recognizes that leadership effectiveness depends on our willingness to interact with others and on developing effective communication skills. Those who engage in skillful communication are more likely to influence others. University of West Virginia communication professors James McCroskey and Virginia Richmond developed the Willingness to Communicate (WTC) scale to measure the predisposition to talk in a variety of situations.[47] Take a few minutes to complete the WTC instrument in box 1.8, and then compute your total score as well as your scores for each of the subscales.

McCroskey, Richmond, and their colleagues report that overall scores on the WTC scale are directly related to communication behavior. Individuals with high WTC scores communicate more frequently and for longer periods of time than people with low WTC scores. Increased communication activity, in turn, leads to a number of positive outcomes in the United States, a society that values individualism and assertiveness (see chapter 10). Speaking up is not viewed as favorably in cultures, such as some Asian societies, that put more emphasis on the needs of the group as a whole.[48] In the United States:

- High WTCs are viewed as more credible and attractive and are more often identified as opinion leaders.

- People who speak frequently in small groups are more likely to hold leadership positions (see chapter 7).

- Talkative people are more likely to be hired and promoted. They also stay with organizations longer than their quiet colleagues.

- High WTCs are rated as more socially and sexually attractive by members of the opposite sex.

- Those who are more willing to communicate are also more open to change and enjoy tasks that require thought.[49]

Box 1.8 Self-Assessment

Willingness to Communicate Scale (WTC)[50]

Directions: Below are twenty situations in which a person might choose to communicate or not to communicate. Presume you have completely free choice. Indicate in the space at the left what percentage of the time you would choose to communicate in each type of situation. You can choose any percentage ranging from 0% (never communicating) to 100% (always communicating).

_30_ 1. Talk with a service station attendant.

_80_ 2. Talk with a physician.

_10_ 3. Present a talk to a group of strangers.

_70_ 4. Talk with an acquaintance while standing in line.

_70_ 5. Talk with a salesperson in a store.

_90_ 6. Talk in a large meeting of friends.

_70_ 7. Talk with a police officer.

_40_ 8. Talk in a small group of strangers.

_100_ 9. Talk with a friend while standing in line.

_90_ 10. Talk with a waiter/waitress in a restaurant.

_90_ 11. Talk in a large meeting of acquaintances.

_70_ 12. Talk with a stranger while standing in line.

_70_ 13. Talk with a secretary.

_50_ 14. Present a talk to a group of friends.

_40_ 15. Talk in a small group of acquaintances.

_10_ 16. Talk with a garbage collector.

_30_ 17. Talk in a large meeting of strangers.

_100_ 18. Talk with a spouse (or girl/boy friend).

_100_ 19. Talk in a small group of friends.

_30_ 20. Present a talk to a group of acquaintances.

The WTC is designed to indicate how willing you are to communicate in a variety of contexts, with different types of receivers. The higher your WTC total score, the more willing you are to communicate in general. Similarly, the higher your given subscore for a type of context or audience, the more willing you are to communicate in that type of context or with that type of audience.

Scoring: The WTC permits computation of one total score and seven subscores. The subscores relate to willingness to communicate in each of four common communication contexts and with three types of audiences. To compute your scores, merely add your scores for each item and divide by the number indicated below.

Subscore Desired	Scoring Formula
Group discussion	Add scores for items 8, 15, and 19; then divide by 3.
Meetings	Add scores for items 6, 11, and 17; then divide by 3.
Interpersonal conversations	Add scores for items 4, 9, and 12; then divide by 3.
Public speaking	Add scores for items 3, 14, and 20; then divide by 3.
Stranger	Add scores for items 3, 8, 12, and 17; then divide by 4.
Acquaintance	Add scores for items 4, 11, 15, and 20; then divide by 4.
Friend	Add scores for items 6, 9, 14, and 19; then divide by 4.

To compute the total WTC scores, add the subscores for stranger, acquaintance, and friend. Then divide by 3.

Norms for WTC Scores

Group discussion	>89 High WTC, <57 Low WTC
Meetings	>80 High WTC, <39 Low WTC
Interpersonal conversations	>94 High WTC, < 64 Low WTC
Public speaking	>78 High WTC, < 33 Low WTC
Stranger	>63 High WTC, < 18 Low WTC
Acquaintance	>92 High WTC, <57 Low WTC
Friend	>99 High WTC, < 71 Low WTC
Total WTC	>82 High Overall WTC
	<52 Low Overall WTC

There are a number of reasons why we may be reluctant to interact with others: we may have inherited a tendency to be shy, introverted, and anxious about communication; put a low value on talk; feel alienated from other people; suffer from low self-esteem; or experience fear or anxiety about specific communication situations. In some cases, we're reluctant to communicate because of a skill deficiency. We don't know how (or think we don't know how) to communicate effectively. This perceived deficiency becomes a vicious cycle. Thinking we can't communicate successfully, we avoid interaction. As a consequence, we don't get the practice we need and therefore can't communicate as well.

We can reverse the cycle by developing our skills. Skill development builds confidence and encourages us to talk. When we communicate, we practice our skills and increase our effectiveness. This results in greater self-assurance, making it even more likely that we'll participate in future interactions.

Functional Communication Skills

Before determining which specific skills we need to develop in order to become more productive leaders, we should be familiar with the functions of human communication. Frank Dance and Carl Larson identify three such functions.[51] First, *symbolic communication links humans to other humans and to the physical environment.* Conversations, parties, weather reports, meetings, and so on tie us to one another and to the world. Second, *symbol usage develops higher mental processes.* Language makes reasoning and conceptualizing possible. Third, *human communication allows for the regulation of our own behavior as well as the behavior of others.* We can suggest, plead, command, or convince—to name a few of the possible means to regulate behavior.

Each of the functions of human communication identified by Dance and Larson plays a critical role in effective leadership. Successful leaders are experts in processing cues from the environment. They attend to current events, to the activities of other groups and organizations, and to their own group norms and cultures, as well as to the physical environment. Most importantly, they solicit feedback from others. Listening that accurately interprets verbal and nonverbal messages is a primary linking skill. Effective leadership also involves the establishment and maintenance of satisfying relationships with group members and nonmembers alike. Creating a trusting cooperative work atmosphere, building an effective team, and collaborating with leaders from other groups are all key linking abilities.

Thinking and reasoning skills are essential to leaders since leaders engage in problem solving and decision making. In addition, they direct groups towards goals. Key cognitive skills include constructing arguments, organizing ideas, identifying faulty assumptions and logic, evaluating alternatives, and thinking creatively. The term "envisioning" describes one additional conceptual activity needed for leadership. As leaders, we must be able to take the inputs we receive from linking with others and the environment and convert them into an agenda or vision for the future.

We noted earlier that influence is an important element in the definition of leadership. Skills that involve regulating the behavior of others are part of the leader's repertoire. In addition, leaders must regulate their own behaviors. To achieve both of these objectives, leaders need to:

1. Build and use power bases effectively.
2. Empower followers.
3. Develop perceptions of credibility.
4. Make effective use of verbal and nonverbal influence cues.
5. Resist inappropriate or unethical influence.
6. Communicate positive expectations for others.
7. Foster creativity and manage change.
8. Gain compliance.

Box 1.9   Research Highlight

How Important Are Communication Skills?[52]

In a survey of 428 personnel managers (the individuals most involved in corporate hiring decisions), respondents listed oral and communication skills as the most important factors in landing a job, successful job performance, and fitting the "ideal management profile." Important communication competencies include: interpersonal/human relations skills, listening, public speaking, writing, information gathering, small group communication, and giving effective feedback. The personnel professionals listed grade point average, résumé, school attended, and letters of recommendation as the least important factors in hiring and promotion decisions.

Table 1 lists the skills that members of the American Society of Personnel Administrators chose as most important in helping college graduates get their first jobs. Table 2 lists the factors that the personnel managers identify as keys to success on the job.

TABLE 1
Factors/Skills Important for Successful Job Search

Rank/Order	Factors/Skills	Rank/Order	Factors/Skills
1	Oral (speaking) communication	11	Grade point average
2	Listening ability	12	Part-time or summer
3	Enthusiasm		employments
4	Written communication skills	13	Accreditation of program
5	Technical competence	14	Leadership in campus/
6	Appearance		community activities
7	Poise	15	Participation in campus/
8	Work experience		community activities
9	Résumé	16	Recommendations
10	Specific degree held	17	School attended

TABLE 2
Factors/Skills Important for Successful Job Performance

Rank/Order	Factors/Skills	Rank/Order	Factors/Skills
1	Interpersonal/human	9	Dress/grooming
	relations skills	10	Poise
2	Oral (speaking)	11	Interviewing skills
	communication skills	12	Specific degree held
3	Written communication skills	13	Physical attractiveness
4	Persistence/determination	14	Grade point average
5	Enthusiasm	15	Résumé
6	Technical competence	16	School attended
7	Personality	17	Letters of recommendation
8	Work experience		

9. Develop argumentative competence.
10. Negotiate productive solutions.
11. Adapt to cultural differences.
12. Shape public opinion.
13. Organize and deliver effective presentations.
14. Engage in self-leadership.
15. Challenge and correct faulty personal assumptions.

Emotional Communication Competencies

Functional communication skills highlight the rational dimension of leadership by focusing on how leaders efficiently gather and process information, make decisions, construct logical arguments, and so on. Forgetting the emotional side of leadership would be a mistake, however. Effective leaders are also skilled at sharing and responding to emotions. For example, they know how to communicate affection, liking, and excitement to followers. In addition, they know how to channel their emotions in order to achieve their objectives and to maintain friendly group relations.

Growing recognition of the importance of emotional leadership is due in large part to the emotional intelligence (EI) movement.[53] Psychologist Daniel Goleman and others argue that emotional intelligence (the ability to recognize, control, and express emotions) is more important to success in life than traditional IQ.[54] This is particularly apparent in the workplace where emotional sensitivity sets excellent performers apart from ordinary ones.[55] For example, store managers who are better at managing stress have higher sales per square foot of floor space. More effective counselors respond calmly to emotional attacks from clients, and the best sales people are sensitive to the emotional desires of their customers.

Emotional intelligence becomes increasingly important with every step up the organizational ladder. Higher-level positions are generally more complex, involve more communication, and have a greater impact on the bottom line. Not surprisingly, then, emotional competence is critical to top executives. They carry out a series of sophisticated tasks, most of which involve interaction with subordinates and other leaders, and are responsible for the performance of the entire group. Their ability to manage emotions is integral to both their personal success and the success of their organizations.

The most significant task of senior leaders, according to Goleman and his colleagues, is to foster a positive emotional climate. They introduce the term "primal leadership" to describe how effective leaders create or "prime" good feelings in followers. Creating a positive emotional climate brings out the best in leaders and followers alike, an effect called *resonance*.[56] The benefits of resonance include more optimism about reaching objectives, increased creativity, greater cooperation, and sustained focus on the task, all of which contribute to higher profits and growth.

Unfortunately, proponents of emotional intelligence appear to overstate its importance to leaders. They go so far as to argue that nearly 90 percent of the competencies that account for executive success are emotional rather than cognitive in nature.[57] They also label some competencies as "emotional" that seem to have more to do with thinking than feeling. For instance, EI researchers identify conflict management and influence as emotional skills, but we included them on our earlier list of functional (rational) leadership communication abilities.

Striking a balance between logic and emotion is safer than making one more important than the other. When it comes to leadership, *both* are essential.[58] An example of the importance of both cognitive and emotional competencies is provided by looking at crisis decision making (see chapter 8). To avoid making a hasty decision in a crisis, leaders must use a variety of cognitive skills, such as rejecting their faulty beliefs and assumptions, gathering facts, identifying stakeholders, soliciting a broad range of opinions, keeping records, and perspective taking. At the same, they must employ such emotional skills as managing stress, overcoming mental and physical fatigue, and resisting group pressures.

The following set of emotional competencies demonstrates that the success of followers and leaders depends on how well are they able to integrate emotion and cognition. Skillfully blending feeling and thinking requires the five skills listed below.[59]

1. *Perception, appraisal, and expression of emotion.* Emotional intelligence begins with the ability to identify, evaluate, and then express emotional states. These skills may seem rudimentary, but some people are "emotionally illiterate." For example, people can be oblivious to the fact that they are irritating everyone else in the group. While most of us are not this insensitive, we frequently suffer from emotional blind spots. There are times when we feel uneasy but can't identify our emotions or when we don't know exactly how to express our affection for friends or loved ones.

2. *Attending to the emotions of others.* Those in a leadership role must understand the feelings of followers in order to connect with them. Consider the case of a CEO who doesn't understand that his employees are feeling overworked and discouraged. If he fails to acknowledge their frustration and tries to inspire them to work harder, they aren't likely to put forth additional effort. Instead, he will appear out of touch.

3. *Emotional facilitation of thinking.* Emotional states impact decision-making styles. Good moods facilitate creative thinking while sad moods slow the decision-making process and encourage more attention to detail. Both emotional states have a role to play in problem solving. Some problems require intuitive, broad thinking; others demand a more linear, logical approach. Emotionally intelligent leaders know how to match the mood with the problem. Further, they recognize the dangers of ignoring risks when in an optimistic frame of mind, or of being too critical when feel-

ing pessimistic. Using emotions to facilitate thinking also means channeling feelings in order to reach goals. For example, moderate fear of failure can spur us to prepare before making a presentation. Remembering past successes can reduce our anxiety before we deliver the speech.

4. *Understanding and analyzing emotional information and employing emotional knowledge.* This cluster of competencies links symbols to emotions. Leaders must be able to label what they feel and recognize the relationship between that label and other related terms. For example, "anger" belongs to a family of words that includes "irritation," "rage," "hostility," and "annoyance." The internal states identified by these labels are connected in specific ways. Irritation and annoyance lead to anger and rage, not the other way around. Understanding this fact can empower leaders. A supervisor may decide to postpone a meeting with a disagreeable employee, for instance, when she senses that her irritation with this individual could escalate into unwanted anger. Recognizing how emotions blend together is also important. Surprise is one example of an emotion that rarely stands alone. When we feel surprised, we generally experience some other emotion, perhaps happiness, disappointment, or anger, at the same time.

5. *Regulation of emotion.* The last component of emotional intelligence puts knowledge into action. This set of competencies enables leaders to create the feelings they desire in themselves and in others. Emotionally skilled leaders know how to maintain positive moods and how to repair negative ones. To do so, they employ such tactics as avoiding unpleasant situations, engaging in rewarding tasks, and creating a comfortable work environment. In addition, they can step back and evaluate their feelings to determine if their responses in a situation were appropriate. Such evaluation can encourage them to remain calm instead of getting upset and to be more supportive instead of only focusing on the task. Effective leaders also help others maintain and improve their moods. They use these skills to create cohesive groups and to inspire and motivate followers.

> *Humans are not, in any practical sense, predominantly rational beings, nor are they predominantly emotional beings. They are both.*
>
> —Peter Salovey

Playing to a Packed House: Leaders as Impression Managers

From a communication standpoint, leaders are made, not born. We increase our leadership competence as we increase our communication skills.

We can compare the leadership role to a part played on stage to illustrate how effective communication skills translate into effective leadership.

Sociologist Erving Goffman adapted Shakespeare's adage that life is a stage and argued that most communication interactions can be viewed as performances complete with actors, dialogues, and dressing rooms.[60] Let's look at a typical date, for example. The date is a performance that may take place on any number of stages: the dance floor, the living room, the movie theater, the football game. The actors (the couple) prepare in their dressing rooms at home before the performance and may return to the same locations for a critique session after the date ends. Particularly on the first date, the interactants may work very hard to create desired impressions—they engage in "impression management." Each dating partner tries to manage the perceptions of the other person by using appropriate behaviors, which might include dressing in the latest fashions, acting in a courteous manner, engaging in polite conversation, and paying for meals and other activities.

To see how impression management works, change one aspect of your usual communication and watch how others respond. If friends have told you that you seem unfriendly because you are quiet when meeting new people, try being more assertive the next time you meet strangers at a party. If you make a conscious effort to greet others, introduce yourself, and learn more about the others at the gathering, you may shake your cool, unfriendly image.

Leaders also engage in impression management, both to secure leadership positions and to achieve their goals. Social psychologists Robert Lord and Karen Mahar report that leadership impression formation begins with followers deciding whether or not they like an aspiring leader.[61] Their initial, emotional reaction then shapes how they process additional information about this individual. Liking leads to more favorable evaluations; dislike has the opposite effect. Those with good feelings toward a leader are more likely to tolerate or excuse his or her failings. Those harboring negative feelings will be much more critical of miscues.

After the initial emotional evaluation, cognitive processing takes place. Judgments of leaders are largely based on images of ideal leaders called prototypes. For instance, the ideal small group leader takes an active role in the discussion through setting goals, giving directions, managing conflict, and summarizing the group's deliberations (see chapter 7). The group member who engages in these prototypical behaviors is most likely to emerge as leader when one has not been appointed ahead of time. In a similar fashion, presidential candidates who create the impression that they are decisive, informed, responsible, dignified, and intelligent (characteristics associated with the prototypical president) are most likely to get elected. Military leaders, too, can succeed only if they present the right image to their troops. (Read the Research Highlight in box 1.10 for more information on commanders as impression managers.)

Performance outcomes also impact the way that followers and outsiders view those in leadership roles. Observers make judgments about a leader's effectiveness based on how well the group performs, and on whether or not they believe the leader is responsible for its successes or failures. For example, we generally infer that the CEO of a highly profitable company is effective due to the success of the corporation. However, leaders don't always get credit for the group's achievements. Professional basketball coach Phil Jackson has more championship rings than any other contemporary coach. Yet some critics dismiss his accomplishments, claiming that his success is almost entirely due to the fact that he had Michael Jordan on his team in Chicago and Shaquille O'Neal and Kobe Bryant as players on the Los Angeles Lakers.

Rosalie Hall and Robert Lord's research provides some important clues as to how we can go about shaping the impressions others have of us as leaders.[62] First, since affective evaluations occur immediately and shape future perceptions, establish friendly relations with followers early on. Treat group members as warmly and fairly as possible. Unfriendly or preferential treatment will create disliking that will cast your future actions in an unfavorable light. Second, determine the leadership prototypes held by the group and act in a way that fulfills those expectations. What followers expect of you, as a leader, will depend on a variety of factors, including organizational and national culture, group history, and elements of the situation. Third, increase your power or discretion to influence events through your knowledge and example (see chapter 5) while establishing coalitions with others in the organization. Finally, recognize that performance counts or, rather, your connection with performance counts. To be effective, you'll need to be perceived as contributing to the group's success.

Remember that when it comes to impression management, as a leader you'll play to a packed house. People in organizations carefully watch the behavior of the CEO for information about the executive officer's character and for clues as to organizational priorities, values, and future directions. They seek answers to such questions as: "Can I trust him/her?" "What kind of behavior gets rewarded around here?" "Is she or he really interested in my welfare?" "Is dishonesty tolerated?" "Are we going to survive the next five years?" "Is this an enjoyable, exciting place to work?"

Outstanding leaders use communication as a tool to reach their ends. If they want to emphasize customer service, they spend more time with customers and reward good service providers. If they want to foster cooperation, they downplay power and status cues and emphasize listening. These leaders promote communication on a first-name basis and refuse such luxuries as executive washrooms and reserved parking places. Effective leaders know what they want to accomplish, what communication skills are needed to reach their goals, and how to put those behaviors into action.[63]

Many people are uncomfortable with the idea of impression management. They equate playing a role with being insincere, since true feelings and beliefs might be hidden. While this is a very real danger, followers continually watch for inconsistencies and often "see through" performances of insincere leaders. Frequently, we have no choice but to play many roles. We are forced into performances as job applicants, students, dating partners, and leaders each day. The real problem is that we often mismanage the impressions we make. Our behaviors may make us appear dull or untrustworthy when we really are interesting and honest.

Some fear that leaders can manipulate impressions to mislead the group. This is a legitimate concern (we'll discuss the ethical dimension of leadership in greater detail in chapter 11). Because impression management can be used to further group goals or to subvert them, it should be judged by its end product. Ethical impression management meets group wants and needs and, in the ideal, spurs the group to reach higher goals. Unethical impression management subverts group needs and lowers purpose and aspiration.

Box 1.10   Research Highlight

Impression Management in the Military

British military historian John Keegan believes that impression management is the key to successful military leadership.[64] All commanders are actors who perform before their troops. However, only those who create the right image or "mask of command" will consistently lead their armies to victory. According to Keegan, "The theatrical impulse will be strong in the successful politician, teacher, entrepreneur, athlete, or divine, and will be both expected and reinforced by the audiences to which they perform."[65] Men and women who must lead others into battle show themselves to followers only through a mask. The mask reveals what followers hope and require; it conceals what they should not know. The mask the leader constructs marks him or her as the leader wanted and needed at a particular time and place.

Keegan examines the careers of Alexander the Great, Wellington, Ulysses S. Grant, and Adolph Hitler to determine the elements that make up the desired mask of command.

1. **Kinship.** Effective commanders select staff members who help them create a bond with their troops. These officers simultaneously carry out two functions. They relay the message that the commander cares about the needs of his/her soldiers; simultaneously they bring the concerns of those on the front line to the leader's attention. Hitler didn't establish kinship with his soldiers because he surrounded himself with advisors who echoed his opinions and had no empathy for the misery of the German army.

2. **Public speaking.** No commander can rely entirely on his/her staff, no matter how effective those officers might be. There are times when he/she must directly address the troops, "raising their spirits in times of trouble, inspiring them at moments of crisis and thanking them in victory."[66] This makes public speaking one of the most important skills of military leadership. Contemporaries of Alexander the Great were so impressed by his battlefield addresses that they recorded his words for future generations.

3 **Sanction.** To maintain an aura of authority, every commander needs to punish those who desert, pillage, or otherwise disobey orders. Yet, physical force should be used sparingly lest the leader become as much an enemy to his/her soldiers as the opposing army. Rewards reduce the need for coercion. Over the centuries military leaders have encouraged obedience by rewarding followers with money, material goods, vacation leaves, medals, and war memorials.

4. **Action.** The image of military commanders rests heavily on what they accomplish on the battlefield. Winning generals combine what Keegan calls *knowing* and *seeing*. Wellington and Grant triumphed because they learned everything they could about the terrain and their enemies before the battle started (knowing). When the fighting began, they periodically visited the front lines to witness developments first hand (seeing). Hitler, while he knew a great deal about military matters, stayed in his bunker. As a result, he didn't really understand (see) battlefield conditions and ended up as one of history's most notable military failures.

5. **Example.** Keegan contends that the greatest imperative of command is to share risks with followers. Military leaders must stay alive to direct the fight but can't completely insulate themselves from danger and discomfort if they hope to earn the respect of their followers. Staying in a luxurious headquarters far from the chaos of the front lines is a prescription for disaster. In World War I, for example, the morale of the French, German, Russian, Italian, and British armies all collapsed when soldiers suffering in the trenches rebelled against elite officers who lived like country gentlemen in comfortable chateaux. With the dangers of "chateau generalship" in mind, the modern Israeli, Vietnamese, and Chinese armies insist that their commanders live with their troops and lead by example.

Summary

Leadership is an integral part of the human experience. There are leaders in every type of human society. In this chapter, we suggested that leadership is best understood as a form of human (symbolic) communication. Human communication is: (1) a process, (2) circular in nature, (3) complex, (4) irreversible, and (5) the characteristic that defines the total personality. Leaders use symbols to modify the attitudes and behavior of others in order to reach group goals. In contrast to managers who value efficiency and focus on maintaining the status quo, leaders value effectiveness and focus on the future of the group or organization. Managers plan and budget, organize and staff, and control and problem solve while leaders establish direction, align people, and motivate and inspire. Both management and leadership are important in the overall success of a group or organization.

Leaders and followers are relational partners who play complementary roles. Leaders exert a greater degree of influence and have more responsibility for the overall direction of the group. Followers are more involved in implementing plans and carrying out the work. Most people act as leader-followers, routinely shifting between leader and follower functions. Following is excellent preparation for leadership, and leading can prepare us for the follower role.

Leadership effectiveness depends on our willingness to communicate as well as on developing effective communication skills. Developing skills builds confidence, which encourages us to interact with others. Effective communication facilitates influence.

There are two sets of communication skills—functional and emotional—that are essential to leaders. Functional communication skills include linking, thinking/reasoning, and regulating. Linking skills involve monitoring the environment, creating a trusting climate, team building, and collaborating with outside groups. Thinking and reasoning skills incorporate problem-solving abilities and creating agendas or visions. Regulating involves influencing others through the wise use of power, compliance gaining, argument, negotiation, and other means. Emotional communication competencies include: (1) perception, appraisal, and expression of emotion; (2) attending to the emotions of others; (3) emotional facilitation of thinking; (4) understanding and analyzing emotional information and employing emotional knowledge; and (5) regulation of emotion.

Successful leaders match their communication behaviors to their goals through a process called impression management. They are liked by others, link their attitudes and behaviors to the prototypes of leaders held by group members, strive to expand their ability to influence events, and are associated with high performance. Ethical leaders use impression management to reach group objectives rather than to satisfy selfish, personal goals.

Application Exercises

1. Take a trip to a local bookstore and check to see how many books you can find on leadership. Did you find more or less titles than you expected? Report your findings in class.

2. Conduct a debate regarding the importance of leaders. Have one-half of your class argue that leaders are more important than ever and have the other half argue that leaders are less necessary than in the past. As an alternative, debate the relative importance of cognitive and emotional skills to the success of leaders, once again dividing the class in half to argue for the significance of one set of competencies or the other.

3. Develop your own definition of leadership. How does it compare to the one given in the chapter?

4. Make a list of the characteristics of leaders and managers. Are your characteristics the same as those described by Kouzes, Posner, and Kotter? To clarify the differences between leaders and managers, describe someone who is an effective leader and then someone who is an effective manager. How do these two people differ? Share your descriptions with others in class.

5. Select one of your follower roles (student, employee, team member, etc.) and then select one of your leadership roles (team captain, project group leader, coach). Consider the behaviors and qualities you appreciate or dislike in those who lead or follow you. What can you learn from their strengths and weaknesses that you can apply as a leader-follower? What

conclusions can you draw about being an effective leader or follower? Write up your findings.

6. In a small group, determine whether or not the word "follower" is an outdated term. Should we use terms like "stakeholder" or "collaborator" instead? What alternative terms would your group suggest? Report your conclusions.

7. Pair off with someone and compare your overall Willingness to Communicate (WTC) scores as well as your seven subscores. What factors make you and your partner reluctant to communicate in all situations or in particular contexts? What can each of you do to increase your willingness to communicate? What communication skills do you need to sharpen?

Cultural Connections: Developing Intercultural Emotional Competence

Dealing with groups of followers from a variety of cultural backgrounds is a fact of life for modern leaders. Leadership effectiveness increasingly depends upon intercultural emotional competency—the ability to accurately send and receive emotional messages across cultural boundaries. Consider, for instance, the importance of correctly interpreting the mood of a Japanese negotiator when setting up a trade agreement or of knowing how enthusiastic to be when presenting a new company initiative to a group of German employees.

Transferring emotional intelligence to other cultures is difficult because the rules governing the understanding and expression of emotion vary from society to society. Sally Planalp, a communication professor at both the University of Utah and the University of Waikato in New Zealand, offers a number of examples of cultural differences in her book *Communicating Emotion: Social, Moral, and Cultural Processes*.[67] Here are just a few of the ways that emotional communication differs between cultures:

- Utku Eskimos, who live in extreme hardship, are more likely to tolerate negative events and rarely express anger or aggression.
- the Ifaluk of Micronesia believe that unwanted feelings must be expressed or physical or mental illness will result; the Chinese believe that too much expression of emotion produces sickness.
- European-Americans value emotional self-restraint; African Americans value emotional expressiveness.
- among the Wolof people of Senegal, members of the griot (lower) caste act as emotional spokespeople for their noble patrons, sharing the feelings of the nobility in public meetings.
- the Maori of New Zealand value spontaneous, heart-felt speech over carefully prepared remarks.

- the Balinese both laugh and cry in response to death and fall asleep in the face of frightening events.
- in Malaysia, peasants would "run amok," engaging in random attacks as a way of controlling the power of the ruling class.

In the face of such differences, making assumptions about the likely emotional responses of the members of other groups will probably end in cross-cultural disaster. Most people in the United States trust that "a smile coupled with a friendly and enthusiastic attitude can provide the transcultural social lubricant" to make it through any cross-cultural interaction.[68] However, many foreigners find U.S. friendliness shallow and insulting. Even asking questions about others can backfire. Native Hawaiians view such behavior as invasive and rude.

Effective leaders (and followers) set aside their preconceived notions about how to send and interpret emotional messages and seek instead to learn as much as they can about the feeling rules of other cultures. Only then can they begin to develop the intercultural emotional intelligence they need to succeed in a multicultural world.

Leadership on the Big Screen: *Erin Brockovich*

Starring: Julia Roberts, Albert Finney

Rating: R for language and sexual content

Synopsis: Roberts won an Academy Award for her portrayal of Brockovich, a most unlikely real-life hero. The twice-divorced mother of three, Brockovich talks Finney (the lawyer who lost her personal injury lawsuit) into hiring her. She is anything but a model employee, dressing like a streetwalker, swearing like a teamster, alienating her coworkers, and sassing her employer. However, Brockovich emerges as a leader when she discovers that Pacific Gas and Electric Company (PG & E) has been poisoning the drinking water of the small town of Hinckley, California. Brockovich persuades Finney to take the case and convinces hundreds of townspeople to join the suit. Eventually PG & E pays out more than $300 million in restitution.

Chapter Links: leadership as communication, leader/follower relationships, willingness to communicate, functional and emotional leadership communication skills, impression management

Two

LEADERSHIP AND FOLLOWERSHIP COMMUNICATION STYLES

> *Proper words in proper places, make the true definition of a style.*
> —Jonathan Swift

Overview

The Dimensions of Leadership Communication Style
Authoritarian, Democratic, and Laissez-Faire Leadership
Task and Interpersonal Leadership
   The Michigan Leadership Studies
   The Ohio State Leadership Studies
   McGregor's Theory X and Theory Y
   Blake and McCanse's Leadership Grid®
Follower Communication Styles

The Dimensions of Leadership Communication Style

Think of the leaders you have worked with in the past. Chances are you enjoyed interacting with some of these people more than others. The leaders you enjoyed working with were most likely those who created a productive and satisfying work climate. Under their guidance, you probably accomplished a great deal and had a pleasant and memorable experience.

One factor that contributes to variations in leader effectiveness is communication style. Leadership communication style is a relatively enduring set of communicative behaviors that a leader engages in when interacting with followers. A leader's communication style may reflect a philosophical belief about human nature or may simply be a strategy designed to maximize outcomes in a given situation. The communication style a leader selects contributes to the success or failure of any attempt to exert influence. To explore your own leadership style preferences, complete the self-assessment in box 2.1

Researchers have identified a number of leadership communication styles in the past half-century. These varying styles can be pared down to two primary models of communication: one model compares *authoritarian, democratic*, and *laissez-faire* styles of leadership communication; a second model contrasts *task* and *interpersonal* leadership communication. Let's look more closely at these two models of communication.

Box 2.1   Self-Assessment

Leadership Communication Style Preferences Inventory[1]

Directions: Read the twelve statements below. For each statement indicate your level of agreement.

	Strongly Disagree	Disagree	Unsure	Agree	Strongly Agree
1. A leader should set direction without input from followers.	1	2	3	4	5
2. A leader should set direction with input and consultation with followers.	1	2	3	4	5
3. A leader should set direction based on the wishes of followers.	1	2	3	4	5
4. A leader should use a task force or committee rather than making a decision alone.	1	2	3	4	5

5. A leader should evaluate the progress of work with little input from followers.	1	2	3	4	5
6. A leader should leave it up to followers to initiate informal, day-to-day communication.	1	2	3	4	5
7. A leader should encourage followers to initiate decision making without first seeking approval.	1	2	3	4	5
8. A leader should closely monitor rules and regulations—punishing those who break the rules.	1	2	3	4	5
9. A leader should keep followers up to date on issues affecting the work group.	1	2	3	4	5
10. A leader should explain the reasons for making a decision to his/her followers.	1	2	3	4	5
11. A leader should remain aloof and not get too friendly with his/her followers.	1	2	3	4	5
12. A leader should provide broad goals and leave decisions regarding the methods for achieving the goals to followers.	1	2	3	4	5

Scoring: Tally your score on each of the leadership communication styles listed below by totaling your points as indicated.

Authoritarian	**Democratic**	**Laissez-Faire**
Question 1 _____	Question 2 _____	Question 3 _____
Question 5 _____	Question 4 _____	Question 6 _____
Question 8 _____	Question 9 _____	Question 7 _____
Question 11 _____	Question 10 _____	Question 12 _____
TOTAL _____	TOTAL _____	TOTAL _____

The higher your score, the greater your preference for a given leadership communication style. An unequal distribution of scores generally indicates a stronger preference for a certain style. Relatively equal scores indicate a more balanced preference of styles. This likely indicates a blended approach in which styles are used based on situational factors.

Authoritarian, Democratic, and Laissez-Faire Leadership

Kurt Lewin, Ronald Lippitt, and Ralph White undertook one of the earliest investigations of leadership communication style.[2] They studied the impact of authoritarian, democratic, and laissez-faire leadership communication styles on group outcomes.

Each of these styles of communication has unique features that affect how leaders interact with followers. The authoritarian leader maintains strict control over followers by directly regulating policy, procedures, and behavior. Authoritarian leaders create distance between themselves and their followers as a means of emphasizing role distinctions. Many authoritarian leaders believe that followers would not function effectively without direct supervision. The authoritarian leader generally feels that people left to complete work on their own will be unproductive. Examples of authoritarian communicative behavior include a police officer directing traffic, a teacher ordering a student to do his or her assignment, and a supervisor instructing a subordinate to clean a workstation.

Democratic leaders engage in supportive communication that facilitates interaction between leaders and followers. The leader adopting the democratic communication style encourages follower involvement and participation in the determination of goals and procedures. Democratic leaders assume that followers are capable of making informed decisions. The democratic leader does not feel intimidated by the suggestions provided by followers but believes that the contributions of others improve the overall quality of decision making. The adage that "two heads are better than one" is the motto of the democratic leader. A group leader soliciting ideas from group members, a teacher asking students to suggest the due date for an assignment, and a district manager asking a salesperson for recommendations regarding the display of a new product are examples of democratic communicative behavior.

> *I not only use all the brains that I have, but all that I can borrow.*
> —Woodrow Wilson

Laissez-faire, a French word roughly translated as "leave them alone," refers to a form of leader communication that has been called *nonleadership* by some.[3] An ineffective version of this communication style involves *abdication* of responsibility on the part of the leader; leaders withdraw from followers and offer little guidance or support. As a result, productivity, cohesiveness, and satisfaction often suffer. A supervisor nearing retirement or in jeopardy of being laid off or fired may exhibit the abdicating form of the laissez-faire leadership communication style. A more positive form of the laissez-faire leadership communication style affords followers a high degree of autonomy and self-rule while, at the same time, offering guidance and support when requested. The laissez-faire leader providing *guided freedom* does not directly participate in decision making unless requested to do so by followers. Examples of guided-free-dom communicative behavior include a leader quietly observing group deliberations (providing information and ideas only when asked), a teacher allowing students to create their own assignments, and a research and development manager allowing his or her subordinates to work on product designs without intervention. Take a look at box 2.2 and see if you believe the behavior exhibited by Roland Ortmayer is an effective or ineffective use of the laissez-faire leadership communication style.

How can you tell if a leader is using an authoritarian, democratic, or laissez-faire style? Pay close attention to the leader's communication. The following communication patterns will help you recognize the style of leadership:

Authoritarian	**Democratic**	**Laissez-Faire**
Sets goals individually	Involves followers in setting goals	Allows followers free rein to set their own goals
Engages primarily in one-way, downward communication	Engages in two-way, open communication	Engages in noncommittal, superficial communication
Controls discussion with followers	Facilitates discussion with followers	Avoids discussion with followers
Sets policy and procedures unilaterally	Solicits input regarding determination of policy and procedures	Allows followers to set policy and procedures
Dominates interaction	Focuses interaction	Avoids interaction
Personally directs the completion of tasks	Provides suggestions and alternatives for the completion of tasks	Provides suggestions and alternatives for the completion of tasks only when asked to do so by followers
Provides infrequent positive feedback	Provides frequent positive feedback	Provides infrequent feedback of any kind
Rewards obedience and punishes mistakes	Rewards good work and uses punishment only as a last resort	Avoids offering rewards or punishments
Exhibits poor listening skills	Exhibits effective listening skills	May exhibit either poor or effective listening skills
Uses conflict for personal gain	Mediates conflict for group gain	Avoids conflict

Lewin and his colleagues taught these communication styles to adult leaders who supervised groups of ten-year-old children working on hobby projects at a YMCA. The authoritarian leader was instructed to establish and to maintain policy and procedures unilaterally, to supervise the completion of task

---

Box 2.2   Case Study

The Laid-Back Leader[4]

Roland Ortmayer is a most unusual leader. Ort—as he is known to his friends—was head football coach at a small southern California school, the University of La Verne, for 43 years. In a profession in which winning is the measure of success, Ort's teams won only slightly more games than they lost during his coaching career (190 wins, 186 losses, 6 ties). That does not trouble Ort; he truly believes the adage let the better team win, even if that team is the opposition. If Ort's view of competition seems unusual, consider the following:

Ort never required his players to attend practices. "I think there is something wrong with a player if he practices every day," says Ort. When players did attend his practices, Ort offered his own homespun brand of logic. For example, Ort cut short passing drills after eight consecutive incompletions. Conventional wisdom suggests eight missed passes in a row would demand more, not less, practice. Explains Ort, "The problem was all we were practicing was incompletions."

Ort never recruited a player. He believed that athletes should attend La Verne because of its academic programs, not because of the football team. "I don't like recruiting. If you can out-recruit a school you can outplay them. Sports should be fun and play." Ort taught 10 physical education courses per year while at La Verne and considered himself, first and foremost, a teacher. Football is an "educational adjunct," explains Ort. Besides, he adds, there are many different ways to win. Some years Ort had "a miserable football season but a great archery class." He did not measure his success on his won-loss record on the football field.

Ort does not believe that football players should lift weights. There is too much physical work that needs to be done to waste time lifting useless weight. "I don't care if a player can bench press the world," the coach explains. "I just want my players to become the best they can be."

Ort didn't have a playbook. According to Ort, if he scripted all of the plays in advance there would be no incentive to be creative. "If players would rather run something out of the I formation than out of split backs, that's okay with me. I teach that it's all right to use your brains."

Ort had no team meetings and never kicked a player off any of his teams. Practice lasted from 3:45 to 5:30 P.M. Beyond that, a player's time was his own. "Relationships without punishment are most likely to gain in the long run," Ort contends. "I always feel that everyone who wants to play should play. Sometimes I lost because I tried to play too many players."

Ort lined the field before each game and washed the team's uniforms each Sunday. According to Ort, these activities made him "feel closer to the guys." As Ort explains, "I always carry the balls onto the field and off the field. I am interested in all aspects of the game; that is my responsibility and commitment."

Ort's laid-back style of leadership might not be effective at a larger institution where there is pressure to recruit top-notch athletes and to win big games. But at tiny La Verne, Ort was respected by administrators, faculty, and students alike, although he concedes that "sometimes the university president wanted us to win more games." He coached with compassion and understanding and helped his young men learn the value of competing and trying to be the best they can be. Asked to sum up the contribution he made in 43 years of coaching at La Verne, Ort suggests: "None of my players ever quit college to my knowledge. Some fellas are lawyers today, but I don't like lawyers. I think a culture with more lawyers than farmers is sick. I still have real pride in my former players. We all have responsibilities in society, and I just tried to take care of mine."

Discussion Questions

1. Under what conditions is the laissez-faire style of leadership communication most effective?

2. Do you think Ort used the abdication or guided freedom approach to laissez-faire leadership?

3. How should a leader's success be measured? Does it matter that Ort's teams won only slightly more games than they lost over the years?

4. Do you agree with the definition of leadership presented in chapter 1, which claims that leaders help followers achieve their goals and meet their needs? Did Ort do this?

5. How would you rate Ort as a leader? Would you like to play on his team?

assignments directly, and to dictate follower behavior in all situations. The democratic leader was told to encourage the participation of followers in the determination of policy and procedures related to task completion and follower behavior. The laissez-faire leader was instructed to avoid direct involvement in the establishment of policy and procedures by supplying ideas and information only when asked to do so by followers.[5]

The responses of the children in these experiments led to the formation of six generalizations regarding the impact of leadership communication style on group effectiveness.[6]

1. *Laissez-faire and democratic leadership communication styles are not the same.* Groups with laissez-faire leaders are not as productive and satisfying as groups with democratic leaders. The amount and quality of work done by children in laissez-faire groups was less than that of democratic groups. Additionally, the majority of children in laissez-faire groups expressed dissatisfaction despite the fact that more than two-and-a-half times as much play occurred in these groups.

2. *Although groups headed by authoritarian leaders are often most efficient, democratic leaders also achieve high efficiency.* The greatest number of tasks were completed under authoritarian leadership. This productivity depended on the leader's direct supervision. When the authoritarian leader left the room, productivity dropped by nearly 40 percent in some groups. Democratic groups were only slightly less productive. Further, productivity in these groups remained steady with or without direct adult supervision.

3. *Groups with authoritarian leadership experience more hostility and aggression than groups with democratic or laissez-faire leaders.* Hostile and aggressive behavior in the form of arguing, property damage, and blaming occurred much more frequently in authoritarian groups than in other groups.

4. *Authoritarian-led groups may experience discontent that is not evident on the surface.* Even in authoritarian-led groups with high levels of productivity and little evidence of hostility and aggression, absenteeism and turnover were greater than in democratic and laissez-faire groups. Further, children who switched from authoritarian groups to more permissive groups exhibited tension release behavior in the form of energetic and aggressive play.

5. *Followers exhibit more dependence and less individuality under authoritarian leaders.* Children in authoritarian groups were more submissive than those in other groups. These children were less likely to initiate action without the approval of the leader and less likely to express their opinions and ideas than children in the democratic and laissez-faire groups.

6. *Followers exhibit more commitment and cohesiveness under democratic leaders.* Children in democratic groups demonstrated a higher degree of commitment to group outcomes. The climate in democratic groups was generally supportive and friendly.

A number of follow-up studies to the work of Lewin, Lippitt, and White have provided additional information about the effects of authoritarian, democratic, and laissez-faire leader communication. Box 2.3 summarizes these findings.

The findings related to leadership communication style suggest the leader adopting authoritarian communication can expect: high productivity (particularly when he or she directly supervises followers); increased hostility, aggression, and discontent; and decreased commitment, independence, and creativity among followers. This style of communication would seem best suited for tasks requiring specific compliance procedures and minimal commitment or initiative. Routinized, highly structured, or simple tasks are often effectively accomplished under authoritarian leadership. Authoritarian leadership is also recommended when a leader is much more knowledgeable than his or her followers, when groups of followers are extremely large, or when there is insufficient time to engage in democratic decision making. Certainly a military combat leader would not stop to discuss the possibilities of advancing or retreating while under enemy fire.

Democratic leadership communication contributes to relatively high productivity (whether or not the leader directly supervises followers) and to increased satisfaction, commitment, and cohesiveness. This style of communication is best suited for tasks that require participation and involvement, creativity, and commitment to a decision. The only significant drawbacks to democratic leadership are that democratic techniques are time consuming and can be cumbersome with larger groups.

Box 2.3   Research Highlight

The Effects of Authoritarian, Democratic, and Laissez-Faire Leadership Communication Styles

Authoritarian Leadership	Democratic Leadership	Laissez-Faire Leadership
Increases productivity when the leader is present.[7]	Lowers turnover and absenteeism rates.[13]	Decreases innovation when leaders abdicate, but increases innovation when leaders provide guidance as requested.[19]
Produces more accurate solutions when leader is knowledgeable.[8]	Increases follower satisfaction.[14]	
	Increases follower participation.[15]	Decreases follower motivation and satisfaction when leaders abdicate.[20]
Is more positively accepted in larger groups.[9]	Increases follower commitment to decisions.[16]	
Enhances performance on simple tasks and decreases performance on complex tasks.[10]	Increases innovation.[17]	Results in feelings of isolation and a decrease in participation when leaders abdicate.[21]
	Increases a follower's perceived responsibility to a group or organization.[18]	
Increases aggression levels among followers.[11]		Decreases quality and quantity of output when leaders abdicate.[22]
Increases turnover rates.[12]		Increases productivity and satisfaction for highly motivated experts.[23]

The leader adopting the laissez-faire communication style may be accused of leadership avoidance. This communication style results in decreased productivity and less satisfaction for most followers. A number of variables, including the personality, age, and job experience of followers, impact the effectiveness of laissez-faire leadership. (See the research highlight in box 2.4 for a discussion of the impact of age on leadership style preferences.) A group led by a laissez-faire leader, particularly when the leader engages in abdication, may be less innovative than those with leaders employing authoritarian or democratic communication styles. However, laissez-faire leadership can be highly effective with groups of motivated and knowledgeable experts. These groups often do not require direct guidance and produce better results when left alone. A group

> *Treat people as if they were what they ought to be and you may help them to become what they are capable of being.*
> —Johann Wolfgang von Goethe

Box 2.4   Research Highlight

Leadership Style Across Generations[24]

In their book, *Generations at Work*, management consultants Ron Zemke, Claire Raines, and Bob Filipczak suggest that four primary generational groups exist in the United States: veterans (52 million people born between 1922 and 1943), baby boomers (73 million people born between 1944 and 1960), generation Xers (70 million people born between 1961 and 1980), and generation nexters (70 million people and counting born between 1981 and today). Each generation, they suggest, exhibits unique leadership style preferences.

Veterans. The hard work and vision of this generation shaped the United States as we know it today. Veterans built a space program and landed a man on the moon, revolutionized modern medicine, and helped pave the road for U.S. financial supremacy. Veterans are generally thought to be solid, reliable, no-nonsense employees. In leadership roles, veterans tend toward a directive style that was the norm when they entered the world of work. It is not unusual for veterans to lead by taking charge, making most decisions on their own, and delegating tasks to followers.

Baby Boomers. This group grew up in a time of unprecedented expansion and economic growth. Their generation tends to be optimistic, believing they can positively impact the world. Baby boomers live for the present—working long hours to obtain the material goods they desire while saving less and charging more on credit cards than other generations. As leaders, baby boomers tend toward a collegial and consensual style and are genuinely concerned about the welfare of others. Baby boomers work at encouraging participation in the workplace but (having worked for veterans in their formative years) are not always skilled at achieving these ends.

Generation Xers. This generation came of age in an era when political scandal, a struggling economy, soaring divorce rates, and an increasing reliance on technology fundamentally changed society. Many generation Xers became disillusioned, withholding their optimism and excitement as a means for avoiding disappointment. This tendency led some in other generations to label the Xers as "slackers." In fact, the tendency to challenge authority and question the methods of past generations has been a distinct advantage for this group. Like no previous time in history, the leader of today must be adept at dealing with change and uncertainty. As leaders, generation Xers tend to be fair, competent, and honest (sometimes painfully so). They tend to be supportive of diversity in work habits and believe that allowing workers freedom in their jobs helps produce better overall results.

Generation Nexters. These people are multi-culturalists who are comfortable with diversity of race, religion, and social background. They have lived in a world permeated by the home computer and the Internet, which has afforded them the opportunity to develop a comfort with technology and an appreciation for other cultures and viewpoints. The global mindset of the generation nexters has made them the most tolerant of all generational groups. They are also highly organized and rule-oriented. Indeed, they seem to have more in common with their grandparents and great-grandparents, the veterans, than with the baby boomers or generation Xers. Generation nexters put a premium on ethics and manners and are highly committed to their work. As a group, they exhibit the dedication to teamwork of the baby boomers, the can-do attitude of the veterans, and the technological skill of the generation Xers, suggesting their leadership will exemplify a strong commitment to both the value of the individual and to the quality of the task.

Of course, generational differences are not always cut and dried, particularly among those who were born near the generational transition years. Despite this admonition, Zemske, Raines, and Filipczak offer an interesting argument for the impact of age on leadership style preferences.

of medical researchers, for example, might function very effectively when provided with the necessary information and materials without any direct guidance or intervention by a leader. Take a look at the case study in box 2.5 to see what happens when highly motivated and knowledgeable followers are supervised too closely.

Box 2.5   Case Study

The Importance of Leadership Communication Style: SuperNova Microcomputer

Jay Brooks is the project director of a product development team at SuperNova Microcomputer. His team of thirty employees has been assigned to develop a new "highly user friendly" computer system for the home market. This group of thirty consists of the best technicians within the organization.

Unfortunately, Jay's team has been experiencing numerous difficulties and delays in the development of the new computer system. A number of team members have complained to the president of SuperNova, Sam Lowell, that Brooks is stifling creativity within the team and that Laura Martin, the project assistant, would be a much more effective leader. "We could get this project moving if Laura were in charge," claims one team member.

Brooks, who was hired from a major competitor six months ago, is a very directive leader. He holds a daily meeting from 8 to 10 A.M. in which every unit of the entire team presents their latest innovations. All new ideas must be cleared through Brooks. Many team members have complained about these meetings, claiming that "Brooks might as well build this system by himself if he is going to approve every chip." In addition, all team members must complete a worksheet isolating the specific tasks they have undertaken each day. This worksheet, wryly called "form 1984" by members of the team, is a major source of dissatisfaction among team members.

Laura Martin has been with the company since its inception a decade ago. Laura was passed over for the job as project director because Sam Lowell felt that she was not as technically competent as she needed to be. Laura was disappointed, but she accepted the decision because, overall, she has been very happy at SuperNova. Indeed, Laura has been instrumental in promoting the open, democratic, employee-oriented management style that is characteristic of SuperNova. As project assistant she interacts frequently with all members of the team. She has discovered that many of the members feel unappreciated. One team member complains, "We are expected to create one of the most advanced home computer systems in existence, but we are treated like a bunch of rebellious third graders."

Sam Lowell is disturbed because the project is falling way behind schedule. After only six months, major delays have pushed back the target date for the project by a full year. The team members themselves don't seem to be aware that they are falling behind any projected schedule; they only realize that the project is bogging down.

Things have gotten to the point that a number of team members are threatening to quit. If they leave, the entire project will be jeopardized. Further, rumors are spreading through the team that upper management is disappointed with productivity and may replace several key members. All in all, members of the team seem very frustrated. "We just want to build the best product that we can," says one team member, adding, "I only wish they would let us."

Discussion Questions

1. What problems can you identify at SuperNova Microcomputer?
2. Which leadership communication style(s) would be most effective in working with the product development team? Why?
3. How would you suggest a leader might get the product development team back on schedule? What policy and/or personnel changes would you recommend?
4. What recommendations would you make concerning the overall operation at SuperNova Microcomputer?
5. How might the leaders at SuperNova Microcomputer assure that problems like this can be avoided in the future?

In summary, researchers have concluded that the democratic style of leadership communication is often most effective. Generally, the benefits derived from democratic communication far outweigh any potential costs. Democratic leadership is associated with increased follower productivity, satisfaction, and involvement/commitment. The negative element of democratic leadership is that it can become mired in lengthy debate over policy, procedures, and strategies. In most cases, the increase in follower involvement and commitment more than make up for any such delays. Authoritarian leadership is effective in terms of output (particularly when the leader directly supervises behavior) but generally ineffective in enhancing follower satisfaction and commitment. The abdication factor in laissez-faire leadership often damages productivity, satisfaction, and commitment. The laissez-faire style can be effective when it represents guided freedom or when it is used with highly knowledgeable and motivated experts. In many situations, the costs associated with the authoritarian and laissez-faire styles of leadership can seriously hamper a leader's effectiveness.

Task and Interpersonal Leadership

Closely related to the authoritarian, democratic, and laissez-faire model of leadership style is the task and interpersonal model. From the late 1940s until the early 1960s several groups of researchers worked to identify and to label the dimensions of leadership communication. These researchers used different methodologies and measurement techniques but came to similar conclusions. Each of the research teams suggested that leadership consists of two primary communication dimensions: task and interpersonal. Although each group of researchers applied its own unique label to the communication styles discovered, the groups were essentially talking about the same set of communicative behaviors.

Task-oriented communication has been referred to as: production oriented; initiating structure; Theory X management; concern for production. Interpersonal-oriented communication has been called: employee oriented; consideration; Theory Y management; concern for people.

The similarity in findings among these researchers is not surprising. Leadership boils down to two primary ingredients: work that needs to be done and the people who do the work. Without these ingredients there is no need for leadership!

The leader employing the task style is primarily concerned with the successful completion of task assignments. The task-oriented leader demonstrates a much greater concern for getting work done than for the people doing the work. The task leader is often highly authoritarian. In contrast, the interpersonal leader is concerned with relationships. This style, similar to the democratic style, emphasizes teamwork, cooperation, and supportive communication.

Ernest Stech describes the typical communication patterns of task- and interpersonal-oriented leaders in his book, *Leadership Communication.*[25] He lists the following distinctions between these two styles of leadership.

Task Orientation	Interpersonal Orientation
Disseminates information	Solicits opinions
Ignores the positions, ideas, and feelings of others	Recognizes the positions, ideas, and feelings of others
Engages in rigid, stylized communication	Engages in flexible, open communication
Interrupts others	Listens carefully to others
Makes demands	Makes requests
Focuses on facts, data, and information as they relate to tasks	Focuses on feelings, emotions, and attitudes as they relate to personal needs
Emphasizes productivity through the acquisition of technical skills	Emphasizes productivity through the acquisition of personal skills
Most often communicates in writing	Most often communicates orally
Maintains a "closed door" policy	Maintains an "open door" policy

In the next sections, we will focus on four of the most significant attempts to identify the communication patterns of leaders: (1) the Michigan leadership studies, (2) the Ohio State leadership studies, (3) McGregor's Theory X and Theory Y, and (4) Blake and McCanse's Leadership Grid.

The Michigan Leadership Studies

Shortly after World War II, a team of researchers at the University of Michigan set out to discover which leadership practices contributed to effective group performance. To determine the characteristics of effective leaders, the Michigan researchers looked at both high- and low- performing teams within two organizations. Twenty-four groups of clerical workers in a life insurance company and seventy-two groups of railroad workers were studied in an attempt to identify the factors contributing to satisfactory and unsatisfactory group leadership.[26]

From their observations of these work groups, the Michigan researchers noted a distinction between what they called "production-oriented" and "employee-oriented" styles of leadership communication. Production-oriented leaders focus on accomplishing tasks by emphasizing technical procedures, planning, and organization. The production-oriented leader is primarily concerned with getting work done. Employee-oriented leaders focus on relationships between people and are particularly interested in motivating and training followers. Employee-oriented leaders demonstrate a genuine interest in the well-being of followers both on and off the job.

The Michigan researchers believed that the production-oriented and employee-oriented styles were opposing sets of communicative behaviors. They suggested these leadership communication styles could be described along a continuum as illustrated in figure 2.1. A leader could choose either a production-oriented style, an employee-oriented style, or a neutral style of communication. According to the Michigan research, leaders who exhibited employee-oriented styles had more productive and satisfied work groups.

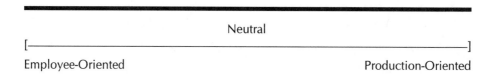

Figure 2.1
Employee- versus Production-Oriented Leadership Communication Styles

This one-dimensional view of leadership communication style was short lived.[27] Follow-up studies performed by the University of Michigan researchers suggested that it was possible for leaders to adopt both production-oriented *and* employee-oriented styles. Further, leaders who demonstrated high concern for both production and people were found to be more effective than leaders who exhibited only employee-oriented or production-oriented communication.[28] Production-oriented and employee-oriented leadership styles were not polar opposites but rather two distinct dimensions of leadership communication style.

The Ohio State Leadership Studies

At the same time that the Michigan researchers were involved in their observations of work groups, an interdisciplinary team of researchers at the Ohio State University attempted to identify the factors associated with leadership communication.[29] The Ohio State researchers developed a questionnaire they called the Leader Behavior Description Questionnaire (LBDQ). The LBDQ was administered to groups of military personnel who were asked to rate their commanders.

Statistical analysis of the LBDQ indicated two primary dimensions of leadership. These dimensions were labeled *consideration* and *initiating structure.* Consideration consisted of interpersonal-oriented communication designed to express affection and liking for followers; the consideration of followers' feelings, opinions, and ideas; and the maintenance of an amiable working environment. Inconsiderate leaders criticized followers in front of others, made threats, and refused to accept followers' suggestions or explanations. Initiating structure referred to task-related behaviors involved in the initiation of action, the organization and assignment of tasks, and the determination of clear-cut standards of performance.

Consideration and initiating structure were believed to be two separate dimensions of leadership. As a result, a leader could rate high or low on either dimension. This representation of leader communication style allowed for the development of a two-dimensional view of leadership. As depicted in figure 2.2, the Ohio State researchers believed that it was possible for a leader to demonstrate varying amounts of task (initiating structure) or interpersonal (consideration) communication.

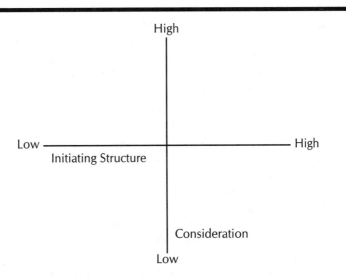

Figure 2.2
A Two-Dimensional View of Leadership Communication Style

Conclusions drawn from the Ohio State research focusing on the use of task and interpersonal styles of leadership communication are complicated by variations in methodology and instrumentation. Over the years, several different versions of the LBDQ have been used to measure task (initiating structure) and interpersonal (consideration) related messages. As a result, the findings of the Ohio State team are inconsistent. In general, both consideration and initiating structure are important to effective leadership. Considerate leadership communication seems to increase follower satisfaction while decreasing hostility and strife. Initiating structure appears important in guiding and organizing the completion of tasks.[30]

McGregor's Theory X and Theory Y

In the late 1950s, Douglas McGregor, a professor of management at the Massachusetts Institute of Technology, attempted to isolate the ways in which attitudes and behaviors influence organizational management. The result of this investigation was McGregor's classic work, *The Human Side of Enterprise*.[31] In his book, McGregor identifies two basic approaches to supervision—Theory X management and Theory Y management.

Theory X and Theory Y represent basic approaches for dealing with followers. Both approaches are based on a set of assumptions regarding human nature. Theory X managers believe that the average person has an inherent dislike for work and will avoid engaging in productive activities whenever possible. Managers must coerce, control, direct, and threaten workers in order to insure performance. Indeed, Theory X management assumes that most people actually desire strict supervision as a means of insuring security. If workers are told what to do, they can have little doubt that they are performing as expected. This approach emphasizes task supervision with little or no concern for individual needs.

Theory Y managers work to integrate organizational and individual goals. Theory Y assumes that work is as natural as play or rest. Work is not viewed as inherently unpleasant but rather as a source of satisfaction. Therefore, threats, punishment, and direct supervision are not necessary to insure productivity. Personal commitment and pride are sufficient to insure quality workmanship. Further, Theory Y argues that the average person seeks responsibility as an outlet for imagination and creativity. This approach emphasizes individual commitment by recognizing individual needs as well as organizational needs.

The leader employing a Theory X orientation adopts a task-oriented approach. This leader focuses on methods for getting work done. Little consideration is given to those doing the work. The Theory Y leader, on the other hand, focuses on the unique characteristics of the individuals performing tasks. The tasks themselves are not ignored but are viewed in terms of the people involved.

The Theory X–Theory Y dichotomy has been criticized for being an overly simplistic attempt to identify polarized extremes of human nature. McGregor responded to his critics by explaining that Theory X and Theory Y are not polar opposites. Rather, they are independent options from which a leader can select, depending on the situation and the people involved.

Blake and McCanse's Leadership Grid®

One of the most commonly cited examples of the task and interpersonal approach to leadership communication style is the Leadership Grid by Robert Blake and Anne Adams McCanse (formerly the Managerial Grid developed by Blake and Mouton).[32] Blake and McCanse identify communication styles based on the degree of concern for production (task orientation) and concern for people (interpersonal orientation) exhibited by a leader. These communication styles are plotted on a graph with axes ranging from one to nine. (See figure 2.3.)

The five plotted leader communication styles are:

1,1 Impoverished Management. The impoverished leader demonstrates a low concern for tasks and a low concern for relationships. The leader with a 1,1 orientation does not actively attempt to influence others but rather assigns responsibilities and leaves followers to complete tasks on their own.

9,1 Authority–Compliance. This leader is highly concerned with the completion of task assignments but demonstrates little concern for personal relationships. The primary function of the 9,1 oriented leader is to plan, direct, and control behavior. Followers are viewed as human resources who facilitate the completion of tasks. Input from followers is not encouraged; the 9,1 oriented leader attempts to dominate decision making.

5,5 Middle-of-the-Road Management. This middle-of-the-road leader is adequately concerned with production and people. In an attempt to involve followers, the 5,5 leader engages in compromise. Middle-of-the-Road leaders do not rock the boat—they push enough to achieve adequate productivity but yield if they believe increasing the workload will strain interpersonal relationships. As a result, the 5,5 leader often achieves mediocre results.

1,9 Country Club Management. The country club leader is more concerned with interpersonal relationships than with the completion of tasks. The 1,9 leader seeks to establish a supportive, friendly environment. Although country club leaders may want tasks to be completed effectively, they will emphasize factors that contribute to the personal satisfaction and happiness of followers. The 1,9 leader believes his or her primary responsibility is to provide a positive working environment.

9,9 Team Management. Team leadership involves a high concern for both production and people. The 9,9 leadership style is the ideal in which the successful execution of task assignments as well as individual support and caring are emphasized. The 9,9 leader nurtures followers so that they are able to achieve excellence in both personal and team goals. Under team leadership, both leader and followers work together to achieve the highest level of productivity and personal accomplishment.

Leaders generally adopt one leadership communication style, which they use in most situations. This is called a *dominant style.* A second orientation from

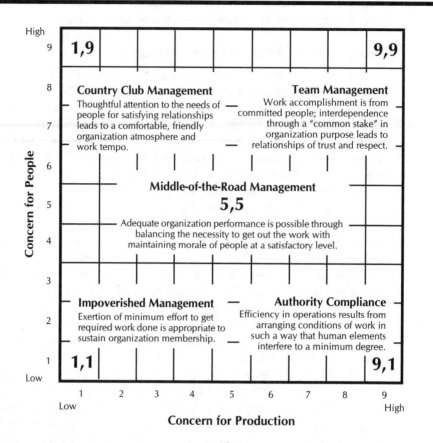

Figure 2.3[33]
The Leadership Grid®

the model may be used as a backup style. For example, a leader might generally adopt a 5,5 leadership communication style but might shift to a 9,1 style when pressured to get orders out to an important customer.

The most effective leadership communication style, according to Blake and McCanse, is team management (9,9). Implementation of the 9,9 style in organizational contexts is associated with increased productivity and profitability, increased frequency of communication, and improved leader-follower relations.[34]

Follower Communication Styles

Robert Kelley believes that followers, like leaders, need to understand their communication styles to carry out their roles successfully.[35] To identify the components that make up follower styles, Kelley asked individuals and focus groups to describe the best, worst, and typical followers in their organizations. He found that followers differ on two dimensions—independent/critical thinking and active engagement. The best followers are people who think for themselves and take initiative. The worst followers have to be told what to do and require constant supervision. Typical followers take direction and complete jobs on their own after being told what is expected of them.

Once he had isolated the key characteristics of followership, Kelley then developed the questionnaire found in box 2.6. Followers fall into one of five categories based on how they respond to the independent thinking and active engagement sections of this test. *Alienated followers* are highly independent thinkers who put most of their energies into fighting rather than serving their organizations because they've become disillusioned with their leaders or feel unappreciated. Alienated followers provide a dose of healthy skepticism for the group but generally come off as cynical. An example of an alienated follower would be Dr. Luka Kovac on *E.R.* In contrast, *conformists* are committed to organizational goals but express few thoughts of their own. These followers (often referred to as "yes men/women" in popular culture) may hold back their ideas out of fear or deference to authority. *Pragmatists* are moderately independent and engaged. Pragmatism is a way of coping with organizational uncertainty caused by frequent changes of leadership, layoffs, and restructuring. These organizational survivors hold on to their jobs but are not likely to be promoted. *Passive followers* demonstrate little original thought or commitment. They rely heavily on the leader's direction and meet only minimal expectations. Their passivity may stem from a lack of skills or be a response to serving under authoritarian leaders. Passive followers can be found at many fast-food restaurants where teenagers with limited job experience work under highly directive supervisors. *Exemplary followers* rate highly as both critical thinkers and active participants, contributing innovative ideas and going beyond what is required.

Kelley outlines three sets of skills and values that characterize exemplary followership. Utilizing these skills can help us shift from the alienated, conformist, pragmatist, and passive styles to the exemplary category. First, exemplary followers add value to the organization by helping it reach its objectives. They know what they want to achieve in life and commit themselves to organizations that share the same purposes. They understand what tasks are most important to achieving an organization's vision and develop the skills necessary to carry out these critical path activities. Second, outstanding followers "weave a web of relationships" through joining teams, building bridges to others throughout the organization, and working as partners with leaders. Third, exemplary followers cultivate a courageous conscience by making the right ethical judgments and then following through on those choices. They anticipate and eliminate ethical problems before they pose a significant threat and disobey leaders who issue directives that put the organization at risk. (For an in-depth discussion of courageous followership, see chapter 11.)

Box 2.6 Self-Assessment

Followership Questionnaire[36]

For each statement, think of a followership situation and how you acted. Choose a number from 0 to 6 to indicate the extent to which the statement describes you. 0 indicates rarely applies and 6 indicates almost always.

____ 1. Does your work help you fulfill some societal goal or personal dream that is important to you?

____ 2. Are your personal work goals aligned with the organization's priority goals?

____ 3. Are you highly committed to and energized by your work and organization, giving them your best ideas and performance?

____ 4. Does your enthusiasm also spread to and energize your co-workers?

____ 5. Instead of waiting for or merely accepting what the leader tells you, do you personally identify which organizational activities are most critical for achieving the organization's priority goals?

____ 6. Do you actively develop a distinctive competence in those critical activities so that you become more valuable to the leader and the organization?

____ 7. When starting a new job or assignment, do you promptly build a record of successes in tasks that are important to the leader?

____ 8. Can the leader give you a difficult assignment without the benefit of much supervision, knowing that you will meet your deadline with highest-quality work and that you will "fill in the cracks" if need be?

____ 9. Do you take the initiative to seek out and successfully complete assignments that go above and beyond your job?

____ 10. When you are not the leader of a group project, do you still contribute at a high level, often doing more than your share?

____ 11. Do you independently think up and champion new ideas that will contribute significantly to the leader's or the organization's goals?

____ 12. Do you try to solve the tough problems (technical or organizational), rather than look to the leader to do it for you?

____ 13. Do you help out other co-workers, making them look good, even when you don't get any credit?

____ 14. Do you help the leader or group see both the upside potential and downside risks of idea or plans, playing the devil's advocate if need be?

____ 15. Do you understand the leader's needs, goals, and constraints, and work hard to help meet them?

____ 16. Do you actively and honestly own up to your strengths and weaknesses rather than put off evaluation?

____ 17. Do you make a habit of internally questioning the wisdom of the leader's decision rather than just doing what you are told?

____ 18. When the leader asks you to do something that runs contrary to your professional or personal preferences, do you say "no" rather than "yes"?

____ 19. Do you act on your own ethical standards rather than the leader's or the group's standards?

____ 20. Do you assert your views on important issues, even though it might mean conflict with your group or reprisals from the leader?

Finding Your Followership Style

Use the scoring key below to score your answers to the questions.

Independent Thinking Items

Question 1. ____
5. ____
11. ____
12. ____
14. ____
16. ____
17. ____
18. ____
19. ____
20. ____

Total Score ____

Active Engagement Items

Question 2. ____
3. ____
4. ____
6. ____
7. ____
8. ____
9. ____
10. ____
13. ____
15. ____

Total Score ____

Add up your scores on the Independent Thinking items. Record the total on a vertical axis, as in the graph below. Repeat the procedure for the Active Engagement items and mark the total on a horizontal axis. Now plot your scores on the graph by drawing perpendicular lines connecting your two scores.

The juxtaposition of these two dimensions forms the basis upon which people classify followership styles.

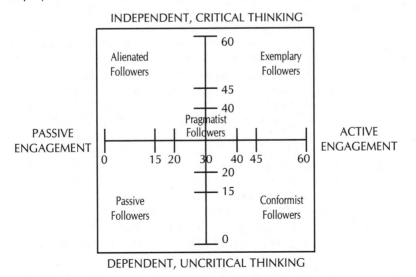

Followership Style	Independent Thinking Score	Active Engagement Score
EXEMPLARY	High	High
ALIENATED	High	Low
CONFORMIST	Low	High
PRAGMATIST	Middling	Middling
PASSIVE	Low	Low

Kelley's typology provides a useful framework for understanding follower communication styles, but there may be other dimensions of followership that he overlooks. Like leaders, some followers may be oriented toward completing the task while others are more concerned about maintaining relationships. Exemplary followership is probably the best approach in most situations, as Kelley suggests. However, other attributes might be necessary if the group faces a dangerous task or an unreasonable leader. (See box 2.7 for an example of how followers can impact a leader.) We'll have more to say about the relationship between situational variables and leading/following in chapter 3.

Box 2.7   Case Study

When Followers Dare

National Insurance Company is a full-service insurance provider with corporate divisions in fifteen locations in the United States. Each division is responsible for writing and servicing policies within its geographic area. For several years the general manager of the Western Division was Fred Jackson. Under Jackson's leadership, the Western Division became the most successful division in the company, achieving a goal of policy sales of $100 million a full eighteen months ahead of projections. The success of the Western Division was directly attributable to Jackson's open, democratic leadership style. Jackson knew all of his 250 employees by their first names and was always willing to talk with an employee who had a question or concern. Jackson, who had worked his way up from an entry-level position in the company, was a tireless cheerleader for his staff and never failed to recognize his employees' achievements. When his division reached its goal of $100 million in policy sales, Jackson hired a local high school band to march through the parking lot and then invited all of his employees to join him for a catered lunch-hour barbecue. Senior management at National recognized Jackson's leadership prowess, and he was promoted to the corporate headquarters in New York.

Jackson's replacement in the Western Division was a recent Stanford MBA graduate named Jason Hirsch. Hirsch's leadership style was very different than his predecessor's. Where Jackson had been open and interactive, Hirsch was closed and private. He spent most of his time alone in his office and made only token appearances at company meetings and functions. Most of Hirsch's communication consisted of directives handed to the senior management team. Within a few months of Hirsch's arrival, the mood at the

Western Division began to change. The energy and team spirit that had been so prevalent under Jackson's leadership was significantly diminished. Sales declined dramatically, and rumors surfaced suggesting the Western Division would be closed with its business moving to other National Insurance Company divisions.

These rumors were the catalyst for a plan among the senior management team in the Western Division. These managers felt that it was their responsibility to communicate their dissatisfaction to Hirsch to save jobs in the Western Division. One morning when Hirsch entered the building, he was greeted by his twelve senior managers dressed in military fatigues. Hirsch was informed that his managers had "taken over the office," and he was escorted to a meeting room. The managers explained to Hirsch that the military uniforms were a joke and that their "coup" was only an attempt to sit down with Hirsch and discuss how to improve the Western Division. Surprisingly (some of the managers fully expected they might be fired for their actions), Hirsch was very open to discussing the situation. As a newcomer to the Western Division, he had felt like an outsider. This bold move by his followers offered an opportunity for communication. Hirsch admitted that he was very nervous about taking charge of the division after the departure of the very popular and successful Fred Jackson. Once Hirsch and his managers began to communicate, they were able to identify strategies for improving the situation in the Western Division. Although it took time, the managers' coup helped to develop a much improved relationship between Hirsch and his staff. Within six months the Western Division was, once again, among the most successful divisions within National Insurance Company.

Discussion Questions

1. Do you think it was appropriate for the followers to approach Jason Hirsch the way they did? Why? Why not?

2. Do followers have a responsibility to take action when a leader's ineffectiveness may have negative consequences on others? How can followers determine when it is time to take action?

3. What can followers do to help a new leader succeed?

4. Robert Kelley suggests that two components make up follower communication styles: independent/critical thinking and active engagement. How would you rate the follower communication of the senior management team in the Western Division? In what category on the Kelley model would you place the followers who organized the "coup"?

5. What impact do you think each of the follower communication styles has on organizational effectiveness? What style followers would you like to lead?

Max DePree, the former chairman of the board of the Herman Miller Company and the author of several best-selling books on leadership, suggests that leaders play an important role in enabling followers to maximize their effectiveness.[37] To allow followers the best opportunity to develop the exemplary follower style, DePree suggests leaders must remember the following:

- When leaders exhibit cynicism, destructive criticism, unnecessary conflict, personal animosity, or gossip, they create an environment where followers cannot flourish.

- Leaders must supply good training and access to all relevant information to enable followers to succeed.

- Leaders must make followers feel needed.

- Change is essential to survival. Followers are good at change when leaders are good at managing change.

- Leaders must listen and be available to help, especially when they don't like what they hear.

- Leaders must be fair with both the division of resources and the evaluation of followers.

> *This business of making another person feel good in the unspectacular course of his [her] daily comings and goings is in my view, the very essence of leadership.*
> —Irwin Federman

Ultimately, the follower styles exhibited within a group, team, or organization are a reflection of the behaviors that are expected, demanded, promoted, or discouraged by formal leaders.[38] Although some followers may thrive working with almost any leader or in almost any context or situation, most followers are powerfully impacted, for better or for worse, by the leaders with whom they work.

Summary

In this chapter, we examined the typical communicative behaviors of leaders adopting the authoritarian, democratic, laissez-faire, task, and interpersonal styles of leader communication. In addition, we described the dimensions of follower communication styles.

Authoritarian leaders maintain strict control over followers by directly regulating policy, procedures, and behavior. Democratic leaders engage in supportive communication that facilitates interaction between leaders and followers. Laissez-faire leaders may engage in either abdication or guided freedom. Leaders exhibiting abdication generally withdraw from followers and offer little guidance or support. Productivity, cohesiveness, and satisfaction often suffer. By contrast, a more positive form of the laissez-faire leadership communication style affords followers a high degree of autonomy and self-rule while, at the same time, offering guidance and support when requested.

The laissez-faire leader providing this guided freedom approach does not directly participate in decision making unless he or she is requested to do so by followers.

The research focusing on leadership communication style suggests the leader adopting authoritarian communication can expect high productivity (particularly when he or she directly supervises followers); increased hostility, aggression and discontent; and decreased commitment, independence, and creativity among followers. Democratic leadership communication contributes to relatively high productivity (whether or not the leader directly supervises followers) and increased satisfaction, commitment, and cohesiveness. Followers under laissez-faire leadership are generally less productive and less satisfied. The only situation in which laissez-faire leadership may be effective is with groups containing highly motivated and knowledgeable experts.

The leader employing the task style is primarily concerned with the successful completion of job assignments. The task-oriented leader demonstrates a much greater concern for getting work done than for the people doing the work. The interpersonal leader is concerned with relationships. This style emphasizes teamwork, cooperation, and supportive communication.

Task- and interpersonal-oriented styles have been observed by (1) the Michigan leadership studies, (2) the Ohio State leadership studies, (3) McGregor, and (4) Blake and McCanse. Although the results are inconsistent at times, generally the use of *both* task- and interpersonal-oriented communication styles is associated with effective leadership.

Two components make up follower communication styles: independent/critical thinking and active engagement. Followers fall into one of five categories based on these characteristics. Alienated followers are highly independent thinkers who rank low on commitment to the organization. Conformists are committed to organizational goals but express few thoughts of their own. Pragmatists are moderately independent and engaged. Passive followers demonstrate little original thought or commitment. Exemplary followers rate highly as both critical thinkers and active participants, contributing creative ideas and going beyond what is expected. Exemplary followers add value to the organization by helping it reach its objectives and by building a network of relationships. These outstanding followers cultivate a courageous conscience that allows them to make and implement ethical choices. Ultimately, the follower styles exhibited within a group, team, or organization are a reflection of the behaviors that are expected, demanded, promoted, or discouraged by formal leaders. Although some followers may thrive when working with almost any leader or in almost any context or situation, most followers are powerfully impacted, for better or worse, by the leaders with whom they work.

Application Exercises

1. Make a list of the qualities that you believe are important for effective leadership. Compare your list with the communicative behaviors listed on page 39. Do effective leaders seem to adopt one leadership communication style more than others?

2. In what types of situations do you believe each of the leadership communication styles identified in this chapter would be most effective? Least effective?

3. Try to think of historical examples of leaders who adopted one of the five grid positions identified by Blake and McCanse. Which of these leaders was most effective? Why?

4. Identify as many alternatives to the styles of leadership communication outlined in this chapter as you can. Discuss with others in class the various styles you identify.

5. In a group, brainstorm examples for each of the five follower categories described in the chapter. Are there other dimensions that categorize follower communication styles besides independent/critical thinking and active engagement? Is exemplary followership always the best approach? Why or why not? Report your conclusions to the rest of the class.

6. Identify your follower communication style using the self-assessment questionnaire found in box 2.6. Why do you think you have adopted this style? What are your strengths and weaknesses as a follower? If you're not an exemplary follower, develop a strategy for becoming one. If you categorized yourself as exemplary, what can you do to become even more effective? Write up your findings.

7. In a group, discuss the relationship between leadership and followership styles. Based on your past experience, identify how leader communication styles have affected your performance as a follower. Try to pinpoint the leadership behaviors you think are most important in promoting exemplary followership.

Cultural Connections: Leadership Communication Styles in Europe[39]

Leaders often exhibit preferences for particular leadership communication styles. These preferences may be based on past successes or failures, the work environment, or the perception that one style may be more effective than another in dealing with a given situation. One factor that appears to impact the selection of leadership communication styles is national culture.

Researchers at the Cranfield School of Management in the United Kingdom surveyed over 2,500 top executives in eight European countries in an attempt to determine if there was a unified leadership communication style that would enable managers to "act European" in their business dealings. The Cranfield results suggested no singular European leadership communication style exists. Indeed, the researchers found distinct cultural differences among leadership style preferences across the countries in their study. They labeled the styles used within Europe as (1) *consensus*, (2) *towards a common goal*, (3) *managing from a distance*, and (4) *leading from the front*. Although the names used by the Cranfield researchers are different, the styles identified in the European study are strikingly similar to the authoritarian, democratic, and laissez-faire styles that have been a part of the leadership literature for more than 60 years.

The consensus style emphasizes open discussion and frequent team meetings, allowing everyone in the organization to be aware of important decisions and developments. Leaders using this style place a high value on effective communication and encourage shared decision making. The consensus style, which has much in common with the democratic approach discussed in this chapter, is most preferred by top managers in Sweden and Finland.

Towards a common goal is based on a strong display of authority. Like those using the authoritarian style, leaders using the common goal style employ strict controls and provide a clear description of roles and responsibilities. The implementation of systems, controls, and procedures is seen as a vehicle for promoting success. The executives in the Cranfield study using this style were more likely to rate themselves and their subordinates as highly disciplined in carrying out their duties. The majority of German and Austrian executives fit into this classification.

The managing-from-a-distance style is similar to the laissez-faire abdication style outlined in this chapter. This style is characterized by the inconsistent communication of key messages and strategies, a lack of discipline, high levels of uncertainty and ambiguity, and the frequent pursuit of personal, rather than group, agendas. This particular classification was unique in the Cranfield study in that only executives from France noted a preference for this style. Indeed, the preference for this style was very strong among French executives, with 83 percent identifying this approach as their primary leadership communication style.

The leading-from-the-front style is centered primarily on an individual's performance. Leaders exhibiting this style are reluctant to create rules or procedures that might hinder individual performance. This style, like the laissez-faire guided freedom approach, is based on the belief that people are self-motivated and skilled and can perform at the highest levels only when organizational structures do not inhibit performance. Among the Cranfield sample, top executives from Spain, Ireland, and the United Kingdom showed the strongest preference for this style.

Although many factors may impact leadership communication style choices, the Cranfield research provides evidence that national culture may be of central importance. Leaders and followers must consider this important factor when assessing the appropriate uses of leadership communication styles around the globe.

Leadership on the Big Screen: *Remember the Titans*

Starring: Denzel Washington, Will Patton, Wood Harris, Ryan Hurst, Donald Faison, Nicole Ari Parker

Rating: PG for language

Synopsis: The plot sounds like it came from Hollywood but *Remember the Titans* is based on actual events. When the Alexandria, Virginia school district is integrated in 1971, African-American football coach Herman Boone (Washington) is hired to replace Bill Yoast (Patton), the successful white coach at T. C. Williams High School. Yoast stays on as an assistant, but the two have an uneasy relationship at first. Boone uses an authoritarian style to break down racial barriers between players and to meld them into a team. The Titans go on to win the state championship, helping to reduce racial division in Alexandria. Along the way, Boone and Yoast become friends and learn to build on one another's strengths.

Chapter Links: authoritarian, democratic, and laissez-faire leadership communication styles, task vs. interpersonal orientations, followership communication styles

Three

TRAITS, SITUATIONAL, AND FUNCTIONAL LEADERSHIP

> *Great leaders are never satisfied with current levels of performance. They are restlessly driven by possibilities and potential achievements.*
>
> —Donna Harrison

Overview

Understanding and Explaining Leadership
The Traits Approach to Leadership
The Situational Approach
   Fiedler's Contingency Model of Leadership
   Path-Goal Theory
   Hersey and Blanchard's Situational Leadership Theory
   Leader-Member Exchange Theory
The Functional Approach to Leadership

Understanding and Explaining Leadership

Much of what was written about leadership prior to 1900 was based on observation, commentary, and moralization. The increasing use of "scientific" procedures and techniques to measure human behavior, which blossomed in the early twentieth century, changed the way scholars looked at leadership. Over the past one hundred years, four primary approaches for understanding and explaining leadership have evolved: the *traits approach*, the *situational approach*, the *functional approach*, and the *transformational approach*.

Early social scientists believed that leadership qualities were innate; an individual was either born with the traits needed to be a leader, or he or she lacked the physiological and psychological characteristics necessary for successful leadership. This approach to leadership, known as the traits approach, suggested that nature played a key role in determining leadership potential. The idea that inherent leadership traits could be identified served as the impetus for hundreds of research studies between the early 1900s and the end of World War II. Since the late 1940s, the popularity of the traits approach has steadily declined. For the most part, present-day researchers no longer accept the notion of the born leader.

The traits approach gave way to a situational explanation of leadership. The situational approach argues that the traits, skills, and behaviors necessary for effective leadership vary from situation to situation. Think of a successful leader you know; perhaps he or she leads a student club, social group, or religious congregation. Now imagine this leader as a union boss, school principal, football coach, lab supervisor, or military commander. Is it difficult to picture this person playing different leadership roles effectively? A leader is not always successful in every situation. A leader's effectiveness depends on his or her personality, the behavior of followers, the nature of the task, and many other situational factors. The eighteenth president of the United States, Ulysses S. Grant, is an example of how a leader's effectiveness varies between situations. Grant was a highly effective military leader but was considered inept as president.

While many researchers have attempted to identify factors influencing leadership effectiveness in various contexts, others have studied the functions of leadership. The functional approach looks at the way leaders behave. The underlying assumption of the functional approach is that leaders perform certain functions that allow a group or organization to operate effectively. An individual is considered a leader if he or she performs these functions. The functional approach has been applied primarily to group leadership. The perspective is important to communication scholars because it attempts to identify specific communicative behaviors associated with leadership.

In this chapter we will explore the traits, situational, and functional approaches to leadership. Another approach to leadership, known as the transformational approach, will be discussed in the next chapter. All four approaches provide perspectives for understanding and explaining leadership—frameworks that guide leadership theory and research. Sometimes the approaches overlap; other times they contradict one another. Currently, no single approach provides a universal explanation of leadership behavior.

The Traits Approach to Leadership

In the early part of the twentieth century, it was widely believed that leaders possessed unique physical and psychological characteristics that predisposed them to positions of influence. Researchers were not completely sure which characteristics were most important, but they assumed that an individual's physical and psychological features were the best indicators of leadership potential. Scores of leadership studies focused on factors such as height, weight, appearance, intelligence, and disposition. Other studies looked at status, social skill, mobility, popularity and other social traits in order to determine which of these characteristics were most strongly associated with leadership. Researchers wanted to know, for example, were leaders: tall or short? bright or dull? outgoing or shy?

In 1948, Ralph Stogdill published a review of 124 studies that examined traits and personal factors related to leadership and had appeared in print between 1904 and 1947.[1] Stogdill's review uncovered a number of inconsistent findings. Leaders were found to be both young and old, tall and short, heavy and thin, extroverted and introverted, and physically attractive as well as physically unattractive. Further, the strength of the relationship between a given trait and leadership prowess varied significantly from study to study. Stogdill concluded, "A person does not become a leader by virtue of the possession of some combination of traits, but the pattern of personal characteristics of the leader must bear some relevant relationship to the characteristics, activities, and goals of the followers."[2]

In 1974, Stogdill again published an exhaustive review of traits research. This time he analyzed 163 traits studies published between 1949 and 1970.[3] Fewer inconsistencies were uncovered in this research, but Stogdill remained convinced that personality traits *alone* did not adequately explain leadership. Once again, Stogdill concluded that *both* personal traits and situational factors influenced leadership.

> *Leaders are made, they are not born. They are made by hard effort, which is the price which all of us must pay to achieve any goal that is worthwhile.*
> —Vince Lombardi

Stogdill's work has sometimes been cited as evidence that personal traits have no bearing on leadership. Stogdill himself did not hold this view. In 1974, he wrote:

[I] have been cited frequently as evidence in support of the view that leadership is entirely situational in origin and that no personal characteristics are predictive of leadership. This view seems to overemphasize the situational and underemphasize the personal nature of leadership. Strong evidence indicates that different leadership skills and traits are required in different situations. The behaviors and traits enabling a mobster to gain and maintain control over a criminal gang are not the same as those enabling a religious leader to gain and maintain a large following. Yet certain general qualities—such as courage, fortitude, and conviction—appear to characterize both.[4]

Recently researchers have used advanced statistical techniques to reanalyze previous reviews of trait research.[5] The updated analyses suggest that personal characteristics do have an influence on leadership perceptions. Certain traits may be important in explaining who is *perceived* as a leader (see box 3.1). These findings do not directly imply that traits predict leadership effectiveness; rather, they suggest that certain traits may enhance the perception that someone has the ability to lead others. (See the discussion of impression management in chapter 1.) These perceptions seem particularly important in gauging political leadership. Research indicates that characteristics such as intelligence, honesty, altruism, and foresight are commonly perceived as qualities of effective political leaders.[6]

The notion that certain personal traits guarantee leadership effectiveness has never been satisfactorily supported. Certain traits can be advantageous in certain situations, but personal traits alone do not predispose individuals to success as a leader. Every tall person will not become a great basketball player, and every outgoing and intelligent person will not become a great leader. While many people possessing desirable personal traits have risen to positions of influence, just as many who lacked the personal characteristics deemed necessary for leadership have been successful leaders. The assumption that leaders are *born* is not accurate. A more reasonable assumption is that leaders are *made* through training and experience.

The Situational Approach

As the traits approach became less accepted as an explanation of leadership behavior, many researchers began to pursue situational explanations for leadership. These approaches, often called contingency approaches, assume that leadership behavior is contingent upon variations in the situation.[7] For example, the strategy for effectively leading a high-tech research and development team is much different from the strategy for effectively leading a military combat unit. The differences in leadership style might be attributed to task and relational structure, superior-subordinate interactions, the motivation of followers, or any one of a number of other situational factors. Four of the most commonly studied situational approaches are Fiedler's contingency model of leadership, path-goal theory, Hersey and Blanchard's situational leadership theory, and leader-member exchange theory.

Box 3.1   Research Highlight

Traits of Successful and Unsuccessful Leaders[8]

Research on the traits of leaders has not been able to demonstrate that any combination of physical and psychological characteristics **guarantee** an individual will be an effective leader in all situations. There does, however, seem to be a set of traits (*competencies* or *skills*, as they have been labeled by some researchers) that appear to differentiate successful leaders from their less successful counterparts. Three sets of traits, in particular, appear to be critical to leadership. These traits are not evident in all successful leaders, but the following attributes do appear to **enhance leadership effectiveness** in many contexts.

1. **Interpersonal factors:** A number of interpersonal competencies appear to be related to leadership effectiveness. These interpersonal factors range from skill-based behaviors, such as the ability to present an effective oral presentation or to manage conflict, to more individual-based factors, such as emotional stability and self-confidence. Among the most common deficiencies of unsuccessful leaders are interpersonal insensitivity and a lack of personal integrity. Successful leaders are highly consistent in their behavior and, therefore, easy to trust. Interpersonal competencies allow leaders to communicate their message and to build relationships with their constituents.

2. **Cognitive factors:** Intelligence appears to be positively related to leadership effectiveness. Traits researchers argue that more intelligent leaders are generally more effective at problem solving and decision making. Intelligent leaders may be better at critical thinking and may also be more creative than leaders with less cognitive ability. It should be noted, however, that some researchers argue there is not a strong correlation between intelligence and creativity.[9] Highly intelligent leaders may have difficulty relating to less intelligent followers or may find they get bogged down in the details of a problem. Further, gifted individuals may be unproductive because they have poor work habits. Generally, though, traits researchers claim intelligence contributes to leadership effectiveness, particularly at higher levels where problems are usually more complex and require more creative solutions.

3. **Administrative factors:** Various administrative or technical factors also contribute to leadership effectiveness. According to scholars adopting a traits perspective, successful leaders are better at planning and organizing and are generally well versed in the methods, processes, procedures, and techniques required for the completion of tasks performed by their followers. Although it is not necessary to be able to complete every task performed by followers, traits researchers believe the most successful leaders have an extensive integrated functional knowledge of the work performed within the group or organization they lead.

Strong interpersonal, cognitive, and administrative skills do not guarantee leadership effectiveness, but leaders who possess these traits may be more effective over time and less likely to have their leadership efforts fail.

Fiedler's Contingency Model of Leadership

One of the earliest, and most often cited, situational models is Fred Fiedler's contingency model of leadership.[10] In the early 1950s, Fiedler became interested in the interpersonal communication in therapeutic relationships. He discovered that competent therapists viewed themselves as more similar to their patients than less competent therapists did. Fiedler wondered how these findings related to group performance and leadership. He decided to assess how workers perceived fellow workers. He developed a measure of assumed similarity between opposites (ASo) to score differences in ratings of most and least-preferred coworkers.

Ratings of least-preferred coworkers (LPC) became the primary element in Fiedler's contingency model of leadership. Fiedler claims that our ratings of others with whom we do not like to work provide us with valuable information about our leadership behavior. This information can help us identify the situations in which we might most effectively lead others. Before continuing with this chapter, take a moment to complete the LPC scale in box 3.2.

Highly negative evaluations of a least preferred coworker result in low LPC scores; favorable evaluations result in higher LPC scores. According to Fiedler, low-LPC leaders are more concerned with tasks, and high-LPC leaders demonstrate greater concern for relationships. The effectiveness of a leader in a given situation is influenced by three primary factors that control the amount of influence a leader has over followers. These are (1) the leader's position power, (2) task structure, and (3) the interpersonal relationship between leader and members.

Position Power. A leader gains power by virtue of his or her position within a group or organization. Positions that afford a leader the ability to reward and punish provide substantial position power. The leader of a classroom problem-solving group has little power to reward or punish group members as compared to an employer who can offer a raise or a bonus, a more appealing work schedule, or long-term job security.

Task Structure. Some tasks are highly structured. These tasks have very specific procedures, agreed-upon outcomes, and are generally easy for leaders to evaluate. The production of a circuit board on an assembly line is an example of a structured task. Other tasks are largely unstructured. These tasks may be accomplished in a number of different ways. In these situations, it is very difficult for a leader to determine the best method of task completion, and evaluations of performance are extremely difficult to make. The writing of a television or movie script would be an example of an unstructured task.

Leader-Member Relations. A leader builds a relationship with his or her followers through interaction. A good relationship is characterized by loyalty, affection, trust, and respect. Poor relationships result in lower motivation and commitment.

Fiedler plotted each of the three situational variables for leaders on a continuum from favorable to unfavorable to create his contingency model (see figure 3.1). The most favorable conditions for leaders exist when the relationship

Box 3.2   Self-Assessment

Least Preferred Coworker (LPC) Scale[11]

										Score
Pleasant	8	7	6	5	4	3	2	1	Unpleasant	____
Friendly	8	7	6	5	4	3	2	1	Unfriendly	____
Rejecting	1	2	3	4	5	6	7	8	Accepting	____
Tense	1	2	3	4	5	6	7	8	Relaxed	____
Distant	1	2	3	4	5	6	7	8	Close	____
Cold	1	2	3	4	5	6	7	8	Warm	____
Supportive	8	7	6	5	4	3	2	1	Hostile	____
Boring	1	2	3	4	5	6	7	8	Interesting	____
Quarrelsome	1	2	3	4	5	6	7	8	Harmonious	____
Gloomy	1	2	3	4	5	6	7	8	Cheerful	____
Open	8	7	6	5	4	3	2	1	Guarded	____
Backbiting	1	2	3	4	5	6	7	8	Loyal	____
Untrustworthy	1	2	3	4	5	6	7	8	Trustworthy	____
Considerate	8	7	6	5	4	3	2	1	Inconsiderate	____
Nasty	1	2	3	4	5	6	7	8	Nice	____
Agreeable	8	7	6	5	4	3	2	1	Disagreeable	____
Insincere	1	2	3	4	5	6	7	8	Sincere	____
Kind	8	7	6	5	4	3	2	1	Unkind	____
									Total	____

Scoring of the LPC

The LPC score is obtained by adding your responses on the item ratings. Your total score should range between 18 and 144. Scores on the LPC are used to identify two types of leadership styles. If your score is **64 or above**, you are a **high LPC leader**. *High LPC leaders tend to be more relationship-oriented.* If your score is **57 or below**, you are a **low LPC leader**. *Low LPC leaders tend to be more task-oriented.* If your score falls **between 58 and 63**, you likely have **both low LPC and high LPC tendencies**; therefore, you *may be either relationship- or task-oriented.*

between the leader and followers is good, the task is highly structured, and the leader's position power is strong. The least favorable conditions exist when the relationship between the leader and followers is poor, the task is highly unstructured, and the leader's position power is weak. According to Fiedler, the effectiveness of a leader in a given situation is influenced by LPC scores. Leaders with low LPC scores (task orientation) are most effective when conditions are either highly favorable or unfavorable for the leader. Notice that in figure 3.1 the tails on each end of the graph represent the correlation between group performance and low leader LPC scores. The hump in the center of the graph indicates a relationship between high LPC scores (relational orientation) and group performance. High-LPC leaders are most effective when situational variables are neither extremely favorable nor unfavorable.

Criticism of Fiedler's contingency model has been fierce.[12] Most of the criticism has focused on the development of the LPC measure and the methods used to distinguish the effect of position power, task structure, and leader-member relations on leader effectiveness. Additional concerns have been expressed regarding the utility of the contingency model. Since LPC scores are relatively consistent personality measures, situations must be adapted to fit leaders, as opposed to leaders modifying behavior to fit situations.

Path-Goal Theory

Path-goal theory is based on a theory of organizational motivation called expectancy theory. Expectancy theory claims that followers are more motivated to be productive when they believe that successful task completion will provide a path to a valuable goal. According to Robert House and his associates, leaders play an important role in influencing follower perceptions of task paths and goal desirability.[13] It is a leader's responsibility to communicate clearly what is expected of followers and what rewards can be anticipated when tasks are successfully completed. Take, for example, a group of students assigned to give a classroom presentation. How might the leader of such a group apply expectancy theory? By providing specific expectations for individual task assignments and reinforcing the group goal (a quality product that will receive a good grade), the group leader can increase the motivation and satisfaction level of followers.

According to House and Terence Mitchell, the ability to motivate followers is influenced by a leader's communication style as well as by certain situational factors. Four communication styles are identified.

1. *Directive leadership:* procedure-related communication behavior that includes planning and organizing, task coordination, policy setting, and other forms of specific guidance.

2. *Supportive leadership:* interpersonal communication focusing on concerns for the needs and well-being of followers and the facilitation of a desirable climate for interaction.

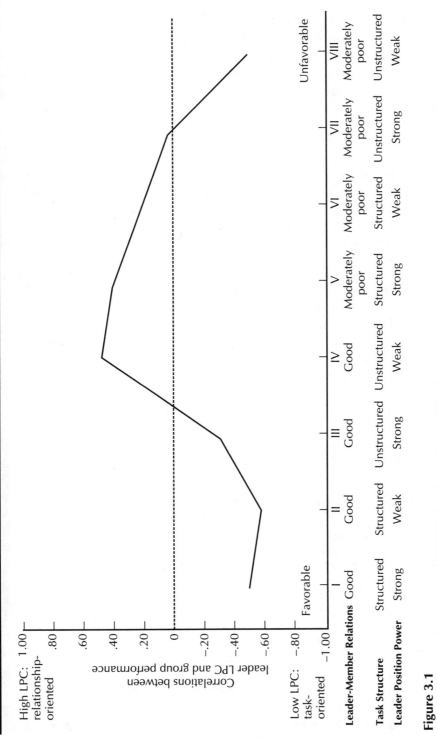

Figure 3.1
Correlations between Leaders' LPC Scores and Group Effectiveness under Conditions Ranging from Favorable to Unfavorable for Leaders[14]

3. *Participative leadership:* communication designed to solicit opinions and ideas from followers for the purpose of involving followers in decision making.

4. *Achievement-oriented leadership:* communication focusing on goal attainment and accomplishment, emphasizing the achievement of excellence by demonstrating confidence in the ability of followers to achieve their goals.

In path-goal theory, two situational variables are most influential in the selection of an appropriate leadership communication style: the nature of followers and the nature of the task. Follower characteristics thought to be important include follower needs, abilities, values, and personality. Important task factors include task structure and clarity. These factors influence motivation and satisfaction levels among followers and determine the most effective leader communication style. Box 3.3 diagrams the use of particular leader communication styles depending on follower abilities and task structure.

Directive leader communication is most effective when followers are inexperienced or when the task is unstructured. In these situations, followers might have a low expectation of their ability to perform satisfactorily. This expectation can lead to decreased motivation and satisfaction. In general, when expected behavior and task assignments are ambiguous, such as in a new position or job function, followers need directive leadership. On the other hand, if behavioral expectations are clearly understood and followers are competent in performing tasks, directive leadership lowers motivation and satisfaction. Nobody likes to have someone looking over her or his shoulder when the task is clear and performance is not problematic.

Box 3.3

Path-Goal Theory Factors

Leader Communication Style	Directive	Supportive	Participative	Achievement-Oriented
To enhance motivation and satisfaction use when:	Followers are inexperienced or unsure.	Followers are skilled, but lack confidence or commitment.	Followers are unsure (particularly if uncertainty prompts apprehension).	Followers possess necessary skills.
	Task is unstructured.	Task is structured (particularly if task is stressful, tedious, frustrating, difficult, or dissatisfying).	Task is unstructured.	Task is unstructured.

When followers confront structured tasks that are stressful, tedious, frustrating, difficult, or dissatisfying (such as working on an assembly line), a leader can make the situation more tolerable by engaging in supportive leader communication. In situations such as these, followers might have the necessary skills to complete tasks effectively, but they may lack confidence or commitment. This lack of confidence or commitment can produce a low self-expectation, resulting in poor performance. Supportive communication bolsters confidence and commitment and offers social rewards that can enhance motivation and satisfaction. Simply recognizing the difficulty of a task and expressing your appreciation for a follower's efforts can increase motivation and satisfaction levels. Supportive communication will contribute less to motivation and satisfaction when tasks are already stimulating and enjoyable.

> *Good leadership consists of showing average people how to do the work of superior people.*
> —John D. Rockefeller

Situations in which tasks are unstructured and behavior expectations are ambiguous are good opportunities for participative leader communication. Participating in decision making allows followers to think critically about expected behavior and task performance. Becoming more intimately involved with an unclear task can increase understanding and motivation. A follower struggling to develop a program to simplify a new computerized accounting system might benefit from participative communication. When uncertainty is uncomfortable for followers, participative communication stimulates understanding and clarity and can increase satisfaction. In situations where the task is highly structured and followers are aware of behavior expectations, participative leadership will have a minimal effect on motivation and satisfaction, according to path-goal theory.

Achievement-oriented leader communication increases a follower's confidence in his or her ability to realize challenging goals. By emphasizing excellence and demonstrating confidence in a follower's abilities, a leader can create a positive performance expectation. We are more likely to produce excellent results when others have expressed confidence in our ability to excel. The expectations of his coach and teammates might offer a partial explanation for the incredible success of Michael Jordan when he played for the Chicago Bulls. When the coach was asked what his game plan was, he claimed, "We give the ball to Michael and get out of his way." Achievement-oriented communication is most effective in unstructured situations. Followers performing highly structured tasks will not be as effectively motivated by achievement-oriented messages.

Path-goal theory attempts to explain follower motivation and satisfaction in terms of leader behavior and task structure. Although the theory neglects many situational variables that might potentially be important (such as power, organizational climate, and group cohesiveness), path-goal theory provides a viable explanation of the relationship among leaders, followers, and tasks.

Hersey and Blanchard's Situational Leadership Theory

Paul Hersey and Kenneth Blanchard suggest that the maturity level of followers plays an important role in selecting appropriate leadership behavior.[15] As in the Fiedler model and path-goal theory, Hersey and Blanchard divide leader behavior into task and relationship dimensions. The appropriate degree of task and relationship behavior exhibited by a leader depends on the maturity level of followers.

According to Hersey and Blanchard, follower maturity consists of two major components that can be plotted along a continuum: job maturity and psychological maturity. Job maturity refers to demonstrated task-related abilities, skills, and knowledge. An intern making rounds for the first time has low job maturity. A budget officer preparing a yearly financial statement for the twentieth consecutive year has high job maturity. Psychological maturity relates to feelings of confidence, willingness, and motivation. A factory worker bored and unchallenged by a repetitive task has low psychological maturity, while a teacher committed to excellence in the classroom has high psychological maturity. Maturity levels can fluctuate as a follower moves from task to task or from one situation to another.

Four combinations of job maturity and psychological maturity indicate follower readiness:

Readiness Level 1: Low job maturity and low psychological maturity (follower lacks skills and willingness)

Readiness Level 2: Low job maturity and high psychological maturity (follower lacks skills but is willing)

Readiness Level 3: High job maturity and low psychological maturity (follower is skilled but lacks willingness)

Readiness Level 4: High job maturity and high psychological maturity (follower is skilled and willing)

According to situational leadership theory, the maturity level of followers dictates effective leader behavior (see figure 3.2). By adapting the Blake and McCanse Leadership Grid® discussed in chapter 2, Hersey and Blanchard suggest appropriate task and relational orientations for each of the four levels of follower maturity. Immature, R1 followers require specific guidance. The most effective leader behavior with R1 followers is high task-directed communication and low relationship-directed communication. Task-related messages direct and guide follower behavior. The use of supportive, relationship-directed communication should be avoided at this level, as such messages might be interpreted as a reward for poor performance.

R2 and R3 followers are moderately mature. R2 followers lack skills but are willing. Because they do not possess necessary task skills, they need direct guidance. Because they are putting forth effort, they need support. Thus, the most effective leader behavior with R2 followers is high task/high relationship. At this level, the leader is "selling" the belief that the necessary skills can be acquired. R3 followers are skilled but lack the willingness to perform. Leaders need to promote follower participation in decision making. Task guidance is not necessary since performance has been demonstrated, but leaders must

LEADER BEHAVIOR

(Supportive Behavior)
RELATIONSHIP BEHAVIOR → (HIGH)

PARTICIPATING

SELLING

S3 Share ideas and facilitate in decision making

S2 Explain decisions and provide opportunity for clarification

DELEGATING

TELLING

S4 Turn over responsibility for decisions and implementation

S1 Provide specific instructions and closely supervise performance

(LOW) ←——— **TASK BEHAVIOR** ———→ (HIGH)
(Guidance)

FOLLOWER READINESS

HIGH	MODERATE		LOW
R4	**R3**	**R2**	**R1**
Able and Willing or Confident	Able but Unwilling or Insecure	Unable but Willing or Confident	Unable and Unwilling or Insecure

FOLLOWER DIRECTED — LEADER DIRECTED

Figure 3.2
Hersey and Blanchard's Situational Leadership Theory[16]

encourage R3 followers to discuss problems or fears hampering commitment or confidence. The most effective leader behavior facilitates involvement by using low task and high relationship behavior.

R4 followers are skilled and willing. Delegating authority to these mature performers is the best strategy. Since task skills are well developed, task guidance is not necessary. Relationship behavior is not required, since commitment and confidence are not a problem. This does not mean that relationship behavior should be completely ignored. Certainly a leader needs to offer support and recognition periodically to maintain the level of excellence of the R4 follower.

> *Things do not change, we change.*
> —Henry David Thoreau

By engaging in appropriate leadership behavior, Hersey and Blanchard suggest a leader can influence follower behavior. The manipulation of task and relationship behaviors in accordance with follower maturity can facilitate growth and development among followers. If leaders carefully diagnose the situation, communicate accordingly, and maintain flexibility as the situation changes, situational leadership theory claims that they will be more effective in influencing followers. (Practice applying Hersey and Blanchard's situational leadership theory by reading the case study in box 3.4.)

Leader-Member Exchange Theory

Leader-member exchange (LMX) theory describes how leaders develop relationships with followers. The theory focuses on how leaders and followers coordinate their actions to accomplish goals.[17] According to George Graen, this process of coordination involves playing roles developed through interaction.[18] The basic idea of the theory is that leaders generally establish two different types of relational role exchanges with followers. Some followers will be members of the "in-group." These followers will play the role of assistant, lieutenant, or advisor to a leader. The remaining followers will be members of the "out-group." Leader-follower exchanges differ in each group. *High levels of trust, mutual influence, and support characterize in-group exchanges.* In-group exchanges allow for wider latitude in task development; followers are granted more responsibility and influence in decision making. *Low levels of trust and support characterize out-group exchanges.* Authoritarian and task-oriented leadership communication is often evident in out-group exchanges.

According to LMX theory, in-group and out-group relationships are established soon after a follower joins a group or organization. Leaders make choices regarding the inclusion of followers in both the in-group and the out-group. These choices may be contingent on the situation or the personal characteristics of followers. Such factors as compatibility, competence, and depend-

Box 3.4   Case Study

Leadership at *The Campus News*

Maryanne Norton is the faculty advisor to *The Campus News*, the student newspaper at Algonquian University. She oversees production of the weekly publication and advises the newspaper's editor, Mark Lee, and his staff. Mark is a junior political science major with little experience in journalism. He is, however, enthusiastic and excited about his role as editor of *The Campus News*. Mark is typical of many of the staff in his lack of journalist's training. In fact, many of *The Campus News* reporters have no background in news writing. As a faculty member in the Department of Communication, Maryanne teaches four courses per semester and is responsible for several other projects, including supervision of the internship program. Maryanne has a keen interest in student journalism and has long been an advocate of the rights of student reporters. Although Maryanne is very busy, she takes time to meet with the staff of *The Campus News* each week prior to publication and often hosts social gatherings for the students at her home. Although the staff of *The Campus News* is comprised of students, Maryanne believes the most effective approach to leading is to treat followers as peers and colleagues; she is most comfortable serving as a confidant and a friend to her advisees. She rarely criticizes a story and feels it is not her place to correct the work of the student reporters. She is quick to offer suggestions or guidance when asked for advice, but mainly she tries to make the experience of working for *The Campus News* enjoyable and rewarding for students.

Although there have been minor problems in the past during Maryanne's term as advisor, *The Campus News* has been heavily criticized recently. The inexperience of Mark and his staff have been evident in the last few issues of the student newspaper. In one headline, the name of the Dean of Engineering was misspelled, and details have been inaccurately reported in several stories. The most troubling error occurred in a story about Algonquian's attempt to settle a dispute with a faculty member who had been denied tenure. The story did not present the situation accurately and contained several quotes attributed to administrators at Algonquian that were later determined to have been taken out of context. One of the statements was so inflammatory that the administrator quoted was subpoenaed and asked to explain his comments in a deposition.

Shortly after that incident Maryanne was called into the university president's office to discuss the situation at *The Campus News*.

Discussion Questions
1. What is the problem at *The Campus News*?
2. How would you rate Maryanne Norton as a leader? How would you rate Mark Lee as a follower?
3. Which leadership style discussed in the Hersey and Blanchard situational leadership theory does Maryanne exhibit? How would you rate the readiness level of the student followers at *The Campus News*?
4. What Hersey and Blanchard situational leadership style would be most effective with the students working for *The Campus News*? Why?
5. What would you advise Maryanne to tell the president of Algonquian University she will do to improve the situation at *The Campus News*?

ability may influence in-group/out-group determinations.[19] Once these determinations are made, patterns of communication begin to differ. In-group relationships exhibit greater levels of mutual influence during conversation.[20] Leaders are more dominant in conversations with followers with whom they have an out-group relationship.[21]

To fulfill leader expectations, members of the out-group must meet formal role expectations, such as following company procedures, meeting deadlines, or submitting work containing few errors. In-group members are afforded greater autonomy and control. In return, in-group members are expected to work harder, be more committed, take on more administrative duties, and be more loyal to the leader than out-group members.

The assistance of committed followers can be very useful to a leader. However, the leader must be mindful of maintaining the in-group relationship by paying attention to the needs of in-group followers. An in-group relationship is reciprocal; it must be maintained by both the leader and the follower. By adapting relational role exchanges, leaders can shape the performance of followers. Research suggests followers in an in-group are often more satisfied and perform better than followers in an out-group.[22]

LMX theory has evolved through a series of stages.[23] In stage 1, validation of differentiation, Graen and his colleagues identified the in- and out-group relationships described above. They initially believed that leaders could only maintain a few high quality relationships with trusted assistants due to limited time and resources. In stage 2—leader member exchange—researchers confirmed that differentiated relationships do exist and that in-group followers are better performers. However, LMX investigators then concluded that leaders could build high quality partnerships with *all* their followers, not just a chosen few. In stage 3, leadership making, they began to study how these relationships develop over time as leaders and followers move from strangers to acquaintances to maturity. Followers in mature relationships begin to act as leaders themselves, shouldering more responsibility for the success of the group. The greater the number of leader-follower partnerships, the higher the performance of an organizational unit. In stage 4, the team building competence network, investigators adopt a system-wide perspective to determine how group members could develop a network of high-quality relationships throughout the organization. The instrument Graen designed to measure in- and out-group relationships is found in box 3.5.

Box 3.5   Self-Assessment

Recommended Measure of Leader-Member Exchange (LMX-7)[24]

Directions: Rate your relationship as a follower with a leader of your choice by circling the numbers preceding your responses to these seven items. You can also rate your relationship as a leader with a follower of your choice (leader items are in parentheses).

1. Do you know where you stand with your leader; that is, do you usually know how satisfied your leader is with what you do? (Does your member usually know?)

    (1) Rarely   (2) Occasionally   (3) Sometimes   (4) Fairly Often   (5) Very Often

2. How well does your leader understand your job problems and needs? (How well do you understand the problems and needs of your member?)

    (1) Not a Bit   (2) A Little   (3) A Fair Amount   (4) Quite a Bit   (5) A Great Deal

3. How well does your leader recognize your potential? (How well do you recognize member potential?)

    (1) Not at All   (2) A Little   (3) Moderately   (4) Mostly   (5) Fully

4. Regardless of how much formal authority he/she has built into his/her position, what are the chances that your leader would use his/her power to help you solve problems in your work? (What are the chances that you would use your power to help a member solve problems?)

    (1) None   (2) Small   (3) Moderate   (4) High   (5) Very High

5. Again, regardless of the amount of formal authority your leader has, what are the chances that he/she would "bail you out," at his/her expense? (What are the chances that you would use your power to cover a member's shortcomings?)

    (1) None   (2) Small   (3) Moderate   (4) High   (5) Very High

6. I have enough confidence in my leader that I would defend and justify his/her decision if he/she were not present to do so. (Your member would support your decisions.)

    (1) Strongly Disagree   (2) Disagree   (3) Neutral   (4) Agree   (5) Strongly Agree

7. How would you characterize your working relationship with your leader? (How would your member characterize your working relationship?)

    (1) Extremely Ineffective   (2) Worse Than Average   (3) Average
    (4) Better Than Average   (5) Extremely Effective

Total the numbers preceding your responses. The higher the score, the better your perceived relationship with your leader. To determine if your view matches that of your relational partner, compare your rankings with those of your leader or follower.

The Functional Approach to Leadership

Traits and situational approaches focus primarily on the individual characteristics of leaders and followers. The functional approach looks at the communicative *behavior* of leaders. The functional approach suggests that it is the ability to communicate like a leader that determines leadership. Imagine that while driving you witness an accident. Several motorists, including you, stop to offer assistance. Who will become the leader in this emergency situation? Will the leader be the person with the most knowledge regarding first aid? Perhaps. Will the leader be the person with the right combination of motivation and maturity for the situation? Maybe. Most likely the leader will be the person who starts behaving like a leader. Leadership functions in this situation might include assigning tasks ("You call 911"), initiating action ("I'll put my jacket on him so he'll be warm"), giving support ("The ambulance will be here in just a few minutes"), and mediating conflict ("Let's not worry about whose fault it was until everyone is feeling better"). By performing the functions of leadership, an individual will be viewed as a leader by others.

Many ordinary people took on leadership functions during the horrific events of September 11, 2001. Office workers carried injured colleagues down the stairs of the World Trade Center, while firefighters rushed up to help victims. Those in buildings near Ground Zero pulled pedestrians off the street and out of harm's way. Staff at Starbucks and other businesses organized to provide food to relief workers. Employees at many firms in Manhattan refused to be cut off from their jobs, finding new ways to get to work by kayaking the East River, renting buses, and hiking.

One of the earliest contributions to the functional approach was Chester Barnard's 1938 classic, *The Functions of the Executive*.[25] Barnard's work isolated communication as the central function of organizational leadership. Since then, a number of researchers have attempted to identify the various behaviors associated with leadership in organizations and groups. Kenneth Benne and Paul Sheats were pioneers in the classification of functional roles in groups.[26] After analyzing group communication patterns, they identified three types of group roles: *task-related, group building and maintenance,* and *individual.*

Task-related roles contribute to the organization and completion of group tasks. Six task-related roles are listed below.

The initiator defines the problem, establishes the agenda and procedures, and proposes innovative strategies and solutions. The initiator makes statements such as: "I see our problem as maintaining our market share," or "Let's begin by just throwing out some possible ways to approach this problem."

The information/opinion seeker solicits ideas, asks questions about information provided by others, and asks for evaluations of information and procedure. The information/opinion seeker makes statements such as: "Why do you think our production costs will increase in the next quarter?", or "Do you think we are spending enough time discussing possible solutions?"

The information/opinion giver presents and evaluates facts and information and evaluates procedure. The information/opinion giver makes statements such as: "I think we will serve our students better by offering more night courses next semester," or "I learned in my group communication course that we shouldn't offer solutions until we have thoroughly analyzed the problem."

The elaborator provides examples and background as a means for clarifying ideas and speculates how proposed solutions might work. The elaborator makes statements such as: "A bake sale may be an effective way to raise money. Last year, the Ski Club made $500 from its bake sale."

The orienter/coordinator summarizes interaction, looks for relationships among ideas and suggestions and focuses group members on specific issues and tasks. The orienter/coordinator makes statements such as: "That suggestion seems to fit with Glenn's idea about training," or "Maybe if we all come to the next meeting with a few pages of notes we could put together an outline for our presentation."

The energizer stimulates or arouses the group to achieve excellence and promotes activity and excitement. The energizer makes statements such as: "If we can get this product out on schedule, I think it will revolutionize the industry."

Group building and maintenance roles contribute to the development and maintenance of open, supportive, and healthy interpersonal relationships among group members. Four group building and maintenance roles appear below.

The encourager supports and praises the contributions of others, communicates a sense of belonging and solidarity among group members and accepts and appreciates divergent viewpoints. The encourager makes statements such as: "I agree with Susan," or "I am confident that our group will do a great job next week," or "I can appreciate your concern about reaching a decision too quickly. We must be careful not to jump to premature conclusions."

The harmonizer/compromiser mediates conflict, reduces tension through joking and attempts to bring group members with opposing points of view closer together. The harmonizer/compromiser makes statements such as: "What's the worst thing that could happen if we don't get this project done on time? Okay, what's the second worst thing that could happen?", or "Is there any way both you and Brett can get what you want from this decision?"

The gatekeeper encourages the involvement of shy or uninvolved group members and proposes regulations of the flow of communication through means such as time and topic limitation. The gatekeeper makes statements such as: "I'd be interested to hear what Meg has to say about this," or "Why don't we limit our discussion of the budget to twenty minutes."

The standard-setter expresses group values and standards and applies standards to the evaluation of the group process. The standard-setter makes statements such as: "Our goal has always been to develop user-friendly products," or "Let's try to be critical of ideas, not people. That has always been our policy in the past."

Individual roles not supportive of task or group relationships can minimize group effectiveness. Although a certain degree of individuality is healthy, individual-centered behaviors do not contribute to task completion or relationship development and maintenance. Five possible disruptive individual roles are included here.

The aggressor attacks the ideas, opinions, and values of others; uses aggressive humor; makes personal judgments. The aggressor makes statements such as: "It is better to keep your mouth shut and appear stupid than to open it and remove all doubt," or "Pete's concern for equal workloads is the reason this group is so unproductive."

The blocker resists the ideas and opinions of others and brings up "dead" issues after the group has rejected them. The blocker makes statements such as: "I don't care if we already voted on it; I still think the traits approach offers the best explanation of leadership."

The recognition-seeker relates personal accomplishments to the group and claims to be more expert and knowledgeable than other group members on virtually every topic. The recognition seeker makes statements such as: "I know I am not a nurse, but I might as well be, considering how much time I spent with my husband when he was ill."

The player maintains a noncaring or cynical attitude and makes jokes at inappropriate times. The player makes statements such as: "We can't get much accomplished in one hour. Let's knock off early and get a beer."

The dominator lacks respect for the views of others, disconfirms the ideas and opinions of others, and frequently interrupts. The dominator makes statements such as: "Steve's idea doesn't seem worthwhile to me. The way to get this program to run is to do what I have suggested."

Roles associated with the successful completion of the task and the development and maintenance of group interaction help facilitate goal achievement and the satisfaction of group needs. These roles serve a leadership function. Roles associated with the satisfaction of individual needs do not contribute to the goals of the group as a whole and are usually not associated with leadership. By engaging in task-related and group-building/maintenance role behaviors (and avoiding individual role behavior), a group member can perform leadership functions and increase the likelihood that he or she will achieve leadership status within the group. (For more information on group leadership, see chapter 7.)

In addition to the Benne and Sheats categories, several other communicative behaviors associated with leadership have been identified. Box 3.6 provides a listing of three sets of proposed leadership functions.

The functional approach provides guidelines for the behavior of leaders by suggesting the necessary functions that a leader should perform. In its present form, the functional approach does not provide a clear, well-developed prescription for leader behavior. Many of the identified leader behaviors are vague, and some are contradictory. *How*, for example, can a leader increase interdependence among group members? What specific leader behavior will facilitate work? Still, the functional approach does provide a useful framework for identifying communication behaviors that contribute to the exercise of leadership.

Box 3.6   Research Highlight

The Functions of Leadership

Krech and Crutchfield (1948)[27]

- executive
- planner
- policy-maker
- expert
- external group representative
- facilitator of internal relationships
- supplier of rewards and punishments

- arbitrator
- role model
- group symbol
- surrogate for individual responsibility
- ideologist
- parental figure
- scapegoat

Bowers and Seashore (1966)[28]

- supporter of others
- interaction facilitator

- goal emphasizer
- work facilitator

Cartwright and Zander (1968)[29]

- goal achievement (including: initiating action, focusing on goals, clarifying issues, developing procedural plans, and evaluating outcomes)
- maintenance behavior (including: keeping interpersonal relationships pleasant, mediating disputes, providing encouragement, involving reticent followers, and increasing interdependence among members)

Summary

Four primary approaches for understanding and explaining leadership have emerged over the past ninety years. In this chapter, we examined three of these approaches.

The traits approach suggests that leaders are born with specific characteristics that predispose them to positions of influence. Traits research, conducted primarily in the early part of the twentieth century, has failed to find a clear connection between personal and physical traits and leadership. However, certain traits may enhance the perception that someone has the ability to lead others.

The situational approach claims that situational conditions influence leadership effectiveness. Four of the most commonly cited situational approaches are Fiedler's contingency model of leadership, path-goal theory, Hersey and Blanchard's situational leadership theory, and leader-member exchange theory. Fiedler claims that rating those with whom we do not like to work will provide valuable information about how to lead more effectively. Three situational factors influence whether conditions are favorable or unfavorable between leaders and followers: the leader's position power, the task structure, and the relationship between the leader and his or her followers. Path-goal theory focuses on a leader's communication style related to the nature of the task and to followers.

Hersey and Blanchard suggest that the maturity level of followers determines the selection of appropriate task and relational orientations for leaders. Leader-member exchange theory claims leaders make choices regarding the inclusion of followers in either in-groups or out-groups. Followers in an in-group are more satisfied and perform better than those in an out-group. Followers in high quality relationships with leaders shoulder more responsibility for the success of the group. The greater the number of leader-follower partnerships, the higher the performance of an organizational unit.

The functional approach offers suggestions for behaving like a leader. Leaders play task-related and/or group building and maintenance roles. They avoid selfish, individual roles that do not support the task or group relationships.

Application Exercises

1. Make a list of traits that might be perceived as characteristic of leadership. Determine the accuracy of your list by comparing it with the actual traits of some of the effective leaders you have seen.

2. Review the LPC scale on page 69. See if your LPC score is indicative of a task or relational orientation. Do you agree with Fiedler's assertions?

3. Complete the LMX scale on pages 78–79. What factors contribute to your ratings on each of the items? What can you do to improve your relationship with this leader or follower?

4. Either alone, or in a group, make a list of leadership functions. Try to engage in these behaviors the next time you participate in a group. See if others look to you for leadership.

5. Describe a time when you or someone you know became a leader by communicating like a leader. Identify the specific behaviors that led to you or the person you observed becoming the leader. What can you learn from the situation to apply to other leadership situations? Write up your analysis and conclusions.

6. Conduct interviews with several effective leaders. Try to identify which approach to leadership provides the best explanation for their success. Share your results with your classmates.

Cultural Connections: Are Leadership Theories Culturally Bound?

Nearly all the leadership theories discussed in the first section of this text were developed in the United States. U.S. teachers and consultants frequently export these ideas to Europe, Africa, Asia, Latin America, and other regions. According to cross-cultural expert Geert Hofstede, the transfer of organizational theories across boundaries, whether from the U.S. or any other culture, is dangerous.[30] Ideas about how to plan, motivate, evaluate, and reach goals are culture specific, reflecting the particular value system of the country of origin. As a result, what works in one region may not work in another. Transfer is possible but demands "prudence and judgment."[31]

Hofstede offers the following examples of U.S. leadership theories that are culturally bound.

- Expectancy theories of motivation are based on the premise that individuals operate according to their self-interest. In more collectivist or group-oriented cultures, the relationship between workers and organizations is moral in nature. For example, layoffs are a common way to cut costs in the United States. In Japan, companies have an ethical obligation to retain their employees no matter what the economic climate.

- In Maslow's hierarchy (see figure 4.1), self-actualization (a very individualistic motive) is the ultimate human need. Only U.S. participants seem to follow the hierarchy (security, social, esteem, self-actualization) outlined by Maslow.

- Both Theory X and Theory Y are based on the assumption that work is good and desirable and should serve the goals of the organization. Southeast Asian societies view work as a necessity and are more concerned with tradition and their place in society.

- U.S. researchers and writers focus on the deeds of the individual leader who makes important decisions. The Dutch expect to be involved in consensus decision making.

- The Leadership Grid® and related theories promote participative management but assume that the leader will take the initiative to solicit employee input. In Sweden, Norway, Germany, and Israel, subordinates take the initiative, expecting to participate in the decision process. In societies that accept large differences in power and status, such as Greece, workers don't expect leaders to ask them for feedback; they expect leaders to tell them what to do.

Leadership on the Big Screen: *Dave*

Starring: Kevin Kline, Sigourney Weaver, Frank Langella, and Ben Kingsley
Rating: PG-13 for language and sexual situations
Synopsis: Kevin Kline is Dave Kovic, a presidential look-alike hired from a temp agency to stand in for the chief executive at an official luncheon. The philandering president (also played by Kline) uses the occasion to engage in a tryst with an aide, during which he suffers a stroke and falls into a coma. At the insistence of the president's chief of staff, Bob Alexander (Langella), Dave finds himself stuck in the role of president indefinitely. While Alexander plots

to elevate himself to the White House, Dave finds himself enjoying his time in office. His inside look at politics inspires him to balance budgets, hold other officials accountable, expose unethical members of the White House staff, and eventually run for office on his own merits.

Chapter Links: leadership traits, situational leadership, and functional leadership

Four

Transformational and Charismatic Leadership

> *The new leader is one who commits people to action, who converts followers into leaders, and who may convert leaders into agents of change.*
>
> —Warren Bennis

Overview

The Transformational Approach to Leadership

Beginning in the late 1970s, the transformational approach emerged as a new perspective for understanding and explaining leadership. The transformational approach was first outlined by James MacGregor Burns. He compared traditional leadership, which he labeled as *transactional*, with a more "complex" and "potent" type of leadership he called *transformational*.[1] The motivational appeals of the transactional leader are designed to satisfy basic human needs; the appeals of the transformational leader go beyond those basic needs to satisfy a follower's higher-level needs.

According to Abraham Maslow, five hierarchically arranged human needs exist: physiological, safety, belonging and love, self-esteem, and self-actualization.[2] (See figure 4.1.) The most basic human needs are physiological. Before we can concern ourselves with other needs, we must secure the basic necessities: oxygen, food, water, and sleep. If you study for several days without sleeping, the need for sleep takes precedence over any other concern. Once physiological needs are satisfied, we can turn our attention to the second level of the hierarchy, safety needs. Humans seek predictability and protection. We are generally most comfortable in environments that are familiar and free from danger. If you become lost in the desert in the heat of the day, one of your first priorities will be finding a safer, cooler environment. After environmental factors are satisfied, social belonging and love needs surface. Humans desire affiliation with others. Whether you are a member of a group or an organization, involved in a friendship or an intimate relationship, all these situations involve seeking social connections with others.

Self-esteem needs become important after the first three levels have been reasonably well satisfied. Self-esteem needs relate to our desire to feel good about ourselves. Self-esteem consists of internal feelings of competence, respect, and self-worth as well as external feedback and recognition that support positive esteem. The feeling of satisfaction you get when you finish a difficult assignment, and the "A" your instructor gives you for your hard work, help to satisfy your self-esteem needs.

When all other needs are satisfied, we can turn our attention to self-actualization needs. Self-actualization is the process of applying your own unique set of interests and abilities to become the best person you can possibly become. If you are self-actualized, Maslow claims you will feel a sense of fulfillment and purpose. He also suggests those who achieve self-actualization have a strong urge to help others satisfy their self-actualization needs.

For Burns, the distinction between transactional and transformational leadership is dichotomous—leaders are either transactional or they are transformational. Subsequent research proposed that transformational leadership augments the effects of transactional leadership.[3] Similar to the hierarchy Maslow described, lower-level transactional leadership is the foundation for higher-level transformational leadership. As leadership expert Bernard Bass explains: "Many

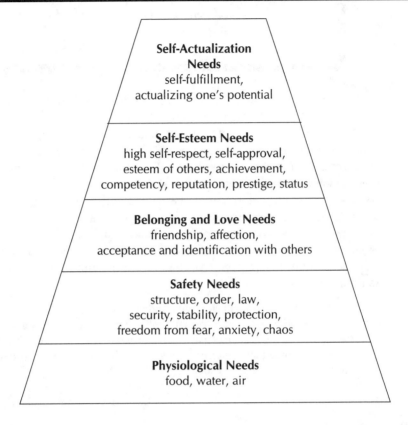

Figure 4.1
Maslow's Hierarchy of Needs

of the great transformational leaders, including Abraham Lincoln, Franklin Delano Roosevelt, and John F. Kennedy, did not shy away from being transactional. They were able to move the nation as well as play petty politics."[4]

The transactional leader is most concerned with the satisfaction of physiological, safety, and belonging needs. To meet these needs, a transactional leader exchanges rewards or privileges for desirable outcomes—much the way a Marine drill sergeant would trade a weekend pass for a clean barracks. Transformational leaders also attempt to satisfy the basic needs of followers, but they go beyond mere exchange by engaging the total person in an attempt to satisfy the higher-level needs of self-esteem and self-actualization. Transformational leadership is empowering and inspirational; it elevates leaders and followers to higher levels of motivation and morality. According to Burns, "The result of transforming leadership is a relationship of mutual stimulation and elevation that converts followers into leaders and may convert leaders into moral agents."[5]

> *The function of leadership is to produce more leaders, not more followers.*
>
> —Ralph Nader

In a series of research studies involving groups of military leaders, university students, corporate managers, and educators, Bernard Bass and his associates looked at the factors of transactional and transformational leadership.[6] These researchers identified seven leadership factors: two dimensions of transactional leadership, four dimensions of transformational leadership, and one nonleadership dimension (see box 4.1). Transactional leadership is primarily passive. The behaviors most often associated with transactional leadership are establishing the criteria for rewarding followers and maintaining the status quo. Those leaders who went beyond transaction and engaged in transformational leadership demonstrated active behaviors that included providing a sense of mission, inspiration, emotional support, and intellectual stimulation. As Bass explains:

> Unlike the transactional leader who indicates how current needs of followers can be fulfilled, the transformational leader sharply arouses or alters the strength of needs that may have lain dormant. . . . It is leadership that is transformational that can bring about the big differences and big changes in groups, organizations, and societies.[7]

Box 4.1

Dimensions of Transactional and Transformational Leadership[8]

Transactional Leadership Factors

Contingent reward: Provide rewards for effort; recognize good performance.

Management-by-exception: Maintain the status quo; intervene when subordinates do not meet acceptable performance levels; initiate corrective action to improve performance.

Transformational Leadership Factors

Charisma: Provide vision and a sense of mission; inspire; build trust and respect.

Individualized consideration: Exhibit considerate and supportive behavior directed toward each individual subordinate; coach and advise.

Inspiration: Communicate high expectations; use symbols to focus efforts and enhance understanding of goals.

Intellectual stimulation: Promote innovative ways of viewing situations; stimulate intelligent problem solving and decision making.

Nonleadership Factor

Laissez-faire (abdication): Abdication of leadership responsibility; avoidance of problem solving and decision making.

Whether or not a leader exhibits transformational behavior may be directly related to his or her communication skills. Ted Zorn discovered a relationship between the complexity of a leader's communication system and the tendency to exhibit transformational leadership behavior.[9] Zorn found those leaders with the most developed cognitive and communicative abilities were the most likely to be perceived as transformational by their followers.

The Characteristics of Transformational Leadership

Several other researchers have attempted to describe the characteristics of transformational leaders. Tom Peters and Robert Waterman prompted a renewed interest in organizational leadership with the publication of their best seller, *In Search of Excellence.*[10] Peters and Waterman studied 62 successful American companies. They discovered that excellent companies were most often blessed with extraordinary leadership. Later, Peters and Nancy Austin extended the exploration of the phenomenon of extraordinary leadership in *A Passion for Excellence.*[11] Peters expanded his discussion of transformational leadership in *Liberation Management*, in which he described the adaptable and flexible leadership practices required to deal with the necessary disorganization of the rapidly changing business environment.[12] Warren Bennis and Burt Nanus studied 90 successful leaders from business, government, education, and sport in an attempt to identify the strategies used by transformational leaders.[13] James Kouzes and Barry Posner of Santa Clara University surveyed over 1,300 managers in order to discover practices common to successful transformational leaders.[14] Thomas Neff and James Citrin attempted to identify the best business leaders in the United States, and Bruce Avolio and Bernard Bass developed a series of leadership case studies suggesting the most successful leaders exhibit transformational leadership behaviors.[15]

The characteristics of transformational leaders identified by all of these researchers are strikingly similar. Five primary characteristics appear, in one form or another, in all of the classification systems dealing with extraordinary leaders. Transformational leaders are *creative, interactive, visionary, empowering*, and *passionate*. Further, since transformational leadership can convert followers into leaders themselves, these characteristics are often filtered throughout transformed groups and organizations.

Creative

Transformational leaders are innovative and foresighted. They constantly challenge the status quo by seeking out new ideas, products, and ways of performing tasks. Transformational leaders recognize that satisfaction with the status quo poses a serious threat to a group or organization's survival. Resting on past achievements can blind members to new opportunities and potential problems. As organizations such as Netscape, AOL TimeWarner, and Sears have discovered, the most successful organizations are often in the most danger. Transformational leaders ignore the adage, "If it ain't broke, don't fix it." Instead, the transformational leader adopts the attitude, "If it ain't broke, you're not looking hard enough."[16] Iwao Isomura, chief of personnel for Toyota, explains, "Success is the best reason to change."[17]

The Process of Creativity

To clarify the relationship between creativity and leadership, we first need to understand how the creative process works. Creativity, like leadership, is based on our capacity for creating and manipulating symbols. Not only does creative problem solving involve abstract thought (which is made possible by language), but creative ideas nearly always take a particular symbolic form—as chemical formulas, sentences, drawings, ad slogans, and so on.

Experts suggest that creativity involves making new combinations or associations with existing elements. Educator Sidney Parnes, for example, describes creating as "the fresh and relevant association of thoughts, facts, ideas, etc. in a new configuration."[18] Psychologist Sarnoff Mednick defines creativity as "the forming of associative elements into new combinations which either meet specified requirements or are in some way useful."[19]

Creative thinking is frequently referred to as divergent or lateral thinking because it requires looking at problems from a number of different perspectives, thinking in broad categories, and producing a variety of solutions. Once a creative idea is generated through lateral thinking, however, the concept is refined through analysis, evaluation, and other convergent (vertical) thinking strategies. For example, to develop his theory of relativity, Einstein used lateral thinking to visualize himself as a passenger holding a mirror as he rode on a ray of light. He determined that his image would never reach the mirror because both he and the glass would move at the speed of light. In contrast, a stationary observer could catch Einstein's reflection in a mirror as the scientist passed by. Einstein started work on his theory of relativity as a result of this visualization. In order to complete the task, he worked for a decade using such vertical thought processes as calculation and reasoning.

One widely used description of creative problem solving was developed by George Graham Wallas. Based on research done with problem solvers, Wallas claimed that there are four steps to the creative process.[20]

1. *Preparation.* Creativity often begins with a conscious attempt to define and solve a problem. The preparation stage involves days, months, and even years of reading, gathering information, and repeated experiments. Composers, for example, may spend over ten years in study before their first important compositions are finished. The more extensive the preparation, the more likely the creative solution. As two-time Nobel Prize winner Linus Pauling once pointed out: "The best way to get a good idea is to get lots of ideas." In addition, valuable new insights often come from unrelated fields of study. Take the case of Steven Jobs who co-developed the Apple Com-

puter. Before starting Apple, Jobs designed video games at Atari. He attributes his success in developing the game Breakout to what he learned about movement and perception in a college dance class.[21]

2. *Incubation.* During the incubation period, the conscious mind shifts to other interests and the subconscious has an opportunity to make new associations, which lead to creative problem solving. To see how the incubation process works, build in an incubation period as you write your next major paper. Work as hard as you can for a few hours, and then turn your attention to other matters. When you return to write, you may find that ideas come more easily.

3. *Illumination.* Ideas may appear as sudden inspirations during the creative process. These flashes of insight come during the illumination stage, often when a person is alone and more sensitive to intuitive messages. Carol Orsag Madigan and Ann Elwood compiled the stories of many such inspirational moments in a book called *Brainstorms and Thunderbolts.*[22] Here are a few examples of famous flashes of illumination:

   - While in the bathtub, the ancient Greek scientist Archimedes discovered the principle that "a body immersed in liquid loses as much in weight as the weight of the fluid it displaces." Afterwards he celebrated his discovery by running naked through the streets, shouting "Eureka!" ("I have found it.")

   - The formula for the structure of benzene came to German chemist Friedrich August Kekule (1847) in a dream. Dreams were also a source of story plots for Robert Louis Stevenson. Mary Shelley, on the other hand, got her inspiration for the novel *Frankenstein* during a sleepless night.

   - William Booth, the founder of the Salvation Army, came home after a walk through the slums of London to announce to his wife, "Darling, I have found my destiny."

   - Mary Baker Eddy used her recovery from a fall on the ice to launch a new faith—Christian Science.

4. *Verification.* In this last stage, the creator develops the ideas that have come through preparation, incubation, and illumination. Verification can include writing poetry and novels, testing mathematical theorems, or checking with suppliers and running cost data.

Creative Roadblocks

The belief that only a few people are blessed with creative ability is one common misconception about creativity. According to this view, some outstanding individuals like William Shakespeare, Marie Pasteur, Bill Gates, or artist Georgia O'Keefe have large amounts of creative talent while most people have little or none. Research suggests, however, that everyone can think creatively—not just a few creative superstars. Studies of creative people reveal that they do not fit a single profile. Creative individuals are both aggressive and passive, introverted and extroverted, unstable and adjusted. Creative people share only three characteristics: (1) they are hardworking and persevering; (2) they are independent and nonconformist in their thinking; and (3) they are comfortable with complexity and ambiguity.[23] If we all have creative potential, then we need to identify those factors that keep us from being effective as creative problem solvers. James Adams identifies four types of creative blocks in his book *Conceptual Blockbusting*.[24]

1. *Perceptual blocks.* According to Adams, "Perceptual blocks are obstacles that prevent the problem solver from clearly perceiving either the problem itself or the information needed to solve the problem." Such blocks can include seeing what you expect to see (stereotyping), difficulty in isolating the problem, putting too many constraints on the problem, being unable to see the problem from many different viewpoints, being too close to the problem (saturation), and failure to use all the senses to understand the problem.

2. *Emotional blocks.* Our fears and emotions can also keep us from using our creative potential. We may fear risk, failure, or uncertainty; we might be unenthusiastic and too quick to judge new ideas, or we might confuse fantasy with reality.

3. *Cultural and environmental blocks.* Not all blocks to creativity come from within. Society often imposes stringent guidelines that inhibit the creative process. Cultural taboos eliminate certain solutions, and societal norms frequently emphasize reason to the exclusion of other methods of problem solving. Reliance on tradition ("We never did it that way before") also inhibits creative thinking. Ours is a rational society that emphasizes vertical thinking. When was the last time you took a course in creativity, for example, or talked about intuition in class? The result of a study of Oregon teachers demonstrates how little time is devoted to creative activities in the classroom. The teachers spent 67 percent of their time teaching cognitive learning skills like reading, writing, and math, while another 15 percent of their school day was devoted to administrative tasks. Most of their instructional methods were analytical, centering on lecture, discussion, recitation, and drill/practice.[25]

4. *Intellectual and expressive blocks.* Intellectual blocks come from using the wrong strategies to solve problems, from being inflexible, or from not having enough (or correct) information. Expressive blocks keep us from communicating ideas effectively. Using words, for instance, is not always the best way to share ideas with others. To demonstrate the limitations of language, Adams suggests that you have someone place an unfamiliar object in a bag so that you can feel the item but not see it. Describe the object while others try to draw a picture based on your description. You will find this task to be extremely difficult if you rely on common verbal symbols ("the top is circular with a piece cut out, and the longest side comes down from this cut off area"). You will be more successful if you describe the object in coordinates or geometric terms.

Becoming a Creative Leader

Becoming a creative leader means thinking more creatively yourself, while at the same time helping followers develop their creative abilities. To achieve these goals, leaders need to adopt a problem-finding perspective, learn to tolerate failure, and focus collective attention on innovation.

Identifying new problems is called the ***problem-finding orientation*** to creativity.[26] In order to develop a problem-finding orientation, keep in constant touch with sources both inside and outside the organization or group—employees, members of other task forces, customers, stockholders, government officials, media outlets, industry officials, and others. These linkages will reveal gaps between what the organization is and should be doing, shifts in the political or social climate, and so on. In addition, go looking for "trouble" by posing questions that challenge current products, practices, procedures, and beliefs. Psychologists Robert Kriegel and David Brandt call this process hunting for sacred cows.[27] Sacred cows are outmoded, usually invisible ways of doing things that blind organizations to new opportunities. For example, many reports, proposals, and publications could be eliminated because nobody reads them. To round up sacred cows, listen to complaints, identify and analyze basic assumptions, and form cow-hunting groups. Pay particular attention to the way you spend your time. Keep a daily log for an average week and then eliminate the sacred cows by asking yourself: (1) Why am I doing this activity, and what would happen if it didn't exist? (2) Is someone else doing this task? (3) How and when did this practice come into being, and who started it? and (4) Can another person, department, or company do it faster, better, or more easily?

> *A leader is someone who can take a group of people to a place they don't think they can go.*
>
> —Bob Eaton

Because every creative idea carries with it the risk of failure, we need to tolerate mistakes if we hope to foster creativity in ourselves and those we lead. Creative leaders concentrate on the task rather than on what can go wrong. They recognize that failure is a significant learning tool; the only people who don't fail are those who don't try. The founder of the Johnson & Johnson Company once declared: "If I wasn't making mistakes, I wasn't making decisions."[28] IBM's first president, Thomas Watson, took this philosophy to heart. After making a ten-million-dollar blunder, a young executive walked into his office and began the conversation by saying, "I guess you want my resignation." Watson replied: "You can't be serious. We've just spent $10 million educating you!"[29] Microsoft's Bill Gates likes to hire people who have made mistakes: "It shows they take risks. The way people deal with things that go wrong is an indicator of how they deal with change." [30] (See box 4.2 for a discussion of how the transformational leader approaches failure.)

If you want to encourage creativity, you need to help your group focus on generating new products, ideas, and procedures. In an organizational setting, invest your own time in project start-ups and other innovative activities. Encourage creativity by measuring and rewarding creative efforts. At 3M, for instance, 30 percent of each division's profits must be generated by products developed in the past four years (see the case study in box 4.3).

> *Creative activity is one of the few self-rewarding activities.*
> *Being creative is like being in love!*
>
> —Woody Flowers

Box 4.2   Research Highlight

The Wallenda Factor[31]

Warren Bennis and Burt Nanus interviewed ninety successful public and private leaders. Although the leaders Bennis and Nanus studied were different in many respects, they were similar in the way they responded to failure. They simply didn't concern themselves with failing. Indeed, many of these extraordinary leaders created euphemisms such as "glitch," "bollix," and "setback" to refer to their mistakes. As far as these leaders were concerned, their mistakes served as a learning tool. Bennis and Nanus called this positive approach to failure the "Wallenda factor."

The Wallenda factor originates from the famed tightrope aerialist, Karl Wallenda. Wallenda fell to his death in 1978 traversing a 75-foot high wire in downtown San Juan, Puerto Rico. The walk was among the most dangerous Wallenda had ever attempted. For months prior to the walk he worried about failing. He was so concerned about his safety that he personally supervised the installation of the tightrope for the first time in his career. Wallenda focused all of his energies on not falling, rather than on walking.

Focusing on what can go wrong virtually guarantees failure. Transformational leaders put their energies into the task and don't concern themselves with potential failures. Although these leaders do not ignore possible failure, they also don't fear failure. As one leader quoted by Bennis and Nanus explained: "There isn't a senior manager in this company who hasn't been associated with a product that flopped. That includes me. It's like learning to ski. If you're not falling down, you're not learning."

Box 4.3   Case Study

Encouraging Innovation at 3M[32]

Many of us associate innovation with computer manufacturers, software developers, robotics, and other high-tech industries. Yet one of the most innovative companies in the United States manufactures products as mundane as tape and sandpaper. At the Minnesota Mining and Manufacturing Company (3M), innovation has been essential to the company's success since its earliest days. 3M started when a group of investors bought a piece of land so they could mine corundum, the abrasive that makes sandpaper scratchy. When the investors discovered the land didn't hold any corundum, they had to create new products or quit. The firm's first successful inventions were an abrasive cloth for metal finishing and waterproof sandpaper used for polishing exterior auto finishes. From the outset, innovators at 3M learned from their mistakes. Early inventor Francis Okie initially suggested that sandpaper could be sold to men as a replacement for razor blades! Despite this dubious suggestion, Okie kept his job and went on to invent the waterproof sandpaper that helped the company survive. Today, 3M is a $15 billion manufacturing company with over 70,000 employees worldwide and more than 60,000 products, including Post-it notes, Scotchgard fabric protector, overhead projectors, heart-lung machines, insulating materials, and light fixtures. Innovation is so important at 3M that it is central to the company's vision--*to be the most innovative company in the markets it serves.* How does a company as diverse as 3M maintain its creative edge?

1. *Challenging People.* The goal at 3M is for 30 percent of sales to come from products introduced within the past four years. Not every 3M division achieves this target, but managers are judged on the number of new products as well as on the expansion of existing product lines.

2. *Using Sponsors.* Most successful creators have a sponsor in upper management. Senior executives must be willing to help innovators gain access to resources and offer protection when projects fail.

3. *Providing Rewards.* Rewarding innovation is a tricky matter. Most successful innovators find gratification in seeing their ideas turned into reality and are less motivated by financial rewards and promotions. The best reward for a successful idea is most often the freedom to work on other projects. At 3M, being a successful innovator is like playing an arcade game—if you win you get to play again!

4. *Guaranteeing Time.* Creative staff at 3M are encouraged to spend up to 15 percent of their time on projects of their own choosing. Known as "bootlegging," this concept enables innovators to work on pet projects without first gaining management approval.

5. *Communicating.* 3M doesn't allow creative personnel to work in isolation. The company requires its scientists to attend seminars where they meet their counterparts in other departments and discuss applications for new research. Annual private trade shows encourage technology sharing by showcasing new ideas being developed in every laboratory in the company. Communication is facilitated by sending engineers to 3M labs in other countries and through the use of computer-mediated forums, teleconferences, and an internal television network.

6. ***Recognizing Outstanding Performance.*** When a product is successful, leaders at 3M recognize those responsible. The Carlton Society, a company hall of fame, honors the achievements of outstanding scientists; the Golden Step Award honors teams of people who have successfully developed and marketed new products.

7. ***Accepting (Original) Mistakes.*** Failure is a major concern for innovators, since it will happen to most of them at one time or another. 3M is very insightful in realizing that nothing inhibits creativity like the fear of punishment for failure. More than 60 percent of new product ideas developed at 3M ultimately fail. This figure does not include the countless failures occurring on a daily basis in 3M research and development labs. However, successes like the Post-it note (found in virtually every office in the world) more than compensate for 3M's product failures. Post-its were developed by adapting materials from a failed venture. The compound used for the adhesive on the back of the Post-it note was initially deemed useless because of its limited adherence to other objects—the very quality that made Post-it notes a success! Today, there are more than 400 Post-it products sold in over 100 countries around the world, and a product born from failure generates over $300 million per year for 3M.

Discussion Questions

1. Does a company have to have a history of innovation like 3M in order to be highly creative? If not, how can an innovative climate be fostered?

2. What type of reward do you feel is most effective in motivating creative people? Are financial rewards important?

3. What advantages/disadvantages do you see in the 3M policy of "bootlegging?"

4. Do you agree with the 3M philosophy that all original mistakes should be accepted without punishment? Under what conditions should people be punished for failure?

5. How could the seven methods for fostering creativity employed at 3M be used in an organization with which you are familiar?

Interactive

Transformational leaders are masterful communicators able to articulate and define ideas and concepts that escape others. As suggested earlier, the process of leadership depends on the existence of symbols that facilitate coordinated action. Transformational leaders transmit their ideas through images, metaphors, and models that organize meanings for followers. Extraordinary leadership is a product of extraordinary communication. To communicate successfully, a transformational leader must be aware of the needs and motivations of his or her followers. Only when a leader is involved with followers can he or she find ways to do things better. Tom Peters and Nancy Austin suggest that "managing by wandering around" (MBWA) is one way to become involved with followers.[33] MBWA involves walking the floor, interacting with followers on a regular basis. The transformational leader engaging in MBWA does not play the role of a cop on patrol but acts as a coach whose primary activities are listening, teaching, and helping followers with problems.

One organization that embodies the transformational philosophy is Johnsonville Foods of Sheboygan, Wisconsin. At Johnsonville, traditional organizational structure was replaced in the early 1980s by self-directed work teams. Middle managers adopted the leadership roles of coordinators and coaches rather than the traditional roles of supervisors and disciplinarians. Leaders were responsible for teaching team members how to lead themselves more effectively. In short, the primary job responsibility of organizational leaders at Johnsonville Foods became one of interacting with team members (see box 4.4).

Thomas Neff and James Citrin, senior executives at Spencer Stuart, one of the most well regarded executive search firms in the world, surveyed over 500 leaders in business and education to identify the 50 best public and private sector business leaders in the United States. Among their top-rated leaders were Michael Dell (Dell Computer), Elizabeth Dole (at the time with the Red Cross), Michael Eisner (Disney), Bill Gates (Microsoft), Lou Gerstner (IBM), and Howard Schultz (Starbucks).[34] One common trait among the 50 top-rated business leaders was the ability to communicate effectively. As Neff and Citrin explain, "Nowhere is it more critical to be a strong communicator than in leading people."

One of their most powerful examples is Mike Armstrong, the former CEO of AT&T. Every Monday, Armstrong brought together the company's top executives—eight to 10 people—who met for the entire day to make sure the company was on track. Armstrong said the key was to "Communicate, communicate, communicate. You cannot be a remote image. You've got to be touched, felt, heard, and believed."[35] This is particularly important in times of change. In the days following the September 11 terrorist attacks, Continental Airlines CEO Gordon Bethune recorded a daily voice-mail message to keep all of his employees fully informed about the rapidly changing situation in their industry.[36] These examples illustrate the importance of communication to successful leadership. Indeed, the more leadership responsibility an individual has, the more likely it is there will be a significant communication component to his or her job. Political and social leaders, CEOs, and senior executives all devote a great deal of energy to clearly communicating their message to followers.

By encouraging open communication, a leader allows followers to share their ideas and insights. The experience of the U.S. Forest Service provides a good example of how simplifying the communication process can help foster employee participation. The Eastern Region of the U.S. Forest Service had a system for suggestions that required employees to fill out a four-page form each time they had an idea. In a four-year period the region's 2,500 employees submitted 252 ideas for consideration, or about one idea per person every forty years. To see if they could improve participation, the Forest Service officials changed the process to make it easier for employees to communicate

---

Box 4.4   Case Study

The Revolution at Johnsonville Foods[37]

Ralph Stayer joined his family's sausage-making business in Sheboygan, Wisconsin, after graduating from Notre Dame in 1965. In 1978, he replaced his father as president of Johnsonville Foods. Stayer inherited a stable company with annual growth averaging around 20 percent. Johnsonville was a successful company by all accounts, yet Stayer sensed problems. He noticed workers were operating far below their potential. Employees were disinterested. Most who worked at Johnsonville Foods appeared to be doing no more than meeting minimum performance expectations. Few seemed concerned with excelling in their work. Stayer felt there had to "be a better way."

After attending a series of seminars by University of Wisconsin communication professor Lee Thayer, Stayer became inspired to revolutionize leadership practices at Johnsonville Foods. In 1982, Stayer wrote a six-page letter to his employees. Leadership at Johnsonville Foods was going to change. Employees would be asked to take far more responsibility for the work they performed. Further, the compensation system would be overhauled. Instead of across-the-board annual raises, employees would be paid for performance. Those who learned new skills and developed their talents would receive the largest salary increases and profit-sharing bonuses.

The traditional organizational structure was dismantled. First-line employees were organized into self-directed work teams. These employees, known as members, were given a wide array of responsibilities ranging from budgeting, scheduling, quality control, and marketing to strategic planning and personnel, including the hiring *and* firing of their fellow team members. Middle managers, formerly responsible for the tasks turned over to the first-line workers, now focused their efforts on teaching and on coaching members to lead themselves. Meanwhile, Ralph Stayer turned his attention away from the day-to-day operation of Johnsonville Foods and began to focus more energy on maintaining his philosophy of transformational leadership. Slowly, members working on the production line began to take over more of the responsibility for operating Johnsonville Foods.

The watershed moment came in 1985 when Johnsonville was asked to produce a new line of meats for another manufacturer. To make the venture work successfully, employees at Johnsonville would have to make tremendous sacrifices. During the start-up phase, members would have to work six- and seven-day workweeks for months on end. Further, quality would have to be maintained at the highest level to insure that the contract continued. In the past, Stayer would have consulted with his senior management team before making a decision of this importance. This time, however, Stayer continued with his plan to revolutionize leadership practices at Johnsonville Foods. He conducted a forum with all members in the plant and presented the problem to them. Two weeks later the members decided, almost unanimously, to take the business.

The venture was a great success! Quality rose on the new product line as well as on the original Johnsonville product line. The reject rate dropped from 5 percent to less than one-half of one percent. Revenues increased nineteenfold in a ten-year period. All this occurred at a time when people were eating healthier, and most other sausage products were experiencing declining sales.

In recent years, members have taken so much responsibility that Stayer has moved away from the day-to-day leadership of Johnsonville. He now works primarily on other projects, including the development of a line of pasta products and a successful leadership consulting business. Although it took over a decade to fulfill his promise, Ralph Stayer did revolutionize leadership practices at Johnsonville Foods.

Discussion Questions
1. Is it fair to ask employees to take more responsibility for their work without offering a significant increase in pay? What should Johnsonville Foods do about employees who don't want more responsibility?
2. Are there some responsibilities that should not be given to first-line workers?
3. What are the advantages/disadvantages of having members hire and fire (if necessary) their own teammates?
4. Why do you think Johnsonville Foods was so successful in producing a new line of meats in 1985? Do you think this venture would have been as successful if the senior management team had made the decision to take on this project?
5. What conditions do you believe are necessary for this revolutionary approach to leadership to work elsewhere?

with their superiors. The new system allows anyone with an idea to submit a brief description by e-mail. Under the new system, employees sent in 6,000 new ideas in the first year, an average of more than two ideas per employee each year![38]

Visionary

Communicating a vision to followers may well be the most important act of the transformational leader. A vision is a concise statement or description of the direction in which an individual, group, or organization is headed. Compelling visions provide people with a sense of purpose and encourage commitment. Followers achieve more and make more ethical decisions when they pursue a worthy goal. To be compelling, a vision must be both desirable and attainable. Uninspiring or unachievable visions are ineffective and may demoralize followers.

Warren Bennis and Burt Nanus found that transformational leaders spend a good deal of time talking with employees, clients, other leaders, and consultants before developing a vision for their organization.[39] They study the history of their organization to determine the reasons for past successes and failures; they study the present to determine current strengths, weaknesses, and resources; and they look to the future to identify possible long-term social, political, and environmental changes. The leaders then interpret the information and construct a realistic vision that fits the norms of the group and inspires followers to put forth more effort.

Burt Nanus lists four characteristics of effective visions.[40]

1. *An effective vision attracts commitment and energizes people.* People are willing, even eager, to commit to worthwhile projects. An effective vision inspires people by transcending the bottom line. Whether it involves something that improves conditions for others (such as the development of new medical technology) or something that allows for growth and development on the part of the follower (such as increased autonomy), people are motivated to meet challenges that make life better.

2. *An effective vision creates meaning for followers.* People find meaning in their work lives. When groups and organizations share a vision, individuals see themselves not just as sales clerks or assembly workers or whatever else their job demands, but as part of a team providing a valuable product or service.

3. *An effective vision establishes a standard of excellence.* Most people want to do a good job. A shared commitment to excellence provides a standard for measuring performance. Establishing a standard of excellence helps followers identify expectations and provides a model for the distinctive competence of a group or organization.

4. *An effective vision bridges the present and the future.* A vision is a mental model of a desirable and idealistic future. By bridging the present and the future, an effective vision transcends the status quo by linking what is happening now with what should happen in the future.

Extraordinary leaders at every level communicate compelling visions. Whether the vision is to have the best customer service in the industry or the fewest defects on an assembly line, a sense of direction and purpose is essential to inspired leadership. The behavior exhibited by a transformational leader provides the basis for reinforcing a vision. When the plant manager jumps into a delivery truck to rush an order to an important customer, people notice. This kind of dramatic behavior reinforces priorities and values and sets a standard for follower behavior. As James Collins and Jerry Porras explain in their book *Built to Last*, organizations with a well-articulated vision that permeates the company are most likely to prosper and have long-term success.[41] Visionary companies such as Boeing, General Electric, Hewlett-Packard, Nordstrom, Wal-Mart, and Walt Disney tend to be the premier market leaders in their industries. Collins and Porras found that visionary companies were more likely to prosper over long periods of time even through multiple product cycles and changes in corporate leadership.

According to John Kotter, an effective vision is specific enough to provide real guidance to people, yet vague enough to encourage initiative and remain relevant under a variety of conditions.[42] If a vision is too specific it may leave followers floundering once the goals it articulates are achieved. An example of an overly narrow vision statement was President John F. Kennedy's vision for NASA. In 1962, Kennedy defined NASA's vision as "landing a man on the moon and returning him safely to earth before this decade is out." When a vision this specific is achieved (as it was in 1969), followers may feel a sense of confusion regarding what to do next (as NASA did in the 1970s and 1980s).[43]

> *If you do not know where you are going, every road will get you nowhere.*
> —Henry Kissinger

More effective vision statements offer general guiding philosophies without detailing specific end results. The following vision statements are examples of well-conceived organizational visions:

Amazon.com	To be Earth's most customer-centered company.
AT&T	We are dedicated to being the world's best at bringing people together—giving them easy access to each other and to information and services they want and need—anytime, anywhere.
Bristol-Myers Squibb	To extend and enhance human life by providing the highest-quality health and personal care products.
British Airways	To be the world's favorite airline.
Ford Motor Company	To become the world's leading consumer company for automotive products and services.
McDonald's	To provide the world's best quick service restaurant experience consistently satisfying customers better than anyone else through outstanding quality, service, cleanliness, and value.
Sheraton Hotels and Resorts	Building lasting relationships with people around the world.
Walt Disney	We create happiness by providing the finest in entertainment for people of all ages, everywhere.[44]

These vision statements provide a general philosophy that guides the actions of members of the organization while simultaneously reflecting key organizational values. Well-conceived vision statements evolve directly from the core values shared by members of a group or organization. (To see how the process of developing a personal vision statement works, try the self-assessment activity in box 4.5.)

A company's vision is not the same as its mission. While the vision provides a sense of direction and an idea or image of a desirable future, the mission is a description of the organization and how it is aligned to achieve its vision. As author and consultant Laurie Beth Jones explains, "The mission statement is centered around the process of what you need to be doing."[45] Ernst & Young consultant Ira Levin goes on to add, "Mission describes who the organization is and what it does. It is a statement of purpose, not direction."[46] Simply stated, a mission is a statement that identifies the scope of an organization's operations—it defines a company's core values and reason for

Box 4.5   Self-Assessment

Developing a Personal Vision Statement[47]

Values are at the core of individual, group, or organizational identity. Values are relatively enduring conceptions or judgments about what we consider to be important. According to Milton Rokeach there are two types of personal values:

Terminal values   Lifelong goals (e.g., freedom, inner harmony, salvation).

Instrumental values Behaviors that help people achieve lifelong goals (e.g., independence, ambition, obedience).

Values guide and direct behavior. There is substantial research suggesting that a number of positive effects result from agreement between personal values and the values most prized in the organization at which we work. Agreement between personal and organizational values result in increased personal identification with the organization, higher levels of job satisfaction, greater team effectiveness, and lower turnover rates. Values play a key role in the development of vision. Try to identify your own personal vision by ranking the values on the lists below. These two lists represent key terminal and instrumental values as identified by Rokeach. There are 18 values on each list. Rank order each from 1 (most important) to 18 (least important). Remember to consider the values on each list separately. You are to create two rank-ordered lists. Many people find this to be a very difficult process. Remember, you are ranking values from most important to least important—not from important to unimportant. Because values are so central to our personality there are few unimportant values.

TERMINAL VALUES	INSTRUMENTAL VALUES
___ **Freedom** (independence, free choice)	___ **Loving** (affection, tenderness)
___ **Self-respect** (self-esteem)	___ **Independent** (self-reliant, self-sufficient)
___ **Mature love** (sexual and spiritual intimacy)	___ **Capable** (competent, effective)
___ **An exciting life** (activity)	___ **Broad-minded** (open-minded)
___ **A comfortable life** (prosperity)	___ **Intellectual** (intelligent, reflective)
___ **Family security** (taking care of loved ones)	___ **Honest** (sincere, truthful)
___ **True friendship** (close companionship)	___ **Responsible** (dependable, reliable)
___ **Social recognition** (respect, admiration)	___ **Ambitious** (hardworking, aspiring)
___ **Wisdom** (an understanding of life)	___ **Imaginative** (daring, creative)
___ **Happiness** (contentedness)	___ **Helpful** (working for the welfare of others)
___ **A world at peace** (free of war and conflict)	___ **Forgiving** (willing to pardon others)
___ **A world of beauty** (beauty of nature and art)	___ **Logical** (consistent, rational)
___ **Pleasure** (an enjoyable, leisurely life)	___ **Cheerful** (lighthearted, joyful)
___ **Equality** (brotherhood, equal opportunity for all)	___ **Self-controlled** (restrained, self-disciplined)
___ **A sense of accomplishment** (lasting contribution)	___ **Courageous** (standing up for your own beliefs)
___ **Inner harmony** (freedom from inner conflict)	___ **Polite** (courteous, well-mannered)
___ **National security** (protection from attack)	___ **Obedient** (dutiful, respectful)
___ **Salvation** (saved, eternal life)	___ **Clean** (neat, tidy)

When you complete your rankings, write down the top-rated five or six values from each of your lists in the space below.

Terminal Values	**Instrumental Values**
1.	1.
2.	2.
3.	3.
4.	4.
5.	5.
6.	6.

Carefully examine the list of your top-rated terminal and instrumental values. Look for similarities, patterns, and themes. Using this as a starting point, try to create your own personal vision statement. Remember, this vision statement should emerge from the top-rated core values you identified. Your vision statement should be concise (usually a single sentence). Look back at the examples of well-conceived organizational vision statements on page 103 if you need a reminder of what a vision statement looks like.

My Personal Vision Statement:

Once you have developed your personal vision statement, try to shorten your statement into a slogan. A slogan is a shorter version of the vision statement you previously created. Slogans are most often associated with corporate advertising (e.g., Just Do it—Nike; Because I'm Worth It—L'Oreal; We Try Harder—Avis). Write your slogan below and share it with others in your class.

My Personal Slogan:

Discussion Questions
1. How does your personal vision statement and slogan match that of your present or past employer? How do think your personal vision statement might impact your job satisfaction?
2. Based on the slogans presented, what values do you perceive to be most prized in your class?
3. How can learning what is import to ourselves (as well as to others) help organizations operate more effectively?
4. What is the most significant thing you learned about yourself in this exercise?

being, while a vision mobilizes people into action by presenting an image of the desired future.

Empowering

Transformational leaders empower others. Even an extraordinary leader cannot accomplish a great deal without capable followers. Transformational leaders encourage participation and involvement. The exchange of ideas between leader and follower does not pose a threat to the transformational leader. Extraordinary leaders realize that individual achievement and success is the basis for team achievement and success. Transformational leaders know how to give power away and how to make others feel powerful. Transformational leaders give followers access to the funds, materials, authority, and information needed to complete tasks and develop new ideas (see chapter 5 for an in-depth discussion of empowerment). These leaders allow others to make decisions rather than insisting on making all the decisions themselves. Implicit in the concept of empowerment is the fact that such autonomy encourages employees to take ownership for their work. This ownership is exemplified by Disney which encourages its employees to treat every customer like a guest in their own home. To provide such service employees must be empowered to make decisions without management approval. An astonishing indication of the depth of employee empowerment at Disney is the fact that customer service representatives, the people who take the tickets at the theme park entrances, have $500,000 in tickets and cash at their disposal to give out to guests who lose or forget their tickets, run out of money, or encounter any other problem. [48]

> *The growth and development of people is the highest calling of leadership.*
> —Harvey S. Firestone

Followers will only take ownership of their jobs when there is sufficient trust within the organization. Without such trust, followers will be reluctant to make decisions for fear of possible reprisals. Researchers Pam Shockley-Zalabak, Kathy Ellis, and Ruggero Cesaria suggest that product and service quality critically depend on employees' trust in their organization and its leaders. [49] Collecting data from around the world, the researchers identified five key dimensions of organizational trust:

- *Competence*: The extent to which leaders, co-workers, and the organization as a whole are viewed as effective.
- *Openness and Honesty*: The extent to which the amount, accuracy, and sincerity of communication is perceived as appropriate.

- *Concern for Employees*: The extent to which feelings of caring, empathy, tolerance, and concern for safety are exhibited.
- *Reliability*: The extent to which leaders, co-workers, and the organization as a whole is perceived as consistent and dependable.
- *Identification*: The extent to which we share common goals, norms, values, and beliefs with those associated with the organization's culture.

Leaders hoping to successfully empower their followers need to be aware of perceptions of trust and should work to enhance overall trust levels.

> *Many hands, and hearts, and minds generally contribute to anyone's notable achievements.*
>
> —Walt Disney

Max DePree, former chairman of the board of the Herman Miller furniture company, goes so far as to suggest that leaders act as "servants" to their followers.[50] The leader serves followers by providing necessary resources and encouragement, empowering followers to complete assignments in the most productive manner. (See the case study in box 4.6 for an example of how empowerment and servant leadership can contribute to outstanding customer service.) In the words of Jan Carlzon, the former CEO of Scandinavian Airline Systems, "If you're not serving the customer, you'd better be serving someone who is."[51] This philosophy is exemplified by another retired airline CEO, Herb Kelleher of Southwest Airlines. Since Thanksgiving is a popular travel day, the staff at Southwest Airlines often has to be away from their families on this holiday. Kelleher made it a tradition to work along with his staff on Thanksgiving Day—taking tickets and handling bags along with his rank and file employees. As Kelleher explains, "You have to be willing to subjugate your ego to the needs of your business . . . and your people."[52] (For more information on servant leadership see chapter 11.)

Box 4.6   Case Study

Working by the Rule Book at Nordstrom

Nordstrom began as a small shoe store in Seattle in 1901 and has grown into a retail giant with more than 80 large department stores and 50 outlet clearance centers (Nordstrom Rack) in the United States, four boutiques in Europe (Faconnable), and one of the top-rated online customer apparel companies (Nordstrom.com). Together they generate some $6 billion per year in sales. Although other retailers may be larger, few engender so much enthusiasm and loyalty from both customers and employees.

From the beginning, Nordstrom incorporated the idea that outstanding customer service offers a competitive advantage. Stories abound concerning the almost mythic levels of assistance offered by Nordstrom staff. This (well deserved) reputation has turned the opening of new Nordstrom stores into civic events. When the first Nordstrom was built in Denver in the 1990s, hundreds of shoppers camped overnight in the parking lot in anticipation of the store's grand opening. Nordstrom capitalizes on this customer devotion, producing sales of about $400 per square foot—nearly double the sales for an average department store.

The key to Nordstrom's success is its leadership philosophy based on empowering employees to do whatever it takes to satisfy customers. As in many companies, new hires at Nordstrom attend a day-long employee orientation before they begin work on the sales floor. Unlike other companies, however, the training focuses almost exclusively on customer service. Each new hire is given a 5" X 7" card entitled, Nordstrom Rule Book, which reads:

> WELCOME TO NORDSTROM
> We're glad to have you with our company.
>
> Our number one goal is to provide
> **outstanding customer service.**
>
> Set both your personal and
> professional goals high.
> We have great confidence in your
> ability to achieve them.
>
> Nordstrom Rules:
> Rule #1: **Use your good
> judgment in all situations.**
>
> There will be no additional rules.
>
> Please feel free to ask your department manager,
> store manager, or division general manager
> any questions at any time.[53]

This entrepreneurial spirit allows Nordstrom sales associates to perform at levels that often exceed customers' expectations. For example, a Nordstrom sales associate in suburban Washington, D.C., received a letter from a Swedish business executive who had purchased $2,000 worth of shirts and ties from Nordstrom while in the United States. After returning to Sweden, he washed the shirts in hot water; they shrank. He wrote to Nordstrom to ask for advice on how he might deal with his problem. The Nordstrom sales associate immediately put through a call to Sweden and told the customer he would replace the shirts with new ones at no charge. He asked the customer to mail the damaged shirts to the store—at Nordstrom's expense—so he could send back the appropriate replacements. Such a move would likely require several levels of approval—if it would happen at all—at most stores, but as the Nordstrom sales associate explained, he "didn't have to ask for anyone's permission. . . . Nordstrom would rather leave it up to me to decide what's best."[54] In another example, a woman brought a pair of shoes purchased at Bloomingdale's into a New York area Nordstrom. The customer explained the shoes were too small. She had purchased them because she liked the style, but Bloomingdale's didn't have her size. After being fitted with the same shoe in the proper size (the average Nordstrom store carries over 150,000 pairs of shoes!), the customer started to pay for the shoes. The salesperson suggested the customer simply exchange the too-small shoes and take the correctly fitting pair for free. When the customer reminded the sales associate she had purchased the shoes at Bloomingdale's, the Nordstrom salesperson explained, "If I take these shoes for you, you won't have any reason to return to Bloomingdale's."[55] These liberal return and exchange policies might invite abuse, but the company's unconditional money-back guarantee is designed for the 98 percent of customers that Nordstrom finds to be honestly seeking fair treatment.

Developing this level of customer service can be challenging. Nordstrom prefers to hire people without previous sales experience. As Jim Nordstrom, the late co-chairman of the company once explained, those with little sales experience, "haven't learned to say 'no' to customers, because they haven't worked for anybody else."[56] Nordstrom expects its sales staff to exhibit high levels of professionalism and initiative. As such, Nordstrom sales associates are paid about 20 percent above industry standards. Salespeople receive either a base salary of $10 per hour, or a commission on sales of roughly 6.75 percent—whichever is greater. This allows Nordstrom staff the opportunity to earn handsome salaries as their sales increase, benefiting both the employee and the bottomline at Nordstrom. As Nordstrom has learned, financial outcomes are best for the staff and for the company when employees are empowered to offer the highest imaginable levels of customer service and attention.

Discussion Questions
1. What constitutes outstanding customer service? What are the best and worst customer service experiences you have had?
2. What is the relationship between empowerment and customer service?
3. What do you think of the Nordstrom Rule Book? Would you like to work for a company like this? Why? Why not?
4. Do you think the Nordstrom return and exchange policies might be abused by more than the two percent of its customers?
5. If a company expects people to take on more responsibility at work, what, if anything, should an employer be expected to offer in return?

Passionate

Transformational leaders are passionately committed to their work. They love their jobs and have a great deal of affection for the people with whom they work. This passion and personal enthusiasm motivates others to perform to their highest levels as well. Transformational leaders are able to encourage others because they, first and foremost, encourage themselves.

One organization that has received cult-like recognition for the passion exhibited by its employees is the Pike Place Fish Market in Seattle. Documented in books and training videos, the seafood store has become a tourist attraction. Thousands flock each day to watch the employees perform their jobs. The onlookers are treated to a spectacle that includes ongoing banter with customers, fish flying through the air as they are tossed to the cashier, and countless other zany antics. [57]

Organizational consultant Richard Chang suggests that passion is the single most important competitive advantage an organization can have.[58] Passion is a reflection of the organization and its leaders. In the book *Good to Great*, Jim Collins investigates elite companies that have exhibited sustained greatness over a period of at least fifteen years, such as Circuit City, Gillette, Walgreens, and Wells Fargo. One of his key findings was that great companies focus their energies on what they can get passionate about. For example, when Gillette executives made the choice to build sophisticated and more expensive shaving systems rather than enter the low-margin disposable market, they did so in large part because they had little enthusiasm for developing cheap disposable razors. For executives at Gillette the technical design of shaving systems sparks the same type of excitement that might be expected from an aeronautical engineer working on the latest advancements in aviation. People who aren't passionate about Gillette are not welcome in the organization. One top business school graduate wasn't hired by the company because she simply didn't show enough passion for deodorant. [59]

> *Nothing great in the world has ever been accomplished without passion.*
>
> —Georg Friedrich Wilhelm Hegel

By demonstrating the characteristics of transformational leaders, individuals can begin to transform themselves and their organizations. By encouraging creativity, fostering open communication, demonstrating forward thinking, sharing responsibility, and exhibiting commitment, leaders can help construct organizations prepared to meet the challenges of the future.

Most of the observations of transformational leaders have been made in organizational settings. Many questions remain to be answered concerning the viability of transforming leadership in less permanent contexts (such as a group that meets only once). Regardless, the transformational approach represents a bold and exciting perspective for understanding and explaining leadership. The assumption that effective communication is a key to extraordinary leadership will undoubtedly be tested by researchers in the years to come.

Perspectives on Charisma

Charismatic leaders are the "superstars" of leadership. We usually reserve the label "charismatic" for well-known political, social, and business leaders who have had significant impact on the lives of others. Notable historical figures such as Joan of Arc, Queen Elizabeth I, Henry Ford, John F. Kennedy,

Martin Luther King, Jr., and Walt Disney likely come to mind when we think of charisma. More recent conceptions of charisma, however, suggest that charismatic leadership can be found at all levels—not just among those in senior positions. By discovering how charismatics communicate, we can increase our effectiveness as leaders. In this section of the chapter, we'll summarize five approaches to the study of charismatic leadership. We'll also examine the dark side of charisma by exploring the potential abuses of charismatic leadership.

The Sociological Approach

German sociologist Max Weber, writing in the early twentieth century, was one of the first scholars to use the term charisma to describe secular leaders. The word charisma, which Weber borrowed from theology, means "gift" in Greek.[60] Early Christians believed that God gave special gifts or abilities to church leaders. Weber expanded the definition of gifted leadership to include all leaders, both religious and nonreligious, who attracted devoted followers through their extraordinary powers. In summarizing the nature of the charismatic leader, Weber wrote:

> . . . he [she] is set apart from ordinary men [women] and treated as endowed with supernatural, superhuman, or at least specifically exceptional powers or qualities. These [powers] are such as are not accessible to the ordinary person, but are regarded as of divine origin or as exemplary and on the basis of them the individual concerned is treated as a leader.[61]

According to Weber, a leader retains charismatic status as long as he or she is seen as charismatic. A charismatic must periodically demonstrate his or her exceptional personal gifts in order to maintain power over followers. Harrison Trice and Janice Beyer found five key components in Weber's conception of charisma.

1. A leader with extraordinary, almost magical, talents.
2. An unstable or crisis situation.
3. A radical vision for providing a solution to the crisis.
4. A group of followers attracted to the extraordinary leader because they believe they are linked through the leader to powers that exceed usual limits.
5. A validation, through repeated success, of the extraordinary leader's talents and power.[62]

> *Great crises produce great deeds of courage.*
> —John F. Kennedy

A number of important details are missing from Weber's pioneering theory of charismatic leadership. Weber never describes the origin or exact nature of the charismatic leader's extraordinary powers, nor does he clarify how charismatic authority rests both on the traits of the leader and on the perceptions of followers. Much debate is also generated by the claim that instability or crisis is a necessary condition for charismatic leadership. Many scholars argue that charisma can be demonstrated in the absence of crisis, noting that charismatic leaders with compelling visions often appear in the business world in times of stability and calm.[63] Because Weber left much to be discovered, clarified, and expanded, investigators from a number of disciplines have added insights to his discussion of charisma. Psychoanalysts, in particular, have been interested in the unique psychological characteristics of charismatic leaders and followers.

The Psychoanalytic Approach

The leading advocate of a psychoanalytic approach to leadership is Abraham Zaleznik of Harvard University. In 1981 Zaleznik was awarded the chair in leadership at Harvard, the first faculty position devoted entirely to the study of leadership at any major business school in the United States. Using the theories of Sigmund Freud, Zaleznik argues that leaders differ significantly from managers (a distinction we also make in chapter 1). According to Zaleznik, leaders introduce change, take risks, and arouse emotions. These same elements can be found in Weber's definition of charismatic leadership. Zaleznik also identifies some of the communication behaviors of leaders. Leaders focus on what events mean for followers rather than on how to get things done. Unlike managers who send vague "signals" that promote compromise, leaders send clear messages that may anger others.[64]

Other psychoanalysts use Freudian concepts to describe the motivation of those who follow charismatic leaders. Followers often have an intense attraction to charismatic leaders that is beyond ordinary admiration. This attraction can best be described in terms of "devotion, awe, reverence, and blind faith."[65] Intense follower identification is explained by the psychoanalytic approach in terms of regression, transference, and projection.[66] *Regression* involves a return to feelings and behaviors more typical at a younger age. Charismatic leaders in cults often control basic aspects of follower activity, including eating and drinking behavior, sleep patterns, and sexual conduct. This broad level of control enables a follower to regress to a point where he or she no longer has to deal with the stress of adult decision making. *Transference* occurs when a follower responds to a leader as if he or she were an important figure, such as a parent or teacher. Some charismatic leaders profess to provide care for followers. Charles Manson, for example, referred to his followers as his "family," just as many gang members claim a familial bond with gang leaders. *Projection* involves a process of attributing feelings or motives to someone else, thereby shifting attention away from one's own feelings and motivations. Ralph Hummel uses Freud's projection theory to explain why the Israelites rallied behind the biblical prophets. In projection theory, individuals who suffer loss project their love on an outside object or person. Hummel contends that when the ancient nation of Israel came under attack from foreign enemies, citizens turned to a group they had once scorned—the prophets. The Israelites coped with the loss of their traditional way of life by making the prophets the recipients of their love.[67]

Through regression, transference, and projection, charismatic leaders may help followers cope with their own feelings of inadequacy. In validating a charismatic leader's extraordinary ability, followers may experience feelings of empowerment by submerging their own identities in that of a seemingly superior leader. In this way, the charismatic leader becomes the embodiment of the follower's aspirations. The follower may feel unable to influence others, perceiving himself or herself as powerless and inadequate. Yet, followers may feel as though they are able to change the world when riding on the coattails of the charismatic leader.

The Political Approach

A number of political scientists, sociologists, and others apply Weber's definition of charisma to political figures. However, they don't always put the charismatic label on the same people. One extensive list of charismatic figures from this century was developed by Arthur Schweitzer.[68] He calls the twentieth century "The Age of Charisma" since so many charismatic leaders emerged during that period. Schweitzer believes there are different types of charismatic political leaders. *Charismatic giants* control the governments of world powers. Franklin Roosevelt, Benito Mussolini, Indira Gandhi, and Adolph Hitler fall into this category. *Charismatic luminaries* are leaders who have political authority in small countries (i.e., Gamal Nasser in Egypt or Muammar Gaddafi in Libya). *Charismatic failures* (such as Senator Joseph McCarthy) try for political control but fail. *Charismatic aspirants* are still striving for leadership positions.

Ruth Ann Willner's list of charismatic figures is shorter than Schweitzer's. She names only six people—Ayatollah Khomeini, Mahatma Gandhi, Adolph Hitler, Franklin Roosevelt, Fidel Castro, and Sukarno of Indonesia—as charismatic leaders.[69] Willner defines charisma on the basis of the leader-follower relationship. Charismatic followers: (1) attribute divine or semi-divine qualities to their leaders; (2) believe that their leaders have supernatural abilities to do magic, to prophesy or to escape from injury; (3) offer absolute devotion and obedience; and (4) are extremely loyal. Letters written to Franklin Roosevelt reveal the deep devotion followers have for their charismatic leaders. One highly committed follower, an Iowa congressman, told Roosevelt: "I will do anything you ask. You are my leader." A citizen wrote to say: "I have never had the urge to write to any President before, but with you it is different. . . . To me you're a god in disguise."[70] All in all, those who study charisma from a political perspective view charismatics as rare individuals able to exert great influence over the behavior of their followers.

The Behavioral Approach

Unlike political scientists who limit their discussion of charisma to famous social leaders, behavioral scientists argue that organizational leaders, like Thomas Watson of IBM and George Johnson of Endicott-Johnson Shoes, can also be described as charismatic. Behavioralists try to quantify the differences between charismatic and noncharismatic leaders. By describing charisma as a set of behaviors, they hope to clarify what charisma is and predict the effects of charismatic leadership.[71]

> *Do what you can, with what you have, where you are.*
> —Theodore Roosevelt

Based on a behavioral model of charisma, Robert House and Bernard Bass developed a set of propositions or conclusions about charismatic leaders.[72] These propositions fall into three major categories:

- *Leader behaviors.* Charismatic leaders have strong power needs, display high self-confidence, demonstrate competence, serve as role models, communicate high expectations, engage in effective argumentation, and create transcendent goals.

- *Leader-follower relations.* Charismatics serve as targets for follower hopes, frustrations, and fears. They also create a sense of excitement and adventure. While charismatics lead groups toward new visions, they build their appeals to followers on widely shared beliefs, values, and goals.

- *Elements of the charismatic situation.* Charismatic leaders are most likely to appear when groups are under stress. For a corporation, stress might involve bankruptcy or the loss of a major market. Chrysler's financial problems, for example, set the stage for Lee Iacocca's emergence as a charismatic figure. Societies experience tension when they move from an agricultural to an industrial economic base, fight a war, or face a depression. Ironically, the charismatic's success in rallying support in response to an emergency may also explain the strong resistance she or he faces. Charismatic leaders generate intense feelings of love or hate. Charismatic movie czar Louis B. Mayer convinced members of the financial community to back his movies at a time when the future of the film industry was in doubt, yet many considered him to be a vain tyrant. In fact, Samuel Goldwyn claimed that the reason so many people came to Mayer's funeral was to make sure he was really dead![73]

The Attribution Approach

Closely linked to the behavioral approach is the attribution approach. Jay Conger and Rabindra Kanungo view charismatic leadership as an attributional process.[74] In this approach, charisma is defined in terms of the perceptions of followers. Conger and Kanungo claim certain leader behaviors motivate followers to regard individuals as charismatic. Five behaviors that encourage followers to attribute charismatic characteristics to leaders are:

- *Possess a vision that is unique, yet attainable.* A charismatic leader's vision differs markedly from the status quo. It is unique, innovative, and energizing. At the same time, the charismatic leader's vision is not too radical. A vision that challenges conventional wisdom too greatly (for example, a presidential candidate claiming it is possible to balance the federal budget in one year) will promote distrust. Through the achievement of a unique vision, followers attribute powers of observation and insight to a leader.

- *Act in an unconventional, counternormative manner.* By engaging in behaviors that are outside traditional normative bounds, a charismatic demonstrates he or she is different from other leaders. When such behaviors produce successful outcomes, a leader appears to transcend the existing societal, organizational, or group order.

- *Demonstrate personal commitment and risk taking.* Trust is an important component of charisma, and followers have greater trust for a leader who is personally committed to his or her own vision. Most impressive is a leader who is willing to risk losing such things as power, status, or money.

- *Demonstrate confidence and expertise.* Leaders who appear confident and knowledgeable are far more likely to be viewed as charismatic than those who seem unsure and confused. A leader's confidence can be infectious. When a leader believes in his or her decision making, followers are likely to be more confident in their judgments as well. This shared confidence increases the likelihood of success for both leaders and followers and enhances the status of a leader among his or her followers. At the same time, when a leader demonstrates a high level of expertise, followers may believe the leader has privileged knowledge. The leader's successes will be attributed to expert decision making as opposed to chance.

- *Demonstrate personal power.* Followers are more likely to attribute charisma to leaders who use personal power to meet the objectives of their vision than to those who use authoritarian or democratic approaches. Leaders who use authoritarian means based on position power when implementing a vision are not likely to be perceived as charismatic. Likewise, leaders who delegate responsibility by asking followers to develop their own strategies for achieving a vision are unlikely to be seen as charismatic. Although these democratic leaders are generally well liked, they usually are not considered extraordinary by followers. Those leaders who demonstrate their personal power through the use of compelling oratory or persuasive appeals, however, are likely to be viewed by followers as possessing charismatic characteristics.

The Communication Approach

None of the perspectives on charisma that we have discussed so far view the topic from a communication vantage point. Nonetheless, all of these approaches acknowledge the prominent role that communication plays in charismatic leadership. Sociologist Weber emphasized that charisma is perceived by followers who look to the leader to illustrate his or her charismatic standing through communication. Psychoanalyst Abraham Zaleznik notes that leaders send clear messages and focus on the meaning that events have for followers. Both political scientists and behaviorists recognize the importance of (1) the charismatic leader's command of rhetoric and persuasion, (2) the charismatic's creation of a self-confident, competent image, and (3) the link between symbolic myths and goals and charismatic emergence. Attribution theorists Conger and Kanungo emphasize the importance of articulating a compelling vision through personal communication.

We think that communication is more than an important element of charismatic leadership, however. We believe that *charisma is the product of communication.* We agree with Robert Richardson and Katherine Thayer who point out that "charisma isn't so much a gift as it is a specific form of communication."[75] Richardson and Thayer argue that we can exert charismatic influence by working to improve our communication skills.

In chapter 1 we established that effective leaders must demonstrate communication skills associated with monitoring the environment and building relationships, thinking and reasoning (envisioning), and influencing others. Charismatic leaders excel in all three functions of communication.

Charismatics as Relationship Builders

Charismatic leaders are skilled at linking with others. Their relationships with followers are characterized by strong feelings. As we've seen, such terms as excitement, adventure, loyalty, and devotion are frequently used to describe charismatic leader-follower relations. In addition, charismatics convince followers that as leaders they have a significant impact on the course of events—that they are "at the center of things." [76]

Charismatics as Visionaries

Charismatic leaders can also be defined in terms of their ability to create symbolic visions. Above all, charismatics emphasize the transcendent. According to one scholar, "They provide in themselves and in their visions an opportunity for the follower to imagine himself and his society transformed into something entirely new."[77]

Although the visions of charismatic leaders are new images of the group's future, they are built upon the foundation of previous myths and values. The power of the charismatic grows as larger and larger numbers of people accept his/her symbolic focus. Stressful events like unemployment, war, fear for the future, and racial strife discredit current definitions of reality. This creates a more receptive audience for the charismatic leader's new vision. For example, the Civil Rights movement of the 1960s made many white Americans aware of the extent of racial injustice. Martin Luther King, Jr.'s nonviolent message gained wide acceptance because people of all racial groups could accept King's vision of a world united by love.[78]

Charismatics as Influence Agents

Charismatics are masters at influence and inspiration. In some instances, their influence is so great that followers never question their decisions or directives. Charismatic leaders project an image of confidence, competence, and trustworthiness. They utilize the power of positive expectations to generate high productivity and make effective use of language and persuasion to achieve their goals. Such leaders rely heavily on referent power (their influence as role models) to encourage others to sacrifice on behalf of the group.

If the perception of charisma is the result of communication behaviors, then we all have the potential to act as charismatic leaders. We can generate charismatic effects as small group, organizational, and public leaders. Though we may never influence millions as did Mahatma Gandhi or Martin Luther King, Jr., we can have a strong impact on the lives of others through shaping the symbolic focus of the group, generating perceptions of confidence and competence, communicating high expectations, and inspiring others.

The Dark Side of Charisma

We mentioned the dark side of charisma earlier in this chapter during our discussion of the psychoanalytic approach. Leaders like Charles Manson and Adolph Hitler used their charismatic abilities with horrific results. These leaders directed followers to achieve personal objectives. Jane Howell and Bruce Avolio offer the following guidelines for distinguishing between ethical and unethical charismatic leadership.[79]

The ethical charismatic leader	The unethical charismatic leader
uses power to serve others.	uses power only for personal gain.
aligns vision with followers' needs and aspirations.	promotes his/her own personal vision.
considers and learns from criticism.	censures critical or opposing views.
stimulates followers to think independently and to question the leader's view.	demands that his or her own decisions be accepted without question.
engages in open, two-way communication.	engages in one-way communication.
coaches, develops, and supports followers.	is insensitive to followers' needs.
relies on internal moral standards to satisfy organizational and societal interests.	relies on convenient external moral standards to satisfy self-interests.

> *Charisma becomes the undoing of leaders. It makes them inflexible, convinced of their own infallibility, unable to change.*
> —Peter Drucker

In his book, *The Charismatic Leader,* Jay Conger identifies some of the potential abuses of charismatic leadership in organizations.[80] These include problems related to vision, the misarticulation of goals, and poor management practices. While Conger acknowledges that some of the problems he identifies are common to many leaders, charismatic or not, he suggests the most extreme abuses are likely to be observed among charismatics.

Failures of vision. When vision fails, the cause can usually be traced to errors made by a leader. Ultimately, the success of a leader's vision depends on a realistic assessment of both external and internal environments. While visions may fail for a wide variety of reasons, Conger offers the following as significant factors:

- *The leader's vision projects personal needs rather than the needs of the market or his or her followers.* Edwin Land, the inventor of the Polaroid camera, pushed forward his vision to create the "perfect" instant camera, the SX-70, despite evidence that market demand would be very limited. The camera was an improvement over earlier models, but few consumers were willing to pay the additional cost.

- *The leader seriously miscalculates the resources needed to achieve his or her vision.* Donald Burr, the founding CEO of People Express, took the airline from a start-up company in 1980 to a billion-dollar business by the end of 1985. Two years later, People Express was taken over by a competitor. The primary reasons? Overexpansion into new routes and an ill-advised takeover of the incompatible Frontier airlines. Unable to contain his enthusiasm, Burr's dreams of expansion for People Express led to the company's demise.

- *The leader fails to recognize flaws and to redirect his or her vision.* John DeLorean wanted to design a profitable and popular sports car. His automobile was stylish, with gull-wing doors and a shiny steel body. However, much less effort was dedicated to the reliability and performance of the automobile. Further, the high price of the car resulted in sluggish sales. Before the problems with his venture became fully evident to DeLorean, his new company was too far in debt to be saved.

Misarticulation of goals. Charismatic leaders are generally gifted communicators. In some instances, charismatics misuse this ability. Among the most grievous acts identified by Conger are:

- *Exaggerated self-descriptions and claims for their vision.* According to one source, Apple co-founder Steven Jobs took far more credit for the development of the Macintosh computer than he deserved.[81] The need for personal recognition is so great among some charismatics that they may distort reality to enhance their own personal image.

- *Suppression of negative information.* The making of the box-office flop *Heaven's Gate* provides insight into how a charismatic leader can get caught up in a failing project. *Heaven's Gate* was directed by Michael Cimino. The film was made just after Cimino directed *The Deer Hunter,* a critically and commercially successful film. *Heaven's Gate,* on the other hand, was anything but a success. When the film was submitted for release it was nearly five-and-one-half hours long and 600 percent over budget! Cimino finally edited the film down to two- and-one-half hours, but critics and moviegoers were unimpressed. In the end, the film was removed from distribution. The company responsible for the project, United Artists, suffered a $44 million loss. How did *Heaven's Gate* get so out of hand? Cimino never informed his superiors of the problems he was having. He suppressed negative information about the production of his film for so long that when United Artists finally realized there were significant problems, it was too late to back out of the project.[82]

- *Attribution of failure to others.* In annual reports, for example, executives often use their letters to shareholders to claim responsibility for successes while blaming external forces for problems.

Poor management practices. Charismatic leaders can be excessively impulsive and somewhat authoritarian in their leadership style. The unconventional behaviors that make charismatics highly effective may also contribute to their downfall. Among the most serious concerns identified by Conger are:

- *Difficulty managing others.* Charismatics sometimes get carried away by their success and have difficulty relating to subordinates. In one organization, a charismatic division head routinely returned employee suggestions with the words "Stupid Idea" stamped on them. Similarly, when charismatics sense failure, they are likely to become dictatorial and demanding.

- *Lack of administrative skills.* Some charismatics are so absorbed in the big picture they fail to pay attention to essential deals. For instance, Lee Iacocca, as he became increasingly famous, turned over most of the day-to-day operations at Chrysler to others. He lost touch with the real issues in his company.

- *Failure to plan for succession.* Charismatic leaders often fail to develop competent successors. They leave their followers in jeopardy when they leave their positions.

Summary

The transformational approach focuses on the actions of inspiring leaders as they attempt to meet the higher level needs of followers. Transformational leaders are often creative, interactive, visionary, empowering, and passionate.

Transformational leaders recognize that creativity is an integral part of leadership. Wallas suggests that the creative process occurs in four steps: preparation (defining the problem and gathering background data), incubation (putting the problem on the "back burner" for a period of time), illumination (realization of the solution to the problem), and verification (testing the validity and usefulness of the solution). Overcoming creative roadblocks can help leaders to be more creative. Adams identifies four types of creative blocks: perceptual blocks (obstacles that prevent a problem-solver from seeing what they need to see to solve a problem), emotional blocks (emotions that inhibit creativity), cultural and environmental blocks (blocks imposed by culture or society), and intellectual and expressive blocks (blocks based on inadequate knowledge or the inability to articulate solutions). Strategies for becoming a creative leader include developing a problem-finding orientation and tolerating failure.

Transformational leaders are masterful communicators able to articulate ideas and concepts to others; they interact with followers on a regular basis. Communicating a vision and direction to followers may well be the most important act of a transformational leader. Transformational leaders encourage participation and involvement. These leaders know how to give power away and make others feel powerful. Transformational leaders are also passionately committed to their work. They encourage others because they, first and foremost, encourage themselves.

We ended the chapter with a discussion of charisma—the quality possessed by leaders who exert extraordinary influence over followers. Scholars in many disciplines have been interested in charismatic leadership. Major perspectives on charisma include: (1) sociological, (2) psychoanalytical, (3) political, (4) behavioral, (5) attributional, and (6) communication-based. While the first five perspectives make communication a prominent part of charismatic leadership, only the communication-based approach sees charisma as the product of symbolic activity. Charismatic leaders excel in every function of human communication. They form strong emotional bonds with followers, emphasize transcendent visions, generate perceptions of confidence, communicate high expectations, and inspire others. However, charisma also has a dark side, often reflected in failure of vision, misarticulation of goals, and poor management practices.

Application Exercises

1. Select a particular leader discussed in one of the many books focusing on transformational leadership (*In Search of Excellence, Passion for Excellence, Leaders, The Leadership Challenge, Built to Last, Lessons From the Top, Developing Potential Across a Full Range of Leadership,* or *Good to Great,* for example). Analyze how effectively the leader applies transformational techniques. Does he/she meet the higher level needs of followers? Is he/she an effective communicator? Does he/she have a clearly stated vision?

2. Think of a time when you came up with a creative solution to a major problem. Analyze your problem-solving effort based on the four stages of the creative process identified by Wallas: preparation, incubation, illumination, and verification. Did you experience each stage? Which was most difficult for you? How can you overcome creative blocks and increase your flow of creative ideas in the future? Report your findings.

3. Collect vision statements from several sources. Share your examples with others in class. Identify the common characteristics of the vision statements you think are most effective.

4. Discuss your past experiences with empowerment. Identify factors that let you know that you are truly empowered. Discuss factors that undermine empowerment. Develop a set of guidelines for effective empowerment.

5. Make a list of your passions. How could these passions be used to guide your career and future leadership experiences?

6. Make a list of ten charismatic leaders. Then form a small group and generate a composite list. To make the group's list, a leader must be accepted as charismatic by all the members of the group. Keep a record of those individuals who fail to receive unanimous support. Present your findings to the rest of the class. As part of your report, describe the criteria that the group used to compile its list. In addition, name those individuals who were rejected by the group. Explain why these leaders failed to make the master list.

7. Do an in-depth study of a public charismatic leader. Describe how this person's use of communication resulted in his/her emergence as a charismatic figure. Write up your findings.

Cultural Connections: Is Transformational Leadership a Universal Concept?[83]

As society becomes increasingly global in its focus, it is important to assess the universality of leadership research and theory. Bernard Bass argues that the concept of transformational leadership may be truly universal—transcending organizational and national boundaries. Evidence supporting the viability of the transformational approach has been gathered from all continents except Antarctica. The results suggest leadership, in general, and transformational leadership, in particular, are found in one form or another at all levels and in all cultures. Additional research conducted by Robert House and 170 research associates around the world as part of the Global Leadership and Organizational Behavior Effectiveness (GLOBE) project also supports the notion that transformational leadership has universal features.

Initially Bass and his colleagues believed that transformational leadership was only exhibited by leaders in senior positions. Soon it became apparent that a variety of leaders, including middle managers, community activists, students, housewives, team leaders, salespeople, and members of the clergy exhibited transformational characteristics. Based on this broad application of the approach, Bass and fellow researcher Bruce Avolio offered three corollaries, which have subsequently been supported across a variety of cultures.

1. *Transformational leaders are more effective than leaders adopting a more transactional approach.* This has been verified in research conducted in the United States, Canada, Austria, Belgium, Italy, Germany, Spain, India, Singapore, Japan, China, New Zealand, and several other countries. Based on the perceptions of followers and organizational outcomes, including performance appraisals, career advancement, and performance of the work unit, transformational leaders consistently exceeded the performance of transactional leaders.

2. *Transformational leadership adds value to transactional leadership, but the inverse is not true.* Results supporting this corollary have been obtained in the United States, Canada, the Dominican Republic, India, Singapore, and several other countries. While transformational leadership appears to augment transactional leadership, transactional leadership does not enhance transformational leadership.

3. *Whatever the country, when people think of leadership, their prototypes and ideals are transformational.* Participants in research conducted in the United States, Canada, South Africa, Spain, Austria, Sweden, Italy, Israel, Japan, Taiwan, Sri Lanka, New Zealand, and elsewhere consistently described the ideal leader as possessing the traits and characteristics of transformational leaders.

The researchers in the GLOBE project surveyed over 15,000 middle managers from 60 different cultures. Their research, like that conducted by Bass and his colleagues, suggests that attributes of transformational leadership such as being trustworthy, skilled, encouraging, visionary, communicative, and inspiring are universally endorsed leadership components. Bass acknowledges that there may be cultures in which transformational leadership is not found. In those cultures trust between the leader and the led would be unimportant and followers would have to demonstrate no concern for self-esteem, intrinsic motivation, consistency in the actions of leaders, or meaningfulness in their work and lives. Based on his work and that of the GLOBE project researchers, Bass argues such cultures would be the exception rather than the rule.

Leadership on the Big Screen: *Stand and Deliver*

Starring: Edward James Olmos, Lou Diamond Phillips
Rating: PG
Synopsis: This film, based on a factual story, documents high school mathe-

matics teacher Jaime Escalante and his efforts to transform the lives of a group of inner city Los Angeles high school students. Convinced that his students have potential, Escalante (Olmos) uses unconventional teaching methods to try to turn gang members and potential dropouts into some of the country's top algebra and calculus students. Over the course of the film, Escalante wins over Angel (Phillips) and other class members, eventually convincing 18 of his pupils to take the difficult National Advanced Placement calculus test.

Chapter Links: transformational leadership, charisma

Five

LEADERSHIP AND POWER

> *Leadership begins and ends with the problem of power.*
> —Abraham Zaleznik

Overview

Power: The Last Dirty Word?

Americans have contradictory feelings about power. On the one hand, we are fascinated by the power and wealth we see on television shows. We admire those with "clout," those who move quickly and decisively to get things done. We also loathe the corruption and greed that often comes with power. We're uneasy with exercising power—just discussing the topic can make us uncomfortable. According to Rosabeth Kanter, "Power is America's last dirty word. It is easier to talk about money and much easier to talk about sex than it is to talk about power."[1]

As a society, we pay a high price for our ambivalence towards power. Avoiding the subject makes us more vulnerable to the misuse of power by those in authority. A chilling example is cult leader Jim Jones, who presided over the mass suicide of 800 followers in Guyana. This tragedy might have been prevented if cult members and outsiders had recognized and challenged Jones's unhealthy use of power.[2] Conversely, our discomfort with the subject of power diminishes our capacity as leaders. In chapter 1 we noted that leadership is associated with innovation. Leaders can only bring about change if they skillfully use power to enlist the support of followers, overcome resistance, collect resources, create alliances, and so on. If we ignore the reality of power, we won't learn how to exercise power effectively on behalf of worthy goals.

Power is a given. Treating it as a dirty word won't make it go away. Instead, we need to acknowledge the importance of power and determine how to use it appropriately. In the words of John Gardner:

> To say a leader is preoccupied with power is like saying that a tennis player is preoccupied with making shots his [her] opponent cannot return. Of course leaders are preoccupied with power! The significant questions are: What means do they use to gain it? How do they exercise it? To what ends do they exercise it?[3]

Power and Leadership

Sorting out the relationship between power and leadership can be confusing. Is using power the same as exerting leadership? Does having power automatically make you a leader? Power and leadership are obviously interdependent; however, they are not interchangeable. While power can exist without leadership, leadership cannot exist without power.

Interdependent But *Not* Interchangeable

We define power as *the ability to influence others*. Leadership is impossible without power since a leader must modify attitudes and behaviors. Yet influencing others does not automatically qualify as leadership; power must be used in pursuit of group goals to merit leadership classification. Imagine a terrorist armed with a semiautomatic weapon bursting into a bank, ordering everyone to lie on the floor. The group obeys. The terrorist certainly exerted power—a very negative manifestation of power. We would not label the terrorist a "leader," however. His power was exercised only on behalf of his own interests. In other instances, powerful individuals do not use their power and thus fail to take a leadership role. The small group member who knows the most about a topic would be a natural candidate for group leadership. However, this person may refuse to participate in the group's discussion.

Leadership experts Warren Bennis and Burt Nanus summarize the relationship between power and leadership this way: "Power is . . . the *capacity to translate intention into reality and sustain it*. Leadership is the wise use of this power. . . . Vision is the commodity of leaders, and power is their currency."[4]

Sources of Power

If power is the "currency of leadership," then understanding the sources and uses of power is essential to effective leadership. The ability to influence others can be based on a wide variety of factors. John French and Bertram Raven have isolated five primary sources of power.[5] Chances are you prefer to use one or two of these power bases more than the others (see the self-assessment exercise in box 5.1).

Coercive power is based on the ability to administer punishment or to give negative reinforcements. Examples of coercion range from reducing status, salary, and benefits to requiring others to do something they don't like. In the most extreme form, coercive power translates into brute physical force. Whistleblowers (employees who have pointed out unethical practices like cost overruns and safety hazards) often experience coercion. They may be fired, assigned to distasteful jobs, or socially ostracized.

Coercion is most effective when those subject to this form of power are aware of expectations and are warned in advance about the penalties for failure to comply. Leaders using coercive power must consistently carry out threatened punishments. A parent who punishes without first establishing expectations and the consequences for failure will be less effective than a parent who clearly sets the ground rules. The effective parent says: "I expect you home by 10:00. If you're not home by then, you will be grounded for the rest of the weekend." The user of coercive power must then follow through with the announced consequence. Threatening over and over again to ground a teenager for being late without ever carrying out the punishment significantly diminishes coercive power. The same is true in organizational settings. A supervisor who threatens to take action against a subordinate must carry out the threat if the coercive attempt is to be successful.

> *Concentrated power is not rendered harmless by the good intentions of those who create it.*
>
> —Milton Friedman

Box 5.1   Self-Assessment

Personal Power Profile[6]

Instructions: Below is a list of statements describing possible behaviors of leaders in work organizations toward their followers. Carefully read each statement, thinking about *how you prefer to influence others.* Mark the number that most closely represents how you feel.

I prefer to influence others by	Strongly Disagree	Disagree	Neither Agree nor Disagree	Agree	Strongly Agree
1. increasing their pay level	1	2	3	4	5
2. making them feel valued	1	2	3	4	5
3. giving undesirable job assignments	1	2	3	4	5
4. making them feel like I approve of them	1	2	3	4	5
5. making them feel that they have commitments to meet	1	2	3	4	5
6. making them feel personally accepted	1	2	3	4	5
7. making them feel important	1	2	3	4	5
8. giving them good technical suggestions	1	2	3	4	5
9. making the work difficult for them	1	2	3	4	5
10. sharing my experience and/or training	1	2	3	4	5
11. making things unpleasant here	1	2	3	4	5
12. making work distasteful	1	2	3	4	5
13. helping them get a pay increase	1	2	3	4	5
14. making them feel they should satisfy job requirements	1	2	3	4	5
15. providing them with sound job-related advice	1	2	3	4	5
16. providing them with special benefits	1	2	3	4	5
17. helping them get a promotion	1	2	3	4	5
18. giving them the feeling that they have responsibilities to fulfill	1	2	3	4	5
19. providing them with needed technical knowledge	1	2	3	4	5
20. making them recognize that they have tasks to accomplish	1	2	3	4	5

Scoring: Record your responses to the 20 questions in the corresponding numbered blanks below. Total each column, then divide the result by 4 for each of the five types of influence.

	Reward	Coercive	Legitimate	Referent	Expert
	1____	3____	5____	2____	8____
	13____	9____	14____	4____	10____
	16____	11____	18____	6____	15____
	17____	12____	20____	7____	19____
Total	____	____	____	____	____
Divide by 4	____	____	____	____	____

Interpretation:

A score of 4 or 5 on any of the five dimensions of power indicates that you prefer to influence others by using that particular form of power. A score of 2 or less indicates that you prefer not to employ this particular type of power to influence others. Your power profile is not a simple addition of each of the five sources. Some combinations are more synergistic than the simple sum of their parts. For example, referent power magnifies the impact of other power sources because these other influence attempts are coming from a "respected" person. Reward power often increases the impact of referent power, because people generally tend to like those who can give them things. Some power combinations tend to produce the opposite of synergistic effects. Coercive power, for example, often negates the effects of other types of influence.

Failure to execute threats can produce a cycle of negative behavior. Warnings to punish represent attention. Although humans certainly prefer positive reinforcement, they will select negative reinforcement over no reinforcement at all (apathy). Humans would rather be punished than ignored. If a child is unable to attract positive attention, he or she may begin to misbehave in an attempt to attract negative attention. Employees in organizations are no different. "Problem" employees who receive warning after warning may simply need attention. Following the guidelines regarding the use of coercive power and offering positive reinforcement minimizes the negative behavior.

> *I praise loudly, I blame softly.*
> —Catherine The Great

Reward power rests on the ability to deliver something of value to others. The reward can be tangible (money, health benefits, or grades, for example) or something intangible like warmth and supportiveness. Many organizations use both tangible and intangible rewards to recognize superior performance.

Any reward must be desirable and attractive to serve as a sufficient motivator. One of our students worked in a large organization that decided to change computing systems. The changeover took six months and required employees to work many hours of overtime. When the new system was finally in place, the corporation hosted a Friday afternoon party and rewarded those who had worked such long hours with T-shirts that said, "I Survived the Changeover." The student and her coworkers were insulted. More suitable rewards, like giving workers the day off after so many weeks of overtime, might have been more appreciated and more attractive to employees.

This student's unhappy experience with rewards is all too common, prompting some experts to suggest that leaders should strictly limit their use of rewards as a motivational strategy. A summary of the case against reward power is found in box 5.2.

Box 5.2   Case Study

Alfie Kohn and the Case Against Rewards

In America, we take it for granted that offering a reward is the best way to get someone to do what we want. Parents promise their kids candy for being quiet in the car, professors offer students high grades if they work hard in their courses, and owners of professional sports franchises use incentive clauses to encourage players to score more points or to drive in more runs. On the surface, such tactics seem to work. Noisy children often quiet down when bribed with goodies, students do study hard in pursuit of an "A" grade, and baseball players strive to raise their batting averages in hopes of earning a bonus. However, a growing number of observers question whether the use of rewards really improves performance over the long term. Writer and lecturer Alfie Kohn builds a case against the use of rewards in a book entitled *Punished by Rewards: The Trouble With Gold Stars, Incentive Plans, A's, Praise and Other Bribes*.

In his book Kohn takes on the popular notion, based on the theories of B. F. Skinner and other behaviorists, that positive reinforcements produce positive results. He acknowledges that rewards secure compliance, but he questions the ethics of their use as well as their effectiveness. Rewards are the flip side of punishment, he argues, because both are used to control the behavior of others. Like punishments, rewards reinforce the higher status of those using them and generally benefit the rewarder rather than the rewardee. Not only does the use of rewards raise moral questions, but when it comes to producing lasting change, "the research suggests that they [rewards] fail miserably."[7] For example, people paid to lose weight, to quit smoking, or to use seat belts change their behavior for a short period of time but actually end up gaining more weight, smoking more cigarettes, and driving without their seat belts more often than those who are not bribed. Kohn offers five reasons why rewards fail. First, *rewards punish.* They limit the options of recipients, and many followers don't get the rewards they were expecting.

Second, *rewards rupture relationships.* Rewarding only a few individuals sets people against each other and destroys collaboration. A professional basketball player paid on the basis of how many points he scores, for instance, may hurt his team by shooting when he should pass the ball instead. Also, when we depend on someone for a reward, we want to impress that person instead of being open about the difficulties we're experiencing.

Third, ***rewards ignore reasons.*** Implementing an award system in response to poor performance diverts attention away from the underlying issues that caused the problem. Kohn puts it this way:

> Rewards do not require any attention to the reasons that the trouble developed in the first place. You don't have to ask why the child is screaming, why the student is ignoring his homework, why the employee is doing an indifferent job. All you have to do is bribe or threaten that person into shaping up.[8]

Fourth, ***rewards discourage risk taking.*** If we're focused on rewards, we avoid risks and take the easiest, surest path. After all, taking a risk might endanger the payoff we seek. No wonder we frequently try to avoid taking classes taught by professors who give very few As and Bs. Unfortunately, the safest path is the least creative one:

> "Do this and you'll get that" makes people focus on the "that," not the "this." Prompting employees to think about how much will be in their pay envelopes, or students to worry about what will be on their report cards, is about the last strategy we ought to use if we care about creativity. . . . *Do rewards motivate people? Absolutely. They motivate people to get rewards.*[9]

Fifth, ***rewards undermine intrinsic motivation.*** The motivation generated by the challenge and enjoyment of the task itself suffers when external motivators are put into effect. Rewards deflect our attention from the task itself, and we resent the loss of autonomy that comes when we submit to the rewarder. In other words, we're less interested in what we're doing when we're rewarded for doing it. Consider Pizza Hut's "Book It!" program, for example. Participants receive certificates good for free pizza as rewards for reading books. Unfortunately, school children will probably be less likely to read for pleasure after earning their certificates. Kohn quotes one psychologist who (only partly in jest) predicts that Pizza Hut's well-intended effort would probably result in "a lot of fat kids who don't like to read."[10]

Alfie Kohn is convinced that rewards of all kinds, even praise and the rewards we give ourselves, are harmful. He urges leaders to encourage "authentic motivation" by fostering collaboration; making sure the content (the curriculum, work, rules, etc.) of what followers do is meaningful; and giving students, employees, and children as much choice as possible in deciding which tasks should be completed and how they ought to be done.[11] If we must provide rewards, he says, then offer them as a surprise after the fact and make them less conspicuous. Never pit people against each other to receive them (don't grade on a curve, for example) and link the reward to the task (if a child reads a book, provide her another book, not a pizza). Give potential recipients a choice about how rewards will be given and try to convince followers that the task itself is worthwhile.

Discussion Questions

1. Do you agree with Kohn's argument that rewards are punishing? Why or why not?

2. How do you respond to rewards? Do they most often serve to motivate or to punish?

3. Can you add any additional guidelines to Kohn's list of ways to minimize the negative effects of rewards? How can rewards be used to more effectively motivate followers?

4. Can leaders motivate followers, or do they "tap in" to motivational factors that are already present in followers?

5. Would you want to work in an organization that never expressed encouragement or celebrated group accomplishments?

Legitimate power resides in the position rather than in the person. Persons with legitimate power have the right to prescribe our behavior within specified parameters: judges, police officers, teachers, and parents, for example. Although we may disagree with our supervisor at work, we go along with a decision because that person is "the boss." The amount of legitimate power someone has depends on the importance of the position she or he occupies and the willingness to grant authority to the person in that position. Individuals grant legitimate power based on particular circumstances. An assistant will comply when the boss assigns a word-processing project or requires the phone to be answered because those are legitimate requests. The assistant may not be willing to assent to tasks that are not related to work.

Expert power is based on the person not the position, in contrast to legitimate power. Experts are influential because they supply needed information and skills. In our culture, it is particularly important to be perceived as expert. Those with credentials are more powerful than those without appropriate certification. When visiting a new physician, do you immediately check his/her diploma? Our culture mandates that certain credentials must be obtained before an individual can be considered a professional. Demonstrating practical knowledge and skills can also build expert power. For this reason, members of an organization often have little legitimate power but a great deal of expert power. Receptionists can be extremely influential because of what they learn through talking to employees, managers, customers, and others. School janitors are often powerful because they know how to fix bulletin boards, open locked doors, and so on.

Referent power is role model power. When people admire someone, they confer upon the admired person the ability to influence their behavior. Referent power depends on feelings of affection, esteem, and respect for another individual. This loyalty generally develops over an extended period of time. Since referent power takes so long to nurture, it should be used carefully. A supervisor who asks a subordinate to work overtime as "a personal favor" will succeed if the employee likes and respects the supervisor. Referent power will probably be effective the first weekend and possibly the second, but after several weeks the employee will tire of doing "favors" for his/her supervisor. Once depleted, referent power must be replenished by engaging in behavior that will produce new feelings of affection, esteem, and support.

> *The measure of a [hu]man is what he [she] does with power.*
> —Pittacus

Deciding Which Types of Power to Use

A useful way of determining the relative advantages and disadvantages of each source of power is to view leadership as a transaction between leaders and followers. The relationship between leaders and followers is reciprocal. While leaders exert more influence than other group members, leaders are also influenced by followers. According to social exchange theory, leaders must maintain profitable relationships with followers.[12] They do this by providing rewards like approval, information, or salary in return for such commodities as labor, compliance, and commitment. When the relationship becomes unprofitable to either party (the costs outweigh the benefits), then the relationship is redefined or ended. There are potential costs and benefits associated with using each power type. For example, coercion can be used by followers as well as by leaders. Students may punish instructors who rely heavily on threats and other coercive tactics by giving them low course evaluations. Politicians who legislate unpopular tax measures are often removed from office.

A list of the benefits and costs of each type of power is given below. The list (which incorporates the thoughts of the authors and a number of researchers) is not exhaustive.[13] In fact, we hope that you will add your own costs, benefits, and conclusions (see application exercise 2).

BENEFITS	COSTS
Coercive Power	
Effective for gaining obedience	Drains physical and emotional energy from user
Appropriate for disciplinary actions	Lowers task satisfaction of followers
Achieves quick results	Destroys trust and commitment
	Becomes less effective over time
	Followers may respond in kind
Reward Power	
Culturally sanctioned	Lower task satisfaction than with expert and referent power
Focuses attention on group priorities	Not consistently linked with high task performance
Effective for gaining obedience	Escalating financial and material costs to provide ever-greater tangible rewards
Boosts short-term performance	Some groups, like nonprofit agencies, have limited tangible rewards to give
	Ineffective or destructive if rewards are not desirable or attractive, or if the wrong individuals are rewarded
Legitimate Power	
Culturally sanctioned	Lowers follower task performance
Incorporates weight of entire organization	Lowers follower task satisfaction organization
Effective for gaining obedience	May become less effective over time
Helps large organizations function efficiently	

BENEFITS	COSTS
Expert Power	
High follower task satisfaction	Takes a long time to develop
High follower task performance	Must possess the necessary knowledge and skills
Drains little, if any, emotional energy from the user	Not as effective in gaining obedience as coercion, reward, or legitimate power
	May not be effective if followers do not share the leader's goals
Referent Power	
High follower task satisfaction	Takes a long time to develop
High follower task performance	Can diminish if overused
	Must possess the necessary knowledge and interpersonal skills
	Not as effective for gaining obedience as coercion, reward, or legitimate power

The cost/benefit ratios suggest that leaders should rely heavily on expert and referent power. These forms of power have a positive effect on the performance and satisfaction of those being influenced and are less costly to use. They are most likely to maintain a profitable relationship between leader and follower. Yet, effective leaders need access to all five types of power. Taking charge may require discipline through coercion, the judicious use of rewards, and the power of position. In fact, a leader's impact is enhanced if, for example, she or he combines legitimate power with expert and referent power. A highly respected group member who is appointed the chair of a committee is in a very powerful position.

To summarize, group members seem to prefer leaders who rely on power associated with the unique characteristics of the person (expert and referent) rather than leaders who rely on power related to their position (coercion, reward, legitimate). Since effectiveness is more directly tied to personal performance than to official position, we can manage our communication behaviors to increase our power—which, in turn, can increase our ability to lead. Let's take a closer look at one cluster of communication behaviors—powerful forms of talk—that seem particularly well suited to building both expert and referent power.

Powerful and Powerless Talk

Sociolinguists, anthropologists, communication specialists, and others have long been fascinated with the two-way relationship between language and power. Viewed from the perspective of society, language is a mirror reflecting power differences. Every culture has a "standard language" that is spoken by the highest socioeconomic group in that society. Nonstandard languages are dialects spoken by less advantaged people.[14] Just as language provides a mirror of power, the use of language creates power differentials.[15] In fact, speakers are stereotyped as powerless or powerful based on their word choices.[16]

The fact that speakers are perceived as powerless or powerful based on the way they talk means that language can be an important tool for building power bases. Conversely, inappropriate language can reduce perceived power and leadership potential. Over the past two decades, a number of language features have been identified as "powerful" or "powerless" by researchers. Powerful talk makes speakers seem knowledgeable and confident; powerless talk is tentative and submissive. Most researchers have concentrated on identifying powerless speech forms, while powerful speech has been treated as speech without powerless speech features. Here are some forms of powerless types of talk:

- *Hesitations* ("uh," "ah," "well," "um," "you know") are the most frequently used form of powerless talk and the least powerful speech feature. The characteristic that is most likely to clutter our talk is also the most likely to reduce our power.

- *Hedges* ("kinda," "I think," "I guess") may occasionally be appropriate (when we truly are not sure of our facts, for example), but they greatly reduce the impact of what we say. Compare "I think you should have that report in by Friday" to "Have that report in by Friday."

- *Tag Questions* ("isn't it?"; "wouldn't it?") on the end of a sentence indicate uncertainty. These expressions make a declarative statement much less forceful. For example, "That presentation was unorganized, wasn't it?"

- *Disclaimers* ("Don't get me wrong, but"; "I know this sounds crazy, but") can be a useful conversational tool. Speakers use disclaimers when they are not sure if listeners will accept what they have to say. For instance: "I'm not trying to be critical, but your speech was way too long." They should be used with caution, however, since they can signal that we lack confidence in our statements.

- *Accounts* (excuses or justifications) deny responsibility for what happened. Speakers employ accounts after they say or do the wrong thing: "It was an accident," or "I wasn't ready for the test because I stayed up all night helping my roommate with a problem." A speaker who frequently excuses or justifies his/her behavior will be seen as inept or uncertain.

- *Side Particles* ("like," "simply," "that is") detract from a powerful image. They can be irritating for listeners.

Researchers report that the use of powerless speech in experimental settings significantly lowers source credibility. (We'll have more to say about believability—what communication experts call credibility—in the next chapter). Listeners consistently rate the knowledge and ability (competence) of powerless speakers lower than that of powerful speakers when both deliver the same message. In addition, they find such sources less trustworthy, less dynamic, and less sure of themselves. Powerless speakers are perceived as less attractive and less persuasive. Audiences don't retain as much information from a speech or lecture if the message is delivered in a tentative style.[17]

Language choices clearly have a strong influence on the two bases of power most easily controlled by the communicator: expert and referent power. Powerless speakers often *appear* to be uninformed and unskilled even if they do, in fact, possess the necessary knowledge and abilities. On the other hand, powerful speakers are frequently seen as competent and attractive, and their messages have more persuasive and informational impact. Some evidence suggests that powerful talk can help overcome the disadvantages that come from having low legitimate power.[18] It should be noted, however, that other variables may moderate or override the influence of powerless speech. For example, students are less distracted by an instructor's use of powerless talk if they like that professor or if the information contained in the lecture is important to them.[19] Also, powerful speech is most effective when speakers are trying to be authoritative. There are times when a powerless style may be more appropriate, such as in a conversation between friends or when a superior is trying to establish common ground with a subordinate. The key is to adopt the appropriate style for the situation.

Fortunately, we can eliminate powerless language features if we choose to do so. Lawyers report that they can teach clients to avoid powerless language. Public speaking instructors help their students eliminate powerless talk by noting powerless speech features on speech evaluation forms. To become a more powerful speaker, start by monitoring your powerless speech habits. Record a conversation and count the number of powerless speech features you used, or ask a friend to give you feedback about your powerless speech patterns. Make a conscious effort to eliminate powerless language. Keep track of your progress using the recording and feedback methods described above. Another way to become a more powerful speaker is by monitoring public speakers (including instructors). Evaluating what others do can help to improve your own performance.[20]

Empowerment

Up to this point, we have emphasized how power is the essential currency of leadership. There is no leadership without power, and some forms of power are more effective for leaders than others. However, a leader will frequently want to distribute rather than to maintain power. Reducing power differentials often enhances group performance and may be the key to organizational survival. (Take a look at the case study in box 5.3 to see how empowerment can increase productivity.)

Paradoxically, leaders gain more power by empowering others. There are five major reasons why leaders choose to share power. In an organizational setting, distributing power *increases the job satisfaction and performance of employees.* People like their jobs more and work harder when they feel that they have a significant voice in shaping decisions.[21] Withholding power has the opposite

Box 5.3   Case Study

Empowerment on the Load Line at Techstar Industries

Techstar Industries is one of several companies responsible for assembling the circuit boards used in personal computers. Companies like Techstar compete with many other organizations doing the same type of work. The assembling of circuit boards is tedious and demanding; the work is often repetitive and dull. At the same time, there is tremendous pressure to assemble large numbers of boards with very few rejects. The only competitive advantage a company like Techstar can hope for is to produce a higher quality product at a lower price than its competitors.

Boards at Techstar are assembled on the load line. Parts are loaded by hand onto the board as it travels along a conveyer belt. The most recent Techstar board, the MT2000, has twenty-seven parts that are loaded at six different stations by a team of operators. To be profitable, Techstar must manufacture six hundred usable boards with fewer than ten rejects during each eight-hour shift.

The load line team has averaged fewer than five hundred usable boards with as many as thirty defective boards produced on each shift. The supervisor, Tom Friedman, decided that the only way to improve the situation was to turn the problem over to the operators. Tom called a meeting to announce his intentions. Despite his team's apprehension, he told the operators he wanted them to generate ideas for improving their productivity. To get the team started, Tom chaired the first few meetings. He told the team he would provide all the necessary support required to improve the situation. Further, Tom made it clear that he was willing to turn over control of the load line to the operators if they could meet the production goal for profitability and keep him apprised of their progress.

Over the next two months, the load line team met on a regular basis. They identified twenty ways to improve the process. Among the most important suggestions were: cross-train operators, develop a system for keeping the line stocked with parts, and re-engineer the line to optimize efficiency. The team based these suggestions on several problems that they identified during their meetings. First, each operator was trained to work at only one of six stations. When an operator needed to leave the line for any reason, the entire assembly process came to a halt. Second, when an operator on the line ran out of parts, the line had to be stopped until the parts were replenished. Finally, with six stations operating at once, all members of the load line team were tied to the line. This became even more problematic when the team realized that the demands of each station were very different. Because workloads were unevenly distributed, some operators were rushing to get their parts loaded while those at other stations worked at a much slower pace.

The team presented their plan to Tom. They requested downtime to train each member of the team to work at each station. The team felt the process could be improved if there were only five stations rather than six. This would enable the team to balance the workload so that the demands of each station would be roughly equal. In addition, five workstations would allow one team member to circulate between stations. This team member would be responsible for filling in for other team members when they left the line, for stocking parts, and for troubleshooting before defective boards were produced.

Tom liked the team's ideas and, as he promised, offered his support. Within a few days the line was reconfigured and the load line team began assembling MT2000 boards on their new five-station line. With team members working together and rotating positions on the load line throughout their shift, the number of MT2000 boards produced began to climb. Within three months, the team not only met Tom's production goal, they exceeded it—producing over seven hundred usable boards with an average of only three defective boards per eight-hour shift.

Discussion Questions

1. How do you think the assembly process would have been affected if Tom had decided to reconfigure the load line without consulting the team?

2. What are the major advantages/disadvantages of the type of empowerment strategy Tom used?

3. What advice would you offer Tom for dealing with the load line team if their suggestions for improvement had not resulted in increased productivity?

4. Discuss a time when you have been empowered to make a decision. What were the results?

5. What kinds of tasks do you think should be among the first delegated to followers as part of a leader's empowerment effort? Why?

result. Those who feel powerless often respond by becoming cautious, defensive, and critical.[22]

Sharing power *fosters greater cooperation among group members.* Cooperation, in turn, increases group accomplishment. The effectiveness of any group depends in large part on the cooperation of group members. For instance, a small group cannot get an "A" on a class project if members withhold information from each other or if a number of members refuse to participate at all. The same is true for a sales team or computer project group. The genius of organizing lies in combining individual efforts in order to achieve goals that would be beyond the capability of any one person. The group advantage is lost or diluted when participation is only halfhearted. James Kouzes and Barry Posner report that enabling others is a key to leadership; accomplishment results from the efforts of many people, not just the leader. According to Kouzes and Posner: "We have developed a simple one-word test to detect whether someone is on the road to becoming a leader. That word is *we.*"[23]

> *There is no limit to what you can do if you don't care who gets the credit.*
>
> —John Wooden

Distributing power means *collective survival*; the group endures rather than fails. One of the best ways to stay competitive in a fast-paced environment is to develop a "flat" organizational structure. Flat structures are decentralized and grant a great deal of decision-making authority to lower-level leaders. For instance, branch managers in flat corporations control decisions affecting their operations. They do not have to check with headquarters constantly. In these companies, project groups blur traditional lines of authority in order to develop new ideas. Flat organizations offer two advantages: (1) they can move quickly to meet changing market conditions, and (2) they foster innovation—the development of new products and processes on which a business ultimately depends.

Effective leadership helps *personal growth and learning.* Group members become more mature and productive than they were before. Empowerment is one way to stimulate growth. Sharing power with followers can help them tackle new challenges, learn new skills, and find greater fulfillment.[24] In the end, both the group member and the group are transformed when power is shared. Not only does the individual grow, but the collective gains a more committed and skilled member.

Sharing power *prevents power abuses.* Concentrating power in the hands of a few individuals is dangerous. As Britain's Lord Acton observed, "Power corrupts, and absolute power corrupts absolutely.

Powerful individuals often ignore the needs of others. Compared to the powerless, they typically devote less attention to finding out how other people think and feel. As a consequence, they are more likely to hold and act on harmful stereotypes, particularly of minority group members.[25] Those in power are also tempted to further their own interests at the expense of followers. Tyrannical bosses, for example, seek to maintain their positions by (1) tracking every move of employees, (2) sending conflicting messages about what they want, (3) engaging in angry outbursts, (4) demanding absolute obedience, (5) putting followers down in public, (6) acting arbitrarily, and (7) coercing subordinates into unethical behavior.[26] Leaders who distribute power are less likely to abuse their positions or to take advantage of followers. Empowerment is a key element of servant leadership, an ethical perspective we'll discuss in chapter 11.

> *Oh, it is excellent to have a giant's strength, but it is tyrannous to use it like a giant.*
>
> —William Shakespeare

Making a case for empowering followers is easier than making empowerment happen. Many organizations continue to operate under the traditional, hierarchical model where top executives often get treated like royalty, and middle- and lower-level managers are rewarded for keeping, not sharing, their authority. Giving power away is difficult in these hostile environments. (See the

Research Highlight in box 5.4 for some vivid examples of how organizations create feelings of powerlessness.) Yet, empowerment efforts can and do succeed. Leaders have relinquished much of their legitimate, reward, expert, and coercive power bases at companies like Gore and Associates (makers of Gore-Tex fabric), Johnsonville Foods, Harley-Davidson, McCormick Spice Company, and many other successful organizations. Self-directed work teams (SDWTs), as we'll see in chapter 7, are taking over many of the functions traditionally reserved for lower- and middle-level managers. Power sharing is most likely when leaders understand the components of the empowerment process and are equipped with implementation strategies.

Box 5.4   Research Highlight

The View from the Cubicle[27]

DILBERT reprinted by permission of United Feature Syndicate, Inc.

The popularity of the Dilbert cartoon strip is one indication that empowerment is more of a myth than a reality in many large organizations. Millions of white-collar workers can relate to cartoonist Scott Adams's depiction of company life. Collections of his daily strips and humorous observations about work are best sellers. Adams pokes fun at everyone—middle managers, top executives, consultants, coworkers, engineers—and nearly everything—meetings, training programs, working conditions, memos, and management fads—in corporate America.

In a very real sense, Adams is a researcher. He spent several years gathering data as an employee at a bank and at Pacific Bell before quitting to become a full-time cartoonist. Readers keep him posted on the "dark side" of organizations by e-mailing him with their workplace stories. The real-life examples he receives are often more absurd than anything he can make up. Consider the following:

From: (name withheld)

To: scottadams@aol.com

Shortly after taking my first job, I submitted a trip report and expense account only to have it returned to my desk because one item "violated company policy." Being a concerned employee, I immediately contacted the soon-to-be retired career bureaucrat in charge, expressed my contrition, and requested a copy of the company policies so as to avoid another violation. The bureaucrat informed me that company policies were secret and not for general distribution, as then "everyone would know them."[28]

Other real-world examples of how corporations confuse and humiliate their employees instead of empowering them include:

- Permanently attaching laptop computers (purchased for business trips) to desks so they won't get stolen
- Assigning "Positivity Police" to catch those displaying a "Non-Positive Attitude" (NPA)
- Editing resignation letters and making employees rewrite and resubmit them
- Requiring semi-daily progress reports or asking salaried workers to account for their time in six-minute increments
- Using meaningless technical jargon ("utilize issue clarification processes"; "act in the best interests of achieving the team")
- Consultants taking employee suggestions and presenting them to company executives as their own ideas
- Cost cutting by turning off the down escalator or restricting workers to one donut at weekly meetings (enforced by the use of a "donut ticket")
- Putting employees about to be laid off into the "mobility pool" or enrolling them in the new "Career Transition Plan"
- Instituting a random drug testing program and "Individual Dignity Enhancement Program" at the same time
- Refusing to list the extension numbers of Human Resources representatives
- Adopting confusing slogans like "Our innovation makes us first, our quality makes us last!"

Components of the Empowerment Process

We'll take the remainder of the chapter to outline the important elements of empowerment. In the final section, we will describe two models that take a systematic approach to giving power away.

Modifying the Environment

Environment refers to the setting where work occurs. Important elements of the environment include reward systems, job tasks, organizational structure and workflow, rules, charts, and physical layout. The first step in the empowerment process is often the elimination of situational factors that create feelings of powerlessness, like inappropriate rewards, authoritarian supervision, and petty regulations (see box 5.5). Next, the environment is redesigned to shift decision-making authority to followers. Those assigned to do the work get a great deal of say in how the job gets done.

Box 5.5   Research Highlight

Situational Factors Leading to a Potential State of Powerlessness[29]

Organizational Factors
Significant organizational changes/transitions
Start-up ventures
Excessive, competitive pressures
Impersonal, bureaucratic climate
Poor communications and limited network-forming systems
Highly centralized organizational resources

Supervisory Style
Authoritarian (high control)
Negativism (emphasis on failures)
Lack of reasons for actions/consequences

Reward Systems
Noncontingency (arbitrary) reward allocations
Low incentive value of rewards
Lack of competence-based rewards
Lack of innovation-based rewards

Job Design
Lack of role clarity
Lack of training and technical support
Unrealistic goals
Lack of appropriate authority/discretion
Low task variety
Limited participation in programs, meetings, and decisions that have a direct impact
  on job performance
Lack of appropriate/necessary resources
Lack of opportunities to form networking
Highly established work routines
Too many rules and guidelines
Low advancement opportunities
Lack of meaningful goals/tasks
Limited contact with senior management

Supplying Resources

Empowerment increases the demand for resources. No follower, no matter how motivated, can complete a task if she/he doesn't have adequate funds and supplies, enough time to devote to the job, and a place to work. Political support—the approval of important individuals—is essential for the completion of major projects. Leaders supply this resource when they publicly endorse the work of stakeholders and encourage other leaders to "buy in" to initiatives.[30]

Information is a particularly important resource for newly empowered followers. Consider the machine operator who has just joined a self-directed work team, for example. Under the old system, she had to know how to run a single piece of equipment. Now she's part of a group that makes decisions for an entire department: planning, scheduling, hiring, quality control. In addition to operating her machine, she must learn how to work in a team, set objectives, measure results, read a profit-and-loss statement, conduct a hiring interview, and so forth. She can only succeed if she receives adequate training and if company management supplies the team with financial and performance data for planning and measurement.

Building a Sense of Personal Power

Empowerment also means helping followers believe in their own abilities—to develop what psychologist Albert Bandura calls the *efficacy expectation*. Followers who believe that they can deal with the people, events, and situations in their environments and who have a sense of self-efficacy or personal power are more likely to take initiative, set and achieve higher goals, and persist in the face of difficult circumstances. Constituents who believe that they have limited self-efficacy and feel powerless dwell on their failures. They are less inclined to offer new ideas, to set and meet challenging standards, or to continue when they encounter obstacles.[31] Leaders can build followers' perceptions of their personal power by:[32]

- providing positive emotional support, particularly during times of stress and anxiety. Stress, fear, depression, and other negative factors reduce feelings of personal efficacy. The impact of these factors can be diminished if a leader clearly defines the task, offers assistance, engages in play to create a positive emotional climate, and uses films, speakers, seminars, and other devices to build excitement and confidence.

- expressing confidence. The most effective leaders spend time everyday encouraging others and expressing confidence in their abilities at meetings, during speeches, in the lunchroom, in hallways, and in offices.

- modeling successful performance themselves or providing opportunities to observe others who are successful. Knowing that someone else can handle a task makes it easier for a worker to continue to learn the same task even after repeated failures.

- structuring tasks so that followers experience initial success. Initial victories build expectations for future triumphs. Effective leaders structure tasks so that they become increasingly complex. Completing one part of the job is followed by training and then greater responsibilities. The same strategy can be used to introduce large-scale change. A new marketing strategy or billing system can be started in one region or plant and then adopted by the organization as a whole.

Empowerment Models

Leaders who empower followers take on different tasks than they do under the traditional, hierarchical model. According to James Belasco and Ralph Stayer, an empowering leader acts more like a lead goose than a head buffalo.[33] As head buffalo, a leader takes charge while loyal followers look on, waiting for direction. In contrast, geese flying in a V formation on their annual migrations frequently shift leaders and roles in response to travel conditions. (See box 5.6 for an example of a highly successful organization that routinely rotates members in and out of leadership roles.)

> . . . *[B]ecause buffalo are loyal to one leader; they stand around and wait for the leader to show them what to do. When the leader isn't around, they wait for him to show up. That's why the early settlers could decimate the buffalo herds so easily by killing the lead buffalo. The rest of the herd stood around, waiting for their leader to lead them, and were slaughtered.*
>
> —James Belasco & Ralph Stayer

Leading the Journey

Belasco and Stayer call their model for a systematic approach to empowerment "Leading the Journey." In this model, leaders (acting as lead geese) are responsible for determining vision and direction, removing obstacles, developing ownership, and stimulating self-directed action.

- *Determining focus and direction.* Leaders at all levels of an organization are responsible for setting vision and direction. Staying in touch with customers (those who use an organization's products and services) is the key to determining direction. Your goal is to put on an outstanding performance for the end user, not just an adequate one.

- *Removing obstacles.* Eliminate obstacles that keep followers from providing outstanding performances. Help ensure that all systems (compensation, information, procedures) support this one objective. At Johnsonville Foods, product quality improved when customer complaint letters, which used to go to the marketing department, went directly to line workers instead. The people on the line responded to the complaints and then took responsibility for measuring product quality. Soon these measurements led to improvements in production processes.

- *Developing ownership.* Refuse to accept responsibility for problems that can be solved by followers. Use questions to coach followers instead of providing answers. Coaching questions include:

- "In the best of all worlds, what is great performance for your customers?"
- "What do you want to achieve in the next two or three years?"
- "How will you measure your performance?"
- "What things do you need to learn in order to reach your goals?"
- "What work experience do you need to help you learn what is needed to achieve your goals?"

- *Stimulate self-directed actions.* Decide what you do best and give your other responsibilities away. Change systems and structures so that followers are rewarded for solving their own problems and not for bringing their problems to you. Hire the best performers and fire or transfer those who aren't contributing.

Belasco and Stayer argue that the only way to master the leadership tasks described above is to learn by doing. Test these behaviors and learn from your failures. Use mistakes, fear of failure, anger, terminations, and other obstacles and setbacks as teachers. In sum: "Leading requires learning. Learning requires doing. So get on with the doing. Then study how you did it."[34]

Box 5.6   Case Study

The Empowered Orchestra[35]

The Orpheus Chamber Orchestra is one of the country's premiere classical musical ensembles. This symphony orchestra, based at New York City's Carnegie Hall, is made up of musicians who teach at prestigious schools like Juilliard and the Manhattan School of Music. What makes Orpheus unique, and its success all the more remarkable, is the fact that the orchestra has no conductor. Members have shared artistic power since the group was founded in 1972. The orchestra as a whole, not a conductor, chooses which pieces to play and how they should be performed.

Some observers refer to Orpheus as a leaderless orchestra. That would be a mistake. The group has many leaders, not just one. A leadership team of five to ten players is chosen for each piece of music. This committee then selects a concertmaster to be in charge of the practices and the performance. During rehearsals, members of the entire orchestra offer suggestions and criticisms. Any disagreements are worked out on the spot. When a concert is complete, members suggest further refinements before presenting the program again.

Orpheus has drawn the attention of a number of large corporations and nonprofit groups for the way it utilizes the talents of its employees. Orchestra members (like engineers, software developers, and bankers) are knowledge workers. Their information and skills are critical to the group's success. Like highly trained professionals in other fields, musicians often feel stifled by top down leadership. Orpheus actively seeks the input of its knowledge workers and is rewarded by a high level of commitment and performance. Other organizations (Morgan Stanley, The Ritz-Carlton Hotel Company, Gore Associates, the San Diego Zoo) are discovering that the same model can work for them. They are utilizing some or all of the following eight Orpheus principles.

1. Put power in the hands of the people doing the work. Orpheus disperses power throughout the organization, giving individuals the authority to make significant decisions.

2. Encourage individual responsibility. With authority comes responsibility. Each orchestra member insures that his or her individual performance and the group's performance is the best possible. At Orpheus, there are no supervisors to take charge of fixing problems; individuals must do so on their own.

3. Create clarity of roles and functions. Orpheus is very clear about the duties of the core group, concertmaster, and support staff. Clarity reduces unnecessary conflict and makes people accountable by identifying who is responsible for each task.

4. Share and rotate leadership. Everyone must lead in Orpheus. Players in each section routinely rotate positions, for example, so that everyone in that section takes a turn as leader.

5. Foster horizontal teamwork. Core groups are made up of individuals who play a variety of instruments.

6. Learn to listen, learn to talk. Members must learn from one another. They can only do so when every player both listens to and expresses opinions. Anyone keeping silent hurts the orchestra as a whole.

7. Seek consensus. Consensus doesn't translate into total agreement among chamber members but means achieving a "critical mass" that allows the group to go forward. If Orpheus can't reach agreement, it may call upon an outside expert or take a vote. However, consensus is almost always achieved. The musicians make thousands of joint decisions every year; yet only two or three issues are divisive enough to be put to a vote.

8. Dedicate passionately to your mission. The mission of Orpheus isn't imposed from above; it is continually developed and reinforced by the players.

Discussion Questions

1. Would you like to perform with Orpheus (assuming that you had the necessary skills)? What might be frustrating for you as an orchestra member? What might be particularly rewarding?

2. Why don't other large musical groups go without conductors? What factors might hold them back?

3. In what ways is an orchestra like a company? What is its "product," for example? What business decisions must it make? What competitive and other pressures does it face?

4. Would the Orpheus model transfer to the organizations of which you are a part? Why or why not?

5. Can you think of organizations that use some or all of the Orpheus principles? What have been the results?

Superleadership/Self-Leadership

Management professors Henry Sims and Charles Manz argue that the ultimate goal of leadership is empowering followers to take charge of their thoughts and behaviors. Sims and Manz use the term "superleaders" to describe those who help followers learn to lead themselves. They use the label "self-leaders" to refer to followers who act on their own.[36]

Guiding followers from dependence to independence (see box 5.7) is a process that begins with the leader modeling the desired behaviors. Followers then work under the guidance of the leader who encourages and rewards initiative and provides the necessary resources and training. In the final stage, followers act on their own with minimal direction from the leader.

Superleaders use three strategies to create a climate that promotes independent thought and action. (1) *Changing organizational structures.* They reconfigure roles, functions, and responsibilities to reduce hierarchy and specialization; create self-managing teams; remove layers of organizational structure; and reduce job and pay classifications. (2) *Changing organizational processes.* Superleaders redesign the way that communication and materials flow in the organization. They push decisions down to the lowest possible level, encourage teams to solve their own problems, and reengineer jobs so that followers have the responsibility for the whole project, not just part of it. (3) *Changing interpersonal communication patterns.* Effective leaders use verbal and nonverbal behaviors to build follower

---

Box 5.7

Shifting Followers to Self-Leadership[37]

FROM (DEPENDENT)	TO (INDEPENDENT)
External observation	Self-observation
Assigned goals	Self-set goals
External reinforcement for task performance	Internal reinforcement plus external reinforcement for self-leadership behavior
Motivation mainly based on external compensation	Motivation also based on the "natural" rewards of the work
External criticism	Self-criticism
External problem solving	Self-problem solving
External job assignment	Self-job assignments
External planning	Self-planning
External task design	Self-design of tasks
Obstacle thinking	Opportunity thinking
Compliance with the organization's vision	Commitment to a vision that the employee helped to create

confidence. They listen more and command less, ask followers to solve their own problems, express confidence in employees, and compliment initiative.

According to Manz and Sims, followers can learn to lead themselves without the guidance of those in authority if they become self-disciplined, find rewards in the task, and adopt positive thought patterns. We'll illustrate these self-leadership tactics by applying them to a common classroom assignment: the term paper.

The first set of self-leadership strategies involves self-behavior modification. Most of us complete jobs we enjoy, but we often miss deadlines when tackling difficult or unpleasant tasks like research papers. To succeed we need self-discipline. Self-discipline can be fostered by deliberately taking actions that enhance our performance on challenging assignments. Goal setting is one such self-behavior modification strategy. Chances are you already engage in goal setting by keeping a to-do list or a record of upcoming assignments for class. Effective goals, whether as simple as a daily list or as complicated as a five-year plan, put specific completion dates and benchmarks in writing. Goal setting for a term paper project would mean breaking the assignment into a series of smaller sections or tasks and making up a schedule of due dates.

Seeking out opportunities to observe and evaluate your actions is the best way to determine if you're reaching your goals. Don't wait for feedback from others; instead, watch your own behavior to determine what factors raise or lower your performance. Track how frequently you carry out a desired behavior, such as going to the library or completing sections of your paper. When self-observation indicates you're achieving your objectives, reward yourself (take a break, go to a movie, fix your favorite meal). Avoid self-punishment because it focuses on past failures rather than on improvement (see the discussion of the Wallenda factor in chapter 4).

Modifying the physical environment through cueing strategies is another important self-behavior modification strategy. Determine those conditions that encourage peak performance and build those elements into the work setting. If you write best in a quiet location, take your laptop computer to the library or work when your roommates or family members are gone. Use rehearsal strategies to prepare for particularly important communication performances like speeches, interviews, sales calls, or presenting your research paper to the rest of the class. Identify the key elements of the situation and rehearse by visualizing the setting and a successful performance. Practice out loud whenever possible. (Box 5.8 provides additional information on how to reach optimal performance.)

The second set of self-leadership strategies focuses on the task itself. We achieve more when we are pulled or attracted to a project. The key is in finding enjoyment or pleasure in the job itself. Naturally rewarding activities make us feel competent and in control and contribute to our sense of purpose. You may enjoy mastering a difficult subject, setting your own work pace for a project, or learning material that will further your career and benefit others. The setting also plays an important role in how we feel about a task. Whenever possible,

---

Box 5.8

World Class Performance[38]

Top leaders have much in common with world class athletes. Like tennis players, golfers, and speed skaters, executives have to focus their energy and skills to perform at their best over long periods of time, what psychologists call the *Ideal Performance State* (IPS). IPS is built on the principle of oscillation, the continual shift between expending energy and energy recovery. The mind and body need time to recover from stressful (energy expending) situations. Skipping rest periods leads to burn out.

Outstanding athletes use recovery rituals in order to recharge their energy levels. During match play, for example, professional tennis players lower their heart rates between points by staring at their racquet strings and assuming a ready posture. Leaders can recover their energy through periodic workouts, good nutrition, eating several small meals a day, and taking periodic breaks (the body and mind need to recover every 90 to 120 minutes).

Physical capacity lays the groundwork for high performance, but emotional, mental, and spiritual capacities also come into play. Athletes performing at their best feel calm, confident, and focused. Corporate athletes achieve the same frame of mind through managing negative emotions, using their body language to shape their emotions (striking a confident pose can generate a coordinating feeling of confidence, for example), and separating work and home responsibilities. They also meditate, take frequent breaks, and reduce their work hours in order to increase their mental ability to focus on their tasks. Finally, they draw sustaining energy from their deeply held values and strong sense of personal purpose by journal writing, prayer, service to others, and other means.

---

pleasurable features should be built into the work environment. Put on your favorite music when writing, for instance, or settle in to read with your favorite drink or snack.

The final set of self-leadership strategies fosters self-confidence through positive thinking. Think in terms of opportunities rather than limitations. Begin by using mental rehearsal as a preparation tool (see the discussion above). Eliminate critical and destructive self-talk, and challenge unrealistic beliefs and assumptions. In the case of a term paper, damaging self-statements like "I can't complete this project" can be changed to "There's no reason I can't finish if I set my goals and follow my timeline." Irrational beliefs like "I must get an A on this paper or I'm a failure" can be reframed as "I'm going to give this paper my best effort, but I can't expect to excel in every situation."

Former president Ronald Reagan provided one of the best examples of opportunity thinking when he was wounded in an assassination attempt. He tried to relieve the tension of the nation rather than focusing on his own condition. Reagan told his wife: "Honey, I forgot to duck." He pleaded with his doctors: "Please say you're Republicans." To the medical staff, he quipped: "Send me to L.A. where I can see the air I'm breathing."

Summary

In this chapter, we examined the relationship between power and leadership. Power, the ability to influence others, is the "currency of leadership." Leadership is not possible without power, although not everyone who exercises power is a leader. There are five sources or types of power: (1) coercive, (2) reward, (3) legitimate, (4) expert, and (5) referent. Personal forms of power (expert and referent) are less costly to use and generate higher satisfaction and job performance. Because expert and referent power are more tied to personal characteristics than to position, developing our communication skills and abilities can increase these power bases and improve our leadership potential. Adopting powerful speech is one way to build expert and referent power. Avoid the use of such powerless speech features as hesitations, hedges, tag questions, disclaimers, accounts, and side particles. Powerful speakers are seen as authoritative, persuasive, and informative.

Leaders frequently want to distribute rather than to maintain power. Five reasons for empowering others are: (1) to increase follower task satisfaction and performance, (2) to foster greater cooperation in the group, (3) to ensure the survival of the group or organization, (4) to encourage the personal growth and learning of group members, and (5) to prevent power abuses. Components of the empowerment process include modifying the work environment, supplying resources, and building a sense of personal power (self-efficacy). Leaders eliminate situational factors that create feelings of powerlessness, shift decision-making authority to those doing the work, and supply information and other resources. They help followers believe in their own abilities by providing positive emotional support, expressing confidence, modeling successful performance, and structuring tasks so that followers experience initial success.

Leading the Journey and Superleadership/Self-Leadership are two systematic approaches to empowering followers. In the Leading the Journey model, leaders set the overall direction in consultation with end users, remove obstacles that lower performance, help constituents develop ownership, and stimulate self-directed actions. Proponents of Superleadership argue that the leader's ultimate goal is to help followers learn to lead themselves. Empowering followers to become self-leaders (those who take charge of their own thoughts and behaviors) involves modeling the desired behaviors, providing guidance, and creating a climate that promotes independent thought and action. Followers can become self-leaders without the help of their superiors if they engage in such self-behavior modification strategies as goal setting, rewarding themselves, creating positive physical cues, and rehearsal. Aspiring self-leaders should also find enjoyment or pleasure in the task itself and replace destructive self-talk with opportunity thinking.

Application Exercises

1. Is power the last dirty word? Discuss your answer to this statement in class or in a reflection paper.

2. Create your own cost/benefit ratios for each type of power. Do you agree that leaders should strive for expert and referent power?

3. Develop a strategy for overcoming your powerless talk using the techniques discussed in the chapter. Report on your progress to another person in the class.

4. Brainstorm a list of strategies for eliminating environmental factors that cause powerlessness.

5. Write a paper describing why an empowerment effort succeeded or failed based on the components and models of empowerment presented in the chapter.

6. Select a major task or project facing you this term (a major speech, a professional exam, getting in shape, training for a long race) and apply the self-leadership strategies described in this chapter to completing this task. Develop specific goals and determine how you will observe and evaluate your behavior, reward yourself, modify the physical environment, and rehearse. Consider the elements of the project that might be naturally rewarding and how you can think in terms of opportunities instead of limitations. Turn in your preliminary plan. At the end of the quarter or semester, after the project has been completed, reflect on your performance. Did using these tactics produce better results? How would you rate yourself as a self-leader? Record your conclusions and submit them to your instructor.

Cultural Connections—A Different View on Power: The South African Concept of Ubuntu[39]

As we have discussed in this chapter, using power effectively is critical to the success of leadership. Whether power is centralized or distributed, its use or misuse has much to do with overall leadership outcomes. This becomes more complex, however, when crossing cultural boundaries. Inhabitants of different countries have sometimes radically dissimilar viewpoints on power. In some countries such as Israel, Denmark, and New Zealand, workers often expect that power will be shared. In countries like Malaysia, India, and the Philippines, followers are generally much more willing to be directed. One country with a very unique view on power is South Africa.

Since the collapse of the oppressive apartheid system, black empowerment has been a priority. Over three-fourths of the population in South Africa is black, yet many of these indigenous people live in poverty in rural settlements outside major cities. The South African government has been working to integrate traditional black African cultural values into mainstream society. One option for development that has gained popularity embraces the traditional African concept of ubuntu. In Zulu, ubuntu roughly translates as: "a person is a person through other persons." As such, ubuntu is based on caring for the well-being of others through a spirit of mutual support and the promotion of individual and societal well-being. Ubuntu basically views an enterprise as a community of relationships that reflect group solidarity. The ubuntu philosophy of democracy is not based simply on majority rule; rather it focuses on building consensus through shared power. The ubuntu philosophy helps to create a community built upon interdependent and equal participation.

This can be seen in the nearly one million South African collectives known as stokvels. These joint undertakings—savings clubs, burial societies, and other cooperatives—offer community-based services to members and are led through a process of shared decision making based on the ubuntu philosophy. Power is distributed within South African society in ways that place the good of the collective above the needs of the individual. For the stokvels, making a profit is important, but never if it involves the exploitation of others. Although similar practices are found in many other cultures, this approach would be quite different than the view of power held by many in Western industrialized society, which often focuses on maximizing profits whatever the costs.

Leadership on the Big Screen
The Lord of the Rings: Fellowship of the Ring

Starring: Ian McKellen, Elijah Wood, Ian Holm, Sean Astin, Cate Blanchett

Rating: PG-13, for intense battle scenes and frightening special effects

Synopsis: Based on the first volume of J. R. R. Tolkein's popular *Lord of the Rings* fantasy trilogy. Hobbit Frodo Baggins (a short fellow with large, hairy feet played by Wood) inherits a ring of incredible magical power from his Uncle Bilbo. The evil Lord Sauron wants the ring in order to complete his conquest of Middle Earth. To thwart Sauron and his minions, the ring must be taken to the desolate land of Mordor and destroyed in the fires of Mount Doom where it was created. Nine brave souls, including a dwarf, an elf, two humans, the wizard Gandalf (played by McKellen), Frodo, and three hobbit companions, take on this mission. The Fellowship of the Ring faces orc warriors, an evil sorcerer, a giant troll, and other obstacles on its trek to Mordor. Team unity crumbles when group members fight over ownership of the ring, seeking to keep and use its power instead of destroying it.

Chapter Links: the corrupting force of power, coercive vs. role model and expert power bases, self-leadership

Six

LEADERSHIP AND INFLUENCE

> *Leadership is serious meddling in other people's lives.*
> —Max DePree

Overview

Exercising influence is the essence of leadership. Leading means influencing since leaders must shape the attitudes and behavior of others to help groups reach their goals. In the last chapter, we examined the sources and uses of power. In this chapter, we continue our discussion of influence by taking a closer look at how leaders modify the behavior of others through symbolic communication. We will focus on four sets of influence tools particularly significant to leaders: (1) credibility building behaviors, (2) compliance-gaining strategies, (3) argumentation skills, and (4) negotiation tactics. We'll conclude by examining ways to resist unethical influence attempts.

Credibility: The Key to Successful Influence

Credibility is the foundation for successful influence because the success or failure of a particular influence strategy ultimately depends on the credibility of the influencer. The results of a survey of 15,000 managers from North America, Mexico, Asia, Europe, and Australia demonstrate how important credibility is to leaders. When the managers were asked what characteristics they admired most in their leaders, the answers were honest, forward-looking, inspiring, and competent. Taken together, these elements comprise what researchers label as believability or credibility.

> Above all else, people want leaders who are credible. We want to believe in our leaders. We want to have faith and confidence in them as people. We want to believe that their word can be trusted, that they have the knowledge and skill to lead, and that they are personally excited and enthusiastic about the directions in which we are headed. Credibility is the foundation of leadership.[1]

Credibility has always been central to the study of communication and leadership. The ancient Greeks studied the public speaking techniques of leaders and used the term "ethos" for what we now call credibility. Ethos consisted of high moral standards, intelligence, and other speaker character traits for Plato, Aristotle, and others.[2] An orator swayed an audience through logic (logos), emotion (pathos) and, most importantly, personal characteristics (ethos). Interest in credibility remains high today, ranking as one of the most popular topics of communication study.[3]

The strong tie between credibility and influence is the reason why scholars have been interested in ethos through the ages. No matter what the setting, credible sources are more effective. Consider the following:

- Highly credible public speakers are more likely to convince audiences to accept their arguments. By citing credible sources, speakers build their own credibility and generate greater attitude change.[4]
- Successful counselors first earn the trust of their clients.[5]
- Salespeople are more productive if they sell themselves (build their credibility) before they sell their products.
- Editorials are more persuasive if they come from highly credible newspapers like the *New York Times* or the *Chicago Tribune*.[6]

> *Leader credibility is the cornerstone of corporate performance and global competitiveness.*
>
> —Tom Peters

Dimensions of Credibility

Modern investigators no longer treat credibility as a set of speaker traits. Instead, they isolate factors that audiences use to evaluate the believability of speakers. The most significant elements or dimensions of credibility are *competence, trustworthiness*, and *dynamism*.[7]

Competence can be defined as knowledge of the topic at hand, intelligence, expertise, skill, or good judgment. The term "value-added" best describes the kind of competence that leaders need to demonstrate.[8] A leader must provide the skills that the group needs at a particular time. For example, a new facilities manager may know little about carpentry, plumbing, or painting. However, he/she can become an effective leader through using communication skills to build a cohesive work unit.

Trustworthiness (Character) is another name for honesty and consistency.[9] This dimension of credibility is critical to effective leadership since the leader-follower relationship is built on trust. Managers rate honesty as the most important leader quality; the most influential public opinion leaders are also the most trustworthy. Unfortunately, the collapse of the Enron Corporation (which wiped out employee retirement accounts) and the shady practices of its auditing firm Arthur Andersen and other companies have undermined worker trust. Nearly half of those responding to a *USA Today* poll said that corporations can be trusted only a little, or not at all, to care for the best interests of their employees.[10] Over 40% of the sample believed that executives care solely about meeting their own needs.

Dynamism refers to perceptions of a source's confidence, activity, and assertiveness. Dynamic leaders communicate confidence in their visions for the future. They inspire others to work harder and to make greater sacrifices. Dynamism appears to be an integral part of what many people call charismatic leadership, a topic we discussed in detail in chapter 4.

Credibility Effects

Perceptions of credibility vary over time. Consider a typical college classroom. At the beginning of a course, students are most concerned about a teacher's competence. At the end of the quarter or semester, they are more interested in the instructor's character. They want to know if the professor will grade fairly.[11] Credibility evaluations also vary between situations. For instance, listeners hearing a speech from a social organization are likely to evaluate the presenter's competence. Those listening to a sermon put more emphasis on the speaker's trustworthiness.[12]

To have the greatest impact, highly credible communicators need to be identified at or near the beginning of messages. On the other hand, if a source with poor credentials is named first, then the audience is on guard against the message that the source will bring.[13] However, a message can change attitudes and behavior even if it comes from a source with low credibility. As time passes, the source is forgotten, but the message is remembered and judged on its own merits. This is called the "sleeper effect."[14] The sleeper effect may explain the success of persuasive messages such as the advertising campaign for cough medicine in which an actor states, "I am not a doctor, but I play one on TV." When you are in the supermarket shopping for cough medicine months after exposure to this commercial, you might select this product because you remember the message but not the source. You recall that "a doctor recommends this brand."

> *A single lie destroys a whole reputation for integrity.*
> —Baltasar Gracian

Building Your Credibility

Discovering how others assess your competence, trustworthiness, and dynamism is an excellent way to begin to build your credibility. Rate yourself on the credibility scales found in the first application exercise on page 181 in this chapter. Then ask someone else to rate you and compare the responses. You will probably rank higher on one dimension of credibility than on others. In addition, your self-ratings might be either above or below the ratings you receive from your partner. Once you've targeted the dimension(s) of credibility most in need of improvement, you can start to change your behaviors in order to generate more favorable impressions. In chapter 1, we called this process impression management. Since initial impressions are largely based on nonverbal cues, pay particular attention to nonverbal behaviors such as appearance, voice, posture, and eye contact to increase your credibility:[15]

- Make sustained **eye contact** when communicating with others. Avoid shifting the eyes, looking away, keeping your eyes downcast, or excessive blinking.

- Use **gestures** to add emphasis to the points that you make. Try to appear spontaneous and unrehearsed; let your gestures convey the depth or intensity of your emotions. Hand wringing, finger tapping, tugging at clothing, and tentative movements undermine credibility.

- Maintain a relaxed, **open posture** when talking with others. Lean forward and smile when answering a question in order to establish rapport. Change your posture frequently and forcefully to communicate responsiveness. Try to avoid those behaviors that make you look timid or non-assertive—holding your body rigid, keeping arms and hands crossed and close to the body, and so on.

- Pay attention to your **voice**. Strive to sound confident by using a conversational speaking style and vary your rate, pitch, and volume. Sounding nasal, tense, or flat can make you appear significantly less credible. In addition, frequent pauses, speaking too rapidly, repeating words, and stuttering have a negative impact on credibility.

- Watch what your **clothing** communicates. Dress to draw attention away from physical features that are associated with negative stereotypes. For instance, avoid darkly tinted contacts or glasses. The stereotype holds that untrustworthy people wear dark eyeglasses. Since the endomorphic (round) body type is perceptually linked with low self-confidence and low competence, wear neutral colors rather than bright colors if weight is a problem. Bright colors draw attention to body size while neutral colors do not.

Modifying behaviors to make the desired impression on others is the first step to building your credibility. However, James Kouzes and Barry Posner point out that over the long term our credibility as leaders depends on the quality of the relationships we maintain with followers. They describe the following practices to build perceptions of credibility over time.[16]

Discovering Yourself. Perceptions of trustworthiness are largely the product of consistency. Followers trust leaders who clearly articulate what they believe and then "walk their talk." In order to behave in a consistent manner, you first must identify your values. As we noted in chapter 4, values represent what we consider to be important. They also serve as principles or standards by which we evaluate our actions and the actions of others. Writing your personal credo or leadership philosophy is a way to clarify what you believe. To develop your credo, imagine that you'll be going on a six-month sabbatical to a location where you cannot be reached by phone, letter, fax, or e-mail. Write a short memo before you go in which you identify the values and beliefs you think should guide the decision making and actions of colleagues when you're gone. (Turn to application exercise 2 on pages 181–182 for a complete description of this project.)

Increase your skill and confidence. A well-defined leadership philosophy is not sufficient in and of itself. You must also possess the necessary skills or competencies to put your beliefs into action and have the confidence to do so. Skill and confidence levels can be built by taking classes or training seminars, reading, mastering current tasks and adding new ones, following effective role models, and seeking out support from others.

Appreciating Constituents. Credible leaders have a deep understanding of the values, needs, and beliefs of constituents. In particular, they appreciate the perspectives of an increasingly diverse workplace (see chapter 10 for a discussion of leading diversity). To cultivate an in-depth understanding of followers, listen (visit the sales force, hold feedback sessions, call customers), be willing to learn from others, solicit feedback from superiors and subordinates, encourage dissent or controversy about ideas, and put your trust in others at the same time you live up to the trust they put in you.

Affirming Shared Values. Kouzes and Posner refer to shared values as the "common language with which we can collaborate." Speaking this common language increases job satisfaction, promotes unity, encourages loyalty, enables individuals to make decisions on their own, and increases productivity. We've already seen how important it is for a leader to have a clear set of personal values. However, you must not unilaterally impose your values on others. Instead, work together with followers through discussion groups and other forums to develop shared values statements. Additional ways to encourage shared beliefs and actions include advocating cooperation, assigning projects that require individuals to work together to achieve success, and developing hiring procedures, orientation programs, and other organizational structures that highlight organizational values.

Developing Capacity. Like leaders, followers need to develop skills and self-confidence to put their beliefs into action. You can help constituents increase their capacity by (1) providing educational opportunities, (2) giving followers the latitude and authority to make significant decisions, and (3) helping followers believe in their own abilities (for a discussion of empowerment strategies, see chapter 5). The most credible leaders create a climate where risk taking is encouraged, and they promote an atmosphere of sharing information. At the Springfield Remanufacturing Company, for example, managers teach new hires how to read financial statements; then they supply employees with weekly updates that tell them how the company is performing and how their departments can help improve the company's financial picture.

Serving a Purpose. Serving a purpose refers to creating a sense of direction for the group. Leaders can communicate direction by:

- *going first.* Demonstrate commitment by taking the initial step, like being the first to volunteer to work overtime to get a product out on schedule.

- *staying in touch.* Maintain daily, personal contact with constituents.

- *making meaning on a daily basis.* Send consistent messages about attitudes and values through how you respond to routine events like interruptions, stress, meetings, and complaints.

- *teaching during moments of learning.* In the life of any group there are key moments called critical incidents that test the credibility of leaders and teach important lessons. To pass these tests, you must act on your principles, often at a significant cost. For instance, if as a shift manager you say that quality comes first, then you must let line workers reject products that are substandard even if such rejections lower production numbers and threaten your bonus.

- *storytelling.* Stories (discussed in more detail in chapter 8) are vivid reminders of what the group or organization thinks is important.

- *handling failure and the loss of credibility.* Every leader, no matter how conscientious or successful, will fail on occasion. The effects of such failures do not have to be permanent, however. Restoring your credibility involves the six "As" of leadership accountability: accept responsibility, admit mistakes, apologize, take immediate remedial action, make amends or reparation (you should share in any penalty for the mistake), and pay close attention to the reactions of followers.

- *establishing systems.* Rewards, team meetings, performance reviews, presentations, and other organizational practices should be designed to help you create a sense of institutional purpose.

> *Example is not the main thing in influencing others. It is the only thing.*
>
> —Albert Schweitzer

Sustaining Hope. Leaders play a critical role in boosting the spirits of followers in a world marked by rapid change. As employees at Xerox, K-Mart, Motorola, and Compaq Computer have discovered, even the most successful organizations are vulnerable to new competitors and technologies, mergers, government deregulation, and other changes. If you want to keep hope alive in an uncertain economic and social climate, you must demonstrate optimism, inspiration, and supportiveness. Optimistic leaders believe that the future offers many opportunities for success and take the necessary steps to see that they achieve their goals. They treat failures as temporary setbacks that are out of their control (see chapter 4). When things go wrong, optimists don't blame themselves or followers. Instead, they take steps to reduce the likelihood of failure in the future. Inspirational leaders share in the suffering of followers. Their salaries and benefits are frozen along with those of other employees when company earnings drop, for example. Supportive leaders show genuine concern for others by listening to their problems, offering words of encouragement, and helping out when needed.

Compliance-Gaining Strategies

Compliance-gaining strategies are the verbal tactics that leaders and others use to get their way in face-to-face encounters. These strategies are based on the types of power we described in chapter 5. Attempts to get others to do what we want are a frequent occurrence in everyday life. Requesting notes from a classmate, convincing a friend to take a cab rather than driving home drunk from a party, enlisting volunteers for a fund drive, and persuading a neighbor to keep her dog chained up are all examples of interpersonal compliance-gaining situations.

John Hunter, Franklin Boster, and others suggest that persuaders in interpersonal settings select and reject compliance-gaining strategies based on the impact they have on the emotional state of both the compliance seeker and the target of the request.[17] Compliance gainers prefer "friendly persuasion"—messages that put both parties in a positive frame of mind.[18] Tactics that produce a positive emotional climate are:

- *Supporting Evidence*: giving reasons why the target of the request should comply (arguments, evidence, appeals to rules, fairness, tradition, etc.)

- *Other Benefit*: emphasizing how the target of the request will benefit by complying with the request ("You'll feel good about yourself if you help in the cleanup project on Saturday.")

- *Exchange*: offering to trade or exchange things of value like favors, money, and services

- *Referent Influence*: appealing to how much the target and actor (persuader) have in common ("We both need to pass this course, so why don't we study together.")

Strategies likely to generate negative feelings include deceit, coercion, and making the target feel guilty, sad, or selfish for not going along.

In chapter 5 we developed a cost/benefit ratio for each of the five types of power. The same approach can be used to determine the best compliance-gaining strategy for an interpersonal situation. Conduct an emotional cost/benefit analysis when choosing a compliance-gaining strategy. Whenever possible, select the strategy that is most likely to generate positive feelings for both you and the target of your request. (For a closer look at one group of leaders who rely heavily on friendly persuasion, see box 6.1.)

Organizational compliance seekers face a number of constraints not present in the interpersonal context. First, they have less freedom to decide whether or not to engage in persuasion. Middle managers and supervisors must influence others if they are to perform their roles. Second, the statuses of both the compliance seeker and the target of the request in an organization are clearly defined. Third, organizational influence agents aren't free to pursue their personal goals only; they must direct most of their efforts at achieving organizational objectives like increasing productivity, reducing tardiness, and improving service. Fourth, the rules and culture of the organization may favor some influence methods while discouraging others.

Since 1980 researchers have tried to determine how, given the constraints described above, managers influence others at work. David Kipnis, Stuart Schmidt, and their colleagues found that managers are most likely to use reason and the support of coworkers when approaching superiors.[19] Making direct demands or appealing to a higher authority are the least popular strate-

Box 6.1 Research Highlight

Compliance in the Classroom[20]

Instructors are well aware of the importance of influence to successful teaching. In addition to creating a positive learning climate, a teacher must persuade students to focus their attention on classroom activities, to turn assignments in on time, to enjoy the subject matter, and to conform to classroom regulations. A teacher's choice of compliance-gaining tactics can have a significant impact on student learning as well as on the teacher's satisfaction with her or his job.

James McCroskey and his associates at West Virginia University measured teacher power strategies based on the power topology developed by French and Raven. They found that teachers rely most heavily on expert, reward, and referent power. Instructor use of expert and referent power enhances student learning, while the use of coercive and legitimate power has the opposite effect. Later, McCroskey and his colleagues identified specific techniques and messages that teachers use to implement each type of power. For example, to employ reward power, a teacher might tell a student that he/she will enjoy doing an assignment (reward from behavior) or will get approval from classmates for complying (reward from others). Specific messages associated with expert and referent power ("You will feel good about yourself if you do." "Because I need to know how well you understand this.") are positively associated with learning. In addition, the West Virginia researchers and other investigators report that:

- The most effective messages (labeled as prosocial) are those that identify good reasons for compliance, while the least effective messages (called antisocial) concentrate on the consequences of noncompliance. Students may see messages that emphasize negative consequences as a "challenge" and become more resistant.

- Instructors engage in more compliance-gaining attempts as the semester goes on.

- Effective teachers use prosocial messages more frequently than poor teachers.

- Experienced teachers use a wider variety of compliance-gaining techniques than inexperienced teachers.

- Those teachers who use nonverbal communication behaviors that reduce physical and psychological distance—frequent head nods, close distance, and open posture—face less resistance from students no matter what type of verbal message they use.

- Teachers are most likely to use antisocial tactics like punishment or relying on authority in response to active misbehaviors (talking frequently, disrupting the class); they will also respond more forcefully to frequent misbehaviors. In addition, male teachers rely more heavily on punishment techniques.

- Teacher job satisfaction is directly related to the instructor's choice of classroom influence strategies. College instructors are more satisfied with teaching and with students if they rely on prosocial influence techniques. Among secondary and elementary teachers, those who use antisocial messages are less content with their professional careers.

- Professors in China use more punishment-oriented, antisocial compliance messages than U.S. instructors because of their role as respected authority figures in Chinese culture.

gies. When influencing subordinates, managers also rely heavily on reason, but they are much more likely to be direct and forceful (insisting, setting timelines, etc.). The relative power of the compliance seeker and the target of the request often determines the strategy selected. Kipnis and Schmidt speculate that there is an "Iron Law of Power" that dictates that the greater the difference in power between the influencer and the target of the request, the greater the probability that directive strategies will be used. Large power differences tempt managers to use coercive tactics with subordinates even when positive strategies could be more appropriate.

Kipnis and Schmidt also found that managers have different influence profiles. Shotgun managers, generally those with the least experience, make indiscriminate use of all types of influence strategies to achieve their goals. Tactician managers rely heavily on reason but revert to other tactics when needed. They usually have the most expert power in the organization and are the most satisfied and successful. Bystander managers make fewer compliance-gaining attempts and exercise less organizational influence. Based on their findings, the researchers argue that successful organizational leaders (those who fit the tactician profile) take a careful, rational, and flexible approach to influencing superiors and subordinates. Rather than employ any tactic that comes to mind, they carefully consider which strategy to use. They prefer reason (which, like the use of supportive evidence in the interpersonal context, helps to promote a positive emotional climate), but they shift tactics when appropriate.

While Kipnis and Schmidt were the first scholars to take an in-depth look at compliance gaining in organizations, Gary Yukl of the State University of New York at Albany has directed the most extensive research program. Yukl and his associates identified the following common managerial influence tactics.[21] For specific suggestions on how to use each of the nine organizational influence tactics, see box 6.2.

Rational persuasion: use of logical arguments and factual evidence

Inspirational appeals: arousing enthusiasm by appealing to values, ideals, aspirations; building the self-confidence of the target

Consultation: seeking input for planning an activity, strategy or change; modifying a proposal in response to target concerns

Exchange tactics: trading favors; promising to reciprocate later or to share the benefits when the task is completed

Personal appeals: appealing to feelings of loyalty and friendship when asking for something

Ingratiation: use of flattery, praise, and friendly/helpful behavior to put the target in a good mood before making a request

Legitimating tactics: claiming the right or authority to make a request; aligning the request with organizational policies, rules, traditions, etc.

Pressure tactics: demanding, threatening, checking up; persistent reminders

Coalition tactics: soliciting the aid of others or using the support of coworkers to convince the target to go along

Box 6.2

Guidelines for Organizational Influence Tactics[22]

Rational Persuasion
- Explain the reason for a request or proposal.
- Explain how the person would benefit from your proposal.
- Provide evidence that your proposal is feasible.
- Explain why your proposal is better than competing ones.
- Explain how problems or concerns would be handled.

Inspirational Appeals
- Appeal to the person's ideals and values.
- Link the request to the person's self-image.
- Link the request to a clear and appealing vision.
- Use a dramatic, expressive style of speaking.
- Use positive, optimistic language.

Consultation
- Ask for suggestions on how to improve a tentative proposal.
- State your objective and ask what the person can do to help you attain it.
- Involve the person in planning how to attain an objective.
- Respond to the person's concerns and suggestions.

Exchange Tactics
- Offer to share the benefits.
- Offer an incentive unrelated to the task.
- Offer to help the person carry out the request.
- Offer to do some of the person's regular work.
- Modify your request to make it easier to do.
- Indicate you will "owe" the person a favor.

Personal Appeals
- Appeal to friendship for a personal favor.
- Explain why the request is important to you.
- Say that you are counting on the person's help.
- Say you need to ask for a favor before saying what it is.

Ingratiation
- Compliment the person on past achievements.
- Emphasize the person's unique qualifications.
- Be sympathetic about problems caused by your request.
- Be sensitive to the person's moods.

Legitimating Tactics
- Refer to organization policies and rules.
- Verify legitimacy by referring to a written document.
- Say your request is approved by someone with authority.
- Invoke tradition or precedent.

Pressure Tactics
- Use persistent requests.
- Remind the person that he or she agreed to do something for you.
- Check frequently on the person's progress.
- Ask the person for a specific date when the task will be done.

Coalition Tactics
- Mention credible people who support your proposal.
- Bring someone along to help you in an influence attempt.
- Get other people to provide evidence or an endorsement.
- Ask someone with higher authority to help you.

In evaluating the effectiveness of individual managerial influence tactics, Yukl concludes that any given strategy is more likely to be successful if: (1) the target perceives the influence attempt as socially acceptable; (2) the influencer has the position and personal power to use the tactic; (3) the strategy can make the request seem more desirable to the target; (4) the tactic is used skillfully; and (5) the request is legitimate and doesn't violate the needs and values of the recipient.[23] Strong forms of rational persuasion (providing a detailed plan, responding in a memo) are more effective than weak forms (making a claim without support or offering only a brief explanation). Consultation and inspirational appeals are most likely to generate commitment to the task, whether the target is a superior, peer, or subordinate. "Hard tactics" (pressure, coalitions, legitimating tactics), on the other hand, gain compliance at the expense of long-term commitment.

Combinations of tactics also vary in effectiveness. "Soft tactics" (consultation, ingratiation, inspirational appeals) work better when combined than when used alone. Combining a soft tactic with supporting evidence generally increases the chances of success. However, there is no similar cumulative impact for hard tactics. Using several hard tactics in a compliance-gaining attempt is no more effective than using just one. Further, mixing incompatible strategies (i.e., pressuring someone while asking them to do a favor based on loyalty or friendship) can derail a request.

Yukl reminds us that we can't take effective influence for granted. Subjects in his studies report many examples of when they originated or received "inept influence attempts."[24] Managers may combine incompatible tactics, make clumsy attempts at being helpful or friendly, fail to recruit allies, try to gain compliance for an improper or unethical request, and so forth. One common mistake is using hard tactics when softer ones would have been more successful.

> *The humblest individual exerts some influence, either for good or evil, upon others.*
>
> —Henry Ward Beecher

Developing Argumentative Competence

When two or more people take different sides on a controversial issue like national health care or how to reduce the local crime rate, they generally try to establish the superiority of their positions through argument. To be successful, arguers must build a strong case for their positions while simultaneously refuting the arguments of those who take other positions. The introduction of controversy and dialog sets argumentation apart from compliance-gaining strategies, which also rely on reason and evidence. Compliance gainers may provide evidence even when there is no significant disagreement, and compliance-gaining messages often take only a few seconds to deliver. Argumentation always involves controversy and extended discussion.

Argumentation is important to leaders at every level. In small groups, argumentative individuals are more likely to emerge as leaders, and groups that argue about ideas generate higher quality solutions.[25] In organizations, supervisors must defend their own ideas and argue on behalf of subordinates.[26] In the public arena, political leaders, public relations specialists, or social activists engage in argument to support new government regulations, promote industry interests, or defend the rights of disadvantaged groups. (Complete the Argumentativeness Scale in box 6.3 to determine how likely you are to engage in arguments.)

While argumentation is an essential leadership activity, many of us view arguments with suspicion. Although you have probably had enjoyable arguments that stimulated your thinking, chances are you've also been in unpleasant arguments that resulted in hurt feelings and broken relationships. Dominic Infante suggests that the key to understanding the mix of good and bad experiences we've had while arguing lies in distinguishing between argumentativeness and verbal aggression.[27] Argumentativeness involves presenting and defending positions on issues. Verbal aggressiveness is hostile communication aimed at attacking the self-concepts of others instead of (or in addition to) their positions on the issues.

Box 6.3   Self-Assessment

Argumentativeness Scale[28]

Instructions: This questionnaire contains statements about arguing controversial issues. Indicate how often each statement is true for you personally by placing the appropriate number in the blank to the left of the statement. If the statement is almost never true for you, place a "1" in the blank. If the statement is rarely true for you, place a "2" in the blank. If the statement is occasionally true for you, place a "3" in the blank. If the statement is often true for you, place a "4" in the blank. If the statement is almost always true for you, place a "5" in the blank.

_4_ 1. While in an argument, I worry that the person with whom I am arguing will form a negative impression of me.

_3_ 2. Arguing over controversial issues improves my intelligence.

_2_ 3. I enjoy avoiding arguments.

_4_ 4. I am energetic and enthusiastic when I argue.

_1_ 5. Once I finish an argument I promise myself that I will not get into another.

_2_ 6. Arguing with a person creates more problems for me than it solves.

_5_ 7. I have a pleasant, good feeling when I win a point in an argument.

_3_ 8. When I finish arguing with someone I feel nervous and upset.

_4_ 9. I enjoy a good argument over a controversial issue.

_1_ 10. I get an unpleasant feeling when I realize I am about to get into an argument.

_4_ 11. I enjoy defending my point of view on an issue.

_1_ 12. I am happy when I keep an argument from happening.

_3_ 13. I do not like to miss the opportunity to argue a controversial issue.

_3_ 14. I prefer being with people who rarely disagree with me.

_4_ 15. I consider an argument an exciting intellectual challenge.

_4_ 16. I find myself unable to think of effective points during an argument.

_3_ 17. I feel refreshed and satisfied after an argument on a controversial issue.

_3_ 18. I have the ability to do well in an argument.

_1_ 19. I try to avoid getting into arguments.

_3_ 20. I feel excitement when I expect that a conversation I am in is leading to an argument.

Argumentativeness Scoring:
1. Add your scores on items: 2, 4, 7, 9, 11, 13, 15, 17, 18, 20. 36
2. Add 60 to the sum obtained in step 1. 96
3. Add your scores on items: 1, 3, 5, 6, 8, 10, 12, 14, 16, 19. 22
4. To compute your argumentativeness score, subtract the total obtained in step 3 from the total obtained in step 2. 74

Interpretation:
73–100 = High in Argumentativeness ✗
56–72 = Moderate in Argumentativeness
20–55 = Low in Argumentativeness

Aggressive tactics include:

- *Character attacks*
- *Background attacks*
- *Insults*
- *Teasing*
- *Ridicule*
- *Profanity*

- *Threats*
- *Competence attacks*
- *Physical appearance attacks*
- *Nonverbal indicators that express hostility*
  (looks of disgust, clenched fists, rolling eyes, demeaning tone of voice

If our arguments have been unpleasant, it is probably because one or both parties engaged in verbal aggression. We can encourage genuine argument rather than aggression if we avoid the behaviors listed above and sharpen our argumentation skills. Infante outlines five skills that, collectively, constitute argumentative competence: stating the controversy in propositional form; inventing arguments; presenting and defending your position; attacking other positions; and managing interpersonal relations.[29]

Stating the controversy in propositional form. Productive arguments begin with a clear understanding of the argumentative situation. Stating the problem in the form of a proposition or proposal is the best way to clarify what the conflict is about. Propositions of fact deal with what happened in the past ("The college grew in the 1990s largely due to its president's leadership."), the present ("Enrollment is down due to higher tuition."), or future ("Unless the college cuts its rate of tuition increase, it will be in financial trouble within five years."). Propositions of value deal with issues of rightness or wrongness: "It's unethical to lay off employees when profits are rising;" "Everyone ought to do their part on the group project." Propositions of policy are concerned with what course of action should be taken, such as how to reduce the number of homeless people in a city or how to market a new financial service. By framing an argument in the form of a proposal, we identify the sides that people are likely to take on the issue, clarify where we stand, and determine who has the burden of proof. Those who favor a proposition must demonstrate that the status quo ought to be changed.

Inventing arguments. Careful examination of the proposition is the key to developing a case either for or against the proposal. The set of questions in box 6.4 can help us analyze controversies systematically. To illustrate how this system works, we'll use the example of a student government faced with the following proposition: "Student activity fees should be increased to help pay for a new fitness center on campus." Proponents of this idea might argue that long waiting lists for racquetball courts, weight rooms, gyms, and physical education classes are signs that current facilities are too small. Overcrowding means that students can't exercise when they want and can't get the classes they need for graduation (specific harm). The problem appears widespread because of the large number of students who express frustration with the current situation.

In answering questions related to blame and possible solutions, proponents might conclude that the problem of overcrowding stems from the fact that student enrollment has outgrown current facilities. A change is in order because current facilities are inadequate (sub-issues b and c). More efficient scheduling

---

Box 6.4

Inventional System[30]

Major Issues and Sub-Issues:

1. Problem
    a. What are the signs of a problem?
    b. What is the specific harm?
    c. How widespread is the harm?
2. Blame
    a. What causes the problem?
    b. Is the present system at fault?
    c. Should the present system be changed?
3. Solution
    a. What are the possible solutions?
    b. Which solution best solves the problem?
4. Consequences
    a. What good outcomes will result from the solution?
    b. What bad outcomes will result from the solution?

---

and sharing community facilities might help relieve some of the pressure, but the best solution appears to be to build a new, larger building on campus. Since the college does not currently have enough money to build the center, student activity fees must be raised to pay for the project.

Possible positive outcomes or consequences of using fees for the building include more health and human performance classes, an expanded intramural program, additional recreational opportunities, and a higher level of fitness on campus. These positive benefits, proponents might suggest, should outweigh the negative consequence—having to pay higher fees.

Those who oppose the idea of using student fees to pay for a new fitness center could use the same set of questions to generate arguments for opposing the project (the problem does not affect that many students, other solutions can be found, the hardship caused by the additional fees would outweigh any benefits, etc.).

Presenting and defending your position. Most arguments involve four parts— claim, evidence, reasons, and summary. Begin by stating what you want others to accept—the conclusion or claim of your argument. Provide evidence in the form of statistics, examples, or testimonials from others and supply reasons or logic for taking your position. Common patterns of logic include: (1) inductive (generalizing from one or a few cases to many), (2) deductive (moving from a larger category to a smaller one), (3) causal (one event causes another), and (4) analogical (argument based on similarities). All four types of reasoning could be used in the fitness center argument. If you supported this idea, you could argue that the frustration experienced by some students is typical of the student body at large (inductive), that most colleges have developed new fitness facilities in the past ten years (deductive), that building a new fitness center will improve student retention (causal), or that billing students for a new fitness center worked well for a similar college in the next town (analogical). End your presentation with a summary that shows what you've established. Be prepared to supplement your position with further evidence and reason once it comes under attack.

Attacking other positions. This argumentative skill is based on identifying weaknesses in the evidence and reasoning of the other party. Questions to ask when attacking evidence include: Is the evidence recent enough? Was enough evidence presented, and was it from reliable sources? Is the evidence consistent with known facts? Can it be interpreted in other ways, and is it relevant to the claim of the argument? When evaluating reasoning, look for these common reasoning fallacies or errors.[31]

- *False Analogy.* The differences in the two items being compared outweigh their similarities.

- *Hasty Generalization.* Drawing conclusions based on a sample that is (a) too small or (b) isn't typical of the group as a whole.

- *False Cause.* Assuming that one event caused another just because it happened first, or using only one cause to explain a complex problem like school shootings or the crime rate.

- *Slippery Slope.* Assuming that an event (requiring background checks for purchasing firearms, for example) is the first in a series of steps that will inevitably lead to a bad outcome (outlawing gun ownership). No proof is offered for the claim that the subsequent events will actually take place.

- *Begging the Question (Circular Reasoning).* Using the premise of the argument to support the claim instead of bringing in outside evidence. (For example: "The latest Star Wars film is popular because so many people have seen it.")

- *Non-Sequitur ("It Does Not Follow").* The evidence doesn't support the arguer's claim.

- *Misdirection.* Diverting attention from the central argument to an irrelevant argument. This includes attacking the opponent instead of his/her position, appealing to popular opinion or tradition, and destroying a weak or false version of an opponent's case (a "straw" or "strawperson" argument).

Managing interpersonal relations. There are a number of tactics that can be used to keep an argument from deteriorating into verbal aggression. When others are not as skilled in argument as you, don't humiliate them by showing off your argumentative skills. Save your best efforts for those times when you are matched with someone of equal ability. Reaffirm the sense of competence of other participants through appropriate complements ("Though I don't agree, I can see that you've studied this issue thoroughly."). Emphasize what you have in common and show that you're interested in their views. Let your opponents finish what they're saying instead of interrupting, and deliver your messages in a calm voice at a deliberate pace. If opponents become verbally aggressive, you can point out the differences between argument and verbal aggression, ask them to justify their use of aggression, or appeal to them to act in a rational manner. You may need to leave if these tactics fail. As a general rule of thumb, never respond to verbal aggression with aggressive tactics of your own.

The Leader as Negotiator

Like argumentation, negotiation comes into play when leaders must influence those who actively disagree with them. However, while the goal of argumentation is to establish the relative superiority of one position over another, the goal of negotiation is to reach a conclusion that is satisfying to both sides. Negotiation consists of back-and-forth communication aimed at reaching a joint decision when people are in disagreement. A mix of compatible and incompatible interests marks all negotiation situations. Negotiators must have some common goal or they wouldn't negotiate. On the other hand, at least one issue must divide them or they wouldn't need to negotiate to reach an agreement. Consider the relationship between members of the production and marketing departments. Although both share a common interest in seeing company sales increase, marketing wants fast product turnaround to capture a new market; production wants to minimize costs while maintaining quality. These departments must resolve their differences through negotiation in order to be successful. Similar disagreements can be found in small groups. Everyone working in your class project group probably wants a high grade. However, some group members may prefer to spend their time relaxing or studying for other classes instead of meeting with the group or gathering research. The amount of work each does for the group then becomes a matter for negotiation.

> *The very essence of all power to influence lies in getting the other person to participate.*
> —Harry A. Overstreet

The significance of negotiation to leading becomes particularly apparent when a leader introduces change. Take the case of a law originating in the House of Representatives. The author of the legislation may have to negotiate for cosponsors and then negotiate passage through one or more committees and the House. Once the bill passes, any differences in the House version of the bill must be reconciled with the Senate's version in another committee. Changes must be ratified by both bodies before the bill goes to the president, who may or may not sign the legislation. A presidential veto may mean further negotiations as the House and Senate try to enact the bill without a presidential signature. To complicate matters, this whole process takes place under the scrutiny of special interest groups, the media, and the public—all of whom may try to negotiate their own changes to the bill.

Creating a Cooperative Climate

Our discussion of compliance gaining and argumentation emphasized the activities of the persuader. The outcome of the negotiation process depends on the *joint* efforts of the parties involved. As we indicated earlier, negotiators have compatible and incompatible goals. Since they have both similar and different interests, the two parties simultaneously possess the incentive to cooperate and to compete. Participants must foster cooperation and reduce competition if they are to reach a mutually satisfying solution. According to conflict expert Morton Deutsch, there are sharp differences between cooperative and competitive negotiation climates:[32]

Cooperation	Competition
Open and honest communication	Very little communication; messages often negative and misleading
An emphasis on similarities	An emphasis on differences
Trusting, friendly attitudes	Suspicion, hostility
Mutual problem solving	One party wins over the other
Reduction of conflicting interests	Escalation of conflict and negative emotions

Those who want others to cooperate act in a cooperative manner. Conversely, those who compete meet resistance. Both cooperation and competition get "locked in" to a negotiation relationship at an early stage and persist throughout the negotiation process.[33] One way to foster cooperation is by using the Tit for Tat strategy. The three rules of Tit for Tat are (1) be nice, (2) respond to provocation, and (3) be forgiving. Begin the negotiation by offering to cooperate. If the other negotiator tries to take advantage of you, respond in kind. When he or she switches to a cooperative approach, begin to cooperate again.[34] Promises and concessions are two ways to signal that you are willing to cooperate. Offer to share important information, for example, or back away from one of your initial demands. If the other party responds in kind, make further concessions. However, if the other party does not match your concession, he or she may be looking to compete rather than to cooperate. In this case, follow the rules of the Tit for Tat strategy and make no further concessions until the other negotiator becomes more conciliatory.

Threats hinder the development of cooperation. Threats gain compliance, but they intensify the conflict because they invite retaliation. A threat puts both the threatmaker and the recipient in a bad position. The negotiator who makes a threat gives up other options and must be willing to carry out the threat. The recipient of the threat may not want to retaliate, but failure to do so signals weakness.[35]

Perspective-Taking Skills

Understanding the other negotiator's perspective is a valuable leadership skill. A negotiator with high perspective-taking ability anticipates the goals and expectations of the other party. He/she can encourage concessions that lead to agreement. Perspective taking reduces the defensiveness of the other negotiator and makes him/her more conciliatory. The result is faster, more effective negotiations.[36] However, trying to see the other person's point of view in a negotiation is difficult for these reasons:

- strong emotions, such as anger, may be aroused
- both parties may be highly committed to their positions
- negotiators may have significantly different values, beliefs, and experiences
- interactants may be unequal in power, which increases uncertainty about how the other person will respond.

Perspective taking begins before any actual negotiation. Start by gathering information about the issues and individuals involved in the future negotiation. For example, if you want to negotiate for more funding for your organization from the student government, find out the amount of money available, past grants to your group and other campus organizations, the interests of those serving on the funding committee, and other relevant facts.

It is also important to identify the negotiating style of the other party. Interpersonally-oriented negotiators are sensitive to relational aspects of the negotiation. They want to get to know the other negotiator before they do business. (See Cultural Connections at the end of the chapter for a description of one group of negotiators who take a highly interpersonal approach to bargaining.) In contrast, high task negotiators do not want coffee, doughnuts, or small talk; they want to attack the issues right away. Cooperative negotiators have an interest in others, while competitive bargainers only seek benefits for themselves. Knowing where the other party falls on these orientations can help you target your approach more effectively. A high task/competitive negotiator will want to focus solely on task issues and may try to intimidate you at first. A cooperative/high interpersonal/high task bargainer will expect you to be enthusiastic and highly involved.[37]

Once you've gathered as much information as you can, role play the negotiation by taking the part of the other negotiator. This should give you a greater understanding of that person's vantage point. For instance, if you are a manager preparing for labor negotiations, act out the role of the union negotiator. Do symbolic role playing if you can't physically role play. Imagine how the other party thinks and feels in the situation. As a manager in contract negotiations, consider the relationship between the union negotiator and the union membership. This person may have to make unreasonable demands at first in order to satisfy union members.

Active listening skills are critical once the negotiation begins. Ask for clarification when needed and paraphrase the speaker's comments. By making an effort to listen actively to the other negotiator, you demonstrate that you want to understand his or her point of view. This makes conciliation more likely.[38]

Negotiation as Joint Problem Solving

As we've seen, effective negotiators create a cooperative atmosphere and take the perspective of others. The most productive approaches to negotiation incorporate these two elements by viewing negotiation as a problem-solving process rather than as a competitive tug of war. In contrast to the win-lose approach, problem-solving negotiation fosters cooperation and focuses on generating solutions that will meet the interests of both sides. Perhaps the best known example of the problem-solving style of negotiation is the principled negotiation model developed by Roger Fisher, William Ury and associates of the Harvard Negotiation Project.[39] Following the four steps of principled negotiation will help you reach a solution that is satisfactory to both you and the other party. After you've read the description of the four steps, apply them to the case study in box 6.5.

(1) Separate the people from the problem. Avoid defining the situation as a test of wills. Focus instead on working side by side on a common goal—resolving the issues at hand. Build trust to defuse strong emotions and to keep conflict from escalating. Colonial activist John Woolman is an excellent example of a negotiator who was able to tackle tough issues without attacking the people with whom he disagreed.[40] Woolman, a prominent Quaker cloth merchant in Philadelphia, spent thirty years negotiating the end of slavery in Pennsylvania. Woolman assumed that there was good in everyone, including slave owners. He believed that slaveholders, rather than being evil, were "entangled" in a corrupt system. They had been socialized to believe that blacks were lazy and didn't want to oppose the practice of slavery for fear of alienating their parents and the rest of the community. Woolman was friendly and cheerful when he confronted slave owners and encouraged consensus building and experimental learning. As a group, Woolman and local farmers designed an experiment that freed a few slaves to sharecrop. The productivity of the sharecroppers was higher than that of the slaves, proving that blacks could be just as industrious as whites. Woolman's "friendly disentangling" strategy paid off. By 1770 Quakers were forbidden to own slaves, and by 1800 Pennsylvania became the only state south of New England to make slavery illegal.

(2) Focus on interests, not positions. A negotiating position is the negotiator's public stance (i.e., "I want $50,000 a year in salary from the company."). An interest, on the other hand, is the reason why the negotiator takes that position ("I need to earn $50,000 so that I can save the down payment for a house."). Focusing on positions can blind you and the other negotiator to the fact that there may be more than one way to meet the underlying need or interest. The company in the example above might pay less in salary and yet meet the employee's need for housing by offering a low-cost home loan. The Camp David peace treaty between Egypt and Israel demonstrates how making a distinction between interests and positions can generate productive settlements. When the two nations first sat down to negotiate with the help of President Jimmy Carter in 1978, they argued over the return of the Sinai Peninsula, which had been seized by Israel from Egypt during the Six-Day War in 1967. Egypt took the position that all occupied lands should be returned, while Israel

---

Box 6.5   Case Study

Negotiating Homes for Students

Higgins College is a private, residential four-year liberal arts school located in a small rural community in the Northeast. Over the past three years it has experienced a surge in enrollment, growing from 1,400 to 1,900 students. Unable to build student housing fast enough to meet demand, the college has purchased houses in the adjoining neighborhood as a temporary solution to its housing crisis. Unfortunately, resentment toward the college grows with each additional house it buys. Neighbors complain that student tenants are noisy and that the college lets the condition of its properties deteriorate. Some individuals who sold their homes to the school believe that they were paid less than full market value.

Imagine that you are the special assistant to the president at Higgins, newly hired with special responsibility for property acquisition. You must negotiate the purchase of two additional homes to help house this fall's incoming freshman class, the largest in the college's history. Higgins' president, a forceful personality largely credited with the college's rapid growth, has made it clear that this is to be your top priority. You've also received several e-mail messages from the student housing director, who says she needs to know if you can complete the deal in three weeks so she can complete housing assignments. The two most desirable properties are located next to each other right across the street from the college's science building. Other options are located much farther away from campus in a more expensive area. Fearful of being "ripped off," the owners of the homes near the science building have hired a real estate agent to represent them in this transaction. When you call the realtor to set up a meeting, you learn that members of the neighborhood association have urged the homeowners to sell to private individuals, not to the college. You have three days to get ready for the first negotiation session.

Discussion Questions
1. What steps will you take to build a cooperative climate?
2. Describe the perspectives of all the parties, including yourself.
3. What are the interests of both sides and how can they be met?
4. What solutions could meet the needs of both parties?
5. What objective criteria could be used to determine the terms of the settlement?
6. What alternatives does each side have to reaching a settlement? How will this influence the likely outcome of the negotiation?

took the position that only some of the Sinai should be returned to Egyptian control. As a result, the talks stalled. However, once the negotiators realized that Israel's real interest was national security and Egypt's interest lay in regaining sovereignty over her land, an agreement was reached. Israel gave back the occupied territory in return for pledges that Egypt would not use the Sinai for military purposes.[41] Despite recent unrest in the region, the two nations remain at peace.

(3) Invent options for mutual gain. Spend time brainstorming solutions that can meet the needs of both negotiators. Obviously, this is impossible unless you first separate the people from the problem and focus on interests rather than on negotiating positions. Fisher and Ury offer the following example of a creative solution, which met the interests of both parties.

> Consider the story of two men quarreling in a library. One wants the window open and the other wants it closed. They bicker back and forth about how much to leave it open: a crack, halfway, three quarters of the way. No solution satisfies them both. Enter the librarian. She asks one why he wants the window open: "To get some fresh air." She asks the other why he wants it closed: "To avoid the draft." After thinking a minute, she opens wide a window in the next room, bringing in fresh air without a draft.[42]

(4) Insist on objective criteria. Find a set of criteria on which you both can agree when determining the terms of the settlement. This reduces the possibility that one party will force the other into accepting an unsatisfactory solution. In most cases, negotiators will be comfortable with an agreement that corresponds to widely accepted norms. Such standards can range from used car price books to legal precedents for insurance settlements to industry standards for wages.

Resisting Influence: Defending Against the Power of Mental Shortcuts

Up to this point in the chapter we've focused on how leaders exercise influence to carry out their roles. However, leaders must resist influence as well as exert it. Succumbing to dishonest or poorly reasoned persuasive appeals can be costly to leaders and to their groups and organizations. Among the possible negative consequences are paying too much for goods and services, giving to unworthy causes, and engaging in illegal activities.

Arizona State University social psychologist Robert Cialdini believes that mental shortcuts leave leaders and others vulnerable to unethical influence.[43] In the modern age it is impossible to carefully evaluate every piece of information that comes our way through cable television, cell phones, Palm Pilots, the Internet, and other channels. Faced with a flood of data, we often make decisions based on a single piece of information that we believe accurately represents the total situation—we use shortcuts to save time.[44] Automatic responses produce poor choices if advertisers and others manipulate information to their advantage. Cialdini believes in the adage "forewarned is forearmed." If you are aware of the following tactics, you are more likely to resist persuasive attempts and avoid negative consequences.[45]

Reciprocation (give and take). The rule of reciprocity (that people are obligated to return favors) appears to be a universal guideline, which encourages individuals of every culture to cooperate with one another. Solicitors and advertisers take advantage of this basic standard of human behavior. The March of Dimes and other charities send out free address labels in hopes that recipients will return the favor by making donations. Other examples of this strategy (known as "foot-in-the-door") are the product representatives who line supermarket aisles on weekends handing out samples of cheese, sausage, pizza, and other foods. Shoppers often respond by buying the items, partly out of a sense of obligation. One sobering example of the effectiveness of the foot-in-the-door strategy came during the Korean War. People were shocked by the fact that many captured U.S. soldiers readily informed on one another and offered other help to the enemy. This collaboration was not forced through torture or harsh treatment; it was the product of a series of small commitments. First, the captors convinced their prisoners to agree to such statements as "the United States is not perfect." Interrogators then asked these same men to make a list of problems in the United States and to sign their names. These lists were shown to other prisoners, and the prisoners wrote essays expanding on the nation's weaknesses. Later the names and essays were broadcast to other POW camps and U.S. soldiers still fighting in South Korea. Now the prisoners were publicly identified as collaborators. Knowing that they had written their statements without strong coercion, the captives began to live up to the "collaborator" label, giving further aid to their jailers.

The reciprocal concessions strategy (referred to as the "door-in-the-face" technique) is an interesting variation on the theme of give and take. In this strategy, persuaders make an extreme request and then back off, asking for less. Making a smaller request is viewed as a concession and, as a result, targets are more likely to comply with the second attempt. Also, the follow-up request appears more reasonable in contrast to the original one. Cialdini and his colleagues first tested this procedure by asking strangers to make a two-year commitment as youth volunteers. The researchers then followed up their initial request by asking these same individuals to take children to the zoo for two hours. To create a comparison group, they approached a separate group of strangers with only the second request. Those who had first been asked to make the long-term commitment were more likely to agree to go to the zoo.[46]

The reciprocity rule can result in unwanted debts and trigger unequal exchanges. Concerns about dangers of reciprocity are behind attempts to reform the campaign finance system. Large contributions put elected officials in debt to wealthy individuals and large corporations. Generous donors may not be able to buy votes per se, but they do gain greater access as a result of their donations. For example, Enron executives made a number of calls to federal officials just before filing for bankruptcy. While Cabinet officials apparently did not honor the company's requests for help, there can be little doubt that Enron's political contributions made it more likely that government leaders would listen to their pleas.

Cialdini outlines three strategies for resisting the power of reciprocity. One, turn down initial favors. Some political candidates refuse large contributions, for instance, and universities return contributions from controversial donors. Two, do not feel obligated to return favors that are tricks, not genuine favors. Three, turn the tables on unethical influencers by exploiting the exploiters. Take the free gift (a cracker, a free weekend visit at a time-share resort, a road atlas) and walk away without giving anything in return.

Commitment and Consistency. This shortcut is based on the desire to appear consistent with previous choices and actions. Consistency prevents feelings of dissonance while reducing the need to think carefully about an issue after making a choice. Commitment goes hand in hand with the drive for consistency. Once we've made a commitment, no matter how small, we want to remain consistent with that decision or action.

Voluntary, public decisions increase the commitment of people who made the choice. They can't attribute their behavior to outside pressures. Consider the popularity of college hazing rituals, for example. Sorority and fraternity pledges (of their own free will) publicly commit themselves to a particular Greek affiliation. When they are subsequently subjected to strenuous (and perhaps dangerous) initiation ceremonies, they become even more committed. Despite the efforts of many college administrators, the new inductees continue the tradition and insist that future pledges go through similar initiation rites. Voicing concern about the initiation hazing could be interpreted as inconsistent with the previous commitment to the sorority or fraternity. Having endured an unpleasant experience, there is a desire to embrace the commitment even more strongly.

Your best defense against the pull of commitment and consistency is listening to internal signals. Being trapped into complying with an undesirable request produces a tight, queasy stomach and generates negative emotions. Respond to these feelings by drawing the attention of the persuader to the tactic being used and to the faulty logic of being consistent for consistency's sake. Also, ask yourself: "If I could go back in time, would I make the same choice again?" If you wouldn't make the same decision twice, then don't make it in the first place.

> *Moderation in temper is always a virtue, but moderation in principle is always a vice.*
> —Thomas Paine

Social Proof. Social proof refers to deciding how to act based on what others are doing. Television producers use laugh tracks, for example, to convince viewers that situation comedies are funny. Campaign managers hope to pick up additional support by trumpeting the fact that their candidates are leading in the polls. Social proof exerts the most influence in ambiguous situations when observers don't know how to interpret information. Take the case of someone lying on a busy city sidewalk. This individual could be drunk, asleep, or sick. A drunk or sleepy person can be ignored; an individual with a medical emergency needs help. To determine how to respond, pedestrians look around and see how others react. If other passers-by stop to help, they are more likely to offer assistance as well. The influence exerted by social proof can be deadly. Members of the People's Temple (Jim Jones) and Heaven's Gate (the Hale-Bopp cult) committed mass suicide in response to social pressure from other members of their group.

Social proof has less impact when you recognize that influencers are making false claims and/or creating false impressions. For instance, producers of infomercials pay actors to participate in "spontaneous" demonstrations designed to convince us that juicers and other products are effective and easy to use. Supporters of the president pack the gallery during the State of the Union Address and applaud at every opportunity, hoping to make the chief executive look more popular. In addition to being on the look out for misleading influence attempts, you can also increase your resistance to this shortcut by periodically testing the crowd's reactions against established facts as well as against your past experiences and personal judgments.

Liking. As targets of influence, we are more swayed by people we like. The Tupperware Company, Avon, and other marketers take advantage of this fact by having their representatives sell directly to friends and neighbors. Liking is based on a variety of factors, including: (1) physical attractiveness; (2) similarity (in appearance, attitude, nonverbal behavior, ethnic background); (3) compliments; (4) familiarity and frequent cooperative contact; and (5) association with positive events and people (the Olympics, winning sport teams, celebrities).

Preventing liking is almost impossible. The key, according to Cialdini, is to determine if you like someone too much given the circumstances and to separate the merits of the proposal from the person. Ask yourself, for example: "Am I ignoring a lower bid just because I like another contractor better?" "Do I support an applicant for a job opening only because he/she shares the same ethnic background as me?" "Do I find it hard to say 'no' to a request when I've received compliments first?" If you say "yes" to any of these questions, you need to reconsider your choices.

Authority. Receivers frequently overlook the content of the message and respond instead based on status cues like titles, clothes, nice jewelry, and fine automobiles. The higher the perceived status of the persuader, the more likely it is that targets will comply. In one investigation, for example, hospital nurses were telephoned by a "doctor" (really an experimenter) they had never met who told them to administer a large amount of an unauthorized drug to a patient. Despite the fact that prescribing medications over the phone was expressly forbidden by hospital policy and the drug was not cleared for use, 95% of the nurses went straight to the patient's room to administer the dosage, only to be stopped by the researchers.[47]

The best way to undermine the influence of authority is to engage in critical thinking. Consider whether the person is truly an expert on the topic at hand. Consider too whether this person will likely be truthful in this situation. Be on guard against those who will benefit personally if you go along with their recommendations.

Scarcity. Scarcity appeals are a staple of advertising. Television offers are good only if viewers call now, supermarket ads run for one week only, the most popular holiday toys always seem to be in short supply, and some furniture outlets always seem to be going out of business. Retailers recognize that items appear more valuable when they appear to be less available. Two principles underlie this mental shortcut. The first is the belief (often supported by experience) that items in short supply are better than common ones. The second is that people react against any attempt to limit their freedoms, particularly when something is newly scarce or when competition develops. Notice how fast lines form at service stations at the first hint that supplies of gas will be running low, for example, and how shoppers fight over limited supplies of Beanie Babies and PlayStation II.

Scarcity generates physical arousal (i.e., increased blood pressure and adrenaline), making a rational response difficult. The best way to defend against physiological arousal is to calm the nervous system. Take a break in the negotiations or refuse to commit to a major decision until thinking about it overnight (see chapter 7 for further discussion of vigilant decision making). Realize, too, that limited availability doesn't make an object any better. If you want the car, property, or service for its function to you or your organization, its ultimate usefulness should determine how much you pay for it, not its scarcity. Forgetting this principle has been costly to television executives. Bidding against other networks encourage these leaders to pay too much for the rights to broadcast sports and movies. Often they lose sight of the fact that, despite its scarcity, no sports programming or film is worth the cost if it doesn't generate enough advertising revenue, viewers, or prestige to justify the expenditure.

Summary

In this chapter, we examined some of the ways that leaders exert influence. We began with a look at credibility, the key to any successful influence attempt. Credibility is built on perceptions of competence, trustworthiness, and dynamism. These perceptions, in turn, can be modified by adopting credibility-building behaviors: discovering yourself, appreciating constituents, affirming shared values, developing capacity, serving a purpose, and sustaining hope.

Next, we identified verbal compliance-gaining strategies used to make requests in face-to-face encounters. In the interpersonal context, prosocial strategies that put the compliance seeker and target in a positive frame of mind are most popular. In the organizational setting, successful leaders take a rational yet flexible approach to influencing superiors and subordinates. They generally offer reasons for compliance first but switch tactics when appropriate. Hard tactics, like applying pressure, forming coalitions or appealing to authority, gain compliance at the expense of long-term commitment. Soft tactics, such as consulting with others, putting the other person in a good mood, and arousing enthusiasm, work better when combined than when used alone. Mixing incompatible strategies greatly decreases the likelihood of compliance.

In the second half of the chapter we identified argumentation and negotiation skills that are essential to managing conflict. When two or more people take different sides on controversial issues, they often try to establish the superiority of their positions through argument. Argumentative competence consists of: stating the controversy in propositional form, inventing arguments, presenting and defending your position, attacking other positions, and managing interpersonal relations.

The goal of negotiation is to reach a conclusion that is satisfying to both parties. Successful negotiators build a cooperative atmosphere, take the perspective of the other person, and work together to reach a joint solution. Joint problem-solving negotiation involves separating the people from the problem, identifying the interests of each party, brainstorming options for mutual gain, and basing the settlement on objective criteria.

Leaders must resist influence as well as exert it. We ended the chapter by outlining mental shortcuts that lead to poor choices. Manipulative influence tactics appeal to: the principle of reciprocation (give and take), the desire for consistency, social proof (looking to others), liking, authority, and the principle of scarcity. Being aware of the dangers of these unethical strategies reduces their power over our decisions.

Application Exercises

1. Evaluate Your Credibility

   Rate your credibility on form 1 below. You may want to evaluate yourself based on your image in a particular situation. For example: how competent, trustworthy, and dynamic do you appear in class or at your job? Next, have someone else rate you on form 2, while you evaluate that person. After you have finished your evaluations, discuss your reactions to this exercise. Were you surprised at how your partner rated you? Pleased? Displeased? Why did you rate yourself as you did? Would others rate you the same way?

Form 1: Self-Analysis[48]

Competence

Experienced	—	—	—	—	—	—	—	Inexperienced
Informed	—	—	—	—	—	—	—	Uninformed
Skilled	—	—	—	—	—	—	—	Unskilled
Expert	—	—	—	—	—	—	—	Inexpert
Trained	—	—	—	—	—	—	—	Untrained

Trustworthiness

Kind	—	—	—	—	—	—	—	Cruel
Friendly	—	—	—	—	—	—	—	Unfriendly
Honest	—	—	—	—	—	—	—	Dishonest
Sympathetic	—	—	—	—	—	—	—	Unsympathetic

Dynamism

Assertive	—	—	—	—	—	—	—	Hesitant
Forceful	—	—	—	—	—	—	—	Meek
Bold	—	—	—	—	—	—	—	Timid
Active	—	—	—	—	—	—	—	Passive

Form 2: Partner Rating

Competence

Experienced	—	—	—	—	—	—	—	Inexperienced
Informed	—	—	—	—	—	—	—	Uninformed
Skilled	—	—	—	—	—	—	—	Unskilled
Expert	—	—	—	—	—	—	—	Inexpert
Trained	—	—	—	—	—	—	—	Untrained

Trustworthiness

Kind	—	—	—	—	—	—	—	Cruel
Friendly	—	—	—	—	—	—	—	Unfriendly
Honest	—	—	—	—	—	—	—	Dishonest
Sympathetic	—	—	—	—	—	—	—	Unsympathetic

Dynamism

Assertive	—	—	—	—	—	—	—	Hesitant
Forceful	—	—	—	—	—	—	—	Meek
Bold	—	—	—	—	—	—	—	Timid
Active	—	—	—	—	—	—	—	Passive

2. Credo Memo

To help you develop your leadership philosophy, complete the following exercise developed by James Kouzes and Barry Posner.

Imagine that your organization has afforded you the chance to go to a beautiful island where the average temperature is about eighty degrees Fahrenheit during the day. The sun shines in a brilliant sky, with a few wisps of clouds. A gentle breeze cools the island in the evening, and a light rain clears the air. You wake up in the morning to the smell of tropical flowers.

You may not take any work with you on this sabbatical, and you will not be permitted to communicate with anyone at your office, plant, or school—not by letter, phone, fax, e-mail, or other means. There will be just you, a few good books, some music, and your family or a friend. But before you depart, those with whom you work or go to school need to know something. They need to know the principles that you believe should guide their actions in your absence. They need to understand the values and beliefs that you think should steer their decision making and action taking. However, do not write a long report; just a one-page memorandum.

If given this opportunity, what would you write for your one-page credo memo? Take out a piece of paper and write the memo.

Once you've completed your memo, identify the values that appear. Use key words or phrases and rank them in order of importance to you. Reflect on what you've learned through this exercise. Write down your insights and share your memo and conclusions with a partner or in a small group.

3. Analyze your effectiveness as a compliance gainer both in an interpersonal and in an organizational setting. Describe a recent situation in which you were the persuader in an interpersonal encounter and as an organizational leader or follower. Which strategy or combination of strategies did you use in each situation? Did they differ? Why did you choose those tactics? How successful were your efforts? Were you more effective in one context than the other? What would you do differently next time?

4. Think of a time when you had an enjoyable argument with someone over a controversial issue, one that stimulated your thought and interest. Briefly describe that argument. Now think of a time when you had an unpleasant argument that resulted in hurt feelings and may have damaged the relationship. Briefly describe that situation. Was the first discussion an example of genuine argument and the second a case of verbal aggression? Why or why not?

5. Participate in a debate in class. Your instructor will give you the topic and ground rules. Use the inventional system presented in box 6.4 to construct your argument. When the debate is complete, evaluate your performance using the guidelines presented in the chapter.

6. Tape a political talk show and then evaluate the evidence and reasoning of the host and callers. Identify examples of faulty evidence and reasoning and share your tape and analysis in class.

7. Analyze an infomercial to identify its unethical, poorly reasoned persuasive appeals. As an alternative, identify similar appeals found in all the commercials that appear during a one hour television broadcast.

Cultural Connections: Negotiating Credibility in Swaziland[49]

Swaziland is a small African state (about the size of New Jersey) surrounded by South Africa and Mozambique and inhabited by the Bantu-speaking Swazi people. Reaching agreements with the Swazi demonstrates the challenges of cross-cultural negotiation. Meeting these challenges, whether in Swaziland or in other cultures, depends on building credibility and sensitivity to cultural expectations.

The Swazi are a hospitable people but approach every negotiation with a skeptical attitude because they have been victimized in the past by colonial powers and neighboring South Africa (all of whom stole their land and natural resources). Foreigners are considered guilty of deception until they prove themselves innocent through their conduct. Such suspicion puts a premium on establishing legitimacy in the eyes of Swazi bargainers. To build their credibility and achieve their goals, visiting negotiators should:

- employ a Swazi intermediary (or someone familiar with Swazi culture) to make the initial contact (to "clear the way").
- create the impression that they are humble but competent. They must avoid appearing proud and "pushy" but, at the same time, should not remain too calm or quiet.
- build relationships through personal visits to dignitaries, attendance at ceremonies, and other events. The Swazi are high relationship negotiators who don't get down to business until personal connections are established.
- be patient (the Swazi don't like to be rushed or to limit negotiations to a particular time frame). Impatience can provoke the Swazi into suspending negotiations indefinitely.
- listen. Expect long pauses and silences that are uncomfortable by Western standards. These allow the Swazi to analyze proposals.
- keep open disagreements to a minimum. Vocal conflict is viewed as a threat to negotiator relationships.
- use formal titles, not informal first names.
- adopt an African view of time, which is more attuned to the rhythms of nature. Expect less concern for punctuality based on the belief that people are the masters of time, not (as in the West) the other way around.

Leadership on the Big Screen: *12 Angry Men*

Starring: Henry Fonda, Lee J. Cobb, Jack Klugman

Rating: Not rated, but probably worthy of a PG-13 ranking because of the film's emotional intensity

Synopsis: This 1957 classic courtroom drama focuses on the deliberations in a murder trial. The action takes place almost exclusively in the jury room where eleven jurors are convinced the defendant is guilty of murdering his father. The twelfth (Henry Fonda) believes the young man accused of the crime is innocent. Fonda's character influences the others to reconsider their positions and eventually triumphs in persuading the members of the jury to listen to reason.

Chapter Links: credibility, compliance-gaining strategies, negotiation, resisting influence

Seven

LEADERSHIP IN GROUPS AND TEAMS

> *The well-run group is not a battlefield of egos.*
> —Lao Tzu

Overview

Fundamentals of Group Interaction
  Viewing Groups from a Communication Perspective
  Group Evolution
Emergent Leadership
  How *Not* to Emerge as a Leader
  Useful Strategies
  Idiosyncratic Credits
  Appointed vs. Emergent Leaders
Leadership in Meetings
Group Decision Making
  Functions and Formats
  Avoiding the Pitfalls: Counteractive Influence/Preventing Groupthink
Team Leadership
  When Is a Group a Team?
  Developing Team-Building Skills
Self-Directed Work Teams

Small groups play a major role in all of our lives. Every week we are members of planning committees, dorm councils, social clubs, condominium associations, and countless other groups. Often our most enjoyable memories are of group experiences like playing on a winning softball team or developing a new product on a task force. Yet, at the same time, some of our greatest frustrations arise out of group interaction. Many classroom project groups, for example, get low grades because group members dislike one another. In other instances, members fail to show up for meetings, leaving one person to do most of the work on the project at the last minute.

The purpose of this chapter is to improve your chances of having a productive group experience by building your understanding of group and team leadership. There are no formulas to guarantee that you will become a group leader or that your group will be successful. However, learning about how group leadership works can increase the likelihood that both will happen. We'll start by looking at some fundamentals of group behavior and then talk about emergent leadership, leading meetings, decision making, and team leadership.

Fundamentals of Group Interaction

As you read this book you may be learning a number of new terms, or you may be discovering new meanings for familiar terms. The symbols we master during our academic training focus our attention on some parts of the world and away from others. Kenneth Burke calls this focusing influence of language the "terministic screen."[1] Phillip Tompkins describes the following case of terministic screens in action:

> For example, suppose we assemble an economist, a psychologist, and a sociologist in the college cafeteria and ask each to give explanations of food choices made by a customer. Suppose further that the customer we observe happens to select custard rather than either cake or pie. The economist might explain that, because custard is less "labor intensive" and therefore cheaper than the other desserts, it was the only dessert the customer could afford. The psychologist might explain the choice by means of the customer's history; for instance, he or she might say that the customer's "past reinforcement schedule" provides the answer. The sociologist might explain the choice by pointing to the "ethno-social background" of the customer and showing how different classes of people favor different desserts. . . . Thus, the terministic screen of vocabulary causes each to focus on elements and interpretations of the situation to the exclusion of others.[2]

Viewing Groups from a Communication Perspective

The terministic screens of academic languages operate when scholars from different disciplines study groups. Psychologists, for example, are often interested in the "personalities" of group members and focus on how these characteristics shape group behaviors and outcomes. Sociologists pay attention to other factors like the "social status" of group members. Communication scholars are most interested in the communication that occurs within groups, which they label as "interaction." They argue that group success or failure often rests most heavily on what group members say and do when the group is together rather than on what group members bring with them to the discussion.

Supreme Court decisions are good examples of how group outcomes can't necessarily be predicted by knowing the characteristics of members. Presidents often try to influence Supreme Court decisions by appointing justices who favor either a conservative or liberal point of view. They are frequently surprised when their appointees violate their expectations after deliberating with other justices. In your own experience, there probably have been times when you went into a group meeting with your mind made up only to change your opinion as a result of the discussion. From a communication perspective, then, any definition of a group must take into account that communication is the essential characteristic of a group. A survey of small group communication texts reveals that the following elements define small groups:[3]

A common purpose or goal. A group is more than a collection of individuals. Several people waiting for a table at a restaurant would not constitute a group. Group members have something that they want to accomplish together, whether it is to overcome drug dependency, to decide on a new site for a manufacturing plant, or to study for an exam. As an outgrowth of this common goal and participation in the group, a sense of belonging or identity emerges. For example, a number of strangers enrolled in an evening class that met weekly; seven months later class members felt such a strong sense of group identity that they bought shirts with the name of the class imprinted on the back.

> *Cooperation can be set up, perhaps, more easily than competition.*
>
> —B. F. Skinner

Interdependence. The success of any one member of the group depends on everyone doing his or her part. When student group members fail to do their fair share of the work, the grade of even the brightest individual goes down. Interdependence is reflected in the roles that members play in the group. One person may gather materials for the meeting; another may take notes; a third may keep the group focused on the task.

Mutual influence. Not only do group members depend on each other, they influence each other through giving ideas, challenging opinions, listening, agreeing, and so on.

Face-to-face communication. In order for a group to exist, members must engage in face-to-face communication. For example, although employees working on an assembly line share the common goal of producing a product, they do not constitute a group unless they interact with one another.[4] Workers at different sites who communicate via e-mail, teleconference, fax, and telephone still need to meet periodically at the same location for face-to-face conversation in order to clarify their goals and to resolve complex issues. (See the Cultural Connections section at the end of the chapter for a closer look at the special challenges faced by geographically distributed groups.)

Specific size. Groups range in size from 3 to 20 people. The addition of a third person makes a group more complex than a dyad. Group members must manage many relationships, not just one. They develop coalitions as well as sets of rules or norms to regulate group behavior. The group is also more stable than a dyad. While a dyad dissolves when one member leaves, the group (if large enough) can continue if it loses a member or two. Twenty is generally considered the maximum size for a group because group members lose the ability to communicate face-to-face when the group grows beyond this number.

John Cragan and David Wright summarize the five elements described above in their definition of a small group: "a few people engaged in communication interaction over time, usually in face-to-face settings, who have common goals and norms and have developed a communication pattern for meeting their goals in an interdependent manner."[5]

Group Evolution

Groups change and mature over time. A number of models that describe the evolution of groups, particularly the development of decision-making groups, have been offered. One early model was developed by Thomas Scheidel and Laura Crowell.[6] These two researchers suggested that group decisions are not made through a linear, step-by-step process. Instead, an idea is introduced, discussed, and then dropped. Later that same idea is reintroduced and developed further. After several such starts and stops, agreement is reached and the decision emerges. This process is called the spiral model because the discussion spirals in greater and greater loops as the discussion continues.

B. Aubrey Fisher relied heavily on the spiral model when developing his influential theory of group decision making.[7] As they listened to groups communicate, Fisher and his coworkers noted what each group member said (labeled a speech act) and how the next person responded. This pairing of speech acts is called an interact. A group interact might look something like this:

Kathy: I think we ought to get away from the office for a day and do some planning for next year.
Tim: I don't think we can cover everything in one day.

By looking at series of interacts, Fisher discovered four phases in group decision making.

(1) *Orientation phase.* Participants are uncertain and tentative when groups first get together. They are not sure how to tackle the group's task or what kind of behavior will be accepted in the group. Individuals may be asking them-

selves such questions as, "What kinds of jokes can I tell?" or "What happens when I disagree with the rest of the group?" In this initial stage, statements about what the group should do are ambiguous, and members try hard not to offend others.

(2) *Conflict phase.* In the second phase, members are no longer tentative and ambiguous. Instead, they express strong opinions about decision proposals and provide evidence to support their positions. Members who support the same ideas band together. Interacts frequently reflect disagreement in this stage. A statement of support for an idea will often be followed by a negative opinion.

(3) *Emergence phase.* At this point the group begins to rally around one solution or decision. Coalitions formed during the second phase disband while dissent and social conflict die out.

(4) *Reinforcement phase.* Consensus develops during the final stage. Interacts are positive in nature, reflecting support for other group members and for the solution that emerged in phase three. Tension is gone, and the group commits itself to implementing the decision.

Not everyone is convinced that groups develop through a single series of phases. For example, Marshall Scott Poole argues that groups go through multiple stages of development.[8] Poole suggests that at any given time a group may be at one point in its social development and at another in its task development. One group might start by proposing solutions and stop later to socialize, while another group might build relationships before tackling the task. Important moments of change in a group's development are called *breakpoints*. These breakpoints can involve naturally occurring topic changes, moments of delay or, most seriously, disruptions caused by conflict or failure. Consensus about who the leader is will result in fewer delays and disruptions in the group's decision-making process.

Though scholars may describe the process in different ways, the concept of group evolution has important implications. First, timing is critical. It's not just what you say, it's when you say it. A good proposal made too early in the discussion, for instance, may not be accepted. Second, since groups take time to develop successfully, any attempt to rush a group's development is likely to meet with failure. Third, effective groups are characterized by a high degree of cohesion and commitment. Consensus both speeds the development of groups and is the product of effective group interaction. Finally, the evolution of groups suggests that group leadership also develops in stages or as a process.

Emergent Leadership

Ernest Bormann and others at the University of Minnesota studied emergent or "natural" leadership in small groups.[9] The researchers found that the group selects its leader by the *method of residues*. Instead of choosing a leader immediately, the group eliminates leader contenders until only one person is left. This procedure is similar to what happens in the presidential primary system. Many candidates begin the race for their party's presidential nomination; gradually the field shrinks as challengers lose the primaries, run out of money, get caught in ethics violations, and so forth. Eventually, only one candidate remains. This same principle of selection by elimination operates in the small group. Although all members enter the group as potential leaders, contenders are disqualified until only one leader emerges.

According to Bormann and others, the elimination of potential leaders occurs in two phases. In the first phase, those deemed unsuitable for leadership are quickly removed from contention. Unsuitable candidates may be too quiet or they may be too rigid and aggressive. Many would-be leaders stumble because they appear to be unintelligent and uninformed. Once these cuts have been made, the group then enters the second phase. At this point, about half the group is still actively contending for leadership. Social relations are often tense during this stage. Communication behaviors that lead to elimination in phase two include dominating other group members and talking too much. Such factors as social standing outside the group may be used to eliminate other aspiring leaders.

Four major patterns of leader emergence were found in the Minnesota studies. In the first pattern, the ultimate winner recruits an ally or "lieutenant" who helps him/her win out over another strong contender. In the second pattern, each of the remaining contenders has a lieutenant and, as a result, the leadership struggle is prolonged, or no strong leader emerges. In the third pattern, a crisis determines leader emergence. The successful leader is the person who helps the group handle such traumatic events as unruly members or the loss of important materials. In the fourth pattern, no one emerges as a clear leader. The result is a high level of frustration. Bormann says that people find such groups to be "punishing."[10]

The Minnesota researchers seem to rule out the possibility that more than one person can act as a group leader or that leadership tasks can be shared among group members. While the emergence of a single leader may be the norm for most groups, there are times when two or more individuals share the functions of leadership, as described in chapter 3. Shared leadership, as we'll see later in this chapter, is one of the defining characteristics of groups that function as teams.

How *Not* to Emerge as a Leader

Since natural leaders emerge through the process of elimination, it can be useful to identify those behaviors that virtually guarantee you won't become the group's leader. B. Aubrey Fisher and Donald Ellis offered the following "rules" for those who want to secure a low-status position in the group.[11]

Rule 1: Be absent from as many group meetings as possible. Don't explain why you didn't attend.

Rule 2: Contribute very little to the interaction.

Rule 3: Volunteer to be the secretary or the record keeper of your group's discussion. This is an important role, but a recorder or secretary rarely ends up as the group's leader.

Rule 4: Indicate that you are willing to do what you are told. While disinterest guarantees avoiding leadership responsibilities, subservience is not perceived as a leadership quality.

Rule 5: Come on [too] strong early in the group discussions. Be extreme; appear unwilling to compromise.

Rule 6: Try to assume the role of joker. Make sure your jokes are off the topic and never let on that you are serious about anything.

Rule 7: Demonstrate your knowledge of everything, including your extensive vocabulary of big words and technical jargon. Be a know-it-all and use words that others in the group won't understand.

Rule 8: Demonstrate a contempt for leadership. Express your dislike for all kinds of leaders and the idea of leadership itself.

Avoiding the behaviors identified by Fisher and Ellis works in the reverse and increases the possibility of eventually emerging as the leader of a group.

Useful Strategies

Identifying negative behaviors that eliminate leader contenders is easier than isolating positive behaviors that are essential to leadership emergence. However, the following communication strategies can boost your chances of emerging as a group leader:

Participate early and often. The link between participation and leadership is the most consistent finding in small group leadership research.[12] Participation demonstrates both your motivation to lead and your commitment to the group. Impressions about who would and would not make a suitable leader begin to take shape almost immediately after a group is formed.[13] Begin contributing in the group's first session.

Focus on communication quality as well as quantity. Frequent participation earns you consideration as a leader. However, communicating the wrong messages (rigidity, contempt, irrelevance) can keep you from moving into the leadership position. Communication behaviors that are positively correlated with emergent leadership include: setting goals, giving directions, managing tension and conflict, and summarizing.[14] Not only is quality communication essential to becoming a leader, but effective leadership communication helps the group as a whole. Groups are most likely to make good decisions when their most influential members facilitate discussion by asking questions, challenging poor assumptions, clarifying ideas, and keeping the group on track.[15] (We'll have more to say about group decision making later in the chapter.)

Demonstrate your competence. Not surprisingly, the success of would-be leaders depends heavily on their ability to convince others that they can successfully help the group complete the job at hand. Doing your homework in preparation for a project, for example, gives your leadership bid a major boost. Along with competence, you will also need to demonstrate your character and dynamism. Group members want to know that the leader candidate has the best interests of the group in mind and is not manipulating the group for personal gain. Being enthusiastic and confident makes other members more receptive to your suggestions and ideas. As we noted in chapter 6, nonverbal communication plays an important role in building perceptions of all three dimensions of credibility. One study of the nonverbal behaviors of emergent small group leaders found that they gestured frequently, established good eye contact, and expressed agreement through nodding and facial expressions.[16]

Help build a cohesive unit. You must also demonstrate that you want to cooperate with others if you want to become a group leader. Successful leader candidates pitch in to help, work to build the status of others, and don't claim all the credit for decisions.

> *The path to greatness is along with others.*
> —Baltasar Gracian

Idiosyncratic Credits

Another useful tool for understanding group leadership is Edwin Hollander's notion of idiosyncratic credits. The process of accumulating idiosyncratic credits is similar to starting an account at a bank. Members generate positive impressions in the group that are then deposited in their accounts.[17] Those with the highest idiosyncratic balances emerge as leaders. Credits are accumulated two ways. The first and most important way to build credits is by contributing to the completion of the group's task. The second is by conforming to group expectations. These expectations involve (1) general group norms (not being rude or overly emotional, for example), and (2) role expectations for a leader (such as representing the group well in front of other groups). Idiosyncratic credits are lost through incompetence and norm violations.

Leaders, because they have accumulated a large number of idiosyncratic credits, have greater freedom to deviate from group norms than do other group members. The right to deviate is granted only after leadership has been achieved, however. To demonstrate the important relationship between timing and the acceptance of deviance, one group of researchers planted confederates in groups who would either support or violate group norms such as speaking in turn and majority rule. Confederates who deviated early in the group process had more trouble convincing others to accept their opinions than those who deviated later in the session.[18] Although group leaders have more freedom to disobey rules, they should be very careful not to violate expectations associated with the leader role. A group leader may get away with being late to meetings or interrupting; she or he probably will not be able to act unfairly or selfishly regardless of the number of idiosyncratic credits earned.[19]

Appointed vs. Emergent Leaders

By this time you may wonder if anyone has paid any attention to groups who have appointed rather than emergent leaders. In many cases, a leader is assigned to a group before it meets for the first time. As you might have discovered from personal experience, groups are often successful in spite of, not because of, their official leaders. Many appointed leaders fail to function as leaders; in addition, an incompetent leader slows group progress because members must spend time and energy developing alternative leadership. Groups spend less time on leadership issues if the appointed leader earns the leader label by doing an effective job.[20]

Researchers comparing the impact of assigning or choosing leaders have discovered that followers expect more from natural leaders than appointed leaders. Since they have more invested in leaders that they have selected for themselves, members have higher expectations and tolerate less failure. Yet, at the same time, group members give natural leaders more room to operate. Emergent leaders have greater freedom to make decisions on behalf of the group.[21] One of the most common assignments for appointed group leaders is to plan and to preside over meetings, the subject of the next section.

Leadership in Meetings

For many people, the thought of attending a meeting conjures up images of long, boring sessions spent doodling on a note pad while endless amounts of useless information are presented. The reason for this negative impression of meetings is simple: most meetings are poorly planned and ineptly led. That's unfortunate because U.S. workers spend lots of time in meetings. As many as 11 million meetings take place each day, and some managers spend up to 80% of their time in group sessions.[22] Effective meeting leaders plan and prepare before a meeting to be certain that the content is both informative and useful. Adopting the following guidelines can help to insure that your meetings are successful.

Determine if a meeting is necessary before calling people together. The first step before calling a meeting is to determine if you are justified in taking people away from other activities. Bert Auger, a supervisor with the 3M corporation for over thirty years, provides a checklist outlining when you should and should not call a meeting.[23]

When to Call a Meeting

- Organizational goals need clarification.
- Information that may stimulate questions or discussion needs to be shared.

- Group consensus is required regarding a decision.
- A problem needs to be discovered, analyzed, or solved.
- An idea, program, or decision needs to be sold to others.
- Conflict needs to be resolved.
- It is important that a number of different people have a similar understanding of the same idea, program, or decision.
- Immediate reactions are needed to assess a proposed problem or action.
- An idea, program, or decision is stalled.

*When **Not** to Call a Meeting*

- Other communication networks, such as telephone, fax, e-mail, letter, or memo will transmit the message as effectively.
- There is not sufficient time for adequate preparation by participants or the meeting leader.
- One or more of the key participants are not available.
- Issues are personal or sensitive and could be handled more effectively by talking with each person individually.

Have a clear agenda. A leader should outline the items he or she wishes to address before a meeting begins. A copy of this agenda should be circulated in advance of the meeting. Participants should be encouraged to add items to the agenda (within reason) that they feel are important. The agenda should be constructed with time constraints in mind. Additions that greatly increase the number of topics to be discussed should be tabled or scheduled for a separate meeting. Remember, it is the leader's responsibility to decide how much meeting time is available and to keep the meeting on schedule. As with writing a report or delivering a presentation, a meeting leader should always have a clear purpose and a plan for achieving his or her goals. Always ask: "Why are we having this meeting?"

Maintain focus on the agenda throughout the meeting. Unless leaders maintain sharp focus, meetings have a tendency to drift away from the intended agenda. When the meeting digresses significantly, the leader needs to redirect the group. Comments like, "I think we're getting away from the real issue here. Sam, what do you think about . . ." steer the discussion back to the original agenda. A meeting leader must engage in communication behaviors that help stimulate and maintain group interest and attention. Effective meeting leaders use language that is precise yet understandable. They speak loudly and clearly (not in a mumble), and they avoid distracting gestures or movements.

Listen to others. Effective meeting leaders are active, attentive listeners. Listening involves more than merely hearing what others say; it involves incorporating the meaning of messages. University of Minnesota professor Ralph Nichols pioneered the research on effective listening. Nichols suggests several strategies for improving listening skills.[24]

- *Focus on the content of the message, not the speaker's delivery.* Information is contained in the symbols the speaker uses. Although certain habits or mannerisms such as pacing, pushing up eyeglasses repeatedly, or the excessive use of powerless forms of language (see chapter 5) can be distracting, the content of the message should be the most important focal point. Effective listeners focus on the information that is important and useful while ignoring distracting elements of delivery.

- *Listen for ideas, not just facts.* Good listeners focus on the big picture. Effective listeners don't just collect facts; they listen for concepts. If you miss some of the facts but understand the main idea, it is easy to conduct research to fill in the missing details. On the other hand, a listener who tries to incorporate all the facts may miss the larger and more important issues being addressed. It's always much more difficult to fill in the big picture later.

- *Don't let yourself get distracted.* Avoid distractions by any means possible. If you are distracted by a talkative group member, get up and move. If you are hungry, bring a snack with you to the meeting. Don't let external or internal distractions get in the way of your listening. One of the most common distractions experienced in meetings is complex or technical information. Many listeners simply tune out when information becomes difficult to comprehend; whereas effective listeners concentrate even harder. A good listener works to avoid all forms of distraction that interfere with effective listening.

- *Be open-minded.* Most of us respond instantly when someone says something with which we disagree. We may not blurt out our rebuttal immediately, but we almost always begin thinking of our response. The problem with this habit is that it interferes with our ability to listen intently to the other person's point of view. Effective listeners are open-minded and don't overreact to divergent points of view.

- *Use thought speed to your advantage.* Various researchers have suggested that we think from four to twenty times as fast as we speak.[25] This capability sometimes causes us to lose concentration while listening—everyone daydreams! Effective listeners use the ability to think more rapidly to their advantage. They use internal thought processes to anticipate the next point, to summarize or paraphrase information that has already been presented, or to focus on nonverbal behaviors such as facial and body movements that help to illustrate key ideas.

> *We have been given two ears and but a single mouth in order that we may hear more and talk less.*
> —Zeno of Citium

Involve all participants. Effective meeting leaders encourage the involvement of all participants. Meetings are designed as a forum for the exchange of information and ideas. Remember, a leader calls a meeting because he or she is eager to receive immediate information. Don't stifle participants. Always encourage an atmosphere in which discussion flourishes. When making particularly important decisions, you may want to poll each person individually to make sure the group hears from every member.

Keep a record. A written record serves as the group's memory. The minutes of a meeting generally include: (1) when and where the session took place, (2) the names of those attending, and (3) a summary of the discussion and important decisions. Action plans focus on implementation by recording *what* the group decided, *who* will carry out the action or decision, and *when* the task will be completed. For example:

What	Who	When
Key Actions/Decisions	Person(s) Responsible	Target Date
Set a timeline for spending cuts	Tom/Pam	June 1
Decided to have movie night	Jane	March 23

Evaluate Your Performance. Stopping periodically to talk about the effectiveness of your group's meetings is a good way to improve your collective performance over time. Be sure to include everyone when evaluating the agenda as well as the behavior of the chair and other participants.[26]

Group Decision Making

Decision making and problem solving, as we noted earlier, are important reasons for calling group members together for a meeting. Groups are often charged with making choices because they have access to more information than do individuals. Members bring a variety of perspectives to the problem and challenge errors in thinking that might go unrecognized by a lone decision-maker. Groups don't always make effective decisions, of course. But they are more likely to succeed when leaders and other members carry out important problem-solving functions, while avoiding the pitfalls that contribute to faulty solutions.

Functions and Formats

Group experts Dennis Gouran and Randy Hirokawa believe that high quality solutions emerge from group deliberations when participants use communication to complete four tasks or functions: problem analysis, goal setting, identification of alternatives, and evaluation of possible solutions.[27] We'll use the example of a group made up of homeless shelter staff members to demonstrate the role that each of these functions plays in the decision-making process. The shelter team is meeting to discuss a year-long decline in the number of individuals and families seeking temporary housing at their facility.

(1) A*nalysis of the problem*. Clearly identifying the nature and extent of the dilemma is critical to resolving it. Analysis includes recognizing that there is a problem, determining its size and scope, isolating causes, figuring out who is impacted by the problem, and so on. Analysis is a critical first step because initial decisions shape the rest of the group's deliberations. Our shelter team might decide that last year's decline in demand was a random occurrence, not a trend. If this is the case, then the situation doesn't need to be addressed for now. Even if the group determines that housing fewer residents poses a problem that must be solved, members could identify a variety of causes, each of which calls for a different solution. For example, low visibility in the community means more publicity is needed. If run-down facilities are discouraging potential clients, then the shelter house needs to be upgraded.

(2) *Goal setting*. Outlining goals and objectives clarifies what the group wants to accomplish in addressing the problem. To succeed, members must formulate clear objectives and set goals that, if achieved, will produce a reasonable solution. Identifying criteria or standards for evaluating solutions is also part of goal setting. The group from the homeless shelter may agree that it wants to come up with a plan to rebuild numbers over the course of the next year, without a significant increase in the budget.

(3) *Identification of alternatives*. The greater the number of potential solutions, the better the chances of coming up with a workable plan. Shelter staff members could consider a variety of options to draw more clients, including advertising their services, building better relations with social service agencies and religious groups, renovation of facilities, and more staff training designed to improve service to residents.

(4) *Evaluation of solutions*. In this function, decision makers evaluate the merits and demerits of each possible solution using the criteria developed earlier. Advertising would probably attract more people to the homeless shelter, for instance, but would be expensive. Renovation of the facilities would also be too costly. On the other hand, establishing better relations with social service agencies and religious congregations who refer clients would likely increase occupancy rates without the high costs that are associated with advertising and remodeling.

Using a decision-making format is one way to encourage a group to carry out the functions described above. Following a set of predetermined steps increases the likelihood that members will carefully define the problem and develop criteria instead of rushing to potential solutions. There is no consensus as to which format is best, but evidence suggests that groups following a structure are generally more effective than those who don't.[28]

The oldest and most widely used decision-making format is the Standard Agenda. Originally developed by educator John Dewey to describe the process that individuals follow when making choices, the Standard Agenda consists of the following steps:[29]

1. *Problem identification*. Formulate the problem in the form of a question. A question of fact addresses whether or not something is true ("Is the

defendant guilty?). A question of value asks for a judgment involving right or wrong, good or bad ("Is it fair to only allow upperclassmen to live off campus?"). A question of policy asks what course of action should be followed ("Should taxes be raised to maintain public services?"). Questions of policy are the most common problems faced by groups. (See our earlier discussion of propositions of fact, value, and policy in chapter 6.)

2. *Problem analysis.* Determine the cause(s), scope, and impact of the problem (number of people affected, costs to the organization or town, etc.).

3. *Develop criteria.* Criteria should in place before entering the solution phase since these standards play a critical role in sorting through proposals.

4. *Generate possible solutions.* Strive for quantity. Produce a variety of alternatives without passing judgment.

5. *Evaluate and select a solution.* In this stage, apply the criteria generated earlier to eliminate options and to identify the best choice. The final solution may combine elements of several proposals.

6. *Implement the solution.* This seems like an obvious step but all too often groups make a decision only to fail to follow through on their choice. Before disbanding, determine who will take action (see our earlier discussion of action plans), if future meetings are needed, and so forth.

An alternative to the Standard Agenda is the Single Question Format. This procedure incorporates the communicative functions of effective group decision making by asking participants to formulate, analyze, and then solve the problem through a series of questions. A description of this procedure is found in box 7.1

Avoiding the Pitfalls: Counteractive Influence/ Preventing Groupthink

Using a format is the first step to effective problem solving; avoiding common decision-making pitfalls is the second. Groups make significant mistakes at every stage of the decision-making process. Members fail to recognize that there is a problem or come up with the wrong cause(s), for example. They set unclear or inappropriate goals that fail to adequately address the situation and misjudge the negative and positive consequences of alternative solutions. Faulty information and/or the faulty use of information also derail group deliberations. Problem solvers often ignore important details or rely on inaccurate information. Even if their information is sound, they may misinterpret or misapply the data.[30]

In light of the logical pitfalls of group decision making, Gouran and Hirokawa argue that *counteractive influence* (statements that highlight problems in reasoning and get the group back on track) is particularly important to group success. Leaders and followers exercising counteractive influence draw attention to faulty problem definitions, information, assumptions, and inferences. They challenge the group when it deviates from its mutually agreed upon procedures and aren't afraid to take issue with high status members who are leading the rest of the participants astray.[31]

Poor logic isn't the only cause of faulty decision making. The relationships between members, referred to as the social or emotional dimension of the

---

Box 7.1

The Single Question Format[32]

1. Identify the Problem

What is the *single question*, the answer to which is all the group needs to know to accomplish its purpose for meeting?

2. Create a Collaborative Setting

a. Agree on principles for discussion.

What principles should we agree on in order to maintain a reasonable and collaborative approach throughout the process?

Examples: We will:

1. Invite and understand all points of view.
2. Remain fact-based in our judgments.
3. Be tough on the issues, not on each other.
4. Put aside any personal agenda.

b. Surface any assumptions and biases.

What assumptions and biases are associated with the single question identified in step 1, and how might they influence the discussion?

Examples:

1. We tend to assume we know our customers needs.
2. We believe we have efficient processes.
3. We think our level of customer service is acceptable.
4. We assume our past approach should be our future strategy.

3. Identify and Analyze the Issues (Subquestions)

Before responding to the single question in Step 1, what *issues,* or *subquestions, must be answered* in order to fully understand the complexities of the overall problem?

- Limit opinions by focusing on the facts.
- If facts are unavailable, agree on the *most reasonable* response to each subquestion.

4. Identify Possible Solutions

Based on an analysis of the issues, what are the two or three most reasonable solutions to the problem? Record the advantages/disadvantages of each.

	Advantages	Disadvantages
Solution 1		
Solution 2		
Solution 3		

5. Resolve the Single Question

Among the possible solutions, which one is *most desirable?*

group, can also lead to poor choices.[33] Members who don't trust each other aren't likely to share important information, for instance, or to work hard on a project. On the other hand, too much emphasis on strong relationships (which puts cohesion above performance) can also be detrimental.

Social psychologist Irving Janis developed the label *groupthink* to characterize groups that put unanimous agreement above all other considerations.[34] Groups that suffer from this syndrome fail to: consider all the alternatives, reexamine a course of action when it doesn't seem to be working, gather additional information, weigh the risks of their choices, work out contingency plans, or discuss important ethical issues. Janis noted faulty thinking in groups of ordinary citizens but is best known for his analysis of major U.S. policy disasters like the failure to anticipate the attack on Pearl Harbor, the Bay of Pigs invasion of Cuba, the invasion of North Korea, and the escalation of the Vietnam War. In each case, some of the smartest political and military leaders in U.S. history made poor choices.

Janis identified the following as symptoms or signs of groupthink:

Signs of Overconfidence

1. *Illusion of invulnerability.* Members are overly optimistic and prone to take extraordinary risks

2. *Belief in the inherent morality of the group.* Participants ignore the ethical consequences of their actions and decisions.

Signs of Closedmindedness

3. *Collective rationalization.* Group members invent rationalizations to protect themselves from feedback that would challenge their assumptions.

4. *Stereotypes of outside groups.* The belief that members of other groups are evil, weak or stupid; underestimating their capabilities.

Signs of Group Pressure

5. *Pressure on dissenters.* Coercing dissenting members to go along with the prevailing opinion in the group.

6. *Self-censorship.* Individuals keep their doubts about group decisions to themselves.

7. *Illusion of unanimity.* The mistaken assumption that the absence of conflicting opinions means that the entire group agrees on a course of action.

8. *Self-appointed mindguards.* Group members take it upon themselves to protect the leader from dissenting opinions that might disrupt the group's consensus.

A number of factors contribute to the emergence of groupthink, including failing to follow a decision-making procedure, group isolation, time pressures, homogenous members (same background and values), external threats, and low individual and group esteem caused by previous failure. (Refer to the Leadership on the Big Screen section at the end of the chapter for an example of one group that successfully resisted groupthink despite the presence of many of these conditions.) However, leadership may be the most important influence contributing to groupthink.[35] Directive leaders who push for a particular solution cut off discussion and reduce the number of alternatives considered by the group.

Fortunately, leaders can prevent groupthink as well as promote it.[36] As a leader, don't express your preference for a particular solution; urge members to participate in the deliberations and to look at a variety of alternatives. Encourage every group member to be a critical evaluator and assign individual participants the role of "devil's advocate" to argue against prevailing opinion. Follow a set of decision-making guidelines like those outlined earlier. Divide regularly into subgroups and then come back to negotiate differences. Invite outside experts or colleagues to the group's meetings to challenge the group's ideas. Keep in regular contact with other groups in the organization. Role-play the reactions of rival organizations and groups to reduce the effects of stereotyping and rationalization. Visualize successful collective performance and eliminate negative talk and thought ("we can't succeed"; "the task is too difficult") within the group. Help members challenge the assumption that whatever they do is right and discuss the moral implications of choices.

After the decision has been made, give members one last chance to express any remaining doubts about the solution. The ancient Persians provide one example of how to revisit decisions. They made every major decision twice—once when sober and again when under the influence of wine!

Team Leadership

We noted earlier that two of the distinguishing features of groups are commonality of purpose and interdependence. Members of every small group rely on each other as they work toward their objectives. Yet, some groups are more focused than others. Members of these groups are much more dependent on one another. Compare, for example, a task force designing a software product due on the market in six months to a board of directors that oversees a business. The task force has a narrow goal that cannot be achieved unless members coordinate their activities on a daily basis. The board can reach its broad objective by meeting a few times a year and by assigning ongoing tasks to individual members.

> *When a team outgrows individual performance and learns team confidence, excellence becomes a reality.*
> —Joe Paterno

When Is a Group a Team?

In recognition of the fact that groups such as task forces and boards of directors function in different ways, some observers argue that we ought to differentiate between groups and teams. They suggest that while every team is a group, not every group is a team. The two leading proponents of this position, Jon Katzenbach and Douglas Smith, draw the following contrasts between working groups and teams:[37]

Working Group	Team
Individual work products	Collective work products
Individual accountability	Individual and group accountability
Group's purpose is the same as the broader organizational mission	Specific team purpose
Measures performance indirectly by how it influences others (e.g., financial performance of the business)	Measures its effectiveness directly by assessing collective work products
Runs meetings and active problem-solving meetings	Encourages open-ended discussion
Discusses, decides, and delegates	Discusses, decides, and does real work together
Strong, clearly focused leader	Shared leadership roles

Katzenbach and Smith believe that the key difference between a working group and a team lies in what each produces. In a working group, members meet to share information, discuss ongoing projects, and make decisions. They don't produce anything collectively and are judged largely on their individual efforts. In a team, on the other hand, members work together to produce a joint product, such as an assigned class paper, a science experiment, or a marketing strategy. While the working group shares the overall mission of the organization and measures its effectiveness by how well the whole organization does, the team has a unique purpose and clearly defined performance goals ("cut working defects on the assembly line by 25 percent"; "recommend a new site for the plant by August"). Leaders of formal working groups often control the agenda and make most of the decisions and assignments. Team leaders share decision-making responsibilities, let team members take the initiative in their areas of expertise, and are active participants in the work.

Common types of teams include (1) teams that recommend things (choosing a new computer system; planning a reorganization), (2) teams that make or do things (sell or service products, for example), and (3) teams that run things (managing the development of a product line). There are many potential advantages to taking a team approach.

- Teams are more flexible than departments or organizations.
- Teams are more productive and fun than working groups.
- Teams help the organization adapt to change.
- Teams encourage individual learning and foster new behaviors.
- Teams build trust and confidence between members.
- Teams focus attention on the group agenda rather than on individual agendas.

Despite their many advantages, teams aren't the answer in every situation. Top-level executives are one category of employees who generally function in working groups because their goals overlap those of the entire organization, their rewards are based on individual efforts, and their performance is measured indirectly through the success of their units.[38] The director of a government agency, for instance, will likely take a group approach to running her organization, asking department heads to meet regularly to coordinate their activities. However, when she wants to make a major change in the structure or operations of the agency, a team approach will probably produce better results. The crucial decision for a leader, then, is to determine whether a group approach or a team approach is best. If performance levels can be met through individual activities, then stick with working groups. Make the shift from groups to teams only when the potential payoff outweighs the costs (effort, disruption, expense, etc.) of making the change.

Katzenbach and Smith use the team performance curve diagrammed in figure 7.1 to describe how an existing working group becomes a team. The first stage in the curve—the pseudo-team—reflects a decline in performance. When a group decides to become a team, but hasn't yet set performance standards, individual performance declines without any corresponding increase in group performance. Or, to put it another way: "In pseudo-teams, the sum of the

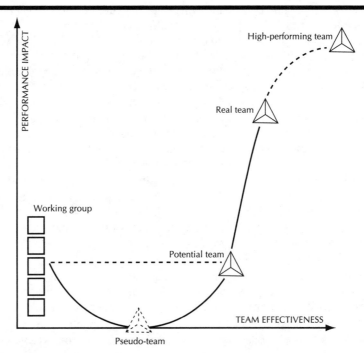

Figure 7.1
The Team Performance Curve[39]

whole is less than the potential of the individual parts."[40] The second stage of the curve reflects a sharp increase in performance as the group makes a strong effort to improve its output, even though members have yet to establish collective accountability. Performance increases still further when the group becomes a real team, which Katzenbach and Smith define as "a small number of people with complementary skills who *are equally committed to a common purpose, goals, and working approach for which they hold themselves mutually accountable.*"[41] (To determine if your group is a pseudo or real team, see the self-assessment exercise in box 7.2.) The peak of the performance curve comes when the group evolves into a high-performance team made up of members who are very committed to each other's growth and success.

Box 7.2   Self-Assessment

Evaluating Your Team's Talk[42]

Sociolinguist Anne Donellon believes that analyzing how members talk is the best way to determine if a group is acting as a pseudo-team (nominal) rather than as a real team. She identifies six dimensions of conversation that distinguish between nominal and real teams. Read the description of each dimension and then assess your group's performance by putting a check mark along the corresponding continuum in the diagram. Your pattern of check marks will give you a picture of your team's status. The more marks you put on the left-hand side of the diagram, the more likely it is that members are thinking and acting as individuals rather than as team members.

- *Identification.* Members of real teams identify themselves with the team through their conversations. They talk at least as much about the team as they do about other groups, using the words "we" and "us" to refer to the team. Members of nominal/pseudo teams talk more about their departments and other functional groups; their personal pronouns refer to those other groups.

- *Interdependence.* In high-functioning teams, members reflect their dependence on one another by expressing mutual interests, making proposals for joint action, and by soliciting the views of other team members. In low-functioning teams, members express their personal needs and independence and may not respond to questions.

- *Power Differentiation.* Differences in positional power exist in nearly every organizational team. Influential individuals in real teams minimize these power differences through apologies, making indirect requests, and politeness. The most powerful individuals in nominal teams highlight status differences by dominating the discussion, interrupting, issuing orders, and so on.

- *Social Distance.* Members of real teams express feelings of closeness through informal speech, demonstrating concern for others, expressions of liking, and humor. Members of nominal teams keep their distance by failing to respond to the comments of others or by using formal forms of address and being overly polite.

- *Conflict Management Tactics.* In real teams, participants try to integrate their differences through collaboration and by getting input from everyone. They welcome dissent but try to reach a consensus. In nominal teams, members force others to go along, give in, or avoid conflict completely.

- *Negotiation Process.* When trying to reach a mutual agreement about problems, members of real teams explore the ideas of others and reevaluate and adjust their ideas accordingly. Individuals on nominal teams engage in win-lose negotiation by focusing on the positions that divide them, by using power differences to get their way, and by talking about winners and losers.

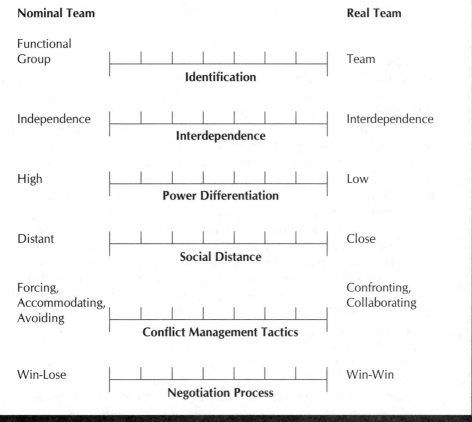

Nominal Team		Real Team
Functional Group	**Identification**	Team
Independence	**Interdependence**	Interdependence
High	**Power Differentiation**	Low
Distant	**Social Distance**	Close
Forcing, Accommodating, Avoiding	**Conflict Management Tactics**	Confronting, Collaborating
Win-Lose	**Negotiation Process**	Win-Win

Developing Team-Building Skills

Successful leaders use team-building skills to help groups move up the performance curve. Carl Larson and Frank LaFasto spent nearly three years studying more than seventy-five diverse teams.[43] Larson and LaFasto interviewed key members of these teams, including the leader of the Boeing 747 project, a person who served on several presidential cabinets, members of cardiac surgery teams, the founder of the U. S. Space Command, a member of a Mount Everest climbing expedition, and several players from the 1966 Notre Dame championship football team. From their groundbreaking work, Larson and LaFasto identified eight strategies that they believe are essential to effective team performance.

Establish clear and inspiring team goals. Effective teams are clearly focused on goals that maximize team outcomes. Further, these goals inspire the team to perform at peak levels. The team leader is primarily responsible for defining and articulating goals and for motivating followers. Team failure can be caused by a lack of clarity in the identification of a team agenda, the loss of focus from the agenda, or from distractions associated with individual demands at the expense of the group.

Maintain a results-oriented team structure. Within effective teams, each member clearly understands his or her role in the overall successful functioning of the group. Further, team members are accountable for their behavior in all situations. Every member of a successful team knows what is expected and takes responsibility for making sure tasks are done correctly. Members of a surgical team, for example, all play an important role in the overall success of an operation. The anesthesiologist monitors the patient's breathing, the nurse prepares the instruments, and the surgeon performs the procedure. Each member of the team must perform his or her task in concert with others in order to achieve a successful outcome. Communication within results-oriented teams is open and honest. Effective team leaders communicate in a highly democratic manner. (You may want to refer back to chapter 2 to reacquaint yourself with the qualities of the democratic leadership communication style.) Information is easily accessible, and questions and comments are always welcomed from all members of the group. Successful team leaders also provide frequent evaluation and feedback to members. Identifying strengths and weaknesses of group members is necessary in order to reward excellence and to suggest strategies for improving deficiencies. Finally, results-oriented teams base their decisions on sound factual data. Although "gut" feelings and hunches may produce positive results on occasion, successful decision making is based on objective criteria.

Assemble competent team members. Effective teams are comprised of competent team members. Both technical and interpersonal competencies are essential to team success. Technical competence refers to the knowledge, skills, and abilities relevant to the team's goals. Interpersonal competence relates to the ability of team members to communicate feelings and needs, to resolve conflict, and to think critically. Hewlett-Packard has a reputation as one of the most innovative organizations in the electronics industry. One reason for the company's success is that Hewlett-Packard hires only the most highly regarded research and development engineers.

Strive for unified commitment. The members of successful teams are wholly committed. Leaders seeking this type of unified commitment must work to create a team identity. Team identity is enhanced when team members are involved in decision making, policy implementation, and analysis. Indeed, involvement begets commitment. The president's cabinet and staff are examples of unified teams with a collective identity. Members of these groups feel such a strong sense of duty that they are literally on-call to handle any crisis that may arise.

Provide a collaborative climate. Cooperation and teamwork are essential to allow teams to function smoothly. Teams that work well together perform most effectively. Trust is the key ingredient in teamwork. An open, honest environment in which team members trust and respect one another promotes collaboration. In such an atmosphere, team members feel free to express dissenting opinions, thus avoiding groupthink.

Encourage standards of excellence. Successful teams have high expectations regarding outcomes. These standards of excellence define acceptable performance. High standards mean hard work, and top performing teams spend a great deal of time preparing and practicing. They are ready for virtually any contingency. The cockpit crew of United Airlines Flight 232 performed an almost impossible task in July 1989 during a crash landing at Sioux City, Iowa. Although over one hundred passengers died, aviation experts lauded the crew for maneuvering the plane under the most extreme emergency—a complete failure of the hydraulic system. Fortunately for the surviving 185 passengers, the crew expected that they could do the impossible. Standards of excellence are found everywhere within successful teams. Individual team members expect excellence from themselves and others. Perhaps most importantly, the leaders of highly effective teams demand that a standard of excellence be upheld. They will accept nothing less from themselves or the team.

Furnish external support and recognition. External support in the form of material or social rewards is important to the success of teams. These rewards alone do not guarantee success, but the absence of any form of external recognition or support appears to be detrimental to a team's overall effectiveness. According to Larson and LaFasto, recognition and support are most critical when the team is performing either extremely well or extremely poorly.

Apply principled leadership. The leaders of effective teams employ transformational leadership techniques. As discussed in chapter 4, the transformational leader is creative, interactive, visionary, empowering, and passionate. Larson and LaFasto found that three qualities seemed most important to effective team leadership: (1) establishing a vision; (2) creating change; and (3) unleashing talent. Effective team leaders have a clear vision for the team. The specific actions required to achieve this vision are clearly presented to team members. Further, this vision represents an inspiring and desirable goal for the group. Effective leaders also create change. Change is essential to improving and progressing. Effective team leaders encourage team members to seek out new and better ways to perform tasks and solve problems. Successful team leaders are not completely satisfied with the present level of achievement; they are always looking to the next challenge. Finally, effective team leaders empower their followers by unleashing the talent of all members of the team.

> The most effective leaders, as reported by our sample, were those who subjugated the needs of their ego in favor of the team's goals. They allowed team members to take part in shaping the destiny of the team's effort. They allowed them to decide, to make choices, to act, to do something meaning-

ful. The result of this approach was the creation of the "multiplier effect." It created a contagion among team members to unlock their own leadership abilities.[44]

> *When building a team, I always search first for people who love to win. If I can't find any of those, I look for people who hate to lose.*
>
> —H. Ross Perot

LaFasto and Larson extended their exploration of successful teams in 2001 with *When Teams Work Best*.[45] In this book, the authors report the results of data collected from 6,000 team members over a 14-year period. They conclude that five dynamics—*the team member, team relationships, team problem solving, team leadership,* and *the organizational environment*—are fundamental to team success.

The team member. Successful teams are most often a collection of effective individuals. Six factors differentiate effective from ineffective team members. (1) Experience—they know the task, are technically competent, and have a clear sense of vision. (2) Problem-Solving Ability—they proactively assist the team in resolving critical problems. (3) Openness—they address issues in a straightforward manner and promote an open exchange of ideas within the team. (4) Supportiveness—they provide encouragement and demonstrate a willingness to help others succeed. (5) Action Orientation—they are willing to take action and prod others on the team to take initiative as well. (6) Personal Style—they display behavior that is energetic, optimistic, engaging, fun-loving, and confident.

Team relationships. Although the individual qualities of each team member form the basic building blocks of team success, how well the team works together is critical in determining overall team effectiveness. LaFasto and Larson suggest the most significant barrier in building effective team relationships is the inability to give and receive feedback. To improve feedback ability and to strengthen existing interpersonal relationships, they recommend following the seven steps in The Connect Model. The first letter of each of the steps form the acronym CONNECT.

Step 1: **C**ommit to the relationship. Let the other person know that you are interested in strengthening your relationship with them. Tell the other person why you believe it is worth having a conversation and reinforce your willingness to work to improve the relationship.

Step 2: **O**ptimize safety. After you commit to the relationship, help the other person feel safe by letting them know you will try your hardest not to make him or her feel defensive. This means you will commit to making every effort to understand and appreciate the other person's point of view and try to suspend judgment.

Step 3: Narrow to one issue. After creating a safe environment for discussion, the next step is to identify a single issue to be addressed. The issue might be the scheduling of breaks, statements that have been made in team meetings, the level of trust in the relationship, or your roles on an upcoming project.

Step 4: Neutralize defensiveness. Before the conversation begins, think about the types of words, statements, or behaviors that might cause a defensive reaction in the other person. Avoid these provoking actions. While engaging in discussion, ask the other person to let you know if they are feeling defensive at any point. Use this feedback to work to diffuse defensive reactions.

Step 5: Explain and echo. Explain what you observe, how it makes you feel, and the long-term consequences. For example:

> What I observe, Sally, is that you have a tendency to interrupt me in group meetings. In the budget meeting the other day, for instance, I had an idea that I tried to bring up a couple of times, and each time you interrupted me, and I had to wait. Eventually, the idea came out, but maybe we could have gotten to it sooner if I had been given a chance. It makes me feel less valued, like my ideas don't have a lot of merit. It makes me feel frustrated because I can't seem to get my ideas on the table. And I am starting to feel resentful. The consequences are, if we don't change this, I don't think I'm going to want to be in meetings with you in the future.[46]

After providing the explanation, ask the other person to echo (paraphrase) your concerns. Allow the other person to state his or her concerns and echo back your understanding of those issues.

Step 6: Change one behavior each. Based on the discussions in steps one through five, initiate a conversation about a change that both of you could make to improve the situation. Agree on one behavior each person will initiate or terminate.

Step 7: Track it. Monitor progress on the agreement by selecting some specific follow-up times to give one another feedback on the effectiveness of the agreements reached in step six.

Team problem solving. A major part of any team's work consists of solving problems to advance the team toward its goals. The team members in LaFasto and Larson's research suggest three key factors are critical to effective team problem solving—the degree to which team members are focused and clear about what they are trying to accomplish; the creation of a team climate that emphasizes a relaxed, comfortable, and accepting atmosphere; and open and honest communication. Team problem solving is further enhanced by the use of a systematic strategy like the Standard Agenda and Single Question Format approaches presented earlier in this chapter.

Team leadership. Successful team leaders share six consistent leadership competencies. (1) Focus on the goal—establish a common goal for the team and continue to reinforce that goal to keep the team on track. (2) Ensure a collaborative climate—promote a safe environment where team members can openly discuss issues. (3) Build confidence—work to strengthen the self-confidence of team members by building and maintaining trust and offering meaningful levels of responsibility. (4) Demonstrate sufficient technical know-how—be technically competent in matters relating to team tasks and goals. (5) Set priorities—keep the team focused on a manageable set of priorities. (6) Manage performance—offer clear performance expectations, recognize and reward superior performance, and provide developmental feedback to team members.

The organizational environment. The organizational environment is the psychological atmosphere that permeates the broader organization within which a team operates. Like the concept of organizational culture we will discuss in chapter 8, the environment can enhance or inhibit the achievement of successful outcomes. A productive work environment depends on the effectiveness of three organizational dimensions: management practices that set direction, align effort, and deliver results; structure and processes that ensure the best decisions are made as quickly as possible by competent people; and systems that provide relevant information and drive behavior toward desired results.

Self-Directed Work Teams

One type of team seen with increasing frequency in organizations is the self-directed work team (SDWT)—an intact, interdependent group of approximately six to ten highly-trained employees who are responsible for managing themselves and their work.[47] SDWTs are generally responsible for a complete product or process. Unlike traditional group or team structures, where an organizational segment may be divided by functional specialties (for example, accounting or marketing), SDWTs are usually responsible for the delivery of an entire service or product. In this way, SDWTs operate like small businesses within a larger organization.

Several characteristics typically distinguish SDWTs from other types of teams:

- SDWTs consist of multi-skilled, cross-trained employees who are responsible for an entire job.
- Quality and process control are an ongoing, key SDWT responsibility.
- SDWTs are empowered to share a wide variety of management and leadership functions, including: scheduling, budgeting, purchasing, inventory control, and, in many cases, hiring and firing.
- Leadership is shared by the SDWT, rather than assigned to a supervisor. (If there is a designated team leader he or she plays the role of facilitator, supporting the group as a coach, rather than acting as a boss.)
- SDWTs meet regularly to diagnose and to solve their own problems.
- Customer satisfaction and overall business needs are the primary focus of SDWTs. Information generally reserved for management is passed on to the team, so members can make informed decisions.
- SDWTs engage in ongoing training as a means for enhancing team skills.[48]

> *As we look ahead into the next century, leaders will be those who empower others.*
>
> —Bill Gates

In practice, SDWTs can be classified by their degree of empowerment. Figure 7.2 illustrates responsibilities delegated to a team at four levels of empowerment. The first level on the continuum describes the responsibilities generally assigned to a newly formed team. These team duties include such tasks as running meetings ("housekeeping"), cross-training, and scheduling. As the team matures and the level of empowerment increases, members may take responsibility for continuous improvement of their processes, monitoring external customer relationships, recruiting and selecting new members, and making decisions about capital expenditures and budgeting. Finally, at level four, the mature self-directed team assumes the responsibilities related to performance appraisal, discipline, and even compensation. At this level the team controls about 80 percent of their total work responsibilities. The remaining responsibilities, mostly administrative and strategic in nature (e.g., establishing administrative policies, long-range planning), are generally performed by leaders outside the team.[49]

Although the SDWT approach has only recently begun to receive widespread attention, SDWTs have been successfully used in organizations for many years. In 1951, management professor Eric Trist and his student Kenneth Bamforth trained British coal miners to work in SDWTs.[50] The miners were taught to assist one another with key tasks and to trade jobs when workloads became unbalanced or tedious. Further, each work team was permitted to set its own rate of production and was responsible for handling its own conflicts. The output of these self-directed teams was compared with that of groups in the same organization using traditional hierarchical management. Trist and Bamforth discovered clear indications of higher productivity and job satisfaction among those workers in the self-directed teams. The miners in SDWTs outperformed their hierarchically managed counterparts by approximately 34 percent, or 1.8 tons of coal per shift.

Application of self-direction didn't begin in the United States until the early 1960s. The earliest SDWT experiment was undertaken by Procter and Gamble. The results of this experiment with self-direction were so successful that the company declared them trade secrets, with all the restrictions and security precautions associated with product development.[51] In 1990, 26 percent of all organizations in the United States had employees working in SDWTs.[52] By 1992, the percentage of organizations using SDWTs had climbed to 35 percent.[53] Over the past decade a wide variety of large (Boeing, Bristol-Myers Squibb, Corning, General Electric, Hewlett-Packard, IBM, and Xerox) and small (Ampex, Johnsonville Foods, Lake Superior Paper, and Sterling Win-

Figure 7.2
Team Empowerment Continuum[54]

throp Limited) companies have had success with SDWTs.[55] These numbers will likely continue to increase as more organizations become aware of the dramatic results of self-directed work teams (see the chart in box 7.3).

Making the transition from a traditional organizational structure to a SDWT environment can be difficult. The transition is, perhaps, most difficult for managers who must make the switch from playing the role of supervisor to playing the role of facilitator. The key differences between the traditional manager and the SDWT facilitator are outlined in box 7.4. As a facilitator, emphasis is placed on developing the leadership skills of team members while, at the same time, serving as an advocate for the team by enabling team members to free themselves from internal and external obstacles to group effectiveness.[56] Making this change can be difficult, as Kenneth Labich notes.

> Managers are often directly on the firing line when a company begins experimenting with a new management method. They are asked to learn entirely new ways of behaving, and their worth to the company can sud-

denly depend on their willingness to do something adults generally hate to do: change. The pressures can be intense, leading at times to a professional identity crisis.[57]

Management consultant Kimball Fisher suggests four primary reasons why it is difficult for managers to make the transition to SDWT facilitation.[58] (See the case study in box 7.5 for an example of how difficult this transition can be.)

1. *Perceived loss of power and status.* Equality is emphasized in the SDWT environment. As a result, managerial titles and perks (such as preferred parking and office space) are generally relinquished. Although these symbols of power do little to engender respect among subordinates, they are often perceived by managers themselves as important indicators of organizational status. The egalitarian approach to leadership in SDWTs

---

Box 7.3   Research Highlight

The Effectiveness of Self-Directed Work Teams

An increasing number of organizations have implemented the self-directed work team approach. Research suggests self-directed team members are more innovative, able to share information, involved, and task-skilled than those in more traditional organizational structures.[59] These outcomes appear to relate directly to increased productivity and satisfaction. Consider the following examples:

Organization	Results
AT&T Credit Corporation	Teams process 800 lease applications per day vs. 400 per day before SDWTs.[60]
Carrier	Reduced unit turnaround time from two weeks to two days.[61]
Corning	Decrease in defect rate from 1,800 parts per million to 9 parts per million.[62]
Federal Express	Reduced service errors (incorrect bills and lost packages) by 13 percent in one year.[63]
General Mills	Productivity 40 percent higher than traditional factory.[64]
Hewlett-Packard	Cut financial transaction processing costs by 27 percent, realizing a savings of nearly $14 million.[65]
Honeywell	Output increased 280 percent.[66]
Miller Brewing Company	Reduced labor hours needed to produce a barrel of beer by 30 percent.[67]
Shenandoah Life Insurance	Case handling time reduced from 27 days to 2 days, resulting in $200,000 savings per year.[68]
Xerox	Teams are 30 percent more productive than traditionally managed counterparts.[69]

is problematic for some. In one organization using SDWTs, prospective employees are asked if they can work in an environment where there are no promotions (there are pay raises, but there are no increasing levels in which job titles change). The answer for many is, "No."

2. *The role of team facilitator may feel ambiguous.* Acting as a facilitator is an unfamiliar role for many managers. To be successful, supervisors at all levels need to have a clear understanding of the team facilitator role and how the role differs from traditional management.

3. *Job security concerns may frustrate supervisory change.* The phrase "self-directed" leads many managers to fear that supervisors are unnecessary. Although some companies have used the transition to SDWTs as an excuse for downsizing, the most successful transitions have capitalized on managerial experience by using former managers as team leaders and facilitators, trainers, consultants, and, in some cases, team members.

4. *Facilitators may be victims of a management "double standard."* Even if a manager successfully adapts to the role of facilitator, she may be caught in a double bind. The facilitator's superiors may still be using traditional management practices in dealing with her. For instance, the team may be responsible for its own performance appraisals and salary reviews based on team goals, while the facilitator is likely to be evaluated by her superiors using traditional appraisal standards that are based on individual, rather than team, performance. This "double standard" makes it difficult to successfully play the role of team facilitator.

Box 7.4

The Self-Directed Work Team Facilitator as Leader[70]

Typical behaviors of the traditional manager and the self-directed work team (SDWT) facilitator.

The Traditional Manager	The SDWT Facilitator
Supervise	Empower
Direct	Develop
Focus on tasks	Focus on people
Make decisions for others	Assist with decision making
Set policies and procedures	Remove barriers for team
Tell people what to do	Listen to team members
Control people	Trust people
Meet with staff when necessary	Be visible and available
Punish mistakes	Reward risk taking
Manage change	Embrace change
Focus on the bottom line	Focus on the customer and the employee
Set limits	Believe there are no limits

While making the transition from a supervisor to facilitator role may be challenging, organizational leaders can smooth the way by screening out those who are unwilling to share power; by providing training that carefully outlines the responsibilities of facilitators; by ensuring job security during the transition period; and by adopting appraisal standards that evaluate team achievements. The time, money, and effort leaders invest in the transition process will likely be rewarded with significant increases in productivity, quality, efficiency, and profits.

Box 7.5   Case Study

Learning to Let Go: The Role of the Self-Directed Work Team Facilitator

Martin Kelly spent four years working as a sales representative in the marketing department at Aircom Industries. He traveled around the globe meeting with customers considering the purchase of various airplane components. Although Martin enjoyed this job, he decided he needed to gain additional experience to advance his career. The vice president of marketing and several of Martin's colleagues suggested he should seek an opportunity that would enable him to develop his skills as a manager. Martin applied for several positions in other Aircom departments. After two interviews he was offered a position in financial services.

The vice president of financial services, Judy Morton, was impressed with Martin's energy and eagerness. Though Martin had no previous experience managing others, Judy hired him as a manager in her department of 50 employees. Judy was certain that Martin would be a good choice to help her implement a new organizational structure—self-directed work teams (SDWTs). Martin was introduced to the staff at a luncheon. His enthusiasm was a breath of fresh air in a department that had experienced little turnover in the past decade. Shortly after he joined the department, Judy and Martin announced that employees would be re-organized into eight SDWTs. Martin would be the facilitator for four of the teams and another manager in the department, Anna Garcia, would be facilitator for the remaining teams.

Judy, Martin, and Anna consulted with other managers in Aircom who had successfully implemented SDWTs. They kicked off the project with a five-day training session that provided instruction regarding the use of SDWTs and the role of the SDWT facilitator. After the training, most people in the department were eagerly anticipating the change in their work environment.

It was quickly apparent that Anna was better prepared to serve as a facilitator than Martin. Anna encouraged her teams to make their own decisions; when approached with an idea or suggestion, she told team members to "give it a try." Martin, on the other hand, was much more controlling. When one of his teams approached him with the suggestion that a particular order management form was redundant and should be eliminated, he accused the team of trying to "get out of work" and called those who presented the idea "immature" and "irresponsible." Within a matter of months Anna's teams were developing process improvements, setting their own work schedules, managing daily work flow, and implementing training plans. Martin's teams were still closely supervised.

Each day Martin would send several e-mails to his teams outlining what he considered to be the most urgent tasks to be completed. Since Martin was new in the department, his priorities were not always on target, and customers' needs were sometimes not met. Many on Martin's teams were dissatisfied, and morale was steadily declining.

Nearly a year after the introduction of SDWTs in financial services, Anna's teams had improved their productivity by nearly 15 percent. Those on Martin's teams were operating at levels 10 percent below where they were prior to the introduction of SDWTs. The problem became critical when three team members working for Martin transferred to other departments. In their exit interviews with Judy, the team members complained they were treated with a lack of respect. They added that they felt as if there was *less* autonomy working with Martin than there had been *before* the introduction of SDWTs. The productivity numbers and the information gained in the exit interviews convinced Judy it was time to discuss the situation with Martin.

Discussion Questions
1. What are the characteristics of an effective SDWT facilitator? How do these behaviors differ from those of a traditional manager?
2. Do you think anyone can learn to be an effective SDWT facilitator? Why? Why not? Are there any factors that Judy should have considered before hiring Martin?
3. Research suggests the effective use of SDWTs generally results in increased productivity and satisfaction. Why do you think this occurs? What made Anna's teams more successful than Martin's?
4. If you were Judy, what would you say to Martin?
5. What should be done to improve the morale on Martin's teams? How would you advise Martin to re-establish his credibility in the financial services department?

Summary

To start our study of group leadership, we defined a group from a communication perspective. Communication scholars are more interested in the interaction between group members than in the characteristics that members bring with them to the group. From a communication viewpoint, a small group has five essential elements: (1) a common purpose or goal, (2) interdependence, (3) mutual influence, (4) face-to-face communication, and (5) a size of three to twenty members.

Groups evolve over time. Both group decisions and group leaders emerge as the group changes and matures. Emergent group leaders (leaders who aren't appointed by someone outside the group) emerge by a process of elimination—the *method of residues*. Leader contenders are eliminated until only one remains. To emerge as a leader, avoid actions that lower your status. Instead, participate frequently in the group discussion, make constructive contributions, demonstrate your competence, and help build a cohesive unit. Another way to think of establishing leadership credentials is through *idiosyncratic credits*. Potential leaders build their credits in the eyes of other group members by demonstrating that they can help the group complete its task. They also conform to group norms. Followers expect more from emergent than from appointed leaders. On the other hand, they are willing to give emergent leaders more freedom to act on behalf of the group.

Leading meetings is an important task for both emergent and appointed leaders. To provide effective leadership in meetings: (1) determine if a meeting is necessary before calling people together; (2) have a clear agenda; (3) maintain focus on the agenda throughout the meeting; (4) listen to others; (5) involve all participants; and (6) keep a record.

Groups charged with making decisions are more likely to succeed when they use communication to fulfill key problem-solving functions—analysis of the problem, goal setting, identification of alternatives, and evaluation of solutions—through the use of such formats as the Standard Agenda and Single Question model. They also avoid logical pitfalls through *counteractive influence*—highlighting problems in reasoning and getting the group back on track. Leaders of these groups help members combat groupthink—the tendency to put cohesion above performance. Better decisions emerge when leaders solicit input rather than push for their own choices and when they take steps to encourage diverse opinions and constructive group thought patterns.

There are significant differences between working groups and teams. A working group shares the overall mission of the organization and measures its effectiveness by how well the organization as a whole performs. Group members meet to share information and ideas, but they are judged on their individual efforts. In contrast, a team has a unique purpose and clearly defined performance standards. Members work together to produce a joint product, and the team is accountable for achieving its objectives. Teams are often more productive than working groups and encourage personal growth and organizational change. When they determine that a team approach is best, successful leaders use team-building skills to help working groups move up the performance curve. Eight characteristics essential to effective team performance include: clear and inspiring team goals; results-oriented team structure (clear roles and responsibilities, an effective communication network, frequent feedback, objective criteria); competent team members; unified commitment; a collaborative climate; standards of excellence; external support and recognition; and principled (transformational) leadership. Five additional dynamics—the team member, team relationships, team problem solving, team leadership, and the organizational environment—are fundamental to team success.

We ended the chapter with an examination of self-directed work teams (SDWTs) that are empowered to operate like small businesses within a larger organization. Leaders can help managers who must switch from a supervisory to a facilitator role deal with perceived loss of power and status, feelings of ambiguity, job security concerns, and outdated appraisal standards by screening out unsuitable candidates, by providing training, by ensuring job protection, and by developing team-oriented evaluation guidelines.

Application Exercises

1. Brainstorm a list of possible group norms. Which norms do leaders always have to follow? Which can they violate?

2. Discuss the pattern of leadership emergence in a group to which you belong. First, describe the communication patterns that eliminated members from leadership contention. Next, describe the communication behaviors of the leader (if one emerged) that contributed to that person's success. Evaluate your own performance. Why did you succeed in your attempt to become the leader or why did you fail? Finally, choose the leadership pattern that describes your group from the four identified in the Minnesota studies. Write up your findings.

3. Add to the list of reasons why you should or should not hold a meeting. What happens if you have a meeting when there isn't a valid reason for doing so?

4. Form a group and use the Standard Agenda or Single Question Format to solve one of the following problems.

   • Due to a budget shortfall, one of your college or university's sports teams must be cut. The president of the school will act on the recommendation of your student panel. Decide which sport will be eliminated.

   • A wealthy donor has given $5 million to your institution "to be spent by students for the benefit of students." As members of student government, come up with recommendations for spending this gift.

   • Your college/university task force has been charged with developing a plan for improving relationships with the surrounding community. Outline a strategy for achieving this goal.

5. Evaluate the talk of a group you belong to using the Self-Assessment on pages 204–205 and write up your findings. If members tend to act more like individuals than as team members, include a strategy for helping the team move up the performance curve.

6. Analyze the performance of a team using the eight characteristics of effective teams described in the chapter. Which elements are present? Which are missing? What can the team do to become more productive?

7. Describe a high performing team of which you have been a member. What made this team so successful? Why do you think other teams you were on were less successful?

8. Interview someone who has been a member of a self-directed work team. Report your findings in class.

Cultural Connections: Leading Geographically and Culturally Distributed Work Groups[71]

Distributed work groups play an important role in many modern organizations. These teams work on joint projects in a variety of locations from the headquarters to the most distant branches, coordinating their efforts through audio and video conferencing, e-mail, simultaneous computer chats, and other means.

The potential benefits of distributed work teams are obvious. Communicating electronically greatly reduces the cost and time of travel. Team members can draw upon the expertise of colleagues from around the world who have a better sense of how local markets will respond to new products and services. Yet, these advantages must be balanced against a host of potential problems. Electronic communication is not as "rich" as face to face interaction that allows participants to send messages through both verbal and nonverbal behaviors. It is difficult, for example, to tell if someone is being sarcastic or serious in an e-mail message. Physical separation is also a barrier, encouraging the growth of organizational subcultures. Further, team members in different countries have a variety of perspectives on teamwork, rewards, management styles, and other issues.

The experience of one *Fortune 100* U.S. based computer company provides some important insights into the challenges faced by dispersed groups and how they can be addressed through effective leadership. David Armstrong and Paul Cole studied a computer firm's distributed software and product development groups, which were made up of members located on the East and West coasts, the United Kingdom, France, Germany, Italy, Israel, Hong Kong, Taiwan, and Japan. They found that these teams had special problems with misunderstandings and "strangely escalating conflicts." Misunderstandings resulted when members were left off e-mail distribution lists, failed to return calls, and interpreted messages differently, depending upon their location. Conflicts were more intense and took longer to manage because members had no chance to resolve them informally before they escalated. There were also significant cultural variations between sites. Some of these differences were related to country of origin (the Europeans had more formal relationships with their managers, for example), but even engineers at locations in the United States had conflicting values and procedures.

Effective leaders played a key role in helping distributed groups span both geographical and cultural gaps. They used face-to-face meetings, particularly when forming groups, to promote commitment to a common purpose and procedures for working together. These leaders regularly traveled from site to site, repeatedly encouraged their groups to deal with miscommunication and cultural differences, made sure everyone received essential information, and modeled cross-cultural sensitivity. They also adopted a highly structured leadership approach to conducting electronic conferences by (1) carefully planning the agenda, (2) providing participants at every location with all the supporting materials well in advance of the meeting, and (3) following through on action plans generated during the session.

Leadership on the Big Screen: *Thirteen Days*

Starring: Kevin Costner, Bruce Greenwood, Steven Culp, Michael Fairman

Rating: PG-13 for language

Synopsis: Costner plays the role of a fictional presidential advisor during the thirteen days of the Cuban Missile crisis. During this period (which extended from the discovery of nuclear warheads in Cuba to Kruschev's decision to withdraw them), John Kennedy (Greenwood) and his brother Robert (Culp) face a series of critical decisions. They have to figure out how to get more intelligence about the launching sites, just how firm to be with the Cubans and Russians, and how to respond to conflicting messages from the Soviet leader. All of these deliberations take place in a highly charged atmosphere. Top military officers push for a quick, armed response but JFK resists. Through skillful use of the group process, he averts nuclear disaster. UN ambassador Adlai Stevenson (Fairman) plays an important role in preventing groupthink by offering unpopular options at significant risk to his reputation.

Chapter Links: decision-making functions, avoiding groupthink, faulty reasoning, counteractive influence, meetings, listening

Eight

LEADERSHIP IN ORGANIZATIONS

> *The final test of a leader is that he [she] leaves behind in others the conviction and will to carry on.*
>
> —Walter Lippmann

Overview

Leaders and organizations: it's hard to talk for very long about either topic without mentioning the other. Although this chapter is devoted to a discussion of leadership in organizations, we've already talked at length about organizational leadership in this book. For example, most of the leadership theories presented in chapters 3 and 4 were developed by organizational scholars. Interest in organizational leadership is not surprising when you consider that leaders are extremely important to the health of organizations and that we spend a good deal of our time in organizations. Amitai Etzioni sums up the importance of organizations this way:

> We are born in organizations, educated by organizations, and most of us spend much of our lives working for organizations. We spend much of our leisure time paying, playing, and praying in organizations. Most of us will die in an organization and when the time comes for burial, the largest organization of all—the state—must grant official permission.[1]

In the pages that follow we will focus, first of all, on the nature of organizations and symbolic leadership. Then we'll examine leadership in crisis situations. We'll end the chapter by exploring the ways that leader expectations can either increase or decrease follower performance.

Symbolic Leadership in the Organization

Organizational experts have traditionally taken a "container approach" to organizational life. When the organization is seen as a container, communication becomes only one of many variables that determine the health of the organization.[2] Textbooks written from this perspective talk about how leaders design organizational structures, manage information, oversee tasks and relationships, use technology, and so forth. The container approach understates the role of communication in organizing.

Communicating and Organizing

Earlier we noted that humans have the ability to create reality through their use of symbols. Nowhere is this more apparent than in the organizational context. Organizations are formed through the process of communication. As organizational members meet and interact, they develop a shared meaning for events. Communication is not contained within the organization. Instead, communication *is* the organization.

In recent years communication scholars and others have borrowed the idea of culture from the field of anthropology to describe how organizations create shared meanings.[3] From a cultural perspective, the organization resembles a tribe. Over time, the tribe develops its own language, hierarchy, ceremonies, customs, and beliefs. Because each organizational tribe shares different experiences and meanings, each develops its own unique way of seeing the world or culture. Anyone who joins a new company, governmental agency, or nonprofit group quickly recognizes unique differences in perspectives.

New employees often undergo culture shock as they move into an organization with a different language, authority structure, and attitude towards work and people. Even long-term members can feel out of place if they move within an organization. Each department or branch office may represent a distinct subculture. Salespeople, for example, generally talk and dress differently than engineers employed by the same firm.[4]

Elements of Organizational Culture

Dividing organizational culture into three levels—assumptions, values, and symbols—provides important insights into how culture operates. Members of every organization share a set of assumptions that serve as the foundation for the group's culture. Assumptions are unstated beliefs about: human relationships (are relationships between organizational members hierarchical, group oriented, or individualistic?); human nature (are humans basically good or evil or neither?); truth (is it revealed by authority figures or discovered on one's own through testing?); the environment (should we master the environment, be subjugated to it, or live in harmony with it?); and universalism/particularism (should all organizational members be treated the same, or should some individuals receive preferential treatment?).[5] How an organization answers these questions will determine the way it treats employees and outsiders, whether or not members will respond favorably to directives from management, what sorts of products a company manufactures, and so on.

Values make up the next level of organizational culture. Frequently (but not always) recognized and acknowledged by members, values reflect what the organization feels it "ought" to do. They serve as the yardstick for judging behavior. One way to identify important values is by examining credos, vision and mission statements, and advertising slogans. Words like "concern," "quality" and "corporate responsibility" articulate the official goals and standards of the organization. At times, however, the official or espoused values conflict with what people actually do, as in the case of an organization that touts its commitment to the environment but engages in illegal dumping.

Symbols and symbolic creations called artifacts make up the top level of an organization's culture. By analyzing these visible elements, used in everyday interaction, we gain insights into an organization's assumptions and values.[6] Common organizational symbols and artifacts include:

language	buildings
stories and myths	products
rites and rituals	technology
written materials	heroes
metaphors	logos
dress and physical appearance	office decor

While there are far too many symbols to examine each in detail, experts pay particularly close attention to the first three symbols when they analyze organizational culture. We will review them briefly.

A good way to determine how an organization views itself and the world is by listening carefully to the *language* that organizational members use. Word choices reflect and reinforce working relationships and values. The selection of the word "we" is revealing. It reflects a willingness to share power and credit and to work with others (see chapter 5). The choice of terms to describe followers also provides important insights into organizational life. For example, using the term "associates" rather than "employees" suggests that all organizational participants are important members of the team. Workers at Disney are called "cast members" to emphasize that they have significant roles to play in the overall performance for visitors who are, in turn, called "guests".

Language is a powerful motivator that focuses attention on some aspects of experience and directs it away from others. Those who speak of customer service or quality workmanship ("At Target, Guest Service is Job One") are generally more likely to provide good service and quality products. In addition, a common language binds group members together. To demonstrate this fact, brainstorm a list of terms that you use frequently at school and on the job. Many verbal symbols like "student union" or "all nighter" that you take for granted as a student might not be familiar to those at your workplace. On the other hand, some of the terms you use at work might be new to other students.

Organizational *stories* carry multiple messages. They reflect important values, inspire, describe what members should do, and provide a means to vent emotions. In many cases, organizational members are more likely to believe the stories they hear from coworkers than the statistics they hear from management.[7] For example, workers at Intel tell the story of a manager who was fired after receiving an average performance evaluation. She was dismissed because "there are no average employees at Intel." This story makes it clear that the company has high expectations of its members.

Rituals, rites, and *routines* involve repeated patterns of behavior: saying "hello" in the morning to everyone on the floor; an annual staff retreat; or disciplinary procedures. Harrison Trice and Janice Beyer identify some common organizational rites:[8]

- *Rites of passage.* These events mark important changes in roles and statuses. When joining the army, for instance, the new recruit is stripped of his or her civilian identity and converted into a soldier with a new haircut, uniform, and prescribed ways of speaking and walking.
- *Rites of degradation.* Some rituals are used to lower the status of organizational members, such as when a coach or top executive is fired. These events are characterized by degradation talk aimed at discrediting the poor performer. Critics may claim, for example, that the coach couldn't get along with the players or that the executive was overly demanding.

- *Rites of enhancement.* Unlike rites of degradation, rites of enhancement raise the standing of organizational members. Giving medals to athletes, listing faculty publications in the college newsletter, and publicly distributing sales bonuses are examples of such rituals. Recall the example of Mary Kay Cosmetics in chapter 1. The Mary Kay Cosmetic Company is one organization that makes effective use of enhancement rituals. At Mary Kay seminars, high performers are rewarded with jewelry, fur stoles, and pink Cadillacs in front of cheering audiences. The pink Cadillac is a clear symbol of high status for the Mary Kay sales force, since this is the type of car that Mary Kay herself drove.

- *Rites of renewal.* These rituals strengthen the current system. Many widely used management techniques like management by objectives and organizational development are rites of renewal because they serve the status quo. Such programs direct attention toward employee evaluation, goal setting, long-range planning, and other areas that need improvement.

- *Rites of conflict reduction.* Organizations routinely use collective bargaining, task forces, and committees to resolve conflicts. Even though committees may not make important changes, their formation may reduce tension since they signal that an organization is trying to be responsive.

- *Rites of integration.* Rites of integration tie subgroups to the large system. Annual stockholder meetings, professional gatherings, and office picnics all integrate people into larger organizations.

- *Rites of creation.* These rites celebrate and encourage change, helping organizations remain flexible in turbulent environments marked by rapid shifts in markets and technology. Some groups rotate individuals in and out of the role of devil's advocate to challenge the status quo, for example. One company went so far as to appoint a "vice-president for revolutions." Every four years he made dramatic changes in the organization's structure and personnel in order to introduce new perspectives.

- *Rites of transition.* Meetings, speeches, and other strategies can help organizational members accept changes that they didn't plan, as in the case of an unexpected merger. Addressing what the group has lost (past values, symbols, heroes) can ease the transition to a new culture.

- *Rites of parting.* When organizations die, parting ceremonies are common. Members meet to reminisce and to say goodbye, often over meals. These events help participants understand and accept the loss and provide them with emotional support.

The Nature of Symbolic Leadership

Viewing organizations as the product of symbol using suggests that organizational leaders play an important role in the creation of organizational meaning or culture. In particular, the organizational leader is actively involved in "symbolic leadership" by using symbols to determine meaning and the direction of the organization. Leaders can't always control what happens in organizations, but they can exert significant influence over how events are understood. Helping followers interpret events like mergers, market shifts, and new programs is an important task of organizational leadership. According to organizational experts Gail Fairhurst and Robert Sarr:

> Leadership is about taking the risk of managing meaning. We assume a leadership role, indeed we become leaders, through our ability to decipher and communicate meanings of complex and confusing situations. Our communications actually do the work of leadership; our talk is the resource we use to get others to act.[9]

Fairhurst and Sarr use the term "framing" to describe how leaders encourage constituents to adopt one particular interpretation or frame instead of alternative explanations. To translate a new corporate vision into action, for example, lower-level leaders must: (1) help followers understand the new concepts associated with the vision, (2) show followers how the new vision is relevant to their jobs, (3) demonstrate enthusiasm for the vision, (4) relate new ideas with established programs and practices, and (5) help stakeholders see the next steps in implementing the vision.[10]

> *Those who give voice and form to our search for meaning, and who help us make our world purposeful, are leaders we cherish, and to whom we return gift for gift.*
> —Margaret Wheatley

Another important task of symbolic leadership is directing people's attention to future goals. At any given time, an organization can veer in many different directions. Even a successful company must: decide on new products and services, react to new government regulations, and maintain or change production methods. Rosabeth Moss Kanter calls these choices "action possibilities."[11] A successful leader uses his or her vision (created with the input of constituents) to guide the organization down one particular path—in Kanter's words, to one particular action possibility that meets both individual and collective needs. In doing so, a leader provides direction for an organization and, at the same time, may strengthen employee identification with the company. Complete the self-assessment in box 8.1 to determine how strongly you identify with a particular organization.

Symbolic leaders concern themselves with much more than organizational charts, information management systems, and all the other traditional subjects of management training. They pay close attention to the assumptions, values, and symbols that create and reflect organizational culture. Organizational psychologist

Box 8.1   Self-Assessment

Organizational Identification Questionnaire[12]

Think of an organization you currently work for or have worked for in the past. For each item below, select the answer that best represents your attitude toward or belief about the organization.

7 = **agree very strongly**   3 = **disagree**
6 = **agree strongly**   2 = **disagree strongly**
5 = **agree**   1 = **disagree very strongly**
4 = **neither agree nor disagree**

1. ____   I would probably continue working for _____ even if I didn't need the money.
2. ____   In general, the people employed by _____ are working toward the same goals.
3. ____   I am very proud to be an employee of _____.
4. ____   _____'s image in the community represents me as well.
5. ____   I often describe myself to others by saying, "I work for _____." or "I am from _____."
6. ____   I try to make on-the-job decisions by considering the consequences of my actions for _____.
7. ____   We at _____ are different from others in our field.
8. ____   I am glad I chose to work for _____ rather than another company.
9. ____   I talk up _____ to my friends as a great company to work for.
10. ____   In general, I view _____'s problems as my own.
11. ____   I am willing to put in a great deal of effort beyond that normally expected in order to help _____ be successful.
12. ____   I become irritated when I hear others outside _____ criticize the company.
13. ____   I have warm feelings toward _____ as a place to work.
14. ____   I would be quite willing to spend the rest of my career with _____.
15. ____   I feel that _____ cares about me.
16. ____   The record of _____ is an example of what dedicated people can achieve.
17. ____   I have a lot in common with others employed by _____.
18. ____   I find it difficult to agree with _____'s policies on important matters relating to me.
19. ____   My association with _____ is only a small part of who I am.
20. ____   I like to tell others about projects that _____ is working on.
21. ____   I find that my values and the values of _____ are very similar.
22. ____   I feel very little loyalty to _____.
23. ____   I would describe _____ as a large "family" in which most members feel a sense of belonging.
24. ____   I find it easy to identify with _____.
25. ____   I really care about the fate of _____.

Scoring:
1. Reverse your scores on items 18, 19, and 22 so that 7 becomes 1; 6 becomes 2; 5 becomes 3; 3 becomes 5; 2 becomes 6; and 1 becomes 7 (4s remain unchanged).
2. Tally your reversed scores on these items.
3. Compute your scores on the remaining items.
4. Add your scores from steps 2 and 3 to come up with your grand total.

If your total score is **137 or above** you have a strong identification with the organization you evaluated; if your total score is **113 to 136** you have moderate identification; if your total score is **112 or below** you have a weak identification.

Discussion Questions
1. Do you think the results you obtained on this questionnaire were accurate? Why? Why not?
2. Do you believe there is a link between organizational identification and organizational culture? If so, what is the connection?
3. How can organizational identification be strengthened?
4. How well do you identify with your college or university? How does this impact your performance as a student?

Edgar Schein highlights the significant role that leaders play in the creation of organizational culture:

> Neither culture or leadership, when one examines each closely, can really be understood by itself. In fact, one could argue that the only thing of real importance that leaders do is to create and manage culture and that the unique talent of leaders is their ability to understand and work with culture.[13]

Schein notes that the responsibilities of symbolic leaders shift as the organization matures. The founder/owner, in addition to determining the group's purpose, imparting values, and recruiting followers, provides stability and reduces the anxiety people feel when an organization is just starting out.[14] A new organization often struggles with meeting payroll, developing a market niche, and managing growth. The seeds of future problems are often sown during the organization's initial stage of development. For example, the founder/leader might emphasize teamwork but continue to make all major decisions. Other founders do not perform as effectively as leaders once the organization has been firmly established. Founder/leaders often lay the groundwork for future change by promoting people who will share some, but not all, of their values. Once the organization reaches mid-life and maturity, leaders (frequently someone other than the founder) become change agents who intervene to challenge cultural assumptions, reinforce key values, or create new symbols. (For one example of a company that is intent on maintaining its core values as it expands, see box 8.2).

Box 8.2   Case Study

Imprinting and Maintaining Cultural Values at Starbucks

Starbucks is one of the world's fastest growing retail chains. The specialty coffee retailer, which began in Seattle with a single store in 1971, now has nearly 6,000 outlets in 28 countries employing more than 47,000 people.[15] The company's rapid expansion helped create the gourmet coffee craze and introduced lattes, cappuccinos, mochas, and other European coffee drinks to the United States.

Former Starbucks CEO Howard Schultz (now director of overseas development) is the driving force behind the firm's expansion. Schultz joined the company in 1982 as a salesman. A visit to Italy convinced him that the coffee bar culture, an important part of Italian social life, could be recreated in the United States. The company's founders and a number of outside investors were skeptical, but by 1987 Schultz had raised enough money to buy the firm. In 1992 the company began selling shares to the public. Starbucks stock value soared more than 2200 percent in the 1990s, surpassing Wall Street giants such as General Electric, Microsoft, and IBM in total return.[16]

Schultz attributes the company's success to a variety of factors—early financial supporters, a solid business plan, dedicated employees, a talented management team, risk taking, and sophisticated operating systems. However, he gives most of the credit to the corporation's values. From the moment he took over, Schultz was very conscious of the fact that one of the major tasks of an entrepreneur is imparting or "imprinting" values.

> Whatever your culture, your values, your guiding principles, you have to take steps to inculcate them in the organization early in its life so that they can guide every decision, every hire, every strategic objective you set. Whether you are the CEO or a lower-level employee, the single most important thing you do at work each day is communicate your values to others, especially new hires. Establishing the right tone at the inception of an enterprise, whatever its size, is vital to its long-term success.[17]

The following are the values that Schultz tried to imprint at Starbucks when the firm consisted of a handful of stores in the Northwest:

- a passion for quality coffee products and educating consumers
- outstanding customer service that creates a bond with consumers
- creation of a comfortable atmosphere for casual social interaction
- recognition that employees (referred to as "partners") are the company's greatest asset
- concern for local communities and the environment
- continuous innovation

Ironically, rapid global growth threatens the very value system that fueled the company's expansion. The greater the number of employees and stores around the globe, the harder it is for Schultz to communicate his passion for coffee and his values to employees. Critics have accused Starbucks of becoming just another "soulless" large chain that takes advantage of small coffee farmers. Some communities have resisted the opening of Starbucks outlets, fearing that the retailer will drive out local businesses.[18]

Schultz and other executives have tried to "stay small" as the company gets bigger. To encourage employee identification with the corporation and its values, Starbucks pays higher-than-average wages, offers stock options, provides health insurance for part-time workers, recognizes outstanding partners, and holds quarterly open forums. The company has responded to criticisms by supporting local charity programs, contributing to the CARE international relief agency, offering Fair Trade coffee (shade-grown beans that guarantee a living wage to growers), and placing more of its stores in middle- and lower-class neighborhoods.

Some observers are skeptical that Starbucks will be able to maintain its values as it continues to expand. Yet, Schultz is committed to a strategy that holds fast to core values while fostering flexibility and innovation:

> No matter how many avenues Starbucks pursues, and no matter how much we grow, our fundamental core values and purpose won't change. I want Starbucks to be admired not only for *what* we have achieved but for *how* we achieved it. I believe we can defy conventional wisdom by maintaining our passion, style, entrepreneurial drive, and personal connection even as we become a global company.[19]

Discussion Questions

1. Can Starbucks maintain its values as it continues to expand? Why or why not?
2. What additional strategies could the company use to "stay small" as it grows big?
3. Would you want to work for Starbucks? Do you or would you shop at its stores? Why?
4. If you were to found a corporation or nonprofit organization, what values would you try to imprint on its culture?
5. What challenges do you think Starbucks faces as it becomes increasingly global in its focus?

Shaping Culture

Your effectiveness as a symbolic leader will depend in large part on how well you put your "stamp" on an organization's culture or subcultures either as a founder or as a change agent. Perhaps you want to introduce more productive values and practices or encourage innovation as part of your vision or agenda. Cultural change, while necessary, is far from easy. Some organizational consultants sell programs that promise to modify organizational culture in a quick and orderly fashion. Such claims, which treat culture as yet another element housed in the organizational container, are misleading.

> *Nothing is inevitable until it happens.*
>
> —A. J. P. Taylor

Change is difficult because cultures are organized around deeply rooted assumptions and values that affect every aspect of organizational life. Current symbols and goals provide organizational and individual stability, so any innovation can be threatening. However, knowing how culture is embedded and transmitted can help you guide the cultural creation and change process. According to Edgar Schein, there are six primary and six secondary mechanisms you can use to establish and maintain culture. Primary mechanisms create the organization's "climate" and are the most important tools for shaping culture. Secondary mechanisms serve a supporting role, reinforcing messages sent through the primary mechanisms.[20]

Primary Mechanisms

1. *Attention.* Systematically and persistently emphasize those values that undergird your organization's philosophy or plan. If your vision emphasizes customer service, for example, then you need to focus the organization's attention on service activities. Your claim that service should be the company's first priority will not be taken seriously unless you as a leader perform service, honor good service, and penalize those who fail to respond to customer needs. In this way, others are encouraged to act as you do, to share your meaning that good service is important, and to believe service activities are critical. Some, like Ren McPherson of the Dana Corporation, argue that paying attention is the key activity of leader/managers. In McPherson's words: "When you assume the title of manager, you give up doing honest work for a living. You don't make it, you don't sell it, you don't service it. What's left? Attention is all there is."[21] Focused attention takes on even more importance when undertaking major transformation efforts (see box 8.3).

2. *Reactions to critical incidents.* The way you respond to stressful events sends important messages about underlying organizational assumptions. Compare the way that organizations handle financial crises, for example. Some use layoffs as an efficient way to balance the books. Others, who put cooperation ahead of efficiency, cut costs by asking everyone to work fewer hours. (See the discussion of leadership in crisis later in this chapter for more information on how to prepare for a crisis situation.)

3. *Resource allocation.* How an organization spends its money is a key indicator of where it is headed. Looking at projected expenses reveals whether a company will invest in new product lines, for example. Further, the process of budgeting reveals a great deal about organizational values and assumptions. The greater the organization's faith in the competence of its employees, for instance, the more likely it is to involve people from all levels of the organization in setting financial targets. Because budgeting sends such strong cultural signals, think carefully about what you want to communicate when deciding how to create the departmental or organizational spending plan.

4. *Role modeling.* Effective leaders work to develop others who share their vision. Become a coach and teacher to followers, particularly to those

Box 8.3   Research Highlight

Leading Transformation[22]

Introducing significant change is one of the toughest challenges facing organizational leaders. Harvard business professor John Kotter studied 100 companies in the United States and abroad who launched a variety of change initiatives under such labels as "restructuring," "downsizing," and "total quality management (TQM)." He found that only a handful of these firms succeeded at transforming the way they do business. The rest were only partially successful or total failures.

Why do so few transformation efforts succeed? Kotter identifies eight common errors, any one of which can slow a change effort.

Error 1: Not establishing enough sense of urgency. Creating motivation for change is critical. Without a sense of urgency, organizational members don't have any reason to take on the extra work and psychological discomfort associated with change. Top executives often underestimate how hard it is to get people to abandon their current behaviors, or they start the transformation process without the buy-in of their management teams. In Kotter's sample, successful reform movements were sparked by such factors as poor financial results, changing markets, and customer complaints. Three-quarters or more of the managers in the transformed companies supported the change efforts.

Error 2: Not creating a powerful guiding coalition. A top executive can spearhead transformation but he or she must soon be joined by other powerful leaders (senior managers, union leaders, board members, key customers). This coalition typically operates outside the normal chain of command because, by definition, reform threatens the status quo. Companies fail in their change efforts when they don't assemble enough influential leaders who can work as a team, or assign the responsibility for the change effort to one department instead of including members from many different units.

Error 3: Lacking a vision. One of the change coalition's most important tasks is coming up with a clear, achievable vision that is easily communicated to internal and external constituencies. All too often, lists, plans, and programs replace a compelling picture of the end result. The change initiative then disintegrates into a series of fragmented projects that confuse and alienate employees.

Error 4: Undercommunicating the vision by a factor of ten. A single meeting, speech, or memo will not encourage the kind of sacrifice needed for transformation. Instead, the vision needs to be constantly communicated in every kind of forum and through every channel (e-mail, newsletters, annual reports, department meetings, company celebrations, advertising). Leaders also need to model the desired new behaviors (i.e., commitment to quality, cost cutting, team building)—backing their rhetoric with action.

Error 5: Not removing obstacles to the new vision. The organization's current structure, compensation guidelines, and performance appraisal systems can all undermine renewal. For instance, the current pay and evaluation structure may reflect past, not current, values. The greatest danger to transformation, though, comes from those who actively resist change. They must be won over to the change effort or be removed from the organization.

Error 6: Not systematically planning and creating short-term wins. Major change efforts take years to complete. Members lose their sense of urgency when leaders focus solely on the end results of the change program. Setting intermediate goals marks the progress of the group and provides opportunities to reward gains through money, public recognition, promotions, and other means.

Error 7: Declaring victory too soon. Initial victories, while important for sustaining momentum, don't signal the end of the change battle. In fact, confusing short-term wins with long-term transformation puts change supporters at ease and emboldens resisters, bringing change to a halt. Major transformations take 5–10 years to complete.

Error 8: Not anchoring changes in the corporation's culture. Changes may seem solidly in place, but they can be undone unless they become part of the group's deeply held norms and values. Drawing attention to how the new systems and behaviors have improved collective performance is one way to anchor changes; making sure the next generation of leaders champions the reforms is another.

who are directly underneath you on the organizational ladder. You can also instill organizational philosophy through formal training programs. Hewlett-Packard estimates that one-third of its initial training session is devoted to discussing the "Hewlett-Packard Way." Employee evaluation is partially based on how well workers adhere to the HP philosophy.

5. *Rewards.* Rewards and punishments go hand in hand with the mechanism of attention described earlier. If service is your goal, then honor those who provide good service (through expanded job responsibilities, pay raises, etc.) and discipline those who don't.

6. *Selection.* Since organizations tend to perpetuate existing values and assumptions by hiring people who fit into the current system, reform the culture by recruiting members who share your perspective rather than the old one. Promote those who support your vision; if necessary, help those who won't or can't change find employment at another organization.

Secondary Mechanisms

1. *Structure.* Organizational design and structure affect how leaders divide up such things as product lines, markets, and work responsibilities. Some structures emphasize the interdependence of organizational units, for example, while others encourage each department or branch to operate as independently as possible. With this in mind, determine what your current structure says about your underlying premises and make changes when appropriate.

2. *Systems and procedures.* Quarterly reports, monthly meetings, work routines, and other recurring tasks occupy much of our time in organizations. You can use these organizational routines to reinforce the message that you care about certain activities. For example, requiring a weekly sales report is a reminder that you are concerned about marketing results.

3. *Rites and rituals.* To encourage change, nonessential rituals (those with little meaning for participants) can be dropped, essential rituals can be adapted to new purposes, and new rituals can be created. For instance, the annual Christmas party that has been a source of discomfort can become an annual banquet in which the organization promotes cooperation and teamwork. Harrison Trice and Janice Beyer suggest that rites of passage and enhancement are the best ways to encourage change.[23] Develop new ways to help organizational members pass from one status to the next and publicly celebrate the accomplishments of those who meet the new standards.

4. *Physical space.* The physical layout of your organization's facilities can transmit your values, but only if you pay close attention to the messages you send through these elements. Restaurants are good examples of how physical settings can communicate important themes. The harsh lights, stainless steel counters, bright colors, and uncomfortable seats of fast-food restaurants invite customers in for a cheap, pleasant, and quick meal. The muted lighting, plush carpeting, and linen tablecloths at fancy restaurants encourage customers to linger over expensive dinners complete with drinks and dessert. Determine what type of message you want to send through your use of physical space (collegiality, stability, familiarity) and design accordingly.

5. *Stories.* Consider creating new stories and changing old ones. If you are faced with a negative story that is already part of the organizational culture (perhaps a tale of how management is insensitive to worker needs), work to change the behaviors that made the story believable.

6. *Formal statements.* Most of what an organization believes never makes it into a formal statement. Nonetheless, as we noted earlier, credos and mission statements do reflect important values. Writing such statements can help you and your constituents clarify your thinking. If members understand the philosophy of the organization and have a statement of its goals, they can quickly make decisions about what actions will help their company or nonprofit group. (Remember the example in chapter 1 of the Procter and Gamble employee who bought all the mislabeled Jif peanut butter jars he found at the store.)

> *We must be the change we wish to see in the world.*
> —Mahatma Ghandi

Leadership in Crisis

Crises can bring out the best or the worst in organizations and their leaders.[24] Some organizations respond quickly and forcefully when a crisis strikes and emerge stronger than ever. A case in point is the Johnson & Johnson Company, the makers of Tylenol. When six people died after taking extra-strength Tylenol capsules laced with cyanide, the firm, led by CEO James Burke, immediately recalled the capsules and later replaced them with caplets. Company officials cooperated fully with the press and government authorities. Public confidence in Johnson & Johnson was restored, and Tylenol sales are higher now than they were before the tampering incident.

Unfortunately, for every positive example of crisis management there are many instances where leaders and organizations stumble. Bridgestone/Firestone, for example, has "become a textbook case of how **not** to manage a corporate crisis."[25] The company was aware of problems with its Wilderness tires six months before announcing a recall. Even then, the company wanted to stagger the replacement schedule, forcing some customers to risk their lives for months while they waited their turn for safer tires. As a consequence of the firm's sluggish response, its future was put in danger. In another case of crisis mismanagement, the Jack-in-the-Box restaurant chain waited nearly a week before admitting that it was responsible for an *E.coli* bacterial outbreak that caused the deaths of four children and made over one thousand people sick.

Preparation is the key to managing a crisis rather than falling victim to it; organizations and leaders who triumph over tragedy prepare in advance. To be ready when trouble strikes requires understanding how a crisis develops and creating a set of crisis management tools.

Anatomy of a Crisis

A crisis is any unpredictable event that has the potential to damage an organization and, in extreme cases, to threaten its survival.[26] Researchers at the Center for Crisis Management at the University of Southern California report that crises generally fall into the following categories:[27]

- *Criminal attacks:* employee violence, product tampering, sexual harassment
- *Economic attacks:* boycotts, hostile takeovers, stock devaluation, strikes
- *Loss of proprietary information:* false rumors, copyright infringement, counterfeiting
- *Industrial disasters:* contamination, explosions, fires, spills
- *Natural disasters:* blizzards, earthquakes, floods, tornadoes
- *Breaks in equipment and plants:* product defects and recalls, computer breakdowns, security breakdowns
- *Legal:* major lawsuits, class action suits, product liability
- *Reputational/perceptual:* rumors that damage an organization's operations and image
- *Human resources/occupational:* executive succession, employee violence, sexual harassment
- *Health: AIDS,* environmental contamination, job-related injuries and death
- *Regulatory:* adverse government regulations, hostile special-interest groups

Stephen Fink compares an organization faced with a crisis to a body fighting a disease.[28] Crises pass through a series of stages just as illnesses do. Some unexpected events, like an upset stomach, last only a short time and do very little damage. Others, like heart attacks or strokes, have lingering, life-threatening consequences. In keeping with his medical metaphor, Fink dissects the anatomy of a crisis into four phases or stages (see figure 8.1).

The *prodromal* (warning) *phase* is the first stage in the crisis cycle. Prodomes (taken from the Greek meaning "running before") are warning signs that something is seriously amiss. FBI officials, for example, were warned that they had a spy in their agency long before Counterintelligence Chief Robert Hanson was arrested for espionage. Catholic cardinals and bishops knew that priests were sexually abusing children decades before victims began suing for damages. Catching problems in the prodromal stage, before they turn into full-blown crises, is the ultimate goal of crisis management. Crisis prevention requires constant vigilance and the determination to respond immediately to prodromes once they are identified. However, even if your organization doesn't correct a problem you spot, the forewarning will help you identify the exact nature of a crisis if it occurs.

The **acute crisis stage** marks "the point of no return" when the focus shifts from prevention to damage control. At this juncture, the crisis erupts into pub-

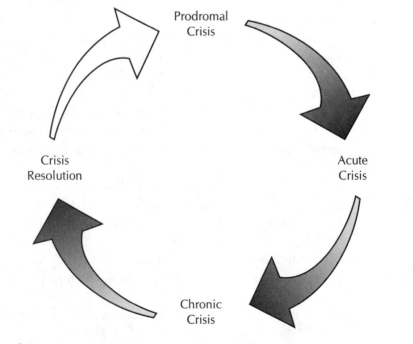

Figure 8.1
Crisis Cycle[29]

lic consciousness, and events move at lightning speed. Mercifully, the acute crisis stage lasts only a short time. For instance, the acute crisis phase of the Three Mile Island incident (when the reactor was in danger of melting down) lasted about a week.

In contrast to the acute crisis stage, the *chronic crisis phase* can linger indefinitely. During this period, the organization deals with the long-term consequences produced by the crisis events. These consequences can include lawsuits, criminal or congressional investigations, financial losses, management turnover, newspaper exposés, hostile mergers, and bankruptcy. Repairs at Three Mile Island and investigations of the plant's operators dragged on for years. Exxon is still settling claims with individuals and groups damaged by the grounding of its tanker, the *Exxon Valdez*. Having a crisis management plan can shorten the chronic crisis stage, however. Fink found that *Fortune 500* companies without crisis management plans suffered from the lingering effects of a crisis up to two-and-a-half times longer than companies with contingency plans.

The *crisis resolution stage*, when the organizational patient is healthy again, marks the final stage of the crisis cycle. Yet, resolution of one crisis doesn't mean that another one isn't on the way. Crisis development is cyclical. Even as one crisis fades into memory, others are in the prodromal stage, requiring leaders and organizations to maintain a constant state of alertness.

Crisis Management Tools

Few of us would take an extended driving vacation without taking such essentials as a jack, a spare tire, a few basic medical supplies, and a blanket. These items could literally mean the difference between life and death if the car breaks down in a remote location. Like prudent motorists, farsighted leaders develop emergency tool kits to deal with crises before they happen, converting their organizations from crisis prone to crisis prepared.[30] Well-stocked crisis management kits contain vigilant problem-solving strategies, action plans, crisis management teams, designated spokespersons, cooperative media strategies, honesty and compassion, and image insurance. Let's examine each one of these tools in more detail.

Vigilance

Poor decisions lead to crises and/or make them worse. Some crisis situations—criminal activities, biased hiring practices, sexual harassment—are the direct result of the unethical or unwise decisions of managers. In other cases, leaders decide to ignore warning signs or respond in a way that intensifies the crisis. Increased vigilance is the best way to avoid the errors that generate crisis situations and make them worse. Vigilant decision making begins with recognizing potential errors or biases in our thinking processes. According to David Messick and Max Bazerman, many organizational leaders make poor choices, not because they are greedy or callous but because they hold faulty beliefs or theories about the world, other people, and themselves.[31] Theories of the world include the following activities: (1) determining the possible consequences of decisions, (2) assessing the risks involved in choices, and (3) determining the causes of a problem. Theories about other people are based on how we think our group ("we") differs from other groups ("they"). Faulty theories about the self are unrealistic beliefs about our contributions, abilities, and judgment. Box 8.4 summarizes the ways in which these theories can undermine problem solving.

Messick and Bazerman argue that leaders can make more effective decisions if they focus on quality, breadth, and honesty. The likelihood of making a high quality decision increases if you base decisions on facts rather than

---

Box 8.4

Decision-Making Biases[32]

Theories of the World
- ignoring low-probability events even when they could have serious consequences later
- limiting the search for stakeholders and thus overlooking the needs of important groups
- ignoring the possibility that the public will find out about an action
- discounting the future by putting immediate needs ahead of long-term goals
- underestimating the impact of a decision on a collective group, industry, city, profession, etc.
- acting as if the world is certain instead of unpredictable
- failing to acknowledge and confront risk
- framing risk differently than followers
- blaming people when larger systems are at fault
- excusing those who fail to act when they should

Theories about Other People
- believing that our group is normal and ordinary (good) while others are strange and inferior (bad)
- giving special consideration and aid to members of the "in group"
- judging and evaluating according to group membership (stereotyping)

Theories about Ourselves
- rating ourselves more highly than other people
- underestimating the likelihood that negative things will happen to us like divorce, illness, accidents, and addictions
- believing that we can control random events
- overestimating our contributions and the contributions of departments and organizations
- being overconfident, which prevents us from learning more about a situation
- concluding that the normal rules and obligations don't apply to us

hunches, stop to consider how you might be wrong, and keep detailed records to correct errors in memory. To make broad decisions, identify all stakeholders and take their perspectives into account. Make honest decisions by rejecting the temptation to deceive others or yourself. If you wouldn't want your decision to appear on the front page of the local newspaper, for example, don't do it. Consider whether the people with the most to lose would agree with the reasons for your decision. (We'll have more to say about the ethics of decision making in chapter 11.)

Once a crisis strikes, resisting premature closure becomes the most important consideration for vigilant decision makers. The stress of a crisis puts incredible demands on organizational leaders. Lives may have been lost, property damaged, or products recalled from the shelves. Mental and physical fatigue sets in. Under such conditions, both individual leaders and groups of decision makers are tempted to make quick decisions. Be sure to carry out the decision-making functions described in the last chapter—analyze the problem, set goals, and then identify and evaluate alternatives—whether working alone or with others. When deciding in a group, be particularly attuned to symptoms of groupthink (which are more likely to appear when groups are under pressure). Remember the steps outlined in chapter 7 to prevent cohesion from taking priority over a well reasoned, defensible choice.

> *I take it we are all in complete agreement on the decision here. . . . Then I propose we postpone further discussion of this matter until our next meeting to give ourselves time to develop disagreement and perhaps gain some understanding of what the decision is all about.*
>
> —Alfred P. Sloan

Action Plans

Identifying potential trouble spots is the first step in preparing an action plan. As a department or organization, brainstorm a list of possible crises based on warning signs originating from within your organization or from the experiences of organizations similar to yours.[33] Here, for example, are some potential crises that might strike your college or university (see application exercise 3).

- asbestos contamination
- dramatic decrease in enrollment
- earthquake
- explosion in the science lab
- faculty member or administrator accused of illegal or immoral conduct

- food poisoning in the cafeteria
- financial problems
- fire
- flood
- lawsuits against the university
- staff or faculty strike
- student protests
- students arrested for serious crimes
- controversial speaker or art exhibit
- students hurt or killed while participating in school-sponsored activities

After identifying what might happen, develop a plan of action to cope with each potential emergency. In the case of a fire or flood in a dormitory, for instance, how will students be evacuated? Where will they live? How will the media be notified and by whom? What will switchboard operators say when anxious parents and friends call? The plan should be reviewed periodically to keep up with changes in personnel and to make sure that the addresses and phone numbers of television and radio stations are up to date.

Crisis Management Teams

The crisis management team carries out the action plan when disaster strikes. The typical crisis team is headed by a member of senior management and includes representatives from public relations, finance, the legal department, human relations, and technical operations. This core group can be supplemented with other members as needed, depending on the particular crisis. Each member of the team should have a designated replacement in case he or she isn't available. To train the team, create simulations that ask team members to role play in response to crisis scenarios.

Designated Spokespersons

In case of an emergency, one person should speak on behalf of the entire organization in order to eliminate conflicting messages and to prevent the spread of misinformation. Generally the chief operating officer should fill this role, receiving assistance from others when needed. This leader's performance in front of the media will have a significant impact on public perceptions, for better or for worse. Successful spokespersons communicate in a clear, succinct, and forthright manner under pressure and handle hostile questions without getting angry or flustered. Taping and evaluating mock interviews and press conferences is one way to prepare for this role.

Cooperative Media Strategies

Plan to cooperate with the media in order to encourage more accurate and favorable coverage. Make sure the spokesperson is available to the press at all times. Compile press kits that describe the organization and its officers. Set up a crisis center with additional phone lines, copiers, and fax machines. Conduct press conferences well before newspaper and television deadlines.

Honesty and Compassion

When it comes to a crisis, honesty is the best policy. If your company is at fault, take responsibility. Don't try to hide damaging information (chances are it will be discovered anyway), and correct your mistakes when necessary. At the beginning of the Tylenol tampering crisis, the Johnson & Johnson company stated that cyanide was not utilized in the manufacturing process. When the company later discovered that small amounts of the chemical were used, it admitted the error. Never respond to a question with "no comment" because this statement makes you appear as if you have something to hide. If you don't know the answer, offer to check further and to get back to the questioner later. Demonstrate genuine concern by acting as quickly as possible to repair the damage and by communicating your compassion for victims. Don't appear aloof and detached, as NASA did when it proclaimed that there was "an apparent malfunction" in the *Challenger* spacecraft as millions watched replays of the explosion on television. Sadly, NASA had occasion to apply what it had learned when the shuttle *Columbia* disintegrated upon reentry in 2003. Officials expressed shock and sadness immediately after the tragedy.

> *Adversity is the first path to truth.*
>
> Lord Byron

Image Insurance[34]

The established image of an organization can be one of its greatest assets in a dangerous situation. Companies with a reputation for integrity and social and environmental concern are better equipped to weather a crisis. When reports surfaced of needles in cans of Pepsi, for instance, few consumers panicked because the company has a reputation for producing safe, high-quality products. Work hard to establish a positive image by supporting community activities, conducting an ongoing, active public relations program (see chapter 9), and being a responsible steward of the environment.

The Power of Expectations: The Pygmalion Effect

What a leader expects is often what a leader gets. This makes the communication of expectations one of a leader's most powerful tools. Our tendency to live up to the expectations placed on us is called the Pygmalion Effect. Prince Pygmalion (a figure in Greek mythology) created a statue of a beautiful woman whom he named Galatea. After the figure was complete, he fell in love with his creation. The goddess Venus took pity on the poor prince and brought Galatea to life. The Pygmalion Effect has been studied in a number of settings. Consider the following examples of the power of expectations in action:

- Patients often improve when they receive placebos because they believe they will get better.

- The expectations of teachers can influence the test and IQ scores of students. The most widely publicized investigation of the Pygmalion Effect in education was conducted by Robert Rosenthal and Lenore Jacobson, who randomly assigned students in a San Francisco area elementary school to a group labeled as intellectual "bloomers." These investigators told teachers to expect dramatic intellectual growth from these students during the school year. The "bloomers" made greater gains on intelligence tests and reading scores than the other children.[35]

- Military personnel perform up to the expectations of their superiors. At an Israeli army training base, for example, instructors were told that trainees had high, regular, or unknown command potential. The high-potential soldiers (who really had no more potential than the other trainees and who were not told that they were superior) outperformed the members of the other groups, were more satisfied with the training course, and were more motivated to go on for further training.[36] In an investigation conducted in the U.S. Navy, the performance of problem sailors improved significantly after they were assigned to mentors and given a special training seminar designed to promote personal growth.[37]

Patterns created through expectations tend to persist. One long-term study of 500 students revealed that their standardized math test scores in the twelfth grade were influenced, in part, by the expectations that teachers had of their mathematical abilities in the sixth grade.[38] David Berlew and Douglas Hall examined the careers of two groups of AT&T managers and found that new managers performed best if they worked for supervisors who had high but realistic expectations.[39] These new employees internalized positive attitudes and standards and were entrusted with great responsibilities. Six years later, they were still highly productive. On the other hand, managers who worked for bosses who expected too much or too little performed poorly throughout the test period. These workers either failed to develop high standards or didn't get recognition for the work that they did complete. As a result, they may have decided to perform at minimal levels. Berlew and Hall conclude that the first twelve to eighteen months are critical to the career success of any new employee. Patterns set during this initial period often continue throughout a worker's tenure at a company.

There can be little doubt that leader expectations exert a long lasting influence on performance. Yet, it would be a mistake to conclude that the Pygmalion Effect has a dramatic impact on all followers. Disadvantaged groups (those stereotyped as low achievers) tend to benefit most from positive expectations, as do those who lack a clear sense of their abilities or find themselves in a new situation. Men seem to be more influenced by the expectancies of their managers than do women.[40]

Two characteristics of leaders moderate the impact of their expectations. The first is their level of self-esteem. Even when placed with subordinates with superior abilities, some leaders fail to communicate positive expectations because they lack confidence in their own abilities. One study of sales managers at a Metropolitan Life Insurance agency demonstrates the important relationship between leader self-confidence and the Pygmalion Effect. Sales agents were randomly divided into high, average, and poor performance groups. Sales of the high performer unit dramatically increased, while sales of the weakest unit declined and members dropped out. Significantly, the performance of the "average" group went up because the leader of this group refused to accept the fact that he or his sales force were any less capable than the supposedly outstanding sales unit. In summarizing the results of this study, J. Sterling Livingston writes:

> Superior managers have greater confidence than other managers in their own ability to develop the talents of their subordinates. Contrary to what might be assumed, the high expectations of superior managers are based primarily on what they think about themselves—about their own ability to select, train, and motivate their subordinates.[41]

The superior manager's confidence in his or her ability to develop and stimulate high levels of performance results in the belief that expectations will be met. Doubts about one's ability lead to lowered expectations and less confident interactions.

A second characteristic of leaders that moderates the influence of the Pygmalion Effect is their level of expectations. As we saw in the case of the AT&T managers, expectations must be high, but realistic. Setting standards too low does not challenge the abilities of followers since there is little satisfaction to be gained by fulfilling minimal expectations. Yet, setting expectations too high guarantees failure and may start a negative self-fulfilling prophecy. Having failed once, the organization member expects to fail again. Goal-setting theorists argue that high performance comes from setting specific, challenging objectives, not vague, easy ones. (Being told to "try your best" is not very motivating, for instance.) Employees must be adequately trained for their tasks and then rewarded when they reach their targets.[42]

> *We are not only our brother's keeper; in countless large and small ways, we are our brother's maker.*
> —Bonaro Overstreet

To summarize, followers often perform up to expectations, whether in the classroom, the military, or the corporation. Leaders must have confidence in their own abilities and set realistic goals for followers in order for the positive

Pygmalion Effect to operate. However, the confidence that leaders have in themselves and their followers will have no impact on group behavior unless group members know that this confidence exists. Leaders must clearly communicate their expectations to followers. With this in mind, we turn now to a description of how expectations are communicated.

The Communication of Expectations

Telling others that they have ability, offering them compliments, and saying that you expect great things from them communicates high expectations. Subordinates also get the message that leaders have high or low expectations of them even when expectancies are not explicitly stated. Expectations are communicated through four important channels.[43]

1. *Climate.* Climate refers to the type of social and emotional atmosphere leaders create for followers. When dealing with people whom they like, leaders act in a supportive, accepting, friendly, and encouraging manner. Nonverbal cues play a major role in creating climates. Communication experts John Baird and Gretchen Wieting recommend that organizational managers use nonverbal behaviors that emphasize concern, respect, equality, and warmth—while avoiding behaviors that communicate coolness, disinterest, superiority, and disrespect.[44] (See box 8.5 for a summary of nonverbal cues that communicate positive expectations.)

2. *Input.* In an organizational setting, positive expectations are also communicated through the number and type of assignments and projects given employees. Those expected to perform well are given more responsibility, which creates a positive performance spiral. As employees receive more tasks and complete them successfully, they gain self-confidence and the confidence of superiors. As a result, these star performers are given additional responsibilities and are more likely to meet these new challenges as well.

3. *Output.* Those expected to reach high standards are given more opportunities to speak, to offer their opinions, or to disagree. Superiors pay more attention to these employees when they speak and offer more assistance to them when they need to come up with solutions. This is similar to what happens in the classroom when teachers call on "high achievers" more than "low achievers," wait less time for low achievers to answer questions, and provide fewer clues and follow-up questions to low achievers.[45]

4. *Feedback.* Supervisors give more frequent positive feedback when they have high expectations of employees, praising them more often for success and criticizing them less often for failure. In addition, managers provide these subordinates with more detailed feedback about their performance. However, superiors are more likely to praise minimal performance when it comes from those labeled as poor performers. This reinforces the perception that supervisors expect less from these followers.

The Galatea Effect

Our focus so far has been on the ways that leaders communicate their expectations to followers. Once communicated, these prophecies can have a significant impact on subordinate performance. The same effects can be generated by expectations that followers place on themselves, however. Earlier we noted the example of Israeli army trainees who performed up to instructor expectations. In a follow-up experiment, a psychologist told a random group of military recruits that they had high potential to succeed in a course. These trainees did as well as those who had been labeled as high achievers by their instructors. In this case, the trainees became their own "prophets."[46] The power of self-expectancies has been called the Galatea effect in honor of Galatea, the statue who came to life in the story of Pygmalion.

Figure 8.2 depicts the relationship between supervisor and self-expectations. In the positive Pygmalion Effect, the chain starts with the manager's expectancy (circle A) which causes him/her to allocate (arrow 1) more effective leadership behavior (circle B). These leadership behaviors then positively influence (arrow 2) the expectations that followers have of themselves, particularly their sense of self-efficacy or personal power (circle C). This increases motivation (arrow 3), leading to more effort (circle D), greater performance (arrow 4), and higher achievement (circle E). Subordinate performance then

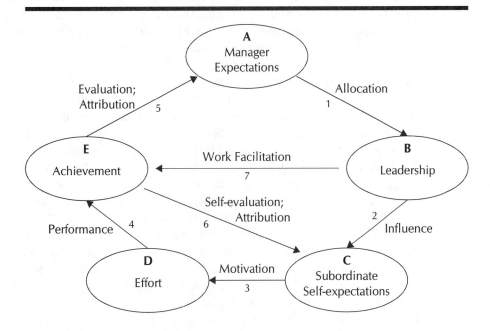

Figure 8.2
A Model of the Self-Fulfilling Prophecy at Work[47]

completes the chain because employee behavior raises or lowers the supervisor's expectations for future assignments (arrow 5). A manager with high expectations may also structure the subordinate's job to facilitate performance by eliminating obstacles, shielding him/her from outside interference (arrow 7). This leads to higher achievement without necessarily impacting follower motivation. Circles A & B and arrows 1 and 2 are eliminated in the Galatea effect. Subordinates perform better if they set high standards for themselves (circles C, D, & E). When they reach their goals, they expect to achieve even more in the future (arrow 6).

> *We usually see only the things we are looking for—so much that we sometimes see them where they are not.*
> —Eric Hoffer

Putting Pygmalion to Work

Since expectations can have a powerful influence on performance, we need to know how to put the power of Pygmalion to work. As leaders, we often aren't conscious of the expectations we have for others, or we don't realize how we communicate these expectations. We may assume that we treat all followers alike. Nevertheless, we've already noted that there are significant differences in how managers, teachers, and others treat high and low performers. Take inventory of how you communicate expectations using the four channels we discussed earlier: climate, input, output, and feedback. Analyze your nonverbal communication: do you engage in the behaviors described in box 8.5? Take a look at how assignments are distributed, how frequently some employees are given the opportunity to offer their opinions, whom you help most often, and the type of feedback you provide. Finally, identify the steps that you can take to communicate high expectations to your subordinates; try to put these behaviors into action.

In addition to taking steps as an individual leader to "harness" the power of Pygmalion, there are strategies that your organization can use to institute a positive expectation/performance cycle.[48] All supervisors should learn about the power of expectations. Eliminate organizational labels ("dumbbells," "fast trackers") that reflect low expectancies or suggest that only a few individuals are capable of outstanding performance. Because the patterns of high expectations/ high success and low expectations/low success are established early in organizational careers, try to insure that new employees work under effective managers. Often new subordinates are exposed to the worst leadership the organization has to offer—inexperienced supervisors or those who are trapped in low-level management positions because of poor past performance. Try instead to place new workers with the best leaders in the organization—those with high self-confidence who set stringent, yet realistic, goals. The positive

Box 8.5

Nonverbal Cues that Communicate Positive Expectations[49]

Nonverbal Category	Positive Behaviors
Time	Don't keep employees waiting, give adequate time, make frequent contacts.
Setting	Meet in pleasant, attractive surroundings and avoid using furniture as a barrier.
Physical Proximity	Sitting or standing close to an employee promotes warmth and decreases status differences.
Gestures	Make frequent use of open palm gestures.
Head Movements	Use head nods, but do not indicate suspicion by cocking the head or tilting it backward while the other person is speaking.
Facial Expression	Smile frequently.
Eye	Make frequent, direct eye contact.
Voice	Combine pitch, volume, quality, and rate to communicate warmth. Avoid sounding bored or disinterested.

patterns new subordinates establish under the guidance of these supervisors will pay off for both the individual and the organization for years to come. Consider moving established low performers to new situations where they can break the influence of old, negative self-fulfilling prophecies.

We can also put the power of Pygmalion to work as followers. Dov Eden argues that as subordinates we can protect ourselves from the force of negative leadership expectations by being aware of how such expectancies operate. We can also encourage supervisors to have high expectations of us by meeting and exceeding standards. In essence, this approach uses the Galatea effect to create positive expectations in leaders. Eden summarizes subordinate use of expectations this way:

> Subordinates could be taught how to behave in a manner that would evoke more effective leadership from their supervisors. This would be harnessing Pygmalion in reverse, subordinates "treating" their supervisors in such a way that they mold their supervisory behavior in accordance with subordinate desires. Similarly, awareness of interpersonal expectancy effects might help immunize certain subordinates against the debilitating effects of poor leadership from supervisors who harbor low expectations toward them.[50]

Summary

In this chapter we looked at leaders in the organizational context. We began by defining organizations as the product of communication. As organizational members communicate, they develop shared meanings that form the organization's unique way of seeing the world—an organization's culture. Cultures are made up of underlying assumptions, values, and symbols called artifacts. Since the organization is the product of symbol using, organizational leaders are really symbolic leaders who use symbols to interpret events and to help determine the direction of the group. They play an important role in the formation of organizational meaning or culture.

You can embed and transmit culture by primary and secondary mechanisms. Primary mechanisms are the most important elements for shaping culture: what you pay attention to; how you react to critical incidents; the way you spend budgeted monies; how you role model; the criteria you select for allocation of rewards; and the criteria you use for selection. Secondary mechanisms reinforce primary messages: how you mold the organizational structure; how you utilize organizational systems and procedures; your use of rites and rituals; how you design physical space to reinforce key values; the stories you tell about important events and people; and the way you communicate organizational philosophy.

Preparation is the key to leading in a crisis. The typical crisis passes through prodromal (warning), acute crisis, chronic crisis, and crisis resolution phases. Effective leaders help their organizations develop emergency tool kits to deal with crises before they happen. Crisis management tools include a vigilant problem solving style, action plans, crisis management teams, designated spokespersons, cooperative media strategies, honesty and compassion, and image insurance.

In the final section we described how expectations shape motivation and performance. The Pygmalion Effect refers to our tendency to live up to the expectations of others. Generally, the higher the expectancy, the higher the performance. Leaders communicate expectations through climate (social and emotional atmosphere), input (the number and type of assignments they give to employees), output (the number of opportunities that followers have to voice opinions), and feedback (the frequency of praise or criticism). To create a high expectations/high performance cycle, effective leaders build a warm climate, delegate important responsibilities, solicit ideas, and provide frequent positive feedback. Self-expectations (called the Galatea effect) also influence performance. Followers who set high standards for themselves are more productive.

Application Exercises

1. As a major research paper, conduct your own organizational culture analysis. Be sure to identify the following:
   - the role of the founder and current leadership
   - assumptions
   - values

- important symbols, such as myths and stories, rituals, and language
- efforts at change

2. Framing Scenario
   Imagine that you work for the public relations office of Lake Okiboji University (L.O.U.). Your college is merging with a smaller school that was just about to close its doors for good. Your frame is that the merger will help both schools. The student body at L.O.U. will grow (increasing tuition revenue), and the merger will create an attractive new branch campus. Students at the smaller college (who would have been forced to transfer) can now finish their degrees without leaving town. The presence of a stronger university will also benefit the community as a whole. In addition to offering classes and cultural and athletic events, L.O.U. will become the area's largest employer when the merger is complete. Not everyone agrees with your perspective, however. You've heard the following comments from students, faculty, donors, and others in the community:

   - L.O.U. is getting too big and impersonal
   - the leaders of L.O.U. are "empire builders"
   - the needs of students have been ignored in the rush to merge
   - L.O.U. is more interested in collecting more tuition and acquiring property than in meeting the needs of the community

   Generate some possible responses to these competing frames and then pair off with a classmate. Take turns playing the role of the public relations professional and a stakeholder who is critical of the merger. When you're done, evaluate how well each of you constructed and communicated the university's frame to the hostile stakeholder.

3. In a group, create your own list of possible crises that could strike your college or university. Then take two or three of the items on the list and develop action plans for these emergencies.

4. Evaluate the crisis preparedness of an organization of your choice. Is the organization alert to warning signs? How many crisis management tools are in place? What kind of training has been done to prepare for unexpected events?

5. Form a small group and brainstorm ways that teachers, managers, and others communicate both low and high expectations. Report your findings during class discussion.

6. Develop a strategy for communicating high expectations to someone you lead but do not like. Analyze what expectations you have for that person now and how you communicate these expectancies. Identify steps that you can take to create a positive Pygmalion Effect. Is it possible to modify your expectations? To mask your negative feelings? Write up your conclusions.

Cultural Connections: McDonald's Serves Up a Global Approach to Organizational Culture[51]

One multinational company that has been very adept at honoring local customs is McDonald's. While the signature McDonald's sandwich, the Big Mac, is served in much the same way around the globe, McDonald's also serves regional items such as kosher hamburgers in Israel, vegetable McNuggets in India, sandwiches on rye bread in Finland, Teriyaki beef in Japan, and the Kiwi Burger in New Zealand—a local favorite featuring a fried egg and beetroot. Unlike many other large global corporations, McDonald's restaurants are mostly locally owned—affording restaurant franchisees an intimate understanding of regional culture. In Muslim countries McDonald's offers prayer rooms, while in Greece it significantly alters its menu during Lent. In Asia, students often sit in McDonald's for hours—turning the restaurants into youth clubs—a practice that would not be tolerated in the United States but is encouraged by local owners in places like Hong Kong, Seoul, and Beijing.

Of course, much of the McDonald's experience is standardized around the globe—from the golden arches to the core menu items—making dining at McDonald's much the same from Atlanta to Nairobi to Warsaw. Entrepreneurs from all over the world are taught McDonald's product and service-quality principles at one of four Hamburger Universities. Yet, these local owners are given wide latitude to adapt the McDonald's concept to their native cultures. The results have been positive. Despite a recent decline in McDonald's sales in the United States, restaurants in other countries are doing well. France, of all places, is outpacing performance in most markets around the world. McDonald's has been so successful in winning over French consumers, with restaurants featuring barstools made from bicycle seats and wood-and-stone interiors reminiscent of a chalet, that the company opened a new outlet in France every six days in 2003. Further, French customers spend an average of $9 per visit compared to only $4 in the United States, even though a Big Mac costs roughly the same in Paris and New York.

McDonald's financial future will depend on its continuing ability to connect with global customers. The company serves 46 million people every day in about 30,000 restaurants in 121 countries. With sales in the core U.S. market on the decline, McDonald's will rely on its more than 15,000 restaurants in other countries to generate increasing sales while suiting the tastes of customers by acknowledging local cuisine and cultures.

Leadership on the Big Screen: *Startup.com*

Starring: Kaleil Tuzman, Tom Herman
Rating: R for language
Synopsis: This documentary chronicles the meteoric rise and fall of an Internet firm started by boyhood friends Kaleil Tuzman and Tom Herman.

They created a Web site called govWorks that enabled citizens to pay parking tickets and other fees on-line. Along the way, they raised $60 million in venture capital and hired 120 employees. Unfortunately, managing a rapidly growing company in a highly competitive marketplace causes a split between Tuzman, the CEO, and Herman, the firm's technology chief. A year and a half after it started, govWorks fails. Not all is lost, however. The two entrepreneurs manage to reestablish their friendship and now run a consulting firm that helps troubled dotcom companies.

Chapter Links: organizational symbols and artifacts, cultural transmission, founder/owners as symbolic leaders, crisis management

Nine

PUBLIC LEADERSHIP

> *A leader is a dealer in hope.*
>
> —Napoleon Bonaparte

Overview

The Power of Public Leadership

Public leadership is one of the most visible and dynamic forms of social influence. Religious and political authorities, educators, social activists, and other public leaders attempt to modify the attitudes and behaviors of mass audiences. The influence of public leaders on the course of history is a matter of conjecture. Some scholars adopt the viewpoint of Thomas Carlyle, suggesting that history is essentially the story of "heroic" leaders.[1] Others agree with Herbert Spencer that no single leader is capable of changing the evolutionary development of history.[2]

Conventional wisdom supports Carlyle's notion that powerful leaders shape history. Many public leaders have had a profound effect on human affairs. Robert Tucker, a Princeton University political scientist, argues that the atrocities committed under the leadership of Adolph Hitler in Nazi Germany and Joseph Stalin in the Soviet Union were directly attributable to the "paranoid" personalities of those two ignoble public leaders.[3]

There are many different types of public leadership. For example, historian Garry Wills identifies the following 16 categories of pubic leaders and representatives of each type, which he calls archetypes.[4]

- *Electoral* (political, democratic). Archetype: Franklin Roosevelt
- *Radical* (single-minded leadership aimed at righting wrongs and lifting the status of a particular group of people). Archetype: Harriet Tubman of the Underground Railroad
- *Reform* (moderate leadership that operates within existing laws to bring gradual improvement). Archetype: Eleanor Roosevelt
- *Diplomatic* (fosters cooperation among competing factions). Archetype: Andrew Young, former UN ambassador
- *Military* (overcomes follower's inhibitions about killing and dying to create a fighting force). Archetype: Napoleon Bonaparte
- *Charismatic* (authority focused on the person; founds a new social order). Archetype: King David
- *Business* (mobilizes a sales team to sell products). Archetype: Ross Perot
- *Traditional* (authority based on religious and other traditions that have been handed down through the generations). Archetype: Pope John XXIII
- *Constitutional* (authority based on rules agreed to by members of society). Archetype: George Washington
- *Intellectual* (takes knowledge and makes it accessible to a wide audience). Archetype: Socrates
- *Church* (forms a body of religious belief that meets the needs of the times). Archetype: Mary Baker Eddy, founder of Christian Science
- *Sports* (organizes and promotes sports activities). Archetype: Carl Stolz, founder of Little League

- *Artistic* (advances an artistic cause). Archetype: dancer Martha Graham
- *Rhetorical* (use of public speaking to inspire and sway audiences). Archetype: Martin Luther King, Jr.
- *Opportunistic* (flexible leadership that takes advantage of rapidly changing conditions to promote good or evil). Archetype: Cesare Borgia (Italian Duke)
- *Saintly* (serves a large transcendent goal; seen as highly moral or holy). Archetype: Catholic Workers Movement founder Dorothy Day

Wills provides a number of famous historical figures to illustrate his leadership categories, but it is important to note that public leadership is not limited to nationally known political, religious, or social figures. John Gardner, former Secretary of Health, Education, and Welfare in the Lyndon Johnson administration and the founder of Common Cause, used the term "dispersed leadership" to describe how leaders are found at all levels, including social agencies, universities, the professions, businesses, and minority communities.[5] Gardner believed that dispersed leadership is essential to the health of complex organizations and societies. Lower-level leaders can deal more effectively with local problems. When local leaders take initiative, they encourage higher-level leaders to do the same. At times the efforts of lower-level leaders trigger events that change society as a whole. For example, Lech Walesa (an electrician) and Vaclav Havel (a writer) mobilized public sentiment against communist regimes in Poland and the Czech Republic and were later elected as the democratic leaders of those two nations.

Every public leader, from the president of the United States (see Box 9.1) down to the president of a local chamber of commerce, must influence the attitudes and behaviors of groups within a social system. This process of influence is called opinion leadership. Since public leaders deal with large audiences, they often use different tactics than leaders in other contexts. In an interpersonal encounter, a leader can target a persuasive message to the special needs of one follower using face-to-face communication. In a public setting, a leader must address messages to what groups of people have in common—health and financial worries, political beliefs, age, ethnic heritage—through both mediated and interpersonal channels.[6] Effective public leaders shape public opinion through public relations activities, public speaking, and persuasive campaigns.

Box 9.1   Case Study

Rating the Presidents[7]

The President of the United States receives more scrutiny than any other world leader. His actions and policies are described and dissected daily in thousands of news stories, editorials, and commentaries at home and abroad. Later, after he has left office, historians compare his accomplishments to those of his predecessors.

Despite all the attention, it is not always clear what makes a "good" president. Our view of the person who occupies the office tends to be biased by our party affiliation. David Gergen, co-director of Harvard University's Center for Public Leadership, is one observer who tries to look beyond the president's label as a Republican or Democrat to draw some conclusions about the characteristics of effective presidencies. Gergen began his career as the chief of Richard Nixon's speechwriting team. He then helped Gerald Ford as a special counsel and served as Ronald Reagan's first director of communications. Gergen came to the White House one more time to serve as a counselor to Democrat Bill Clinton.

In his book *Eyewitness to Power*, Gergen provides an overview of the strengths and weaknesses of each of his presidential bosses. Among his conclusions:

- Nixon was a farsighted leader who was able to predict and shape world trends through his foreign policy. He also had a number of domestic policy successes, such as giving more power to the states, establishing the Environmental Protection Agency, and supporting desegregation efforts. Unfortunately, his "inner demons" overcame the good side of his personality.

- Gerald Ford restored integrity to the presidency but was slow to take charge of his administration and mishandled the Nixon pardon.

- Ronald Reagan had excellent instincts and intuition as a leader and used his emotional intelligence, rather than polls, to guide his policies and reactions to events. He may have been the best presidential speaker since Franklin Roosevelt. Reagan concentrated on a few themes, like shrinking the federal government, cutting taxes, and opposing Communism, but left it to subordinates to work out the details. Because he focused on the big picture, it was easier for others around him (such as Oliver North in the Iran-Contra Scandal) to engage in illegal acts and put him at the mercy of whoever was serving as his chief of staff.

- Bill Clinton is a "mass of contradictions." One of the brightest men ever to serve as president, he nonetheless became entangled in stupidities such as trying to hide his Whitewater dealings and engaging in inappropriate sexual behavior with his intern, Monica Lewinsky. Clinton succeeded in boosting the economy and passing the North America Free Trade Agreement but lost his biggest initiative—a new national health care plan. A resilient man, he was able to synthesize the ideas of many advisors and sense the mood of his audiences. However, he failed more than he should have because he never developed a clear sense of his values and character before he became president.

Gergen concludes his analysis of the four former chief executives by offering seven keys to good presidential leadership.

1. *Leadership starts from within.* Both Nixon and Clinton failed to master their characters and suffered as a result. Intelligence is not enough for a successful presidency; good judgment and courage are also required.

2. *A central, compelling purpose.* Presidents need to have clear goals, ones that are tied to the core values of the country as a whole.

3. *A capacity to persuade.* Effective presidents know how to use the medium of television to persuade the public. However, they don't dull their impact by speaking too often.

4. *An ability to work within the system.* Achieving goals depends on working effectively with the general public, Congress, the press, foreign governments, special interest groups, and cultural elites.

5. *A quick, sure start.* The first months in office are critical because the power of the presidency evaporates over time. A fast start helps a president pass his legislative program.

6. *Strong, prudent advisors.* "The best presidents are ones who surround themselves with the best advisors." George Washington, for example, got advice for his third annual message to Congress from Thomas Jefferson, James Madison, and Alexander Hamilton.

7. *Inspiring others to carry on the mission.* An effective president leaves behind followers who carry on his mission. Franklin Roosevelt left such a legacy. His successors, regardless of their party affiliation, worked to fulfill the New Deal. Even Reagan, a champion of smaller government, looked to Roosevelt as a political role model.

Discussion Questions

1. What standards do you use to evaluate the performance of a president?

2. Do you concur with Gergen's evaluation of each of the four presidents for whom he worked? Why or why not?

3. Which of the seven keys to an effective presidency is most important? Why?

4. What factors increase a president's power? Diminish it?

5. What can we learn about leadership from studying the performance of presidents past and present?

Leading Public Opinion through Public Relations

Communication professionals use the term public relations to describe how groups and organizations influence important audiences (publics) through a cluster of coordinated activities. Sparked by the growth of the mass media and the rising importance of public opinion, the practice of public relations has become a multibillion-dollar industry employing as many as 400,000 people.[8] Common public relations tasks include:

- working with media representatives
- researching public attitudes
- disseminating financial information
- lobbying government agencies
- publicizing company events
- creating internal communication programs aimed at organizational members
- supporting marketing programs

- maintaining positive relationships with community groups
- advising top management
- responding to customer concerns
- fund raising
- planning promotional events
- writing and delivering speeches and presentations
- organizing persuasive campaigns

The mix of activities that leaders use to influence public opinion will vary depending on the needs of the group. The leader of a private charity may concentrate on fundraising and attracting donors. The leader of a publicly held corporation will likely devote attention to marketing and, by law, must provide information about the company's financial condition to important news sources.

Whatever their differences, the best public relations programs share a number of elements.[9] First, performance precedes publicity in any effective public relations campaign. Attempts to shape public opinion are counterproductive if the group hasn't performed as advertised. An Internet provider that touts its reliability, for example, must deliver uninterrupted service or lose customers and be criticized in the press. Second, good public relations serves the interests of the public as well as the needs of the organization. Siemens International, Exxon Mobil, and other companies that sponsor public television programs like *Nature* and *Mystery!* boost their corporate images by providing quality programming for viewers. Third, successful public relations involves two-way communication. Such communication enables leaders to learn what audiences know and believe so that they can either modify their objectives and/or better target their clients.[10] Fourth, policy is informed by public relations. Wise leaders consider their audiences before they raise their fees, furlough employees, or build new facilities. Fifth, effective public relations programs take a proactive stance, anticipating changes (new regulations, competitors' products, demographic shifts) in the larger environment before they happen. For instance, proactive leaders are already taking steps to cope with the changes that will occur as the population ages. As baby boomers approach retirement, they may become increasingly conservative, reduce their support for local schools, put more demands on the Social Security and health care systems, buy fewer consumer goods, and so on. These changes will have a significant impact on nearly every type of institution in society, including political parties, local and federal governments, school districts, hospitals, businesses, and social service agencies.

Of all the elements that go into a public relations program, public speaking and persuasive campaigns deserve special attention because they play such a critical role in shaping public opinion. In the next two sections of the chapter, we'll take a closer look at the relationship between public address and public leadership and outline ways to use persuasive campaigns to full advantage.

Influencing Audiences through Public Address

To command a public audience is to have influence. Just by listening to a public figure we acknowledge his or her leadership.

> *Of all the talents bestowed upon men[women], none is so precious as the gift of oratory . . . Abandoned by his[her] party, betrayed by his[her] friends, stripped of his[her] offices, whoever can command this power is still formidable.*
> —Winston Churchill

A Key Leadership Tool

Public speaking is a significant tool for all types of public leaders, from student body officers to environmental activists and religious figures. As a matter of fact, it is hard to think of effective leaders who don't have at least some public speaking ability.[11] (See box 9.2 for examples of the wide variety of leaders who used public address to influence U.S. society during the past century.)

As an exercise in discovering the essential role of public address in public life and public leadership, clip out all the news stories about public speakers from an edition of your newspaper (see application exercise 3). Included below are stories that appeared in just one issue of a metropolitan daily.[12]

- The chair of the *Columbia* Accident Investigation Board announced that NASA management and safety system failures contributed to the shuttle crash.
- Citizens from around the state testified at a series of legislative hearings dealing with tax reform.
- Administration officials defended the president's decision to use a false intelligence report in his State of the Union address in briefings with reporters.
- Former commanders at the Air Force Academy testified that they hadn't punished women cadets who claimed that they had been sexually assaulted.
- William Gates Sr., father of Bill Gates, urged members of the City Club to support a larger estate tax.
- Friends and family eulogized a marine killed in Iraq.

Developing Effective Public Speeches

Because public address is such an important skill for leaders, we need to understand the key elements that go into effective public messages. Regardless

---

Box 9.2   Research Highlight

Words That Shaped a Century[13]

Words don't merely record historical events, they make history. That's the thesis of a book edited by former New Jersey Senator Robert Torricelli and Andrew Carroll, founder of the Legacy Project (a national organization dedicated to preserving historically significant correspondence and documents). *In Our Own Words* is a collection of speeches that demonstrates the power of public address in U.S. society. Citizens from all walks of life can have an impact through public communication, according to Torricelli and Carroll.

> From some more distant perspective the century might appear to be punctuated solely with the grandiloquence of Roosevelt, Kennedy, or Reagan. But the most lasting impression we hope to leave with this collection is that the power of words is not reserved for the powerful. The use of language to effect change or communicate ideas is limited only by imagination, not birthright. . . . The sound track of democracy, as it is recorded here, emanates from well beyond the Oval Office or the gilded halls of Congress. Indeed, it is all around us. (p. xxix)

The 150 speeches found in the book include messages delivered in traditional settings (policy speeches, commencement addresses, eulogies) and in other contexts (testimony before Congress, courtroom summations, radio broadcasts). The speakers come from a variety of ethnic and cultural backgrounds and include famous politicians, a drug addict, an AIDS victim, ministers, actors, judges, lawyers, poets, coaches, military officers, civil rights activists (and their opponents), and others. Here are some of the speakers and speeches that appear in the collection. This sample makes it clear that public speaking is a significant tool for all kinds of leaders, whatever their position in society.

1900–1909	Social worker Jane Addams pays tribute to George Washington on the anniversary of his birthday
	Civil rights activist W. E. B. Du Bois issues a call to arms to fellow African Americans
1910–1919	A union organizer uses a memorial service for seamstresses killed in an industrial fire to criticize society's apathy toward workers
	Suffragette Carrie Chapman Catt urges Congress to extend voting rights to women
1920–1929	Preacher Billy Sunday condemns alcohol as "God's worst enemy"
	Helen Keller endorses communism and the Russian Revolution when addressing a crowd of socialists
1930–1939	Radio broadcaster Herb Morrison reports live on the crash of the *Hindenburg* dirigible
	Baseball star Lou Gehrig, suffering from a fatal illness, thanks his fans and declares himself the "luckiest man on the face of the earth"
1940–1949	General George S. Patton extols the virtues of war to his troops
	U.S. Attorney General Robert Jackson demands guilty verdicts for Nazi war criminals at the Nuremberg trials

1950–1959	Architect Frank Lloyd Wright encourages his students to create buildings that benefit humankind
	Environmentalist Rachel Carson reflects on the beauty of the Earth and its impact on the human spirit before a women's group
1960–1969	George Wallace, in his inaugural address as governor of Alabama, declares that his state will practice segregation forever
	Robert F. Kennedy calms an angry black crowd after telling them that Martin Luther King, Jr. had just been assassinated
1970–1979	An inmate reads prisoner demands during a hostage crisis at Attica Prison in New York state
	A soldier describes to army investigators the atrocities committed at the Vietnamese town of My Lai
1980–1989	Sixteen-year-old AIDS victim Ryan White describes to a presidential commission the hatred directed at him because of his illness
	President Ronald Reagan honors the memory of the astronauts killed in the *Challenger* explosion
1990–1999	Supreme Court nominee Clarence Thomas denies charges of sexual harassment during confirmation hearings
	Singer Barbra Streisand defends the role of the arts in society to an audience of Harvard students

of where you speak—whether in the classroom, at a political rally, or in a business meeting—you will discover that the delivery of an effective public speech enhances audience perceptions of your personal power and leadership potential. The effectiveness of a public speech depends on six primary elements: pre-speech planning, organization, language, rehearsal, delivery, and responding to questions.

Pre-speech Planning

Planning is essential in the development of successful public messages. The following factors should be considered before delivering a public presentation. In particular, think carefully about possible modes of delivery and audience analysis.

The principal modes of delivery are *impromptu*, *extemporaneous*, and *manuscript*. Impromptu speeches are delivered "off the cuff," with little advance preparation. Situations that might require an impromptu presentation include responding to an unexpected disaster or crisis, accepting an award, or participating in a meeting. One of President George W. Bush's most memorable speeches was an impromptu message delivered to rescue workers through a bullhorn at Ground Zero in New York City. When speaking in the impromptu mode, try to maintain a clear focus or theme. Always avoid long, rambling impromptu messages.

Speaking from a prepared outline or set of notes is known as extemporaneous speech. This is the most common mode of public address. Extemporaneous speech gives you an opportunity to develop a clear presentational purpose or goal and adequate reasoning and support. The extemporaneous speech also offers you freedom in the construction of the message. Since your notes consist of an outline or a few key phrases, you have greater flexibility.

Working from a manuscript—a written transcript of the speech—allows for the greatest control of subject matter. Many political leaders use the manuscript mode of delivery. Manuscripts are most effective when the content of the message must be very precise, such as when the president announces the details of a treaty or when law enforcement officials reveal the results of an investigation. Because the manuscript mode does not allow a speaker to be spontaneous, it is advisable to use a teleprompter or similar mechanical device so that eye contact with the audience is not disrupted.

Regardless of the delivery style chosen, it is essential that you have an understanding of the attitudes and expertise of your listeners. Although size may vary from a small group to a worldwide audience, an understanding of the needs, aspirations, experiences, and intellectual abilities of listeners helps to create a more effective message. For example, a political candidate addressing a group of union employees will be more effective if he or she is aware of the issues that have the greatest impact on union members. A well-prepared speaker will seek information about the audience from a variety of sources. The speaker might research the previous positions of audience members; observe current actions; or question, interview, or survey selected audience members as a means of uncovering information.

Organization

The logic and structure of the ideas presented within a public speech are critical. Successful presentations are organized around a central theme with supporting points. Developing a thesis, arranging ideas, and linking those primary points are the three most important factors in organizing a public speech.

The purpose or objective of a speech is known as the thesis. In general terms, the thesis identifies your goals (to inform, persuade, entertain, etc.). More specifically, the thesis outlines exactly what you hope to achieve in your presentation. A thesis statement is prepared in the initial stages of speech organization and usually consists of one declarative sentence. The thesis statement itself should be as specific as possible in identifying the feelings, knowledge, or understanding you wish to convey to your audience. For example, "My speech is on John F. Kennedy," is ineffective. This thesis provides no explanation regarding the specific purpose of the speech. A better thesis would be, "John F. Kennedy was one of the most effective public communicators of the twentieth century." This thesis statement provides a detailed description of the argument you wish to make.

As a leader, you may be called upon to frame your organization's vision through a public presentation (see chapter 8 for more information on organizational framing). Your goal in this type of speech should be to generate enthusiasm and commitment for the vision, not merely to explain it. You're more likely to inspire audiences if you can tie the vision to a meaningful cause—serving customers, helping others, addressing injustices, etc. Box 9.3 provides several examples of leaders who were able to place the purpose of their organizations into broader, more meaningful contexts.

> *Many leaders, in all fields, are too quick to patronize their public, assuming that people are selfish, dull, or uninterested in global or universal questions. Quite the contrary, the public is eager to hear, eager to engage, and eager to act when called to contribute to just causes that are larger than themselves.*
>
> —Terry Pearce

Box 9.3

Inspirational Speech Samples[14]

We're an army going out to set other men free. . . . Here you can be *something*. Here's a place to build a home. It isn't the land—there's always more land. It's the idea that we all have value, you and me, we're worth something more than the dirt. . . . What we're fighting for, in the end, is each other.

Joshua Lawrence Chamberlain, 2nd Maine regiment, prior to the Battle of the Little Round Top at Gettysburg

My expectations for Lotus are very simple. I want you to win in the marketplace. I want you to beat our competitors. I want you to grow fast. I want you to execute a set of strategies brilliantly to deliver what we all want, which is leadership for our customers.

IBM Chief Executive Louis Gerstner speaking to the employees of the newly-acquired Lotus Corporation

One of my largest wishes is that we build NEXT from the heart. And the people that are thinking about coming to work for us, or buying our products or who want to sell us things feel that we're doing this because we have a passion about it. We're doing this because we really care about the higher educational process, not because we want to make a buck, not because, you know, we just want to do it.

Steven Jobs' comments to the staff of the NEXT computer company

Now if this blind pursuit of licentious trade continues, political instability will return big time. The rise of fascism, brutal nationalism, and the ethnic racism we see on continent after continent are not an accident.

Demagogues *prey* on insecurity and fear; they breed in the darkness of poverty and desolation. If we do not build an economic growth that helps sustain communities, cultures, and families, the consequences will be severe. Even if our politics somehow survives, our globe will not.

Body Shop President Anita Roddick, advocating that the International Chamber of Commerce become more socially responsible

Once the thesis has been developed, arrange the main points you have selected to support your thesis. The number of main points should be kept to a minimum, and each main point should be supported with statistics, examples, illustrations, anecdotes, or other forms of evidence. Main points can be arranged in chronological order (from the earliest to the most recent event), spatial order (by some physical or geographical relationship), in order of size or impact (from largest to smallest or vice-versa), or, when no other logical pattern seems appropriate, in what is known as a topical arrangement pattern. Topical arrangement involves creating an organizational pattern that fits the ideas presented. For example, a persuasive speech describing the benefits of a particular university would be difficult to organize chronologically, spatially, or in relation to size. Developing a series of arguments strung together in a topical pattern would be more effective. Topics could include tuition and housing costs, location, and the quality of the faculty. (Additional organizational patterns more appropriate to other cultures can be found in the Cultural Connections section at the end of the chapter.)

Statements that link ideas together are known as transitions. Be careful to include transitions in your presentation so that audience members can follow your message. Phrases such as, "now that we have discussed the affordable housing at State University, let's focus on the desirability of the surrounding area," help to shift an audience's attention from one main point to the next.

Language

The effective use of language is the key to producing memorable and moving public speeches. We remember Martin Luther King, Jr.'s "I Have a Dream" speech as one of the greatest of the twentieth century primarily because of the way King used words to create dramatic images. King spoke of coming to cash in on the promise of equal rights at the "bank of justice" and urged followers to refuse to drink from "the cup of bitterness and hatred." At one point he declared his hope that his children would "one day live in a nation where they will not be judged by the color of their skin, but by the content of their character." Successful speakers follow the example set by King by using language that is clear, vivid, and appropriate.

The best rule of thumb in a presentation is to use clear, specific, understandable language. Technical and complicated words should be used sparingly, particularly when dealing with mass audiences. Further, avoid the use of jargon and euphemisms. Government officials often try to create pleasant descriptions for unpleasant events, referring to missiles as "peace-keepers," taxes as "revenue enhancements," and death as "exceeding survivability."[15] This type of "doublespeak" confuses and distracts audience members. The more you complicate your message by using technical or convoluted language, the more likely it is that your message will be misunderstood.

Clear language does not have to be dull. Public speeches should be descriptive and distinctive. The use of affect and imagery enliven public address. Affective language sparks emotion, while imagery creates visual connections for the audience. Franklin Roosevelt's Declaration of War following the Pearl Harbor attack of 1941 began as follows:

> Yesterday, December 7, 1941—a date which will live in infamy—the United States was suddenly and deliberately attacked by naval and air forces of the Empire of Japan.

Roosevelt's words expressed the shock of a nation. To this day, many people look at the calendar on December 7th and are transported back to the attack. The mark of effective public speakers is their ability to create vivid, stirring representations for audiences. While a picture may paint a thousand words, it is equally true that a gifted speaker can fashion a word into a thousand pictures.

Avoid using language that might offend members of the audience. The use of inappropriate, profane, or obscene language can irreparably damage a speaker's image. In 2002, Mississippi Senator Trent Lott offended many and lost his position as majority leader of the Senate when he claimed that the United States might have been better off if the racist segregation policies outlined in the 1948 presidential campaign of Strom Thurmond had been adopted.

Some types of humor lower a speaker's credibility. One type of humor that can be detrimental involves making oneself or others the brunt of a joke. Disparagement focusing on personal shortcomings (such as height, weight, complexion, or social skills) does not enhance a speaker's image. Speakers who belittle themselves are rated as less competent, less expert, and less likable, while speakers who belittle others are rated as having lower character.[16] Other research suggests that a speaker's use of milder forms of disparaging humor aimed at one's occupation or profession are not as harmful.[17] Most evidence suggests that public speakers should generally avoid using disparaging humor.

Rehearsal

Practicing gives you the opportunity to simulate a public presentation. This experience helps you refine content and increase your confidence level. Just as a dress rehearsal makes a marriage ceremony or theater production less confusing and stressful, a speech rehearsal helps polish a public presentation.

The most important thing to remember when rehearsing a speech is that you must practice out loud. We think more rapidly than we speak. As a result, internal thought and external speech operate differently. Thought is characterized by condensed grammar and syntax, which makes the structure of internal thought incomplete. Our thoughts are composed of fleeting images and words. External speech, on the other hand, is grammatically and syntactically complete. Speech consists of fully constructed messages that follow a distinctive organizational pattern. Since presentations are delivered in external speech, the external form of communication must be used during rehearsal. Rehearsing only in internal thought (just thinking about what you will say without saying it out loud) may contribute to the same feelings of anxiety that are associated with inadequate speech preparation.[18]

Delivery

Delivery refers to the physical aspects of speechmaking. A speaker's delivery should not be awkward or distracting. The delivery of a message is most effective when it appears natural. Physical appearance, gestures, movement, eye contact, and voice quality all directly affect the delivery of public messages.

Public speakers should be appropriately groomed and clothed. Audience expectations regarding hygiene and dress vary from one situation to another. For example, it is usually acceptable to deliver a classroom presentation dressed in jeans and a t-shirt, but this casual attire would not be acceptable for a speech to a group of civic leaders. In general, it is best to tailor your appearance to the situation, region, or culture in which you will be speaking. Your audience analysis should help you decide what will be acceptable.

Gestures occur naturally in conversation, and that tendency should be followed in public address. When did you last worry about gesturing while conversing casually with your best friend? Unfortunately, many speakers are uncomfortable about body language during their presentations. Instead of allowing the natural tendency to gesture to operate, they plan where to insert gestures in the speech. As a result, their movements are awkward and distracting. Pay attention to your natural pattern of gestures. When rehearsing, include natural gestures in your presentation. You'll then be more relaxed and natural when you make your appearance in front of an audience.

Movement can be used to heighten interest in a speech. Movement that minimizes physical distance between speaker and audience also creates a sense of psychological closeness that communication scholars call "immediacy." Audiences are more receptive to speakers who signal warmth, liking, and friendliness through movement and other nonverbal behaviors. You can assess how well you communicate a sense of immediacy as a public speaker by completing the self-assessment exercise in box 9.4.

In Western culture, looking others in the eyes is a sign of respect and honesty. Effective public speakers maintain eye contact with audience members. Staring at your notes or letting your eyes dart around leads to the perception that you are not trustworthy. Use your notes sparingly. Maintain focus for a few seconds on individuals seated in one section of the audience and then sustain eye contact with another section. Avoid monotonous or strident tones. An expressive voice conveys emotion and interest without being harsh. Most unpleasant vocal patterns can be improved with training and practice.

Responding to Questions

The delivery of a speech is often followed by a question and answer session. Responding to questions can be stressful; speakers must "think on their feet." The advantage of taking questions is that it provides immediate feedback about how the audience reacted to the presentation and gives the speaker an opportunity to clarify misunderstandings. Effective responses can help a leader establish a stronger bond with the audience.[19]

Box 9.4   Self-Assessment

Nonverbal Immediacy Scale[20]

Instructions

Originally developed to assess the nonverbal immediacy of teachers, this scale has been revised to reveal nonverbal immediacy in all types of public presentations. For each item, indicate how likely you would be to engage in the nonverbal behaviors while speaking before a large group. Use the following scale:

5-extremely likely   4-likely   3-maybe/unsure   2-unlikely   1-extremely unlikely

_____ 1. I would sit behind a table or desk while speaking.

_____ 2. I would use a lot of purposeful gestures while talking to the group.

_____ 3. I would use a monotone/dull voice when speaking.

_____ 4. I would look directly at my audience while presenting.

_____ 5. I would smile at the group while talking.

_____ 6. My entire body would feel tense and rigid while giving my speech.

_____ 7. I would approach or stand beside individual audience members.

_____ 8. I would move around the room while speaking.

_____ 9. I would avoid looking at individual audience members during my speech.

_____ 10. I would look at my notes frequently during my presentation.

_____ 11. I would stand behind a podium or desk while giving my speech.

_____ 12. I would have a very relaxed body position while talking to the group.

_____ 13. I would smile at individual members in the audience.

_____ 14. I would use a variety of vocal expressions while talking.

_____ 15. I would engage in a lot of nervous gestures or body movements, such as shuffling my note cards or switching my weight from one foot to the next.

Calculating Your Score

Step 1: Total your responses to items 1, 3, 6, 9, 10, 11, and 15 _____.
Step 2: Total your responses to items 2, 4, 5, 7, 8, 12, 13, and 14 _____.
Complete the following formula:

42 minus total from step 1 = _____

Plus total from step 2 = _____

YOUR TOTAL SCORE _____

Interpreting Your Score

Your score should fall between 15 and 75. The average or midpoint is around 45. If your score totals 50 or higher, you are high in nonverbal immediacy and are likely to be seen as approachable and likable. If your score falls below 40, you might want to learn and practice the specific immediacy behaviors reflected in the items listed in step 2. Nonimmediate speakers are perceived as cold and distant and are more likely to bore their audiences.

Try to anticipate possible questions when preparing a speech and learn to distinguish between types of questions. Some questions are really statements of support that elaborate on points you made in your speech. They're easy to handle—just agree when the response is appropriate to what you've said. Other questions ask for additional information and clarification and should be acknowledged and answered as directly as possible. The most difficult queries are disputes or challenges offered in the form of a question. In these cases, listen to the questioner's words, tone of voice, and body language to determine her/his true intent. The question "When will we get our next raise?" might really be a criticism of the fact that employees in some departments got pay increases while members of other departments did not. Try to address both the stated question and the speaker's intention, acknowledging the feelings behind the dispute or challenge. For example, in response to the question about raises, a corporate executive might answer:

> Linda, you've asked about upcoming raises but I also sense that you have some frustration about unequal pay. Let me speak to both your question and other concerns you might have. It's true that union employees recently received pay increases even though we instituted a hiring and wage freeze in January. We were legally obligated to pay these increases to union employees under the previous contract. However, like many of you, I don't think that's fair. Now that the freeze has been lifted, the next round of raises is scheduled for July 1. At that time we will give top priority to increasing the salaries of nonunion staff.

Persuasive Campaigns

As we've seen, public speaking is an important tool for public leaders. However, much like a single television advertisement or a single newspaper editorial, a single speech does not always change the attitudes or behaviors of large numbers of people. For this reason, public leaders frequently put together persuasive campaigns in order to influence public opinion.

Characteristics of Successful Campaigns

Persuasion expert Herbert Simons defines campaigns as "organized, sustained attempts at influencing groups of people . . . through a series of messages."[21] Campaigns use both the mass media and interpersonal communication networks to achieve their goals. There are five types of persuasive campaigns: (1) product/commercial (selling goods and services), (2) political (electing candidates to office), (3) issue (changing or implementing government or corporate policy), (4) image (building positive images for individuals or organizations), and (5) social action (influencing attitudes and behaviors for the public good).[22]

Not all campaigns are successful. The failure of many heavily promoted Hollywood movies and Web sites (Pets.com, homegrocer.com, eToys.com, Webvan) demonstrates how even well planned and well-financed commercial campaigns can go astray. Other types of campaigns often suffer a similar fate. For example, the popular DARE (Drug Abuse Resistance Education) program for elementary school children has had no measurable long-term effect on drug usage. Teens who participated in campaign activities when they were younger are just as likely to take illegal substances as those who didn't go through the program.[23]

While many campaigns fail, others meet their objectives. One of the longest running and most successful campaigns is the Smokey Bear fire prevention program. Since the campaign began in 1942, the number of acres lost to wildfires has dropped from 30 million to five million a year. One survey found that 98% of the population knows who Smokey is and Smokey Bear headquarters has its own zip code to handle the volume of cards and letters requesting fire prevention kits.[24] Another successful campaign encourages the use of designated drivers. The number of drinkers who choose designated drivers has risen dramatically since the program began in 1988. The belief that drivers should not drink has now become a widely accepted norm in society.[25]

Why do some campaigns have a significant impact on public attitudes and behavior while others have little influence at all? In order to answer this question, Everett Rogers and Douglas Storey surveyed forty years of campaign research.[26] Rogers and Storey identified the following as characteristics of successful campaigns. Subsequent research has confirmed their conclusions.[27]

Pretest messages and identify market segments. Organizers of effective campaigns rely on research to help them shape their messages. Doing market research prior to a campaign reveals what audiences currently believe, if receivers understand campaign advertisements and themes, and which messages are best suited to particular segments of the market. Soul City, a nonprofit health organization in South Africa, is one group that uses research to identify issues and audiences. The group's leaders conduct focus groups, interviews, and pretesting to identify important national health concerns (HIV prevention, alcohol abuse, domestic violence) and public attitudes about these issues. The mix of campaign media activities and materials is then adapted to target audiences. Television reaches urban populations while radio programs are directed at rural listeners. Education packets for youths consist of a comic book and set of workbooks. Education packets for adults include a health booklet, audiotapes, and *Soul City* posters.[28]

Expose a large segment of the audience to clear campaign messages. Message exposure is a prerequisite for campaign success. Audiences must be aware of campaign messages before they can act on the information contained in those messages. Similarly, in most cases it is important that messages be clear. Consider the AT&T "M Life" campaign, for example. The company sparked public curiosity through a series of ads that introduced the name M Life but didn't identify the product. Later advertisements revealed that M Life is AT&T's name for its mobile wireless service. However, the campaign has not clearly identified the unique features of the service.

Use the most accessible media for target groups. Successful campaigns utilize those media that are most accessible to audiences. In some countries few people have access to either television or newspapers. In these situations, campaign organizers must rely on radio and other media. The timing of messages is also critical. Effective campaigns reach audiences when they are most receptive. For example, when the Olympic Games are in session (and public interest in the Olympics is at its peak), corporations use media spots to trumpet the fact that their products are endorsed by the U.S. Olympic Committee.

Use the media to raise awareness. The media are most effective when they are used to provide important information, stimulate interpersonal conversations, and recruit additional people to participate in the campaign. Media messages raise awareness and get people talking about the merits of politicians, products, organizations, and causes. In addition, many people volunteer for food drives, fundraisers, clean-up campaigns, and other projects after hearing about them through advertisements or news stories.

Rely on interpersonal communication, particularly communication between people of similar social backgrounds, to lead to and reinforce behavior change. Interpersonal communication networks play a particularly important role in persuasive campaigns designed to change people's behaviors. Behavioral change is more likely when the desired behaviors are modeled by others. Rogers and Storey note, "While the mass media may be effective in disseminating information, interpersonal channels are more influential in motivating people to act on that information."[29] The national crime prevention campaign that urges listeners and viewers to "Take a Bite Out of Crime" is one example of how media and interpersonal channels can complement each other. Although many people learn about crime prevention behaviors through the campaign's media spots, listeners often put these behaviors into action only after they become involved in neighborhood watch groups. The groups reinforce the message and demonstrate that crime prevention activities are socially acceptable.

Certain individuals—called opinion leaders—play a major role in convincing others to adopt new products, techniques, or ideas. Enlisting the participation of these individuals greatly increases a campaign's chances for success. Opinion leaders share four characteristics: (1) they have greater exposure to the media, outside change agents, and other key external communication sources; (2) they participate in a variety of social networks and rapidly spread new ideas to others; (3) they generally have higher socioeconomic status than opinion followers; and (4) they are more innovative when the norms of the social system favor change.[30] (Turn to Box 9.5 for more information on how a few individuals can bring about major social changes.)

Use high credibility sources. Successful campaigns use highly credible representatives. (Refer to chapter 6 for more information on the dimensions of credibility.) For instance, many people criticized the Nestlé company for taking advantage of the credibility of medical personnel by using women dressed as nurses to promote the use of infant formula in Third World countries. Infant formula is extremely expensive in developing areas and is unsafe when mixed with dirty water. Audiences keep the motives of sources in mind when evaluating their credibility. An actor who promotes AIDS prevention as a public service is generally seen as more credible than an actor paid to promote a product.

Box 9.5   Research Highlight

Starting Positive Epidemics[31]

New Yorker staff writer Malcolm Gladwell believes that products, behaviors, and ideas are contagious and spread like viruses. In his book *The Tipping Point,* he argues that social trends ranging from clothing styles to crime rates are transmitted in the same way as the flu or AIDS. The "tipping point" refers to the critical moment when a social epidemic becomes highly contagious, bringing rapid change. For example, 1998 marked a tipping point for cellular phones in the United States. By that year mobile phones had become cheap and easy to use. The number of cellular users then exploded. Gladwell offers three rules of social epidemics.

The first is the "law of the few" which describes the types of people who play a key role in spreading trends. *Connectors* know lots of people from a variety of social groups and spread information about ideas through their social networks. *Mavens* are eager to share information to help others; they are experts on topics like supermarket prices, movies, and cars. *Salespeople* actively persuade those who are reluctant to buy a new product or adopt a new behavior.

The second rule is "the stickiness factor." For information to have an impact, it must "stick" or be retained. The producers of *Sesame Street* (who were out to create a literacy epidemic among 3–5 year-olds) used this principle to make their show memorable to children. They made sure that human actors always appeared on screen with Muppet characters after they discovered that young viewers tuned out when the adults were shown on their own.

The third law is the power of context. Environment plays a critical role in shaping human activity, and small modifications in the setting can bring about significant behavioral changes. For instance, the rapid drop in the New York City crime rate between 1992 and 1997 is attributed in large part to crackdowns on such minor offenses as graffiti tagging and cheating on subway fares.

The fact that a few people introducing small changes can produce major effects is good news for leaders who want to start positive epidemics like lowering teen pregnancy or school drop-out rates. Gladwell introduces San Diego nurse Georgia Sadler as one example of someone who is making a significant difference through a series of small steps. Sadler wanted to increase awareness of breast cancer and diabetes in her African-American community. When she didn't make much progress contacting church groups, she took her message to area beauty salons. Sadler trained stylists in how to present breast cancer information through stories and kept supplying new anecdotes for them to share. Information was written in large print on laminated sheets so stylists could refer to it when needed. Follow-up evaluation revealed that women who went to the salons were having more mammograms and diabetes testing.

Direct messages at the individual needs of the audience. Audiences are most influenced by messages aimed directly at personal needs. Effective political campaigns emphasize how the candidate will help the voter by lowering taxes, providing more jobs, building better roads, lowering crime, and so on. Campaigns for popular products link the purchase of the item with a specific need felt by the audience. (i.e. smoke detectors for safety, cosmetics to enhance physical appearance, frozen dinners for convenience).

Emphasize positive rewards rather than prevention. Many campaigns (such as the one urging us to wear our seat belts) try to help audiences avoid future, unwanted events. These campaigns often fall short of their goals because the consequences of noncompliance are uncertain. In the case of safety belts, many of us drive without them because we believe that we will never be in a serious auto accident. Effective campaigns emphasize the immediate positive rewards that come from adopting a value, belief, or behavior. Campaign planners may use our fear of suffering a heart attack to encourage us to start a regular exercise program. However, we are more likely to adopt a regular exercise routine if campaign messages emphasize weight loss, stress reduction, and other *immediate* benefits.

Campaign Stages

Even with an understanding of the factors that contribute to successful campaigns, organizing a campaign can seem like an overwhelming task. Successful campaigns involve research, the careful construction of messages, and effective use of both the media and interpersonal networks. To make the campaign process more manageable, Gary Woodward and Robert Denton suggest that you follow the six steps described in box 9.6.[32]

Situation analysis is the foundation for the rest of the campaign. In this first stage, begin by identifying key audience characteristics. These include: (1) demographic variables (age, education, occupation), (2) geographic variables (urban vs. suburban, West vs. Midwest), and (3) psychographic variables (lifestyle, interests, activities and opinions). If your campaign is product oriented, then size up the competition and determine attitudes toward your product. Your research can be both informal and formal. Informal research is the process of gathering information from libraries, personal contacts, industry publications, and other sources. Formal research is based on the statistical analysis of data collected through surveys and interviews.

Once the preliminary research is complete, goals should be set in stage 2. *Objectives* can center on increased awareness, attitude change, or changes in behavior. Many campaigns fail because they are too ambitious. When you seek significant behavioral change, set more modest goals. For example, you might be able to convince a large percentage of your audience that recycling reduces our dependence on landfills. Yet, only a portion of those who believe in recycling will actually participate in recycling programs.

Box 9.6

Campaign Implementation Overview[33]

Stage	Components
1. Situation analysis	target audience product/issue/idea competition or opponent
2. Objectives	mission goals outcomes
3. Strategies	messages media presentation activities
4. Budget	labor material media talent production
5. Implementation	timing follow-up
6. Evaluation	what people say what people think what people do

---

The third stage of the campaign is concerned with *strategies* to get things done. Structure messages to appeal to market segments, determine how you will use the media to reach audiences, and plan presentational activities like press conferences, rallies, and conventions.

In the fourth stage, prepare a *budget*. Financial resources will frequently determine the scope of your campaign. Labor, material, media, talent, and production costs must all be taken into consideration.

Implementation is the fifth stage. The campaign goes into action during this stage. Monitor your progress and determine the timing of messages through ongoing research. Poll voters to test attitudes; check and recheck reactions. By periodically gathering data, you will know if your campaign is on target or if you should modify your campaign messages and strategies.

The *evaluation* stage completes the ongoing campaign and lays the groundwork for future projects. In order to determine if you reached the campaign objectives you set earlier, you will need to survey target audiences, measure sales, and determine if favorable attitudes translate into desired action. What you learn from the successes and failures of one persuasive campaign can serve as the foundation for the next.

Collaborative Leadership

In a pluralistic society such as ours, encouraging groups to cooperate on behalf of the common good is often a public leader's greatest challenge.[34] Attempts to restore salmon and steelhead runs in the Pacific Northwest are a case in point. Billions of dollars have been spent to bolster these fish populations, but their numbers continue to decline due to dams, overgrazing, urban pollution, logging, irrigation, fishing, and other factors. Reversing this trend will take the cooperative efforts of biologists, government agencies, power companies, ranchers, barge owners, water districts, tribes, city councils, environmental activists, governors, and congressional representatives. Unless these groups look beyond their individual interests and work together, many species (which used to return to the region's rivers by the millions) will become extinct.

Fortunately, collaborative efforts can succeed if led effectively. Collaborative leaders focus on the process of decision making rather than on any particular outcome.[35] They believe that diverse groups will generate reasonable solutions if interested parties work together in constructive ways. These leaders have little formal power but function as "first among equals" who encourage their peers to take ownership in the collaborative process. They convene the discussions, help the group reach agreement, and work with other participants to implement the solution.

David Chrislip and Carl Larson conducted a comprehensive investigation of successful collaborative public leadership efforts in Phoenix, Denver, Baltimore, and other cities. Each produced concrete, tangible results and was hailed as a success by those involved. The collaborative efforts brought together diverse members of communities with varied (and often contradictory) needs and interests to tackle problems such as homelessness, decaying city infrastructure, poor school performance, and racism. Based on their observations, Chrislip and Larson identified ten factors necessary for successful collaboration.[36]

- *Good timing and a clear need.* Stakeholders must be ready to act in response to a clear need. Whether the issue is roads in need of repair or programs for pregnant teens, collaborative leadership will not be successful until people in a community feel it is time to address a problem.

- *Strong stakeholder groups.* The ability to voice public opinion accurately is an important ingredient in successful collaboration. Strong stakeholder groups can represent their constituents effectively. Successful collaborative leadership depends on strong stakeholder groups who are able to voice public opinion accurately. When a group such as the chamber of commerce speaks and acts credibly for its members, collaborative leadership is more likely to succeed.

- *Broad-based involvement.* Collaborative efforts are most successful when participants from different segments of the community are involved. Successful collaborative initiatives often involve people from government, business, education, and other key community groups.

- *Credible and open process.* At the beginning of almost any broad-based collaborative process there is suspicion and cynicism. Participants in successful collaborative efforts work to create an atmosphere of trust and openness. This is accomplished by actions such as treating all stakeholder groups fairly and consistently, establishing ground rules for engaging in civilized disagreement, and working to de-politicize the decision-making process.[37]

- *Participation of high level, visible community leaders.* The support of leaders such as mayors, city council members, CEOs of local organizations, and school administrators gives visibility to collaborative goals. Although these leaders need not always be directly involved in every step of the process, their commitment to the collaborative venture is critical.

- *Formal support.* Support from established authorities such as government agencies, city councils, and school boards is critical to the success of community-based collaborative decision making. For example, the mayor of Phoenix, Paul Johnson, assigned each member of the Phoenix city council the task of implementing a recommendation made by a citizen task force. The task force had no power to put its recommendations into action, and Mayor Johnson realized that support from the formal power structure was a mandatory ingredient.

- *Ability to overcome mistrust and skepticism.* Many participants begin the collaborative process with little hope that substantive progress can be made. They worry that certain stakeholders will behave poorly or that the collaborative effort will be derailed. Successful collaborative groups overcome their mistrust and skepticism, particularly in the early stages of their deliberation.

- *Strong leadership of the process.* As we noted earlier, successful collaborative efforts are characterized by strong leadership of the process. This leadership is exhibited in many ways: keeping stakeholders at the table through periods of frustration and skepticism, helping stakeholders negotiate difficult points, and enforcing group ground rules.

- *Celebration of ongoing achievement.* Whether it involves reaching an interim goal, overcoming a difficult obstacle, attracting new resources, or bridging a gap with a reluctant stakeholder, highly effective collaborative groups acknowledge their successes. From the use of pizza parties to formal award ceremonies, small signs of progress are celebrated.

- *Shift to broader concerns.* As collaborative efforts progress, successful groups focus less on narrow issues and more on the broader interests of the community.

Chrislip and Larson emphasize that collaborative leadership both produces tangible results and creates effective problem-solving mechanisms for the future. The process of collaboration changes the way organizations and communities function. Thus, collaborative leadership is effective in dealing with current problems and in setting the stage for addressing future issues. It helps create an energized constituency primed to address the problems of an organization or community.

Summary

In this chapter we examined the nature of public leadership. Public leaders influence the attitudes and behaviors of large audiences at all levels of society. These leaders use public relations activities, public address, and persuasive campaigns to shape public opinion. Outstanding public relations programs share a number of elements. They recognize the necessity of effective performance before any publicity campaign. They also serve the interests of the public, involve two-way communication, shape policy, and take a proactive stance.

Effective public speeches are based on careful pre-speech planning (deciding on a mode of delivery, audience analysis); clear organization (developing a thesis statement, arranging and linking ideas); clear, vivid, and appropriate language; extensive rehearsal; delivery that appears natural and creates a sense of immediacy; and skillful anticipation and response to questions after the presentation is over.

A persuasive campaign consists of a series of messages aimed at changing the beliefs and behaviors of others. To have a significant impact, campaigns must pretest their messages and identify market segments; expose a large portion of the audience to campaign messages; use the media most accessible to target groups; rely on the media to raise awareness; utilize interpersonal communication to bring about behavior change; employ high credibility sources; direct messages at individual needs; and emphasize positive rewards rather than prevention. There are six steps or stages to any type of persuasive campaign: (1) situation analysis, (2) objectives, (3) strategies, (4) budget, (5) implementation, and (6) evaluation.

We ended the chapter with a discussion of collaborative leadership. Collaborative leaders focus on the decision-making process instead of promoting a particular solution. They have little formal power but get discussions started, help the group reach agreement, and work with other participants to implement the solution. Ten necessary conditions for successful collaborative public ventures include: (1) good timing and a clear need; (2) strong stakeholder groups; (3) broad-based involvement; (4) a credible and open process; (5) committed, high-level, visible community leaders; (6) formal support; (7) an ability to overcome mistrust and skepticism; (8) strong leadership of the process; (9) celebration of ongoing achievement; and (10) shift to broader concerns.

Application Exercises

1. Consider the impact of public leaders on history. Do you agree with Carlyle's perspective that history is shaped by powerful leaders or with Spencer's claim that history develops according to patterns that cannot be altered by a single individual? Think of some examples that support your position.

2. In a small group, identify emerging issues or trends that will likely have an impact on your college or another organization of your choice. How should the organization respond in order to lead public opinion?

3. Locate all the articles related to public speaking from one newspaper. Classify the news stories as local, regional, national, or international. What conclusions can you draw about the relationship between public address and public leadership based on your sample?

4. Use the techniques discussed in the chapter to prepare a speech. Concentrate on pre-speech preparation, organization, language, rehearsal, and delivery. After the speech, evaluate your performance and record ways that you can make your future presentations more effective. As an alternative assignment, evaluate a speech delivered by someone else.

5. In a major research paper describe the public speaking techniques of a well-known leader (e.g., Abraham Lincoln, Winston Churchill, Margaret Thatcher, Martin Luther King, Jr., or Eleanor Roosevelt). What made this individual an effective speaker? What can we learn about public address from this person?

6. Analyze a recent persuasive campaign based on the characteristics of successful campaigns presented in the chapter. Based on these elements, why did the campaign succeed or fail? Write up your findings.

7. Analyze the effectiveness of a collaborative public venture using Chrislip and Larson's ten characteristics of successful collaborative groups. Report your findings in a class presentation.

Cultural Connections: Configural Speech Organization Patterns[38]

The organizational patterns we outlined in this chapter are found in most public speaking texts published in the United States. All of these structures arrange ideas according to a linear design. In the linear approach, a presenter previews, presents one idea at a time, relies heavily on facts and data, uses phrases to guide listeners between major points, and then summarizes. Linear organizational structures are best suited for Euro-American speakers and audiences who reason in a systematic, step-by-step fashion. Configural patterns may work better in Native American, Latino, and Eastern cultures. In a speech organized according to a configural pattern, the presenter does not preview or spell out major points one by one but subtly implies or suggests them. She or he may approach the subject from a variety of angles, leaving it to audience members to create their own meanings. Configural organizational patterns include:

- *narrative.* The entire speech is presented as a story with main characters and plot development. May begin with a statement like "Once upon a time."
- *web.* Several ideas emanate from the core or central point. The speaker begins at the core, explores one of the radiating ideas, returns to the core again, introduces another idea, and so on.
- *problem-no solution.* The problem (suicide, crime rate, terrorism) is examined in detail but no solution is offered. Instead, the presenter may encourage the audience to come up with a solution.
- *multiple perspective.* One topic is analyzed from a variety of perspectives, such as moral, legal, social, and political.
- *wave.* Each major point acts like the crest of a wave. Examples and illustrations lead up to each crest and a series of waves make up the speech. This is the pattern used by Martin Luther King, Jr. in his "I Have a Dream" speech.
- *spiral.* Presents a series of examples or narratives, each more dramatic than the one before, leading up to the most dramatic point or story. Good for controversial issues like abortion, capital punishment, or doctor assisted suicide.
- *star.* Visualizes the major points of the speech as a star. The speaker then chooses which points to emphasize and their order of presentation. Politicians often use this pattern when campaigning, adapting their approach to particular audiences. For example, a candidate running for Congress has a campaign platform that includes prescription drug benefits for retirees, environmental protection, and education. She emphasizes Medicare drug coverage when speaking to seniors, conservation initiatives when in front of environmental groups, and plans for better schools when addressing parents of school age children.

Leadership on the Big Screen: *The Insider*

Starring: Russell Crowe, Al Pacino, Christopher Plummer

Synopsis: Jeffrey Wigand (played by Russell Crowe) was director of research at the Brown and Williamson tobacco company until he was fired for urging his superiors to make a safer cigarette. *60 Minutes* producer Lowell Bergman (Pacino) convinces Wigand to appear on the program to reveal that tobacco executives lied under oath when they testified before Congress that nicotine is not addictive. For blowing the whistle on Big Tobacco, Wigand loses his generous severance package, is the target of a smear campaign, and goes through a divorce. CBS cancels his interview when threatened with a lawsuit. Bergman defends Wigand's reputation and uses his contacts at *The New York Times* and *Wall Street Journal* to get the papers to publicize the researcher's testimony. *60 Minutes*, urged by Mike Wallace (Plummer), then relents and broadcasts the piece. Wigand was the ultimate insider, and the airing of his story on major media outlets led to a major shift in popular and legal opinion. Before Wigand, tobacco companies had successfully resisted liability lawsuits. Since Wigand, they have paid out millions to both state governments and private individuals.

Chapter Links: public opinion, public relations, media effects, dispersed leadership

Ten

LEADERSHIP AND DIVERSITY

> *There are truths on this side of the Pyrenees which are false-hoods on the other.*
>
> —Blaise Pascal

Overview

Managing Diversity—The Core of Leadership
Understanding Cultural Differences
   Defining Culture
   Classifying Cultures
   Cultural Synergy
Fostering Diversity
   The Benefits of Diversity
   Obstacles to Diversity
   Promoting Diversity: Best Practices
The Gender Leadership Gap
   Male and Female Leadership Behavior: Is There a Difference?
   Creating the Gap
   Narrowing the Gap

Managing Diversity—The Core of Leadership

Cultural diversity is a growing force both at home and abroad. In the United States, minorities generated two thirds of the nation's population growth between the 1990 and 2000 census. Most of the growth in the work forces of other industrialized nations is coming from immigrants or groups currently underrepresented in the work place. Along with these demographic trends, four main forces—known as the four T's—have brought the world into a global age: *technology, travel, trade, and television.* The Internet, satellite hookups, and fiber optic lines; increased international travel with millions of people visiting other nations each year; multinational organizations and open markets; and rapidly expanding broadcasting bandwidth foster diversity by enabling members of different cultures to have more frequent contact and exposure to one another. Large firms like IBM, Nokia, Coca-Cola, Honda, and McDonald's are part of a global, free-market, capitalist system that crosses national boundaries.[1] (See the Cultural Connections section at the end of this chapter for more information on the modern global economy.)

Taylor Cox concludes that managing diversity is the "core" of modern organizational leadership.[2] To Cox, managing diversity means taking advantage of the benefits of a diverse labor force while coping with the problems that arise when people from different backgrounds work together. The goal is to enable all employees, regardless of ethnicity, gender, age, or physical ability to achieve their full potential and to contribute to organizational goals. While Cox focuses his attention on the organizational work setting, managing diversity is essential to leaders in group and public contexts as well. In this chapter we will explore the topic of leadership and diversity by identifying important cultural differences, by examining the impact of culture on leadership behavior, by outlining ways to overcome diversity barriers, and by discussing the gender leadership gap.

Understanding Cultural Differences

In chapter 8 we defined an organization's culture as a unique way of seeing the world, based on particular assumptions, values, rituals, stories, practices, artifacts, and physical settings. These same elements make up the cultures of larger groups.

Defining Culture

Everett Rogers and Thomas Steinfatt define culture as "the total way of life of a people, composed of their learned and shared behavior patterns, values, norms, and material objects."[3] Because cultures are human (symbolic) creations, they take many different forms. Cultural teachings result in very different assumptions, expectations, and rules for interaction. If we are not aware of these cultural differences, we can ascribe meanings to behaviors that are inaccurate and divisive.

Communication patterns are the verbal and nonverbal codes used to convey meanings in face-to-face encounters; these patterns vary from culture to culture. One important ingredient is language. Languages help people organize their perceptions and shape their worldviews. The grammar of Spanish, for instance, reflects a number of levels of respect that reinforces status distinctions. English reinforces individualism by being the only language that capitalizes the pronoun "I" in writing.

Nonverbal codes help individuals interpret the meaning of gestures, posture, facial expressions, time, touch, and space. Again, culture teaches the meanings of nonverbal behaviors. A simple action like sticking out the tongue can be interpreted many different ways. Tongue protrusion can signal everything from polite deference (Tibet), to embarrassment (south China), negation (Marquesa Islands), and contempt (United States).[4] Patterns of relationships are strongly influenced by the culture in which one was raised. A son or daughter in the United States has much more freedom than in South Korea. In Korean families, the oldest male relative has the right to determine where children go to school, what careers they pursue, and whom they marry.

Formal organizations structure the activities of significant numbers of people. Important institutions include governments (which sponsor schools to teach cultural knowledge and values), social and professional organizations, work organizations, and religions. Religious faiths organize people differently. In Christianity or Judaism, adherents attach themselves to a particular church or synagogue, which sponsors a program of worship activities. Followers of Hinduism, on the other hand, worship whenever they want at the most convenient temple. Religions hold conflicting views about the meaning of existence, salvation, sin, and other questions.

Cultures create or borrow inventions necessary to maintain or enhance day-to-day functions. *Artifacts* is the term frequently used to describe the tools used by a culture. The personal computer is one technological creation that has greatly impacted U.S. culture. PCs have increased office productivity, encouraged more people to work at home, shortened the production time of books and other written materials, increased the flow of information, linked users from around the world, and introduced new terms like "hackers," "computer virus," and "e-commerce" into the national vocabulary.

The *collective wisdom* of a culture is shaped by historical events such as immigration, invasions, wars, economic crises, legal decisions, legislative acts, and the decisions of prior leaders. For example, the rise of communism in Vietnam was spurred by the oppression of French colonialism. In the United States, the Social Security system and other entitlement programs are a legacy of the Great Depression.

A culture's external *environment*, including climate, geographical features, and natural resources, influences a wide variety of cultural elements, such as interaction patterns and population density. People from warm climates (the Middle East or the Mediterranean, for example) are more involved with each other, maintain closer distances, and engage in more touch than individuals from cold-weather climates like Scandinavia and Great Britain. In the United States, most major cities are located near lakes and rivers because they provide drinking water, serve as sources of hydroelectric power, and act as transportation corridors. The most sparsely populated regions of the country (portions of the Dakotas, Nebraska, Nevada, Oregon, Kansas, and Texas) generally receive very little rainfall.

Classifying Cultures

Researchers group cultures according to common characteristics. These commonalities help leaders recognize and respond to the needs of diverse groups.

Five cautions should be kept in mind when studying cultural categories. First, cultures change over time, so older groupings may not be as accurate as newer ones. Second, scholars disagree about how to categorize some nations and have not studied some regions (such as Africa and the Middle East) as thoroughly as others. Third, not every member of a cultural group will respond the same way. Statements about cultural patterns are generalizations that don't account for the behavior of every individual on every occasion. Americans are generally regarded as highly individualistic, but some groups in the United States (religious orders, communes) are much more collectively oriented. Fourth, political and cultural boundaries are not always identical, as in the case of the Basque people, who live in both Spain and France. Fifth, Westerners have developed most of the cultural category systems and may have overlooked values that are important to non-Western societies. (See box 10.1 for an Eastern approach to leadership currently attracting considerable interest in North America.)

There are a number of cultural classification systems; Edward Hall and Geert Hofstede developed two of the most notable.

> *To lead the people, walk behind them.*
>
> —Lao Tzu

High- and Low-Context Cultures

Hall, an anthropologist and nonverbal communication expert, categorizes cultures as high or low context based on the way people in the culture communicate.[5] In high-context cultures such as Japan, China, and South Korea, most of the information about the meaning of a message is contained in the context or setting. Group members assume that they share common meanings and prefer indirect or covert messages that rely heavily on nonverbal codes. In low-context cultures such as Germany and Great Britain, much more meaning is embedded in the words that make up the verbal message, and speakers are

Box 10.1   Research Highlight

Taoism: Leadership Insights from Nature

Scholars in the United States and Europe developed nearly all of the theories presented in this and other Western leadership texts. However, there is one non-Western approach to leadership that is becoming increasingly popular in the United States. Advocates of Taoism (pronounced Daoism) claim that leaders who follow its principles achieve better results with less stress.[6]

The original Taoists were a group of philosophers who offered advice to the rulers of warring city-states in China during the years 600–300 B.C. Taoist teachers hoped to restore peace and order by encouraging leaders to follow natural principles. The *Tao Te Ching* is Taoism's most important text. Over the centuries this book has been translated more often than any other book except the Bible. Many believe that a royal librarian named Lao-Tzu was the author, but most experts conclude that this short volume (approximately 5,000 words long) is a collection of the teachings of several sages.[7]

Taoists emphasize simplicity and integrity in life and in leadership based on their understanding of nature. Ideal leaders resemble uncarved blocks of stone or wood. They reject wealth, status, and cleverness. Instead, they accept what comes—success or failure, life or death—and do not intrude in the lives of followers. Such leaders demonstrate integrity or character *(te)* that comes from living in harmony with natural processes. They are in tune with how the universe works because they are as innocent and honest as children. The power of a childlike character can be seen in the life of Mahatma Gandhi. Gandhi dressed simply, owned almost nothing, and did not seek political office. Yet, he was one of the twentieth century's most influential leaders.[8]

Central to the Taoist approach to leadership is the notion of *wu wei* or positive inaction. Nature can't be rushed but takes its own course. The wise leader, then, knows when to intervene and when to step back. According to the *Tao Te Ching*:

> He [she] who takes action fails.
> He [she] who grasps things loses them.
> For this reason the sage takes no action and therefore does not fail.
> He [she] grasps nothing and therefore he [she] does not lose anything.[9]

The martial art called T'ai Chi is based on the principle of *wu wei*. Practitioners of this art never attack; instead they wear their enemies out by yielding, deflecting the force of their opponents' attacks back to them. In the same way, wise leaders seldom take aggressive action to get their way. Instead, they are sensitive to the natural order of things (circumstances, the needs and interests of followers, stages of group development) and work with events instead of against them. They use less energy but get more done.

Along with advocating positive inaction, Taoism also encourages leaders to be weak rather than strong. To the Taoists (and to many other Chinese), the universe is made up of two forces: the yin (negative, dark, cool, female, shadows) and the yang (positive, brightness, warmth, male, sun). While our culture highlights the yang or masculine side of leadership, the Taoists draw more attention to the yin. They urge leaders to be valleys (which reflect the yin) instead of prominent peaks (which reflect the yang). The *Tao Te Ching* describes the action of water to illustrate that weakness overcomes strength:

There is nothing softer and weaker than water,
And yet there is nothing better for attacking hard and strong things.
For this reason there is no substitute for it.
All the world knows that the weak overcomes the strong and the soft overcomes the hard.[10]

Just as water cuts the hardest rock over time, the weak often overcome the powerful in human society. For example, authoritarian governments in Soviet Russia, Argentina, and the Philippines were overthrown through the efforts of ordinary citizens. Leaders who use "soft" tactics (listening, empowering, collaborating) rather than "hard" ones (threats and force) are more likely to overcome resistance to change in the long term.

Flexibility is an important attribute of weakness. Weak things are more likely to survive because they can adapt. Pliability is a sign of life; stiffness signals death. Like young grass and saplings, successful leaders bend rather than break, adjusting their strategies to meet changing conditions. The *Tao* sums up the advantages of flexibility and adaptability this way:

When a man is born, he is tender and weak.
At death, he is stiff and hard.
All things, the grass as well as trees, are tender and supple while alive.
When dead, they are withered and dried.
Therefore the stiff and the hard are companions of death.
The tender and the weak are companions of life.
Therefore if the army is strong, it will not win.
If a tree is stiff, it will break.
The strong and the great are inferior, while the tender and the weak are superior.[11]

more direct. Other differences between high- and low-context cultures center on group membership, interpersonal relationships, and orientations toward time. A summary of the differences between high- and low-context cultures is found in box 10. 2.

Leaders can run into serious difficulties when dealing with followers who prefer a different communication style. Take the case of the German manager who deals with conflict by confronting his Japanese employees directly. The supervisor's low-context culture encourages him to be honest and straightforward. However, his followers, who have been raised in a high-context society, would rather ignore tensions or deal with them indirectly through hints and nonverbal cues like making less eye contact.

Geert Hofstede of the Netherlands conducted the largest study of cultural patterns. In order to determine important values that are "programmed" into members of various cultures, Hofstede surveyed 116,000 IBM employees in 72 countries. He then validated his findings by correlating his results with data collected by other investigators in many of the same nations.[12] Hofstede found four values dimensions that characterize cultures in his original research. Later,

---

Box 10.2

Characteristics of High- and Low-Context Cultures[13]

High-context cultures	Low-context cultures
Covert and implicit	Overt and explicit
Messages internalized	Messages plainly coded
Much nonverbal coding	Details verbalized
Reactions reserved	Reactions on the surface
Distinct ingroups and outgroups	Flexible ingroups and outgroups
Strong interpersonal bonds	Fragile interpersonal bonds
Commitment high	Commitment low
Time open and flexible	Time highly organized

---

with Michael Harris Bond, he identified a fifth category that has its roots in Eastern culture.[14] These dimensions and some of their implications for leader/follower relations are described below.[15]

Power Distance. The first value dimension identified by Hofstede looks at the importance of power differences in a culture. "All societies are unequal," Hofstede states, "but some are more unequal than others."[16] In high power-distance cultures, inequality is considered to be a natural part of the world. Superiors are a special class of people who deserve special privileges. However, at the same time, they are obligated to take care of their less fortunate subordinates. High-status individuals try to look as powerful as possible and exert influence through coercive and referent power bases. In contrast, low power-distance cultures are uncomfortable with differences in wealth, status, power, and privilege; they promote equal rights. Members of these groups emphasize interdependence and rely on reward, legitimate, and expert power. Superiors are similar to subordinates and may try to appear less powerful than they actually are. Citizens of the Philippines, Mexico, Venezuela, India, and Singapore ranked among the highest in power distance; residents of New Zealand, Denmark, Israel, Austria, and Sweden the lowest. Power distance has a number of implications for leadership.

- The larger the power-distance between leaders and followers, the greater the fear of disagreeing with a superior, and the closer the supervision of follower activities.

- Followers in high power-distance countries expect managers to give direction and feel uncomfortable when asked to participate in decision making.

- Coercive, authoritarian leadership is more common in high power-distance countries; democratic leadership is more often the norm in low power-distance cultures.

- Organizations operating in low power-distance countries are less centralized and distribute rewards more equally.

Individualism-Collectivism. The second of Hofstede's value dimensions distinguishes cultures by their beliefs about individuals or groups. Individualistic cultures emphasize that the needs and goals of the individual and his or her immediate family are most important. Decisions are based on what benefits the person rather than the group. Collectivist cultures emphasize group identity. Individuals do not function as independent agents, rather, they define themselves and make decisions on the basis of their connection to an extended family, tribe, clan, or organization. The United States ranked as the most individualistic culture in Hofstede's sample, followed by Australia, Great Britain, Canada, and the Netherlands. Colombia, Mexico, Pakistan, Taiwan, and South Korea were among the most collectivistic. The following are implications for leadership of the individualism-collectivism continuum.

- Followers in individualistic societies generally respond well to material rewards that honor individual effort (commissions, bonuses for winning sales contests). Followers in collectivistic cultures don't feel comfortable with individual recognition and prefer team rewards instead.

- Members of collectivist societies expect mutual loyalty between organizational leaders and followers and feel betrayed when companies furlough or fire employees.

- To be accepted, new ideas in collectivist countries must come from the group as a whole rather than from any individual.

- Decision making is identified with a single leader in individualistic societies. Leaders in collectivist groups rely more heavily on group norms and social values to manage the behavior of followers.

- The ideal leader for individualists is someone who provides autonomy and opportunities for personal growth. The ideal leader for collectivists takes an active role in nurturing followers and fostering the growth of the group as a whole.

- Followers with a collectivist orientation prefer indirect criticism while followers with individualistic values expect to be confronted directly about poor performance and conflicts.

Masculinity-Femininity. The third value dimension looks at roles assigned to the sexes. In masculine cultures, men are thought to be assertive, decisive, competitive, ambitious, and dominant. They are concerned with material success and "respect whatever is big, strong, and fast." Women are encouraged to serve; responsibilities include caring for interpersonal relationships, the family, and weaker members of society. In feminine cultures, sex roles overlap. Neither sex is expected to be competitive, ambitious, or caring at all times. These cultures stress intuition, interdependence, and concern; there is respect for the small, weak, and slow. Japan, Austria, Venezuela, and Italy were the most masculine cultures surveyed while Sweden, Norway, the Netherlands, and Denmark were the most feminine. The masculinity-femininity implications for leadership including the following.

- Females in masculine cultures have a harder time emerging as leaders and are more likely to be segregated into a few specialized occupations.
- Decision makers in feminine cultures put a greater emphasis on intuition and consensus.
- Leaders and constituents in masculine cultures put a higher priority on work (they "live to work"); leaders and constituents in feminine cultures put more emphasis on the quality of life (they "work to live").
- Leaders in feminine societies are more likely to demonstrate an interpersonally-oriented leadership style.
- Members of masculine cultures are more motivated by achievement, recognition, and challenge.

> *If a [hu]man can be gracious and courteous to strangers, it shows he[she] is a citizen of the world.*
> —Francis Bacon

Uncertainty Avoidance. The fourth dimension measures (1) the extent to which people feel uncomfortable in unstructured or unpredictable situations, and (2) the lengths to which they will go to avoid ambiguity by following strict codes of behavior or by believing in absolute truths. Members of high uncertainty-avoidance cultures view uncertainty as a threat, are less tolerant, face high stress, seek security, believe in written rules and regulations, and readily accept directives from experts and those in authority. Individuals in low uncertainty-avoidance cultures accept uncertainty as a fact of life, are more contemplative, experience less stress, take more risks, are less concerned about rules, are more likely to trust their own judgments or common sense rather than experts, and believe that authorities serve the citizens. Citizens of Greece, Portugal, Belgium, and Japan reported some of the highest uncertainty-avoidance ratings; residents of Jamaica, Denmark, Sweden, and Ireland among the lowest. Uncertainty-avoidance has several implications for leadership.

- High uncertainty-avoidance cultures give more weight to age and seniority when selecting leaders.
- Managers in low uncertainty-avoidance societies emphasize interpersonal relations and are more willing to take risks. Managers in high uncertainty-avoidance countries seem unapproachable and are more likely to try to control the activities of followers.
- Organizational constituents in high uncertainty-avoidance cultures prefer clear instructions, are more willing to follow orders, disapprove of competition between employees, and are more loyal than their low uncertainty-avoidance counterparts.

Long-Term-Short-Term Orientation. The fifth value dimension is concerned with how citizens view the past, present, and future. Cultures with a long-term orientation (LTO) encourage norms and behaviors that lead to future rewards. Members of these societies sacrifice immediate gratification (leisure time, luxuries, entertainment) for long-term benefits. They put a high value on persistence and perseverance, spend sparingly, and save a lot. Status relationships (teacher-student, manager-worker, parent-child) are clearly defined and honored. Feelings of shame come from violating social contracts and commitments. Cultures with a short-term orientation (STO) focus on the past and the present, respecting tradition and expecting quick results. Members of these groups put much less importance on persistence, spend freely, and have lower savings rates. China, Hong Kong, Taiwan, Japan, and South Korea ranked highest on long-term orientation; Pakistan, Nigeria, the Philippines, Canada, and Zimbabwe ranked lowest. Long-term or short-term orientations have the following implications for leadership.

- Leaders in LTO cultures can expect greater sacrifice from followers on behalf of long-term goals. Leaders in STO societies are under greater pressure to demonstrate immediate progress.
- Feelings of shame can be powerful motivational tools to encourage follower compliance in LTO nations.
- Short-term orientation, with its emphasis on spending instead of saving, interferes with economic development in emerging countries, making the task of national leaders and aid agencies more difficult.

Understanding cultural differences lays the groundwork for leading groups in a variety of cultures as well as for leading groups made up of diverse members. The successful leader recognizes and responds to cultural differences; the leader who fails to appreciate cultural influences is doomed to frustration and failure. Consider, for example, the interaction described in box 10.3.

> *A [hu]man's feet must be planted in his[her] country, but his[her] eyes should survey the world.*
> —George Santayana

Cultural Synergy

Cultural synergy is the ultimate goal of recognizing and responding to cultural variations. Synergy refers to the production of an end product that is greater than the sum of its parts. In cultural synergy, decision-makers draw on the diversity of the group to produce a new, better than expected solution. According to cross-cultural management expert Nancy Adler, culturally synergistic problem solving is a four-step process.[17]

Box 10.3

When Cultural Values Clash: American Leader-Greek Follower[18]

Bob is a U.S. manager from a low power-distance/low uncertainty-avoidance culture. His Greek subordinate, Ari, ranks high on both these dimensions.

Verbal Conversation	Attribution
Bob: How long will it take you to finish this report?	Bob: I asked him to participate.
	Ari: His behavior makes no sense. He is the boss. Why doesn't he *tell* me?
Ari: I do not know. How long should it take?	Bob: He refuses to take responsibility.
	Ari: I asked him for an order.
Bob: You are in the best position to analyze time requirements	Bob: I press him to take responsibility for own actions.
	Ari: What nonsense! I better give him an answer.
Ari: 10 days	Bob: He lacks the ability to estimate time; this time estimate is totally inadequate.
Bob: Take 15. Is it agreed you will do it in 15 days?	Bob: I offer a contract.
	Ari: These are my orders—15 days.

In fact the report needed 30 days of regular work. So Ari worked day and night, but at the end of the 15th day, he still needed one more day's work.

Verbal Conversation	Attribution
Bob: Where is the report?	Bob: I am making sure he fulfills his contract.
	Ari: He is asking for the report
Ari: It will be ready tomorrow.	
Bob: But we had agreed it would be ready today.	Bob: I must teach him to fulfill a contract.
	Ari: The stupid, incompetent boss! Not only did he give me wrong orders, but he does not even appreciate that I did a 30-day job in 16 days.
Ari hands in his resignation.	Bob is surprised.
	Ari: I can't work for such a man.

The first step is identifying the dilemma or conflict facing the dyad or group. Due to differing cultural perspectives, some communicators may not realize that there is a problem. In the U.S. manager-Greek employee interaction described in box 10.3, Bob didn't think that asking for input would cause difficulties. After all, involving employees in decision making is what a "good" leader would do in the United States. Bob can't begin the synergistic process until he recognizes that soliciting participation is problematic for his follower. Further, he needs to identify the conflict without making negative value judgments about Ari's response. Ari will need to approach Bob in the same nonjudgmental fashion.

In step two, communicators try to determine why members of other cultures think and act as they do. The underlying assumption is that all people act rationally from their culture's point of view. Communicators identify both similarities and differences in cultural perspectives and recognize that cultural values can cluster together in different ways. For instance, some collectivist societies are low in power distance. Others, such as Malaysia, are characterized by "vertical collectivism"—a combination of collectivism and high power distance.[19] Constituents in all collectivist cultures expect to work in groups, but vertical collectivists try to insure that group decisions are acceptable to persons in authority.[20]

Step three begins by asking the question: "What can people from one culture contribute to people from another culture?" Problem solvers then generate alternatives and come up with a creative answer that incorporates the cultural assumptions of all group members but also transcends them.

Consider the dilemma faced by a male Uruguayan doctor and a female Filipino nurse employed by a California hospital.[21] The physician noticed that the nurse was giving poor treatment to a patient because she couldn't operate a piece of medical equipment. He gave the nurse instructions on how to operate the machinery and asked if she understood his directions. She replied that she did. When the doctor returned two hours later, he found the nurse still unable to use the machine effectively. The hospital administrator was able to find a creative, synergistic solution. After reflecting on the problem, the administrator concluded that the nurse didn't want to ask questions of the doctor because Filipinos are reluctant to contradict superiors. She couldn't tell him that she didn't understand without implying that he had given faulty instructions and causing him to lose face. He, on the other hand, expected her to ask questions if she didn't understand and took it as a sign of incompetence when she kept on giving ineffective treatment using the equipment. The hospital administrator asked the doctor to give instructions to the nurse who would then describe the procedure she would follow back to the doctor. The physician would quickly find out if the nurse understood his directions, but she would not be forced to contradict him. The patient received better care without violating the cultural norms of either party.

Effective implementation of a solution in step four also requires synergistic thinking based on cultural awareness. Synergistic implementation of a sales reward system at a multinational corporation, for example, would give managers in host countries plenty of leeway in distributing awards appropriate for the specific cultural settings.[22] As we noted earlier, stakeholders in individualistic societies expect to be compensated for their personal efforts, but a greater share of the rewards will go to the group in collectivistic cultures. Shell Nigeria took the collectivist orientation of its employees into account when it rewarded a group of workers by building a well in their village. The new water system helped the community and, at the same time, raised the status of the Shell employees.

Fostering Diversity

So far we've highlighted the importance of responding to cultural differences. We've seen that leaders improve their effectiveness if they recognize and incorporate differences into their problem solving. However, the best leaders go beyond simply responding to cultural differences; they actively promote diversity in the groups they lead. In this section of the chapter we provide a rationale for fostering diversity, discuss some of the obstacles that keep members of minority groups from reaching their full potential, and suggest ways to promote diversity in the organizational context.

The Benefits of Diversity

Perhaps the best reason for encouraging diversity is that it is the right thing to do. Fostering diversity reduces inequities and gives everyone a chance to make a meaningful contribution. While ethical considerations alone should be sufficient motivation for promoting diversity, there are also a number of practical benefits that come from making maximum use of the members of various constituencies.[23]

- *Cost Savings.* Absenteeism and turnover rates in organizations are often higher for women and ethnic minorities than they are for white males. Finding temporary substitutes and permanent replacements is expensive. Addressing diversity concerns lowers the number of absences and resignations and reduces the likelihood of sexual harassment and racial discrimination lawsuits.

- *Resource Acquisition and Utilization.* Organizations with reputations for managing diversity will attract the best personnel out of a shrinking labor pool. They will also help talented minority employees break out of low-level positions.

- *Keeping and Gaining Market Share.* Diverse organizations are in the best position to take advantage of markets both at home and abroad. Such organizations understand the needs of a variety of target audiences and have minority representatives who can appeal to members of many different cultural groups. The Avon company illustrates how diversity can boost the bottom line. The corporation gave African-American and Hispanic managers authority over unprofitable inner-city markets. These territories are now among the company's most productive.

- *Better Decision Making.* Earlier we argued that cultural differences can be the basis for higher quality solutions. Forming heterogeneous groups is one way to stimulate cultural synergy. Members of diverse groups are also less likely to succumb to groupthink (see chapter 7). Having a variety of opinions forces group members to pay more attention to all aspects of an issue, consider more viewpoints, and use a wider variety of problem-solving strategies.[24]

- *Greater Innovation.* Nurturing a variety of cultural perspectives makes an organization more open to ideas. Innovative organizations employ more women and minorities and work harder at eliminating racism and sexism.[25]

Organizations experience more of the benefits of diversity when their senior leaders strive for the cultural synergy we described earlier. These executives adopt a *learning-and-effectiveness* approach that recognizes cultural differences as valuable organizational assets.[26] Drawing on the insights of diverse members can dramatically improve how organizations carry out their tasks—helping them to think in new ways about markets, products, goals, and organizational structures. This synergistic approach stands in sharp contrast to the diversity paradigms adopted by the leaders of most organizations. Executives in some groups view diversity initiatives solely as a way to provide equal opportunity; they strive to treat everyone the same way and try to ignore cultural differences rather than building on them. Executives in other groups value minorities solely as marketing agents who can sell to their ethnic groups. Diversity in those two situations has little impact on the way that these organizations conduct their core businesses.

Obstacles to Diversity

While the benefits of fostering diversity are substantial, so too are the barriers that prevent leaders and followers from reaching cultural synergy. According to Taylor Cox, diversity barriers can be found at every level of society—personal, group, and institutional. Barriers found at the individual level include prejudice, discrimination, and stereotyping.[27] The term prejudice refers to negative attitudes toward people from other backgrounds. Surveys reveal that whites, for example, typically believe that minorities are less intelligent, do not work as hard, and are less patriotic.[28] These negative attitudes produce discriminatory behavior, which likely accounts for the fact that minorities receive fewer organ transplants, are underrepresented in the media, serve on fewer corporate boards, earn less money than whites, and so on. Stereotyping is the process of classifying group members according to their perceived similarities, either good or bad. According to widely held stereotypes in U.S. culture, disabled workers are seen as less productive, and Asian Americans are seen as excelling at technical but not managerial skills. As a consequence of these stereotypes, organizations are reluctant to hire disabled persons and hire Asian Americans primarily for technical positions. Stereotypes also influence the evaluation of performance. For instance, when minorities perform well, their success is often attributed to help from others rather than to their individual ability and effort.

> *What is repugnant to every human being is to be reckoned as a member of a class and not an individual person.*
> —Dorothy Sayers

On a group level, ethnocentrism—the attitude (conscious or unconscious) that regards one's own culture as the measure by which all others should be judged—is a significant barrier to incorporating diversity. Ethnocentrism is less hostile than prejudice, but it still leads to preferential treatment for insiders. Most of us would rather socialize with people from similar backgrounds and prefer to recruit, promote, and reward those who share our values. Intergroup conflicts also serve as diversity obstacles. Religious, social, political, and economic differences generate tensions that tear groups and societies apart. To identify your own diversity profile, complete the self-assessment in box 10.4.

At the institutional level, large power differences between cultural groups reduce the motivation of minority group members and make it more difficult for them to be perceived as leaders. Many organizations (often without meaning to do so) engage in practices that keep minority groups from fully participating. Here are some of the practices that Cox believes are organizational barriers to diversity. You may be able to identify others (see application exercise 1).[29]

Practice	Impact
Fifty-hour plus workweeks with weekend and evening meetings	Increases stress for working mothers who have more responsibility for children and home chores.
Self-promotion (selling oneself) and self-evaluations	Uncomfortable for people from cultures that value modesty (i.e., Japanese, Chinese).
Informal networks	Women, the disabled, and others may be excluded from "old boy networks" that are important sources of information and contacts for promotion.
Inaccessible facilities	Despite passage of the American Disabilities Act some schools, businesses, and houses of worship remain inaccessible to disabled workers.

Box 10.4   Self-Assessment

Diversity Profile[30]

Complete each sentence by placing a check in the appropriate box(es).

	African American	Asian American	Caucasian	Hispanic	Native American	Other
I am						
Most of the students in this class are						
Most of my friends on campus are						
Most of my professors are						
Most of the people I work with at my most recent job are (were)						
My boss is (was)						
My high school was predominantly						
My neighbors when I was growing up were						
My dentist is						
My doctor is						
People who live in my home are						
People who regularly visit my home are						
The music I listen to is generally performed by artists who are						
My favorite actor or actress is						
My favorite author is						
My personal hero is						

Discussion Questions

1. Are you involved primarily with members of only one ethnic group?
2. Identify any patterns in your diversity profile (e.g., school, work, home, social) that divide along ethnic boundaries? Do these patterns contribute to prejudice or ethnocentrism?
3. How could you expand your involvement with members of ethnic groups under-represented in your diversity profile?
4. What advantages or disadvantages could you envision from interacting regularly with members of diverse ethnic groups?
5. Does a diverse membership make an organization more or less effective?

Promoting Diversity: Best Practices

Two facts must be kept in mind when encouraging diversity, particularly in an organizational setting. First, no single approach can possibly fit every situation; the mix of cultural groups and the needs of followers vary from organization to organization. Second, no group is perfect. Even the best organizations continue to struggle with diversity issues. While there are no universal approaches or perfect models, we can gain important insights into leadership and diversity by studying the techniques of the most successful organizations.

> *Leadership has a harder job to do than just choose sides. It must bring sides together.*
> —Jesse Jackson

In this section of the chapter we'll look at the results of two research projects that used this "best practices" approach. The Center for Creative Leadership (a well-regarded international leadership training institution) created Guidelines On Leadership Diversity (GOLD). Ann Morrison and other researchers at the GOLD project did an in-depth analysis of sixteen larger organizations (twelve businesses, two government agencies, and two educational institutions) to identify promising strategies for fostering diversity at the managerial level. Harvard professors David Thomas and John Gabarro conducted an in-depth study of three demographically diverse organizations (a law firm, bank, and consulting firm), and collected data at nine additional companies and nonprofits that were more homogeneous. They compared the careers of African-American, Asian, and Hispanic executives with minorities who had plateaued in their careers to identify the organizational and personal factors that promote the development of minority leaders.

The GOLD Project

In their analysis of diverse organizations, Morrison and her colleagues discovered a variety of common practices that they grouped under the headings of accountability, development, and recruitment.[31]

Accountability starts with the top leaders in an organization. Unless they are committed to holding lower-level leaders accountable for fostering diversity, any diversity effort will fail. However, responsibility for diversity is neither limited to CEOs and vice presidents nor relegated to the human resources department. Every manager must help develop nontraditional leaders as a routine part of her or his job description. Important accountability tools include:

- *Internal advocacy groups*—collectives of similar employees (women, Asian Americans, Hispanics) who act as lobbyists within their organizations. The most effective advocacy networks focus on organizational policy, not on individual cases of discrimination. They have access to top managers as well as to information about job openings, promotions, and pay scales. Some executives share information with advocacy networks because these groups help generate solutions to diversity problems and act as sounding boards before changes are made. Others are wary of such groups because they can fragment the work force. These executives prefer to use demographically mixed task forces instead.

- *Administrative practices*—structured to encourage managers to foster diversity. Managers from every department are evaluated on how well they treat nontraditional workers. They must include women and people of color on promotion lists. Charges of sexual harassment and racism are taken seriously, with offenders being fired or demoted.

Development has been the missing link in many diversity efforts. Too many leaders have mistakenly assumed that nontraditional workers would automatically work their way up the organizational hierarchy. Managed development opportunities produce better results. These opportunities are directed both at making traditional managers more aware of and responsive to diversity issues and at helping nontraditional employees prepare for greater leadership responsibilities. Development strategies include:

- *Diversity training programs.* These programs are an important tool for attacking three of the most important obstacles to diversity—prejudice, discrimination, and stereotyping. Participants learn about the perspectives of other groups; this knowledge helps them break their stereotypes and change discriminatory behavior. An important element of any effective training program is instruction about the organization's specific diversity policies.

- *Development programs* These programs help nontraditional managers move up the organizational ladder by providing challenging job assignments, education, coaching, and assessment and feedback. Managers identified as having "high potential" regularly interact with influential leaders and develop career goals and peer networks. Participants are often paired with mentors (see chapter 11) who act as sponsors and coaches. In some cases, development opportunities are limited to women and minorities. In other cases, these programs are open to both traditional and nontraditional managers. Whites often have trouble giving negative verbal feedback to members of other ethnic groups. Best practices organizations overcome this problem by asking superiors, peers, and subordinates to provide written feedback to minorities using structured assessment instruments.

Recruitment of nontraditional members remains a problem for many organizations. Lower salaries can make it difficult for governments, educational institutions, and charities to compete with businesses for qualified candidates. Many organizations have little contact with minority populations. Some job criteria, such as height or weight limits for police and fire personnel, may screen out women and some men of color (Asian Americans, for instance). To recruit more diverse members, successful organizations:

- develop relationships with schools with a high percentage of minority students
- create internship and work-study programs for students of color and women
- recruit key managers from the outside
- publicize diversity efforts to interest potential employees
- provide incentives for nontraditional candidates

One troubling aspect of the best practices report is its emphasis on identifying, training, and promoting employees labeled as "high potentials." As we noted in our discussion of the Pygmalion Effect in chapter 8, labeling some people as high performers suggests that only a few individuals can do an outstanding job. We then expect less, and often get less, from everyone else. When this happens, many people do not participate to the fullest extent of their abilities.

Breaking Through to the Executive Ranks

Leaders at every level of the organization (human resource staff, department heads, sales managers, etc.) can use the guidelines provided by the GOLD researchers. Thomas and Gabarro, on the other hand, limit their recommendations to top level leaders and to those minority employees who want to join their ranks.[32] They offer the following seven "lessons" (divided into three categories) for executives interested in developing and promoting minorities to upper management and executive posts.

Creating an Enabling Organizational Context

- *Lesson 1: Become personally involved in diversity initiatives.* Executives must champion the diversity process, mentor and sponsor minority managers, outline the way that diversity initiatives relate to the organizational mission and strategy, and so forth.

- *Lesson 2: Build partnerships to ensure long-term success of diversity efforts.* Top leaders must remain involved, rather than shifting the responsibility to a diversity office or human relations department. If diversity initiatives become compartmentalized, they are quickly jettisoned when costs must be cut. Partnerships should include members of minority groups who are most directly impacted by diversity initiatives and need to help implement them.

- *Lesson 3: Understand that diversity initiatives will both maintain and change corporate culture.* Diversity efforts imply change, meaning that top leaders and others act as change agents. However, successful initiatives are tied to an organization's unchanging core values.

Ensuring Opportunity

- *Lesson 4: Monitor the distribution of and pathways to opportunity.* Tournament models that quickly label people as "executive material" work to the disadvantage of both minorities and talented whites who are not identified as potential high achievers. (See our earlier criticism of the GOLD recommendations.) Understand the norms or rules that determine rewards as well as the pathways that lead to top-level positions.

- *Lesson 5: Spotlight the threshold between upper-middle management and executive level positions.* Determine which positions lead to executive appointments and make sure that qualified minorities are placed in these threshold jobs. In many cases, a technical position doesn't develop the skills necessary to function effectively as a vice-president, a position that requires many emotional as well as cognitive competencies.

Ensuring the Development Takes Place

- *Lesson 6: Facilitate the formation of developmental relationships.* Finding a mentor early in a career is particularly important to people of color (we'll have more to say about developmental relationships in chapter 12.)[33] Make sure that minorities are given assignments that pair them with people who are skilled at developing others.

- *Lesson 7: Directly address attitudes that create low expectations for minority performance.* White managers should not accept substandard work as the price of diversity efforts. High expectations lead to high performance that benefits minorities and organizations alike.

Thomas and Gabarro, based on their analysis of the career paths of high performers, also offer seven lessons for aspiring minority leaders.

- *Lesson 1: Choose work and an organization that suit your personality.* Hating the job or the company will cause you to leave too soon, before you can take advantage of the opportunities the position has to offer. Minorities, in particular, pay a high price for making poor career choices because biased observers interpret premature job changes as evidence of low ability. According to Thomas and Gabarro, most of the minority candidates for CEO positions have spent the majority of their careers at one firm.

- *Lesson 2: Choose high quality experiences over fast advancement.* Quality experiences build credibility and confidence. Early in a career they are superior to so-called "fast track" experiences for which you are unprepared.

- *Lesson 3: Build a network of developmental relationships.* Find those who can help your career, whether they be sponsors, mentors, or peers.

- *Lesson 4: The organization matters.* Avoid companies that have a poor track record of minority advancement. Chances are, one individual is not going to have much impact on the entire organizational system. Be on guard against organizations that set low expectations for minorities or that have failed to align their diversity strategies with their cultures and values. Minorities in these organizations rarely get promoted to the executive suite. Expect, too, to play a role in promoting corporate diversity efforts.

- *Lesson 5: Take charge of your own career.* People of color cannot count on the system working on their behalf. As a result, they set personal goals, seek to learn, solicit feedback, and so forth. Remember that commitment to high performance is important whatever the position.

- *Lesson 6: Race matters, but it alone does not determine your fate.* Minority executives are comfortable with who they are and talk freely about racial issues. They have integrated their racial identities with their professional roles. As a result, these executives solve race-related problems the same way they handle other dilemmas. Race may play a role in a conflict with a boss, for example, but other factors like personality and communication styles also come into play. An effective minority manager is able to talk to a superior about all the issues that may be interfering with effective communication.

- *Lesson 7: Make sure it is worth the price.* Success comes at a price—long hours, time away from children, moves. Determine if you are willing to endure these costs while, at the same time, meeting your personal needs and maintaining important personal relationships.

> *Luck is when opportunity meets preparation.*
> —Denzel Washington

The Gender Leadership Gap

Over the past century, the number of women occupying leadership positions has risen dramatically. In 1900, women held only 4 out of 100 managerial positions. By the beginning of the new millennium, nearly half of all managerial and professional positions in the workforce were held by females. Women are also playing a larger role in politics. They hold 23 percent of the seats in state legislatures, 62 seats in the House of Representatives, and 13 seats in the Senate.

Despite these gains, a gender leadership gap still exists. Males in the same occupations earn more than their female counterparts, and males dominate occupations with higher pay scales. Very few women have moved into top management or government positions. Twelve percent of Fortune 500 officers and corporate directors are female. Of the women executives, only six are CEOs. There are just four female governors, and despite some progress women remain underrepresented in Congress.[34]

The existence of the gender leadership gap raises three significant questions: (1) Are there differences in how males and females lead? (2) What factors hinder the emergence of women as leaders? (3) Can the gender leadership gap be narrowed? To answer these questions, we'll begin by taking a look at what researchers have discovered about female and male leadership behavior.

Male and Female Leadership Behavior: Is There a Difference?

There has been much debate about whether differences between male and female leadership behaviors are genuine or merely a matter of perception. Judy Rosener, for instance, argues that female leaders are more likely to use an interactive style of leadership that encourages participation, shares power and information, and enhances the self-worth of others.[35] (See the case study in box 10.5 for an example of how one woman's approach to leadership has proven successful).

Box 10.5   Case Study

Applying Feminist Ideals at the Body Shop[36]

In March 1976, Anita Roddick opened a small cosmetics shop in Brighton, England. Despite a threatened lawsuit from two neighboring funeral parlors unhappy with her choice of store name, Roddick dubbed her venture The Body Shop. The initial product line consisted of 15 natural-based skin and hair care products packaged in reusable bottles with handwritten labels. These products were inspired by Roddick's previous travels where she observed how women in other cultures, without access to expensive cosmetics, cared for their bodies naturally. On the shop's first day, Roddick took in $225.

Within seven months a second Body Shop was opened in Chichester, England. By 1984, The Body Shop went public on the London Stock Exchange with a value of over $12 million. Today, it has a stock market value of some one billion dollars and offers over 400 products in its 1900 company-owned and franchised stores located in over 50 countries. On average, The Body Shop sells a product every 0.4 seconds. The brand is nearly everybody's darling. It was recently identified as the second most trusted brand in the United Kingdom and the 28th most respected company (second in retailing) in the world.

The key to The Body Shop's success is twofold—a powerful social conscience and a commitment to feminist ideals. All products sold at The Body Shop use natural-based and biodegradable ingredients, packaging is kept to a minimum, recyclable materials are used whenever possible, and customers are encouraged to bring bottles back to be refilled when making subsequent purchases. All this is in response to Roddick's claim that her rivals in the cosmetics industry produce mostly "packaging and garbage."

The Body Shop's model of commerce-with-a-conscience also extends to important social issues. The Body Shop strictly forbids the testing of any of its products on animals. Further, through window displays, pamphlets, posters, and messages on shopping bags, each Body Shop retail outlet highlights issues ranging from AIDS awareness to preservation of the rain forests.

Conventional business practices used by others in the cosmetics industry are generally ignored at The Body Shop. Products are not hyped. The word "beauty" is not used in conjunction with any Body Shop product. Packaging is plain and practical, and there has never been one cent spent on product-based advertising. When the first franchise opened in the United States in 1988, the *Wall Street Journal* quoted a Harvard Business School professor as saying that a major advertising campaign would have to be launched for The Body Shop to succeed in the United States. In response, Roddick stated she would "never hire anybody from Harvard Business School."

Roddick's greatest disdain, however, is reserved for the cosmetics industry itself. She believes that women are "enslaved by the images of beauty and glamour" portrayed by her competitors. She explains:

It is immoral to trade on fear. It is immoral to constantly make women feel dissatisfied with their bodies. It is immoral to deceive a customer by making miracle claims for a product. It is immoral to use a photograph of a glowing sixteen-year-old to sell a cream aimed at preventing wrinkles in a forty-year-old.[37]

The Body Shop is also guided by feminist philosophy. Honesty, caring, intuition, and a concern for women are core company values. In 1990, The Body Shop opened a day-care center at its corporate headquarters. The facility took nearly two years to build and cost over $1 million. The Body Shop pays a subsidy for employees using the center, and the facility has been made available to those who work elsewhere in the community but are unable to afford reliable, high quality day care. Further, employee training whether related to work or merely of a personal interest is paid for by the company. As Roddick explains, "Most businesses today are concerned with maximizing profits for the few. We try to create a humanized workplace that is joyful to be in, creative, and encourages brilliance."[38]

Also grounded in feminist ideology is The Body Shop approach to retailing. The objective of employees is not only to sell merchandise, but also to educate customers. "The idea that everyone should walk out of our shops having bought something is anathema to me," Roddick insists. "We prefer to give staff information about the products, anecdotes about the history and derivation of the ingredients, and funny stories about how they came [to be] on The Body Shop shelves. We want to spark conversations with our customers, not brow-beat them to buy."[39] This manner of customer interaction (which emphasizes conversation over control, coercion, and hierarchy) represents a practical application of feminist principles.

Commitment to The Body Shop values is the cornerstone of the organization. Before a potential franchisee is offered a Body Shop outlet, she or he must work in an existing store so that the store's staff can evaluate how well the prospect fits into The Body Shop culture. Then the potential franchisee must go through extensive interviews at corporate headquarters with Roddick and other top executives before being invited to join The Body Shop family.

Some detractors argue that The Body Shop is "off-beat" and "loony." To those critics Roddick explains: "The big mistake they make is to equate our feminine values with weakness and inefficiency. We know how to run a business. We do it differently, but we do it well."[40]

Discussion Questions
1. Do you think The Body Shop would be more or less successful if it were led in a more "traditional" manner?
2. What is the impact of Roddick's social conscience and commitment to feminist ideals on employees? Customers? Competitors?
3. Do you agree with Roddick that the "feminine values" of The Body Shop are often misinterpreted?
4. Can you identify other organizations that demonstrate a commitment to feminist ideals? Would you like to work for such a company?
5. Are there any types of organizations that could not be effectively led using feminist ideals?

Other researchers argue that differences in male/female leadership are a matter of perception. These investigators note that most of the data supporting differing leadership patterns among males and females come from laboratory studies. Such controlled environments are more likely to yield results supporting stereotypical views of gender behavior because the research models are often biased.[41] These studies assume that men, being masculine, will be higher in task-oriented behavior and women, being feminine, will demonstrate greater interpersonally-oriented behavior. In actual leadership situations, such differences are not generally evident.

For example, in studies of cadet leaders at the Air Force Academy, cadets rated female leaders less favorably before they saw the women in action. After serving with the women leaders over a period of time, the cadets gave female and male leaders equal evaluations.[42] Related findings have been reported in large-scale investigations. In a survey of nearly 3,000 employees from *Fortune* 500 companies, respondents gave men and women managers similar ratings on such criteria as fairness, keeping workers informed, and providing recognition and support.[43]

Alice Eagly uses the concept of gender spill-over to explain why there are usually only slight differences in female/male leadership patterning in organizational settings.[44] She argues that variation in the behavior of men and women is greatest in contexts where there are few constraints, such as when friends interact informally. In these settings, gender role expectations are more likely to "spill over" and influence behavior. In contrast, when there are clear guidelines about how to act, there is less room for variation and less gender role spill-over. In managerial positions there will be relatively fewer gender differences because both males and females receive similar training, carry out the same job responsibilities, and work toward similar goals.

Creating the Gap

The gender leadership gap is the product of the obstacles to diversity identified earlier in this chapter. One way to visualize the development of the gender leadership gap is to think of women and men competing against each other on a track. Both are running in a 440-yard race. However, women run the 440 hurdles while men run the 440 dash. With each hurdle, more women fall behind, and the gap between male and female leadership aspirants widens. These hurdles have eliminated most of the female competitors by the time both contenders reach the finish line.

A study of female executives conducted by the Center for Creative Leadership illustrates the difficulties shared by women who had reached significant leadership positions within organizations.[45] The researchers discovered that all 76 of the successful female executives relied on the assistance of a senior mentor while making their climb to the top of the corporation. Mentors offered wide-ranging advice from assistance with key projects to support for promotions. (See chapter 12 for further discussion of mentoring.) Although mentors are valuable to both men and women, the investigators discovered that it was absolutely necessary for a woman to have a mentor to reach the highest levels of organizational leadership.

The study also found that successful female executives reported a willingness to take career risks and a desire for success that exceeded that of their male colleagues. These female executives, in many instances, felt a need to sacrifice family and relationships as the price for success. To overcome the hurdles to leadership success, women needed influential mentors and a commitment to exceed the standards usually set for males striving to reach the same top leadership positions.

Of all the barriers to diversity, stereotyping has the greatest negative impact on female leaders. Gender stereotypes are based on cultural definitions of what it means to be male or female. Sex is biologically based, but gender orientation—the way we think about acting female and male—is the product of symbolic communication. Julia Wood summarizes the relationship between sex, gender, and culture this way:

> There is nothing a person does to acquire her or his sex. It is a classification based on genetic factors and one that is enduring. Gender, however, is neither innate nor necessarily stable. It is acquired through interaction in a social world, and it changes over time. One way to understand gender is to think of it as what we learn about sex. We are born male or female—a classification based on biology—but we learn to be masculine and feminine. Gender is a social construction that varies across cultures, over time within a given culture, and in relation to the other gender.[46]

In the United States (which ranks toward the masculine end of Hofstede's masculine-feminine typology), masculine characteristics are equated with strength, aggression, ambition, independence, stoicism, and rationality. Feminine characteristics are associated with sensitivity to the needs of others, concern for family and relationships, emotionality, and nurturing. Gender expectations are communicated to us from the moment we're born. Girl babies are dressed in pink, boy babies in blue. Parents engage in more rough-and-tumble play with their infant sons than with their infant daughters. Boys are encouraged to engage in adventurous activities and to avoid tears while girls are encouraged to be careful, to share, and to look pretty.

These expectations shape the roles we play in society. Despite a recent shift to greater role flexibility, women remain the primary caregivers (in a dual career family, for instance, the mother is the parent who generally leaves work to pick up a sick child). Men are still considered the primary breadwinners and are most likely to build their identities around their careers.

Unfortunately, cultural expectations work against women who aspire to leadership. Not only are women and men viewed in different ways, but those characteristics defined as masculine are given higher status. As a culture, we put more value on decisiveness, assertiveness, competition, and other characteristics traditionally associated with males.[47] Compounding the problem of gender bias is the notion that the prototypical leader is masculine.

The damaging impact of gender typing can be seen at every step in leadership development. Many women never seriously consider becoming leaders because the process of socialization has taught them that leadership is the province of males or that some professions are open to men but not to women. Negative stereotypes and discrimination lower the self-confidence of some females, making them reluctant to take risks and to strive for leadership positions.[48] Because our culture highlights the nurturing role of women, most females enter service professions (teaching, nursing) or work in departments (such as human resources) that support the larger organization.[49] Female-dominated careers like clerical support, day care, and library science have less status than comparable male-dominated fields.

Women who do enter departments or professions that are overwhelmingly male face difficulties common to all who act as token representatives of their social groups.[50] Female tokens often find themselves treated as mothers or daughters. They may turn against other women as a result of the perceived need to adopt the attitudes of the dominant male culture. There is also a more narrow range of acceptable behavior for female leaders. Women who act "too aggressive," for example, risk being criticized for behaving in an unfeminine manner.[51]

In her book *Beyond the Double Bind,* Kathleen Jamieson explores a number of the traps and restrictions women confront. She describes a double bind as a rhetorical concept "that posits two and only two alternatives, one or both penalizing the person being offered them. . . . The strategy defines something 'fundamental' to women as incompatible with something the woman seeks—be it education, the ballot, or access to the workplace."[52] Thus, for example, it is often assumed that women cannot be both female and competent.

Other examples of double binds are plentiful. Historically, women were forbidden to speak, yet are now criticized for not producing great oratory. In mid-century (and continuing in moderated form), the trap was that women could choose either parenting or intellectual/economic pursuits. Discussions of similarities and/or differences between men and women use men as the standard, skewing the discussion from the start or, at a minimum, assuming that a "gain" for one "side" is a "loss" for the other. Jamieson points out that the double bind is "durable, but not indestructible."[53] She urges us to examine the binds as rhetorical forms to understand them, to manipulate them, and then to dismantle them.

Narrowing the Gap

The best practices for fostering diversity outlined earlier in this chapter address many of the barriers generated by negative gender stereotypes. Aggressive recruitment, greater accountability for developing female leaders, formation of advocacy groups, mentorship, and executive development programs can help bridge the gender leadership gap.

Overlooked in many strategies for bridging the gender leadership gap is the important role that communication competencies and communication styles play in the leadership advancement of both women and men. In chapter 1 we cited a survey in which personnel managers rated communication skills as the most important factor for gaining employment, performing successfully on the job, and managing effectively. Being recognized for these communication competencies can be problematic for women, however. They often have difficulty being recognized for their communication abilities. While they see themselves as competent communicators, their supervisors (the people most directly responsible for judging performance and recommending promotions) and others may not.[54]

Linguist Deborah Tannen believes female communication patterns are keeping women from getting the credit they deserve in organizational settings. Tannen begins by suggesting that communication styles are developed through childhood interactions with same-sex peer groups in which girls foster cooperation and boys promote competition. Female children are encouraged to play indoors in small groups or best-friend pairs and to build a sense of closeness and equality with their playmates. They are discouraged from boasting and giving orders, announcing their achievements, or expressing their preferences. Instead, girls are socialized to express their feelings and desires as helpful suggestions. Boys, on the other hand, are encouraged to play outdoors in large, hierarchically structured groups. They create and follow strict rules for competition where there are clearly defined winners and losers. Boys achieve status and maintain a degree of independence by giving orders, boasting, telling jokes and stories, and challenging the assertions of other boys in the group.[55]

The result of this early childhood training, according to Tannen, is a set of conversational patterns or rituals that contribute both to confusion on the job and to the gender leadership gap. Some of the more important differences in communication practice are listed below.[56]

- *Apologies.* Women often say "I'm sorry" to express understanding rather than to apologize for doing something wrong. Sharing the blame fosters equal positions for both parties. Men are reluctant to apologize because they perceive admitting mistakes as a subordinate act. Problems arise in conversations when women apologize to create equal status. Women expect a response like "It's partially my fault, too." Instead, they generally receive a response from men such as "I accept your apology." This pattern of interaction places women in an inferior position.

- *Softening criticism.* To foster cooperation, women soften their criticism by injecting positive comments ("I really like the first section of the article, but the second section needs some more work"), while men are more likely to address only the critiques ("The second section of this article is poorly done").

- *Saying thanks.* Politeness enhances feelings of goodwill and closeness. Women frequently say thanks as a way to signal the end of a conversation. Men, on the other hand, believe that expressions of gratitude place them in a subordinate position and will not respond in kind. This lack of "appropriate" response may be perceived by women as rude and can create confusion and conflict.

- *Ritual fighting.* Males are socialized to express their preferences through open challenge and criticism; women are socialized to offer helpful suggestions in a spirit of camaraderie. Females are discouraged from ritual fighting and find open challenge and criticism alien to the sense of cooperation they strive to foster.

- *Giving compliments.* Striving for equality, women are more willing to risk lessening their position of control by recognizing others' strengths and complimenting them on those strengths. Men associate giving compliments with low status and are less likely to respond in kind. These perceptions create one-up and one-down positions that place women at a disadvantage in male-dominated workplaces.

- *Complaining.* Females are trained to nurture and support. Listening and sharing problems and feelings foster an environment where rapport is highlighted. Males perceive complaints and problems as something that must be fixed by those in charge. Women who share problems and feelings may be perceived by men as difficult.

- *Humor.* Early childhood socialization of male humor involves teasing and hostility while female humor in childhood focuses on self-deprecation. Men are apt to take women's self-deprecation literally and fail to understand that it is actually understatement. When men accept this form of humor at face value, women are placed in an adverse position.

- *Boasting.* Females are discouraged from publicly acclaiming their efforts; they are encouraged to focus on the welfare of the group. Males, on the other hand, are encouraged to trumpet their accomplishments in order to achieve higher individual recognition and status. Organizational standards that encourage personal acclaim place women at a disadvantage.

- *Downplaying authority.* In order to create feelings of equality, women are less likely than men to remind subordinates of their lower status or to behave in an authoritarian manner.

Tannen is careful to note that there is no one best conversational style and that not all men and women fit the descriptions she provides. Gender socialization is only one of many cultural influences on conversational styles. Ethnic background, regional differences, family influences, and personality variables also determine how we interact. However, Tannen suggests that the gender gap may be largely a "wall of words." Ritual apologies, thank yous and compliments, frequent complaints, soft criticism, self-deprecating humor, the preference for modesty, and downplaying authority are often perceived as lower-status behaviors—making women and their ideas invisible. As a consequence, women are less likely to be rewarded or considered for advancement.

Kathleen Kelley Reardon supports the belief that differing communication styles are keeping women from advancing to the top levels of many organizations.[57] She notes that men are more comfortable with self-promotion, verbal sparring, and the language of team sports. The contrasting male/female communication styles have created a number of dysfunctional communication patterns (DCPs) that belittle women and reinforce male bias. Common DCPs include (1) excluding women from the decision-making process; (2) dismissing their contributions by interrupting, talking over, or ignoring ideas expressed; (3) retaliation based on male fear of female competence; and (4) patronizing responses such as treating female participation as unimportant or as an afterthought. Reardon encourages women managers (who often opt for silence) to confront these patterns head on. They should draw attention to the fact that they've been excluded from important meetings, claim credit for good proposals, challenge retaliatory statements, refuse to honor patronizing comments, and so on (see the case study in box 10.6).

Critics suggest that focusing on gender communication differences is counterproductive. Highlighting differences reinforces sexual stereotypes; too often male communication is seen as the norm and female communication as deviant. This, skeptics argue, negates the unique and valuable contributions of women.[58] Further, there are many more similarities than differences in male and female communication patterns. While popular culture has embraced the notion that men and women are from different planets (Mars and Venus), in reality it may be more appropriate to suggest "men are from South Dakota and women are from North Dakota."[59] South Dakotans and North Dakotans may believe that they are significantly different, but to the rest of the world the residents of the two states look and act very much alike. There are differences in how the sexes communicate due to cultural and biological factors, but these variations are frequently exaggerated. A more productive approach highlights the potential of women's communication to increase leadership effectiveness. Many of the behaviors Tannen identifies—softening criticism, being polite, recognizing achievement, and downplaying status differences—are qualities of exceptional leadership. As Carole Spitzack and Kathryn Carter explain, we should "begin to question the qualities proposed for leadership and conduct investigations which do not begin by assuming that female behaviors impede group progress. Female leadership may, in fact, promote cohesiveness, openness, trust, and commitment."[60]

Indeed, leaders perceived as transformational, whether male or female, exhibit gender balance—displaying characteristics traditionally regarded as masculine and feminine.[61] These leaders are emotional and nurturing as well as independent and ambitious—cooperative as well as competitive. The most effective leaders narrow the gender gap by combining the talents traditionally thought of as masculine and feminine to create a well-balanced leadership style.

Box 10.6   Case Study

The Memo in Every Woman's Desk[62]

The following case appeared in the *Harvard Business Review* and the *Washington Post* and was broadcast on National Public Radio. Readers and listeners were sharply divided over whether Liz should send the memo to her boss. Read the case and decide for yourself.

TO: Mr. John Clark, CEO
FROM: Elizabeth C. Ames, Director of Consumer Marketing

I've been working in the marketing department at Vision Software for more than ten years, where I've had my share of challenges and successes. I've enjoyed being part of an interesting and exciting company. Despite my general enthusiasm about the company and my job, however, I was taken aback when I received your memo announcing the resignations of Miriam Blackwell and Susan French, Vision's two most senior women. This is not the first time Vision has lost its highest-ranking women. Just nine months ago, Kathryn Hobbs resigned, and a year before that, it was Susanne LaHaise. The reasons are surprisingly similar: they wanted to "spend more time with their families" or "explore new career directions."

I can't help but detect a disturbing pattern. Why do such capable, conscientious women who have demonstrated intense commitment to their careers suddenly want to change course or spend more time at home? It's a question I've thought long and hard about.

Despite Vision's policies to hire and promote women and your own efforts to recognize and reward women's contributions, the overall atmosphere in this company is one that slowly erodes a woman's sense of worth and place. I believe that top-level women are leaving Vision Software not because they are drawn to other pursuits but because they are tired of struggling against a climate of female failure. Little things that happen daily—things many men don't even notice and women can't help but notice—send subtle messages that women are less important, less talented, less likely to make a difference than their male peers.

Let me try to describe what I mean. I'll start with meetings, which are a way of life at Vision and one of the most devaluing experiences for women. Women are often talked over and interrupted; their ideas never seem to be heard. Last week, I attended a meeting with ten men and one other woman. As soon as the woman started her presentation, several side conversations began. Her presentation skills were excellent, but she couldn't seem to get people's attention. When it was time to take questions, one man said dismissively, "We did something like this a couple of years ago, and it didn't work." She explained how her ideas differed, but the explanation fell on deaf ears. When I tried to give her support by expressing interest, I was interrupted.

But it's not just meetings. There are many things that make women feel unwelcome or unimportant. One department holds its biannual retreats at a country club with a "men only" bar. At the end of the sessions, the men typically hang around at the bar and talk, while the women quietly disappear. Needless to say, important information is often shared during those casual conversations.

Almost every formal meeting is followed by a series of informal ones behind closed doors. Women are rarely invited. Nor are they privy to the discussions before the formal meetings. As a result, they are often less likely to know what the boss has on his mind and therefore less prepared to react.

My female colleagues and I are also subjected to a daily barrage of seemingly innocent comments that belittle women. A coworker of mine recently boasted about how much he respects women, saying, "My wife is the wind beneath my wings. In fact, some people call me Mr. Karen Snyder." The men chuckled; the women didn't. And just last week, a male colleague stood up at 5:30 and jokingly informed a group of us that he would be leaving early: "I have to play mom tonight." Women play mom every night, and it never gets a laugh. In fact, most women try to appear devoid of concern about their families.

Any one of these incidents on its own is a small thing. But together and in repetition, they are quite powerful. The women at Vision fight to get their ideas heard and to crack the informal channels of information. Their energy goes into keeping up, not getting ahead, until they just don't have any more to give.

I can assure you that my observations are shared by many women in the company. I can only speculate that they were shared by Miriam Blackwell and Susan French.

Vision needs men and women if it is to become the preeminent educational software company. We need to send stronger, clearer signals that men are not the only people who matter. And this kind of change can work only if it starts with strong commitment at the top. That's why I'm writing to you. If I can be of help, please let me know.

Discussion Questions
1. Would you send this memo? Why or why not?
2. How might CEO Clark respond to this memo?
3. Could you revise the memo to be more effective? If so, how would you change it?
4. What other strategies (besides sending the memo) could Liz use to address the problems she identifies?
5. Have you ever faced dysfunctional communication patterns (DCPs) like those faced by the women at Vision Software? If so, how did you respond?

The new leader is a facilitator, not an order giver.
—John Naisbitt

Summary

In this chapter we explored the topic of leadership and diversity, beginning with a look at significant cultural differences. In high-context cultures, members prefer indirect or covert messages and determine meaning based largely on the context or setting. In low-context cultures, members communicate through overt messages and embed much more information in the language used to construct the message. Five values dimensions have been used to analyze cultures: power distance (how societies deal with inequities); individualism-collectivism (the relative emphasis on the individual or the group); masculinity-femininity (the definition and differentiation of sex roles); uncertainty avoidance (the extent to which people feel uncomfortable in unstructured situations); and long-term-short-term orientation (the extent to which societies sacrifice immediate gratification). Successful leaders recognize and respond to cultural differences, striving for cultural synergy. In cultural synergy, decisionmakers draw upon the diversity of the group and cultural awareness to produce and implement a better than expected solution.

Next we described ways that leaders can encourage diversity. The benefits of fostering diversity include cost savings, improved resource acquisition and utilization, greater market share, better decision making, and higher creativity. Obstacles to diversity operate at the personal, group, and institutional levels. Individuals engage in prejudice, discrimination, and stereotyping. Group members often suffer from ethnocentrism and experience conflicts based on cultural differences. Institutions sponsor practices that limit the progress of minorities. Organizations that have been the most successful at promoting diversity rely on a variety of strategies aimed at making existing leaders accountable for diversity progress, helping nontraditional employees develop leadership skills, and recruiting more diverse members. Aspiring minority executives need to choose high quality experiences over fast advancement in organizations that match their goals and have good diversity track records.

In the final section we focused on female leaders. The percentage of women in leadership positions shrinks with every step up the organizational and societal ladder, creating a gender leadership gap. This gap is not the result of differences in male and female leadership behavior; it is generated largely by gender role stereotypes. Gender typing keeps some women from seeking leadership positions, lowers the self-confidence of others, limits females to service roles, encourages tokenism, and limits the range of acceptable behavior for females. To narrow the gender leadership gap, women may need to confront differences in male and female communication styles that keep them from getting the credit they deserve. However, it is important to remember that outstanding leaders of both sexes display both masculine and feminine characteristics.

Application Exercises

1. In a research paper, compare and contrast the cultural classification systems described in the chapter with others not mentioned in the text. What common themes and differences do you note? What generalizations can you draw? How do your conclusions relate to leaders and followers?

2. Which of the Taoist leadership principles described in box 10.1 is most helpful to you? Least helpful? What other metaphors or images from nature might provide useful insights into leadership? How do Taoist leadership principles compare to those found in other philosophical/religious traditions like Christianity, Judaism, Islam, or Buddhism? Discuss your thoughts in a group or write up your conclusions.

3. As a small group, develop a culturally synergistic solution for the conflict involving Bob and Ari in box 10.3.

4. Create your own list of organizational practices that serve as barriers to diversity either on your own or in a small group. Share your findings with the rest of the class.

5. In a small group, class discussion, or reflection paper, evaluate the recommendations of one or both of the diversity best practices research projects described in the chapter.

6. Analyze the current diversity efforts of your college or work organization. What is the composition of the membership? The surrounding area? What steps have been taken to promote diversity'? How effective have they been? Write up your findings.

7. Divide into debate teams and argue for or against each of the assertions listed below. Your instructor will determine the debate format.

   • There is too much emphasis on the differences in the ways that men and women communicate.

   • Gender stereotypes will change significantly in the next ten years.

   • Prejudice and discrimination are a natural part of the human condition.

8. Interview a successful female leader. Share your findings with the rest of the class.

Cultural Connections: Living in an Integrated World[63]

Pulitzer Prize winning foreign affairs correspondent Thomas Friedman believes that the modern world was born in 1989, the year that the Berlin Wall fell and the Cold War ended. The Cold War divided nations into warring camps. Now integration, not division, marks international relations. Driven by capitalism, countries are deregulating their economies and opening up their markets to the rest of the world. The United States, as the most powerful capitalist society, is the dominant force in this new world-order.

Computers, the Internet, fiber optics, and other technologies increase the speed of communication and increase international interdependency. The collapse of Thailand's currency provides one example of just how integrated the global economy has become. When the value of the Thai baht plummeted in 1997, Southeast Asia went into a recession, which, in turn, drove down world commodity prices. This sharp decline led to the collapse of the Russian economy that is largely based on exports of oil and other raw materials. In the meantime, investors sold their holdings to cover their losses in Southeast Asia and Russia. This sell-off forced the Brazilian government to raise interest rates to as high as 40% to retain economic capital. Many frightened investors fled to the relative safety of U.S. treasury bonds, driving down interest rates and hurting many U.S. banks and mutual funds.

Friedman uses the metaphor of the Lexus and the olive tree to illustrate the tension between the new international economy and local traditions. The Lexus represents the drive toward modernization and globalization. The olive tree represents what "roots" us—family, community, local traditions, religion. While many nations have embraced the Lexus, many others, particularly in the Middle East, want to stay close to the olive tree. U.S. domination causes resentment. Many people oppose everything from U.S. "secular" values to Hollywood movies and fast food. In addition, the world economy makes losers out of former winners and often increases the gap between the rich and poor. The greatest threat to the Lexus will not come from nation states, according to Friedman, but from super-empowered angry men like Osama Bin Laden who use their wealth and the Internet to rally followers and to plot against those who threaten their values and traditions.

Is there any way to reconcile globalization with respect for the needs of local peoples—returning to Friedman's metaphor, to park the Lexus under the olive tree? The author suggests three economic strategies. One, encourage nations to provide more access to capital that will allow the poor to get into business for themselves. Two, provide retraining for new jobs to help those hurt by rapid change to recover. Three, provide assistance when needed (welfare, food aid, subsidized housing). These economic tactics must be accompanied by political changes if they are to make a difference, however. Government leaders must provide basic services, eliminate corruption, and foster democracy. As citizens in developing countries such as Kenya, Haiti, Liberia, and Afghanistan will attest, it is hard to participate in the global economy without reliable telephone systems, good roads, decent schools, involved citizens, honest bureaucrats, and trustworthy police and military forces.

Leadership on the Big Screen: *Tea with Mussolini*

Starring: Cher, Maggie Smith, Judi Dench, Lili Tomlin, Baird Wallace, Joan Plowright

Rating: PG for language and some suggestive sexual content.

Synopsis: A group of eccentric and artsy British women expatriates living in Florence, Italy during the 1930s take a young Italian boy under their collective wing. When World War II comes, the women (dubbed "The Scorpioni") and their U.S. counterparts are taken into custody. Their "adopted" son, now a young man, comes to their aid. This is no ordinary group of captives, however. The Scorpioni maintain their collective dignity and continue to support the arts even while in detention. Overcoming their differences, they unite to save the most controversial member of the group, a wealthy Jewish actress played by Cher. A comedy-drama loosely based on a true story.

Chapter Links: cultural differences, ethnocentrism, cross-cultural communication in conflict, gender stereotypes, assertive female leadership

Eleven

ETHICAL LEADERSHIP AND FOLLOWERSHIP

> *Most people wish to be good, but not all of the time.*
> —George Orwell

Overview

The Importance of Ethics

As we have suggested throughout this book, effective leadership is the product of the creation and delivery of inspiring and compelling messages. Humans, unlike other species, are capable of shaping reality through the manipulation of symbols. We do not passively react but rather *act* to change the world around us.

The power of human communication means that the question of ethics, in the words of Gerald Miller, is "inextricably bound up with every instance of human communication."[1] Ethics refer to standards of moral conduct, to judgments about whether human behavior is right or wrong.[2] The investigation of ethics is critical when focusing on leadership. A leader communicates a plan of action to his or her followers. The ethical implications of a leader's plans must be considered, since the exercise of unethical leadership can have devastating results. If you consider, for example, the negative impact of leaders such as Adolph Hitler, Joseph Stalin, Saddam Hussein, and Osama Bin Laden, you begin to see how important the relationship between leadership and ethics is.

Whether a leader is guiding a problem-solving group, a small business, a multimillion-dollar organization, or a national government, he or she exerts significant influence. Leaders must consider the impact they have on their followers as well as on others external to the group, organization, or society.

Educational writer and consultant Parker Palmer introduces a powerful metaphor to highlight the importance of leadership ethics and to dramatize the difference between moral and immoral leadership. According to Palmer, the distinction between ethical and unethical leaders is as sharp as the contrast between light and darkness, between heaven and hell.

> A leader is a person who has an unusual degree of power to create the conditions under which other people must live and move and have their being, conditions that can either be as illuminating as heaven or as shadowy as hell. A leader must take special responsibility for what's going on inside his or her own self, inside his or her consciousness, lest the act of leadership create more harm than good.[3]

The Ethical Challenges of Leadership: Casting Light or Shadow

Functioning as a leader means taking on a unique set of ethical challenges in addition to a set of tasks and expectations. These dilemmas involve issues of deceit, responsibility, power, privilege, loyalty, and responsibility. How leaders respond to these ethical challenges will determine if they cast more light than shadow.[4]

The Challenge of Deceit

Leaders typically have more access to information than do followers. They participate in decision-making groups, receive financial data, keep personnel files, network with managers from other units, and so on. Being "in the know" raises a number of complicated ethical dilemmas. Sissela Bok, in her book *Lying: Moral Choice in Public and Private Life*, defines lies as messages designed to make others believe what we ourselves don't believe.[5] The adage states that honesty is the best policy, but we have all probably told a lie (even it was merely "little" or "white"). Leaders also practice deception, either to further their own interests or the interests of the group. Newly appointed Notre Dame football coach George O'Leary claimed false credentials on his resume and was fired before he could coach a game. Bernadine Healy of the American Red Cross promised that all donations to the 9/11 relief fund would go directly to victims but then withheld a portion of the money for other projects. Enron officers misled investors by hiding debts through a series of partnerships that didn't show up on the company's balance sheet.

Determining whether or not to tell or conceal the truth is not the only dilemma surrounding access to data. Leaders also must choose whether or not to reveal that they possess important knowledge and when to release information and to whom. Law enforcement officials wrestle with both these issues when solving major crimes. Citizens have a right to know what their officials are doing, and tips from the public are instrumental in bringing many offenders to justice. However, releasing too much information too soon can jeopardize cases by alerting perpetrators to hide incriminating evidence. Releasing details about the crime to the media disperses knowledge previously known only to the perpetrator—and investigators lose one of their tools for assessing guilt.

How leaders get information can be a concern too. For example, civil libertarians protested George W. Bush's proposal to eavesdrop on conversations between suspected terrorists and their lawyers, discussions usually considered privileged. E-commerce firms routinely gather information about those who visit their sites to better target their advertisements. This data is often sold to other companies without the knowledge of the consumer.

When it comes to the challenge of deceit, leaders cast more shadow than light when they:

- lie, particularly for selfish ends;
- use information solely for personal benefit;
- deny having knowledge that is in their possession;
- gather data in a way that violates privacy rights;
- withhold information that followers legitimately need;
- share information with the wrong people;
- put followers in moral binds by insisting that they withhold information that others have a right to know.

The Challenge of Responsibility

Followers are largely responsible for their own actions, but leaders are held accountable for the actions of others. They must answer for the performance of the entire group, whether an academic department, a business, a nonprofit, a government agency, or sports franchise. This challenge is particularly important given the fact that leaders set the ethical tone for an entire organization. One study of the ethical practices of *Fortune 1000* companies found that the commitment of senior level executives determines whether or not a corporation takes its moral responsibilities seriously.[6] Nearly all of the nation's largest firms have taken steps to address ethical problems (i.e., adopting codes of ethics, appointing ethics officers, setting up complaint systems). However, in many cases these programs have little impact on day-to-day operations. CEOs rarely talk about ethics with employees or their ethics officers; workers rarely refer to the policies or call the complaint lines, and so on. Only when top leaders personally commitment themselves to social responsibility do ethical considerations take precedence over profit and efficiency; ethical performance becomes part of evaluation and promotion decisions.

While few would disagree with the fact that leaders are responsible for the actions of followers, determining the extent of a leader's responsibility is far from easy. For example: Can we hold the editor of the school newspaper responsible for the racist comments of a guest writer? Should the Champion Corporation and other manufacturers of college apparel be held accountable for working conditions in overseas factories run by subcontractors? Do these employers "owe" their followers safe working conditions, humane supervision, and a living wage? Can we blame professional football coaches when their players commit crimes during the off season? Should military officers receive the same or harsher penalties when their subordinates are punished for following their orders? Religious leaders urge their congregations to avoid sexual immorality. Should they to be fired if they visit pornographic web sites?

Answers to these questions can vary depending on the particular situation. Nonetheless, there are some general expectations of leaders. Responsible leaders:

- acknowledge and try to correct ethical problems;
- admit that they have duties to followers;

- take responsibility for the consequences of their orders and actions;
- take reasonable steps to prevent crimes and other abuses by followers;
- hold themselves to the same standards as their followers.

The Challenge of Power

A leader must decide what types of power to use and how much power she or he wishes to exert over followers. These decisions have moral implications. Is it ethical, for instance, to dominate followers and demand action, or should power be distributed? Is it ethical for a leader to demand compliance when a follower has a moral objection to the leader's request? The U.S. government, for example, allows those with a moral objection to war to register as conscientious objectors. Those who register for military service in this category are not assigned to combat units but serve in noncombative environments, such as hospitals.

Is it ever appropriate for a leader to insist that a follower behave in a way that he or she finds unacceptable? What if an employee finds a particular task morally objectionable or physically dangerous? Can a leader ethically insist that a follower perform the task? Some medical practitioners, for instance, refuse to participate in the performance of certain medical procedures such as abortions, sterilization, or euthanasia. Should these practitioners be punished for their views? Followers who choose not to perform certain tasks, of course, must live with the consequences of their convictions: a demotion, a narrowing of responsibility, or reassignment to another unit. Under what conditions should a leader respect a follower's right to determine his or her own behavior?

How leaders respond to ethical questions surrounding the use of power will go a long way to determining if they cast light or shadow over the lives of followers. As we noted in chapter 5, power can exert a corrupting influence over those who possess it and the greater the power, the greater the potential for abuse.

> *Lust for power is the most flagrant of all passions.*
> —Cornelius Tacitus

The Challenge of Privilege

Positions of leadership are associated with social and material rewards. Leaders may reap social benefits such as status, privilege, and respect, as well as material benefits such as high salaries and stock options. Is it ethical for a leader to take advantage of his or her position to achieve personal power or prestige? Should a leader's concern always be for the good of the collective? In Kenya, one of the most corrupt and poorest nations in the world, political leaders have traditionally taken advantage of their positions to enrich themselves at the expense of the general population. Government officials seize public property and use international loans and relief funds to purchase villas and luxury cars. At the same time, the majority of Kenyans live on approximately $300 a year.[7] Kenyan leaders are clearly abusing the benefits that come with their positions. However, such abuses are not limited to developing countries. Corporate executives in the United States often live like royalty; they are the highest paid in the world and enjoy such perks as chauffeur driven limousines, private jets, and executive dining rooms. In the 1960s the compensation of U.S. CEOs was 40 times that of the average employee. By 2002 CEO compensation had increased to nearly 600 times the salary of the average worker. At the same time stock prices plummeted, causing investors (including many employees who had investments linked to the performance of their employers) to lose billions.[8]

The Challenge of Loyalty

Leaders have to balance a variety of loyalties or duties when making decisions. Officers of a publicly held corporation, for example, must weigh their obligations to stockholders, employees, suppliers, other businesses, local communities, the societies where the company does business, and the environment. These loyalties often conflict with one another. For example, converting salespeople, insurance adjusters, and other workers to independent contractors reduces company expenditures for payroll taxes and benefits packages. While this decision benefits stockholders, it comes at the expense of workers. Employees may earn less under the new system while paying more in social security taxes and funding their own health and retirement plans.

Admirable leaders put the needs of others above selfish concerns. Executives at Tom's of Maine (a consumer products company) and Ben and Jerry's Ice Cream draw praise for giving to deserving causes, supporting local communities, and protecting the environment. In contrast, trial attorneys were criticized for keeping their suspicions about the safety of Firestone tires to themselves in order to increase their chances of winning lawsuits against the company. Their silence delayed the recall of the defective tires and may have resulted in additional injuries and deaths.[9]

Broken loyalties can also cast shadows. Employees at Enron felt betrayed by the firm's president, Kenneth Lay. He assured workers that the company was prospering even as he sold large quantities of his own stock. When the value of Enron stock evaporated, the retirement savings of many workers disappeared along with their jobs. On the other hand, well-placed loyalty can make a powerful moral statement. This happened in the case of Pee-Wee Reese, the Brooklyn Dodger who publicly demonstrated loyalty to Jackie Robinson, the first black player in the major leagues. In one particularly vivid display of support, Reese put his arm around Robinson's shoulders in front of a extremely hostile crowd in Cincinnati.[10]

The Challenge of Consistency

Leaders deal with a variety of followers, relationships and situations, making it difficult to behave consistently. In fact, situational leadership theory,

LMX, and other contingency models discussed in chapter 3 are based on the premise that a leader's behavior will vary depending on such factors as the readiness levels of followers, the nature of the task, and whether subordinates are members of the in-group or out-group. Nonetheless, acting inconsistently raises significant ethical dilemmas. Those in a leader's in-group probably have no problem with the leader's favoritism; those in the out-group probably resent the preferential treatment. For example, you probably felt cheated when a professor ignored or devalued your contributions while showering attention on his or her favorite students. Deciding when to bend the rules and for whom is also problematic. A strict policy about being on time for work, for instance, may have to be relaxed during bad weather. Some coaches let their star players skip practices to rest up for big games. Resident assistants are tempted to overlook the rules infractions of friends who live on their dormitory floors.

> *Wrong is wrong, no matter who does it or says it.*
> —Malcolm X

Some degree of inconsistency appears inevitable, but leaders cast shadows when they appear to act arbitrarily and unfairly. Leaders should try to be equitable with followers, making exceptions only after careful thought. In addition, they need to be evenhanded in their dealings with those outside the organization. Concerns about favoritism are at the heart of attempts to reform campaign financing. "Buying" access to political officials means that those who make large campaign contributions generally receive better treatment in the form of favorable legislation. The rest of us end up bearing a larger portion of the total tax burden and pay more for goods and services because of laws that protect everyone from farmers to automobile manufacturers and prescription drug companies.[11]

Meeting the unique ethical challenges of leadership is difficult, and we may disagree on what courses of action are appropriate. However, because moral judgments are critical to the practice of leadership, we have a responsibility to make reasoned, ethical decisions and to act on those choices. We can better fulfill this responsibility if we understand the components of ethical behavior and study some widely accepted ethical perspectives for guidance.

Components of Ethical Behavior

James Rest and his colleagues at the Center for the Study of Ethical Development at the University of Minnesota believe that ethical behavior is the product of four intrapersonal and interpersonal communication processes.[12] The first component is *moral sensitivity.* Moral sensitivity involves recognizing that our behavior impacts others, identifying possible courses of action, and determining the consequences of each possible strategy. The second component of the model, ***moral judgment***, is deciding which course of action identified in the first component is the right one to follow. The third component is ***moral motivation***. The desire to do the right thing generally comes into conflict with other values like security, wealth, and social acceptance. Ethical behavior results if moral values take precedence over other considerations. The fourth component is ***moral action***—the implementation stage of the model. Opposition, fatigue, and other factors are formidable barriers to ethical action. Overcoming these obstacles takes strong character and interpersonal skills.

The author is careful to point out that even though he numbers the elements of his four component model and presents them in a logical sequence, they don't necessarily occur in this order in real life. For example, how a person defines what is morally right or wrong (component 2) often determines moral sensitivity (component 1). What is a matter of preference for one individual may be a matter of conscience for another. Consider this seemingly routine decision: Should I have a hamburger or a salad for lunch? This is not an ethical choice for most consumers, but it is for many vegetarians. They refuse to eat meat on the grounds that killing animals for food is immoral. (The Research Highlight in box 11.1 provides an in-depth look at how one group of leaders ignored the moral implications of their choices with tragic consequences.)

Ethical failure occurs when one of the intrapersonal processes malfunctions. Often the problem stems from insufficient motivation and character. We can demonstrate moral sensitivity and judgment but fail to follow through if

---

Box 11.1   Research Highlight

Anatomy of an Ethical Failure[13]

The recent Bridgestone/Firestone/Ford scandal, which involved accidents of Ford Explorers equipped with Wilderness ATV tires, is not the first time that the Ford Motor Company has been accused of ignoring serious safety problems. In the late 1970s, the automaker faced a serious crisis based on its refusal to recall and repair gas tanks on Pinto subcompacts manufactured between 1970–1976. Gas tanks on these models were located behind the rear axle. In low-speed, rear end collisions, bolts from the differential housing (the large gear that transfers power from the driveshaft to the rear axle) could puncture the tank, causing a leak. At the same time, the filler pipe that carries gas to the tank often tore loose, causing additional leaks. Any spark would then ignite the gas and the car would be engulfed in flames.

Despite the fact that fixing the problem would only cost $11 per vehicle, the company failed to act, based in part on the belief that all small cars were inherently unsafe and that "safety wouldn't sell." The company also conducted a cost-benefit analysis and determined that the costs in human life (at $200,000 per fatality and $67,000 per injury) were substantially less than the costs to repair the problem on twelve and a half million vehicles. In 1978, the National Highway and Transportation Administration declared the Pinto defective, and Ford reluctantly issued a recall. That same year, the company lost a major lawsuit brought by a burn victim and was indicted by a grand jury for criminal negligence in the deaths of three teens who died in a rear end crash in Indiana (Ford was acquitted in the subsequent trial). This marked the first time that a major firm had faced criminal, not civil, charges for manufacturing faulty products. Ford stopped producing the Pinto in 1980.

Business professor Dennis Gioia was Ford's Recall Coordinator between 1973–1975. This put him in the research role of a participant-observer. Gioia initiated a discussion about recalling the Pinto but voted with the rest of the safety committee in recommending against any further action. Most of the criticism of Ford came after Gioia left the automaker, when the gas tank problem had been clearly identified, and Ford stonewalled its critics. Yet professor Gioia wonders why he didn't define the defective tanks as an ethical problem rather than as a business decision. Somehow his high moral standards (which included trying to make Ford more socially responsive) did not translate into action.

Gioia offers a number of explanations for his failure to act, including company pressure and personal moral weakness. In the end, however, he lays the blame on his moral insensitivity. He concludes that his typical way of processing information or *script* blinded him to the ethical dimension of the problem. Scripts, like other mental shortcuts, enable decision-makers to process data rapidly and to make quick choices. At the first signs of trouble with the Pinto, Gioia was dealing with as many as 100 possible recalls. His script (shared by others at Ford) defined problems based on their size and costs. To attract the attention of the safety group, there had to be lots of reports about a particular defect. The decision about how to respond to the faulty part was based on balancing the costs against the potential benefits. In the case of the Pinto, only a few exploded, so the problem didn't seem as pressing as defects in other models, which occurred much more frequently. Further, the expense of fixing the gas tank didn't appear to be justified. Sadly, ethical considerations were not part of the standard script. Gioia and his colleagues didn't question the morality of putting a dollar value on human life and allowing customers to die in order to save money.

Gioia argues that organizations should strive to integrate ethics into the scripts of organizational members. Codes of ethics and written policies will not be enough. Instead, ethical responsibilities should be included in job descriptions, and ethics ought to be an important theme in training and mentoring. Experienced employees may have to revise their scripts through training and experiences that explicitly focus on ethical issues. Unless ethics becomes part of the cognitive structure that decision-makers use everyday, they are likely to remain insensitive to the existence of moral problems. According to Gioia:

> Most models of ethical decision making in organizations implicitly assume that people recognize and think about a moral or ethical dilemma when they are confronted with one. I call this seemingly fundamental assumption into question. The unexplored ethical issue for me is the arguably prevalent case where organizational representatives are not aware that they are dealing with a problem that might have ethical overtones. If the case involves a familiar class of problems or issues, it is likely to be handled via existing cognitive structure or scripts—*scripts that typically include no ethical component in their cognitive content.*[14]

(1) other values become more important than moral values, and/or (2) we lack the will and skills to implement our decision. For example, our commitment to telling the truth may be overshadowed by our desire to avoid conflict and our inability to manage confrontation. As a result, we keep unpleasant truths to ourselves.

Researchers have conducted over a thousand studies of Rest's four component model using an instrument called the Defining Issues Test. Respondents read moral dilemmas (Should a model escaped prisoner be reported to the police? Should a doctor help a dying patient take her own life?) and then rank a series of items that reveal what they take into consideration when making ethical choices. According to Rest, the highest form of ethical reasoning is based on broad principles like justice, cooperation, and respect for others.[15]

Results from the Defining Issues Test indicate that we can increase our ethical competence. There is a strong link between higher education and reasoned decision making. Those in college and graduate school demonstrate the greatest gains in moral development. You can maximize the ethical benefits of your college education by taking courses on ethics, by participating in internships that raise real-life ethical dilemmas, and by developing interpersonal and problem-solving skills that can help you overcome barriers to implementing your ethical choices.[16]

Ethical Perspectives

Over the centuries philosophers and other scholars have developed a variety of theories or approaches that can be applied to ethical issues. These perspectives impact all four of the components of ethical behavior described above. They can raise our ethical awareness, guide our decision making, help us prioritize our values, and strengthen our moral character. In this section of the chapter we'll look at five ethical approaches that are particularly relevant to leadership.

Kant's Categorical Imperative

Immanuel Kant argued that individuals ought to do what is morally right, no matter what the consequences. The term *categorical* means *without exception*.[17] This standard can be applied by asking a simple question: Would we want everyone to make the same decision we did? If the answer is "no," then we have made the wrong choice. Based on this reasoning, leaders should never engage in such behaviors as cheating, lying, and murder. For instance, if we're tempted to make up statistics to boost donations to the nonprofit group we lead, we need to ask ourselves what would happen if every charity lied in order to raise funds. A climate of suspicion and hostility might be created that would bankrupt many worthy organizations. Our duty, then, is to present accurate information—even if misleading statistics might convince people to give more to our particular cause.

Utilitarianism

Utilitarianism uses the premise that ethical choices should be based on their consequences. Jeremy Bentham and John Stuart Mill argued that the best decisions are those that (1) generate the most benefits as compared to their disadvantages, and (2) benefit the largest number of people. The end result is that utilitarianism is attempting to do the greatest good for the greatest number of people.[18]

Leaders commonly weigh outcomes when making decisions. Franklin Roosevelt, for instance, lied to Congress and U.S. citizens in order to help Great Britain in World War II. He began to send ships and materials to the embattled nation before he received Congressional approval, judging that saving England justified his deceit. Harry Truman decided to drop the atomic bomb on Japan after determining that the benefits of shortening the war in the Pacific outweighed the costs of destroying Hiroshima and Nagasaki and ushering in the nuclear age.

Identifying and evaluating possible consequences can be difficult. Take the case of the CEO of a publicly owned corporation who is deciding whether or not to close one of the corporation's manufacturing plants. Many groups have a stake in this decision, and each will reach a different conclusion about potential costs and benefits. Stockholders may see the value of their shares go up if the company consolidates its operations. Employees will lose their jobs or be forced to move. The town losing the plant will see a drop in tax revenue, while other cities may see a boost in tax receipts if the corporation expands its operations in their communities. Unanticipated consequences further complicate the decision. If demand for the company's products skyrockets, the organization may need additional manufacturing capacity and regret closing the plant. If demand drops, keeping the plant open could jeopardize the future of the corporation.

Based on the difficulty of determining potential costs and benefits in situations like the one described above, utilitarian decision makers sometimes reach different conclusions when faced with the same dilemma. Some historians, for example, criticize Truman for his decision to drop the atomic bomb. They argue that the war would have ended soon without the use of nuclear weapons and that no military objective justifies such widespread destruction.

Virtue Ethics

As we've seen, there are significant differences between the categorical and utilitarian perspectives. However, both theories involve the application of universal rules or principles to specific situations. Dissatisfaction with rule-based approaches to ethical decision making is growing. Some ethicists complain that these guidelines are applied to extreme situations, not the types of choices we typically make.[19] Few of us will be faced with the extraordinary scenarios (stealing to save a life or lying to the secret police to protect a fugitive) that are frequently used to illustrate principled decision making. Our dilemmas are generally less dramatic. For instance: Should I lie to protect someone's feelings? Tell my employer about another job offer? Confront a coworker about a sexist joke? Ethical decision makers also deal with time pressures and uncertainty. In crisis situations they don't have time to carefully weigh consequences or to determine which abstract principle to apply.[20]

Recognizing the limitations of the utilitarian and categorical approaches, some scholars are turning back to one of the oldest ethical traditions—virtue ethics. Virtue ethicists highlight the role of the person or actor in ethical decision making. They argue that individuals with high moral character are more likely to make wise ethical choices. Virtue theorists seek: (1) to develop a description of the ideal person, (2) to identify the virtues that make up the character of this ethical prototype, and (3) to outline how individuals can acquire the required virtues.[21] Let's take a closer look at each of these objectives as they apply to leadership.

Definitions of *the ideal leader* will differ to some degree depending on the context. We may value kindness and consideration in a religious figure but want toughness in a military leader. Nevertheless, descriptions of the ideal leader show a high degree of consistency, no matter what the setting. The most admired leadership characteristics (honest, forward looking, inspiring, competent) that emerged in the study of fifteen thousand managers described in chapter 6 bear a striking resemblance to the things we look for in political leaders. We want elected officials who act with integrity, exercise good judgment, restrain their impulses, respect others, rally followers, persist in the face of strong opposition, and so forth.[22] President Clinton's affair with Monica Lewinsky demonstrated poor character. He took advantage of the power of his position, acted recklessly, and lied to cover up his unethical behavior. (See the Self-Assessment in box 11.2 for one tool designed specifically to measure the honesty and consistency of those in leadership roles.)

The *virtues of the ethical leader* are "deep-rooted dispositions, habits, skills, or traits of character that incline persons to perceive, feel, and act in ethically right and sensitive ways."[23] Aristotle provided one of the first comprehensive lists of virtues in Western culture. He described the ideal citizen/leader as someone who possesses characteristics such as courage, moderation, justice, generosity, hospitality, a mild temper, truthfulness, and proper judgment. Most, if not all, of these virtues appear on the lists of contemporary ethicists and leadership scholars. Other common virtues include love, empathy, compassion, and strength.[24]

> *Love is the virtue of the heart. Sincerity the virtue of the mind. Courage the virtue of the spirit. Decision the virtue of the will.*
>
> —Frank Lloyd Wright

Box 11.2   Self-Assessment

Perceived Leadership Integrity Scale (PLIS)[25]

This scale asks you to assess the integrity of your supervisor. However, you can also use this instrument to assess the image others have of your character. You might distribute the survey to a group of followers and ask for anonymous responses or estimate how you think others would rate you on each item. The higher the total score on the scale (31 is the lowest possible score, 124 the highest), the lower the perception of integrity of the person being rated.

The following items concern your immediate supervisor—the person who has the most control over your daily work activities. Use the following numbers to indicate how well each item describes your immediate supervisor.

1 = Not at all; 2 = Somewhat; 3 = Very much; 4 = Exactly

_____ 1. Would use my mistakes to attack me personally

_____ 2. Always gets even

_____ 3. Gives special favors to certain "pet" employees, but not to me

_____ 4. Would lie to me

_____ 5. Would risk me to protect himself/herself in work matters

_____ 6. Deliberately fuels conflict among employees

_____ 7. Is evil

_____ 8. Would use my performance appraisal to criticize me as a person

_____ 9. Has it in for me

_____ 10. Would allow me to be blamed for his/her mistake

_____ 11. Would falsify records if it would help his/her work situation

_____ 12. Lacks high morals

_____ 13. Makes fun of my mistakes instead of coaching me as to how to do my job better

_____ 14. Would deliberately exaggerate my mistakes to make me look bad when describing my performance to his/her superiors

_____ 15. Is vindictive

_____ 16. Would blame me for his/her own mistake

_____ 17. Avoids coaching me because (s)he wants me to fail

_____ 18. Would treat me better if I belonged to a different ethnic group

_____ 19. Would deliberately distort what I say

_____ 20. Deliberately makes employees angry at each other

_____ 21. Is a hypocrite

_____ 22. Would limit my training opportunities to prevent me from advancing

_____ 23. Would blackmail an employee if (s)he thought (s)he could get away with it

_____ 24. Enjoys turning down my requests

_____ 25. Would make trouble for me if I got on his/her bad side

_____ 26. Would take credit for my ideas

_____ 27. Would steal from the organization

_____ 28. Would risk me to get back at someone else

_____ 29. Would engage in sabotage against the organization

_____ 30. Would fire people just because (s)he doesn't like them if (s)he could get away with it

_____ 31. Would do things that violate organizational policy and then expect his/her subordinates to cover for him/her

Exemplars or role models play a critical role in the *development of high moral character*. Virtues are more "caught than taught" in that they are acquired through observation and imitation. We learn what it means to be just, generous, and honest by seeing these qualities modeled in the lives of exemplary leaders. Exemplary leaders can be people we work for; political, religious, or military leaders; historical figures (see the case study in box 11.3), and even fictional characters. Any story about leaders, whether it is an item in the morning newspaper, a segment on CNN, a novel, a play, a biography, or a movie, can provide insights into ethical (and unethical) leader behavior. Communities encourage the formation of moral character by telling and retelling stories that illustrate and reinforce ethical values.[26]

Box 11.3   Case Study

Moral Exemplars in the Holocaust[27]

If, as the virtue ethicists claim, we learn how to be virtuous by observing others, then it is important to identify examples of moral leadership. Leaders such as Mother Teresa, Archbishop Desmond Tutu, or Mahatma Gandhi fit neatly into the category of exemplary leader. Others, however, seem to blur the line between virtue and vice.

Lawrence Blum points to Oskar Schindler as someone who defies easy moral classification. The story of his life is familiar to those who have read the book *Schindler's List* by Thomas Keneally or have seen the film by the same name. Schindler was a German industrialist who hoped to get rich off the Nazi war machine in World War II. He went to Poland during the German occupation to set up an enamelware factory. He later used his position as factory manager to save the lives of 1,100 Jews who faced death through slave labor and extermination camps. In the process he was arrested several times and lost his entire fortune. None of his business ventures succeeded after the war and he had to depend on the generosity of those he had rescued in Poland.

There are several features of Schindler's character that contribute to what Blum calls his "moral ambiguity." Schindler loved fast cars, fine clothes, and alcohol. He had two mistresses in Poland and made little effort to hide this fact. An accomplished liar, he enjoyed misleading the Nazis. Part of his motivation for rescuing his workers may have been his addiction to adventure and risk. At times he seemed too enamored of his role as a "savior" of Jews.

Blum argues that Schindler should still be considered a moral hero despite his weak-nesses and ethical complexities. He brought about a great good (or prevented a great evil). While his motives were mixed, there can be no doubt that he found Nazi policies abhorrent and felt compassion for his workers. He carried out his rescue efforts at great personal cost, and his concern for others appeared to be stronger than his need for power.

While labeling Schindler a hero, Blum concedes that there are better models of behavior. He calls these individuals "moral paragons" or "saints." Such leaders live exemplary lives, demonstrating the virtues of integrity, moderation, and good judgment that appear to be missing in Oskar Schindler. They are motivated by high ideals that call forth their best efforts no matter what the situation. In contrast, moral heroes like Schin-dler seem to emerge only during times of crisis.

Blum points to Andre and Magda Trocme as prototypical moral saints. Andre was a pastor in the small town of Le Chambon in occupied France in World War II. He and his wife Magda convinced their congregation to shelter Jews, provided Jewish fugitives with food and shelter, and arranged for many to escape. Like Schindler, their efforts brought about a great good. However, unlike Schindler, they only engaged in deception because they had to and were motivated by a lifelong devotion to nonviolence. Schindler seemed to lose his purpose in life after the war and faded into moral obscurity. Andre Trocme continued to work on the behalf of nonviolence, becoming the European Secre-tary of the Fellowship of Reconciliation. Throughout his life Andre Trocme was able to accept (not condemn) others and, at the same time, bring out the moral best in them.[28]

Discussion Questions

1. What should the criteria be for determining if someone is an exemplary moral leader?

2. Based on your criteria, is Oskar Schindler such a leader?

3. Why does a crisis bring out the ethical best in some leaders like Schindler and the worst in others? What accounts for the difference?

4. Do you agree with Blum's distinction between moral heroes (Schindler) and moral saints (Andre and Magda Trocme)? Why or why not?

5. What can we learn from Schindler's example, whether or not you consider him an exemplary moral leader? What can we learn from the Trocmes?

Communitarianism

The goal of the communitarian movement is to build strong, moral com-munities that foster the development of ethical character. Led by sociologist Amitai Etzioni, communitarians argue that we ought to be less concerned about our individual rights and more concerned about our collective responsi-bilities. These responsibilities include: (1) staying informed about public issues, (2) becoming active in community affairs, (3) working with others on common projects, (4) caring for the less fortunate, (5) cleaning up corruption, and (6) urging families and schools to provide moral education.[29]

> *Who would want to live in a society in which everyone was positively indecent to another and at the same time positively scrupulous in respecting another's rights?*
>
> —Philip Abbott

There is a sense of urgency in the communitarian message. Proponents point to the growing power of special interest groups, the polarization of political parties, self-absorption, and high divorce and crime rates as evidence that U.S. society is fragmenting and in a state of moral decline. This downward slide can be halted, however, if citizens create local, regional, national, and international communities characterized by "people deciding together, face to face, conversing with and respecting each other in a setting which is as equal as possible."[30] In this type of community, members: care about and trust one another; engage in dialogue that involves speaking and listening; manage conflict through rational discussion and collaboration; commit themselves to core values; and debate what constitutes the common good.[31] (For a closer look at the role of trust in society, see box 11.4.)

Robert Putnam uses the label "civic community" to describe the networks and norms that are created when citizens actively participate in public life.[32] His study of the northern and southern regions of Italy illustrates how civil societies differ from "uncivil" ones. In civil northern Italy, residents belong to more social groups, read about community events, get involved in public issues, trust one another, and believe in equality. Values like solidarity, engagement in civic affairs, honesty, and cooperation are important. In uncivil southern Italy, fewer residents belong to civic and social associations, and they leave public affairs to a few political bosses. Greed is more important than the common good; citizens are unwilling to compromise and don't respect the law; corruption is rampant. Not surprisingly, citizens of the healthy communities in northern Italy are more content, enjoying a higher standard of living and better government. Those in southern Italy feel powerless and unhappy, suffering from ineffective government and a lower standard of living.

The communitarian movement has its share of critics. Some observers fear that focusing on the needs of the community will lead to authoritarianism and the erosion of individual rights. Others take issue with the evangelistic fervor of some communitarians and their emphasis on promoting one set of values in a pluralistic society.[33] (Refer to the Cultural Connections section at the end of the chapter for a list of values that might be common to all cultures.)

Despite the controversy, communitarianism is a promising new perspective on ethical decision making. First, the movement addresses many of the dangers of

---

Box 11.4   Case Study

The Case of the Lost Wallet[34]

Read the following description and answer the two questions either "yes" or "no."

Suppose you are walking down the street and you find a wallet containing $50, some credit cards, and a driver's license. Do you think you would try to return the wallet and all its contents to its owner? Do you think most people would try to return the wallet and its contents to its owner?

Alex Michalos used this scenario to measure the trust level of university students. He found that 91% of the students he surveyed would return everything in the wallet, but only 49% thought that most people would do the same. Those who wouldn't return the wallet were even more skeptical about the honesty of others. Based on responses to this case and others like it (scenarios that ask respondents if they would stop for a stranded motorist or give blood during a campus blood drive, for example), Michalos and his fellow researchers draw two conclusions. One, we should have more confidence than we do in others. Two, lack of trust is a self-fulfilling prophecy. If we don't believe that fellow citizens are as decent as we are, we aren't as responsive to the needs of others, and the quality of life declines. On the other hand, placing trust in other individuals encourages them to be more trustworthy, helping to build healthy communities.

Discussion Questions

1. How trusting are you based on your answers to the questions above? Is this an accurate reflection of how much trust you generally have in others?

2. How would you define trust?

3. What factors do you take into consideration when deciding when to trust others?

4. How important is trust to the health of groups, organizations, and communities? How is it developed? How is it lost?

5. What are some ways that you can act in a more trusting manner? Encourage others to do the same?

---

individualism (such as loneliness, polarization, crime, and divorce) by arguing for a better balance between individual rights and collective needs. Second, an emphasis on the common good discourages selfish, unethical behavior on the part of individuals and groups. Lying, polluting, or manufacturing dangerous products may serve the immediate needs of a leader or organization, but such actions are unethical because they rarely benefit society as a whole. Third, communitarianism encourages the collaborative approach to social problems discussed in chapter 9. The practice of public relations is a case in point. Traditionally, organizations have used public relations strategies to persuade outside audiences to support their programs and to buy their products. Communication generally flows from the organization to the public, and managers rarely modify their objectives in response to community concerns. In contrast to the traditional model, a communitarian approach to public relations encourages professionals to view themselves as community builders. In this role, public relations practitioners share information with outsiders, engage in dialogue with organizational publics, build long-term relationships with constituencies, listen and respond to community concerns, and collaborate to resolve disputes and solve problems.[35]

Leaders as Servants

This ethical perspective specifically addresses the behavior of leaders. Contemporary interest in leaders as servants was sparked by Robert Greenleaf. He coined the term "servant-leader" in 1970 to describe a leadership model that puts the concerns of followers first. Greenleaf later founded a center to promote servant-leadership. His ideas have been adopted by businesses (Southwest Airlines, Synovus Financial Corporation, The Container Store, AFLAC), nonprofit organizations, and community and service-learning programs.[36] Servant-leaders put the needs of followers before their own needs. Because they continually ask themselves what would be best for their constituents, servant-leaders are less tempted to take advantage of followers, act inconsistently, or accumulate money and power for themselves. Five principles serve as the foundation for servant leadership.

The first principle is a concern for people—an extension of the ethical principle of altruism. Servant-leaders believe that healthy societies and organizations care for their members. They use such terms as *love, civility,* and *community* to characterize working relationships. Advocates of altruism believe that we should help others whatever the cost to us. Altruism is particularly important to leaders because they exercise influence on behalf of others and may have to take risks and sacrifice personal gain.[37] Servant-leaders argue that the measure of a leader's success lies in what happens in the lives of followers—not in what the leader has accomplished. Greenleaf suggests that we gauge a leader's effectiveness by asking the following questions: "Do those served grow as persons? Do they, while being served, become healthier, wise, freer, more autonomous, more likely themselves to become servants?"[38]

The second principle of servant leadership is stewardship. Servant-leaders hold their positions and organizations in trust for others. They act on behalf of followers who have entrusted them with leadership responsibilities; they act on behalf of society by making sure that their organizations serve the common good. Stewards are accountable for results but reach their goals by serving others, not by controlling or coercing them.[39]

> *The highest of distinctions is service to others.*
> —George VI

The third principle of servant leadership is equity or justice. Servant-leaders make a concerted effort to create a level playing field by distributing results fairly. For example, the Herman Miller company, a highly profitable commercial furniture manufacturing firm, allows every employee with a year or more of service to own stock in the company and limits the compensation of its CEO to 20 times the salary of the lowest-paid factory worker—a sharp contrast to the typical CEO salaries noted earlier in this chapter.[40] The principle of equity extends to the distribution of power. Servant-leaders view followers as partners. They practice empowerment by giving followers the space to develop and exercise their talents, by delegating authority for important tasks, and by sharing information. Former Herman Miller chairman of the board Max DePree urges organizational leaders to engage in "lavish" communications, sharing information about every aspect of the operation. "Information is power," says DePree, "but it is pointless power if hoarded. Power must be shared for an organization or a relationship to work."[41] At Herman Miller, top executives report monthly to employees on company profits and productivity.

> *At the heart of strong democracy is talk.*
> —Benjamin Barber

The fourth principle of servant leadership is indebtedness. For those who view leadership as a form of service, both leaders and followers "owe" each other certain responsibilities. According to DePree, followers can expect the following rights from their leaders.

- *Right to be needed.* Followers have the right to use their gifts and be connected in a meaningful way to the mission of the organization.
- *Right to be involved.* Everyone has a right to participate and to have input. In addition, leaders must respond to suggestions and work with followers to meet the needs of customers.
- *Right to a covenantal relationship.* Contractual relationships are based on legal agreements that define pay, working conditions, vacations, etc. Covenantal relationships are based on a commitment to common goals and values; such relationships meet deeper needs and help provide meaning to work.
- *Right to understand.* Followers have a right to know and understand the following elements: organizational mission, personal career paths, the competition, the working environment, terms of employment.
- *Right to affect one's own destiny.* Followers should always be involved in their performance evaluations and in promotion and transfer decisions that impact their careers.
- *Right to be accountable.* Accountability includes contributing to the achievement of group goals and sharing ownership in group problems and risks. Contributions should be evaluated according to clear, acceptable criteria.

- *Right to appeal.* Everyone should have the right to appeal decisions that might threaten one or more of the rights described earlier.
- *Right to make a commitment.* In order to make a commitment, followers must know that they can do their best and not be held back by leaders, particularly leaders who act in an irrational manner.

Followers, in turn, have responsibilities to their leaders. DePree suggests that followers owe the following to their leaders and institutions.[42]

- understand the institution and its goals, customers, limitations, etc.
- take responsibility for reaching personal goals
- be loyal to the idea behind the organization even when not in agreement with all of the organization's goals and procedures
- resist fear of the new and unknown
- understand the value of others as members of the group and their contributions
- make a personal commitment to be open to change
- build constructive relationships
- ask a great many questions of leaders, including what they believe, how they have prepared themselves for leadership, and whether they can help followers reach their potential

The fifth principle of servant leadership is self-understanding. Like the virtue ethicists, proponents of servant leadership believe that ethical choices should be based on character rather than on codes of conduct. Servant-leaders analyze their motives, seek out opportunities for personal growth, and regularly take time to examine their attitudes and values. They create a positive ethical climate for followers by striving to be trusting, insightful, open to new ideas, strong, and courageous.[43]

Following servant leadership principles can have a significant impact on how organizational leaders think and act. For a summary of the differences between traditional bosses and those who seek to serve, see box 11.5.

Box 11.5

Traditional Bosses vs. Servant Leaders: A New Kind of Leadership[44]

Traditional Boss	Servant as Leader
Motivated by personal drive to achieve.	Motivated by desire to serve others.
Highly competitive; independent mindset; seeks to receive personal credit for achievement.	Highly collaborative and interdependent; gives credit to others generously.
Understands internal politics and uses them to win personally.	Sensitive to what motivates others and empowers all to win with shared goals and vision.

Traditional Boss	Servant as Leader
Focuses on fast action. Complains about long meetings and about others being too slow.	Focuses on gaining understanding, input, buy-in from all parties.
Relies on facts, logic, proof.	Uses intuition and foresight to balance facts, logic, proof.
Controls information in order to maintain power.	Shares big-picture information generously.
Spends more time telling, giving orders. Sees too much listening or coaching as inefficient.	Listens deeply and respectfully to others—especially to those who disagree.
Feels that personal value comes from individual mentoring.	Feels that personal value comes from talents and working collaboratively with others.
Sees network of supporters as power base and titles as a signal to others.	Develops trust across a network of constituencies; breaks down hierarchy.
Eager to speak first; feels his/her ideas are more important; often dominates or intimidates opponents.	Most likely to listen first; values others' input
Uses personal power and intimidation to leverage what he/she wants.	Uses personal trust and respect to build bridges and do what's best for the "whole."
Accountability is more often about who is to blame.	Accountability is about making it safe to learn from mistakes.
Uses humor to control others.	Uses humor to lift others up and make it safe to learn from mistakes.

Courageous Followership

So far we have focused our attention on the ethical responsibilities of leaders. However, followers also make moral choices.[45] As business and government consultant Ira Chaleff notes, being a follower does not justify unethical behavior. He points to the Nuremberg trials held after World War II as proof that we must take ownership of our actions as followers. Convened to try Nazi war criminals, the international tribunal rejected the argument that German officials should be exempt from punishment because they were "following orders."

> The bottom line of followership is that we are responsible for our decision to continue or not to continue following a leader . . . we have the choice of supporting an anathema to our values or not. This is the Nuremberg trials principle. The fact that we are following orders absolves us from nothing.[46]

Chaleff believes that courage is the most important virtue for followers. He defines courage as accepting a higher level of risk. It is risky, for instance, for a student to confront a professor about an unfair grading policy, for a vice-president to oppose the pet project of the CEO, or for a congressional chief of staff to challenge the position of a member of the House or Senate. Exhibiting courage is easier if followers recognize that their ultimate allegiance is to the purpose and values of the organization, not to the leader. Chaleff outlines five dimensions of courageous followership.

The Courage to Assume Responsibility

Followers must be accountable both for themselves and for the organization as a whole. Taking responsibility utilizes many of the strategies outlined in our discussion of self-leadership in chapter 5. Courageous followers take stock of their skills and attitudes, seek feedback and personal growth, maintain a healthy private life, and care deeply about the organization's goals. They take initiative to change organizational culture by challenging rules and mindsets and by improving processes.

The Courage to Serve

Courageous followers support their leaders through hard, often unglamorous, work. This labor takes a variety of forms, including:

- helping leaders conserve their energies for their most significant tasks
- organizing the flow of information from and to the leader
- controlling access to the leader
- defending the leader from unjust criticism
- relaying a leader's messages in an accurate, effective manner
- acting in the leader's name when appropriate
- shaping a leader's public image
- helping the creative leader focus on the most useful ideas generated
- presenting options during decision making
- encouraging the leader to develop a variety of relationships
- preparing for crises
- helping the leader and the group cope with the leader's illness
- mediating conflicts between leaders
- promoting performance reviews for leaders

The Courage to Challenge

Inappropriate behavior damages the relationship between leaders and followers and threatens the purpose of the organization. Leaders may break the law; scream at or use demeaning language with employees; display an arrogant attitude; engage in sexual harassment; abuse drugs and alcohol; and misuse funds. Courageous followers need to confront leaders acting in a destructive manner. In some situations, just asking questions about the wisdom of a policy decision is sufficient to bring about change. In more extreme cases, followers may need to disobey unethical orders. (For examples of leaders who took the initiative to influence their bosses, see box 11.6.)

Box 11.6   Research Highlight

Courage in Action: Leading Up[47]

University of Pennsylvania leadership scholar Michael Useem uses the phrase "leading up" to describe leader/followers who take the initiative to influence their bosses as well as their subordinates. These individuals move beyond their assigned responsibilities, taking charge when they see a need and persuading their superiors to support their efforts. According to Useem, as organizations decentralize authority, modern managers must increasingly lead up as well as down. However, he cautions that while some organizations want followers to speak up, many do not. Leading up in these situations takes courage.

> To come forward when an organization or superior does not encourage it can be both tremendously rewarding and extremely risky. If the upward leadership works, we can help transform incipient disaster into shining triumph. If handled poorly, such upward courage may prove little more than reckless abandon, a career-shortening or even career-ending move. Either way, though, we will have embraced a responsibility whose absence we deplore in others.[48]

In his book *Leading Up*, Useem describes a number of contemporary and historical leaders who either succeeded or failed in their attempts to influence their superiors. He then draws implications from their experiences. Some of his examples of leading up (or failing to lead up) include:

- Charles Schwab president David Pottruck. Through careful planning and reasoning, he convinced the firm's founder to move his brokerage onto the Internet.
- Civil War generals Joseph Johnson, George McClellan, and Robert E. Lee. Johnson and McClellan were replaced because they failed to keep their superiors—Jefferson Davis and Abraham Lincoln—informed. Lee, on the other hand, succeeded in keeping his post because he regularly communicated with Davis and treated him with respect.
- Belgian United Nations peacekeeper Romero Dallaire. Dallaire tried to convince his superiors to intervene in the 1994 genocide in Rwanda but failed because he didn't effectively communicate the gravity of the situation. Even without the permission of the UN Secretary General, he could have taken additional steps to curb the bloodshed.
- CEOs Robert Ayling of British Airways, Eckerd Pfeiffer of Compaq computer, and Thomas Wynan of CBS. All three lost their jobs when they forgot that they worked for their boards of directors and kept their superiors in the dark about profits and business strategies.
- Old Testament patriarchs Abraham, Moses, and Samuel. These prophets were able to intercede with God, persuading the Supreme Being to modify His decrees to better serve His chosen people.

Chaleff offers a number of suggestions for those who must stand up to their leaders. First, recognize that leaders are particularly prone to self-delusion because they have strong egos and their strategies have been successful in the past. The very traits that elevated them to positions of responsibility—decisiveness, independence, and attention to detail—may now be weaknesses in light of current organizational realities (see our discussion of organizational leadership in chapter 8). Next, confront destructive behavior when it first occurs—before it becomes a habit that undermines the organization and the leader. Defuse defensiveness by prefacing comments with statements of support and respect. Finally, aim negative feedback at a behavior or policy, not at the person. Be specific about what the problem behavior is, its negative consequences, and the potential long-term impact if it continues.

The Courage to Participate in Transformation

Negative behavior, when unchecked, often results in a leader's destruction. Yet overcoming ingrained habits and communication patterns is a long, difficult process. Leaders may deny the need to change, or they may attempt to justify their behavior. They may claim that whatever they do for themselves (embezzling, enriching themselves at the expense of stockholders, etc.) ultimately benefits the organization. To succeed in modifying their behavior patterns, leaders must admit they have a problem and acknowledge that they should change. They need to take personal responsibility and visualize the outcomes of the transformation process—better health, more productive employees, higher self-esteem, restored relationships. Followers can aid in the process of transformation by: drawing attention to what needs to be changed; providing honest feedback; suggesting resources; creating a supportive environment; modeling openness to change and empathy; and providing positive reinforcement for positive new behaviors.

The Courage to Leave

When leaders are unwilling to change, courageous followers may take principled action by resigning from the organization. Departure is justified when the leader's behaviors clash with the leader's self-proclaimed values or the values of the group, or when the leader degrades or endangers others. Sometimes leaving is not enough. In the event of serious ethical violations, the misbehavior of the leader must be brought to the attention of the public by going to the authorities or the press. Such a response would be justified when police commanders order the torture of suspects, corporate executives ask employees to ignore serious safety problems, or the founders of activist groups call for acts that endanger the lives of citizens. Those who decide to leave can reduce the risks by setting contingency funds aside, by having written references on file should the need to change jobs arise, by developing good relations with the media in case they need to go public, and by building support groups.

Summary

In this chapter we examined the link between ethics and our roles as leaders and followers. Standards of moral judgment are critical to the practice of leadership. Leaders face a set of six unique ethical challenges: (1) issues related to truthfulness and the release and collection of information; (2) the extent of their responsibility for the actions of followers; (3) use of power; (4) accumulation of social and material rewards; (5) conflicting and broken loyalties; and (6) inconsistent treatment of subordinates and outsiders. How they respond to these challenges will determine if they cast light or shadow over the lives of followers.

Four communication processes lead to ethical behavior: moral sensitivity, moral reasoning, moral motivation and moral action. Ethical leaders are sensitive to the presence of ethical issues, make principled choices, place a high value on ethical behavior, and implement the decision no matter what the cost.

There are five perspectives or approaches that are particularly relevant to ethical leadership. Kant's categorical imperative argues that decision makers ought to do what is morally right no matter what the consequences. Certain behaviors like exaggeration, lying, stealing, and murder are always wrong because we wouldn't want others to engage in them. The premise of utilitarianism is that ethical choices should be based on their consequences. The best decisions are those that generate the most advantages as compared to disadvantages and that benefit the greatest number of people. Virtue ethics highlight the role of the person making ethical choices. Leaders with high moral character (who display virtues such as courage, integrity, justice, wisdom, and generosity) are more likely to behave in an ethical manner. Communitarianism strives to build strong, moral ("civic") communities that foster character development. Civic leaders place the common good above narrow interests. Servant leadership suggests that viewing leadership as an opportunity to serve others encourages ethical behavior. Servant-leaders put the needs of followers before their own needs.

Courage (accepting a higher level of risk) is critical for those in the follower position. Followers must: take responsibility for themselves and the organization; serve their leaders through hard work; challenge leaders when they engage in destructive behaviors; help leaders overcome destructive patterns and habits; and leave when a leader's behaviors clash with important values or when the leader degrades or endangers others.

Application Exercises

1. Look for examples of unethical leadership behavior in the media and classify them according to the six ethical challenges. Which challenge(s) did the leader fail to meet? What shadows did she/he cast? Do you note any patterns? Are there additional ethical dilemmas unique to leadership beyond those discussed in the chapter?

2. Think of an ethical dilemma you have faced and analyze your response based on Rest's four-component model. Why did you identify this problem as an ethical issue? What considerations played a part in your decision about what to do? What values impacted your motivation to implement your choice? Did you follow through on your decision and take the action you had determined to be appropriate? Why or why not? Write up your analysis in a 3–4 page paper.

3. Select a segment from the television show *60 Minutes* and analyze it from a virtue ethics perspective. Choose a story that raises ethical issues about leadership or followership (an employee who blows the whistle on an unethical organization, a world leader who demonstrates courage). What virtues do the subjects in the story exhibit or fail to exhibit? How would you evaluate their ethical character? What ethical lessons can we learn about leadership and followership from this story? Write up your analysis.

4. Do you agree with the list of universal values on page 341? Are there any values that you would add to the list? Subtract? Should the search for ethical common ground be abandoned? Why or why not? Present your conclusions to other class members.

5. Conduct a class debate concerning whether or not leaders should act as "servants" to their followers.

6. Practice confronting leaders by role playing the following scenarios in class:

- You have been at your new job for six months and really enjoy it. However, you are becoming increasingly uncomfortable with the way that your supervisor touches you. At first he gave you brief pats on the shoulder and back. Now his hand lingers for 2–3 seconds. You are concerned that he will become even more intimate, so you set up an appointment to talk about his behavior.

- Your supervisor at the ad agency is a "hard charger" who has dramatically increased billings for new clients. Unfortunately, this highly competent and confident leader demeans employees who don't meet her high standards. In the most recent incident she screamed obscenities at an account executive during a staff meeting. You decide to confront her in private.

- You admire your supervisor who is kind and generous with all employees. However, she can't seem to stay focused on important tasks. As a result, you get stuck with a lot of last minute details that aren't in your job description. You worry that your supervisor and your department will suffer if she doesn't start finishing projects on time and paying attention to the overall direction of your group. Your weekly appointment with your supervisor is about to begin.

- You are assistant director at a nonprofit organization that serves the developmentally disabled. The director founded the agency twenty-five years ago. He recently suffered a series of strokes and cannot carry out many of his responsibilities, including raising money and setting the budget. He refuses to step down or even to take a temporary leave. You decide to discuss his future with him.

Cultural Connections: Identifying a Global Code of Ethics[49]

Is there such a thing as a global code of ethics, a set of values that all cultures can agree on? According to Rushworth Kidder of the Global Ethics Foundation, the answer to this question is a resounding "yes." He argues that there are common ethical standards that cross political, social, and cultural boundaries. Further, identifying these shared values is more important than ever before due to "worldshrink" and "technobulge." The world is becoming increasingly interdependent due to rapid transportation, the mass media, and international commerce. While the world is shrinking, technology is expanding. Technological progress generates new ethical dilemmas with far-reaching consequences. Development of the atomic bomb raised the specter of global holocaust for the first time in human history. Genetic mapping and weather control raise additional ethical issues for contemporary leaders and ethicists. Kidder believes that finding moral common ground is the way to ensure global survival. Adhering to shared values can bind the international community together and enable diverse cultures to solve world problems jointly.

To identify universal values, Kidder interviewed two dozen "ethical thought leaders" from around the world. These men and women included officials from the United Nations, leaders from the United States and New Zealand, former heads of state from Costa Rica and Lebanon, a Buddhist monk and a Catholic priest, and writers from Sweden, Australia, and England. Each of the interviews began with this question: "If you could create a global code of ethics, what would be on it?" Once the data was collected, Kidder and his colleagues looked for common threads in the tapes and transcripts. What they found were eight core values:

- love (compassion that transcends cultural and political differences)
- truthfulness (honesty, keeping promises, not keeping secrets)
- fairness (even-handedness, fair play, a concern for justice and equality)
- freedom (right to express ideas and act on individual conscience)
- unity (putting emphasis on community, solidarity, cooperation)
- tolerance (respect for the dignity, rights, and ideas of others)
- responsibility (for oneself, others, future generations)
- respect for life (not killing)

The researchers don't claim to have isolated *the* global code of ethics, but they believe that their findings prove that world leaders can find an ethical common ground. The fact that the list contains few surprises is proof that these values are widely shared. According to Kidder:

> This eight-point set of values bears striking resemblance to lists of values derived by participants in numerous ethics seminars conducted recently around the United States by the staff at the Institute for Global Ethics. This is not, in other words, an off-the-wall, unique, bizarre list. It may even strike us as familiar, ordinary, and unsurprising. That's a comforting fact. Codes of ethics, to be practicable, need to have behind them broad consensus. The originality of the list matters less than its consistency and universality.[50]

Leadership on the Big Screen: *The Godfather*

Starring: Al Pacino, Marlon Brando, Dianne Keaton, Robert Duval, Talia Shire, James Caan, Abe Vigoda

Rating: R for violence, language, and sexual content

Synopsis: First installment of the Godfather film trilogy that tells the story of the Corleone crime family. Based on the novel by Mario Puzo and the winner of Oscars for Best Picture, Supporting Actor (Brando), and Screenplay. Michael Corleone (Pacino) is reluctantly drawn into the family's criminal enterprises after the assassination of his brother (Caan) and the retirement of his father (Brando). Michael takes over from his father as Mafia don and restores the family's fortunes through cunning, deceit, intimidation, and murder. He triumphs but, in the process, he deadens his soul, shuts out his wife (played by Keaton), and raises important questions about what it means to be a "successful" leader.

Chapter Links: deceit, betrayal, abuse of power and other leadership shadows, ethical failure, the moral duties of followers

Twelve

LEADERSHIP DEVELOPMENT

> *You have to be careful if you don't know where you are going, because you might not get there.*
>
> —Yogi Berra

Overview

Leadership Development: A Lifelong Journey

Every year thousands of adult learners over the age of twenty-five return to college classrooms to complete their degrees and to upgrade their job skills. These nontraditional students (you may be one of them) believe in lifelong learning. We do, too. Developing leadership communication skills is an ongoing process. The moment we think we have "arrived" as leaders, our progress stops. For this reason, we will use this final chapter to discuss ways to continue your development as a leader.

Although leadership is a complex process, almost anyone can develop the skills necessary to lead effectively. As we noted in chapter 3, leaders are not born to greatness. Leaders are developed through learning, experience, and mentoring. Corporations around the globe have recognized that leadership skills can be developed. Companies like Motorola, Southwest Airlines, General Electric, Hewlett-Packard, Xerox, American Express, and Pepsi, among others, spend millions of dollars each year on training. Much of this training is devoted to improving leadership effectiveness.[1] One estimate suggests that as much as $6.6 billion is spent each year on programs specifically devoted to developing corporate leaders.[2]

Ellen Van Velsor, Cynthia McCauley, and Russ Moxley of the Center for Creative Leadership (see chapter 10 for a discussion of the Center's GOLD project) define leadership development as "the expansion of a person's capacity to be effective in leadership roles and processes."[3] Two elements are central to this definition.

1. Leadership can be learned. Individuals can expand their leadership capacities at any age. People do learn, grow, and change.

2. Leadership development helps to make a person effective in a variety of formal and informal leadership roles. While developing leadership abilities improves leadership effectiveness among those who serve formal leadership roles such as supervisors, managers, and project leaders, it can be equally as important in developing leadership competencies for those who play informal leadership roles in their campus, community, workplace, or religious organization.

Three Components of Leadership Development

Leadership development doesn't happen by accident. If becoming an effective leader is your goal, then you need to map out some strategies for reaching this objective. Three components, in particular, should be part of your plan for personal leadership development.

Leadership Learning

There is no shortage of opportunities to learn about leadership. As a matter of fact, it would be hard to avoid hearing about leaders. We track their successes and failures in the newspaper, read about them in history books, and follow them at school and on the job. Some of the strategies and behaviors we witness are excellent models for our own attempts to lead. Unfortunately, we sometimes learn very little from the examples of other leaders because we merely observe them without understanding the reasons behind their successes and failures.

One way to become a more perceptive student of leadership is to keep current with leadership research. The explosion of leadership knowledge in recent years demonstrates why it is so important to view leadership learning as an ongoing process. A search on Amazon.com in 2003 yielded over 12,500 book titles related to leadership.

> *Leadership and learning are indispensable to one another.*
> —John F. Kennedy

In recent years a growing number of colleges and universities have offered leadership training in various forms. As early as 1987, one source estimated that over 500 institutions of higher education delivered some form of leadership instruction.[4] Further, leadership topics are integrated into the curriculum in many courses. Over three-quarters of the communication departments we surveyed include material on leadership in at least one course.[5] At the dawn of the twenty-first century, an increasing number of colleges and universities are offering minors, majors, and even graduate degrees in leadership studies.[6]

Within organizations, formal training programs are widely used to improve leadership effectiveness. Jay Conger and Beth Benjamin surveyed a dozen organizations that offer innovative in-house training programs and identified three approaches to leadership development.[7] Chances are, you'll participate in one or more of the following types of programs during your career.

1. *Individual Preparation*. Historically, training programs have focused on developing the individual leader in the belief that improving a leader's effectiveness will improve the organization as a whole. *Conceptual awareness* workshops develop cognitive understanding. Trainers use case studies, lecture, and discussion to present leadership models or to introduce participants to the differences between leadership and management. *Feedback sessions* provide information to participants about leadership behaviors. Armed with this knowledge, they can address their weaknesses and build on their strengths. Feedback comes from trainers who observe in-class exercises, from fellow trainees, and from self-assessment instruments like those found in each chapter of this text. *Skills-based training* helps leaders master such skills as public speaking, listening, and conflict management through modeling and hands on practice. *Personal growth* programs put leaders into challenging situations that encourage

reflection about working relationships and personal priorities while building confidence. Completing a ropes course, whitewater rafting, rappelling, and other strenuous activities are designed to get trainees thinking about teamwork, risk taking, creativity, and goal setting in hopes that they will take these insights back to their workplaces and homes.

2. ***Socializing Company Vision and Values.*** Transmitting a group's culture, as we saw in chapter 8, is one of the most important responsibilities of organizational leaders. In recognition of this fact, Federal Express, Intel, Nordstrom, and the U.S. Army use leadership training as a socialization tool. Their training programs highlight corporate vision and values, encourage commitment to organizational priorities, develop a shared interpretation of the group's culture, and provide a forum for dialogue between new and established leaders.

3. ***Strategic Leadership Initiatives.*** In this approach, participants learn how to lead change while working toward actual corporate objectives. Strategic programs involve leaders at every level of the organization, and concepts and knowledge covered in training sessions relate directly to the problem at hand. Philips Electronics and Ernst & Young are two examples of firms that have used strategic leadership initiatives to clarify their corporate visions and to reach new markets.

Conger and Benjamin believe that the action learning focus of the strategic initiatives approach will soon become the centerpiece of most corporate leadership programs.[8] Action learning benefits both the individual and the organization. Adults learn best when they immediately apply concepts to the problems they face at work, while companies see visible results from these initiatives. Effective action learning programs involve: (1) careful selection of projects—significant ones that build the skills of individuals; (2) clearly defined objectives and results; (3) periodic opportunities for individuals and groups to discuss and reflect on what they are learning about the project and their personal strengths and weaknesses; (4) sponsorship, participation, and review by top management; and (5) expert facilitation and coaching, generally by outside consultants.

Leadership Experience

Any opportunity to master your communication skills (whether at home, at work, or at school) is preparation for leadership. The most useful experiences, though, are those that put you in the leader role. Since leadership experience is so vital, seek out chances to act as a leader. Volunteer to coordinate a campus or community activity, be a crew manager, teach a skill to a group, or offer to serve in any capacity to further your leadership skills. What you learn from your successes—and perhaps more importantly, your failures—is preparation for future leadership assignments. Warren Bennis notes that leaders engage in "innovative learning." While others often feel trapped by their experiences, leaders build on the past to anticipate and to shape future events. According to Bennis, innovative learning involves reflection:

> Experiences aren't truly yours until you think about them, analyze them, examine them, question them, reflect on them, and finally understand them. The point, once again, is to use your experiences rather than being used by them, to be the designer, not the design, so that experiences empower rather than imprison.[9]

Certain kinds of experiences are extremely helpful in developing leadership abilities. Patricia Ohlott, a research associate at the Center for Creative Leadership, calls these types of experiences developmental job assignments.[10] The key characteristic in all developmental job assignments is challenge. These ventures involve risk and require people to leave their comfort zones. Ohlott identifies five broad types of developmental job opportunities.

- *Job transitions.* Moving from one position to another puts people in new situations where job responsibilities are often unfamiliar. Transitions require people to alter their routines and to find new ways to frame and to solve problems. The greater the change in job function, the more opportunity for leadership development.

- *Creating change.* Job experiences that require a person to create change challenge individuals to find new ways to face ambiguous circumstances. A leader may be asked to develop a new product or process, reorganize a work unit, or develop a strategy for dealing with a crisis. Such situations provide fertile experiences for leaders to develop and enrich leadership skills.

- *High level of responsibility.* Leadership assignments with high levels of responsibility offer potent learning opportunities. These jobs generally involve complex, strategic issues that have a significant impact on an organization. Although these assignments may be stressful, they offer an opportunity for greater visibility and can be a great boon to a leader's self-confidence.

- *Nonauthority relationships.* Most leaders are accustomed to managing downward. When they have to work with peers, clients, or others with whom they do not have direct authority, they must learn to work collaboratively. Leaders in these assignments must develop skills in relationship building, problem solving, negotiation, and conflict resolution.

- *Obstacles.* Difficult situations provide leadership development opportunities. Obstacles may result from situations within the organization (such as a difficult boss) or from external factors such as adverse economic conditions. (See box 12.1 for examples of each of the developmental job assignments).

Another type of developmental experience is **hardship.** Hardships differ from the other developmental opportunities because people encounter them with little or no warning. Popular author and speaker John Maxwell argues

Box 12.1

Developmental Challenges and Examples of Assignments Where They May Be Found[11]

Challenge	**Examples of Assignments**
Job transitions	Being the inexperienced member of a project team
	Taking a temporary assignment in another function
	Moving to a general management job
	Managing a group or discipline you know little about
	Moving from a line job to a corporate staff role
	A lateral move to another department
Creating change	Launching a new product, project, or system
	Serving on a reengineering team
	Facilitating the development of a new vision or mission statement
	Dealing with a business crisis
	Handling a workforce reduction
	Hiring new staff
	Breaking ground on a new operation
	Reorganizing a unit
	Resolving subordinate performance problems
	Supervising the liquidation of products or equipment
High level of responsibility	A corporate assignment with tight deadlines
	Representing the organization to the media or influential outsiders
	Managing across geographic locations
	Assuming additional responsibilities following a downsizing
	Taking on a colleague's responsibilities during his or her absence
Nonauthority relationships	Presenting a proposal to top management
	Corporate staff job
	Serving on a cross-functional team
	Managing an internal project such as a company event or office renovation
	Working on a project with a community or social organization
Obstacles	Working with a difficult boss
	Working in a situation where there is little or unclear direction from senior management
	Taking responsibility for a business or product line that faces intensely competitive markets
	Starting a new project with few resources

that the difference between average and exceptional leaders lies in their response to adversity and failure.[12] Typical leaders "fail backward" by blaming others, repeating their errors, setting unrealistically high expectations, internalizing their disappointments, and quitting. Successful leaders "fail forward" by taking responsibility for their errors and learning from them, maintaining a positive attitude, taking on new risks, and persevering. To learn from adversity, Maxwell suggests that you ask yourself the following questions every time you encounter failures or mistakes.

What caused the failure: The situation, someone else, or myself? You must identify what went wrong before you can put it right. Don't confuse failure with being a failure. Instead, view what happened as a learning experience and start by locating the source of the problem.

Was this truly a failure, or did I just fall short? Some "failures" are really attempts to meet unrealistic expectations (generally those we put on ourselves). Falling short of an unrealistic goal is not a failure.

What successes are contained in the failure? Failures often contain the keys to future success. For example, Kellogg's Corn Flakes is the result of accidentally leaving boiled wheat in a baking pan overnight, and Ivory soap floats because excess air was pumped into a batch when the mixer was left on too long.[13]

What can I learn from what happened? Failure can teach us more than success. When we succeed, we generally use the same approach again. When we fail, we look for different, better ways to proceed.

Am I grateful for the experience? Gratitude can be the key to a teachable mindset. If nothing else, falling short teaches us how to live with disappointments.

How can I turn this into a success? Mistakes teach us how avoid future miscues and (as we saw above) can lead to important discoveries. Bernie Marcus provides one example of the principle of turning failure into success. After being fired from the Handy Dan hardware chain, Marcus and a partner opened their own home improvement store called The Home Depot. The Home Depot now generates over $30 billion in sales annually.

Who can help me with this issue? Learning from adversity is easier with the help of mentors, families, peers, and others. The best advice comes from those who have successfully dealt with their own failures.

Where do I go from here? You can't claim to have learned from an experience unless it leads to a change in behavior.

Research suggests that there are five primary types of hardship events. (These hardships and the lessons they can provide are outlined in box 12.2.)[14]

- *Business mistakes and failures.* These take the form of lost advertising clients, disgruntled employees, failed mergers, discontinued product lines, bankruptcies, and other organizational mishaps. They offer excellent opportunities for failing forward, teaching important lessons about how to manage others, coping with adversity, and the need for humility.

- *Career setbacks.* An individual's career can be derailed in a number of ways: not getting a promotion, being stuck in a dead-end job, or even

---

Box 12.2

Five Types of Hardships and the Lessons They Teach[15]

Hardship	Lessons Learned
Business mistakes and failures	Handling relationships
	Humility
	How to handle mistakes
Career setbacks	Self-awareness
	Organizational politics
	What one really wants to do
Personal trauma	Sensitivity to others
	Coping with events beyond one's control
	Perseverance
	Recognition of limits
Problem employees	How to stand firm
	Confrontation skills
	Coping skills
Downsizing	Taking stock
	Recognition of what's important

---

being demoted or fired. Such career setbacks should be viewed as a wake-up call. They offer the opportunity to see how others perceive you and your contributions. For those who are willing to learn, career setbacks can provide valuable information that can enhance readiness for future leadership endeavors. (See the case study in box 12.3).

- *Personal trauma.* In many instances a personal trauma such as an illness, death in the family, divorce, or difficulties with children can provide a powerful jolt to a leader. These traumas may prompt a leader to soften his or her behavior, focus more attention on work-life balance, or learn the value of perseverance.

- *Problem employees.* Dealing with difficult employees offers an opportunity for leadership development. Whether it is the employee who behaves in a fraudulent or unethical manner, has a poor work ethic, or is just difficult to get along with, problem employees teach a leader how to deal directly with problem situations.

- *Downsizing.* Being downsized is a hardship that offers a leader a chance to reflect on his or her current situation and to make choices for the future. Although many victimized by downsizing feel a powerful sense of anger, distrust, and loss, those who use the time to take stock and to consider anew what's important in life and career can ultimately improve their effectiveness.

Box 12.3   Case Study

Profile in Hardship: Abraham Lincoln[16]

The leaders we admire the most are often the ones who have endured the greatest hardships. William Wilberforce, for example, fought for 46 years to eliminate slavery in Great Britain. Nelson Mandela, Alexander Solzhenitsyn, and Vaclav Havel served prison sentences. Mother Teresa lived in poverty in order to serve the poor. Franklin Roosevelt had to conquer the ravages of polio.

When it comes to rising above hardship, few can match the record of Abraham Lincoln. Lincoln was a small-town lawyer from Illinois who lost two bids for the Senate before his election to the Presidency in 1860. He received only forty percent of the popular vote in a field of four candidates. Assassination threats forced him to sneak into Washington, D. C. to take his oath of office. He then presided over a war that cost the lives of one out of every five male citizens between the ages of fifteen and forty. Some members of Lincoln's extended family fought for the South, and his beloved son Willie died from illness during his first term.

Instead of breaking under the strain, Lincoln grew in stature. He gained confidence and became more committed to the cause of maintaining the Union. The Emancipation Proclamation is one example of how Lincoln matured as a moral and political leader. He bypassed congressional opposition to freeing blacks by issuing the proclamation as a military order. Later, members of the House and Senate followed his example and passed the Thirteenth Amendment, the measure that permanently outlawed slavery in the United States. Few leaders can match Lincoln's generous spirit. He specifically instructed Ulysses S. Grant to offer lenient surrender terms to the Confederate army. On the very day he was shot, Lincoln urged his Cabinet to welcome Robert E. Lee and other Confederate leaders back into the Union fold.

What was the secret of Lincoln's grace under pressure? No one can say for sure, but three factors seem particularly important. (1) Lincoln tried to understand the meaning underlying the tragic events around him. He was convinced that there was a moral pattern in history and that the suffering of the nation was its punishment for slavery. (2) Lincoln was committed to the cause of continuing the "American experiment" in democracy. He believed that the United States was a model for other nations. (3) Lincoln found a spiritual anchor, placing his confidence in God and seeing himself as an imperfect servant of God's will. Never a member of any particular religious group, he nonetheless devoted himself to prayer and to the study of scripture and has been described as the nation's most spiritual president. Lincoln's search for meaning, belief in the American cause, and spiritual understanding are reflected in his second inaugural address. This message, which is etched on his memorial, is considered by some to be the finest political statement of the 1800s. Lincoln concludes his address with these words:

Fondly do we hope, fervently do we pray, that this mighty scourge of war may speedily pass away. Yet, if God wills that it continue until all the wealth piled by the bondsman's two hundred and fifty years of unrequited toil shall be sunk, and until every drop of blood drawn with the lash shall be paid by another drawn with the sword, as was said three thousand years ago, so still it must be said "the judgements of the Lord are true and righteous altogether."

With malice toward none, with charity for all, with firmness in the right as God gives us to see the right, let us strive on to finish the work we are in, to bind up the nation's wounds, to care for him who shall have borne the battle and for his widow and his orphan, to do all which may achieve and cherish a just and lasting peace among ourselves and with all nations.

Discussion Questions
1. Can you think of other leaders, famous or not, who endured significant hardship?
2. What role has hardship played in your development as a leader?
3. Why do some people mature when faced with hardship while others become bitter and disillusioned?
4. What can we learn from Lincoln's struggle with adversity?
5. What role should spirituality play in leadership?
6. How does Lincoln demonstrate the principle of failing forward?

Never, never, never, never give up.
—Winston Churchill

Developmental Relationships

Establishing connections with those who can help you achieve your goals will greatly increase your chances of emerging as a leader in an organizational context. Some of these supportive relationships can be established with peers.[17] *Information peers* are casual acquaintances who provide useful information. *Collegial peers* help with career strategies and provide job-related feedback as well as friendship. *Special peers* act like best friends—giving confirmation, emotional support, and personal feedback. However, the most beneficial relationships will pair you with senior leaders. An established leader can help you by serving as an example that you can emulate from a distance or by taking an active role in your development through acting as your mentor.[18]

The term "mentor" originated from the character Mentor who was the friend of the ancient Greek king Ulysses in Homer's *Odyssey.* He watched the king's son while Ulysses was away, acting as a personal and professional counselor and guide. Modern mentors perform many of the functions of the original. Mentoring expert Kathleen Kram divides mentor functions into two types: career and psychosocial.[19] Career functions are aspects of the relationship that help protégés in their career advancement. Psychosocial functions build the sense of competence and self-worth of both mentors and protégés.

It is important to note that individuals can serve in a mentor role even if they only carry out only one set of functions. Some men, for example, find it hard to provide emotional support to protégés but are eager to offer career advice.[20] The shifting needs of protégés will also have an impact on the functions that mentors perform. An inexperienced protégé may need more reassurance; a long-time protégé may want more advice about how to achieve career goals.[21] With this in mind, here is a brief description of the specific functions that fall into each category.

Career Functions

- *Sponsorship.* Mentors fight for their protégés by standing up for them in meetings, putting their names in for promotions, and so forth. Protégés also gain power and more chances for advancement through their association with powerful mentors.

- *Coaching.* Mentors help protégés learn the ins and outs of the organization, including how decisions are made, what the key values are, and who holds power. Mentors have been totally immersed in the corporate culture and can help acclimate the protégé. In addition, they make specific suggestions about how to get the work done, give advice about how to achieve career goals, and supply valuable feedback about job performance.

- *Protection.* Mentors shield their protégés when things aren't going well. They take the blame for slow progress on projects, talk to senior officials when their mentees aren't ready to do so, and step in when their junior partners aren't up to the task.

- *Challenging assignments.* As we noted in our discussion of the Pygmalion Effect in chapter 8, the type of assignments that a new manager receives can determine whether that person becomes a low or a high performer. Low expectations communicated through unchallenging or overly demanding assignments can generate a negative performance cycle. Effective mentors set challenging yet realistic goals and work with protégés to help them achieve their objectives. Protégés learn key skills and develop a sense of accomplishment as they master challenges.

Psychosocial Functions

- *Role modeling.* Mentors are role models who demonstrate leadership skills. During their apprenticeships, protégés learn how to manage conflict, build teams, gather information, and make ethical choices by observing the behavior of their senior colleagues.

- *Acceptance-and-confirmation.* Positive regard develops in a healthy mentor-mentee relationship. Each side enjoys the feeling of respect and encouragement that comes from interacting with the other party. When a protégé feels accepted and affirmed, she or he is more willing to take risks and to explore new behaviors.

- *Counseling.* Mentors often become sounding boards for their protégés, helping them work through conflicts that detract from work performance. Three issues are particularly important for those just starting out in a career: (1) how to develop job competence and satisfaction, (2) how to relate to the organization without compromising values and individuality, and (3) how to balance work and family responsibilities.

- *Friendship.* In many successful mentor/protégé partnerships, the parties become friends who develop a mutual liking for one another and engage in informal interaction. The emergence of this function signals that the protégé has become more of a peer than a subordinate. Even when the original relationship ends because of a promotion, job transfer, or some other factor, the friendship often remains.

> *Make yourself necessary to someone.*
> —Ralph Waldo Emerson

Based on what mentors can do for their protégés, it's not surprising that those who have organizational sponsors are generally more successful. They typically earn higher salaries, get promoted more often, enjoy greater recognition, and experience higher job satisfaction.[22] These advantages carry over into the university setting. Instructors who receive mentoring help have higher rank and pay and are more likely to be tenured.[23] Undergraduates who receive individual attention from a faculty member generally do better in school.[24]

Protégés aren't the only ones to profit from the establishment of mentor/protégé partnerships. The organization as a whole benefits because those who have been successfully mentored are more productive and more committed to the institution. Mentors benefit from the help they get with tasks as well as from the affirmation, confirmation, and friendship provided by protégés. They enjoy passing on their values and insights and seeing their protégés develop.

While there are a great many advantages to mentoring, there are potential difficulties as well. Linda Phillips-Jones identified the common problems and possible solutions after interviewing mentors and protégés at companies around the United States.[25]

Problem	**Solution**
Mentor/protégé makes excessive demands on the time and energy of the other person.	Decide in advance how much time you can commit and set limits. Continually monitor time and energy commitments. If one party or the other appears undercommitted, terminate the relationship.
Inappropriate choice of mentor or protégé; i.e., someone who can't help you reach your goals or an individual who might endanger your position in the organization.	Don't rush into a binding relationship; choose carefully. Be willing to break off the arrangement if necessary.
Unrealistic expectations for mentors or protégés; i.e., giving too much responsibility to a protégé too soon.	Check to see if you're expecting perfection from the other person. List the other party's strengths and weaknesses and lower expectations when needed. Monitor verbal and nonverbal messages for signs of tension.
Expectations of protégé failure.	Don't mentor if you have serious doubts about the other individual.
Protégé's feelings of inferiority.	Instead of judging yourself by a mentor's accomplishments, set personal goals and determine how well you've reached those objectives.
Unfair manipulation by a mentor or protégé.	Double check to make sure you really are being treated unfairly. Ask yourself if you have contributed to the problem by hiding your needs or volunteering for extra work. Discuss the issues and break off the relationship if they can't be resolved.
Jealousy from mentors or protégés about the success of the other party.	Try to figure out why you feel jealous or what you're doing that might generate these emotions. Talk about these feelings with your partner.
Jealousy from others.	If the envious individuals are important to you, work together with your partner to determine what might be provoking jealous responses. Make sure the relationship really hasn't become a threat to spouses, business partners, coworkers, and others.
Overdependence on mentors or protégés.	Expect the most dependence at the beginning of the relationship and greater independence as the relationship matures. Maintain a network of other relationships and become more self-reliant (learn to judge your own work, for example).
Unwanted romance and sexual involvement.	Take steps to reduce contact (only meet at work, for instance) and back away to analyze romantic feelings if they develop. Communicate about these feelings and end the relationship if necessary.

AT&T, Bell Labs, Federal Express, the Government Accounting Office, New York University, and a growing number of other organizations sponsor mentorship programs to promote the benefits of mentoring while, at the same time, they try to reduce the risks associated with the mentor/protégé relationship. Well-designed programs generally include the following elements:[26]

- criteria and process for selecting both protégés and mentors
- tools for diagnosing the needs of protégés
- strategies for matching protégés with mentors
- formal, negotiated agreements between mentors and protégés
- a coordinator who trains participants, maintains the program, and monitors the mentor/protégé pairs
- periodic evaluation to make necessary adjustments and to determine outcomes for the protégés, mentors, and organization

Joining an organization that has a mentoring program will simplify your search for a mentor. However, most organizations do not have systematic mentoring efforts. In these cases you'll need to identify the person or persons who might aid in your leadership development. This takes more effort on your part, but research suggests that informal mentor-protégé relationships are generally more productive than those established through formal mentoring programs. Unofficial partnerships last longer and are more supportive than those where protégés are assigned to mentors.[27] Linda Phillips-Jones recommends the following steps when searching for a mentor.[28]

Identify what (not who) you need. Before you zero in on people who can help, think first about the kind of help you need. Do you need to sharpen your public speaking or management skills? Polish your writing? Learn how to close sales deals? Developing a list of needs will help you know what kind of assistance to ask for, and some of the items on the list might be satisfied through reading, training sessions, and other resources.

Evaluate yourself as a prospective protégé. Stop for a moment and complete the protégé checklist in box 12.4. Completing this instrument will help you determine just how prepared you are to be mentored. Not everyone is ready for such a relationship. If you're holding back, try to determine why. It may be that you find it hard to ask for help.

Identify mentor candidates. Go back to the list you generated in step one and think of individuals who can provide the help you seek. Some important questions to consider are: Who are the most influential people I know? Who can help me or would like some help? Where are they in their careers? Have they mentored before and with what results? What's their current job situation?

Prepare for the obstacles. Before you approach anyone, do the same kind of preparation you would do for a job interview. Find out about this person's job responsibilities and special interests and talk to others who know this candidate. Anticipate possible questions and concerns.

Approach possible mentors. Indirect tactics for contacting a mentor candidate include asking for help from a mutual acquaintance and letting him or her see you in action on committees and in other settings. The direct approach is to set up an appointment and spell out exactly what you desire from that individual.

Box 12.4   Self-Assessment

Protégé Checklist[29]

	Very certain	Fairly certain	Uncertain	Absolutely not
1. I know the kind of career mentoring I want.	3	2	1	0
2. I'm willing to accept a mentor's help, if it's appropriate.	3	2	1	0
3. I'm a good listener. I hear what the other person is really saying.	3	2	1	0
4. I'm a good follower.	3	2	1	0
5. I can be counted on to carry out commitments.	3	2	1	0
6. I'd be willing to let a mentor take much of the credit for our accomplishments at first while I do more of the background or routine work.	3	2	1	0
7. I learn most new things quickly.	3	2	1	0
8. I'd be willing to speak up (diplomatically) if I disagreed with a mentor. I'm not a "yes" person.	3	2	1	0
9. I'm good about thanking and otherwise showing appreciation to people who help me.	3	2	1	0
10. I feel that my "career potential" is is high; I'd be a good risk as a protégé.	3	2	1	0

Add up your total number of points. A score of 21–30 means that you'd be an excellent protégé candidate; a score of 11–20 indicates that you are a good candidate but need to spend more time thinking about your abilities and career needs; a score of 10 or less suggests that you are not a strong candidate and may want to analyze the reasons why you don't want to serve in this role.

Leadership Development as an Internal Process

Two acclaimed models view leadership development as a process that occurs *within* an individual.

Stephen Covey's Seven Habits of Highly Effective People

This may be the most popular leadership development program in the United States. The seven habits, developed by business consultant Stephen Covey, are described in the best selling book by the same name. Thousands of businesses, nonprofit groups, and government agencies have participated in workshops offered by the Covey Leadership Center. Covey argues that a leader's effectiveness is based on such character principles as fairness, integrity, honesty, service, excellence, and growth. (Refer to chapter 11 for more information on virtue or character ethics.) He defines a habit as a combination of *knowledge* (what to do and why to do it), *skill* (how to do it), and *motivation* (wanting to do it).[30] Leadership development is an "inside-out" process that starts within the leader and then moves outward to impact others.

Habit 1. Be proactive. Proactive leaders realize that they can choose how they respond to events. For example, when insulted or unfairly criticized, they decide to remain calm instead of getting angry. Proactive individuals also take the initiative by opting to attack problems instead of accepting defeat. Their language reflects their willingness to accept rather than to avoid responsibility. A proactive leader makes such statements as "let's examine our options" and "I can create a strategic plan." A reactive leader makes such comments as "the organization won't go along with that idea," "I'm too old to change," and "that's just who I am."

> *No one can hurt you without your consent.*
> —Eleanor Roosevelt

Habit 2. Begin with the end in mind. Effective leaders always keep their ultimate goals in mind. Creating personal and organizational mission statements is one way to identify end results. Covey urges leaders to center their lives on inner principles rather than on external factors like family, money, friends, or work.

Habit 3. Put first things first. This principle is based on the notion that a leader's time should be organized around priorities. Too many leaders spend their time coping with emergencies and neglect long range planning and relationships. They mistakenly believe that urgent items are always important. Effective leaders carve out time for significant activities by identifying their most important roles, selecting their goals, creating schedules that enable them to reach their objectives, and modifying these plans when necessary. They also know how to delegate tasks and have the courage to say "no" to requests that don't fit their priorities.

Habit 4. Think win/win. Those with win/win perspectives take a mutual gains approach to communication, believing that the best solution benefits both parties. The win/win habit is based on: character (integrity, maturity, and a willingness to share); trusting relationships committed to mutual benefit; performance or partnership agreements that spell out conditions and responsibilities; organizational systems that fairly distribute rewards; and principled negotiation that guarantees that the solution is generated by both parties and not imposed by one side or the other. (For an in-depth look at principled negotiation, turn to chapter 6.)

Habit 5. Seek first to understand, then to be understood. Effective leaders put aside their personal concerns to engage in empathetic listening. They seek to understand instead of evaluating, advising, or interpreting. Empathetic listening is an excellent way to build a trusting relationship. Covey uses the metaphor of the emotional bank account to illustrate how trust develops. Principled leaders make deposits in the emotional bank account by showing kindness and courtesy, keeping commitments, paying attention to small details, and seeking to understand. These strong relational reserves help prevent misunderstandings and increase the likelihood that leaders and followers will quickly resolve any problems that do arise.

Habit 6. Synergize. As we noted in our discussion of cultural differences in chapter 10, synergy creates a solution that is greater than the sum of its parts. Synergistic, creative solutions can only come out of trusting relationships (those with high emotional bank accounts) where participants value their differences.

Habit 7. Sharpen the saw. Sharpening the saw refers to continual renewal of the physical, social/emotional, spiritual, and mental dimensions of the self. Healthy leaders care for their bodies, nurture their inner values through study and/or meditation, encourage their mental development through reading and writing, and generate positive self-esteem through meaningful relationships with others.

Kevin Cashman's Leadership from the Inside Out

Kevin Cashman argues that too many leadership development books focus on the external act of leadership.[31] He believes that leadership comes from within and is an expression of who we are as people. Leadership is not something that one does, it comes from somewhere inside. (A profile of the inner dimension of one group of executives can be found in box 12.5.) Cashman defines leadership as "authentic self-expression that creates value."[32] This form of leadership can be found at all levels in organizations and can be exhibited by anyone.

> *A life without purpose is an early death.*
> —Johann Wolfgang von Goethe

Box 12.5 Research Highlight

The Inner Life of Leaders: A Snapshot[33]

Very few researchers have systematically studied the inner dimension of leadership. Scholars have been more concerned with the leader's *doing* than the leader's *being*. In other words, investigators study what leaders do to achieve results rather than looking at their feelings, values, and spiritual beliefs. One exception to this trend is University of Tennessee management professor William Judge. In *The Leader's Shadow: Exploring and Developing Executive Character*, Judge focuses on the interior side of leadership in the belief that acknowledging and grappling with the inner or shadow dimension of leadership should keep leaders from casting shadows on others. Judge surveyed 91 chief executives (all males between the ages of 30 and 77) in 57 different U.S. industries. Their companies ranged in size from 2 to 65,000 employees. He gave respondents personality tests and questionnaires and developed in-depth case studies based on several participants. Taken together, the survey results and interviews provide a picture of the inner life of one group of leaders. The CEOs in Judge's sample:

- had a variety of personality preferences, but the majority (1) preferred intuition to relying on the senses when collecting data, and (2) relied on thinking rather than feeling when making decisions.

- put a high value on a sense of accomplishment, family, self-respect, and salvation (terminal or end-state values), as well as on being honest, responsible, ambitious, and capable (instrumental values).

- reflected a significant interest in religion and spirituality, an interest generally triggered by a dramatic life event (a major loss, the birth of a child). Many reported having deep, regular, spiritual experiences and believe that God lives within them.

- were trusted by followers largely based on their competence and personal integrity. They received lower ratings from subordinates for their benevolence (concern for others, ability to see both sides of an issue).

Judge notes that it is difficult for leaders to pay attention to their inner or shadow sides. Looking inward means confronting evil tendencies and giving up the illusion of control. In addition, leaders tend to be extroverts who find it hard to pause and reflect. The struggle is worth the cost, however. Grappling with the dark side of the self reduces its power and frees leaders to serve others. Only those who have expanded their own consciousness can help followers expand theirs.

To develop self-leadership skills, Cashman identifies seven pathways that allow a person to lead from the inside out. (See figure 12.1.) These pathways are not stages of development arranged in a sequential or hierarchical order. Rather, they are viewed holistically as integrated pieces of a collective framework.

Pathway One: Personal Mastery. The ongoing commitment to exploring who you are is the key to personal mastery. This understanding allows a person to lead through authentic self-expression. Learning what is important to you will impact how you lead. Cashman suggests exploring such questions as:

- What do I believe about myself?
- What do I believe about other people?
- What do I believe about life?
- What do I believe about leadership?

Questions such as these bring your beliefs to the forefront and help to guide your leadership efforts.

Pathway Two: Purpose Mastery. Learning how you make a difference is key to the second pathway. Purpose mastery focuses on understanding and using your gifts and talents to add value to those around you. This pathway encourages a leader to explore his or her purpose in life by identifying activities that are energizing and exciting. Cashman suggests a leader's journey involves seeking ways to move from doing what you "have to do" to doing what you "want to do."

Pathway Three: Change Mastery. Letting go of old patterns and taking a fresh approach allows a leader to enhance his or her creativity. This pathway emphasizes the need to be adaptable and willing to change. Being open to change allows a leader to be open to the possibilities presented by each situation, whether it is the opportunity to start your own business, go back to school, or simply try a new restaurant. Change challenges current reality and allows a leader to see a new reality.

Pathway Four: Interpersonal Mastery. This pathway focuses on the development of interpersonal competencies. Many leaders are not skilled in building relationships with others. A study of 6,403 middle and upper managers conducted by the Foundation for Future Leadership found that managers receive their highest evaluations for their intellect and technical expertise and their lowest marks for their interpersonal skills.[34] To develop interpersonal mastery, seek feedback from others and use that information to improve personal relationships.

Pathway Five: Being Mastery. Being is at the core of an individual. Being mastery involves using periods of peace and silence to understand one's innermost depths of character and being. Quiet moments, a favorite piece of music, a walk in the country, or inspirational reading can serve as a catalyst for exploring one's being.

Pathway Six: Balance Mastery. Taking time for self, family, and friends is critical to maintaining balance in life. Without balance a leader can become irritable, uninspired, unfocused, and nervous. Achieving balance may be among the most difficult of the pathways to mastery to achieve. Interviews with 53 CEOs and presidents of corporations indicated that 92 percent felt balance mastery was the biggest challenge for them in their professional lives.[35]

> *The number one reason leaders are so unsuccessful is their inability to lead themselves.*
>
> —Truett Cathy

Pathway Seven: Action Mastery. Action mastery involves leading as a whole person. In this pathway, a leader gets in touch with his or her authentic self and expresses it to others. During the 1996 Presidential campaign, Bob Dole appeared as a somewhat tough and ill-at-ease candidate. After he lost the election, many people were surprised to see the calm and funny person who surfaced. As Dole told David Letterman when he appeared as a guest on his show, "After 18 months I can be myself again."[36] It would have been interesting to note the electorate's perception of Dole if he had acted as himself throughout the campaign.

Figure 12.1
Seven Pathways to Mastery[37]

Leadership Transitions

Leadership transitions are critical to both personal and organizational success. Not only do we need to acquire the knowledge and skills necessary to carry out new leadership roles, we also need to help ensure that the group as a whole chooses the right successors when positions open up. Any transition is risky. Estimates are that 40 percent of newly promoted managers and two-thirds of senior leaders appointed from outside the organization have to be replaced within 18 months.[38] A number of prominent CEOS like Jill Barad of Mattel, Douglas Ivester of Coca-Cola, and Robert Ayling of British Airways have been forced out after only a few years on the job. In this final section of the chapter, we will try to help reduce the risk of leadership transitions by outlining how successors master their new roles, describing ways to smooth the transition from one leader to another, and identifying the characteristics of effective succession planning programs.

> *Nothing is permanent but change.*
>
> —Heracleitus

The Process of Taking Charge

John Gabarro uses the term "taking charge" to describe how newly appointed managers become leaders.[39] Gabarro (who developed the process model of succession to leadership found in figure 12.2) notes that new managers rely heavily on legitimate power, which is based on organizational position. If they want to become leaders, they must extend their influence by developing other power bases. Appointees take charge by developing an understanding of the leadership situation, gaining acceptance as leaders, and having an impact on organizational performance. To achieve these outcomes, they engage in three types of work or processes: *cognitive* (learning about the organization and its culture, acquiring technical knowledge, diagnosing problems, understanding issues); *organizational* (developing a set of shared expectations with followers, working out conflicts, and building a cohesive management team); and *interpersonal* (developing good working relationships with superiors, subordinates, and peers).

The cognitive, organizational, and interpersonal work that results in a leader taking charge is accomplished over time. Through interviews with successful and unsuccessful new leaders and their subordinates, Gabarro discovered that taking charge involves five stages.[40]

- *Taking hold.* Taking hold is a period of intense activity lasting from three to six months. Newly appointed managers have a great deal of information to absorb. As they learn, they evaluate the situation and take corrective action to solve pressing short-term problems.

- *Immersion.* This stage (lasting four to eleven months) is less hectic than the first. Instead of making changes, new managers immerse themselves in day-to-day operations and develop a deeper understanding of the organization. In-depth understanding often produces a new plan for improving performance.

- *Reshaping.* During the reshaping phase (three to six months), new leaders implement the concepts they developed during the immersion period, making changes in the organization's structure, processes, and personnel.

- *Consolidation.* In the consolidation phase (three to nine months), leaders follow through on the changes made during the reshaping stage. They identify and deal with remaining implementation problems, correct any unanticipated difficulties produced by changes made during the reshaping period, and implement changes they could not make earlier.

- *Refinement.* Refinement signals the end of the taking charge process. By this time, successors are no longer viewed as new, and their major changes are in place. They continue to learn and to make changes, but they have much less new information to master. Any adjustments they make are minor.

There are a number of variables (summarized in the left column in figure 12.2) that either facilitate or complicate the task of taking charge.[41] Some of these variables have to do with the characteristics of the successor. Those brought in from outside the organization generally make more changes and have more to learn. A close match between the successor's previous experience and the demands of the new position make for a smoother transition, but conflicts will likely develop if the successor's leadership communication style is

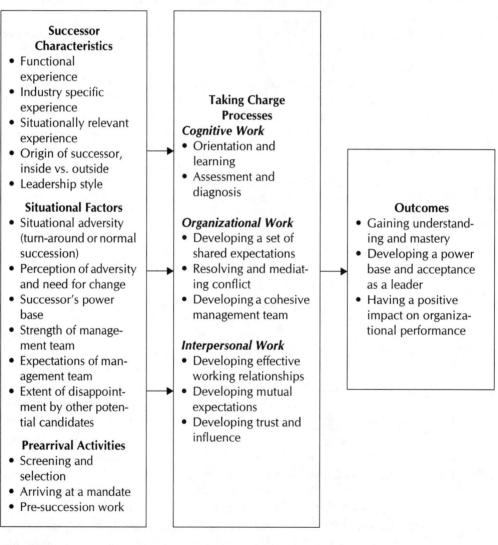

Successor Characteristics
- Functional experience
- Industry specific experience
- Situationally relevant experience
- Origin of successor, inside vs. outside
- Leadership style

Situational Factors
- Situational adversity (turn-around or normal succession)
- Perception of adversity and need for change
- Successor's power base
- Strength of management team
- Expectations of management team
- Extent of disappointment by other potential candidates

Prearrival Activities
- Screening and selection
- Arriving at a mandate
- Pre-succession work

Taking Charge Processes
Cognitive Work
- Orientation and learning
- Assessment and diagnosis

Organizational Work
- Developing a set of shared expectations
- Resolving and mediating conflict
- Developing a cohesive management team

Interpersonal Work
- Developing effective working relationships
- Developing mutual expectations
- Developing trust and influence

Outcomes
- Gaining understanding and mastery
- Developing a power base and acceptance as a leader
- Having a positive impact on organizational performance

Figure 12.2
A Process Model of Succession to Leadership[42]

inconsistent with her or his predecessor's. Other variables are situational in nature. Those faced with significant performance problems must make greater changes. A perceived need for change; a strong power base built on competence, position, and other factors; and a strong, supportive management team make taking charge easier. Disgruntled employees who were turned down for the leader's position make the successor's job harder. The final cluster of variables involves the selection process itself and how the organization prepares for the arrival of the new leader. The successor who clearly understands the expectations of the organization and is given a mandate for change has the greatest chance of success. The new leader's superior can defuse the hostility of disappointed candidates by telling them why they weren't chosen for the position.

Managing Transitions

The process model of leadership succession highlights the fact that taking charge is a complex, difficult, and demanding task. However, Gabarro makes these suggestions to help manage transitions either as a successor or as someone overseeing the succession process.

- *Recognize that taking charge takes time.* It takes over two years to master a new leadership role. Be patient; don't expect instant miracles of yourself or others. Discourage short-term assignments because they don't give new leaders a chance to immerse themselves in the situation and to reshape the department or organization.

- *Develop effective working relationships immediately.* Building strong working relationships with key subordinates and the boss is essential during the taking-hold period. Gabarro found that failure to build effective relationships was "the most prominent characteristic that distinguished between successful and failed succession."[43] To build productive relationships, negotiate specific differences with subordinates and keep superiors informed of changes. Instead of tackling problems on your own (acting as a "Lone Ranger"), seek out the opinions of others and develop a cohesive working group with a common vision.

- *Assess and act on prior experience.* Realistically assess your skills as well as the skills and experience of those you choose for leadership positions. Then develop strategies that reflect these assessments. Build on your strengths as you acquaint yourself with less familiar elements of the job. If you have strong organizational skills but lack technical expertise, for instance, you may want to restructure the department before you tackle problems that require technical solutions. When supervising others, identify the potential problems successors will face and provide the support they will need to overcome these challenges (additional training, key subordinates, etc.). The smoothest transitions, as we noted earlier, are usually made by individuals who have performed similar tasks (accounting, engineering, teaching) in another organization or in another position.

- *Clarify expectations.* Learn exactly what is expected of you and make the "going-in mandate" of a successor as clear as possible. For example, are you to increase market share? Reduce costs? Reorganize? Will the successor you choose have the power to lay employees off? Increase the budget? Develop new systems? After the succession has been made, you or the new appointee should meet with constituents to identify important issues and concerns.

Succession Planning

A growing number of large organizations are developing succession-planning programs that take a systematic approach to identifying and developing future leaders. Taking a proactive stance to leadership transitions makes sense for several reasons. As we saw earlier, the importance of leadership changeover and the high failure rate of new leaders suggests that succession planning should not be left to chance. The need for future leaders is likely to increase as baby boomers reach retirement at the same time that there are fewer younger workers to replace them. Corporate layoffs may also contribute to a leader shortfall by reducing the number of middle management positions that have traditionally served as training grounds for executives. Further, a systematic approach to leadership transitions reduces the likelihood of a mismatch between the person and the position as well as the tendency for job incumbents (who are often white males) to choose successors who resemble themselves (other white males).

Experts report that effective succession-planning programs share the following characteristics:[44]

- Participation and support of top management. When top leaders are involved, others are more likely to devote time and effort to succession concerns.
- Include all leadership levels. Succession planning is important for low level management positions as well as for executive ones.
- Organizational needs assessment. Organizations must decide on the direction in which they are headed before they know what types of skills their future leaders must develop.
- Competency focused. Focusing on competencies means equipping people to take a variety of positions, not just the next one up the organizational ladder.
- Accountability. Accountability comes from appointing one person to oversee the succession program as well as from evaluating current leaders on how well they are preparing potential replacements.
- Development. Future leaders must be developed. Development tools include job rotation, training programs, and mentoring. While organizations provide development opportunities, every employee is ultimately

responsible for acquiring the competencies he or she needs to move into new leadership positions.

Summary

In this chapter we focused on leadership development. Although leadership is a complex process, almost anyone can develop the skills necessary to lead effectively. There are two central elements in the definition of leadership development: (1) leadership can be learned; (2) leadership development prepares a person for both formal and informal leadership roles.

Leadership development is a lifelong process. Three components should be part of a personal plan for improving leadership effectiveness: leadership learning, leadership experience, and developmental relationships. Leadership learning can be achieved through reading, attending college or university courses, or training. Leadership experiences enable us to expand our leadership skills. The richest experiences occur in developmental job assignments. These experiences fall into five categories: job transitions, creating change, taking on a high level of responsibility, nonauthority relationships, and dealing with obstacles. Another type of developmental experience is hardship. Successful leaders "fail forward" by learning from adversity. The most common hardships are business mistakes and failures; career setbacks; personal trauma; problem employees; and downsizing.

Establishing connections with those who can help you achieve your goals will greatly increase your chances of emerging as a leader in an organizational context. The most beneficial relationships are with mentors. Mentors act as sponsors; provide coaching; protect protégés; give challenging assignments; serve as role models; supply acceptance and confirmation; function as counselors or sounding boards; and become friends. To locate a mentor when formal mentoring programs are not available, determine what (not who) you need. After this vital first step, evaluate yourself as a prospective protégé, identify mentor candidates, prepare for the obstacles that might arise, and approach potential mentors.

We looked at two models that view leadership development as an internal process. Stephen Covey prescribes seven habits for effective leadership: (1) be proactive; (2) begin with an end in mind; (3) put first things first; (4) think win/win; (5) seek first to understand, then to be understood; (6) synergize; and (7) sharpen the saw. Kevin Cashman's Leadership From the Inside Out offers a holistic approach consisting of seven pathways to leadership: (1) personal mastery; (2) purpose mastery; (3) change mastery; (4) interpersonal mastery; (5) being mastery; (6) balance mastery; and (7) action mastery.

We concluded the chapter by looking at leadership in transition. Taking charge as a new leader means developing an understanding of the leadership context, gaining acceptance as a leader, and having an impact on organizational performance. The five stages of the taking charge process are: taking hold, immersion, reshaping, consolidation, and refinement. Succession planning programs take a proactive approach to leadership transitions, systematically identifying and developing future leaders.

Application Exercises

1. Talk with someone who is employed in a company that offers leadership training to its workers. Compare your experiences in this class to the training received in the organization. Share your findings in class.

2. Read a book on leadership. Give a presentation to your classmates outlining the major concepts in the book and your evaluation of the strengths and weaknesses of the book you selected.

3. Look at the course catalog at your school and see how many different leadership courses are offered. Compare the results with other schools by viewing their course catalogs online.

4. Profile a famous leader and identify hardships they have suffered. Discuss these examples in class, and try to determine if these experiences were valuable in the leader's development.

5. Pair off with someone and discuss mentor relationships. Have you served as a mentor or protégé? Been a part of a formal mentoring program? How would you evaluate this experience? If you haven't been in this type of relationship, follow the steps outlined in the chapter to identify someone who could serve in this capacity and how you might ask them to be your mentor. Describe peer relationships that have been most helpful to you at work or at school.

6. Read either *The Seven Habits of Highly Effective People* by Stephen Covey or *Leadership From the Inside Out* by Kevin Cashman. Attempt to use either of these models to develop your internal approach to leadership. Report your experiences to your classmates.

7. Attend a leadership-training seminar and measure its effectiveness based on material covered in this text and in class. Write up your conclusions.

8. Develop a taking-charge case study based on the experiences of a new leader. What challenges did this leader face? How did he/she accomplish the three tasks of taking charge? Did she/he pass through the four stages described in the chapter? How successful was the leadership transition? Write up your findings.

Cultural Connections: Leadership Development[45]

All too often corporate trainers and consultants assume that training programs developed for U.S. audiences will automatically work in other countries. Trainers believe that challenge and practical experience promote development and that leaders should periodically measure their progress and get feedback from others. They are disappointed when participants from other nations refuse to enter into discussions, demand a rationale for every activity, or resist giving and receiving feedback. According to Center for Creative Leadership senior associate Michael Hoppe, U.S. trainers operate under a unique set of cultural assumptions. As we've seen in this chapter, leadership development in the United States focuses on the advancement of the individual and is based on the conviction that everyone can develop leadership capacities.

How well training strategies developed in the United States transfer to another country will depend on the overlap between U.S. values and beliefs and those of the host nation. Take the idea of personal advancement, for instance. Trainers in the United States assume that employees want to be promoted. That assumption is not shared in the Far East where managers may fear that they will break community ties by competing for higher positions. In Sweden, promotions are often seen as less desirable because they damage relationships with coworkers and mean less time with family. Promotion in France is based on individual performance as it is in the United States, but career paths are more clearly structured. The use of standardized test instruments is also problematic. Trainers in the United States believe in the power of "objective" measurement and rely heavily on paper and pencil surveys. Germans, on the other hand, put more value on theory and believe that better thinking, not more facts, is the key to progress.

Because leadership development draws upon deeply rooted cultural values and beliefs, Hoppe declares that "there are no shortcuts" when it comes to transferring training models and practices from any one nation to another. Successful cross-cultural leadership development trainers look for cultural similarities and differences. When given an overseas assignment, they learn as much as they can about the host culture, consult cultural insiders when designing programs, and make their content, activities, and assessment methods appropriate for the intended audience.

Leadership on the Big Screen: *The Big Kahuna*

Starring: Kevin Spacey, Danny DeVito, Peter Facinelli
Rating: R for profanity and explicit language
Synopsis: Spacey and DeVito play the roles of Larry and Phil, industrial lubricant salesmen. They are joined at a convention in Wichita by Bob (Facinelli), a recent college graduate who works in the company's research department. Larry is out to make contact with a major new client ("The Big

Kahuna"), newly divorced Phil is taking stock of his life, and Bob is more interested in sharing his religious faith than in selling his firm's products. Bob's religious fervor produces lots of conflict with Larry and presents him with a major ethical dilemma. Larry and Phil offer career and personal advice to their junior colleague at the same time they explore the relationship they have with one another. Adapted from the play *Hospitality Suite*.

Chapter Links: dealing with hardship, developmental relationships, the inner dimension of leadership

ENDNOTES

Chapter 1

[1] For more information on the history of leadership study, see: Bass, B. M. (Ed.). (1990). *Bass and Stogdill's handbook of leadership* (3rd ed., ch. 1). New York: Free Press.

[2] See, for example: Meindl, J. R., Ehrlich, S. B., & Dukerich, J. M. (1985). The romance of leadership. *Administrative Science Quarterly, 30,* 78–102; Meindl, J. R. (1995). The romance of leadership as a follower-centric theory: A social constructionist approach. *Leadership Quarterly, 6,* 329–341; Kiechel, W. (1988, November 21). The case against leaders. *Fortune,* 217–218.

[3] Bass, ch. 1.

[4] Staw, B. M., & Sutton, R. (1993). Macro organizational psychology. In J. K. Murnighan (Ed.), *Social psychology in organizations: Advances in theory and research* (pp. 350–384). Englewood Cliffs, NJ: Prentice-Hall; Meindl (1995).

[5] Fairhurst, G. T., & Sarr, R. A. (1996). *The art of framing.* San Francisco: Jossey-Bass.

[6] Adapted from Tichy, N. M. (1997). *The leadership engine.* New York: HarperBusiness, pp. 215–216. Used by permission.

[7] An IMAX film crew was on Mt. Everest during the 1996 disaster and recorded the rescue efforts. The video and DVD of *Everest* (Miramax Films, 1998) are available for purchase or rental. Krakauer, J. (1997). *Into thin air.* New York: Villard.

[8] Dance, F. E. X. (1982). A speech theory of human communication. In F. E. X. Dance (Ed.), *Human communication theory* (pp. 120–46). New York: Harper & Row, p. 126.

[9] White, L. A. (1949). *The science of culture.* New York: Farrar, Strauss and Cudahy, p. 25.

[10] Information concerning differences among human and animal communication systems is extensive. The following sources serve as a good starting point for reading in this area: Adler, J. J. (1967). *The difference of man and the difference it makes.* New York: Holt, Rinehart and Winston; Pearce, W. B. (1989). *Communication and the human condition.* Carbondale: Southern Illinois University Press; Sebeok, T. A., & Rosenthal, R. (Eds.). (1981). *The clever Hans phenomenon: Communication with horses, whales, apes, and people.* (Annals of the New York Academy of Sciences. Vol. 364). New York: New York Academy of Sciences; Sebeok, T. A., & Umiker-Sebeok, J. (1979). *Speaking of Apes: A critical anthology of two-way communication with man.* New York: Plenum; Terrace, H. S., Pettito, L. A., Sanders, R. J., & Bever, T. G. (1979). Can an ape create a sentence? *Science, 206,* 891–902; Walker, S. (1983). *Animal thought.* London: Routledge & Kegan Paul.

[11] Barnlund, D. C. (1962). Toward a meaning-centered philosophy of communication, *Journal of Communication, 12,* 197–211.

[12] Hersey, P. (1984). *The situational leader.* Escondido, CA: Center for Leadership Studies, p. 14.

[13] Bass, B. M. (1960). *Leadership, psychology, and organizational behavior.* New York: Harper & Row, p. 90.

[14] Alvesson, M. (2002). *Understanding organizational culture.* Thousand Oaks, CA: Sage, p. 105.

[15] Hemphill, J. K. (1949). The leader and his group. *Journal of Educational Research, 28,* 225–229.

[16] Stogdill, R. M. (1950). Leadership, membership and organization. *Psychological Bulletin, 47,* p. 4.

[17] Rost, J. C. (1993). Leadership in the new millennium. *The Journal of Leadership Studies,* 99; Rost, J. C. (1991). *Leadership for the twenty-first century.* New York: Praeger.

[18] Northouse, P. (2001). *Leadership: Theory and practice* (2nd ed., p. 3). Thousand Oaks, CA: Sage.

[19] Yukl, G. (1998). *Leadership in organizations* (4th ed., p. 5). Upper Saddle River, NJ: Prentice-Hall.

[20] Nahavandi, A. (2003). *The art and science of leadership* (3rd ed., p. 4). Upper Saddle River, NJ: Prentice-Hall.

[21] Daft, R. L. (1999). *Leadership: Theory and practice.* Fort Worth, TX: Dryden Press, p. 25.

[22] Witherspoon, P. D. (1997). *Communicating Leadership: An organizational perspective.* Boston, MA: Allyn and Bacon, p. 19.

[23] Kouzes, J. M., & Posner, B. Z. (1987). *The leadership challenge: How to get extraordinary things done in organizations.* San Francisco: Jossey-Bass, pp. 31–32.

[24] Bennis, W., & Nanus, B. (1985). *Leaders: The strategies for taking charge.* New York: Harper & Row, p. 21.

[25] Bennis, W. (1976). *The unconscious conspiracy: Why leaders can't lead.* New York: AMACOM, p. 154.

[26] Kotter, J. P. (1990). *A force for change: How leadership differs from management.* New York: Free Press, p. 6. Used by permission.

[27] Lieber, R. B. (1998, January 12). Why employees love these companies. *Fortune,* pp. 72–74.

[28] Peters, T. (1994). *The pursuit of wow!* New York: Vintage Books, p. 165.

[29] Freiberg, K., & Freiberg, J. (1996). *Nuts! Southwest Airlines crazy recipe for business and personal success.* New York: Broadway Books, p. 288.

[30] Freiberg & Freiberg, p. 148.

[31] Labich, K. (1994, May 2). Is Herb Kelleher America's best CEO? *Fortune,* 46–50.

[32] Herskovitz, J. (2002, June 8-9). Job candidates queue up. *New Zealand Herald,* C7.

[33] Wow, are they that good? (2002, August 5). *Business Week,* 14.

[34] Peters, T. (1992). *Liberation management.* New York: Ballantine, p. 656.

[35] Kotter, pp. 56, 65–67.

[36] Kotter, pp. 6–7.

[37] Kotter, J. P. (1999). *On what leaders really do.* Boston: Harvard Business School Press.

[38] Gardner, J. W. (1986). The tasks of leadership *(Leadership Paper No. 2).* Washington, DC: Independent Sector, p. 7.

[39] Peters, T., & Austin, N. (1985). *A passion for excellence: The leadership difference.* New York: Random House, p. 328.

[40] Rost, Leadership in the new millennium; Gardner, J. W. (1990). *On leadership.* New York: Free Press.

[41] Hollander, E. P. (1992, April). The essential interdependence of leadership and followership. *Current Directions in Psychological Science,* 71–75.

[42] Childress, J. R. (2000). *A time for leadership.* Los Angeles: Leadership Press.

[43] Litzinger, W. & Schaefer, T. (1982, September-October). Leadership through followership. *Business Horizons,* 78–81.

[44] Heenan, D. A., & Bennis, W. (1999). *Co-Leaders: The power of great partnerships.* New York: John Wiley & Sons, p. 6.

[45] Heenan & Bennis, p. 6.

[46] Kelley, R. (1992). *The power of followership: How to create leaders people want to follow and followers who lead themselves.* New York: Doubleday/Currency, p. 41.

[47] Summaries of the development of the Willingness to Communicate construct can be found in: McCroskey, J. C., & Richmond, V. P. (1998). Willingness to communicate. In J. C. McCroskey, J. A. Daly, M. M. Martin, & M. J. Beatty (Eds.), *Communication and personality: Trait perspectives* (pp. 119–131). Cresswell, NJ: Hampton Press; Richmond, V. P., & Roach, K. D. (1992). Willingness to communicate and employee success in U. S. organizations. *Journal of Applied Communication Research, 20,* 95–115; McCroskey, J. C., & Richmond, V. P. (1991). Willingness to communicate: A cognitive view. In M. Booth-Butterfield (Ed.), *Personality and interpersonal communication* (pp. 129–156). Newbury Park, CA: Sage.

48 McCroskey, J. C., & Richmond, V. P. (1990). Willingness to communicate: Differing cultural perspectives. *Southern Communication Journal, 56,* 72–77.

49 Johnson, C., Dixon, B., Hackman, M. Z., & Vinson, L. (1995). Willingness to communicate, the need for cognition and innovativeness: New Zealand students and professionals. In J. E. Aitken & L. J. Shedletsky (Eds.), *Intrapersonal communication processes* (pp. 376–381). Plymouth, MI: Midnight Oil and the Speech Communication Association; Hackman, M. Z., & Johnson, C. (1994). *A cross-cultural investigation of innovativeness, willingness to communicate and need for cognition.* Paper presented at the Speech Communication Association convention, New Orleans, LA.

50 McCroskey, J. C., & Richmond, V. P. (1996). *Fundamentals of Human Communication: An Interpersonal Perspective.* Prospect Heights, IL: Waveland Press, pp. 53–54. Used by permission.

51 Dance, F. E. X., & Larson, C. (1976). *The functions of human communication: Theoretical approach.* New York: Holt, Rinehart and Winston.

52 Curtis, D. B., Winsor, J. L., & Stephens, R. D. (1989). National preferences in business and communication education. *Communication Education, 38,* 6–14. Tables used by permission; for further reading: DiSalvo, V. (1980). A summary of current research identifying communication skills in various organizational contexts. *Communication Education, 29,* 283–290; DiSalvo, V., Larson, D., & Seiler, W. (1976). Communication skills needed by persons in business organizations. *Communication Education, 25,* 269–275, Hanna, M. (1978). Speech communication training needs in the business community. *Central States Speech Journal, 29,* 163–172; Sypher, B. D., & Zorn, T. (1986). Communication-related abilities and upward mobility: A longitudinal investigation. *Human Communication Research, 12,* 420–431.

53 For an overview of the development of the field of emotional intelligence, see Mayer, J. D. (2001). A field guide to emotional intelligence. In J. Ciarrochi, J. P. Forgas, & J. D. Mayer (Eds.), *Emotional intelligence in everyday life: A scientific inquiry* (pp. 3–24). Philadelphia: Psychology Press.

54 Goleman, D. (1995). *Emotional intelligence: Why it can matter more than IQ.* New York: Bantam Books.

55 Goleman, D. (1998). *Working with emotional intelligence.* New York: Bantam Books; Cherniss, C., & Goleman, D. (Eds.). (2001). *The emotionally intelligent workplace: How to select for, measure, and improve emotional intelligence in individuals, groups and organizations.* San Francisco: Jossey-Bass.

56 Goleman, D., Boyatzis, R., & McKee, A. (2002). *Primal leadership: Realizing the power of emotional intelligence.* Boston, MA: Harvard Business School Press.

57 Cherniss, C. (2000). Social and emotional competence in the workplace. In R. Bar-On & J. D. A. Parker (Eds.), *The handbook of emotional intelligence: Theory, development, assessment, and application at home, school, and in the workplace.* San Francisco: Jossey-Bass; Goleman, Working with emotional intelligence; Cooper, R. K., & Sawat, A. (1996). *Executive EQ: Emotional intelligence in leadership and organizations.* New York: Grosset/Putnam; Weisinger, H. (1998). *Emotional intelligence at work: The untapped edge for success.* San Francisco: Jossey-Bass.

58 Johnson, C. (2002). Evaluating the impact of emotional intelligence on leadership performance: Resonance or dissonance? *Selected Proceedings of the 2002 International Leadership Association convention* [online]. Available from http://www.academy.umd.edu/ILA.

59 Salovey, P., Bedell, B. T., Detweiler, J. B., & Mayer, J. D. (2000). Current directions in emotional intelligence research. In M. Lewis & J. M. Haviland-Lewis (Eds.), *Handbook of emotions* (2nd ed., pp. 504–520). New York: Guilford Press.

60 Goffman, E. (1959). *The presentation of self in everyday life.* Garden City, NY: Doubleday.

61 Lord, R. G., & Mahar, K. J. (1991). *Leadership and information processing: Linking perceptions and performance.* Boston: Unwin Hyman.

62 Hall, R. J., & Lord, R. G. (1998). Multi-level information-processing explanations of followers' leadership perceptions. In F. Dansereau & F. J. Yammarino (Eds.), *Leadership: The multiple-level approaches* (Vol. 2) (pp. 159–190). Stamford, CT: JAI Press

63 Social psychologists refer to individuals who are highly skilled at impression management as high self-monitors. For more information on self-monitoring and leadership, see: Synder, M. (1987). *Public appearances/private realities: The psychology of self-monitoring.* New York: W. H. Freeman; Dobbins, G. H., Long, W. S., Dedrick, E. J., & Clemons, T. C. (1990). The role of self-monitoring and gender on leader emergence: A laboratory and field study. *Journal of Management, 16,* 609–618; Ellis, R. J., & Cronshaw, S. F. (1992). Self-monitoring and leader emergence: A test of moderator effects. *Small Group Research, 23,* 113–129.

64 Keegan, J. (1987). *The mask of command.* New York: Viking Penguin.

[65] Keegan, p. 11.

[66] Keegan, p. 318.

[67] Planalp, S. (1999). *Communicating emotion: Social, moral, and cultural processes.* Cambridge, UK: Cambridge University Press.

[68] Planalp, p. 200.

Chapter 2

[1] Adapted from Capezio, P., & Morehouse, D. (1997). *Secrets of breakthrough leadership.* Franklin Lakes, NJ: Career Press; Manning, G., & Curtis, K. (1988). *Leadership: Nine keys to success.* Cincinnati: South-Western; DuBrin, A. J. (1995). *Leadership.* Boston: Houghton Mifflin.

[2] Lewin, K., Lippitt, R., & White, R. K. (1939). Patterns of aggressive behavior in experimentally created "social climates." *Journal of Social Psychology, 10,* 271–299.

[3] See, for example: Bass, B. M. (1990). *Bass & Stogdill's handbook of leadership* (3rd ed., ch. 25). New York: Free Press.

[4] Kriegel, R. J., & Patler, L. (1991). *If it ain't broke . . . break it!* New York: Warner Books; Looney, D. S. (1989, September 4). A most unusual man. *Sports Illustrated,* pp. 118–124; Ortmayer, R. (personal communication, May 13, 1999).

[5] Lewin et al.

[6] White, R., & Lippitt, R. (1968). Leader behavior and member reaction in three "social climates." In D. Cartwright & A. Zander (Eds.), *Group dynamics* (pp. 318–335). New York: Harper & Row.

[7] Shaw, M. E. (1955). A comparison of two types of leadership in various communication nets. *Journal of Abnormal and Social Psychology, 50,* 127–134; Hise, R. T. (1968, Fall). The effect of close supervision on productivity of simulated managerial decision-making groups. *Business Studies, North Texas University,* pp. 96–104.

[8] Cammalleri, J. A., Hendrick, H. W., Pittmen, W. C., Jr., Blout, H. D., & Prather, D. C. (1973). Effects of different leadership styles on group accuracy. *Journal of Applied Psychology, 57,* 32–37.

[9] Vroom, V. H., & Mann, F. C. (1960). Leader authorization and employee attitudes. *Personnel Psychology, 13,* 125–140.

[10] Rudin, S. A. (1964). Leadership as psychophysiological activation of group members: A case experimental study. *Psychological Reports, 15,* 577–578.

[11] Day, R. C., & Hamblin, R. L. (1964). Some effects of close and punitive styles of supervision. *American Journal of Sociology, 69,* 499–510.

[12] Ley, R. (1966). Labor turnover as a function of worker differences, work environment, and authoritarianism of foremen. *Journal of Applied Psychology, 50,* 497–500.

[13] Argyle, M., Gardner, G., & Ciofi, F. (1958). Supervisory methods related to productivity, absenteeism, and labor turnover. *Human Relations, 11,* 23–40.

[14] Mohr, L. B. (1971). Organizational technology and organizational structure. *Administrative Science Quarterly, 16,* 444–459; Bass, B. M., Burger, P. C., Doktor, R., & Barrett, G. V. (1979). *Assessment of managers: An international comparison.* New York: Free Press.

[15] Hespe, G., & Wall, T. (1976). The demand for participation among employees. *Human Relations, 29,* 411–428.

[16] Ziller, R. C. (1954). Four techniques of group decision making under uncertainty. *American Psychologist, 9,* 498.

[17] Farris, G. F. (1972). The effect of individual roles on performance in innovative groups. *R & D Management, 3,* 23–28.

[18] Meyer, H. H. (1968). Achievement motivation and industrial climates. In R. Tagiuri & G. H. Litwin (Eds.), Organizational technology and organizational structure. *Administrative Science Quarterly, 16,* 444–459.

[19] Farris.

[20] Aspegren, R. E. (1963). A study of leadership behavior and its effects on morale and attitudes in selected elementary schools. *Dissertation Abstracts, 23,* 3708.

[21] Baumgartel, H. (1957). Leadership style as a variable in research administration. *Administrative Science Quarterly, 2,* 344–360.

22 Muringham, J. K., & Leung, T. K. (1976). The effects of leadership involvement and the importance of the task on subordinates' performance. *Organizational Behavior and Human Performance, 17,* 299–310.

23 Weschler, I. R., Kahane, M., & Tannenbaum, R. (1952). Job satisfaction, productivity, and morale: A case study. *Occupational Psychology, 26,* 1–14; Meltzer, L. (1956). Scientific productivity in organizational settings. *Journal of Social Issues, 12,* 32–40.

24 Zemke, R., Raines, C., & Filipczak, B. (2000). *Generations at work.* New York: AMACOM.

25 Stech, E. L. (1983). *Leadership communication.* Chicago: Nelson-Hall, ch. 4.

26 See: Katz, D., Maccoby, N., Gurin, G., & Floor, L. (1951). *Productivity, supervision, and morale among railroad workers.* Ann Arbor: University of Michigan, Institute for Social Research; Katz, D., Maccoby, N., & Morse, N. (1950). *Productivity, supervision, and morale in an office situation.* Ann Arbor: University of Michigan, Institute for Social Research.

27 Although the one-dimensional view of leadership communication has been criticized as being overly simplistic, some one-dimensional models are still routinely discussed in leadership courses. For an example of a commonly cited one-dimensional model see: Tannenbaum, R., & Schmidt, W. H. (1958). How to choose a leadership pattern. *Harvard Business Review, 36,* 95–101.

28 Kahn, R. L. (1956). The prediction of productivity. *Journal of Social Issues, 12,* 41–49.

29 Stogdill, R. M., & Coons, A. E. (1957). *Leader behavior: Its description and measurement.* Columbus: Ohio State University, Bureau of Business Research.

30 Stogdill, R. M. (1965). *Managers, employees, organizations.* Columbus: Ohio State University, Bureau of Business Research.

31 McGregor, D. (1960). *The human side of enterprise.* New York: McGraw-Hill.

32 Blake, R. R. & McCanse, A. A. (1991). *Leadership dilemmas—grid solutions.* Houston: Gulf Publishing; Blake, R. R., & Mouton, J. S. (1985). *The managerial grid III: The key to leadership excellence.* Houston: Gulf Publishing.

33 The Leadership Grid Figure for *Leadership Dilemmas—Grid Solutions,* by Robert R. Blake and Anne Adams McCanse (formerly the Managerial Grid Figure by Robert R. Blake and Jane S. Mouton). Austin: Grid International, Inc., p. 29. Copyright 1991 by Grid International, Inc. Reproduced by permission.

34 See: Blake & McCanse, *Leadership dilemmas—grid solutions;* Blake, R. R., Mouton, J. S., Barnes, L. B., & Greiner, L. E. (1964). Breakthrough in organization development. *Harvard Business Review, 42,* 133–155.

35 Kelley, R. (1992). *The power of followership: How to create leaders that people want to follow and followers who lead themselves..* New York: Doubleday/Currency; Kelley, R. (1988, November-December). In praise of followers. *Harvard Business Review, 66,* 142–148.

36 Kelley, *The power of followership,* pp. 89–97. Used by permission.

37 DePree, M. (1992). *Leadership jazz.* New York: Currency/Doubleday, pp. 197–217.

38 Pittman, T. S., Rosenbach, W. E., & Potter, E. H. III. (1998). Followers as partners: Taking the initiative for action. In W. E. Rosenbach & R. L. Taylor (Eds.), *Contemporary issues in leadership* (pp. 107–120). Boulder, CO: Westview Press.

39 Kakabadse, A., Myers, A., McMahon, T., & Spony, G. (1995). Top management styles in Europe: Implications for business and cross-national teams. *European Business Journal, 7,* 17–27.

Chapter 3

1 Stogdill, R. M. (1948). Personal factors associated with leadership: A survey of the literature. *Journal of Psychology, 25,* 35–71.

2 Stogdill, p. 64.

3 Stogdill, R. M. (1974). *Handbook of leadership.* New York: The Free Press.

4 Stogdill, *Handbook,* p. 72.

5 Kenny, D. A., & Zaccaro, S. J. (1983). An estimate of variance due to traits in leadership. *Journal of Applied Psychology, 68,* 678–685 (a reanalysis of Barnlund's consistency of emergent leadership in groups with changing tasks and members published in *Speech Monographs* in 1962); Lord, R. G., De Vader, C. L., & Alliger, G. M. (1986). A meta-analysis of the relation between personality traits and leadership perceptions: An application of validity generalization procedures. *Journal of Applied Psychology, 71,* 402–410 (a reanalysis of Mann's review of the relationships between personality and performance in small groups published in *Psychological Bulletin* in 1959).

[6] Foti, R. J., Fraser, S. L., & Lord, R. G. (1982). Effects of leadership labels and prototypes on perceptions of political leaders. *Journal of Applied Psychology, 67,* 326–333.

[7] See, for example: Burns, T., & Stalker, G. M. (1961). *The management of innovation.* Chicago: Quadrangle Books; Lawrence, P. R., & Lorsch, J. W. (1967). *Organization and environment.* Cambridge: Harvard University Press; Woodward, J. (1965). *Industrial organization: Theory and practice.* Oxford: Oxford University Press.

[8] Boyatzis, R. E. (1982). *The competent manager.* New York: John Wiley; Fiedler, F. E., & Garcia, J. E. (1987). *New approaches to effective leadership: Cognitive resources and organizational performance.* New York: John Wiley; Howard, A., & Bray, D. W. (1988). *Managerial lives in transition: Advancing age and changing times.* New York: Guilford Press; Kirkpatrick, S. A., & Locke, E. A. (1991). Leadership: Do traits matter? *The Executive, 5,* 48–60. Lombardo, M. M., & McCauley, C. D. (1988) *The dynamics of management derailment.* Technical Report No. 34. Greensboro, NC: Center for Creative Leadership; McCall, N. W., Jr., & Lombardo, M. M. (1983). *Off the track: Why and how successful executives get derailed.* Technical Report No. 21. Greensboro, NC: Center for Creative Leadership.

[9] See, for example: Gardner, H. (1983). *Frames of mind.* New York: Basic Books; Johnson, C. E., & Hackman, M. Z. (1995). *Creative communication: Principles and applications.* Prospect Heights, IL: Waveland Press, chapters 2 and 4.

[10] See, for example: Fiedler, F. E. (1967). *A theory of leadership effectiveness.* New York: McGraw-Hill; Fiedler, F. E. (1972). Personality, motivational systems, and the behavior of high and low LPC persons. *Human Relations, 25,* 391–412; Fiedler, F. E. (1978). The contingency model and the dynamics of the leadership process. In L. Berkowitz (Ed.), *Advances in experimental social psychology* (pp. 60–112). New York: Academic Press.

[11] Fiedler, F. E., Chemers, M. M., & Mahar, L. (1976). *Improving leadership effectiveness: The leader match concept.* New York: John Wiley. Used by permission.

[12] See, for example: Ashour, A. S. (1973). The contingency model of leadership effectiveness: An evaluation. *Organizational Behavior and Human Performance, 9,* 339–355; Kerr, S., & Harlan, A. (1973). Predicting the effects of leadership training and experience from the contingency model: Some remaining problems. *Journal of Applied Psychology, 57,* 114–117; Schriesheim, C. A., & Kerr, S. (1977). Theories and measures of leadership: A critical appraisal. In J. G. Hunt & L. L. Larson (Eds.), *Leadership: The cutting edge* (pp. 9–45). Carbondale: Southern Illinois University Press.

[13] See, for example: House, R. J. (1971). A path-goal theory of leader effectiveness. *Administrative Science Quarterly, 16,* 321–338; House, R. J., & Mitchell, T. R. (1974). Path-goal theory of leadership. *Journal of Contemporary Business, 3,* 81–97.

[14] Fiedler, F. E. (1967). *A theory of leadership effectiveness.* New York: McGraw-Hill. Used by permission.

[15] Hersey, P., & Blanchard, K. H. (1996). *Management of organizational behavior: Utilizing human resources* (7th ed.). Englewood Cliffs, NJ: Prentice-Hall.

[16] Paul Hersey and Ken Blanchard, *Management of organizational behavior utilizing human resources, 5/E,* © 1988, p. 171. Reproduced by permission of Prentice-Hall, Inc., Englewood Cliffs, New Jersey.

[17] See, for example: Graen, G. B., & Cashman, J. F. (1975). A role-making model of leadership in formal organizations: A developmental approach. In J. G. Hunt & L. L. Larson (Eds.), *Leadership frontiers* (pp. 143–165). Kent: Kent State University Press; Graen, G. B., & Scandura, T. (1987). Toward a psychology of dyadic organizing. *Research in Organizational Behavior, 9,* 175–208.

[18] Graen, G. (1976). Role-making processes within complex organizations. In M. D. Dunnette (Ed.), *Handbook of industrial organizational psychology* (pp. 1201–1246). Chicago: Rand-McNally.

[19] Graen & Cashman.

[20] Fairhurst, G. T., & Chandler, T. A. (1989). Social structure in leader-member interaction. *Communication Monographs, 56,* 213–239.

[21] Fairhurst, G. T., Rogers, L. E., & Sarr, R. A. (1987). Manager-subordinate control patterns and judgments about the relationship. In M. McLaughlin (Ed.), *Communication Yearbook 10* (pp. 83–116). Beverly Hills: Sage.

[22] See, for example: Graen, G., & Ginsburgh, S. (1977). Job resignation as a function of role orientation and leader acceptance: A longitudinal investigation of organizational assimilation. *Organizational Behavior and Human Performance, 19,* 1–17; Liden, R., & Graen, G. (1980). Generalizability of the vertical dyad linkage model of leadership. *Academy of Management Journal, 23,* 451–465; Vecchio, R. P. (1982). A further test of leadership effects due to between-group variation and within-group variation. *Journal of Applied Psychology, 67,* 200–208.

[23] Graen, G. B., & Uhl-Bien, M. (1998). Relationship-based approach to leadership. Development of leader-member exchange (LMX) theory of leadership over 25 years: Applying a multi-level multi-domain perspective. In F. Dansereau & F. J. Yammariono (Eds.), *Leadership: the multiple-level approaches* (pp. 103–158). Stamford, CT: JAI Press.

[24] Adapted from *Leadership: the multiple-level approaches*, volume 24, George Graen and Mary Uhl-Bien, Relationship-based approach to leadership: Development of leader-member exchange (LMX) theory of leadership over 25 years: Applying a multi-level multi-domain perspective, p. 123, 1998, with permission from Elsevier.

[25] Barnard, C. I. (1938). *The functions of the executive.* Cambridge: Harvard University Press.

[26] Benne, K. D., & Sheats, P. (1948). Functional roles of group members. *Journal of Social Issues, 4,* 41–49.

[27] Krech, D., & Crutchfield, R. (1948). *Theory and problems of social psychology.* New York, McGraw-Hill.

[28] Bowers, D. G., & Seashore, .S. E. (1966). Predicting organizational effectiveness with a four-factory theory of leadership. *Administrative Science Quarterly, 2,* 238–263.

[29] Cartwright, D., & Zander, A. (1968). Leadership and performance of group functions: Introduction. In D. Cartwright and A. Zander (Eds.). *Group dynamics* (pp. 301–317). New York, Harper & Row.

[30] Hofstede, G. (2001). *Culture's consequences: Comparing values, behaviors, institutions, and organizations across nations* (2nd ed.). Thousand Oaks, CA: Sage; Hofstede, G. (1993). Cultural constraints in management theories. *Academy of Management Executive, 7,* 81–94; Hofstede, G. (1980). Motivation, leadership and organization: Do American theories apply abroad? *Organizational Dynamics, 9,* 42–63.

[31] Haire, M., Ghiselli, E. E., & Porter, L. W. (1966). *Managerial thinking: An international study.* New York: John Wiley.

Chapter 4

[1] Burns, J. M. (1978). *Leadership.* New York: Harper & Row.

[2] Maslow, A. H. (1970). *Motivation and personality.* New York: Harper & Row.

[3] See for example: Bass, B. M. (1985). *Leadership and performance beyond expectations.* New York: The Free Press.

[4] Bass, B. M. (1990). *Bass & Stogdill's handbook of leadership* (3rd ed., p. 53). New York: The Free Press.

[5] Burns, p. 4.

[6] Bass, *Leadership*; Bass, B. M., & Avolio, B. J. (1994). *Improving organizational effectiveness through transformational leadership.* Thousand Oaks, CA: Sage.

[7] Bass, *Leadership*, p. 17.

[8] Bass, B. M. (1985). *Leadership and performance beyond expectations.* New York: Free Press; Bass, B. M. (1990). From transactional to transformational leadership: Learning to share the vision. *Organizational Dynamics, 18,* 19–31; Bass, B. M., & Avolio, B. J. (1994). *Improving organizational effectiveness through transformational leadership.* Thousand Oaks, CA: Sage.

[9] Zorn, T. E. (1991). Construct system development, transformational leadership and leadership messages. *Southern Communication Journal, 56,* 178–193.

[10] Peters, T. J., & Waterman, R. H., Jr. (1982). *In search of excellence.* New York: Harper & Row.

[11] Peters, T. M., & Austin, N. K. (1985). *A passion for excellence: The leadership difference.* New York: Warner Books.

[12] Peters, T. (1992). *Liberation management.* New York: Ballantine.

[13] Bennis, W. G., & Nanus, B. (1997). *Leaders: The strategies for taking charge* (2nd ed.). New York: Harper & Row.

[14] Kouzes, J. M., & Posner, B. Z. (1995). *The leadership challenge: How to get extraordinary things done in organizations.* San Francisco: Jossey-Bass.

[15] Neff, T. J., & Citrin, J. M. (1999). *Lessons from the top.* New York: Doubleday; Avolio, B. J., & Bass, B. M. (2002). *Developing potential across a full range of leadership: Cases on transactional and transformational leadership.* Mahwah, NJ: Lawrence Erlbaum Associates.

[16] Snyder, N. H., & Graves, M. (1994). Leadership and vision. *Business Horizons, 37,* 1–7.

[17] Kriegel, R. J., & Patler, L. (1991). *If it ain't broke . . . break it!* New York: Warner Books.

[18] Parnes, S. J. (1975). "Aha!" In I. A. Taylor & J. W. Getzels (Eds.), *Perspectives on creativity* (pp. 224–248). Chicago: Aldine.

[19] Mednick, S. A. (1962). The associative basis of the creative process. *Psychological Review, 69*, p. 221.

[20] Wallas, G. (1926). *The art of thought*. New York: Harcourt.

[21] von Oech, R. (1986). *A kick in the seat of the pants*. New York: Harper & Row, pp. 30, 32.

[22] Orsag Madigan, C., & Elwood, A. (1983). *Brainstorms and thunderbolts*. New York: Macmillan.

[23] Johnson, C. E., & Hackman, M. Z. (1995). *Creative communication: Principles and applications*. Prospect Heights, IL: Waveland Press, ch. 2.

[24] Adams, J. L. (1986). *Conceptual blockbusting* (3rd ed.). Reading, MA: Addison-Wesley.

[25] Sanders, D. A., & Sanders, J. A. (1984). *Teaching creativity through metaphor*. New York: Longman, p. 19.

[26] Getzels, J. W. (1975). Problem-finding and the inventiveness of solutions. *Journal of Creative Behavior, 9*, 12–18; Getzels, J. W. (1973, November 21). Problem finding: The 343rd Convocation Address, the University of Chicago. *The University of Chicago Record, 9*, 281–283; Mackworth, N. H. (1965). Originality. *American Psychologist, 20*, 51–66.

[27] Kriegel, R., & Brandt, D. (1996). *Sacred cows make the best burgers: Paradigm-busting strategies for developing change-ready people and organizations*. New York: Warner Books.

[28] Peters & Waterman, p. 223.

[29] Garvin, D. A. (1993, July-August). Building a learning organization. *Harvard Business Review*, p. 86.

[30] Martin, F. (2002, April). So you failed. . . so what? *Unlimited*, p. 48.

[31] Bennis, W. G., & Nanus, B. (1985). *Leaders: The strategies for taking charge*. New York: Harper & Row.

[32] Conceiao, P., Hamill, D., & Pinheiro, P. (2002). Innovative science and technology commercialization strategies at 3M: A case study. *Journal of Engineering and Technology Management, 19*, 25–38; Dubashi, J. (1992, February 18). 3M: New talent and products outweigh the costs. *Financial World*, p. 19; Katauskas, T. (1990, November). Follow-through: 3M's formula for success. *Research and Development*, pp. 46–52; Lehr, L. W. (1988). Encouraging innovation and entrepreneurship in diversified corporations. In R. L. Kuhn (Ed.), *Handbook for creative and innovative managers* (pp. 211–229). New York: McGraw-Hill; Mitchell, R. (1989, April 10). Masters of innovation: How 3M keeps its new products coming. *Business Week*, pp. 58–63; Mitchell, R. (1989, Innovation Issue). Mining the work force for ideas, *Business Week*, p. 121; Mitsch, R. A. (1992, September-October). R&D at 3M: Continuing to play a big role. *Research Technology Management*, pp. 22–26; Zand, D. E. (1997). *The leadership triad: Knowledge, trust, and power*. New York: Oxford University Press.

[33] Peters & Austin, ch. 2.

[34] Neff & Citrin.

[35] Neff & Citrin, pp. 39–40.

[36] Pasternack, B. A., & O'Toole, J. (2002, second quarter). Yellow light leadership: How the world's best companies manage uncertainty. *Strategy + Business*, pp. 74–83.

[37] Holzman, D. (1993, August). When workers run the show. *Working Woman*, pp. 38–41; 72–74; Managing the journey (1990, November). *Inc.* pp. 45–54; Peters, T. (1992). *Liberation management*. New York: Ballantine, pp. 238–243; Stayer, R. (1990, November-December). How I learned to let my workers lead. *Harvard Business Review*, pp. 66–83.

[38] Guarrero, C. A. (1998, October). The leadership challenge. *Security Management*, pp. 27–29.

[39] Bennis & Nanus.

[40] Nanus, B. (1992). *Visionary leadership*. San Francisco: Jossey-Bass.

[41] Collins, J. C., & Porras, J. I. (1994). *Built to last*. New York: Harper Business.

[42] Kotter, J. P. (1990). *A force for change: How leadership differs from management*. New York: Free Press, p. 36.

[43] The vision thing. (1991, November 9). *The Economist*, p. 89.

[44] The vision statements listed come from the following sources: Abrahams, J. (1995). *The mission statement book*. Berkeley, CA: Ten Speed Press; Collins, J. C., & Porras, J. I. (1996, September-October). Building your company's vision. *Harvard Business Review*, pp. 65–77; Disney Institute. (2001). *Be our guest*. New York: Disney Enterprises; Zaccaro, S. J., & Banks, D. J. (2001). Leadership, vision, and organizational effectiveness. In S. J. Zaccaro and R. K. Kilimoski (Eds.), *The nature of organizational leadership* (pp. 181–218). San Francisco: Jossey Bass.

[45] Jones, L. B. (1996). *The path: Creating your mission statement for work and life*. New York: Hyperion, p. 71.

[46] Levin, I. M. (2000). Vision revisited. *Journal of Applied Behavioral Science, 36*, 91–107.

[47] Rokeach, M. (1973). *The nature of human values*. New York: Free Press.

[48] Capodagli, B., & Jackson, L. (1999). *The Disney way*. New York: McGraw-Hill, p. 87.

[49] Shockley-Zalabak, P., Ellis, K., & Cesaria, R. (2000). *Measuring organizational trust*. San Francisco: International Association of Business Communicators.

[50] DePree, M. (1989). *Leadership is an art*. New York: Doubleday, p. 9.

[51] Carlzon, J. (1987). *Moments of truth*. New York: Harper & Row.

[52] Neff & Citrin, p. 188.

[53] Sanders, B. (1995). *Fabled service*. San Francisco: Jossey-Bass, p. 75.

[54] Spector, R., & McCarthy, P. (1995). *The Nordstrom way*. New York: John Wiley & Sons, p.97.

[55] Heskett, J. L., Sasser, Jr., W. E., & Hart, C. W. L. (1990). *Service breakthroughs*. New York: Free Press, pp. 13–14.

[56] Spector, R. (2001). *Lessons from the Nordstrom way*. New York: John Wiley & Sons, p. 68.

[57] Lundin, S. C., Paul, H, & Chritensen, J. (2000). *Fish!* New York: Hyperion.

[58] Chang, R. (2001). *The passion plan at work*. San Francisco: Jossey Bass, p. 5.

[59] Collins, J. (2001). *Good to great*. New York: HarperBusiness, pp. 109–110.

[60] Bass, *Leadership*, ch. 3. Some contemporary Christian groups also consider their leaders to be gifted by God. The term "charismatic" can also refer to a particular style of religious worship.

[61] Weber, M. (1947). *The theory of social and economic organization* (A. M. Henderson & T. Parsons, Trans.). Glencoe, IL: The Free Press, pp. 358–359.

[62] Trice, H. M., & Beyer, J. M. (1993). *The cultures of work organizations*. Englewood Cliffs, NJ: Prentice-Hall, p. 259.

[63] Bass, *Handbook*, p. 187. Bass summarizes the concerns regarding the centrality of crisis in the definition of charismatic leadership and provides an example of charisma without crisis. Bass notes that financial investment brokers often have devoted, unquestioning followers who perceive them as being charismatic even in times of financial calm.

[64] Zaleznik, A. (1977, May-June). Managers and leaders: Are they different? *Harvard Business Review, 55*, 67–78. See also: Kiechel, W. (1983, May 30). What makes a corporate leader? *Fortune*, pp. 135–140.

[65] Willner, R. A. (1986). *Charismatic political leadership: A theory*. Princeton: Princeton University Center for International Studies, p. 6.

[66] Adapted from: Yukl, G. (1994). *Leadership in organizations* (3rd ed., pp. 328–329). Englewood Cliffs, NJ: Prentice-Hall.

[67] Hummel, R. P. (1975). Psychology of charismatic followers. *Psychological Reports, 37*, 759–770.

[68] Schweitzer, A. (1984). *The age of charisma*. Chicago: Nelson-Hall.

[69] Willner, R. A. (1984). *The spellbinders: Charismatic political leadership*. New Haven: Yale University Press. Although Willner identifies only six pure or true charismatic leaders, she acknowledges that other leaders—like Mussolini and John F. Kennedy—possessed charismatic qualities.

[70] Willner, *Spellbinders*, pp. 20, 29.

[71] Conger, J. A., & Kanungo, R. N. (1987). Toward a behavioral theory of charismatic leadership in organizational settings. *Academy of Management Review, 12*, 637–647.

[72] House, R. J. (1977). A 1976 theory of charismatic leadership. In J. G. Hunt & L. L. Larson (Eds.), *Leadership: The cutting edge* (pp. 189–207). Carbondale: Southern Illinois University Press; Bass, *Handbook*, ch. 3.

[73] Bass, *Leadership*, p. 61.

[74] Conger & Kanungo.

[75] Richardson, R. J., & Thayer, S. K. (1993). *The charisma factor*. Englewood Cliffs, NJ: Prentice-Hall, p. 27.

[76] Geertz, C. (1977). Centers, kings, and charisma: Reflections on the symbolics of power. In J. Ben-David & T. Nichols (Eds.), *Culture and its creation: Essays in honor of Edward Shils* (pp. 150–171). Chicago: University of Chicago Press, p. 151.

[77] Dow, T. (1969). The theory of charisma. *Sociological Quarterly, 10*, 316.

[78] Huggins, N. (1987). Martin Luther King, Jr.: Charisma and leadership. *Journal of American History, 74*, 477–481.

[79] Howell, J. M., & Avolio, B. J. (1992). The ethics of charismatic leadership: Submission or liberation. *Academy of Management Executive, 6*, 43–54.

[80] Conger, J. A. (1989). *The charismatic leader*. San Francisco: Jossey-Bass, ch. 8. Many of the examples of this section come from Conger.

[81] Bucher, L. (1988). *Accidental millionaire*. New York: Paragon House, p. 150.

[82] Bryman, A. (1992). *Charisma and leadership in organizations.* London: Sage, pp. 170–173.

[83] Bass, B. M. (1997). Does the transactional-transformational leadership paradigm transcend organizational and national boundaries? *American Psychologist, 52,* 130–139; Bass, B. M., & Avolio, B. J. (1993). Transformational leadership: A response to critiques. In M. M. Chemers & R. Ayman (Eds.), *Leadership theory and research: Perspectives and directions* (pp. 49–80). New York: Academic Press; Den Hartog, D. N., House, R. J., Hanges, P. J., & Ruiz-Quintanilla, S. A. (1999). Culture specific and cross-culturally generalizable implicit leadership theories: Are attributes of charismatic/transformational leadership universally endorsed? *Leadership Quarterly, 10,* 219–256.

Chapter 5

[1] Kanter, R. M. (1979, July-August). Power failure in management circuits. *Harvard Business Review, 57,* p. 65.

[2] Pfeffer, J. (1992, Winter). Understanding power in organizations. *California Management Review,* pp. 29–50.

[3] Gardner, J. (1990). *On leadership.* New York: Free Press, pp. 55–57.

[4] Bennis, W., & Nanus, B. (1985). *Leaders: The strategies for taking charge.* New York: Harper & Row, pp. 17–18.

[5] French, J. R. P., & Raven, B. (1959). The bases of social power. In D. Cartwright, (Ed.), *Studies in social power* (pp. 150–167). Ann Arbor: University of Michigan, Institute for Social Research. Although there are a number of power typologies, this is the most widely used, generating research in such fields as management, communication, and education.

[6] Modified version of T. R. Hinken and C. A. Schriesheim, "Development and Application of New Scales to Measure the French and Raven (1959) Bases of Social Power." *Journal of Applied Psychology, 74,* 1989, 561–567.

[7] Kohn, A. (1993). *Punished by rewards: The trouble with gold stars, incentive plans, A's, praise and other bribes.* Boston: Houghton Mifflin, p. 37.

[8] Kohn, p. 59.

[9] Kohn, p. 67.

[10] Kohn, p. 73.

[11] For additional information on the relationship between intrinsic motivation and creativity, see: Amabile, T. (1983). *The social psychology of creativity.* New York: Springer-Verlag.

[12] The most popular social exchange theory is that of J. W. Thibault and H. H. Kelley *(Interpersonal relations: A theory of interdependence.* New York: John Wiley, 1978). For one application of social exchange theory to groups, see: Hollander, E. (1978). *Leadership dynamics: A practical guide to effective relationships.* New York: The Free Press.

[13] Information on the costs and benefits of power types are found in the following sources: Bass, B. (1990). *Bass and Stogdill's handbook of leadership* (3rd ed., ch. 13). New York: Free Press; Hersey, P., & Blanchard, K. H. (1996). *Management of organizational behavior: Utilizing human resources* (7th ed.). Englewood Cliffs, NJ: Prentice-Hall; Yukl, G., & Falbe, C. M. (1991). Importance of different power sources in downward and lateral relations. *Journal of Applied Psychology, 76,* 416–423; Baldwin, D. A. (1971). The costs of power. *Journal of Conflict Resolution, 15,* 145–155; Yukl, G. (1998). *Leadership in organizations* (4th ed., ch. 8). Englewood Cliffs, NJ: Prentice-Hall.

[14] Giles, H., & Powesland, P. F. (1975). *Speech style and social evaluation.* London: Academic Press.

[15] O'Barr, W. (1984). Asking the right questions about language and power. In C. Kramarae, M. Schulz, & W. O'Barr (Eds.), *Language and power* (pp. 260–280). Beverly Hills: Sage.

[16] Bradac, J., & Mulac, A. (1984). A molecular view of powerful and powerless speech styles: Attributional consequences of specific language features and communicator intentions. *Communication Monographs, 51,* 307–319.

[17] See, for example: Burell, N. A., & Koper, R. J. (1994). The efficacy of powerful/ powerless language on persuasiveness/credibility: A meta-analytic review. In R. W. Preiss & M. Allen (Eds.), *Prospects and precautions in the use of meta-analysis* (pp. 235–255). Dubuque, IA: Brown & Benchmark; Haleta, L. L. (1996). Student perceptions of teachers' use of language: The effects of powerful and powerless language on impression formation and uncertainty. *Communication Education, 45,* 16–28; Johnson, C.,

Vinson, L., Hackman, M., & Hardin, T. (1989). The effects of an instructor's use of hesitation form on student ratings of quality, recommendations to hire, and lecture listening. *Journal of the International Listening Association, 3,* 32–43.

[18] Johnson, C., & Vinson, L. (1987). "Damned if you do, damned if you don't?": Status, powerful speech and evaluations of female witnesses. *Women's Studies in Communication, 10,* 37–44.

[19] Vinson, L., Johnson, C., & Hackman, M. (1992). *I like you just the way you are: Student evaluations of favorite and least favorite instructors using hesitant speech.* Paper presented at the Speech Communication Association convention, Chicago, IL; Vinson, L., & Johnson, C. (1990). The relationship between the use of hesitations and/or hedges and listening: The role of perceived importance as a mediating variable. *Journal of the International Listening Association, 4,* 116–127.

[20] Sorensen, R., & Pickett, T. (1986). A test of two teaching strategies designed to improve interview effectiveness: Rating behavior and videotaped feedback. *Communication Monographs, 35,* 13–22.

[21] Bass, *Bass and Stogdill's handbook of leadership.*

[22] Kanter, R. M. (1977). *Men and women of the corporation.* New York: Basic Books, ch. 7.

[23] Kouzes, J. M., & Posner, B. Z. (1987). *The leadership challenge: How to get extraordinary things done in organizations.* San Francisco: Jossey-Bass, p. 162.

[24] Bennis, W. (1976). *The unconscious conspiracy: Why leaders can't lead.* New York: AMACOM, p. 167.

[25] Fiske, S. T. (1993, June). Controlling other people: The impact of power on stereotyping. *American Psychologist,* pp. 621–628.

[26] Bies, R., & Tripp, T. M. (1998). Two faces of the powerless: Coping with tyranny in organizations. In R. M. Kramer & M. A. Neale (Eds.), *Power and influence in organizations* (pp. 203–219). Thousand Oaks, CA: Sage; See also, Hornstein, H. A. (1996). *Brutal bosses and their prey.* New York: Riverhead Books.

[27] Adams, S. (1996). *The Dilbert principle: A cubicle's eye view of bosses, meetings, management fads & other workplace afflictions.* New York: HarperBusiness; Adams, S. (1998). The *Dilbert future: Thriving on business stupidity in the 21st century.* New York: HarperBusiness; Adams, S. (1998). *The joy of work: Dilbert's guide to finding happiness at the expense of your co-workers.* New York: HarperBusiness.

[28] Adams, *The Dilbert principle,* p. 325.

[29] Conger, J. (1989). Leadership: The art of empowering others. *The Academy of Management EXECUTIVE, 3,* 17–24, p. 22. Used by permission.

[30] Kanter, Power failure.

[31] Bandura, A. (1977). Self-efficacy: Toward a unifying theory of behavioral change. *Psychological Review, 84,* 191–215; Bandura, A., & Wood, R. (1989). Effect of perceived controllability and performance standards on self-regulation of complex decision making. *Journal of Personality and Social Psychology, 84,* 805–814.

[32] See: Conger, J. A., & Kanungo, R. N. (1988). The empowerment process: Integrating theory and practice. *Academy of Management Review, 13,* 471–482; Conger, *Leadership,* pp. 17–24.

[33] Belasco, J. A., & Stayer, R. C. (1994). *Flight of the buffalo.* New York: Warner Books.

[34] Belasco & Stayer, p. 351.

[35] Seifter, H., & Economy, P. (2001). *Leadership ensemble: Lessons in collaborative management from the world's only conductorless orchestra.* New York: Times Books.

[36] Manz and Sims have described superleadership and self-leadership in a variety of sources. Material for this section was taken from: Sims, H. P., & Manz C. C. (1996). *Company of heroes: Unleashing the power of self-leadership.* New York: John Wiley; Manz, C. C., & Sims, H. P. (1989). *SuperLeadership: Leading others to lead themselves.* New York: Prentice-Hall.

[37] Manz, C. C., & Sims, H. P. (1989). *SuperLeadership: Leading others to lead themselves.* New York: Prentice-Hall, p. 69. Used by permission.

[38] Loehr, J., & Schwartz, T. (2001, January). The making of a corporate athlete. *Harvard Business Review,* pp. 120–128.

[39] Hough, J., & Neuland, E. W. (2000). *Global business.* Oxford: Oxford University Press; Louw, D. J. (2001). *Ubuntu and the challenges of multiculturalism in post-apartheid South Africa* [on-line]. Available: http://www.phys.uu.nl/~unitwin/ubuntu.html; Van der Merwe, W. L. (1996). Philosophy and the multi-cultural context of (post)apartheid South Africa. *Ethical Perspectives, 3,* 1–15.

Chapter 6

[1] Kouzes, J. M., & Posner, B. Z. (1993). *Credibility: How leaders gain and lose, why people demand it*. San Francisco: Jossey-Bass, p. 22.

[2] Sattler, W. M. (1947). Conceptions of ethos in ancient rhetoric. *Speech Monographs, 14*, 55–65.

[3] McCroskey, J. C., & Young, T. J. (1981). Ethos and credibility: The construct and its measurement after three decades. *Central States Speech Journal, 32*, 24.

[4] Haiman, F. S. (1949). An experimental study of the effects of ethos in public speaking. *Speech Monographs, 16*, 190–202; Warren, I. D. (1969). The effects of credibility in sources of testimony and audience attitudes toward speaker and topic. *Speech Monographs, 36*, 456–458.

[5] Strong, S. R., & Schmidt, L. D. (1970). Expertness and influence in counseling. *Journal of Counseling Psychology, 17*, 81–87; Strong, S. R., & Dixon, D. N. (1971). Expertness, attractiveness, and influence in counseling. *Journal of Counseling Psychology, 18*, 562–570.

[6] Hovland, C. I., & Weiss, W. (1951). The influence of source credibility on communication effectiveness. *Public Opinion Quarterly, 15*, 635–650.

[7] Brembeck, W. L., & Howell, W. S. (1976). *Persuasion: A means of social influence* (2nd ed.). Englewood Cliffs, NJ: Prentice Hall.

[8] Kouzes, J. M., & Posner, B. Z. (1987). *The leadership challenge: How to get extraordinary things done in organizations*. San Francisco: Jossey-Bass, p. 19.

[9] Carl Hovland, a pioneer in credibility research, was among the first to argue that a distinction should be made between competence and trustworthiness. He pointed out that a message from a competent source will be rejected if hearers believe that this person is lying. See: Hovland, C., Janis, I., & Kelley, H. H. (1953). *Communication and persuasion*. New Haven: Yale University Press.

[10] Armour, S. (2002, February 5). Employees' new motto: trust no one. *USA Today*, pp. 1A, 1B.

[11] McGlone, E. L., & Anderson, L. J. (1973). The dimensions of teacher credibility. *Communication Education, 22*, 196–200.

[12] Applbaum, R. L., & Anatol, W. E. (1972). The factor structure of credibility as a function of the speaking situation. *Speech Monographs, 39*, 216–222.

[13] Ward, C. D., & McGinnies, E. (1974). Persuasive effects of early and late mention of credible and non-credible sources. *Journal of Psychology, 86*, 17–23; O'Keefe, D. J. (1987). The persuasive effects of delaying identification of high and low-credibility communicators: A meta-analytic review. *Central States Speech Journal, 38*, 63–72.

[14] Kelman, H. C., & Hovland, C. L. (1953). "Reinstatement" of the communicator in delayed measurement of opinion change. *Journal of Abnormal and Social Psychology, 48*, 327–335.

[15] Leathers, D. G. (1997). *Successful nonverbal communication: Principles and applications* (2nd ed.). New York: Macmillan. See also: McMahan, E. M. (1976). Nonverbal communication as a function of attribution in impression formation. *Communication Monographs, 43*, 287–294.

[16] Kouzes & Posner, *Credibility*, p. 221.

[17] Hunter, J. E., & Boster, F. J. (1987). A model of compliance-gaining message selection. *Communication Monographs, 54*, 63–84; Vinson, L. (1988, November). *An emotion-based model of compliance-gaining message selection*. Paper presented at the Speech Communication Association convention, New Orleans, LA; Grant, J. A., King, P. E., & Behnke, R. R. (1994). Compliance-gaining strategies, communication satisfaction, and willingness to comply. *Communication Reports, 7*, 99–108.

[18] Marwell, G., & Schmitt, D. (1967). Dimensions of compliance-gaining behavior: An empirical analysis. *Sociometry, 30*, 350–364. Some researchers use the terms prosocial and antisocial to distinguish between friendly and unfriendly types of compliance gaining. For more information on the differences between pro- and antisocial tactics, see: Falbo, T. (1977). Multidimensional scaling of power strategies. *Journal of Personality and Social Psychology, 35*, 537–547; Kearney, P., Plax, T. G., Sorensen, G., & Smith, V. R. (1988). Experienced and prospective teachers' selections of compliance-gaining messages for "common" student misbehaviors. *Communication Education, 37*, 150–164; Roloff, M. E., & Barnicott, E. F. (1978). The situational use of pro- and antisocial compliance-gaining strategies by high and low Machiavellians. In B. Ruben (Ed.), *Communication Yearbook 2* (pp. 193–208). New Brunswick, NJ: Transaction Books.

[19] Kipnis, D., & Schmidt, S. M. (1988). Upward-influence styles: Relationship with performance evaluations, salary, and stress. *Administrative Science Quarterly, 33*, 528–542; Kipnis, D., Schmidt, S. M.,

Swaffin-Smith, C., & Wilkinson, I. (1984, Winter): Patterns of managerial influence: Shotgun managers, tacticians, and bystanders. *Organizational Dynamics*, pp. 58–67; Kipnis, D., Schmidt, S. J., & Wilkinson, I. (1980). Intraorganizational influence tactics: Explorations in getting one's way. *Journal of Applied Psychology, 65*, 440–452.

[20] Kearney, P., Plax, T. G., Richmond, V. P., & McCroskey, J. C. (1985). Power in the classroom III: Teacher communication techniques and messages. *Communication Education, 34*, 19–28; Kearney, P., Plax, T. G., Smith, V. R., & Sorensen, G. (1988). Effects of teacher immediacy and strategy type on college student resistance to on-task demands. *Communication Education, 37*, 54–67; Kearney, P., Plax, T. G., Sorensen, G., & Smith, V. R. (1988). Experienced and prospective teachers' selections of compliance-gaining messages for "common" student misbehaviors. *Communication Education, 37*, 150–164; Lu, S. (1997). Culture and compliance gaining in the classroom: A preliminary investigation of Chinese college teachers' use of behavior alteration techniques. *Communication Education, 46*, 10–28; McCroskey, J. C., & Richmond, V. P. (1983). Power in the classroom I: Teacher and student perceptions. *Communication Education, 32*, 175–184; McCroskey, J. C., Richmond, V. P., Plax, T. G., & Kearney, P. (1985). Power in the classroom V: Behavior alteration techniques, communication training and learning. *Communication Education, 34*, 214–226; Plax, T. G., Kearney, P., & Downs, T. M. (1986). Communicating control in the classroom and satisfaction with teaching and students. *Communication Education, 35*, 379–388; Plax, T. G., Kearney, P., McCroskey, J. C., & Richmond, V. P. (1986). Power in the classroom VI: Verbal control strategies, nonverbal immediacy and affective learning. *Communication Education, 35*, 43–55; Plax, T. G., Kearney, P., & Tucker, L. K. (1986) Prospective teachers' use of behavior alteration techniques on common student misbehaviors. *Communication Education, 35*, 32–42; Richmond, V. P. (1990). Communication in the classroom. Power and motivation. *Communication Education, 39*, 161–195; Richmond, V. P., & McCroskey, J. C. (1984). Power in the classroom II: Power and learning. *Communication Education, 33*, 125–136; Richmond, V. P., McCroskey, J. C., Kearney, P., Plax, T. (1987). Power in the classroom VII: Linking behavior alternation techniques to cognitive learning. *Communication Education, 36*, 1–12; Roach, K. D. (1991). Graduate teaching assistants' use of behavior alteration techniques in the university classroom. *Communication Quarterly, 39*, 179–188; Roach, K. D. (1994). Temporal patterns and effects of perceived instructor compliance-gaining use. *Communication Education, 43*, 236–245.

[21] Yukl, G., Guinan, P. J., & Sottolano, D. (1995). Influence tactics used for different objectives with subordinates, peers, and superiors. *Group & Organization Management, 20*, 272–296.

[22] Yukl, G. (1998). *Leadership in organizations* (4th ed). Upper Saddle River, NJ: Prentice-Hall, pp. 219–220. Used by permission.

[23] Yukl, G. (1998). *Leadership in organizations* (4th ed). Upper Saddle River, NJ: Prentice-Hall, ch. 9.

[24] Yukl, G., Falbe, C. M., & Youn, J. (1993). Patterns of influence behaviors for managers. *Group & Organization Management, 18*, 5–28.

[25] Hill, T. A. (1976). An experimental study of the relationship between opinionated leadership and small group consensus. *Speech Monographs, 43*, 246–257; Schultz, B. (1982). Argumentativeness: Its effect in group decision making and its role in leadership perception. *Communication Quarterly, 30*, 368–375; Muscovici, S., Migny, G., & Van Avermaet, E. (Eds.) (1985). *Perspectives on minority influence.* Cambridge: Cambridge University Press.

[26] Supervisors who are more argumentative generally fare better in the organizational setting. They have higher salaries and career satisfaction, and subordinates prefer to work for those who are rated high in argumentativeness and low in verbal aggressiveness. Argumentative subordinates are also more successful. See: Infante, D. A., & Gorden, W. I. (1985). Superiors' argumentativeness and verbal aggressiveness as predictors of subordinates' satisfaction. *Human Communication Research, 12*, 117–125; Infante, D. A., & Gorden, W. I. (1985). Benefits versus bias: An investigation of argumentativeness, gender, and organizational outcomes. *Communication Research Reports, 2*, 196–201; Infante, D. A., & Gorden, W. I. (1991). How employees see the boss: Test of an argumentative and affirming model of supervisors' communicative behavior. *Western Journal of Speech Communication, 55*, 294–304; Infante, D. A., & Gorden, W. I. (1989). Argumentativeness and affirming communicator style as predictors of satisfaction/dissatisfaction with subordinates. *Communication Quarterly, 31*, 81–90.

[27] Infante, D. (1988). *Arguing constructively.* Prospect Heights, IL: Waveland Press; Infante, D., & Rancer, A. (1996). Argumentativeness and verbal aggressiveness: A review of recent theory and research. In B. Burleson (Ed.), *Communication Yearbook 19* (pp. 319–351). Thousand Oaks, CA: Sage.

[28] Infante, D. A., & Rancer, A. S. (1982). A conceptualization and measure of argumentativeness. *Journal of Personality Assessment, 46,* 72–80. Used by permission.

[29] Infante, *Arguing constructively,* pp. 33–81.

[30] Infante, *Arguing constructively,* p. 47. Used by permission.

[31] Warnick, B., & Inch, E. S. (1994). *Critical thinking and communication: The use of reason in argument* (2nd ed.). New York: Macmillan.

[32] Deutsch, M., (1973). *The resolution of conflict.* New Haven: Yale University Press.

[33] Rubin, J. Z., & Brown, B. R. (1975). *The social psychology of bargaining and negotiation.* New York: Academic Press.

[34] An impressive demonstration of the effectiveness of the Tit for Tat strategy is found in: Axelrod, R. (1984). *The evolution of cooperation.* New York: Basic Books. Axelrod set up a tournament using a computerized version of the Prisoner's Dilemma game. The Tit for Tat strategy beat all other entries. For more information on variations of this approach, see: Pruitt, D. G., & Carnevale, P. J. (1993). *Negotiation in social conflict.* Pacific Grove, CA: Brooks/Cole, ch. 4.

[35] Putnam, L. L., & Jones, T. S. (1982). The role of communication in bargaining. *Human Communication Research, 8,* 262–280.

[36] Neale, M. A., & Bazerman, M. H. (1983). The role of perspective-taking ability in negotiating under different forms of arbitration. *Industrial and Labor Relations, 36,* 378–388; Bazerman, M. H., & Neale, M. A. (1983). Heuristics in negotiation: Limitations to effective dispute resolution. In M. H. Bazerman & R. J. Lewecki (Eds.), *Negotiating in organizations* (pp. 51–67). Beverly Hills: Sage.

[37] Tenbrusel, A. E., & Messick, D. M. (2001). Power asymmetries and the ethical atmosphere in negotiations. In J. M. Darley, D. M. Messick, & T. R. Tyler (Eds.), *Social influences on ethical behavior in organizations* (pp. 201–216). Mahwah, NJ: Lawrence Erlbaum.

[38] For more information on how to increase perspective-taking skills in interpersonal encounters, see: Kogler Hill, S. E. (1982). The multistage process of interpersonal empathy. In S. E. Kogler Hill (Ed.), *Improving interpersonal competence: A laboratory approach* (pp. 83–89). Dubuque, IA: Kendall/Hunt.

[39] Fisher, R., & Ury, W. (1991). *Getting to yes* (2nd ed.). New York: Penguin Books.

[40] Nielsen, R. P. (1998). Quaker foundations for Greenleaf's servant-leadership and "friendly disentangling" method. In L. Spears (Ed.), *Insights on leadership* (pp. 126–144). New York: Wiley & Sons.

[41] Fisher & Ury, pp. 41–42.

[42] Fisher & Ury, p. 40.

[43] Cialdini, R. B. (2001). *Influence: Science and practice* (4th ed.). Boston, MA: Allyn & Bacon. Some of the examples in this section are drawn from this source.

[44] Richard Petty and John Cacioppo's elaboration likelihood model is also based on the premise that receivers don't have the time, energy, or mental capacity to think carefully about (to elaborate on) all the persuasive messages they receive. Topics deemed important and relevant are carefully processed along the central route of persuasion. All others are processed along the peripheral route, which is heavily influenced by the mental shortcuts identified by Cialdini. See, for example: Petty, R. E., & Cacioppo, J. T. (1986). *Communication and persuasion: Central and peripheral routes to attitude change.* New York: Springer-Verlag. Petty, R., & Wegener, D. (1999). The elaboration likelihood model: Current status and controversies. In S. Chaiken & Y. Trope (Eds.), *Dual process theories in social psychology* (pp. 41–72). New York: Guilford.

[45] Cialdini, R. B., Sagarin, B. J., & Rice, W. E. (2001). Training in ethical influence. In J. M. Darley, D. M. Messick, & T. R. Tyler (Eds.), *Social influences on ethical behavior in organizations* (pp. 137–153). Mahway, NJ: Lawrence Erlbaum.

[46] Cialdini, R., Vincent, J., Lewis, S., Catalan, J., Wheeler, D., & Darby, B. (1975). Reciprocal procedure for inducing compliance: The door-in-the-face technique. *Journal of Personality and Social Psychology, 31,* 206–213.

[47] Hofling, C. K., Brotzman, E., Dalrymple, S., Graves, N., & Pierce, C. M. (1966). An experimental study of nurse-physician relationships. *Journal of Nervous and Mental Disease, 143,* 171–180.

[48] Adapted from the credibility scales of: Berlo, D., Lemert, J., & Mertz, R. (1969). Dimensions for evaluation of the acceptability of message sources. *Public Opinion Quarterly, 33,* 563–576; McCroskey, J., & Young, T. (1981). Ethos and credibility: The construct and its measurements after two decades. *Central States Speech Journal, 22–34.*

[49] Nwosu, P. O. (1998). Negotiating with the Swazis. In J. N. Martin, T. K. Nakayama, & L. A. Flores (Eds.). *Readings in cultural contexts* (pp. 414–422). Mountain View, CA: Mayfield.

Chapter 7

[1] Burke, K. (1968). *Language as symbolic action.* Berkeley: University of California Press.

[2] Tompkins, P. K. (1982). *Communication as action: An introduction to rhetoric and communication.* Belmont, CA: Wadsworth, p. 8.

[3] Books surveyed include: Cragan, J. F., & Wright, D. W. (1999). *Communication in small group: Theory, process, skills* (5th ed.). Belmont, CA: Wadsworth; Fisher, B. A., & Ellis, D. G. (1994). *Small group decision making* (4th ed.). New York: McGraw-Hill; Jensen, A. D., & Chilberg, J. G. (1991). *Small group communication.* Belmont, CA: Wadsworth; Patton, B. P., & Downs, T. M. (2003). *Decision-making group interaction: Achieving quality* (4th ed.). New York: Allyn & Bacon; Rothwell, J. D. (2004). *In mixed company: Small group communication* (4th ed.). Belmont, CA: Wadsworth; Schultz, B. G. (1996). *Communicating in the small group: Theory and practice* (2nd ed.). New York: HarperCollins; Engleberg, I. N., & Wynn, D. R. (2003). *Working in groups: Communication principles and strategies* (3rd ed.). Boston: Houghton Mifflin.

[4] Patton & Downs, p. 3.

[5] Cragan & Wright, p. 9.

[6] Scheidel, T. M., & Crowell, L. (1964). Idea development in small discussion groups. *Quarterly Journal of Speech, 50,* 140–145.

[7] Fisher, B. A. (1970). Decision emergence: Phases in group decision making. *Speech Monographs, 37,* 53–66.

[8] Poole, M. S. (1983). Decision development in small groups II: A study of multiple sequences in decision making. *Communication Monographs, 50,* 206–232; Poole, M. S. (1983). Decision development in small groups III: A multiple sequence model of group decision development. *Communication Monographs, 50,* 321–341.

[9] A summary of the results of these studies can be found in Bormann, E. G. (1975). *Discussion and group methods* (2nd ed., ch. 11). New York: Harper & Row. Leader emergence findings from this research program are also reported in Mortensen, C. D. (1966). Should the discussion group have an assigned leader? *The Speech Teacher, 15,* 34–41; and Geier, J. G. (1967). A trait approach to the study of leadership. *Journal of Communication, 17,* 316–323.

[10] Bormann, p. 261.

[11] Fisher & Ellis, pp. 251–253.

[12] See, for example: Stang, D. J. (1973). Effect of interaction rate on ratings of leadership and liking. *Journal of Personality and Social Psychology, 27,* 405–408; Regula, C. R., & Julian, J. W. (1983). The impact of quality and frequency of task contributions on perceived ability. *Journal of Social Psychology, 89,* 115–122; Riecken, H. (1975). The effect of talkativeness on ability to influence group solutions of problems. In P. V. Crosbie (Ed.), *Interaction in small groups* (pp. 238–249). New York: Macmillan; Daly, J. A., McCroskey, J. C., & Richmond, V. P. (1980). Relationship between vocal activity and perception of communication in small group interaction. *Western Journal of Speech Communication, 41,* 175–187.

[13] Schultz, B. (1980). Communicative correlates of perceived leaders. *Small Group Behavior, 11,* 175–191.

[14] Schultz, B. (1979). Predicting emergent leaders: An exploratory study of the salience of communicative functions. *Small Group Behavior, 9,* 109–114; Knutson, T. J., & Holdridge, W. E. (1975). Orientation behavior, leadership and consensus: A possible functional relationship. *Speech Monographs, 42,* 107–114.

[15] Hirokawa, R., & Pace, R. (1983). A descriptive investigation of the possible communication-based reasons for effective and ineffective group decision making. *Communication Monographs, 50,* 363–379.

[16] Baird, J. E. (1977). Some nonverbal elements of leadership emergence. *Southern Speech Communication Journal, 42,* 352–361.

[17] Hollander developed the idea of idiosyncratic credits over three decades. A summary of this research is found in *Leadership Dynamics: A practical guide to effective relationships* (1978). New York: The Free Press.

[18] This study is described in Jacobs, T. O. (1970). *Leadership and exchange in formal organizations.* Alexandria, VA: Human Resources Research Organization, ch. 3.

[19] Hollander, p. 42.

[20] Poole, Decision development III.

[21] Hollander, pp. 60–64.

[22] Engleberg & Wynn, p. 3.

[23] Auger, B. Y. (1972). *How to run better business meetings.* New York: AMACOM.

[24] Nichols, R. G. (1961). Do we know how to listen? Practical helps in a modern age. *The Speech Teacher, 10,* 120–124.

[25] See, for example: Foulke, E. (1971). The perception of time compressed speech. In D. L. Horton & J. J. Jenkins (Eds.), *The perception of language* (pp. 79–107). Columbus, OH: Charles E. Merrill; Korba, R. J. (1986). *The rate of inner speech.* Unpublished doctoral dissertation, University of Denver; Landauer, T. J. (1962). Rate of implicit speech. *Perceptual and Motor Skills, 15,* 646.

[26] Kline, T. (1999). *Remaking teams: The revolutionary research-based guide that puts theory into practice.* San Francisco: Jossey-Bass.

[27] Gouran, D. S., Hirokawa, R. Y., Julian, K. M., & Leatham, G. B. (1993). The evolution and current status of the functional perspective on communication in decision-making and problem-solving groups. In S. Deetz (Ed.), *Communication Yearbook 16* (pp. 573–600). Newbury Park, CA: Sage. Griffin, E. (2000). *A first look at communication theory* (4th ed., ch. 15). Boston: McGraw-Hill.

[28] Larson, C. E. (1969). Forms of analysis and small group problem-solving. *Speech Monographs, 36,* 452–455.

[29] Dewey, J. (1910). *How we think.* Boston: D.C. Heath. There are a number of variations of Dewey's original model. The version described in this chapter is found in Rothwell, ch. 7.

[30] Hirokawa, R. Y., & Scheerhorn, D. R. (1986). Communication in faulty group decision-making. In R. Y. Hirokawa & M. S. Poole (Eds.), *Communication and group decision-making* (pp. 63–80). Beverly Hills, CA: Sage.

[31] Gouran, D. S., & Hirokawa, R. S. (1986). Counteractive functions of communication in effective group decision-making. In R. Y. Hirokawa & M. S. Poole (Eds.), *Communication and group decision-making* (pp. 81–90). Beverly Hills, CA: Sage.

[32] LaFasto, F., & Larson, C. *When teams work best: 6000 team members and leaders tell what it takes to excel,* p. 85, © 2001 Sage Publications, Inc. Reprinted by Permission of the Publisher.

[33] Druskat, V. U., & Wolff, S. B. (2001, March). Building the emotional intelligence of groups. *Harvard Business Review,* pp. 80–90. Robert Bales developed a coding system based on the task and social dimensions of group interaction that served as the foundation for later theories of group evolution. See: Bales, R. F. (1970). *Personality and interpersonal behavior.* New York: Holt Rinehart & Winston; Bales, R. F., & Cohen, S. P. (1979). *Symlog: A system for the multiple level observation of groups.* London: Collier.

[34] Janis, I. (1971, November). Groupthink: The problems of conformity. *Psychology Today,* 271–279; Janis, I. (1982). *Groupthink* (2nd ed.). Boston: Houghton Mifflin. Janis, I. (1989). *Crucial decisions: Leadership in policymaking and crisis management.* New York: The Free Press; Janis, I., & Mann, L. (1977). *Decision making.* New York: The Free Press. Groupthink has also been identified in other historical events, including the *Challenger* shuttle launch and the Iran-Contra Affair. See: Esser, J. K. (1998). Alive and well after 25 years: A review of groupthink research. *Organizational Behavior and Human Decision Processes, 73,* 116–141.

[35] Chen, Z., Lawson, R. B., Gordon, L. R., & McIntosh, B. (1996). Groupthink: Deciding with the leader and the devil. *Psychological Record, 46,* 581–590.

[36] Janis, *Groupthink.* Manz, C. C., & Peck, C. P. (1995). Teamthink: Beyond the groupthink syndrome in self-managing work teams. *Journal of Managerial Psychology, 10,* 7–15; Moorhead, G., Neck, C. P., & West, M. S. (1998). The tendency toward defective decision making within self-managing teams: The relevance of groupthink for the 21st century. *Organizational Behavior and Human Decision Processes, 73,* 327–351.

[37] Katzenbach, J. R., & Smith, D. K. (1993, March-April). The discipline of teams. *Harvard Business Review,* 111–120; Katzenbach, J. R., & Smith, D. K. (1993). *The wisdom of teams.* Boston: Harvard Business School Press.

[38] Katzenbach, J. R. (1998). *Teams at the top: Unleashing the potential of both teams and individual leaders.* Boston: Harvard Business School Press.

[39] Reprinted by permission of Harvard Business School Press. From *The Wisdom of Teams* by J. R. Katzenbach and D. K. Smith. Boston, MA 1993, p. 84. Copyright © 1993 by the Harvard Business School Publishing Corporation; all rights reserved.

[40] Katzenbach & Smith, *Wisdom,* p. 31.

[41] Katzenbach & Smith, *Wisdom,* p. 45.

[42] Reprinted by permission of Harvard Business School Press. From *Team Talk: The Power of Language in Team Dynamics.* Boston, MA 1996, p. 34. Copyright © 1996 by the Harvard Business School Publishing Corporation; all rights reserved.

[43] Larson, C. E., & LaFasto, F. M. J. (1989). *Teamwork: What must go right/What can go wrong*. Newbury Park, CA: Sage.

[44] Larson & LaFasto, p. 128.

[45] LaFasto, F., & Larson, C. (2001). *When teams work best*. Thousand Oaks, CA: Sage.

[46] LaFasto & Larson, p. 56.

[47] Ray, D., & Bronstein, H. (1995) *Teaming up*. New York: McGraw-Hill. p. 21.

[48] See, for example: Harper, B., & Harper, A. (1992). *Succeeding as a self-directed work team*. Mohegan Lake, NY: MW Corporation; Wellins, R. S., Byham, W. C., & Wilson, J. M. (1991). *Empowered teams*. San Francisco: Jossey-Bass.

[49] Wellins, Byham, & Wilson.

[50] Trist, E. L., & Bamforth, K. W. (1951). Some social and psychological consequences of the longwall method of coal-getting. *Human Relations, 4*, 3–38.

[51] Fisher, K. (1993). *Leading self-directed work teams*. New York: McGraw-Hill, p. 5.

[52] Wellins, R. S., Byham, W. C., & Wilson, J. M. (1991). *Empowered teams*. San Francisco: Joseey-Bass, p. 9.

[53] See: Gordon, J. (1992, October). Work teams: How far have they come? *Training, 59–65*.

[54] Wellins, Byham, & Wilson, p. 26. Used by permission.

[55] Wellins, R. S., Byham, W. C., & Dixon, G. R. (1994). *Inside teams*. San Francisco: Jossey-Bass.

[56] Kayser, T. A. (1994). *Team power*. Burr Ridge, IL: Irwin, p. 36.

[57] Labich, K. (1989, May 8). Making over middle managers. *Fortune*, 58–64.

[58] Fisher, pp. 48–54.

[59] Near, R., & Weckler, D. (1990, September). *Organizational and job characteristics related to self-managing teams*. Paper presented at the International Conference on Self-Managed Work Teams, Denton, TX.

[60] Hoerr, J., & Zellner, W. (1989, July 10). The payoff for teamwork. *Business Week*.

[61] Wyscoki, L. (1990, September). *Implementation of self-managed teams within a non-union manufacturing facility*. Paper presented at the International Conference on Self-Managed Work Teams, Denton, TX.

[62] Sheridan, J. H. (1990, October). America's best plants. *Industry Week, 27–64*.

[63] Dumaine, B. (1990, May 7). Who needs a boss? *Fortune*, 52–55.

[64] Dumaine.

[65] Shockley-Zalabak, P., & Burmester, S. B. (2001). *The power of networked teams*. New York: Oxford University Press.

[66] Sherwood, J. (1988). Creating work cultures with competitive advantage. *Organizational Dynamics, 16*, 4.

[67] Wellins, Byham, & Dixon.

[68] Hoerr, J., & Pollock, M. A. (1986, September 29). Management discovers the human side of automation. *Business Week, 74–77*; O'Dell, C. (1989, November). Team play, team pay: New ways of keeping score. *Across the Board*, 38–45.

[69] Hoerr & Pollock.

[70] Adapted from: Fisher, K.; Harper, B., & Harper, A. (1992). *Succeeding as a self-directed work team*. Mohegan Lake, NY: MW Corporation; Wellins, R. S., Byham, W. C., & Wilson, J. M. (1991). *Empowered teams*. San Francisco: Jossey-Bass.

[71] Armstrong, D. J., & Cole, P. (1995). Managing distances and differences in geographically distributed work groups. In S. E. Jackson & M. N. Ruderman (Eds.), *Diversity in work teams: Research paradigms for a changing workplace* (pp. 187–215). Washington, DC: American Psychological Association; Nohria, N., & Eccles, R. G. (1992). Face-to-face: Making network organizations work. In N. Nohria & R. G. Eccles (Eds.), *Networks and organizations: Structure, form, and action* (pp. 288–308). Boston: Harvard Business School Press. See also: Krauss, R. M., & Russell, S. R. (1990). Mutual knowledge and communicative effectiveness. In J. Galegher, R. E. Kraut, & C. Egido (Eds.), *Intellectual teamwork* (pp. 111–145). Hillsdale, NJ: Lawrence Erlbaum; Walther, J. B., & Tidwell, L. C. (2000). Computer-mediated communication: Interpersonal interaction on-line. In K. M. Galvin & P. J. Cooper (Eds.), *Making connections: Readings in relational communication* (2nd ed., pp. 322–329). Los Angeles: Roxbury.

Chapter 8

[1] Etzioni, A. (1964). *Modern organizations.* Englewood Cliffs, NJ: Prentice-Hall, p. 1.

[2] Hawes, L. C. (1974). Social collectivities as communication: Perspectives on organizational behavior. *Quarterly Journal of Speech, 60,* 497–502.

[3] For an overview of the different ways that communication scholars approach the study of organizational culture, see: Eisenberg, E. M., & Riley, P. (2001). Organizational culture. In F. M. Jablin & L. L. Putnam (Eds.), *The new handbook of organizational communication: Advances in theory, research, and methods* (pp. 291–322). Thousand Oaks, CA: Sage.

[4] The number of cultures an organization has is a matter of some debate. One group of researchers argues that there is only one culture per organization. Others argue that an organization consists of a series of cultural islands or subcultures. A third group contends that there are multiple cultures created by members as they interact. We think that there must be some common cultural elements in order for there to be an organization, but we acknowledge the presence of subcultures and that individuals shape and form culture as they coordinate their actions. For a description of the three perspectives and how each can provide useful insights into organizational behavior, see: Martin, J. (1992). *Cultures in organizations.* New York: Oxford University Press; Martin, J. (2002). *Organizational culture: Mapping the terrain.* Thousand Oaks, CA: Sage.

[5] Dyer, W. G. (1985). The cycle of cultural evolution in organizations. In R. H. Killmann, M. J. Saxton, & R. Serpa (Eds.), *Gaining control of the corporate culture* (pp. 200–229). San Francisco: Jossey-Bass.

[6] Rafaeli, A., & Worline, M. (2000). Symbols in organizational culture. In N. M. Ashkanasy, C. P. M. Wilderom, & M. F. Peterson (Eds.), *Handbook of organizational culture and climate* (pp. 71–84). Thousand Oaks, CA: Sage.

[7] Martin, J., & Powers, M. E. (1983). Truth or corporate propaganda: The value of a good story. In L. R. Pondy, P. J. Frost, G. Morgan, & T. C. Dandridge (Eds.), *Organizational symbolism* (pp. 93–107). Greenwich, CT: JAI Press.

[8] Trice, H. M., & Beyer, J. M. (1984). Studying organizational cultures through rites and ceremonials. *Academy of Management Review, 9,* 653–669; Trice, H. M., & Beyer, J. M. (1993). *The cultures of work organizations.* Englewood Cliffs, NJ: Prentice Hall, ch. 3.

[9] Fairhurst, G. T., & Sarr, R. A. (1996). *The art of framing: Managing the language of leadership.* San Francisco: Jossey-Bass, p. 2.

[10] Fairhurst & Sarr.

[11] Kanter, R. M. (1983). *The change masters: Innovation for productivity in the American corporation.* New York: Simon and Schuster, p. 281.

[12] Adapted from Cheney, G. (1983). On the various and changing meanings of organizational membership: A field study of organizational identification. *Communication Monographs, 50,* 342–362. Used by permission.

[13] Schein, E. H. (1992). *Organizational culture and leadership* (2nd ed., p. 5). San Francisco: Jossey-Bass.

[14] Schein, ch. 10; Schein, E. H. (1983). The role of the founder in creating organizational culture. *Organizational Dynamics, 12,* 13–26.

[15] Statistics taken from: *Standard and Poor's Netadvantage.* Retrieved April 22, 2002; New stores in Spain (2002, April 10). Retrieved April 22, 2002, from http://www.starbucks.com.

[16] Planet Starbucks (2002, September 9). *Business Week,* pp. 100–109.

[17] Schultz, H., & Yang, D. J. (1997). *Pour your heart into it: How Starbucks built a company one cup at a time.* New York: Hyperion, p. 81.

[18] Jones, A. (1999, July 3). Coffee shops leave a sour taste. *The London Times.* Retrieved July 4, 1999, from http://web.lexis-nexis.com/universe; Business Wire (2002, February 26). Starbucks annual shareholder's meeting to highlight new initiatives. Retrieved April 20, 2002, from http://businesswire.com; PR Newswire (2002, February 12). Organic consumer activists will leaflet and protest at Starbucks Coffee shops. Retrieved April 20, 2002, from http://www.prnewswire.com.

[19] Schultz & Yang, p. 332

[20] Schein, *Organizational culture,* ch. 11.

[21] Peters, T., & Austin, N. (1985). *A passion for excellence: The leadership difference.* New York: Warner Books, p. 337.

[22] Kotter, J. (1999). Leading change: The eight steps to transformation. In J. A. Conger, G. M. Spreitzer, & E. E. Lawler III (Eds.), *The leader's change handbook: An essential guide to setting direction and taking action* (pp. 87–99). San Francisco: Jossey-Bass.

[23] Trice, H. M., & Beyer, J. M. (1985). Using six organizational rites to change culture. In R. H. Kilmann, M. J. Saxton, & R. Serpa (Eds.), *Gaining control of the corporate culture* (pp. 370–399). See also: Knittel, R. E. (1974). Essential and nonessential ritual in programs of planned change. *Human Organization, 33*, 394–396.

[24] A number of observers have noted that crises mark organizational highs or lows. See, for example: Barton, L. (1993). *Crisis in organizations*. Cincinnati, OH: South-Western Publishing.

[25] Eisenberg, D. (2000, September 5). Firestone's rough road. *Time*, 39.

[26] Barton, *Crisis*.

[27] Mitroff, I. I., Pearson, C. M., & Harrington, L. K. (1996). *The essential guide to managing corporate crises: A step-by-step guide for surviving major catastrophes*. New York: Oxford University Press.

[28] Fink, S. (1986; 2000). *Crisis management: Planning for the inevitable*. New York: AMACOM; Lincoln, NE: iUniverse.

[29] Fink. Used by permission..

[30] Pauchant, T. C., & Mitroff, I. I. (1992). *Transforming the crisis-prone organization: Preventing individual, organizational, and environmental tragedies*. San Francisco: Jossey-Bass; Pearson, C. M., & Mitroff, I. I. (1993, February). From crisis prone to crisis prepared: A framework for crisis management. *Academy of Management Executive, 7*, 48–60.

[31] Messick, D. M., & Bazerman, M. H. (1996, Winter). Ethical leadership and the psychology of decision making. *Sloan Management Review*, 9–23.

[32] Messick & Bazerman; Bazerman, M. H. (1986). *Management in managerial decision making*. New York: Wiley & Sons. For additional decision-making biases, see: Bazerman, M. H. (2002). *Judgment and managerial decision making* (5th ed.). New York: John Wiley & Sons.

[33] For a list of types of crises that can strike organizations, see: Mitroff, I., & Shrivastava, P. (1987). Strategic management of corporate crises. *Columbia Journal of World Business, 22*, 5–12; Mitroff, I., Shrivastava, P., & Udwadi, F. E. (1987). Effective crisis management. *Academy of Management Executive, 1*, 283–292.

[34] The term "image insurance" is taken from: Gregory, J. R., & Wiechman, J. G. (1991). *Marketing corporate image: The company as your number one product*. Lincolnwood, IL: NTC, p. 181.

[35] Rosenthal, R., & Jacobson, L. (1968). *Pygmalion in the classroom*. New York: Holt, Rinehart and Winston. Many other researchers have verified the findings of Rosenthal and Jackson's groundbreaking study. See, for example: Jussim, L., Madon, S., & Chatman, C. (1994). Teacher expectations and student achievement: Self-fulfilling prophecies, biases, and accuracy. In L. Heath, et al. (Eds.), *Applications of heuristics and biases to social issues* (pp. 303–334). New York: Plenum Press; Barad, E. (1993). Pygmalion—25 years after interpersonal expectations in the classroom. In P. D. Blanck (Ed.), *Interpersonal expectations: Theory, research, and applications* (pp. 125–153). Cambridge: Cambridge University Press.

[36] Eden, D., & Shami, A. B. (1982). Pygmalion goes to boot camp: Expectancy, leadership, and trainee performance. *Journal of Applied Psychology, 67*, 194–199.

[37] Crawford, K. S., Thomas, E. D., & Fink, J. J. (1980). Pygmalion at sea: Improving the work effectiveness of low performers. *Journal of Applied Behavioral Science, 16*, 482–505.

[38] Smith, A. E., Jussim, L., & Eccles, J. (1999). Do self-fulfilling prophecies accumulate, dissipate, or remain stable over time? *Journal of Personality and Social Psychology, 77*, 548–565.

[39] Berlew, D., & Hall, D. (1966). The socialization of managers: Effects of expectations on performance. *Administrative Science Quarterly, 2*, 208–223.

[40] White, S. S., & Locke, E. A. (2000). Problems with the Pygmalion Effect and some proposed solutions. *Leadership Quarterly, 11*, 389–416; McNatt, D. B. (2000). Ancient Pygmalion joins contemporary management: A meta-analysis of the result. *Journal of Applied Psychology, 85*, 314–322; Madon, S., Jussim, L., & Eccles, J. (1997). In search of the powerful self-fulfilling prophecy. *Journal of Personality and Social Psychology, 72*, 791–809. Self-fulfilling prophecy and gender: Can women be Pygmalion and Galatea? *Journal of Applied Psychology, 80*, 253–270.

[41] Livingston, J. S. (1969). Pygmalion in management. *Harvard Business Review, 47*, 85. For another discussion of self-esteem and expectations, see: Hill, N. (1976, August). Self-esteem: The key to effective leadership. *Administrative Management*, 24–25, 51.

[42] Locke, E. A., & Latham, G. P. (1990). *A theory of goal setting & task performance.* Englewood Cliffs, NJ: Prentice Hall.

[43] Rosenthal, R. (1993). Interpersonal expectations: Some antecedents and some consequences. In P. D. Blanck (Ed.), *Interpersonal expectations: Theory, research, and applications* (pp. 3–24). Cambridge: Cambridge University Press.

[44] Baird, J., & Wieting, G. K. (1979, September). Nonverbal communication can be a motivational tool. *Personnel Journal,* 607–610.

[45] Good, T., & Brophy, J. (1980). *Educational psychology: A realistic approach.* New York: Holt, Rinehart and Winston.

[46] Eden, D., & Ravid, G. (1982). Pygmalion vs. self-expectancy: Effects of instructor and self-expectancy on trainee performance. *Organizational Behavior and Human Performance, 30,* 351–364.

[47] Eden, D. (1984). Self-fulfilling prophecy as a management tool: Harnessing Pygmalion. *Academy of Management Review, 9,* 64–73. Used by permission.

[48] Eden, D. (1990). *Pygmalion in management.* Lexington, MA: Lexington Books/D. C. Heath; Eden, D. (1993). Interpersonal expectations in organizations. In P. D. Blanck (Ed.), *Interpersonal expectations: Theory, research, and applications* (pp. 154–178). Cambridge: Cambridge University Press.

[49] Baird & Wieting.

[50] Eden (1984).

[51] Cowan, J. (2002, November). Is McDonald's really so bad? *enRoute,* 79–84; Daniels, J. L., & Daniels, N. C. (1993). *Global vision.* New York: McGraw-Hill; What's this? The French love McDonald's? (2003, January 13). *Business Week,* 50.

Chapter 9

[1] Carlyle, T. (1907). *On heroes, hero-worship, and the heroic in history.* Boston: Houghton Mifflin. (Original work written 1840.)

[2] Spencer, H. (1884). *The study of sociology.* New York: D. A. Appleton. (First published 1873.)

[3] Tucker, R. C. (1965). The dictator and totalitarianism. *World Politics, 17,* 565–573.

[4] Wills, G. (1994). *Certain trumpets: The call of leaders.* New York: Simon & Schuster.

[5] Gardner, J. (1990). *On leadership.* New York: The Free Press, p. xiii.

[6] For more information on the unique features of public communication, see: Hart, R., Friedrich, G., & Brooks, W. (1975). *Public communication.* New York: Harper & Row; Asante, K., & Frye, J. (1977). *Contemporary public communication.* New York: Harper & Row.

[7] Gergen, D. (2000). *Eyewitness to power: The essence of leadership.* New York: Simon & Schuster.

[8] Guth, D. W., & Marsh, C. (2003). *Public relations: A values-driven approach* (2nd ed.). Boston: Allyn and Bacon.

[9] For further information on public relations activities and the characteristics of effective public relations programs, see: Baskin, O., Aronoff, C., & Lattimore, D. (1997). *Public relations: The profession and the practice* (4th ed.). New York: McGraw-Hill; Newsom, D., Van Slyke Turk, J., & Kruckeberg, D. (2004). *This is PR: The realities of public relations* (8th ed.). Stanford, CA: Wadsworth/Thompson Learning; Wilcox, D. L., Cameron, G. T., Ault, P. H., & Agee, W. K. (2003). *Public Relations: Strategies and tactics* (7th ed.). New York: Longman.

[10] Some evidence suggests that the best public relations programs take a symmetrical approach to public relations. Symmetrical practitioners seek information from stakeholders but then use this information to benefit both the organization and its publics. They engage in advocacy but put more emphasis on seeking win-win solutions with publics and building long-term relationships. See: Dozier, D. M., Grunig, L. A., & Grunig, J. E. (1995). *Manager's guide to excellence in public relations and communication management.* Mahwah, NJ: Lawrence Erlbaum; Grunig, J. E., & Grunig, L. A. (1992). Models of public relations and communication. In J. E. Grunig, D. M. Dozier, W. Ehling, L. A. Grunig, F. C. Repper, & J. White (Eds.), *Excellence in public relations and communication management* (pp. 285–325). Hillsdale, NJ: Lawrence Erlbaum Associates.

[11] Whitman, R. F., & Foster, T. J. (1994). *Speaking in public.* New York: Macmillan, ch. 1.

[12] News items were taken from the July 12, 2003 issue of *The Oregonian,* Portland, OR.

[13] Torricelli, R., & Carroll, A. (Eds.) (1999). *In our own words: Extraordinary speeches of the American century*. New York: Kodansha International.

[14] Conger, J. A. (1991). Inspiring others: The language of leadership. *Academy of Management Executive, 5,* 30–45; Pearce, T. (1995). *Leading out loud: The authentic speaker, the credible leader.* San Francisco: Jossey-Bass; Useem, M. (1998). *The leadership moment.* New York: Times Books.

[15] For more examples of this kind of deceptive communication, see: Lutz, W. (1989). *Doublespeak.* New York: Harper & Row. This highly readable and entertaining book describes how government, business, advertisers, and others use language to distort reality. Among the more comical examples: an eighteen-page recipe for fruitcake for army chefs which includes instructions describing how the cake should "conform to the inside contour of the can or can liner," with "no point on the top of the lid greater than ¾-inch from the side of the can where the cake did not touch the lid during baking"; and the U.S. government's description of the 1983 early morning paratroop invasion of Granada as a "pre-dawn vertical insertion."

[16] See: Hackman, M. Z. (1988). Audience reactions to the use of direct and personal disparaging humor in informative public address. *Communication Research Reports, 5,* 126–130; Hackman, M. Z. (1988). Reactions to the use of self-disparaging humor by informative public speakers. *Southern Speech Communication Journal, 53,* 175–183.

[17] Chang, M., & Gruner, C. R. (1981). Audience reaction to self-disparaging humor. *Southern Speech Communication Journal, 46,* 419–447.

[18] For a more complete discussion of the importance of internal thought and external speech in public address, see: Hackman, M. Z. (1989). The inner game of public speaking: Applying intrapersonal communication processes in the public speaking course. *Carolinas Speech Communication Annual, 5,* 41–47.

[19] Pearce, T. (1995). *Leading out loud: The authentic speaker, the credible leader.* San Francisco: Jossey Bass.

[20] Adapted from DeFleur, M. L., Kearney, P., & Plax, T. G. (1993). *Mastering communication in contemporary America.* Mountain View, CA: Mayfield, pp. 418–419.

[21] Simons, H. W. (1986). *Persuasion: Understanding, practice, and analysis* (2nd ed., p. 227). New York: Random House.

[22] Persuasion experts categorize campaigns in different ways. These five categories are adapted from: Woodward, G. C., & Denton, R. E. (2000). *Persuasion & influence in American life* (4th ed., ch. 9). Prospect Heights, IL: Waveland Press; Pfau, M., & Parrott, R. (1993). *Persuasive communication campaigns.* Boston: Allyn & Bacon.

[23] Lynam, D. R., & Milich, R. (1999). Project DARE: No effects at 10 year follow up. *Journal of Consulting Clinical Psychology, 67,* 590–594.

[24] Rice, R. R. (2001). Smokey Bear. In R. R. Rice & C. K. Atkin (Eds.), *Public communication campaigns* (3rd ed., pp. 276–279). Thousand Oaks, CA: Sage.

[25] Winsten, J. A., & DeJong, W. (2001). The designated driver campaign. In R. R. Rice & C. K. Atkin (Eds.), *Public communication campaigns* (3rd ed., pp. 290–294). Thousand Oaks, CA: Sage. Unfortunately, binge drinking among college women is up even as the number of drinking drivers declines. See: Morse, J. (April 1, 2002). Women on a binge. *Time,* 56–61.

[26] Rogers, E. M., & Storey, J. D. (1987). Communication campaigns. In C. R. Berger & S. H. Chaffee (Eds.), *Handbook of Communication Science* (pp. 817–846). Newbury Park, CA: Sage. Some of the examples used in this section of the chapter also come from this article.

[27] See, for example: Atkin, C. K. (2001). Theory and principles of media health campaigns. In R. R. Rice & C. K. Atkin (Eds.), *Public communication campaigns* (3rd ed., pp. 49–68). Thousand Oaks, CA: Sage; Snyder, L. B. (2001). How effective are mediated health campaigns? In *Public communication campaigns* (pp. 181–190).

[28] Singhal, A., & Rogers, E. (1999). *Entertainment-education: A communication strategy for social change.* Mahwah, NJ: Lawrence Erlbaum, ch. 9.

[29] Rogers & Storey, p. 837.

[30] Rogers, E. M. (1995). *Diffusion of innovations* (4th ed., ch. 8). New York: The Free Press.

[31] Gladwell, M. (2002). *The tipping point: How little things can make a big difference.* Boston, MA: Little Brown.

[32] Woodward & Denton, p. 279.

[33] Woodward, G. C., & Denton, R. E. (2000). *Persuasion & influence in American life* (4th ed.). Prospect Heights, IL: Waveland Press, Inc. Used by permission.

[34] Gardner, chs. 9 & 10.

[35] Johnson, C., & Hackman, M. Z. (1998). *Public relations, collaborative leadership and community.* Paper presented at the National Communication Association convention, New York, NY.

[36] Chrislip, D. D., & Larson, C. E. (1994). *Collaborative leadership.* San Francisco: Jossey-Bass. Many of the examples in this section come from Chrislip and Larson.

[37] Acting in a trustworthy fashion is particularly important when participants are angry and hostile. To learn more about dealing with difficult constituents, see: Susskind, I., & Field, P. (1996). *Dealing with an angry public: The mutual gains approach to resolving disputes.* New York: The Free Press.

[38] Kearney, P., & Plax, T. G. (1999). *Public speaking in a diverse society* (2nd ed.). Mountain View, CA: Mayfield; Jaffe, C. (2001). *Public speaking: Concepts and skills for a diverse society* (3rd ed.) Belmont, CA: Wadsworth/Thomson.

Chapter 10

[1] Data taken from: Branch-Brioso, L. (2001, March 13). Minorities fueled growth in last decade, census says: Hispanic population has grown by 13 million. *St. Louis Post-Dispatch*, p. A1; Friedman, T. (2000). *The Lexus and the olive tree* (Expanded Version). New York: Anchor Books; Cox, T. (1993). *Cultural diversity in organizations: Theory research and practice.* San Francisco: Berrett-Koehler; (2000, January 15). Fewer and wrinklier Europeans. *Economist*, 52; Chamie, J. (2001). This new population order. *New Perspectives Quarterly, 18,* 25–27; Marquart, M. J., & Berger, N. O. (2000). *Global leaders for the 21st century.* Albany, NY: State University of New York Press.

[2] Cox, T. (1993). *Cultural diversity in organizations: Theory, research and practice* (ch. 2). San Francisco: Berrett-Koehler.

[3] Rogers, E. M., & Steinfatt, T. M. (1999). *Intercultural communication* (p. 79). Prospect Heights, IL: Waveland Press.

[4] Larrabee, W. (1972). Paralinguistics, kinesics, and cultural anthropology. In L. Samovar & R. Porter (Eds.), *Intercultural communication: A reader* (pp. 172–180). Belmont, CA: Wadsworth.

[5] Hall, E. (1977). *Beyond culture.* Garden City, NY: Anchor.

[6] Books promoting Taoist leadership practices include: Autry, J. A., & Mitchell, S. (1998). *Realpower: Business lessons from the Tao Te Ching.* New York: St. Martin's Press; Heider, J. (1985). *The Tao of leadership.* New York: Bantam Books; Dreher, D. (1995). *The Tao of personal leadership.* New York: HarperBusiness; Messing, B. (1989). *The Tao of management.* New York: Bantam Books.

[7] For additional information on the historical background of Taoism, see: Ching, J. (1993). *Chinese religions.* Maryknoll, NY: Orbis Books; Hopfe, L. M. (1991). *Religions of the world* (5th ed.). New York: Macmillan; Watts, A. (1975). *The Watercourse way.* New York: Pantheon Books; Welch, H. (1965). *Taoism: The parting of the way* (Rev. Ed.). Boston: Beacon Press.

[8] This research highlight is adapted from: Johnson, C. E. (1997, Spring). A leadership journey to the East. *Journal of Leadership Studies, 4,* 82–88.

[9] Chan, W. (1963). *The way of Lao Tzu.* Indianapolis, IN: Bobbs-Merrill, p. 64.

[10] Chan, p. 78.

[11] Chan, p. 76.

[12] Hofstede, G. (2001). *Culture's consequences: Comparing values, behaviors, institutions, and organizations across nations* (2nd ed.). Thousand Oaks, CA: Sage; Hofstede, G. (1991). *Cultures and organizations: Software of the mind.* London: McGraw-Hill; Hofstede, G. (1984). The cultural relativity of the quality of life concept. *Academy of Management Review, 9,* 389–398.

[13] Lustig, M. W., & Koester, J. (2003). *Intercultural competence: Interpersonal communication across cultures* (4th ed., p. 111). Boston: Allyn & Bacon. Used by permission.

[14] Hofstede, G., & Bond, M. H. (1988). The Confucius connection: From cultural roots to economic growth. *Organizational Dynamics, 14,* 483–503; Chinese Culture Connection (1987). Chinese values and the search for culture-free dimensions of culture. *Journal of Cross-Cultural Psychology, 18,* 143–174.

[15] See, for example: Erez, M., & Earley, P. C. (1993). *Culture, self-identity, and work* (ch. 8). New York: Oxford University Press; Hofstede, *Cultures and organizations*; Hofstede, *Culture's consequences*; Offermann, L. R., & Hellmann, P. S. (1997). Culture's consequences for leadership behavior: National values in action. *Journal of Cross-Cultural Psychology, 28,* 342–351; Triandis, H. C. (1993). The contingency

model in cross-cultural perspective. In M. M. Chemers & R. Ayman (Eds.), *Leadership theory and research: Perspectives and directions* (pp. 167–188). San Diego: Academic Press.

[16] Hofstede, *Culture's consequences,* p. 390.

[17] Adler, N. J. (1991). *International dimensions of organizational behavior* (2nd ed.). Belmont, CA: Wadsworth.

[18] Adapted from Harris, P. R., & Moran, R. T. (1993). *Managing cultural differences* (4th ed., p. 30). Houston, TX: Gulf Publishing. Used by permission.

[19] Singelis, T. M., Triandis, H. C., Bhawuk, D. S., & Gelfand, M. (1995). Horizontal and vertical dimensions of individualism and collectivism: A theoretical and measurement refinement. *Cross-cultural Research, 29,* 240–275.

[20] Schermerhorn, R., & Bond, M. H. (1997). Cross-cultural leadership dynamics in collectivism and high power distance settings. *Leadership & Organization Development Journal, 18,* 187–193.

[21] Adler.

[22] Tromprenaars, F. (1994). *Riding the waves of culture: Understanding diversity in global business.* Burr Ridge, IL: Irwin.

[23] Cox, T. (1991). Managing cultural diversity: Implications for organizational competitiveness. *Academy of Management Executive, 5,* 45–56.

[24] For summaries of research on minority influence processes, see: Moscovici, S., Mugny, G., & Van Avermaet, E. (Eds.). (1985). *Perspectives on minority influence.* Cambridge: Cambridge University Press; Maas, A., & Clark, R. D. (1984). Hidden impact of minorities: Fifteen years of minority influence research. *Psychological Bulletin, 95,* 428–450.

[25] Eisenberger, R., Fasolo, P., & Davis-LaMastro, V. (1990). Perceived organizational support and employee diligence, commitment, and innovation. *Journal of Applied Psychology, 75,* 57–59.

[26] Thomas, D. A., & Ely, R. J. (1996, September-October). Making differences matter: A new paradigm for managing diversity. *Harvard Business Review,* 79–90.

[27] Cox, *Cultural diversity,* ch. 13.

[28] Smith, T. W. (1990). *Ethnic images.* National Opinion Research Center, GSS Topical Report No. 19. Chicago: University of Chicago.

[29] Cox, *Cultural diversity,* ch. 13.

[30] Adapted from Dickerson-Jones, T. (1993). *50 activities for managing cultural diversity.* Amherst, MA: HRD Press.

[31] Morrison, A. M. (1996). *The new leaders: Guidelines on leadership diversity in America.* San Francisco: Jossey-Bass.

[32] Thomas, D. A., & Gabarro, J. J. (1999). *Breaking through: The making of minority executives in corporate America.* Boston, MA: Harvard Business School Press.

[33] Thomas, D. A. (2001, April-May). Race matters: The truth about mentoring minorities. *Harvard Business Review,* 99–107.

[34] Statistics taken from: (2001, December 5). More women serving on boards. *Los Angeles Times,* p. C3; Catalyst (2002, March 2). And reach for more of the pie. http://www.fortune.com; Sherman, E. (2001, Fall). Women in political leadership: Reflections on larger social issues. *Leadership,* 4–5; Powell, G. (1993). *Women and men in management* (2nd ed.). Newbury Park, CA: Sage; http://www.4women.gov.

[35] Rosener, J. B. (1990, November-December). Ways women lead. *Harvard Business Review,* 119–125.

[36] Gaines, J. (1993). "You don't necessarily have to be charismatic . . .": An interview with Anita Roddick and reflections on charismatic processes in the Body Shop International. *Leadership Quarterly, 4,* 347–359; Miller, A. (1991, October 14). Reach out and prod someone. *Newsweek,* 50; Peters, T. (1992). *Liberation management.* New York: Ballantine Books; Roddick, A. (1991). *Body and soul.* New York: Crown; Wallace, C. (1990, October). Lessons in marketing—From a maverick. *Working Woman,* 81–84.

[37] Roddick, p. 15.

[38] Birchfield, D. (2002, May). Anita Roddick: In full flight. *New Zealand Management,* 41–43.

[39] Roddick, p. 25.

[40] Roddick, p. 217.

[41] Karsten, M. F. (1994). *Management and gender.* Westport, CT: Praeger.

[42] Adams, J., Rice, R., & Instone, D. (1984). Follower attitudes toward women and judgments concerning performance by female and male leaders. *Academy of Management Journal, 27,* 636–643.

[43] Shellenbarger, S. (1995, September 3). Work-force study finds loyalty is weak, divisions of race and gender are deep. *Wall Street Journal*, pp. B1, B8.

[44] See: Eagly, A. H., & Johnson, B. T. (1990). Gender and leadership style: A meta- analysis. *Psychological Bulletin, 108*, 233–256; Eagly, A. H., & Karau, S. J. (1991). Gender and the emergence of leaders: A meta-analysis. *Journal of Personality and Social Psychology, 60*, 685–710; Eagly, A. H. (1987). *Sex differences in social behavior.* Hillsdale, NJ: Erlbaum.

[45] Morrison, White, & Van Velsor.

[46] Wood, J. T. (1999). *Gendered lives: Communication, gender and culture* (3rd ed., p. 22). Belmont, CA: Wadsworth.

[47] Broverman, I., Broverman, D. M., Clarkson, F. E., Rosenkranz, P. S., & Vogel, S. R. (1970). Sex-role stereotypes and clinical judgments in mental health. *Journal of Consulting and Clinical Psychology, 34*, 1–7.

[48] See: Andrews, P. (1984). Performance, self-esteem and perceptions of leadership emergence: A comparative study of men and women. *Western Journal of Speech Communication, 48*, 1–13; Instone, D., Major, B., & Bunker, B. B. (1983). Gender, self-confidence, and social influence strategies: An organizational simulation. *Journal of Personality and Social Psychology, 44*, 322–333.

[49] Epstein, C. F. (1988). *Deceptive distinctions: Sex, gender, and the social order.* New Haven: Yale University Press.

[50] Kanter, R. M. (1977). Some effects of proportions on group life: Skewed sex ratios and responses to token women. *American Journal of Sociology, 82*, 969–990.

[51] Morrison, A. M., White, R. P., & Van Velsor, E. (1987, August). Executive women: Substance plus style. *Psychology Today*, 18–26.

[52] Jamieson, K. H. (1995). *Beyond the double bind: Women and leadership* (pp. 13–14). New York: Oxford University Press.

[53] Jamieson, p. 20.

[54] See: Shockley-Zalabak, P., Staley, C. C., & Morley, D. D. (1988). The female professional: Perceived communication proficiencies as predictors of organizational advancement. *Human Relations, 41*, 553–567; Staley, C. C., & Shockley-Zalabak, P. (1986). Communication proficiency and future training needs of the female professional: Self-assessment vs. supervisors' evaluations. *Human Relations, 39*, 891–902.

[55] Tannen, D. (1990). *You just don't understand: Women and men in conversation.* New York: Ballantine.

[56] Tannen, D. (1994). *Talking from 9 to 5.* New York: William Morrow and Company.

[57] Reardon, K. K. (1995). *They just don't get it, do they?* New York: Little Brown.

[58] See, for example: Carter, K., & Spitzack, C. (1990). Transformation and empowerment in gender and communication courses. *Women's Studies in Communication, 13*, 92–110; Spitzack, C., & Carter, K. (1987). Women in communication studies: A typology for revision. *Quarterly Journal of Speech, 73*, 401–423; Aries, E. (1998). Gender differences in interaction: A reexamination. In D. J. Canary & K. Dindia (Eds.), *Sex differences and similarities in communication* (pp. 65–81). Mahwah, NJ: Lawrence Erlbaum; Weatherall, A. (1998). Re-visioning gender and language research. *Women and language, 21*, 1–9.

[59] Anderson, P. A. (1998). Researching sex differences within sex similarities: The evolutionary consequences of reproductive behavior. In D. J. Canary & K. Dindia (Eds.), *Sex differences and similarities in communication* (pp. 83–100). Mahwah, NJ: Lawrence Erlbaum, p. 83.

[60] Spitzack & Carter, p. 418.

[61] Hackman, M. Z., Furniss, A. H., Hills, M. J., & Paterson, T. J. (1992). Perceptions of gender-role characteristics and transformational leadership behaviours. *Perceptual and Motor Skills, 75*, 311–319.

[62] Reardon, K. K. (1995). *They just don't get it, do they?* (pp. 18–20). New York: Little Brown. Used by permission.

[63] Friedman, T. (2000). *The Lexus and the olive tree* (Expanded Version). New York: Anchor Books.

Chapter 11

[1] Miller, G. R. (1969). Contributions of communication research to the study of speech. In A. H. Monroe & D. Ehninger, *Principles and types of speech communication* (6th brief ed., pp. 334–357). Glenview, IL: Scott, Foresman, p. 355.

[2] Johannesen, R. L. (2002). *Ethics in human communication* (5th ed.). Prospect Heights, IL: Waveland Press.

[3] Palmer, P. (1996). Leading from within. In L. C. Spears (Ed.), *Insights on leadership: Service, stewardship, spirit, and servant-leadership* (pp. 197–208). New York: John Wiley, p. 200.

[4] Material from this section is adapted from: Johnson, C. E. (2001). *Meeting the ethical challenges of leadership: Casting light or shadow.* Thousand Oaks, CA: Sage.

[5] Bok, S. (1979). *Lying: Moral choice in public and private life.* New York: Vintage Books.

[6] Weaver, G. R., Trivino, L. K., & Cochran, P. L. (1999). Integrated and decoupled corporate social performance: Management commitments, external pressures, and corporate ethics practices. *Academy of Management Journal, 42,* 539–552; Weaver, G. R., Trevino, L. K., & Cochran, P. L. (1999). Corporate ethics practices in the mid-1990s: An empirical study of the *Fortune 1000. Journal of Business Ethics, 18,* 283–294.

[7] Mbaria, J. (2001, July 30). To see corruption, look into the mirror. *The Nation* [East Africa], p. 9; See also surveys published by Transparency International and the World Bank.

[8] Colvin, G. (2001, June 25). The great CEO pay heist. *Fortune,* 64–70; What we learned in 2002 (2002, December 30*). Business Week,* p. 170.

[9] Bradsher, K. (2001, June 24). Firestone tire flaw unreported for 4 years. *The Oregonian,* p. A4.

[10] Ramperstad, A. (1997). *Jackie Robinson.* New York: Knopf.

[11] Bartlett, D. L., & Steele, J. B. (2000, February 7). How the little guy gets crunched. *Time,* 38–41.

[12] Rest, J. R. (1986). *Moral development: Advances in research and theory.* New York: Praeger; Rest, J. R. (1994). Background: Theory and research. In J. R. Rest & D. Narvaez (Eds.), *Moral development in the professions: Psychology and applied ethics* (pp. 1–25). Hillsdale, NJ: Erlbaum.

[13] Gioia, D. A. (1992). Pinto fires and personal ethics: A script analysis of missed opportunities. *Journal of Business Ethics, 11,* 379–389; Birsch, D., & Fielder, J. H. (Eds.). (1994). *The Ford Pinto case: A study in applied ethics, business, and technology.* Albany, NY: State University of New York Press.

[14] Gioia, p. 388.

[15] Rest, *Moral development.*

[16] Rest, J. R. (1993). Research on moral judgment in college students. In A. Garrod (Ed.), *Approaches to moral development* (pp. 201–211). New York: Teachers College Press.

[17] Kant, I. (1964). *Ground work for the metaphysics of morals* (H. J. Ryan, Trans.). New York: Harper & Row.

[18] See, for example: Bentham, J. (1948). *An introduction to the principles of morals and legislation.* New York: Hafner Publishing; Gorovitz, S. (Ed.). (1971). *Utilitariansim: Text and critical essays.* Indianapolis, IN: Bobbs-Merrill.

[19] Meilander, G. (1986). Virtue in contemporary religious thought. In R. J. Nehaus (Ed.), *Virtue: Public and private* (pp. 7–30). Grand Rapids, MI: Eerdmans; Alderman, H. (1997). By virtue of a virtue. In D. Statman (Ed.), *Virtue Ethics* (pp. 145–164). Washington, DC: Georgetown University Press.

[20] Johannesen, p. 11.

[21] Solomon, R. (1988). Internal objections to virtue ethics. *Midwest Studies in Philosophy, 8,* 428–441.

[22] Johannesen, R. L. (1991). Virtue ethics, character, and political communication. In R. E. Denton (Ed.), *Ethical dimensions of political communication* (pp. 69–90). New York: Praeger.

[23] Johannesen, *Ethics,* p. 11.

[24] Luke, J. S. (1994). Character and conduct in the public service. In T. C. Cooper (Ed.), *The handbook of administrative ethics* (pp. 391–412). New York: Marcel Dakker; Hart, D. K. (1994). Administration and the ethics of virtue. In T. C. Cooper (Ed.), *The handbook of administrative ethics* (pp. 107–123). New York: Marcel Dakker.

[25] Bartholomew, C. S., & Gustafson, S. B. (1998). Perceived Leader Integrity Scale: An instrument for assessing employee perceptions of leader integrity. *Leadership Quarterly, 9,* 127–145. Used by permission.

[26] MacIntyre, A. (1984). *After virtue: A study in moral theory* (2nd ed.). Notre Dame, IN: University of Notre Dame Press; Hauerwas, S. (1981). A *community of character.* Notre Dame, IN: University of Notre Dame Press.

[27] Blum, L. A. (1988). Moral exemplars: Reflections on Schindler, the Trocmes, and others. *Midwest Studies in Philosophy, 13,* 196–221; Keneally, T. (1982). *Schindler's list.* New York: Simon and Schuster/Touchstone.

[28] Hallie, P. (1979). *Lest innocent blood be shed: The story of the village of Le Chambon and how goodness happened there.* New York: Harper & Row.

[29] Etzioni, A. (1993). *The spirit of community: The reinvention of American society.* New York: Touchstone; Gardner, H. (1995). Building a responsive community. In A. Etzioni (Ed.), *Rights and the common good: A Communitarian perspective* (pp. 167–178). New York: St. Martin's Press.

[30] Fowler, R. B. (1995). Community: Reflections on definition. In A. Etzioni (Ed.), *New Communitarian thinking: Persons, virtues, institutions, and communities* (pp. 88–95). Charlottesville, VA: University Press of Virginia.

31 Hollenbach, D. (1995). Virtue, the common good, and democracy. In A. Etzioni (Ed.), *New Communitarian thinking: Persons, virtues, institutions, and communities* (pp. 143–153). Charlottesville: University Press of Virginia; Gardner, J. (1995). Building a responsive community. In A. Etzioni (Ed.), *Rights and the common good: A Communitarian perspective* (pp. 167–177). New York: St. Martin's Press.

32 Putnam, R. (1993). *Making democracy work: Civic traditions in modern Italy.* Princeton: Princeton University Press.

33 See, for example: Etzioni, A. (1995). On restoring moral voice. In A. Etzioni (Ed.), *Rights and the common good: A Communitarian perspective* (pp. 271–276). New York: St. Martin's Press; Etzioni, A. (1995). Old chestnuts and new spurs. In A. Etzioni (Ed.), *New Communitarian thinking: Persons, virtues, institutions, and communities* (pp. 16–36). Charlottesville, VA: University Press of Virginia.

34 Adapted from: Michalos, A. (1995). *A pragmatic approach to business ethics* (ch 6). Thousand Oaks, CA: Sage.

35 Culbertson, C., & Chen, N. (1997). Communitarianism: A foundation for communication symmetry. *Public Relations Quarterly, 42,* 36–41; Leeper, K. A. (1996). Public relations ethics and Communitarianism: A preliminary investigation. *Public Relations Review, 22,* 163–179; Johnson, C. E., & Hackman, M. Z. (1998). *Public relations, collaborative leadership and community: A new vision for a new century.* Paper presented at the National Communication Association convention, New York, NY.

36 Spears, L. (1998). Tracing the growing impact of servant-leadership. In L. Spears (Ed.), *Insights on leadership* (pp. 1–15). New York: Wiley & Sons; Ruschman, N. L. (2002). Servant-leadership and the best companies to work for in America. In L. C. Spears & M. Lawrence (Eds.), *Focus on leadership: Servant-leadership for the twenty-first century.* New York: Wiley & Sons.

37 Kanungo, R. N., & Mendonica, M. (1996). *Ethical dimensions of leadership.* Thousand Oaks, CA: Sage.

38 Greenleaf, R. (1977). *Servant leadership* (pp. 13–14). New York: Paulist Press.

39 Block, P. (1993). *Stewardship: Choosing service over self-interest.* San Francisco: Berrett-Koehler.

40 DePree, M. (1989). *Leadership is an art.* New York: Doubleday.

41 DePree, p. 92.

42 DePree, M. (1992). *Leadership jazz.* New York: Currency Doubleday.

43 Fraker, A. (1996). Robert K. Greenleaf and business ethics: There is no code. In L. C. Spears (Ed.), *Reflections on leadership* (pp. 37–48). New York: John Wiley.

44 McGee-Cooper, A., & Trammell, D. (2002). From hero-as-leader to servant-as-leader. In L. C. Spears & M. Lawrence (Eds.), *Focus on leadership: Servant-leadership for the 21st century* (pp. 145–146). New York: John Wiley & Sons. This material is used by permission of John Wiley & Sons, Inc.

45 Perreault, G. (1997). Ethical followers: A link to ethical leadership. *The Journal of Leadership Studies, 4(1),* 78–89.

46 Chaleff, I. (1995). *The courageous follower* (p. 162). San Francisco: Berett-Koehler.

47 Useem, M. (2001). *Leading up: How to lead your boss so you both win.* New York: Crown Business.

48 Useem, p. 1.

49 Kidder, R. M. (1994). *Shared values for a troubled world: Conversations with men and women of conscience.* San Francisco: Jossey-Bass; Kidder, R. M (1994, July-August). Universal human values: Finding an ethical common ground. *The Futurist,* 8–13.

50 Kidder, *Shared values for a troubled world,* p. 312.

Chapter 12

1 Csoka, L. S. (1998). The rush to leadership training. In W. E. Rosenbach & R. L. Taylor (Eds.), *Contemporary issues in leadership* (pp. 230–235). Boulder, CO: Westview Press.

2 DuBrin, A. J. (1998). *Leadership: Research, findings, practice, and skills* (2nd ed., p. 388). Boston: Houghton Mifflin.

3 McCauley, C. D., Moxley, R. S., & Van Velsor, E. (Eds.). (1998). *The Center for Creative Leadership handbook of leadership development.* San Francisco: Jossey-Bass.

4 Spitzberg, I. J. (1987). Paths of inquiry into leadership. *Liberal Education, 73,* 24–28.

5 Johnson, C., & Hackman, M. (1993). The status of leadership coursework in communication. *The Michigan Association of Speech Communication Journal, 28,* 1–13. Leadership material is most often included in small group, organizational, and political communication courses.

[6] A number of colleges and universities offer degree programs in leadership studies, most notably the University of Richmond. An excellent source for exploring offerings in leadership is *The Leadership Education Sourcebook*. The Center for Creative Leadership, 5000 Laurinda Dr., Greensboro, NC 27402–1660.

[7] Conger, J. A., & Benjamin, B. (1999). *Building leaders: How successful companies develop the next generation*. San Francisco: Jossey-Bass.

[8] See also: Brown, P. T. (1999–2000, Winter). New directions in leadership development: A review of trends and best practices. *The Public Manager*, 37–41.

[9] Bennis, W. (1989). *On becoming a leader* (p. 98). Reading, MA: Addison-Wesley. For more information on innovation learning, see: Botkin, J. W., Elmandjra, M., & Malitza, M. (1979). *No limits to learning*. New York: Pergamon Books.

[10] Ohlott, P. J. (1998). Job assignments. In C. D. McCauley, R. S. Moxley, & E. Van Velsor (Eds.), *The Center for Creative Leadership handbook of leadership development* (pp. 127–159). San Francisco: Jossey-Bass.

[11] Ohlott, p. 133. This material used by permission of John Wiley & Sons, Inc.

[12] Maxwell, J. (2000). *Failing forward: Turning mistakes into stepping-stones for success*. Nashville: Thomas Nelson Publishers.

[13] Maxwell, p. 117.

[14] Moxley, R. S. (1998). Hardships. In C. D. McCauley, R. S. Moxley, & E. Van Velsor (Eds.), *The Center for Creative Leadership handbook of leadership development* (pp. 194–213). San Francisco: Jossey-Bass.

[15] Moxley, p. 197. Used by permission of John Wiley & Sons, Inc.

[16] Guinness, O. (Ed.). (1999). *Character counts: Leadership qualities in Washington, Wiberforce, Lincoln, and Solzhenitsyn*. Grand Rapids, MI: Baker Books.

[17] Kram, K. E., & Isabella, L. A. (1985). Mentoring alternatives: The role of peer relationships in career development. *Academy of Management Review, 28*, 110–132.

[18] Crosby, F. J. (1999). The developing literature on developmental relationships. In A. J. Murrell, F. J. Crosby, & R. J. Ely (Eds.), *Mentoring dilemmas: Developmental relationships within multicultural organizations* (pp. 3–20). Mahwah, NJ: Lawrence Erlbaum.

[19] Kram, K. E. (1985). *Mentoring at work: Developmental relationships in organizational life*. Glenview, IL: Scott, Foresman and Company. See also: Hunt, D. M., & Michael, C. (1983). Mentorship: A career training and development tool. *Academy of Management Review, 8*, 475–485; Woodlands Group (1980, November). Management development roles: Coach, sponsor, and mentor. *Personnel Journal, 9*, 18–21.

[20] Crosby; Mullen, E. J. (1998). Vocational and psychosocial mentoring functions: Identifying mentors who serve both. *Human Resource Development Quarterly, 9*, 319–331.

[21] Otto, M. L. (1994). Mentoring: An adult developmental perspective. In M. A. Wunsch (Ed.), *Mentoring revisited: Making an impact on individuals and institutions*. San Francisco: Jossey-Bass.

[22] See, for example: Mullen; Dreyer, G. F., & Ash, R. A. (1990). A comparative study of mentoring among men and women in managerial, professional, and technological positions. *Journal of Applied Psychology, 75*, 539–546; Fagenson, E. A. (1989). The mentor advantage: Perceived career/job experiences of protégés versus non-protégés. *Journal of Organizational Behavior, 10*, 309–320.

[23] Kogler Hill, S. E., Bahniuk, M. H., & Dobbs, J. (1989). The impact of mentoring and collegial support on faculty success: An analysis of support behavior information adequacy, and communication apprehension. *Communication Education, 38*, 15–33.

[24] Jacobi, M. (1991). Mentoring and undergraduate academic success: A literature review. *Review of Educational Research, 61*(4), 505–532.

[25] Phillips-Jones, J. (1983). *Mentors and protégés* (ch. 8). New York: Arbor House; See also: Kram; Myers, D. W., & Humpries, N. J. (1985, July-August). The caveats in mentorship. *Business Horizons*, 9–14.

[26] Murray, M. (1991). *Beyond the myths and magic of mentoring*. San Francisco: Jossey-Bass; Kram, K. E., & Bragar, M. C. (1992). Development through mentoring: A strategic approach. In D. H. Montross & C. J. Shinkman (Eds.), *Career development: Theory and practice*. Springfield, IL: Charles C. Thomas.

[27] Chao, G. T., Walz, P. M., & Gardner, P. D. (1992). Formal and informal mentorships: A comparison on mentoring functions and contrast with nonmentored counterparts. *Personnel Psychology, 45*, 619–636.

[28] Phillips-Jones.

[29] Phillips-Jones, L. (1982). *Mentors and protégés* (p. 99). New York: Arbor House. Used by permission of the William Morrow Company.

[30] Covey, S. R. (1989). *The seven habits of highly effective people*. New York: Simon and Schuster.

[31] Cashman, K. (1998). *Leadership from the inside out*. Provo, UT: Executive Excellence Publishing.

[32] Cashman, p. 20.

[33] Judge, W. Q. (1999). *The leader's shadow: Exploring and developing executive character*. Thousand Oaks, CA: Sage.

[34] Cashman, p. 107.

[35] Cashman, p. 153.

[36] Cashman, p. 184.

[37] Cashman, p. 29. Used by permission.

[38] Gale, S. F. (2001, June). Bringing good leaders to light. *Training*, 38–42; Caudron, S. (1999, September). The looming leadership crisis. *Workforce*, 72–76; Rothwell, W. J. (2001). *Executive succession planning* (2nd ed.). New York: AMACOM.

[39] Gabarro, J. J. (1988). Executive leadership and succession: The process of taking charge. In D. C. Hambrick (Ed.), *The executive effect: Concepts and methods for studying top managers* (p. 258). Greenwich, CT: JAI Press.

[40] Gabarro, J. J. (1985, May-June). When a manager takes charge. *Harvard Business Review*, 110–123.

[41] For further discussion of important variables in the succession process, see: Gordon, G. E., & Rosen, N. (1981). Critical factors in leadership succession. *Organizational Behavior and Human Performance, 27*, 227–254; House, R. J., & Singh, J. V. (1987). Organizational behavior: Some new directions for I/O psychology. In M. R. Rosenzweig & L. Porter (Eds.), *Annual Review of Psychology*, Vol. 38, (pp. 669–717). Palo Alto, CA: Annual Reviews; Lord, R., & Maher, K. (1991). *Leadership and information processing* (ch. 10). Boston: Unwin Hyman.

[42] Gabarro, J. J. (1988). Executive leadership and succession: The process of taking charge. In D. C. Hambrick (Ed.), *The executive effect: Concepts and methods for studying top managers* (p. 258). Greenwich, CT: JAI Press. Used by permission.

[43] Gabarro, J. J. (1987). *The dynamics of taking charge* (p. 131). Boston: Harvard Business School Press.

[44] Rothwell; Gale; Caudron.

[45] Hoppe, M. H. (1998). Cross-cultural issues in leadership development. In C. C. McCauley, R. S. Moxley, & E. Van Velsor (Eds.), *The Center for Creative Leadership handbook of leadership development* (pp. 336–378). San Francisco: Jossey-Bass.

BIBLIOGRAPHY

Abrahams, J. (1995). *The mission statement book.* Berkeley, CA: Ten Speed Press.

Adams, J. L. (1986). *The care and feeding of ideas.* Reading, MA: Addison-Wesley.

Adams, J. L. (2001). *Conceptual blockbusting* (4th ed.). Cambridge, MA: Perseus Publishing.

Adams, J., Rice, R., & Instone, D. (1984). Follower attitudes toward women and judgments concerning performance by female and male leaders. *Academy of Management Journal, 27,* 636–643.

Adler, J. J. (1967). *The difference of man and the difference it makes.* New York: Holt, Rinehart and Winston.

Adler, N. J. (2002). *International dimensions of organizational behavior* (4th ed.). Cincinnati, OH: South-Western College Publishing.

Alderman, H. (1997). By virtue of a virtue. In D. Statman (Ed.), *Virtue Ethics* (pp. 145–164). Washington, DC: Georgetown University Press.

Alvesson, M. (2002). *Understanding organizational culture.* Thousand Oaks, CA: Sage.

Anderson, P. A. (1998). Researching sex differences within sex similarities: The evolutionary consequences of reproductive behavior. In D. J. Canary & K. Dindia (Eds.), *Sex differences and similarities in communication* (pp. 83–100). Mahwah, NJ: Lawrence Erlbaum.

Andrews, P. (1984). Performance, self-esteem and perceptions of leadership emergence: A comparative study of men and women. *Western Journal of Speech Communication, 48,* 1–13.

Applbaum, R. L., & Anatol, W. E. (1972). The factor structure of credibility as a function of the speaking situation. *Speech Monographs, 39,* 216–222.

Aries, E. (1998). Gender differences in interaction: A reexamination. In D. J. Canary & K. Dindia (Eds.), *Sex differences and similarities in communication* (pp. 65–81). Mahwah, NJ: Lawrence Erlbaum.

Armour, S. (2002, February 5). Employees' new motto: trust no one. *USA Today,* pp. 1A, 1B.

Asante, M. K., & Frye, J. K. (1977). *Contemporary public communication.* New York: Harper & Row.

Ashour, A. S. (1973). The contingency model of leadership effectiveness: An evaluation. *Organizational Behavior and Human Performance, 9,* 339–355.

Atkin, C. K. (2001). Theory and principles of media health campaigns. In R. R. Rice & C. K. Atkin (Eds.), *Public communication campaigns* (3rd ed.). Thousand Oaks, CA: Sage.

Atkinson, J. W. (1957). Motivational determinants of risk-taking behavior. *Psychological Review, 64,* 359–372.

Auger, B. Y. (1972). *How to run better business meetings.* New York: AMACOM.

Avolio, B. J., & Bass, B. M. (2002). *Developing potential across a full range of leadership: Cases on transactional and transformational leadership.* Mahwah, NJ: Lawrence Erlbaum Associates.

Axelrod, R. (1984). *The evolution of cooperation.* New York: Basic Books.

Baird, J. E. (1977). Some nonverbal elements of leadership emergence. *Southern Speech Communication Journal, 42,* 352–361.

Baird, J., & Wieting, G. K. (1979, September). Nonverbal communication can be a motivational tool. *Personnel Journal,* 607–610.

Baldwin, D. A. (1971). The costs of power. *Journal of Conflict Resolution, 15,* 145–155.

Bales, R. F. (1970). *Personality and interpersonal behavior.* New York: Holt, Rinehart and Winston.

Bales, R. F., & Cohen, S. P. (1979). *Symlog: A system for the multiple level observation of groups.* London: Collier.

Bandura, A. (1977). Self-efficacy: Toward a unifying theory of behavioral change. *Psychological Review, 84,* 191–215.

Bandura, A., & Wood, R. (1989). Effect of perceived controllability and performance standards of self-regulation of complex decision making. *Journal of Personality and Social Psychology, 84,* 804–814.

Barad, E. (1993). Pygmalion–25 years after interpersonal expectations in the classroom. In P. D. Blanck (Ed.), *Interpersonal expectations: Theory, research, and applications* (pp. 125–153). Cambridge: Cambridge University Press.

Barnard, C. I. (1938). *The functions of the executive.* Cambridge: Harvard University Press.

Barnlund, D. C. (1962). Toward a meaning-centered philosophy of communication. *Journal of Communication, 12,* 197–211.

Barton, L. (1993). *Crisis in organizations.* Cincinnati, OH: South-Western Publishing.

Baskin, O., Aronoff, C., & Lattimore, D. (1997). *Public relations: The profession and the practice* (4th ed.). Madison, WI: Brown & Benchmark.

Bass, B. (Ed.). (1981). *Stogdill's handbook of leadership* (2nd ed.). New York: The Free Press.

Bass, B. (1985). *Leadership and performance beyond expectations.* New York: The Free Press.

Bass, B. M. (1960). *Leadership, psychology, and organizational behavior.* New York: Harper & Row.

Bass, B. M. (Ed.). (1990). *Bass and Stogdill's handbook of leadership* (3rd ed.). New York: The Free Press.

Bass, B. M., & Avolio, B. J. (1994). *Improving organizational effectiveness through transformational leadership.* Thousand Oaks, CA: Sage.

Bauer, T. N., & Greene, S. G. (1996). Development of the leader-member exchange: A longitudinal test. *Academy of Management Journal, 39,* 1538–1567.

Bazerman, M. H., & Neale, M. A. (1983). Heuristics in negotiation: Limitations to effective dispute resolution. In M. H. Bazerman & R. J. Lewecki (Eds.), *Negotiating in organizations* (pp. 51–67). Beverly Hills: Sage.

Belasco, J. A., & Stayer, R. C. (1994). *Flight of the buffalo: Soaring to excellence, learning to let employees lead.* New York: Warner Books.

Benne, K. D., & Sheats, P. (1948). Functional roles of group members. *Journal of Social Issues, 4,* 41–49.

Bennis, W. (1976). *The unconscious conspiracy: Why leaders can't lead.* New York: AMACOM.

Bennis, W. (1994; expanded edition). *On becoming a leader.* Cambridge, MA: Perseus Publishing.

Bennis, W. G., & Nanus, B. (1997). *Leaders: The strategies for taking charge* (2nd ed.). New York: Harper & Row.

Bentham, J. (1948). *An introduction to the principles of moral and legislation.* New York: Hafner Publishing.

Berlew, D., & Hall, D. (1966). The socialization of managers: Effects of expectations on performance. *Administrative Science Quarterly,* 208–223.

Bies, R., & Tripp, T. M. (1998). Two faces of the powerless: Coping with tyranny in organizations. In R. M. Kramer & M. A. Neale (Eds.), *Power and influence in organizations* (pp. 203–219). Thousand Oaks, CA: Sage.

Blake, R. R., & McCanse, A. A. (1991). *Leadership dilemmas—grid solutions.* Houston: Gulf Publishing.

Blake, R. R., & Mouton, J. S. (1985). *The managerial grid III: The key to leadership excellence.* Houston: Gulf Publishing.

Blake, R. R., Mouton, J. S., Barnes, L. B., & Greiner, L. E. (1964). Breakthrough in organization development. *Harvard Business Review, 42,* 133–155.

Block, P. (1993). *Stewardship: Choosing service over self-interest.* San Francisco: Berrett-Koehler.

Bok, S. (1999; updated edition). *Lying: Moral choice in public and private life.* New York: Random/Vintage Books.

Bormann, E. G. (1975). *Discussion and group methods* (2nd ed.). New York: Harper & Row.

Botkin, J. W., Elmandjra, M., & Malitza, M. (1979). *No limits to learning.* New York: Penguin Books.

Bradac, J., & Mulac, A. (1984). A molecular view of powerful and powerless speech styles: Attributional consequences of specific language features and communicator intentions. *Communication Monographs, 51,* 307–319.

Bradsher, K. (2001, June 24). Firestone tire flaw unreported for 4 years. *The Oregonian,* p. A4.

Brembeck, W. L., & Howell, W. S. (1976). *Persuasion: A means of social influence* (2nd ed.). Englewood Cliffs, NJ: Prentice Hall.

Broverman, I., Broverman, D. M., Clarkson, F. E., Rosenkranz, P. S., & Vogel, S. R. (1970). Sex-role stereotypes and clinical judgments in mental health. *Journal of Counseling and Clinical Psychology, 34,* 1–7.

Brown, P. T. (1999–2000, Winter). New directions in leadership development: A review of trends and best practices. *The Public Manager,* 37–41.

Bryman, A. (1992). *Charisma and leadership in organizations* (pp. 170–173). London: Sage.

Bucher, L. (1988). *Accidental millionaire.* New York: Paragon House.

Burell, N. A., & Koper, R. J. (1994). The efficacy of power/powerless language on persuasiveness/credibility: A meta-analytic review. In R. W. Preiss & M. Allen (Eds.), *Prospects and precautions in the use of meta-analysis* (pp. 235–255). Dubuque, IA: Brown & Benchmark.

Burke, K. (1968). *Language as a symbolic action.* Berkeley: University of California Press.

Burns, J. M. (1978). *Leadership.* New York: Harper & Row.

Burns, T., & Stalker, G. M. (1961). *The management of innovation.* Chicago: Quadrangle Books.

Capodagli, B., & Jackson, L. (1999). *The Disney way.* New York: McGraw-Hill.

Carlyle, T. (1907). *On heroes, hero-worship, and the heroic in history.* Boston: Houghton Mifflin. (Original work written in 1840).

Carlzon, J. (1987). *Moments of truth.* New York: Harper & Row.

Carter, K., & Spitzack, C. (1990). Transformation and empowerment in gender and communication courses. *Women's Studies in Communication, 13,* 92–110.

Cashman, K. (1998). *Leadership from the inside out.* Provo, UT: Executive Excellence Publishing.

Caudron, S. (1999, September). The looming leadership crisis. *Workforce,* 72–76.

Chaleff, I. (1995). *The courageous follower.* San Francisco: Berett-Koehler.

Chamie, J. (2001). This new population order. *New Perspectives Quarterly, 18,* 25–27.

Chang, M., & Gruner, C. R. (1981). Audience reaction to self-disparaging humor. *Southern Speech Communication Journal, 46,* 419–426.

Chang, R. (2001). *The passion plan at work.* San Francisco: Jossey Bass.

Chao, G. T., Walz, P. M., & Gardner, P. D. (1992). Formal and informal mentorships: A comparison on mentoring functions and contrast with nonmentored counterparts. *Personnel Psychology, 45,* 619–636.

Chen, Z., Lawson, R. B., Gordon, L. R., & McIntosh, B. (1996). Groupthink: Deciding with the leader and the devil. *Psychological Record, 46,* 581–590.

Cherniss, C. (2000). Social and emotional competence in the workplace. In R. Bar-On & J. D. A. Parker (Eds.), *The handbook of emotional intelligence: Theory, development, assessment, and application at home, school, and in the workplace.* San Francisco: Jossey-Bass.

Cherniss, C., & Goleman, D. (Eds.). (2001). *The emotionally intelligent workplace: How to select for, measure, and improve emotional intelligence in individuals, groups and organizations.* San Francisco: Jossey-Bass.

Childress, J. R. (2000). *A time for leadership.* Los Angeles: Leadership Press.

Chinese Culture Connection (1987). Chinese values and the search for culture-free dimensions of culture. *Journal of Cross-Cultural Psychology, 18,* 143–174.

Chrislip, D. D., & Larson, C. E. (1994). *Collaborative leadership.* San Francisco: Jossey-Bass.

Cialdini, R. B. (2001). *Influence: Science and practice* (4th ed.). Boston, MA: Allyn & Bacon.

Cialdini, R. B., Sagarin, B. J., & Rice, W. E. (2001). Training in ethical influence. In J. M. Darley, D. M. Messick, & T. R. Tyler (Eds.), *Social influences on ethical behavior in organizations* (pp. 137–153). Mahway, NJ: Lawrence Erlbaum.

Cialdini, R., Vincent, J., Lewis, S., Catalan, J., Wheeler, D., & Darby, B. (1975). Reciprocal procedure for inducing compliance: The door-in-the-face technique. *Journal of Personality and Social Psychology, 31,* 206–213.

Collins, J. (2001; 1994). *Good to great.* New York: HarperBusiness.

Collins, J. C., & Porras, J. I. (2002). *Built to last.* New York: HarperBusiness.

Collins, J. C., & Porras, J. I. (1996, September-October). Building your company's vision. *Harvard Business Review,* 65–77.

Colvin, G. (2001, June 25). The great CEO pay heist. *Fortune,* 64–70.

Conger, J. A. (1989). *The charismatic leader.* San Francisco: Jossey-Bass.

Conger, J. A. (1989). Leadership: The art of empowering others. *The Academy of Management Executive, 3,* 17–24.

Conger, J. A., & Benjamin, B. (1999). *Building leaders: How successful companies develop the next generation.* San Francisco: Jossey-Bass.

Conger, J. A., & Kanungo, R. N. (1987). Toward a behavioral theory of charismatic leadership in organizational settings. *Academy of Management Review, 12,* 637–647.

Conger, J. A., & Kanungo, R. N. (1988). The empowerment process: Integrating theory and practice. *Academy of Management Review, 13,* 471–482.

Cooper, R. K., & Sawat, A. (1996). *Executive EQ: Emotional intelligence in leadership and organizations.* New York: Grosset/Putnam.

Copeland, L. (1988, November). Valuing workplace diversity: Ten reasons employers recognize the benefits of a mixed work force. *Personnel Administrator,* 38–40.

Covey, S. R. (1989). *The seven habits of highly effective people.* New York: Simon and Schuster.

Cox, T. (1991). Managing cultural diversity: Implications for organizational competitiveness. *Academy of Management Executive, 5,* 45–56.

Cox, T. (1993). *Cultural diversity in organizations: Theory, research and practice.* San Francisco: Berrett-Koehler.

Cragan, J. F., & Wright, D. W. (1999). *Communication in small group discussion* (5th ed.). St. Paul: West Publishing.

Crawford, K. S., Thomas, E. D., & Fink, J. J. (1980). Pygmalion at sea: Improving the work effectiveness of low performers. *Journal of Applied Behavioral Science, 16,* 482–505.

Crosby, F. J. (1999). The developing literature on developmental relationships. In A. J. Murrell, F. J. Crosby, & R. J. Ely (Eds.), *Mentoring dilemmas: Developmental relationships within multicultural organizations* (pp. 3–20). Mahwah, NJ: Lawrence Erlbaum.

Csoka, L. S. (2001). The rush to leadership training. In W. E. Rosenbach & R. J. Taylor (Eds.), *Contemporary Issues in Leadership* (5th ed., pp. 230–235). Boulder, CO: Westview Press.

Culbertson, C., & Chen, N. (1997). Communitarianism: A foundation for communication symmetry. *Public Relations Quarterly, 42,* 36–41.

Curtis, D. B., Winsor, J. L., & Stephens, R. D. (1989). National preferences in business and communication education. *Communication Education, 38,* 6–14.

Daly, J. A., McCroskey, J. C., & Richmond, V. P. (1980). Relationship between vocal activity and perception of communication in small group interaction. *Western Journal of Speech Communication, 41,* 175–187.

Dance, F. E. X. (1982). A speech theory of human communication. In F. E. X. Dance (Ed.), *Human communication theory* (pp.120–146). New York: Harper & Row.

Dance, F. E. X., & Larson, C. (1976). *The functions of human communication: Theoretical approach.* New York: Holt, Rinehart and Winston.

DePree, M. (1989). *Leadership is an art.* New York: Doubleday.

DePree, M. (1992). *Leadership jazz.* New York: Currency Doubleday.

Deutsch, M. (1973). *The resolution of conflict.* New Haven: Yale University Press.

Dewey, J. (1910). *How we think.* Boston: D.C. Heath.

Disney Institute. (2001). *Be our guest.* New York: Disney Enterprises.

Div, T., & Eden, D. (1995). Self-fulfilling prophecy and gender. Can women be Pygmalion and Galatea? *Journal of Applied Psychology, 80,* 253–271.

Dobbins, G. H., Long, W. S., Dedrick, E. J., & Clemons, T. C. (1990). The role of self-monitoring and gender on leader emergence: A laboratory and field study. *Journal of Management, 16,* 609–618.

Dose, J. J. (1999). The relationship between work values similarity and team-member and leader-member exchange relationships. *Group Dynamics, 3,* 20–32.

Dow, T. (1969). The theory of charisma. *Sociological Quarterly, 10,* 316.

Dozier, D. M., Grunig, L. A., & Grunig, J. E. (1995). *Manager's guide to excellence in public relations and communication management.* Mahwah, NJ: Lawrence Erlbaum.

Dreyer, G. F., & Ash, R. A. (1990). A comparative study of mentoring among men and women in managerial, professional, and technological positions. *Journal of Applied Psychology, 75,* 539–546.

Druskat, V. U., & Wolff, S. B. (2001, March). Building the emotional intelligence of groups. *Harvard Business Review,* 80–90.

DuBrin, A. J. (2001). *Leadership: Research findings, practice, and skills* (3rd ed.). Boston: Houghton Mifflin.

Dyer, W. G. (1985). The cycle of cultural evolution in organizations. In R. H. Killmann, M. J. Saxton, & R. Serpa (Eds.), *Gaining control of the corporate culture* (pp. 200–229). San Francisco: Jossey-Bass.

Eagly, A. H. (1987). *Sex differences in social behavior.* Hillsdale, NJ: Erlbaum.

Eagly, A. H., & Johnson, B. T. (1990). Gender and leadership style: A meta-analysis. *Psychological Bulletin, 108,* 233–256.

Eagly, A. J., & Karau, S. J. (1991). Gender and the emergence of leaders: A meta-analysis. *Journal of Personality and Social Psychology, 60,* 685–710.

Eden, D. (1984). Self-fulfilling prophecy as a management tool: Harnessing Pygmalion. *Academy of Management Review, 9,* 64–73.

Eden, D. (1990). *Pygmalion in management.* Lexington, MA: Lexington Books/D. C. Heath.

Eden, D. (1993). Interpersonal expectations in organizations. In P. D. Blanck (Ed.), *Interpersonal expectations: Theory, research, and applications* (pp. 154–178). Cambridge: Cambridge University Press.

Eden, D., & Ravid, G. (1982). Pygmalion vs. self-expectancy: Effects of instructor and self-expectancy on trainee performance. *Organizational Behavior and Human Performance, 30,* 351–364.

Eden, D., & Shani, A. B. (1982). Pygmalion goes to boot camp: Expectancy, leadership, and trainee performance. *Journal of Applied Psychology, 67,* 194–199.

Eisenberg, E. M. (1984). Ambiguity as strategy in organizational communication. *Communication Monographs, 51,* 227–242.

Eisenberg, E. M., & Riley, P. (2001). Organizational culture. In F. M. Jablin & L. L. Putnam (Eds.), *The new handbook of organizational communication advances in theory, research, and methods* (pp. 291–322). Thousand Oaks, CA: Sage.

Eisenberger, R., Fasolo, P., & Davis-LaMastro, C. (1990). Perceived organizational support and employee diligence, commitments, and innovation. *Journal of Applied Psychology, 75,* 57–59.

Ellis, R. J., & Cronshaw, S. F. (1992). Self-monitoring and leader emergence: A test of moderator effects. *Small Group Research, 23,* 113–129.

Engleberg, I. N., & Wynn, D. R. (2003). *Working in groups: Communication principles and strategies* (3rd ed.). Boston: Houghton Mifflin.

Epstein, C. F. (1988). *Deceptive distinctions: Sex, gender, and the social order.* New Haven: Yale University Press.

Erez, M., & Earley, P. C. (1993). *Culture, self-identity, and work.* New York: Oxford University Press.

Ernster, V. L. (1985, July). Mixed messages for women: A social history of cigarette smoking and advertising. *New York State Journal of Medicine,* 335–340.

Esser, J. K. (1998). Alive and well after 25 years: A review of groupthink research. *Organizational Behavior and Human Decision Processes, 73,* 116–141.

Etzioni, A. (1964). *Modern organizations.* Englewood Cliffs, NJ: Prentice-Hall.

Etzioni, A. (1993). *The spirit of community: The reinvention of American society.* New York: Touchstone.

Etzioni, A. (1995). Old chestnuts and new spurs. In A. Etzioni (Ed.), *New Communitarian thinking: Persons, virtues, institutions, and communities* (pp. 16–36). Charlottesville: University Press of Virginia.

Etzioni, A. (1995). On restoring moral voice. In A. Etzioni (Ed.), *Rights and the common good: A Communitarian perspective* (pp. 271–276). New York: St. Martin's Press.

Fagenson, E. A. (1989). The mentor advantage: Perceived career/job experiences of protégés versus non-proteges. *Journal of Organizational Behavior, 10,* 309–320.

Fairhurst, G. T., & Chandler, T. A. (1989). Social structure in leader-member interaction. *Communication Monographs, 56,* 213–239.

Fairhurst, G. T., & Sarr, R. A. (1996). *The art of framing: Managing the language of leadership.* San Francisco: Jossey-Bass.

Fairhurst, G. T., Rogers, L. E., & Sarr, R. A. (1987). Manager-subordinate control patterns and judgments about the relationship. In M. McLaughlin (Ed.), *Communication yearbook 10* (pp. 83–116). Beverly Hills: Sage.

Falbo, T. (1977). Multidimensional scaling of power strategies. *Journal of Personality and Social Psychology, 35,* 537–547.

Fiedler, F. E. (1967). *A theory of leadership effectiveness.* New York: McGraw-Hill.

Fiedler, F. E. (1972). Personality, motivational systems, and the behavior of high and low LPC scores. *Human Relations, 25,* 391–412.

Fiedler, F. E. (1978). The contingency model and the dynamics of the leadership process. In L. Berkowitz (Ed.), *Advances in experimental social psychology* (pp. 60–112). New York: Academic Press.

Fink, S. (1986; 2000). *Crisis management: Planning for the inevitable.* New York: AMACOM.

Fisher, B. A. (1970). Decision emergence: Phases in group decision making. *Speech Monographs, 37,* 53–66.

Fisher, B. A., & Ellis, D. G. (1990). *Small group decision making* (3rd ed.). New York: McGraw-Hill.

Fisher, K. (1993). *Leading self-directed work teams.* New York: McGraw-Hill.

Fisher, R., & Ury, W. (1991). *Getting to yes* (2nd ed.). New York: Penguin Books.

Fiske, S. T. (1993, June). Controlling other people: The impact of power on stereotyping. *American Psychologist,* 621–628.

Foti, R. J., Fraser, S. L., & Lord, R. G. (1982). Effects of leadership labels and prototypes on perceptions of political leaders. *Journal of Applied Psychology, 67,* 326–333.

Foulke, E. (1971). The perception of time compressed speech. In D. L. Horton & J. J. Jenkins (Eds.), *The perception of language* (pp. 79–107). Columbus, OH: Charles E. Merrill.

Fowler, R. B. (1995). Community: Reflections on definition. In A. Etzioni (Ed.), *New Communitarian thinking: Persons, virtues, institutions, and communities* (pp. 143–153). Charlottesville: University Press of Virginia.

Fraker, A. (1996). Robert K. Greenleaf and business ethics: There is no code. In L. C. Spears (Ed.), *Reflections on leadership* (pp. 37–48). New York: John Wiley.

French, J. R. P., & Raven, B. (1959). The bases of social power. In D. Cartwright (Ed.), *Studies in social power* (pp. 150–167). Ann Arbor: University of Michigan, Institute for Social Research.

Friedman, T. (2000). *The Lexus and the olive tree* (Expanded Version). New York: Anchor Books.

Gabarro, J. J. (1985, May-June). When a manager takes charge. *Harvard Business Review,* 110–123.

Gabarro, J. J. (1987). *The dynamics of taking charge.* Boston: Harvard University Press.

Gabarro, J. J. (1988). Executive leadership and succession: The process of taking charge. In D. C. Hambrick (Ed.), *The executive effect: Concepts and methods for studying top managers* (pp. 237–68). Greenwich, CT: JAI Press.

Gale, S. F. (2001, June). Bringing good leaders to light. *Training*, 38–42.

Gardner, H. (1995). Building a responsive community. In A. Etzioni (Ed.), *Rights and the common good: A Communitarian perspective* (pp. 167–178). New York: St. Martin's Press.

Gardner, J. W. (1986). The tasks of leadership. (*Leadership Paper No. 2*). Washington, DC: Independent Sector.

Gardner, J. W. (1990). *On leadership.* New York, NY: Free Press.

Garvin, D. A. (1993, July-August). Building a learning organization. *Harvard Business Review,* 86.

Geertz, C. (1977). Centers, kings, and charisma: Reflections on the symbolics of power. In J. Ben-David & T. Nichols (Eds.), *Culture and its creation: Essays in honor of Edward Shils* (pp. 150–171). Chicago: University of Chicago Press.

Geier, J. G. (1967). A trait approach to the study of leadership. *Journal of Communication, 17,* 316–323.

Getzels, J. W. (1973, November 21). Problem finding: The 343rd Convocation Address, the University of Chicago. *The University of Chicago Record, 9,* 281–283.

Getzels, J. W. (1975). Problem-finding and the inventiveness of solutions. *Journal of Creative Behavior, 9,* 12–18.

Giles, H., & Powesland, P. F. (1975). *Speech style and social evaluation.* London: Academic Press.

Glazer, M. P., & Glazer, P. M. (1989). *The whistleblowers.* New York: Basic Books.

Goffman, E. (1959). *The presentation of self in everyday life.* Garden City, NY: Doubleday.

Goldberg, A., & Larson, C. (Producers). (1984). *Negotiation and bargaining skills* [Video]. Denver, CO: University of Denver.

Goleman, D. (1995). *Emotional intelligence: Why it can matter more than IQ.* New York: Bantam Books.

Goleman, D. (1998). *Working with emotional intelligence.* New York: Bantam Books.

Goleman, D., Boyatzis, R., & McKee, A. (2002). *Primal leadership: Realizing the power of emotional intelligence.* Boston, MA: Harvard Business School Press.

Good, T., & Brophy, J. (1980). *Education psychology: A realistic approach.* New York: Holt, Rinehart and Winston.

Gordon, G. E., & Rosen, N. (1981). Critical factors in leadership succession. *Organizational Behavior and Human Performance, 27,* 227–254.

Gordon, J. (1992, October). Work teams: How far have they come? *Training,* 59–65.

Gorovitz, S. (Ed.). (1971). *Utilitarianism: Text and critical essays.* Indianapolis: Bobbs-Merrill.

Gouran, D. S., & Hirokawa, R. S. (1996). Counteractive functions of communication in effective group decision making (2nd ed.). In R. Y. Hirokawa & M. S. Poole (Eds.), *Communication and group decision-making* (pp. 81–90). Beverly Hills, CA: Sage.

Gouran, D. S., Hirokawa, R. Y., Julian, K. M., & Leatham, G. B. (1993). The evolution and current status of the functional perspective on communication in decision-making and problem-solving groups. In S. Deetz (Ed.), *Communication Yearbook 16* (pp. 573–600). Newbury Park, CA: Sage.

Graen, G. (1976). Role-making processes within complex organizations. In M. D. Dunnette (Ed.), *Handbook of industrial organizational psychology* (pp. 1201–1246). Chicago: Rand-McNally.

Graen, G., & Ginsburgh, S. (1977). Job resignation as a function of role orientation and leader acceptance: A longitudinal investigation of organizational assimilation. *Organizational Behavior and Human Performance, 19,* 1–17.

Graen, G. B., & Cashman, J. F. (1975). A role-making of leadership in formal organizations: A developmental approach. In J. G. Hunt and L. L. Larson (Eds.), *Leadership frontiers* (pp. 143–165). Kent: Kent State University Press.

Graen, G. B., & Scandura, T. (1987). Toward a psychology of dyadic organizing. *Research in Organizational Behavior, 9,* 175–208.

Graen, G. B., & Uhl-Bien, M. (1998). Relationship-based approach to leadership. Development of leader-member exchange (LMX) theory of leadership over 25 years: Applying a multi-level multi-domain perspective. In F. Dansereau & F. J. Yammarino (Eds.), *Leadership: the multiple-level approaches* (pp. 103–158). Stamford, CT: JAI Press.

Grant, J. A., King, P. E., & Behnke, R. E. (1994). Compliance-gaining strategies, communication satisfaction, and willingness to comply. *Communication Reports, 7,* 99–108.

Greenleaf, R. (1977). *Servant leadership.* New York: Paulist Press.

Gregory, J. R., & Wiechman, J. G. (1991). *Marketing corporate image: The company as your number one product.* Lincolnwood, IL: NTC.

Griffin, E. (2003). *A first look at communication theory* (5th ed.). Boston: McGraw-Hill.

Grunig, J. E., & Grunig, L. A. (1992). Models of public relations and communication. In J. E. Grunig, D. M. Dozier, W. I. Ehling, L. A. Grunig, F. C. Repper, & J. White (Eds.), *Excellence in public relations and communication management* (pp. 285–325). Hillsdale, NJ: Lawrence Erlbaum Associates.

Guarrero, C. A. (1998, October). The leadership challenge. *Security Management,* 27–29.

Guth, D. W., Marsh, C. (2003). *Public relations: A values-driven approach* (2nd ed.). Boston: Allyn and Bacon.

Hackman, M. Z. (1988). Audience reactions to the use of direct and personal disparaging humor in informative public address. *Communication Research Reports, 5,* 126–130.

Hackman, M. Z. (1988). Reactions to the use of self-disparaging humor by informative public speakers. *Southern Speech Communication Journal, 53,* 175–183.

Hackman, M. Z. (1989). The inner game of public speaking: Applying intrapersonal communication processes in the public speaking course. *Carolinas Speech Communication Annual, 5,* 41–47.

Hackman, M. Z., Furniss, A. H., Hills, M. J., & Paterson, T. J. (1992). Perceptions of gender-role characteristics and transformational leadership behaviours. *Perceptual and Motor Skills, 75,* 311–319.

Hackman, M. Z., & Johnson, C. (1994). *A cross-cultural investigation of innovativeness, willingness to communicate and need for cognition.* Paper presented at the Speech Communication Association convention, New Orleans, LA.

Haiman, F. S. (1949). An experimental study of the effects of ethos in public speaking. *Speech Monographs, 16,* 190–202.

Haire, M., Ghiselli, E. E., & Porter, L. W. (1966). *Managerial thinking: An international study.* New York: John Wiley.

Haleta, L. L. (1996). Student perceptions of teachers' use of language: The effects of powerful and powerless language on impression formation and uncertainty. *Communication Education, 45,* 16–28.

Hall, E. (1977). *Beyond culture.* Garden City, NY: Anchor.

Hall, R. J., & Lord, R. G. (1998). Multi-level information-processing explanations of followers' leadership perceptions. In F. Dansereau & F. J. Yammarino, *Leadership: The multiple-level approaches* (Vol. 2, pp. 159–190). Stamford, CT: JAI Press.

Harper, B., & Harper, A. (1992). *Succeeding as a self-directed work team.* Mohegan Lake, NY: MW Corporation.

Hart, D. K. (1994). Administration and the ethics of virtue. In T. C. Cooper (Ed.). (1994). *The handbook of administrative ethics* (pp. 107–123). New York: Marcel Dakker.

Hart, R., Friedrich, G., & Brooks, W. (1975). *Public communication.* New York: Harper & Row.

Hauerwas, S. (1981). *A community of character.* Notre Dame, IN: University of Notre Dame Press.

Hawes, L. C. (1974). Social collectivities as communication: Perspectives of organizational behavior. *Quarterly Journal of Speech, 60,* 497–502.

Heath, R. L. (1988). The rhetoric of issue advertising: A rationale, a case study, a critical perspective—and more. *Central States Speech Journal, 39,* 99–109.

Hemphill, J. K., (1949). The leader and his group. *Journal of Educational Research, 28,* 225–229.

Hersey, P. (1984). *The situational leader.* Escondido, CA: Center for Leadership Studies.

Hersey, P., & Blanchard, K. H. (2001). *Management of organizational behavior: Utilizing human resources* (8th ed.). Englewood Cliffs, NJ: Prentice-Hall.

Hill, N. (1976, August). Self-esteem: The key to effective leadership. *Administrative Management, 51,* 24–25.

Hill, T. A. (1976). An experimental study of the relationship between opinionated leadership and small group consensus. *Speech Monographs, 43,* 246–257.

Hirokawa, R., & Pace, R. (1983). A descriptive investigation of the possible communication-based reasons for effective and ineffective group decision making. *Communication Monographs, 50,* 363–379.

Hirokawa, R. Y., & Sheerhorn, D. R. (1996). Communication in faulty group decision-making. In R. Y. Hirokawa & M. S. Poole (Eds.), *Communication and group decision-making* (2nd ed., pp. 63–80). Beverly Hills, CA: Sage.

Hofling, C. K., Brotzman, E., Dalrymple, S., Graves, N., & Pierce, C. M. (1966). An experimental study of nurse-physician relationships. *Journal of Nervous and Mental Disease, 143,* 171–180.

Hofstede, G. (1980). Motivation, leadership and organization: Do American theories apply abroad? *Organizational Dynamics, 9,* 42–63.

Hofstede, G. (1984). The cultural relativity of the quality of life concept. *Academy of Management Review, 9,* 389–398.

Hofstede, G. (1991). *Cultures and organizations: Software of the mind.* London: McGraw-Hill.

Hofstede, G. (1993). Cultural constraints in management theories. *Academy of Management Executive, 7,* 81–94.

Hofstede, G. (2001). *Culture's consequences: Comparing values, behaviors, institutions, and organizations across nations* (2nd ed.). Thousand Oaks, CA: Sage.

Hofstede, G., & Bond, M. H. (1988). The Confucius connection: From cultural roots to economic growth. *Organizational Dynamics, 14,* 483–503.

Hollander, E. (1978). *Leadership dynamics: A practical guide to effective relationships.* New York: Free Press.

Hollander, E. P. (1992, April). The essential interdependence of leadership and followership. *Current Directions in Psychological Science,* 71–75.

Hollenbach, D. (1995). Virtue, the common good, and democracy. In A. Etzioni (Ed.), *New Communitarian thinking: Persons, virtues, institutions, and communities* (pp. 143–153). Charlottesville: University Press of Virginia.

Hornstein, H. A. (1996). *Brutal bosses and their prey.* New York: Riverhead Books.

Hough, J., & Neuland, E. W. (2000). *Global business.* Oxford: Oxford University Press.

House, R. J. (1971). A path-goal theory of leadership effectiveness. *Administrative Science Quarterly, 16,* 321–338.

House, R. J. (1977). A 1976 theory of charismatic leadership. In J. G. Hunt & L. L. Larson (Eds.), *Leadership: The cutting edge* (pp. 189–207). Carbondale: Southern Illinois University Press.

House, R. J., & Mitchell, T. R. (1974). Path-goal theory of leadership. *Journal of Contemporary Business, 3,* 81–97.

Hovland, C. I., & Weiss, W. (1951). The influence of source credibility on communication effectiveness. *Public Opinion Quarterly, 15,* 635–650.

Hovland, C., Janis, I., & Kelley, H. H. (1953). *Communication and persuasion.* New Haven: Yale University Press.

Howell, J. M., & Avolio, B. J. (1992). The ethics of charismatic leadership: Submission or liberation. *Academy of Management Executive, 6,* 43–54.

Huggins, N. (1987). Martin Luther King, Jr.: Charisma and leadership. *Journal of American History, 74,* 477–481.

Hummel, R. P. (1975). Psychology of charismatic followers. *Psychological Reports, 37,* 759–770.

Hunt, D. M., & Michael, C. (1983). Mentorship: a career training and development tool. *Academy of Management Review, 8,* 475–485.

Hunter, J. E., & Boster, F. J. (1987). A model of compliance-gaining message selection. *Communication Monographs, 54,* 63–84.

Infante, D. (1988). *Arguing constructively.* Prospect Heights, IL: Waveland Press.

Infante, D. A., & Gorden, W. I. (1985). Benefits versus bias: An investigation of argumentativeness, gender, and organizational outcomes. *Communication Research Reports, 2,* 196–201.

Infante, D. A., & Gorden, W. I. (1985). Superiors' argumentativeness and aggressiveness as predictors of subordinates' satisfaction. *Human Communication Research, 12,* 117–125.

Infante, D. A., & Gorden, W. I. (1989). Argumentativeness and affirming communicator style as predictors of satisfaction/dissatisfaction with subordinates. *Communication Quarterly, 31,* 81–90.

Infante, D. A., & Gorden, W. I. (1991). How employees see the boss: Test of an argumentative and affirming model of supervisors' communicative behavior. *Western Journal of Speech Communication, 55,* 294–304.

Infante, D. A., & Rancer, A. (1996). Argumentativeness and verbal aggressiveness: A review of recent theory and research. In B. Burleson (Ed.), *Communication Yearbook 19* (pp. 319–351). Thousand Oaks, CA: Sage.

Instone, D., Major, B., & Bunker, B. B. (1983). Gender, self-confidence, and social influence strategies: An organizational simulation. *Journal of Personality and Social Psychology, 44,* 322–33.

Jacobi, M. (1991). Mentoring and undergraduate academic success: A literature review. *Review of Educational Research, 61*(4), 505–532.

Jacobs, T. O. (1970). *Leadership and exchange in formal organizations.* Alexandria, VA: Human Resources Research Organization.

Jamieson, K. H. (1995). *Beyond the double bind: Women and leadership.* New York: Oxford University Press.

Janis, I. (1971, November). Groupthink: The problems of conformity. *Psychology Today,* 271–279.

Janis, I. (1982). *Groupthink* (2nd ed.). Boston: Houghton Mifflin.

Janis, I. (1989). *Crucial decisions: Leadership in policymaking and crisis management.* New York: The Free Press.

Janis, I., & Mann, L. (1977). *Decision making.* New York: The Free Press.

Jensen, A. D., & Chilberg, J. G. (1991). *Small group communication.* Belmont, CA: Wadsworth.

Johannesen, R. L. (1991). Virtue ethics, character, and political communication. In R. E. Denton (Ed.), *Ethical dimensions of political communication* (pp. 69–90). New York: Praeger.

Johannesen, R. L. (2002). *Ethics in human communication* (5th ed). Prospect Heights, IL: Waveland Press.

Johnson, C. (2001). *Meeting the ethical challenges of leadership: Casting light or shadow.* Thousand Oaks, CA: Sage.

Johnson, C. (2002). Evaluating the impact of emotional intelligence on leadership performance: Resonance or dissonance? *Selected Proceedings of the 2002 International Leadership Association convention* [on-line]. Available from http://www.academy.umd.edu/ILA.

Johnson, C., Dixon, B., Hackman, M. Z., & Vinson, L. (1995). Willingness to communicate, the need for cognition and innovativeness: New Zealand students and professionals. In J. E. Aitken & L. J. Shedletsky (Eds.), *Intrapersonal communication processes* (pp. 376–381). Plymouth, MI: Midnight Oil and the Speech Communication Association.

Johnson, C., & Hackman, M. (1993). The status of leadership coursework in communication. *The Michigan Association of Speech Communication Journal, 28,* 1–13.

Johnson, C., & Hackman, M. (1995). *Creative communication: Principles and applications.* Prospect Heights, IL: Waveland Press.

Johnson, C., & Hackman, M. Z. (1998). *Public relations, collaborative leadership and community: A new vision for a new century.* Paper presented at the National Communication Association convention, New York, NY.

Johnson, C., & Vinson, L. (1987). "Damned if you do, damned if you don't?": Status, powerful speech and evaluations of female witnesses. *Women's Studies in Communication, 10,* 37–44.

Johnson, C., Vinson, L., Hackman, M., & Hardin, T. (1989). The effects of an instructor's use of hesitation form on student ratings of quality, recommendations to hire, and lecture listening. *Journal of the International Listening Association, 3,* 32–43.

Jones, L. B. (1996). *The path: Creating your mission statement for work and life.* New York: Hyperion.

Jussim, L., Madon, S., & Chatman, C. (1994), Teacher expectations and student achievement: Self-fulfilling prophecies, biases, and accuracy. In L. Heath et al. (Eds.), *Applications of heuristics and biases to social issues* (pp. 303–334). New York: Plenum Press.

Kahn, R. L. (1956). The prediction of productivity. *Journal of Social Issues, 12,* 41–49.

Kant, I. (1964). *Groundwork for the metaphysics of morals* (H. J. Ryan, Trans.). New York: Harper & Row.

Kanter, R. M. (1977). Some effects of proportions on group life: Skewed sex rations and responses to token women. *American Journal of Sociology, 82,* 969–990.

Kanter, R. M. (1979, July-August). Power failure in management circuits. *Harvard Business Review, 57,* 65.

Kanter, R. M. (1983). *The change masters: Innovation for productivity in the American corporation.* New York: Simon and Schuster.

Kanter, R. M. (1988). Change-master skills: What it takes to be creative. In R. L. Kuhn (Ed.), *Handbook for creative and innovative managers* (pp. 91–99). New York: McGraw-Hill.

Kanter, R. M. (1993). *Men and women of the corporation* (2nd ed.). New York: Basic Books.

Kanungo, R. N., & Mendonica, M. (1996). *Ethical dimensions of leadership.* Thousand Oaks, CA: Sage.

Karsten, M. F. (1994). *Management and gender.* Westport, CT: Praeger.

Katz, D., Maccoby, N., & Morse, N. (1950). *Productivity, supervision, and morale in an office situation.* Ann Arbor: University of Michigan, Institute for Social Research.

Katz, D., Maccoby, N., Gurin, G., & Floor, L. (1951). *Productivity, supervision, and morale among railroad workers.* Ann Arbor: University of Michigan, Institute for Social Research.

Katzenbach, J. R. (1998). *Teams at the top: Unleashing the potential of both teams and individual leaders.* Boston: Harvard Business School Press.

Katzenbach, J. R., & Smith, D. K. (2003). *The wisdom of teams.* Boston: Harvard Business School Press.

Katzenbach, J. R., & Smith, D. K. (1993, March-April). The discipline of teams. *Harvard Business Review,* 111–120.

Kayser, T. A. (1994). *Team power.* Burr Ridge, IL: Irwin.

Kearney, P., Plax, T. G., Sorensen, G., & Smith, V. R. (1988). Experienced and prospective teachers' selections of compliance-gaining messages for "common" student misbehaviors. *Communication Education, 37,* 150–164.

Kelley, R. (1988, November-December). In praise of followers. *Harvard Business Review,* 142–148.

Kelley, R. (1992). *The power of followership: How to create leaders people want to follow and followers who lead themselves.* New York: Doubleday/Currency.

Kelman, H. C., & Hovland, C. I. (1953). "Reinstatement" of the communicator in delayed measurement of opinion change. *Journal of Abnormal and Social Psychology, 48,* 327–335.

Kenny, D. A., & Zaccaro, S. J. (1983). An estimate of variance due to traits in leadership. *Journal of Applied Psychology, 68,* 678–685.

Kerr, S., & Harlan, A. (1973). Predicting the effects of leadership training and experience from the contingency model: Some remaining problems. *Journal of Applied Psychology, 57,* 114–117.

Kiechel, W. (1983, May 30). What makes a corporate leader? *Fortune,* 135–140.

Kiechel, W. (1988, Nov. 21). The case against leaders. *Fortune,* 217–218.

Kipnis, D., & Schmidt, S. M. (1989). Upward-influence styles: Relationship with performance evaluations, salary, and stress. *Administrative Science Quarterly, 33,* 528–542.

Kipnis, D., Schmidt, S. J., & Wilkinson, I. (1980). Intraorganizational influence tactics: Explorations in getting one's way. *Journal of Applied Psychology, 65,* 440–452.

Kipnis, D., Schmidt, S. M., Swaffin-Smith, C., & Wilkinson, I. (1984, Winter). Patterns of managerial influence: Shotgun managers, tacticians, and bystanders. *Organizational Dynamics,* 58–67.

Kline, T. (1999). *Remaking teams: The revolutionary research-based guide that puts theory into practice.* San Francisco: Jossey-Bass.

Knittel, R. E. (1974). Essential and nonessential ritual programs of planned change. *Human Organization, 33,* 394–396.

Knutson, T. J., & Holdrige, W. E. (1975). Orientation behavior, leadership and consensus: A possible functional relationship. *Speech Monographs, 42,* 107–114.

Kogler Hill, S. E. (1982). The multistage process of interpersonal empathy. In S. E. Kogler Hill (Ed.), *Improving interpersonal competence: A laboratory approach* (pp. 83–89). Dubuque, IA: Kendall/Hunt.

Kogler Hill, S. E., Bahniuk, M. H., & Dobbs, J. (1989). The impact of mentoring and collegial support on faculty success: An analysis of support behavior information adequacy, and communication apprehension. *Communication Education, 38,* 15–33.

Korba, R. J. (1986). *The rate of inner speech.* Unpublished doctoral dissertation, University of Denver.

Kotter, J. P. (1990). *A force for change: How leadership differs from management.* New York: Free Press.

Kotter, J. P. (1999). *On what leaders really do.* Boston: Harvard Business School Press.

Kouzes, J. M., & Posner, B. Z. (2002). *The leadership challenge: How to get extraordinary things done in organizations* (3rd ed.). San Francisco: Jossey-Bass.

Kouzes, J. M., & Posner, B. Z. (2003). *Credibility: How leaders gain and lose, why people demand it* (2nd ed.). San Francisco: Jossey-Bass.

Kram, K. E. (1985). *Mentoring at work: Developmental relationships in organizational life.* Glenview, IL: Scott, Foresman and Company.

Kram, K. E., & Bragar, M. C. (1992). Development through mentoring: A strategic approach. In D. H. Montross & C. J. Shinkman (Eds.), *Career development: Theory and practice.* Springfield, IL: Charles C. Thomas.

Kram, K. E., & Isabella, L. A. (1985). Mentoring alternatives: The role of peer relationships in career development. *Academy of Management Review, 28,* 110–132.

Kriegel, R., & Brandt, D. (1996). *Sacred cows make the best burgers: Paradigm-busting strategies for developing change-ready people and organizations.* New York: Warner Books.

Kriegel, R. J., & Patler, L. (1991*). If it ain't broke . . . break it!* New York: Warner Books.

Labich, K. (1989, May 8). Making over middle managers. *Fortune,* 58–64.

LaFasto, F., & Larson, C. (2001). *When teams work best.* Thousand Oaks, CA: Sage.

Landauer, T. J. (1962). Rate of implicit speech. *Perceptual and Motor Skills, 15.*

Larabee, W. (2003). Paralinguistics, kinesics, and cultural anthropology. In L. Samovar & R. Porter (Eds.), *Intercultural communication: A reader* (10th ed., pp. 172–180). Belmont, CA: Wadsworth.

Larson, C. E. (1969). Forms of analysis and small group problem-solving. *Speech Monographs, 36,* 452–455.

Larson, C. E., & LaFasto, F. M. J. (1989). *Teamwork: What must go right/What can go wrong.* Newbury Park, CA: Sage.

Lawrence, P. R., & Lorsch, J. W. (1967). *Organization and environment.* Cambridge: Harvard University Press.

Leathers, D. G. (1997). *Successful nonverbal communication: Principles and applications* (3rd ed.). New York: Macmillan.

Leeper, K. A. (1996). Public relations ethics and Communitarianism: A preliminary investigation. *Public Relations Review, 22,* 163–179.

Levin, I. M. (2000). Vision revisited. *Journal of Applied Behavioral Science, 36,* 91–107.

Lewin, K., Lippitt, R., & White, R. K. (1939). Patterns of aggressive behavior in experimentally created "social climates." *Journal of Social Psychology, 10,* 271–299.

Liden, R., & Graen, G. (1980). Generalizabilty of the vertical dyad linkage model of leadership. *Academy of Management Journal, 23,* 451–465.

Lieber, R. B. (1998, January 12). Why employees love these companies. *Fortune,* 72–74.

Littlejohn, S. (2002). *Theories of human communication* (7th ed.). Belmont, CA: Wadsworth.

Litzinger, W., & Schaefer, T. (1982, September-October). Leadership through followership. *Business Horizons,* 78–81.

Livingston, J. S. (1969). Pygmalion in management. *Harvard Business Review, 47,* 85.

Locke, E. A., & Latham, G. P. (1990). *A theory of goal setting & task performance.* Englewood Cliffs, NJ: Prentice Hall.

Lord, R. G., De Vader, C. L., & Alliger, G. M. (1986). A meta-analysis of the relation between personality traits and leadership perceptions: An application of validity generalization procedures. *Journal of Applied Psychology, 71,* 402–410.

Lord, R. G., & Maher, K. J. (1991). *Leadership and information processing: Linking perceptions and performance.* Boston: Unwin Hyman.

Louw, D. J. (2001). *Ubuntu and the challenges of multiculturalism in post-apartheid South Africa* [on-line]. Available: http://www.phys.uu.nl/~unitwin/ubuntu.html.

Luke, J. S. (1994). Character and conduct in the public service. In T. C. Cooper (Ed.), *The handbook of administrative ethic* (pp. 391–412). New York: Marcel Dakker.

Lundin, S. C., Paul, H., & Christensen, J. (2000). *Fish!* New York: Hyperion.

Lustig, M. W., & Koester, J. (2003). *Intercultural competence: interpersonal competence across cultures* (4th ed.). New York: Longman.

Lutz, W. (1989). *Doublespeak.* New York: Harper & Row.

Lynam, D. R., & Milich, R. (1999). Project DARE: No effect at 10-year follow-up. *Journal of Consulting & Clinical Psychology, 67*, 590–594.

Maas, A., & Clark, R. D. (1984). Hidden impact of minorities: fifteen years of minority influence research. *Psychological Bulletin, 95*, 428–450.

MacIntyre, A. (1984). *After virtue: A study in moral theory* (2nd ed.). Notre Dame, IN: University of Notre Dame Press.

Mackworth, N. H. (1965). Originality. *American Psychologist, 20*, 51–66.

Madon, S., Jussim, L., & Eccles, J. (1997). In search of the powerful self-fulfilling prophecy. *Journal of Personality and Social Psychology, 72*, 791–809.

Manz, C. C., & Peck, C. P. (1995). Teamthink: Beyond the groupthink syndrome in self-managing work teams. *Journal of Managerial Psychology, 10*, 7–15.

Manz, C. C., & Sims, H. P. (1989). *SuperLeadership: Leading others to lead themselves.* New York: Prentice-Hall.

Marquart, M. J., & Berger, N. O. (2000). *Global leaders for the 21st century.* Albany NY: State University of New York Press.

Martin, F. (2002, April). So you failed . . . so what? *Unlimited*, 48.

Martin, J. (1992). *Cultures in organizations.* New York: Oxford University Press.

Martin, J. (2002). *Organizational culture: Mapping the terrain.* Thousand Oaks, CA: Sage.

Martin, J., & Powers, M. E. (1983). Truth or corporate propaganda: The value of a good story. In L. R. Pondy, P. J. Frost, G. Morgan, & T. C. Dandridge (Eds.), *Organizational symbolism* (pp. 93–107). Greenwich, CT: JAI Press.

Marwell, G., & Schmitt, D. (1967). Dimensions of compliance-gaining behavior: An empirical analysis. *Sociometry, 30*, 350–364.

Maslow, A. H. (1970). *Motivation and personality.* New York: Harper & Row.

Maxwell, J. (2000). *Failing forward: Turning mistakes into stepping-stones for success.* Nashville: Thomas Nelson Publishers.

Mayer, J. D. (2001). A field guide to emotional intelligence. In J Ciarrochi, J. P. Forgas, & J. D. Mayer (Eds.), *Emotional intelligence in everyday life: A scientific inquiry* (pp. 3–24). Philadelphia: Psychology Press.

McCauley, C. D., Moxley, R. S., & Van Velsor, E. (1998). *The Center for Creative Leadership handbook of leadership development.* San Francisco: Jossey-Bass.

McCroskey, J. C., & Richmond, C. P. (1990). Willingness to communicate: Differing cultural perspectives. *Southern Communication Journal, 56*, 72–77.

McCroskey, J. C., & Richmond, V. P. (1991). Willingness to communicate: A cognitive view. In M. Booth-Butterfield (Ed.), *Personality and interpersonal communication* (pp. 129–156). Newbury Park, CA: Sage.

McCroskey, J. C., & Richmond, V. P. (1998). Willingness to communicate. In J. C. McCroskey, J. A. Daly, M. M. Martin, & M. J. Beatty (Eds.), *Communication and personality: Trait perspectives* (pp. 119–131). Cresswell, NJ: Hampton Press.

McCroskey, J. C., & Young, T. J. (1981). Ethos and credibility: The construct and its measurement after three decades. *Central States Speech Journal, 32*, 24.

McGlone, E. L., & Anderson, L. J. (1973). The dimensions of teacher credibility. *Communication Education, 22*, 196–200.

McGregor, D. (1960). *The human side of enterprise.* New York: McGraw-Hill.

McMahan, E. M. (1976). Nonverbal communication as a function of attribution in impression formation. *Communication Monographs, 43,* 287–294.

McNatt, D. B. (2000). Ancient Pygmalion joins contemporary management: A meta-analysis of the result. *Journal of Applied Psychology, 85,* 314–322.

Mednick, S. A. (1962). The associative basis of the creative process. *Psychological Review, 69,* 221.

Meilander, G. (1986). Virtue in contemporary religious thought. In R. J. Nehaus (Ed.), *Virtue: Public and private* (pp. 7–30). Grand Rapids, MI: Eerdmans.

Meindl, J. R. (1995). The romance of leadership as a follower-centric theory: A social constructionist approach. *Leadership Quarterly, 6,* 329–341.

Meindl, J. R., Ehrlich, S. B., & Dukerich, J. M. (1985). The romance of leadership. *Administrative Science Quarterly, 30,* 78–102.

Messick, D. M., & Bazerman, M. H. (1996, Winter). Ethical leadership and the psychology of decision making. *Sloan Management Review,* 9–23.

Michalko, M. (1991), *Thinkertoys.* Berkeley, CA: Ten Speed Press.

Miller, G. R. (1969). Contributions of communication research to the study of speech. In A. H. Monroe & D. Ehninger (Eds.), *Principles and types of speech communication* (6th brief ed., pp. 334–357). Glenview, IL: Scott, Foresman.

Mitroff, I., & Shrivastava, P. (1987). Strategic management of corporate crises. *Columbia Journal of World Business, 22,* 5–12.

Mitroff, I., Shrivastava, P., & Udwadi, F. E. (1987). Effective crisis management. *Academy of Management Executives, 1,* 283–292.

Mitroff, I. I., Pearson, C. M., & Harrington, L. K. (1996). *The essential guide to managing corporate crises: A step-by-step guide for surviving major catastrophes.* New York: Oxford University Press.

Moorhead, G., Neck, C. P., & West, M. S. (1998). The tendency toward defective decision making within self-managing teams: The relevance of groupthink for the 21st century. *Organizational Behavior and Human Decision Processes, 73,* 327–351.

Morrison, A. M. (1996). *The new leaders: Guidelines on leadership diversity in America.* San Francisco: Jossey-Bass.

Morrison, A. M., White, R. P., & Van Velsor, E. (1987). *Breaking the glass ceiling.* Reading, MA: Addison-Wesley.

Morrison, A. M., White, R. P., & Van Velsor, E. (1987, August). Executive women: Substance plus style. *Psychology Today,* 18–26.

Mortensen, C. D. (1966). Should the discussion group have an assigned leader? *The Speech Teacher, 15,* 34–41.

Moscovici, S., Migny, G., & Van Avermaet, E. (Eds.). (1985). *Perspectives on minority influence.* Cambridge: Cambridge University Press.

Moxley, R. S. (1998). Hardships. In C. D. McCauley, R. S. Moxley, & E. Van Velsor (Eds.), *The Center for Creative Leadership handbook of leadership development* (pp. 194–213). San Francisco: Jossey-Bass.

Mullen, E. J. (1998). Vocational and psychosocial mentoring functions: Identifying mentors who serve both. *Human Resource Development Quarterly, 9,* 319–331.

Murphy, S. E., & Ensher, E. A. (1999). The effects of leaders and subordinate characteristics in the development of leader-member exchange quality. *Journal of Applied Psychology, 29,* 1371–1394.

Murray, M. (1991). *Beyond the myths and magic of mentoring.* San Francisco: Jossey-Bass.

Myers, D. W., & Humphreys, N. J. (1985, July-August). The caveats in mentorship. *Business Horizons,* 9–14.

Nanus, B. (1992). *Visionary leadership.* San Francisco: Jossey-Bass.

Neale, M. A., & Bazerman, M. H. (1983). The role of perspective-taking ability in negotiating under different forms of arbitration. *Industrial and Labor Relations, 36,* 378–388.

Neff, T. J., & Citrin, J. M. (1999). *Lessons from the top.* New York: Doubleday.

Newsom, D., Van Slyke Turk, J., & Kruckeberg, D. (2000). *This is PR: The realities of public relations* (7th ed.). Belmont, CA: Wadsworth.

Nichols, R. G. (1961). Do we know how to listen? Practical helps in a modern age. *The Speech Teacher, 10,* 120–124.

Nielsen, R. P. (1998). Quaker foundations for Greenleaf's servant-leadership and "friendly disentangling" method. In L. Spears (Ed.), *Insights of leadership* (pp. 126–144). New York: Wiley.

O'Barr, W. (1984). Asking the right questions about language and power. In C. Kramarae, M. Schulz, & W. O'Barr (Eds.), *Language and power* (pp. 260–280). Beverly Hills: Sage.

Offerman, L. R., & Hellmann, P. S. (1997). Culture's consequences for leadership behavior: National values in action. *Journal of Cross-Cultural Psychology, 28,* 342–351.

Ohlott, P. J. (1998). Job assignments. In C. D. McCauley, R. S. Moxley, & E. Van Velsor (Eds.), *The Center for Creative Leadership handbook of leadership development* (pp. 127–159). San Francisco: Jossey-Bass.

O'Keefe, D. J. (1987). The persuasive effects of delaying identification of high and low-credibility communicators: A meta-analytic review. *Central States Speech Journal, 38,* 63–72.

Orsag Madigan, C., & Elwood, A. (1983). *Brainstorms and thunderbolts.* New York: Macmillan.

Otto, M. L. (1994). Mentoring: An adult developmental perspective. In M. A. Wunsch (Ed.), *Mentoring revisited: Making an impact on individuals and institutions.* San Francisco: Jossey-Bass.

Pacanowsky, M. E., & O'Donnell-Trujillo, N. (1983). Organizational communication as cultural performance. *Communication Monographs, 50,* 126–147.

Palmer, P. (1998). Leading from within. In L. C. Spears (Ed.), *Insights on leadership: Service, stewardship, spirit, and servant-leadership* (pp. 197–208). New York: John Wiley.

Parnes, S. J. (1975). "Aha!" In I. A. Taylor & J. W. Getzels (Eds.), *Perspectives on creativity* (pp. 224–248). Chicago: Aldine.

Pasternack, B. A., & O'Toole, J. (2002, second quarter). Yellow light leadership: How the world's best companies manage uncertainty. *Strategy + Business,* 74–83.

Patton, B. P., Giffin, K., & Patton, E. N. (2003). *Decision-making group interaction* (4th ed.). New York: Harper & Row.

Pauchant, T. C., & Mitroff, I. I. (1992). *Transforming the crisis-prone organization: Preventing individual, organizational, and environmental tragedies.* San Francisco: Jossey-Bass.

Pearce, T. (1995). *Leading out loud: The authentic speaker, the credible leader.* San Francisco: Jossey-Bass.

Pearce, W. B. (1989). *Communication and the human condition.* Carbondale: Southern Illinois University Press.

Pearson, C. M., & Mitroff, I. I. (1993, February). From crisis prone to crisis prepared: A framework for crisis management. *Academy of Management Executive, 7,* 48–60.

Perreault, G. (1997). Ethical followers: A link to ethical leadership. *The Journal of Leadership Studies, 4*(1), 78–89.

Peters, T. (1987). *Thriving on chaos.* New York: Borzoi/Alfred A. Knopf.

Peters, T. (1992). *Liberation management.* New York: Ballantine.

Peters, T. (1994). *The Tom Peters seminar.* London: Macmillan.

Peters, T., & Austin, N. (1985). *A passion for excellence: The leadership difference.* New York: Random House.

Peters, T. J., & Waterman, R. H., Jr. (1982). *In search of excellence.* New York: Harper & Row.

Petty, R. E., & Cacioppo, J. T. (1986). *Communication and persuasion: Central and peripheral routes to attitude change.* New York: Springer-Verlag.

Petty, R., & Wegener, D. (1999). The Elaboration Likelihood Model: Current status and controversies. In S. Chaiken & Y. Trope (Eds.), *Dual process theories in social psychology* (pp. 41–72). New York: Guildford.

Pfau, M., & Parrott, R. (1993). *Persuasive communication campaigns.* Boston: Allyn & Bacon.

Pfeffer, J. (1992, Winter). Understanding power in organizations. *California Management Review,* 29–50.

Phillips-Jones, L. (1983). *Mentors and proteges.* New York: Arbor House.

Pittman, T. S., Rosenbach, W. E., & Potter, E. H. III. (2001). Followers as partners: Taking the initiative for action. In W. E. Rosenbach & R. L. Taylor (Eds.), *Contemporary issues in leadership* (5th ed., pp. 107–120). Boulder, CO: Westview Press.

Poole, M. S. (1983). Decision development in small groups II: A study of multiple sequences in decision making. *Communication Monographs, 50,* 206–232.

Poole, M. S. (1983). Decision development in small groups III: A multiple sequence model of group decision development. *Communication Monographs, 50,* 321–341.

Powell, G. (2003). *Women & men in management* (3rd ed.). Newbury Park, CA: Sage.

Pruitt, D. G., & Carnevale, P. J. (1993). *Negotiation in social conflict.* Pacific Grove, CA: Brooks/Cole.

Putnam, L. L., & Jones, T. S. (1982). The role of communication in bargaining. *Human Communication Research, 8,* 262–280.

Putnam, R. (1993). *Making democracy work: Civic traditions in modern Italy.* Princeton: Princeton University Press.

Rafaeli, A., & Worline, M. (2000). Symbols in organizational culture. In N. M. Ashkanasy, C. P. M. Wilderom, & M. F. Peterson (Eds.), *Handbook of organizational culture and climate* (pp. 71–84). Thousand Oaks, CA: Sage.

Ramperstad, A. (1997). *Jackie Robinson.* New York: Knopf.

Ray, D., & Bronstein, H. (1995). *Teaming up.* New York: McGraw-Hill.

Reardon, K. K. (1995). *They just don't get it, do they?* New York: Little Brown.

Regula, C. R., & Julian, J. W. (1973). The impact of quality and frequency of task contributions on perceived ability. *Journal of Social Psychology, 89,* 115–122.

Rest, J. (1986). *Moral development: Advances in research and theory.* New York: Praeger.

Rest, J. R. (1993). Research on moral judgment in college students. In A. Garrod (Ed.), *Approaches to moral development* (pp. 201–211). New York: Teachers College Press.

Rest, J. R. (1994). Background: Theory and research. In J. R. Rest & D. Narvaez (Eds.), *Moral development in the professions: Psychology and applied ethics* (pp. 1–25). Hillsdale, NJ: Erlbaum.

Rice, R. R. (2001). Smokey Bear. In R. R. Rice & C. K. Atkins (Eds.), *Public communication campaigns* (3rd ed., pp. 276–279). Thousand Oaks, CA: Sage.

Richardson, R. J., & Thayer, S. K. (1993). *The charisma factor* (p. 27). Englewood Cliffs, NJ: Prentice-Hall.

Richmond, V. P., & Roach, K. D. (1992). Willingness to communicate and employee success in U.S. organizations. *Journal of Applied Communication Research, 20,* 95–115.

Riecken, H. (1975). The effect of talkativeness on ability to influence group solutions of problems. In P. V. Crosbie (Ed.), *Interaction in small groups* (pp. 238–249). New York: Macmillan.

Roesner, J. B. (1990, November-December). Ways women lead. *Harvard Business Review,* 119–125.

Rogers, E. M. (1995). *Diffusion of innovations* (4th ed.). New York: The Free Press.

Rogers, E. M., & Steinfatt, T. M. (1999). *Intercultural communication.* Prospect Heights, IL: Waveland Press.

Rogers, E. M., & Storey, J. D. (1987). Communication campaigns. In C. R. Berger & S. H. Chaffee (Eds.), *Handbook of Communication Science* (pp. 817–846). Newbury Park, CA: Sage.

Roloff, M. E., & Barnicott, E. F. (1978). The situational use of pro- and antisocial compliance-gaining strategies by high and low Machiavellians. In B. Ruben (Ed.), *Communication Yearbook 2* (pp. 193–208). New Brunswick, NJ: Transaction Books.

Rosener, J. B. (1990, November-December). Ways women lead. *Harvard Business Review,* 119–125.

Rosenthal, R. (1993). Interpersonal expectations: Some antecedents and some consequences. In P. D. Blanck (Ed.), *Interpersonal expectations: Theory, research and applications* (pp. 3–24) Cambridge: Cambridge University Press.

Rosenthal, R., & Fode, K. L. (1963). The effect of experimenter bias on the performance of the albino rat. *Behavior Science, 8,* 183–189.

Rosenthal, R., & Jacobson, L. (1968). *Pygmalion in the classroom.* New York: Holt, Rinehart and Winston.

Rost, J. C. (1993; 1991). *Leadership for the twenty-first century.* New York: Praeger.

Rost, J. C. (1993). Leadership in the new millennium. *The Journal of Leadership Studies, 1,* 92–110.

Rothwell, J. D. (2001). *In mixed company: Small group communication* (4th ed.). Fort Worth: Harcourt Brace.

Rothwell, W. J. (2001). *Executive succession planning* (2nd ed.). New York: AMACOM.

Rubin, J. Z., & Brown, B. R. (1975). *The social psychology of bargaining and negotiation.* New York: Academic Press.

Ruschman, N. L. (2002). Servant-leadership and the best companies to work for in America. In L. C. Spears & M. Lawrence (Eds.), *Focus on leadership: Servant-leadership for the twenty-first century.* New York: Wiley & Sons.

Salovey, P., Bedwell, B. T., Detweiler, J. B., & Mayer, J. D. (2000). Current directions in emotional intelligence research. In M. Lewis & J. M. Haviland-Lewis, *Handbook of emotions* (2nd ed., pp. 504–520). New York: Guilford Press.

Sanders, D. A., & Sanders, J. A. (1984). *Teaching creativity through metaphor* (p. 19). New York: Longman.

Sandler, L. (1986, February). Self-fulfilling prophecy: Better management by magic. *Training, 60*–64.

Sattler, W. M. (1947). Conceptions of ethos in ancient rhetoric. *Speech Monographs, 14,* 55–65.

Scheidel, T. M., & Crowell, L. (1964). Idea development in small discussion groups. *Quarterly Journal of Speech, 50,* 140–145.

Schein, E. H. (1983). The role of the founder in creating organizational culture. *Organizational Dynamics, 12,* 13–26.

Schein, E. H. (1992). *Organizational culture and leadership* (2nd ed.). San Francisco: Jossey-Bass.

Schermerhorn, R., & Bond, M. H. (1997). Cross-cultural leadership dynamics in collectivism and high power distance settings. *Leadership & Organization Development Journal, 18,* 187–193.

Schriesheim, C. A., & Kerr, S. (1977). Theories and measures of leadership: A critical appraisal. In J. G. Hunt & L. L. Larson (Eds.), *Leadership: The cutting edge* (pp. 9–45). Carbondale: Southern Illinois University Press.

Schultz, B. (1979). Predicting emergent leaders: An exploratory study of the salience of communicative functions. *Small Group Behavior, 9,* 109–114.

Schultz, B. (1980). Communicative correlates of perceived leaders. *Small Group Behavior, 11,* 175–191.

Schultz, B. (1982). Argumentativeness: Its effect in group decision making and its role in leadership perception. *Communication Quarterly, 30,* 368–375.

Schultz, B. G. (1996). *Communicating in the small group: Theory and practice* (2nd ed.). New York: HarperCollins.

Schweitzer, A. (1984). *The age of charisma.* Chicago: Nelson-Hall.

Sebeok, T. A., & Rosenthal, R. (Eds.). (1981). *The clever Hans phenomenon: Communication with horses, whales, apes, and people.* (Annals of the New York Academy of Sciences, Vol. 364.) New York: New York Academy of Sciences.

Sebeok, T. A., & Umiker-Sebeok, J. (1979). *Speaking of apes: A critical anthology of two-way communication with man.* New York: Plenum.

Seitel, F. P. (2001). *The practice of public relations* (8th ed.). Upper Saddle River, NJ: Prentice Hall.

Sherman, E. (2001, Fall). Women in political leadership: Reflections on larger social issues. *Leadership,* 4–5.

Shockley-Zalabak, P., Ellis, K., & Cesaria, R. (2000). *Measuring organizational trust.* San Francisco: International Association of Business Communicators.

Shockley-Zalabak, P., Staley, C. C., & Morley, D. D. (1988). The female professional: Perceived communication proficiencies as predictors of organizational advancement. *Human Relations, 41,* 553–567.

Simons, H. W. (1986). *Persuasion: Understanding practice, and analysis* (2nd ed.). New York: Random House.

Sims, H. P., & Manz, C. C. (1996). *Company of heroes: Unleashing the power of self-leadership.* New York: John Wiley.

Singelis, T. M., Triandis, H. C., Bhawuk, D. S., & Gelfand, M. (1995). Horizontal and vertical dimensions of individualism and collectivism: A theoretical and measurement refinement. *Cross-cultural Research, 29,* 240–275.

Singhal, A., & Rogers, E. (1999). *Entertainment-education: A communication strategy for social change.* Mahwah, NJ: Lawrence Erlbaum.

Smart, T. (1999, July 20). A new presence in the corporate elite; woman crosses gender barrier to be Hewlett-Packard CEO. *The Washington Post,* p. A01.

Smith, A. E., Jussim, L., & Eccles, J. (1999). Do self-fulfilling prophecies accumulate, dissipate, or remain stable over time? *Journal of Personality and Social Psychology, 77,* 548–565.

Smith, T. W. (1990). *Ethnic Images.* National Opinion Research Center, GSS Topical Report No. 19. Chicago: University of Chicago.

Snyder, M. (1987). *Public appearances/private realities: The psychology of self-monitoring.* New York: W. H. Freeman.

Snyder, N. H., & Graves, M. (1994). Leadership and vision. *Business Horizons, 37,* 1–7.

Solomon, R. (1988). Internal objections to virtue ethics. *Midwest Studies in Philosophy, 8,* 428–441.

Sorensen, R., & Pickett, T. (1986). A test of two teaching strategies designed to improve interview effectiveness: Rating behavior and videotaped feedback. *Communication Monographs, 35,* 13–22.

Spears, L. (1998). Tracing the growing impact of servant-leadership. In L. Spears (Ed.), *Insights on leadership* (pp. 1–15). New York: Wiley & Sons.

Spencer, H. (1884). *The study of sociology.* New York: D. A. Appleton. (First published in 1873.)

Spitzack, C., & Carter, K. (1987). Women in communication studies: A typology for revision. *Quarterly Journal of Speech, 73,* 401–423.

Spitzberg, I. J. (1987). Paths of inquiry into leadership. *Liberal Education, 73,* 24–28.

Staley, C. C., & Shockley-Zalabak, P. (1986). Communication proficiency and future training needs of the female professional: Self-assessment vs. supervisors' evaluations. *Human Relations, 39,* 891–902.

Stang, D. J. (1973). Effect of interaction rate on ratings of leadership and liking. *Journal of Personality and Social Psychology, 27,* 405–408.

Star, S. A., & Hughes, H. (1950). Report on an educational campaign: The Cincinnati plan for the United Nations. *American Journal of Sociology, 55,* 389–400.

Staw, B. M., & Sutton, R. (1993). Macro organizational psychology. In J. K. Murnighan (Ed.), *Social psychology in organizations: Advances in theory and research* (pp. 350–384). Englewood Cliffs, NJ: Prentice-Hall.

Stech, E. L. (1983). *Leadership communication.* Chicago: Nelson-Hall.

Stogdill, R. M. (1948). Personal factors associated with leadership: A survey of the literature. *Journal of Psychology, 25,* 35–71.

Stogdill, R. M. (1950). Leadership, membership and organization. *Psychological Bulletin, 47.*

Stogdill, R. M. (1965). *Managers, employees, organizations.* Columbus: Ohio State University, Bureau of Business Research.

Stogdill, R. M. (1974). *Handbook of leadership.* New York: The Free Press.

Stogdill, R. M., & Coons, A. E. (1957). *Leader behavior: Its description and measurement.* Columbus: Ohio State University, Bureau of Business Research.

Strong, S. R., & Dixon, D. N. (1971). Expertness, attractiveness, and influence in counseling. *Journal of Counseling Psychology, 18,* 562–570.

Strong, S. R., & Schmidt, L. D. (1970). Expertness and influence in counseling. *Journal of Counseling Psychology, 17,* 81–87.

Susskind, L., & Field, P. (1996). *Dealing with an angry public: The mutual gains approach to resolving disputes.* New York: The Free Press.

Tannen, D. (1990). *You just don't understand: Women and men in conversation.* New York: Ballantine.

Tannen, D. (1994). *Talking from 9 to 5.* New York: William Morrow and Company.

Tannenbaum, R., & Schmidt, W. H. (1958). How to choose a leadership pattern. *Harvard Business Review, 36,* 95–101.

Tenbrusel, A. E., & Messick, D. M. (2001). Power asymmetries and the ethical atmosphere in negotiations. In J. M. Darley, D. M. Messick, & T. R. Tyler (Eds.), *Social influences on ethical behavior in organizations* (pp. 201–216). Mahwah, NJ: Lawrence Erlbaum.

Terrace, H. S., Pettito, L. A., Sanders, R. J., & Bever, T. G. (1979). Can an ape create a sentence? *Science, 206,* 891–902.

Thibault, J. W., & Kelley, H. H. (1978). *Interpersonal relations: A theory of interdependence.* New York: John Wiley.

Thomas, D. A., & Ely, R. J. (1996, September-October). Making differences matter: A new paradigm for managing diversity. *Harvard Business Review,* 79–90.

Thomas, D. A., & Gabarro, J. J. (1999). *Breaking through: The making of minority executives in corporate America*. Boston, MA: Harvard Business School Press.

Thomas, D. A. (2001, April-May). Race matters: The truth about mentoring minorities. *Harvard Business Review*, 99–107.

Tompkins, P. K. (1982). *Communication as action: An introduction to rhetoric and communication*. Belmont, CA: Wadsworth.

Triandis, H. C. (1993). The contingency model in cross-cultural perspective. In M. M. Chemers & R. Ayman (Eds.), *Leadership theory and research: Perspectives and directions* (pp. 167–188). San Diego: Academic Press.

Trice, H. M., & Beyer, J. M. (1984). Studying organizational cultures through rites and ceremonials. *Academy of Management Review, 9*, 653–669.

Trice, H. M., & Beyer, J. M. (1985). Using six organizational rites to change culture. In R. H. Kilmann, M. J. Saxton, & R. Serpa (Eds.), *Gaining control of the corporate culture* (pp. 370–399). San Francisco: Jossey-Bass.

Trice, H. M., & Beyer, J. M. (1993). *The cultures of work organizations*. Englewood Cliffs, NJ: Prentice-Hall.

Trist, E. L., & Bamforth, K. W. (1951). Some social and psychological consequences of the longwall method of coal-getting. *Human Relations, 4*, 3–38.

Tromprenaars, F. (1994). *Riding the waves of culture: Understanding diversity in global business*. Burr Ridge, IL: Irwin.

Tucker, R. C. (1965). The dictator and totalitarianism. *World Politics, 17*, 565–573.

Van der Merwe, W. L. (1996). Philosophy and the multi-cultural context of (post)apartheid South Africa. *Ethical Perspectives, 3*, 1–15.

VanGundy, A. B. (1992). *Idea power*. New York: AMACOM.

Vecchio, R. P. (1982). A further test of leadership effects due to between-group variation and within-group variation. *Journal of Applied Psychology, 67*, 200–208.

Vinson, L. (1988, November). *An emotion-based model of compliance-gaining message selection*. Paper presented at the Speech Communication Association convention, New Orleans, LA.

Vinson, L., & Johnson, C. (1990). The relationship between the use of hesitations and/or hedges and listening: The role of perceived importance as a mediating variable. *Journal of the International Listening Association, 4*, 116–127.

Vinson, L., Johnson, C., & Hackman, M. (1992). *I like you just the way you are: Student evaluations of favorite and least favorite instructors using hesitant speech*. Paper presented at the Speech Communication Association convention, Chicago, IL.

The vision thing. (1991, November 9). *The Economist*, 89.

von Oech, R. (1986). *A kick in the seat of the pants* (pp. 30, 32). New York: Harper & Row.

von Oech, R. (1992). *Creative whackpack*. Stamford, CT: U.S. Games Systems, Inc.

von Oech, R. (1998; revised edition). *A whack on the side of the head*. New York: Warner Books.

Walker, S. (1983). *Animal thought*. London: Routledge & Kegan Paul.

Wallas, G. (1926). *The art of thought*. New York: Harcourt.

Ward, C. D., & McGinnies, E. (1974). Persuasive effects of early and late mention of credible and non-credible sources. *Journal of Psychology, 86*, 17–23.

Warner, K. E. (1986). *Selling smoke: Cigarette advertising and public health*. Washington, DC: American Public Health Association.

Warnick, B., & Inch, E. S. (1994). *Critical thinking and communication: The use of reason in argument* (2nd ed.). New York: Macmillan.

Warren, I. D. (1969). The effects of credibility in sources of testimony and audience attitudes toward speaker and topic. *Speech Monographs, 36*, 456–458.

Weatherall, A. (1998). Re-visioning gender and language research. *Women and language, 21*, 1–9.

Weaver, G. R., Klebe Trivino, L., & Cochran, P. L. (1999). Integrated and decoupled corporate social performance: Management commitments, external pressures, and corporate ethics practices. *Academy of Management Journal, 42*, 539–532.

Weaver, G. R., Trevino, L. K., & Cochran P. L. (1999). Corporate ethics practices in the mid-1990s: An empirical study of the *Fortune 1000*. *Journal of Business Ethics, 18*, 283–294.

Weber, M. (1947). *The theory of social and economic organization* (pp. 358–359). (A. M. Henderson & T. Parsons, Trans.) Glencoe, IL: The Free Press.

Weisinger, H. (1998). *Emotional intelligence at work: The untapped edge for success.* San Francisco: Jossey-Bass.

Wellins, R. S., Byham, W. C., & Dixon, G. R. (1994). *Inside teams.* San Francisco: Jossey-Bass.

Wellins, R. S., Byham, W. C., & Wilson, J. M. (1991). *Empowered teams.* San Francisco: Jossey-Bass.

White, L. A. (1949). *The science of culture.* New York: Farrar, Strauss and Cudahy.

White, R., & Lippitt, R. (1968). Leader behavior and member reaction in three "social climates." In D. Cartwright & A. Zander (Eds.), *Group dynamics* (pp. 318–335). New York: Harper & Row.

White, S. S., & Lock, E. A. (2000). Problems with the Pygmalion Effect and some proposed solutions. *Leadership Quarterly, 11*, 389–416.

Whitman, R. F., & Foster, T. J. (1994). *Speaking in public.* New York: Macmillan.

Wilcox, D. L., Ault, P. H., & Agee, W. K. (2003). *Public relations: Strategies and tactics* (7th ed.). New York: Longman.

Willner, R. A. (1984). *The spellbinders: Charismatic political leadership.* New Haven: Yale University Press.

Willner, R. A. (1986). *Charismatic political leadership: A theory.* Princeton: Princeton University Center for International Studies.

Wills, G. (1994). *Certain trumpets: The call of leaders.* New York: Simon & Schuster.

Winsten, J. A., & DeJong, W. (2001). The designated driver campaign. In R. R. Rice & C. K. Atkin (Eds.), *Public communication campaigns* (3rd ed., pp. 290–294). Thousand Oaks, CA: Sage.

Wood, J. T. (2003). *Gendered lives: Communication, gender and culture,* (5th ed.) Belmont, CA: Wadsworth.

Woodlands Group (1980, November). Management development roles: Coach, sponsor, and mentor. *Personnel Journal,* 918–921.

Woodward, G. C., & Denton, R. E. (2000). *Persuasion & influence in American life* (4th ed.). Prospect Heights, IL: Waveland Press.

Woodward, J. (1965). *Industrial organization: Theory and practice.* Oxford: Oxford University Press.

Yukl, G. (2002). *Leadership in organizations* (5th ed.). Upper Saddle River, NJ: Prentice-Hall.

Yukl, G., & Falbe, C. M. (1991). Importance of different power sources in downward and lateral relations. *Journal of Applied Psychology, 76*, 416–423.

Yukl, G., Falbe, C. M., & Youn, J. (1993). Patterns of influence behaviors for managers. *Group & Organization Management, 18*, 5–28.

Yukl, G., Guinan, P. J., & Sottolano, D. (1995). Influence tactics used for different objectives with subordinates, peers, and superiors. *Group & Organization Management, 20*, 272–296.

Zaccaro, S. J., & Banks, D. J. (2001). Leadership, vision, and organizational effectiveness. In S. J. Zaccaro and R. K. Kilimoski (Eds.), *The nature of organizational leadership* (pp. 181–218). San Francisco: Jossey Bass.

Zaleznik, A. (1977, May-June). Managers and leaders: Are they different? *Harvard Business Review, 55*, 67–78.

Zorn, T. E. (1991). Construct system development, transformational leadership and leadership messages. *Southern Communication Journal, 56*, 178–193.

INDEX